Applications in Basic Marketing

Clippings from the Popular Business Press

2001-2002 Edition

Applications in Basic Marketing
Clippings from the Popular Business Press

2001-2002 Edition

William D. Perreault, Jr.
University of North Carolina

and

E. Jerome McCarthy
Michigan State University

Boston   Burr Ridge, IL   Dubuque, IA   Madison, WI   New York   San Francisco   St. Louis
Bangkok   Bogotá   Caracas   Kuala Lumpur   Lisbon   London   Madrid   Mexico City
Milan   Montreal   New Delhi   Santiago   Seoul   Singapore   Sydney   Taipei   Toronto

McGraw-Hill Higher Education

A Division of The **McGraw-Hill** Companies

APPLICATIONS IN BASIC MARKETING:
CLIPPINGS FROM THE POPULAR BUSINESS PRESS 2001-2002 EDITION

Published by McGraw-Hill/Irwin, an imprint of The McGraw-Hill Companies, Inc. 1221 Avenue of the Americas, New York, NY, 10020. Copyright © 2002, 2001, 2000, 1999, 1998, 1997, 1996, 1993 by The McGraw-Hill Companies, Inc. All rights reserved. No part of this publication may be reproduced or distributed in any form or by any means, or stored in a database or retrieval system, without the prior written consent of The McGraw-Hill Companies, Inc., including, but not limited to, in any network or other electronic storage or transmission, or broadcast for distance learning.

Some ancillaries, including electronic and print components, may not be available to customers outside the United States.

This book is printed on acid-free paper.

1 2 3 4 5 6 7 8 9 0 QPD/QPD 0 9 8 7 6 5 4 3 2 1

ISBN   0-07-561033-7
ISSN   1099-5579

Publisher: *John E. Biernat*
Executive editor: *Linda Schreiber*
Senior developmental editor: *Nancy Barbour*
Marketing manager: *Kimberly Kanakes Szum*
Associate project manager: *Destiny Rynne*
Senior production supervisor: *Lori Koetters*
Producer, media technology: *Todd Labak*
Director of design BR: *Keith J. McPherson*
Cover design: *Mary Ann Trzyna*
Compositor: *Electronic Publishing Services, Inc., TN*
Printer: *Quebecor World Dubuque Inc.*

www.mhhe.com

Preface

This is the twelfth annual edition of *Applications in Basic Marketing.* We developed this set of marketing "clippings" from popular business publications to accompany our texts—*Basic Marketing* and *Essentials of Marketing.* All of these clippings report interesting case studies and current issues that relate to topics covered in our texts and in the first marketing course. We will continue to publish a new edition of this book *every year.* That means that we can include the most current and interesting clippings. Each new copy of our texts will come shrink-wrapped with a free copy of the newest (annual) edition of this book. However, it can also be ordered from the publisher separately for use in other courses or with other texts.

Our objective is for this book to provide a flexible and helpful set of teaching and learning materials. We have included clippings (articles) on a wide variety of topics. The clippings deal with consumer products and business products, goods and services, new developments in marketing as well as traditional issues, and large well-known companies as well as new, small ones. They cover important issues related to marketing strategy planning for both domestic and global markets. The readings can be used for independent study, as a basis for class assignments, or as a focus of in-class discussions. Some instructors might want to assign all of the clippings, but we have provided an ample selection so that it is easy to focus on a subset which is especially relevant to specific learning/teaching objectives. A separate set of teaching notes discusses points related to each article. We have put special emphasis on selecting short, highly readable articles—ones which can be read and understood in 10 or 15 minutes—so that they can be used in combination with other readings and assignments for the course. For example, they might be used in combination with assignments from *Basic Marketing,* exercises from the *Learning Aid for Use with Basic Marketing,* or *The Marketing Game!* micro-computer strategy simulation.

All of the articles are reproduced here in basically the same style and format as they originally appeared. This gives the reader a better sense of the popular business publications from which they are drawn, and stimulates an interest in ongoing learning beyond the time frame for a specific course.

We have added this component to our complete set of **P**rofessional **L**earning **U**nits **S**ystems (our **P.L.U.S.**) to provide even more alternatives for effective teaching and learning in the first marketing course. It has been an interesting job to research and select the readings for this new book, and we hope that our readers find it of value in developing a better understanding of the opportunities and challenges of marketing in our contemporary society.

William D. Perreault, Jr. and E. Jerome McCarthy

Acknowledgments

We would like to thank all of the publications that have granted us permission to reprint the articles in this book. Similarly, we value and appreciate the work and skill of the many writers who prepared the original materials.

Linda G. Davis played an important role in this project. She helped us research thousands of different publications to sort down to the final set, and she also contributed many fine ideas on how best to organize the selections that appear here.

The ideas for this book evolved from and built on previous editions of *Readings and Cases in Basic Marketing*. John F. Grashof and Andrew A. Brogowicz were coauthors of that book. We gratefully recognize the expertise and creativity that they shared over the years on that project. Their fine ideas carry forward here and have had a profound effect on our thinking in selecting articles that will meet the needs of marketing instructors and students alike.

We would also like to thank the many marketing professors and students whose input have helped shape the concept of this book. Their ideas—shared in personal conversations, in focus group interviews, and in responses to marketing research surveys—helped us to clearly define the needs that this book should meet.

Finally, we would like to thank the people at McGraw-Hill/Irwin, our publisher, who have helped turn this idea into a reality. We are grateful for their commitment to making these materials widely available.

W.D.P. and E.J.M.

Contents

Marketing's Role in the Global Economy and in the Firm

Brazil Cultivates a Spot in Gourmet-Coffee Market

Growers and Foreign Roasters Team Up in Arduous Effort To Brew a Better Blend

By Miriam Jordan

Staff Reporter of The Wall Street Journal

PATROCINIO, Brazil—For decades, Brazil, the world's largest coffee producer, wasn't even on the map for coffee connoisseurs. Among gourmet roasters, Brazilian growers were known for being more concerned with pounds than purity, often adulterating their crops with dust or cornmeal. Brazil was pigeonholed as a supplier of filler coffee for mediocre blends.

"There wasn't coffee in Brazil that Starbucks was interested in buying," says Mary Williams, a buyer for **Starbucks** Corp. in Seattle.

But now, thanks to an arduous campaign by Brazilian producers and international coffee marketers, Brazilian brews are carving out a growing niche in the gourmet market. Italian espresso maker **Illycaffe** SpA, arguably the most fastidious coffee buyer in the world, has tripled imports from Brazil in the past decade after it started helping growers improve their crops. Starbucks has for the first time added a Brazilian variety, Bourbon (pronounced bur-BONE) to a special plantation line, and is buying up other varieties as well. "The quality of Brazilian coffee is getting better all the time," says Ms. Williams.

This year, Brazil expects gourmet-coffee exports, which fetch up to 30% more than regular coffee, to double. While specialty coffee accounts for only a fraction of all Brazilian exports, the segment is growing fast. In December, foreign buyers snapped up every last bean offered by Brazil in its second gourmet-coffee Internet auction, about 230,000 pounds. At a time when coffee prices are at a seven-year low of around 65 cents a pound, the average auction price was $1.38, and the highest price was $3.04. "Absolutely amazing," says Roland Veit, a U.S. importer in White Plains, N.Y., who observed the auction.

Traditionally, Brazilian beans didn't have the cachet of those from Central America, Colombia and some African countries. "For a long time, the market told us 'We want cheap coffee' and that's what we delivered," says Marcelo Vieira, president of the industry trade group Brazilian Specialty Coffee Association. "Today, the message is 'We need quality.' So we're being re-educated."

That re-education began in the early 1990s. The London-based International Coffee Organization, which had guaranteed high prices, ceased to control the global trade after some members sought a free market. Competition from new, low-cost producers, such as Vietnam, changed the global game. In the face of falling prices, a small band of Brazilian producers figured the best way to ensure a good price in the long term was to invest in quality. Then gourmet roasters looking to develop new markets, such as Starbucks and Illycaffe, took an interest in Brazil—unique for having a multitude of bean varieties, industrial infrastructure and scientific expertise. "Brazil has all the elements in the coffee chain," says Maro Sondahl, a Mt. Laurel, N.J., coffee consultant. "Now it's lining them up to make quality coffee."

For instance, a major grower of Arabica coffee, Brazil processes most of its beans as "naturals," or sun-dried, which yields the sweetest, full-body black beverage. But its farmers are also perfecting production of semi-washed or "pulped naturals," where the coffee is peeled and soaked before it's dried. This produces a more mild coffee that suits the palate of Americans.

One of the pioneers of the quality movement in Brazil was Ernesto Illy, nicknamed the espresso evangelist by many coffee aficionados. For the past 10 years, representatives of the family-owned Illycaffe of Trieste, Italy, have scoured Brazilian coffee plantations in the states of Sao Paulo, Minas Gerais and Parana in search of the perfect Arabica bean. Today, several Brazilian farms supply Illycaffe with sun-dried beans capable of delivering an espresso with "just the right body and foam on the top," says Mr. Illy. "It should be naturally sweet and not too bitter."

During a recent visit to three farms in the highlands of Minas Gerais, a southeastern state where the coffee bushes grow thick and seven-feet high, Mr. Illy stops at a warehouse filled with jute sacks of export-quality green coffee. He cups some beans in his hands and raises them to his nose. It takes 55 beans to make one cup of espresso. But, "it takes only one bad bean to spoil the cup," declares the 75-year-old Mr. Illy, Illycaffe's chairman.

Illycaffe gets about 20% of its Brazilian coffee from the farms in Patrocinio owned by **DaTerra Atividades Rurais** Ltda., and works closely with plantation managers. Its experts visit farms and give advice on planting and processing techniques. To further coach producers, Illycaffe founded the University of Coffee with the University of Sao Paulo. It offers courses on coffee planting, processing and marketing.

Rainfall, temperature and soil-quality are important to the development of a coffee tree. But every stage, from cultivating and harvesting to processing and storage, must be carefully monitored. To dry coffee evenly, it must be spread thinly over a patio the size of a football field and raked several times a day under the sun. Only after scrutinizing bean samples in its Trieste laboratories does Illycaffe decide whether to buy an entire lot. "We never know exactly how much Illy will buy from us," says DaTerra manager Leopoldo Ribeiro Santana. "We have to keep improving every stage of coffee production to keep them happy."

The biggest motivation for growers is the premium Illycaffe pays for the coffee, as much as 30% above market price.

Another motivator is an annual contest for the best Brazilian beans, dubbed the Oscars of coffee, that Illycaffe began in 1990. This year, 619 farms sent samples to Italy. The company paid the winning plantation $30,000, offered cash prizes to nine runnersup and bought the entire crop of the top 50 contestants at a premium. As a result, growers are aware of the potential of their production, giving priority to quality rather than quantity.

Starbucks discovered Brazilian coffee in 1997 on Ipanema Farm in southern Minas Gerais. For two years, the company sampled the farm's Bourbon, a mild coffee with a slight cocoa flavor and a nutty aftertaste, in a few stores. "We were extremely pleased and quite surprised at how quickly customers took to this coffee," says Ms. Williams, the buyer.

Last year, Ipanema Farm signed a contract with Starbucks committing its entire Bourbon crop for five years to the chain. Brazil Ipanema Bourbon is now one of four exclusive, pure coffees offered by Starbucks, alongside varieties from Colombia, Costa Rica and Panama. Usually, Bourbon sells out within two months of arriving at Starbucks stores in January. Encouraged by this response, Starbucks is buying other Brazilian coffees for its blends.

"Starbucks opened new markets for us," says Washington Luiz Alves Rodrigues, director of Ipanema Farm. "We ascended to an international-class of suppliers." Ipanema now also sells to Tchibo, a German coffee-bar chain, and Intermarche, a French supermarket chain.

International roasters' interest in Brazil has enhanced coffee's appeal at home, too. Coffee consumption in Brazil—the second-largest coffee-drinking nation in the world, after the U.S.—has more than doubled in the past decade. Coffee bars are flourishing in the country's largest cities, serving homegrown specialty blends. Illycaffe says its sales have grown exponentially here, and Ipanema Farm has signed agreements to supply several boutique coffee shops and top-drawer restaurants, as well as an upscale housewares retailer. In supermarkets, the trade group Brazilian Association of Coffee Industries, is launching an initiative to label coffee according to flavor, body and aroma and region.

"The world is starting to see Brazil as a quality-coffee producer," says Nelson Carvalhaes, a Brazilian exporter. "Now Brazilians are believing in their coffee, too."

Dell Cracks China

No way, the skeptics scoffed, could Dell take its all-American model to China. So why is it being imitated? ■ *by Neel Chowdhury*

It's a wet morning in old Shanghai, and Dell salesman Peter Chan is selling hard. As the Yangtze River flows by the Bund district a few floors below, Chan is getting into a flow of his own. His subject: computers and the unique benefits of Dell's direct-selling model. His customer: Xiao Jian Yi, deputy general manager of China Pacific Insurance, a fast-growing state-owned insurance company. The audience: three of Xiao's subordinates.

China Pacific, a potentially big account, is in the process of computerizing its entire billing system. It already has about 400 desktops and about 70 servers, mainly from IBM and Hewlett-Packard. But Xiao needs more hardware. Much more.

Though Xiao's sleep-heavy eyes suggest he's heard it all before, Chan excitedly says that "direct selling" means China Pacific can order PCs directly through the Internet, the telephone, or salesmen like himself. At the mention of the Internet, still a rare marketing tool in China, the fustily dressed bureaucrat visibly perks up.

Chan goes on to explain that direct selling not only eliminates middlemen—saving Xiao and China Pacific a chunk of change—but also means that Dell can build China Pacific's computers to the firm's exact requirements, from the hardware on the outside to the software on the inside. A murmur of approval ripples through Xiao's subordinates. By the time Chan finishes with a description of Dell's convenient after-sales service, the rain has stopped and Xiao is smiling. "All salesmen from computer companies are aggressive," he says. Then Xiao whispers to FORTUNE: "But the Dell guys are even more aggressive."

That aggressiveness is beginning to pay off. Not only did Dell reel in the China Pacific account, but it is well on its way to becoming a major player in China. Last August, 34-year-old billionaire Michael Dell opened the fourth Dell PC factory in the world in Xiamen, a windswept city halfway between Hong Kong and Shanghai on China's southeastern coast. The point of Dell's push into China seems so obvious as to be a cliche: China is becoming too big a PC market for Dell, or anyone, to ignore. "If we're not in

what will soon be the second-biggest PC market in the world," asks John Legere, president of Dell Asia-Pacific, "then how can Dell possibly be a global player?"

China is already the fifth-largest PC market, behind the U.S., Japan, Germany, and Britain. But if PC shipments in China continue to grow at an average annual rate of 30%—as they have over the past three years—China's PC market will surpass Japan's in only five years. Not even the Asian crisis has slowed down this growth. While crisis-wracked Asian markets like South Korea saw a 46% decline in PC shipments in 1997-98, for example, PC shipments to China surged 48%.

Though the competition is intense, Dell is confident it has a strategy that will pay off. First, it has decided not to target retail buyers, who account for only about 10% of Dell's China sales. That way Dell avoids going head to head against entrenched local market leaders like Legend. "It takes nearly two years of a person's savings to buy a PC in China," notes Mary Ma, the chief financial officer of Legend. "And when two years of savings is at stake, the whole family wants to come out to a store to touch and try the machine." Dell just isn't set up to make that kind of sale yet.

Instead, the company thinks it can make big inroads by selling directly to corporations. Established American PC makers in China—Hewlett-Packard, IBM, and Compaq—depend largely on resellers. Because of the cost savings derived from cutting out the middleman, Dell believes it can sell computers at lower prices than its competitors can—and thus steal market share. Already the gambit seems to be working: At the end of last year Dell's market share tripled to 1.2%, while Compaq's fell from 3.5% to 2.7%.

The outlook wasn't always so rosy. When Dell set up its first Asian factory in Malaysia in 1996, there were serious doubts as to whether its direct-selling model would work. Skeptics fretted that Asia's low Internet penetration and the value Asians put on personal relationships with distributors would punish the Dell model. But in practice Dell has managed to pump up sales during one of Asia's worst economic crises. That has silenced

most of the critics.

In fact, the direct-selling model has almost certainly been a boon, not a barrier, to Dell's plans. "With low-priced, entry-level PCs shaving traditional profit margins, the direct-order model is gaining popularity across Asia," says Archana Gidwani, an analyst with the Gartner Group in Singapore. She figures that starting in 1998, direct sellers like Dell saw shipments in Asia jump 15%, while Hewlett-Packard, IBM, Compaq, and other PC makers that go through resellers saw shipments decline 3%. And she expects 40% of Asia's PC shipments to be ordered directly this year, up from roughly 30% last year. "Dell," she concludes, "is changing the way computers are being sold in Asia."

Though Dell started shipping computers in China only last August, it has already risen to become the country's eighth-largest PC maker; quarter-on-quarter sales are growing 50% on average, admittedly from a very low base. Dell will not say if its operations there are profitable yet.

More impressive is the fact that Dell is starting to rattle Chinese PC makers like Legend and Founder by nibbling into their most valuable client base: state-owned enterprises. These bureaucratic behemoths may seem an odd fit with Dell's fast-as-lightning direct model, but somehow it works. Two-thirds of Dell's corporate customers in China are state-owned enterprises, up from next to none ten months ago. The rest of Dell's customers are multinationals like Ericsson, Nortel, Motorola, and Ford. Dell hopes to keep signing up more Chinese companies—not easy, given the price-slashing tactics of the small shops that sell cheap PCs with bootlegged software. But if it does, then Dell will do something few U.S. companies in China ever manage to do: turn a profit without investing a fortune in manufacturing and without sharing the booty with a Chinese partner or middleman.

Why is Dell's direct model winning in China? First, look at the way Dell is selling to the Chinese. Shredding the myth that to sell in China requires padding the egos (and wallets) of capricious bureaucrats—usually during long and boring banquets—Dell is winning over the chief information officers of state-owned companies the American way: with speed, convenience, and service. "We don't have to change the formula," insists Dell salesman Peter Chan. "It will work in the U.S, China, India, or even in space."

At the heart of that "formula" is the simple tenet that the customer knows best. When Dell's Chan pauses for breath after his sales pitch at China Pacific, for example, the newly awakened Xiao peppers him with questions. How quickly will the computers arrive? Can Excel be loaded onto the hard drive? What kind of service does Dell offer? And, ahem, how much?

What is powerfully clear is that Xiao knows computers. He knows what he needs from Dell. He knows how much he wants to pay. Critically, Xiao knows enough that he does not need to see or touch the machine, or even raise a few glasses of Tsingtao beer with a honey-tongued distributor, before he orders it. All Xiao needs is a phone or, better yet, an Internet connection, to buy what he needs.

Such tech savviness and straightforwardness is increasingly common in China, and that is a terrific advantage for Dell, whose biggest perceived shortcoming was that it lacked the kind of service network that Hewlett-Packard or IBM has. These service networks can provide companies like China Pacific with technical advice and long-term system consultancy. But as Xiao makes clear, Chinese managers are growing more and more tech savvy on their own. They simply don't need that kind of babysitting—and they don't want to pay for it. "We may still need some consulting services, but in our front offices we know how to choose our equipment," says Xiao. "Dell provides exactly what we need, and with Dell we can choose exactly what we want."

In response, IBM, Hewlett-Packard, and other PC makers are changing tactics. Says Dennis Mark, Hewlett-Packard's computer-marketing director in Asia: "We're doing less with smaller local companies and focusing our resources more on big nationwide technology projects." For now, that gives Dell a clean shot at the low end of the PC market. But down the line Dell too may want to go after bigger, more complex sales. At that point competitors like Hewlett-Packard and IBM will have a considerable head start.

In the meantime, Dell will have its hands full in the direct-sales market. Chinese Internet use is spreading like a brushfire. Between 1997 and 1998, according to technical consultants at International Data Corp., the number of Internet users in China jumped 71%, to more than two million. But so far Dell sells

---

We're No. 8!

After only ten months in China, Dell has reached No. 8 in PC shipments.

1. **Legend**
2. **IBM**
3. **Hewlett-Packard**
4. **Founder**
5. **Compaq**
6. **Great Wall**
7. **Toshiba**
8. **Dell**
9. **NEC Japan**
10. **Acer**

FORTUNE TABLE/SOURCE: IDC PC ASIADAT BULLETIN

---

only 5% of its PCs in China through the Net, compared with 25% worldwide. Dell's telephone sales also represent just a small percentage of its total, even though the company advertises aggressively on billboards. Part of the problem is that the Chinese are uncomfortable with credit card sales.

For now, however, Dell's going to have to invest more time and money in door-to-door sales calls to Chinese companies than it might like. For example, Dell's two dozen or so young, gung ho salesmen in Shanghai usually make three to four sales calls a day and spend roughly one-third of their time on the road. Not an easy life, but they are well rewarded for it. Dell will not tell how much they make, but says its sales staff in China is paid salaries and commissions commensurate with those paid in Hong Kong and the U.S. That's expensive, and until China catches up to the West in terms of Internet penetration and credit card use, those costs will take a tidy chunk out of Dell's earnings.

To offset its higher-than-expected marketing costs, Dell is cutting out fat and boosting operational efficiency at its Xiamen plant. In fact, Dell's modest manufacturing operations are a paragon of financial restraint in a country like China, where land and equipment costs can spiral out of control.

In Xiamen the operation is lean and smart. The entire assembly process employs only about 200 workers and is housed in a modest, airy room about the size of a high school gym. Workers scrutinize sales sheets detail-

ing the hardware and software specs of each computer, which is then built according to the buyer's taste (luckily for Microsoft, the Chinese version of Word for Windows is the leading software request).

After the "fully loaded" computer rolls off the line, it goes to Xiamen's sleek and spacious airport to be flown to wherever the customer is located. In China the time it takes for a Dell PC to reach a customer, from order to delivery, is nine days, about the same as in the U.S. "We're leading the entire Dell world in terms of keeping to our promised delivery date," boasts David Chan, president of Dell China.

Behind that boast, of course, is China's increasingly impressive infrastructure of roads, airports, and ports. Belying those horror stories of endless paperwork slowing the traffic of goods or bad phones or potholed roads, most of urban China is relatively well linked. Bureaucratic bottlenecks do arise from time to time, but Dell's just-in-time model is probably easier to execute in China than it would be in, say, the Philippines or India.

Getting the PC to the customer quickly also saves Dell a ton of cash. Because its just-in-time model forces Dell to keep its inventory levels low—about six days' worth of supply, compared with 40 for Chinese PC leader Legend—Dell saves time and money that would otherwise be wasted on warehousing. Shorter inventory cycles also give Dell a greater degree of control over price and profitability than its Chinese competitors have. "The sub-$1,000 PC has been driven by Chinese distributors who have to move obsolete products that have been lying around their warehouses," argues Dell's Legere. "We'll never be driven by those factors, because our inventory cycles in China are so short."

Also greasing the efficiency of Dell in China is money, or to be more precise, stock options. David Chan says the options scheme is meant to "instill a sense of ownership," but most Chinese workers are likelier to see a direct link between their output and the stock price—which is, after all, not a bad way to look at it. Around August every employee in Xiamen got roughly 200 shares of Dell, back when its stock was trading near $60. Three months later Dell's shares had shot up to $110, giving each employee a paper gain of about $10,000. That equals roughly one year's salary for the average Xiamen worker. "Then it dawned on me that they had no idea of the value of the paper in their hands," says Chan. After the worth of the options was explained at a workers' meeting, Chan noticed an uptick in productivity: "They were good before. Now they're better."

So what can go wrong? To some extent, Dell has had to deal with the traditional bugbears of factory life in China: idleness and corruption. The concept of a job for life, though no longer a guarantee in today's China, still attracts workers who expect to spend hours drinking tea or reading the papers on the factory floor—and keep their jobs. Dell China executives acknowledge that at first a little "reeducation" was necessary in Xiamen so that workers understood that their jobs depended on their performance.

Corruption has been a trickier issue. Though Dell vehemently denies that it has ever paid a bribe to get a license or a sales order, David Chan admits he had to "terminate" two Chinese employees suspected of corruption. It's no coincidence, either, that Dell's top salesmen in China are not mainland Chinese but predominantly Overseas Chinese from Hong Kong or Singapore, where the sales culture is defined more by doggedness than by personal favors. Peter Chan, for example, is from Hong Kong.

The company must also grapple with the problem of software piracy. Microsoft estimates that over 95% of the software in use in Chinese corporations is stolen. In fact, setting up a factory in China was Dell's defense against pirates. Concerned that pirates would load bad software onto its machines, ruining its reputation, Dell now controls the process from beginning to end. That quality control is a relief to Dell, its customers, and Microsoft, which collects its Dell-related revenue reliably. But quality costs: No matter how frugal Dell's operations, it cannot compete on price with the small job shops that sell knockoff PCs equipped with bootleg software. Dell computers sell for about the same as in the U.S.—$1,200 to $1,500 each, depending on what is loaded.

Dell's biggest problem, though, is a product of its success: Because the Dell direct model is so simple, it can be copied. And that's just what Legend is doing. "Yes, we're using Dell's direct-selling model when we target Chinese government companies or multinationals in China," admits Mary Ma. For a start, Legend is aping Dell's cash-management model, reducing the time it takes to get payment from its distributors by half, to 30 days. It is also rapidly moving toward Dell's just-in-time delivery model, trying to sell directly to its corporate customers and shaving excess inventory. It is even offering stock options to employees. All these copycat moves will make Legend a more formidable company and should therefore have Dell worrying.

Another cause for concern is China's often nationalistic politics, which can quickly turn against U.S. corporations. Consider, for example, the rash of anti-American demonstrations that swept across China after NATO's accidental bombing of the Chinese embassy in Belgrade in mid-May. Not only were U.S. embassies pelted with eggs and stones, but so were Nike and McDonald's outlets. Given the billions at stake in the telecom and PC markets in China, high-profile U.S. companies like Motorola or Dell could be vulnerable to the ups and downs in Sino-American relations, though retail outlets, not tech factories, seem to be bearing the brunt of patriotic dudgeon so far. "It's not a given for U.S. companies, especially information technology companies, to come into China and grab the entire market," warns Dong Tao of Credit Suisse First Boston Securities in Hong Kong. "The Chinese government has made no secret of the fact that it wants to promote national industries like IT."

Where will Dell be in China five years from now? It will probably never be the No. 1 PC maker in China, or even No. 2, slots that are likely to be occupied by local manufacturers, which will always be able to sell more cheaply to China's masses. Ironically, that seems to suit Dell just fine. Grabbing market share, in the U.S., China, or anywhere else, has never been its highest priority. Profits are. Says John Legere of the estimated $25 billion in revenue that computer sales will generate in China by 2002: "Even if we get 1% of $25 billion, that's a lot. You don't need to be the market leader in China to be profitable."

One thing's for sure: The Dell model is working in China. And as long as China's PC market continues to grow, Dell is ready to grow with it—provided it sticks to that model and continues to execute it better than anyone else.

Innovators Or Copycats? Wal-Mart, Schwab, Southwest Air Were Both

By Marilyn Much
Investor's Business Daily

A few years after Sam Walton opened his first Wal-Mart Discount City, Herb Kelleher began sketching a plan for an airline based on the same concepts: low prices and good service.

Though the two didn't become friends until later, they were kindred spirits. Both came up with huge winners by improving existing models.

The late Walton copied the layout and pricing at Kmart. Kelleher's Southwest Airlines was built on the model of short-haul carrier Pacific Southwest Airlines.

Many great businesses followed similar paths: They were innovators, not inventors. They took existing models and changed them to meet new needs, serve new markets and please customers.

Some key points emerge from a look at such companies:

■ **Liberate customers from models that don't serve them well.**

Charles Schwab didn't invent the discount broker when he started Schwab Corp. in 1974. But doing business solely over the phone wouldn't do. So he opened branches without pushy salesmen.

He sold the firm as a neutral party and took an early lead with fast execution through technology.

"Rather than continue to let the power stay with the brokers, Schwab came up with a standard that put consumers in charge of their own portfolios," said Thomas Kuczmarski, an innovation consultant who works with Schwab.

■ **Analyze the market leaders.**

The best student of Kmart may have been Walton. With a legal pad and tape recorder, he spent days talking to clerks and poking around.

Later, Wal-Mart would do the same at Price Club before launching its own Sam's membership stores.

Walton liked Kmart's model, but didn't want to go head-to-head. To succeed in small towns where Kmart couldn't, he tackled the supply chain so that his stores could make money in smaller markets.

For 25 straight years, Wal-Mart ranked No. 1 in its field for the lowest ratio of expenses to sales.

■ **Think geographically.**

Like Walton, Kelleher and Southwest co-founder Rollin King went for an underserved market. Their idea was to create a cut-rate, short-haul airline to serve Houston, Dallas and San Antonio. Routes and fares weren't regulated. There was no competition.

"There's a geographic dimension to innovation," said Pankaj Ghemawat, a Harvard Business School professor who's studied Wal-Mart and Southwest. "If a model is working well…the argument is for imitating that and applying it to your geography."

"But if your market is being attacked by an existing player, using their business model isn't a good idea unless you have the natural advantage. That's the time to invent."

■ **If a standard works, don't try to change it.**

In 1982, Red Canion, Bill Nutro and Jim Harris founded Compaq Computer. Venture capitalist Ben Rosen joined later.

Others tried to come up with a standard. Compaq copied IBM.

"It would have been a fool's game to invent a new standard," said Adrian Ryans, marketing professor at the Richard Ivey School of Business at Western Ontario University. "Compaq was a start-up without a lot of resources, and there was a lot of confusion in the market."

Compaq sold only to stores and didn't take on the IBM salesmen who called on corporations.

"It gave a powerful momentum for dealers to push Compaq's products, because they weren't competing with a direct sales force as they were with IBM," Ryans said.

Compaq also embraced new technology faster than IBM. In 1986, it was the first to use Intel's i386 chip.

■ **Tackle costs to improve the existing model.**

Both Southwest and Wal-Mart are famous for their assault on costs.

On its first flights in 1971, Southwest's one-way fare was $20 vs. an average $60 for similar flights elsewhere. Today its average fare of $85 compares with the industry's $300-plus, CFO Gary Kelly says.

To get costs down, Kelleher and King knew they had to keep planes flying and generating fares.

> **"A** lot of the innovation came from necessity and the struggle to survive. Competition always makes you better, and in this case it was brutal. They tried to kill the airline and prevent it from getting off the ground."
>
> **—Gary Kelly**
> CFO, Southwest Airlines

Planes had to be reloaded and in the air in 15 minutes vs. the average of 45. In 1973, when they had to sell one of their four planes to raise cash, they cut the turnaround time to 10 minutes. The model they used: pit stops at the Indy 500.

They saved ground time by serving only nuts and using small airports with less traffic.

To drive traffic in slow times, Southwest created peak and off-peak fares. Ticketless flights landed in 1995. Also, Southwest flies only Boeing 737s. Any pilot can fly any plane. Any mechanic can fix it.

Southwest's operating costs are half those of other majors. Its cost to fly one seat one mile is 7 to 7.5 cents vs. 15 or 20 cents for its rivals. It still gets planes up fast—in 20 to 25 minutes. While rivals take heat for poor food and delays, Southwest wins service awards.

Walton's strides in logistics were key. He built stores within a day's drive of a warehouse.

And he was the first major retailer to computerize. Replenishment began at the register. Reorders were sent via satellite. He integrated every step from stock control to checkout.

That data edge let him tailor goods and prices to local markets, lifting volume and inventory turns.

Lost in the Shuffle

As the Telecoms Merge And Cut Costs, Service Is Often a Casualty

One Client's Internet Access Fails—Right After Lines To Its Call Center Go Out

A Bill, but No Repairman

BY REBECCA BLUMENSTEIN AND
STEPHANIE N. MEHTA
Staff Reports of THE WALL STREET JOURNAL

Torrid consolidation in telecom has created soaring stocks, sprawling empires and ever-advancing technology.

Then there's customer service.

One day last summer, the phones stopped working at the national reservations center of LOT Polish Airlines in New York's Queens borough. The airline called the phone company's problem line at about 9 a.m. Eleven hours later, after the reservations center had closed for the day, a repairman arrived. Before all was fixed, the center was without phone service for 33 hours.

Bell Atlantic Corp., which had taken over the service area after merging with Nynex Corp., and which is now merging with GTE Corp., says it followed procedure: It had to check that the problem wasn't in one of its switching facilities before dispatching a technician. Bruce Gordon, group president for Bell Atlantic's Enterprise business unit, says business-customer satisfaction is up since its merger with Nynex.

OK, these glitches happen. But just a few weeks later, Polish Airlines lost its Internet service, too. This time the provider was MCI WorldCom Inc., which, in the wake of one of the 65 mergers that have built it into a colossus, had agreed to sell its Internet "backbone" to another company. Unfortunately, MCI WorldCom neglected to make the transfer, sending the airline and some other business customers into cyberspace limbo.

'Making It a Mess'

A solution was offered, though, to the airline's telecom chief, Jeff Kilpatrick: Just buy an Internet service contract from yet another company with which MCI WorldCom had done a deal.

"MCI WorldCom is one company, but when you get down to the nitty-gritty of who runs things, mergers are making it a mess," Mr. Kilpatrick says. "These telecom companies are killing us. One domino falls and everything falls apart."

MCI WorldCom won't comment on the Internet incident, citing a lawsuit it faces over the matter from the company the accounts were supposed to be transferred to, Britain's Cable & Wireless PLC.

During the past three years, mergers and acquisitions valued at more than $500 billion have rearranged the telecommunications landscape. Phone companies say the corporate customers ultimately benefit: The mergers bring them the latest technology and provide one-stop shopping at the lowest possible prices.

But acquisitions also usually mean layoffs and other cutbacks as companies squeeze costs out of their newly acquired business. Customer-service centers, often seen as overlapping, are among the first operations to be pared. "The morale at the company that is being acquired immediately goes down. Everyone starts throwing their resume around," says Casey Letizia, communications manager for one business customer, Credit Guard of America in Fort Lauderdale, Fla. "At that point, we are orphans."

Business customers can find themselves shuttled between account managers or forced to make multiple phone calls to find someone who can solve their problems. Sometimes the human touch is almost completely lost. AT&T Corp. recently installed an online system that compels many of its business customers to report problems via the Internet.

Rick Roscitt, president of AT&T's Business Services unit, acknowledges that some businesses have expressed concern but says the move saves money and is part of the business evolution toward using the Internet. "We are choosing to keep service levels as high as we possibly can while we take the costs out," Mr. Roscitt says. "AT&T is now an e-enabled company."

It wasn't always like this. Before the consolidation frenzy, client representatives were assigned to take special, goldplated care of business customers. Of course, things were simpler then; one phone company provided local and long-distance calling, and few customers needed special systems for moving bits of data around the country.

And prices were higher. Thanks to competition, the prices on services such as long-distance calling have fallen. "If you are going to charge a nickel, you cannot keep the same cost structure as you did when you were charging 20 to 30 cents a minute," Mr. Roscitt notes.

To keep up with the competition—and to please an increasingly fickle Wall Street—phone companies are cutting fat, automating functions that humans used to provide, and abandoning white-glove services. "That's the old way," says William T. Esrey, chief executive officer of Sprint Corp., which has agreed to merge with MCI WorldCom. "If you do that, you don't get the cost down, and you don't get the ticket to play."

In slashing costs, telecommunications is doing what practically every other business is doing. But in some other businesses—say, a retail store or bank—the customers can manage by themselves if there are fewer people around to help. In the technical world of telecom, a customer without good customer service is helpless.

One reason the merger frenzy makes it harder to deliver good customer service is that companies that are combining don't always communicate with each other. Consider the case of a New York customer called Speedpay Inc. It contracted to get service from Teleport Communications Group, or TCG, a competitive local telephone company. But AT&T acquired that provider in 1998. Speedpay officials claim that since then, AT&T has disavowed responsibility for repairing the line but wants to be paid for it just the same.

Jeff Kilpatrick

"TCG was merged into AT&T, and AT&T is treating it as a separate company," says Darren Manelski, Speedpay's CEO. "Service has become a huge bureaucracy, and the customer is expected to navigate the bureaucracy without a roadmap."

AT&T says it can't discuss confidential customer accounts. But a spokesman, Don Ferenci, says the company tries to provide top service at the best value and adds: "Any company that cares about its customers wouldn't ask them to pay for service they didn't receive."

As the phone companies merge, they have to combine complex networks that often use different equipment and technologies. MCI WorldCom has built an extensive data network through its acquisitions. When the network failed earlier this year, in an outage unrelated to the one that crippled Polish Airlines, the problem shut down numerous bank

(Cont.)

ATMs and paralyzed hundreds of businesses, including the Chicago Board of Trade. Full service wasn't restored for two weeks. "They've gotten so big that they think they don't have to deal with customers like us," says the Board of Trade's CEO, Thomas R. Donovan.

Far from it, reply MCI WorldCom executives, who say the mergers have enabled them to offer customers more services and the latest technology. MCI's status as the fastest-growing company in the industry "speaks volumes about our capability of giving quality service," says CEO Bernard J. Ebbers. He also says the outage "had nothing to do with the merger" between MCI and WorldCom. "We do have hiccups every once in a while. I think most people in business do."

Series of Takeovers

But some of the relationships created by mergers can be vexingly complex. The Board of Trade, for example, picked a company called MFS Communications to handle its telecommunications needs, in part because the small firm was eager to provide red-carpet service. But MFS was taken over by World-Com in 1996. MFS used to guarantee that in an outage, it would restore service to essential lines in about 25 minutes. MCI WorldCom needs an hour, the Board of Trade says.

WorldCom closed an MFS customer-service center in Omaha, Neb., deciding its own center in San Antonio could handle the calls, according to a former MFS manager, who adds that only a small percentage of MFS customer-service people and techicians agreed to move to San Antonio. The former manager says that because customer records were on a couple of different computer systems, service representatives now needed to pull up multiple records, often on different terminals, sometimes leaving the customer on hold for extended periods.

When the Board of Trade outage occurred, MCI WorldCom's Mr. Ebbers blamed it on Lucent Technologies Inc., the equipment maker. Again, a series of mergers shows up as a likely suspect. The faulty software that created the mess had been developed by Cascade Communications Corp., a small company that was later acquired by Ascend Communications Inc.—before Lucent, in turn, acquired Ascend.

The president of Lucent's data networking group, Curtis Sanford, says Lucent is "comfortable that we've worked through any issues that we had with MCI WorldCom."

Bigger Workload

The issues in MCI's sale of its Internet backbone to London's Cable & Wireless are far from resolved. MCI, then in the midst of closing its WorldCom deal, failed to deliver contracts for 3,300 corporate customers on the backbone, according to Cable & Wireless, which is suing MCI; Cable & Wireless also says that of 300 employees who were supposed to help it with sales and customer service, only 50 made the transition.

Sales agents who normally handled five or seven customer accounts were saddled with 500, Cable & Wireless says. It adds that it finally got about 2,000 of the customer contracts—in six different boxes, seven months after the sale closed. "The customers were put through a very difficult time," says Michael McTighe, CEO of global operations for Cable & Wireless. MCI won't comment on the dispute.

Customers' telecom officers often have the impression that the quality of service declines every time one of their providers is involved in a merger. Among those voicing that view is Chris Miller, telecom manager at United Catalysts Inc. in Louisville, Ky., who says that merging companies "talk about synergies, but that is just a bunch of stuff that they say for the stockholders." United Catalysts is among a group of businesses opposing the pending MCI WorldCom takeover of Sprint, because "if they take away Sprint as another option, customer service will just get worse."

Sprint's Mr. Esrey believes things will be different this time. In the wake of World-Com's 1998 acquisition of MCI, officials at the two companies were deeply suspicious of each other, he says: "There was a lot of animosity right from the start, and a lot of infighting in terms of getting things started." But Mr. Esrey says he has studied the mistakes that were made in the integration of those companies in an attempt not to repeat them, adding that avoiding them will be easier because the MCI-Sprint deal is amicable. "Customer service has been ingrained and is part of what we are," he says.

Trying to Get Through

For telecommunications customers, a service glitch is bad enough, but what really annoys them is not being able to talk to anyone about it. Michael Curcio, telecom manager of Western Dental Services Inc. in Orange, Calif., says that was the problem he had with long-distance provider Qwest Communications International Inc. He was so exasperated he finally switched to a different provider.

Not only did Western Dental have to wait months before Qwest provided data-transmission lines to link its 133 offices throughout Southern California and Arizona, Mr. Curcio says, but when it did, hundreds of calls each week were diverted to the wrong numbers. Mr. Curcio tried to call for help.

"I have an account rep to call, and her voice mail says she is out and to call their 800-number," he says. But "their 800-number tells me I have to call the account rep. I don't get any response at all. I can't even report the problem because they keep sending me back to our account rep."

Qwest says Mr. Curcio should have been able to get service from the 800-number and acknowledges some delays in meeting orders in high-demand areas such as California. The company says it is committing significant resources to improving customer service as it integrates operations with a merger partner, U S West Inc.

Still, customer-service woes are now so pervasive in the telecom business that a cottage industry has sprung up to help corporations weed through their bills and services. "The clients do not know who to call for service," says one of these consultants, Bob Morrison of Thousand Oaks, Calif. "And even when they are assigned an account team, these people churn and move on. Everything is in a disarray with these mergers."

Sales smarts rule Internet

Pocket protectors are out, marketing skills are in at tech start-ups

By Greg Farrell
USA TODAY

Forget the geeks and finance people: Marketers are the new rock stars of the Internet. Consider the case of Karen Edwards.

Five years ago, Edwards, a 32-year-old executive with a Harvard MBA, desperately wanted to join an Internet company as head of marketing. She got turned down everywhere for the same reason: She didn't know enough about technology.

Finally, she landed a job, as employee No. 17 at start-up Yahoo. At a time when dot-com companies didn't realize the importance of advertising, she led the way, transforming the search engine with the quirky name into one of the most recognized brands of the Internet economy.

Edwards says that if she were in the same spot with the same resume today as five years ago, she'd have a different problem finding work: "With the marketing background I had then, I wouldn't get my job today. No way!"

So it goes in the wacky world of the Internet economy, where technology smarts and financial acumen are still important, but not as important as a strong background in marketing. Venture capitalists are now insisting that the management team of a start-up include a marketing heavyweight. The result: Headhunters are combing the ranks of the Fortune 500, looking for men and women who know how to build brands.

These start-ups no longer need geniuses in technology and finance; they need people who can sell soap and soft drinks. Marketers are the new "it" people in Silicon Valley.

"This is an enormous position," says Peter Sealey, former head of marketing at Coca-Cola and now an adjunct professor at the University of California at Berkeley. "Companies that want to be the next eBay or Amazon know it's not the technology: It's the marketing position and strategy."

Five years ago, before the Internet was discovered by Wall Street and Main Street, only a few brave young souls like Edwards left comfortable marketing jobs to take a flier on the Web. Now it's a different story: Executives are leaving the biggest marketing jobs in Corporate America for the chance to build Web-based brands. Here are some recent bigwigs who defected:

▲ John Costello, the former head of marketing at Sears, who did a brief stint at AutoNation, joined MVP.com in December as CEO.

▲ David Ropes bolted his position as director of corporate advertising at Ford Motor in November to become head of marketing at zUniversity.com.

▲ Jim Ritts left his perch as LPGA commissioner last March to join the Digital Entertainment Network, where he's CEO.

▲ Michael Beindorff left the top marketing job at Visa last September to become chief operating officer of PlanetRx.

The Web was such an attractive lure for Beindorff that he turned down a job as head of marketing at McDonald's before joining PlanetRx. Of course, money might have had something to do with that decision. Beindorff joined the Internet company with a generous option package just before it went public in October.

"For marketing people, it's too exciting to say no," Beindorff says. "The money is attractive, but only one in 10 will pay out. The real attraction is the opportunity to take a blank sheet of paper and build a business. This is an opportunity that a traditional company can't offer you. McDonald's is a great company, but I've been there and done that."

William Razzouk, CEO of PlanetRx, knew that bringing a top marketer into his organization would help him build his business and impress Wall Street.

"Mike is a huge believer in brands and in how those brands get developed and made," Razzouk said in an interview at the time. "There's no time to waste here. We've got a chance to win."

"A marketer does add value to a company that's seeking funding," says David Powell, a recruiter in Silicon Valley.

"The CEO needs to know how to run a business. But somewhere in the organization you need to have someone who knows marketing."

The Godfather of all these marketers who have taken the plunge is Bob Pittman, president and COO of America Online, and the designated co-COO of the combined AOL Time Warner. Pittman, who helped launch MTV in the early 1980s, left his job as CEO of Century 21 to join AOL in October of 1996. At the time,

AOL was still in a horse race with other Internet service providers. Pittman's marketing skill helped AOL crush competitors to become the dominant brand in its space and one of the most valuable brands in the world.

Before Pittman came along, "I thought AOL was dead," Sealey says.

At the opposite end of the spectrum are young pioneers like Yahoo's Edwards. In 1995, despite the fact that her resume included stints at Clorox, Chevron and ad agency BBDO, Edwards got the cold shoulder in Silicon Valley.

"When I did encounter people at Cisco, At Home and Netscape, they said, 'You don't have enough technology background,' " she recalls. "Nobody was doing consumer marketing at any other consumer Web site I was visiting."

What's in a name?

Her success at Yahoo taught competitors a lesson: In a world with virtually no barriers to entry, a strong brand is the best defense against competition.

"I clearly believe that a brand is the strongest barrier to entry in anything related to consumer/ technology product or service," Edwards says. "It's not technology, because you can leapfrog that or acquire it. At the end of the day, consumers are loyal to brands, not feature frenzy."

Edwards' success helped establish the importance of branding on the Internet, and drew a flurry of imitators. Other marketers crossed the divide; the pace of dot-com ad spending began to pick up; and now the trickle of marketers from soap companies to cyberspace has become a torrent.

"In the early days of the Internet, the search work was in infrastructure," says Jean Bagileo, a managing partner at Powell's recruiting firm. "The pipeline had to get laid.

"The content thing happened two years in, and now we seem to be in this branding phase. Now half my practice relates to young, emerging e-commerce companies looking for CEOs or vice presidents of marketing."

"I think brands will rule in the new decade," says Costello, the former Sears head marketer who's CEO of MVP.com. "Technology is important, but it's the means to an end. The key to success is building a brand that meets customer needs better than anybody else. I find many of the key components of brand building are similar in the Internet space, but taken to the nth degree. Customers are more demanding; competition is more intense; and speed to market has accelerated dramatically."

"The world is becoming this caldron of choices,"

says Ropes, who left Ford for zUniversity.com. "Because of this proliferation of choices, brands will win the day. Before, marketers and manufacturers had control, but the Web opens up more choices. For the first time in the history of marketing, the consumer is in control."

While many of the new e-commerce marketers were lured by stock options, there is heady appeal in shaping a new company in the new economy.

"Your touch probably doesn't change the trajectory of a Pepsi," says Gary Briggs, who helped launch the Aquafina water brand at Pepsi and who is now chief marketing official at Ourhouse.com. "But here, I have the opportunity to take something that had no definition in the consumer's mind and define it and have fun with it."

"Moving to a big, established firm wasn't as interesting as moving to a category on the verge of everything that's happening," says Len Short, head of advertising and brand management at Charles Schwab. "I wanted to be a part of that revolution."

It's in the budget

Perhaps the most alluring aspect of this brave new world is that these marketers don't have to fight to persuade management to increase the ad budget.

"A lot of this is being driven by the recognition that marketing is an investment," says Jerry Gramaglia, chief marketing officer of E- Trade, whose career included stints at Procter & Gamble, Taco Bell and Sprint. "The irony is that these investors are probably more in tune with the role and potential value of marketing than the guys at General Mills and P&G who wrote the book. They're still looking at marketing as a cost and a maintenance."

When Beindorff spoke at the Association of National Advertisers' annual conference in Florida last October, some members of the audience joked that if a marketer hadn't turned down at least one major offer from a dot-com start-up, his or her career was obviously going nowhere.

"This is an absolutely great time for people who have a real interest in marketing," says Paul Ray of Ray & Berenson, who specializes in placing marketing people in top positions. "It's similar to the early 1980s, when the energy business took off like a shot. Suddenly there was this huge demand for land men and geologists. That didn't last long, but this demand will sustain itself for a period of time."

Not for everyone

But for those who do make the leap, success is no guarantee. Most of the start-ups are doomed to failure, and not everyone can adapt to life at dot-com speed.

"I don't think that every person from the offline

(Cont.)

world can adapt," says Annie Williams, who left Conde Nast to become head of marketing at Cnet. "You have to be comfortable making decisions with 80% of the information that's available. The things that were valued in publishing, like what you wore, where you ate lunch and what your office was like—not one of those things mattered in this industry. We eat lunch out of a vending machine."

Even if you adapt to the new lifestyle, the competitive environment is fierce. At Yahoo, success hasn't made Edwards complacent.

"Every time I read one of the press releases about older men with white hair joining Internet start-ups as marketers, it makes us more aggressive," she says. "I'm young; we've got a young team; and we want to win."

6

Target Market

With Recruiting Slow, The Air Force Seeks A New Ad Campaign

Two Agencies Vie for
Deal; At Stake Is
$350 Million And
the Service's Future

Gen. Begert's Big Decision

By Greg Jaffe

Staff Reporter of The Wall Street Journal

RANDOLPH AFB, Texas—A stopwatch clicked. Joan Dufrense, a 38-year-old New York advertising executive, stepped before a panel of stone-faced men and women in crisp sky-blue uniforms.

"What do you do now that there is no Cold War?" she asked. "That's the question."

Ms. Dufrense has created ad campaigns for mouthwash, credit cards, banks and coffee. A few months before she came to this Air Force base near San Antonio, she knew almost nothing about the military. Until a week before, she had never met a soul on active duty. Now she was about to tell a team of Air Force officers and employees what their mission ought to be at the dawn of the 21st century.

For the first time in 14 years, the Air Force was bidding out an ad contract. With recruitment flagging and an unprecedented number of departures thinning its ranks, the service wanted help explaining its role. Air Force surveys showed that most people, including some of the service's own rank and file, don't understand its mission.

For the Air Force, this is a matter of dire importance. Some Pentagon officials say that recruitment shortfalls have begun to jeopardize the service's ability to keep aging jets flying and to protect the country's interests

Joan Dufrense

globally. No one says the U.S. is likely to lose a war as a result, but the risk of endangering men and women in combat could increase.

The top brass believe a big part of the problem is perception. For decades, Americans had a clear image of the Air Force, from its fighter planes jousting with German Fokkers over Europe in World War II to its pummeling of Baghdad in the Gulf War. But as the Communist threat receded, the picture grew fuzzy. Air Force jets shattered Serbia in 1999, saving thousands of Kosovar Albanian refugees without a U.S. casualty. Today, the Air Force polices no-fly zones in Iraq to keep Saddam Hussein from attacking his own people. But many potential recruits don't seem to notice.

"We're a victim of our own success," says Air Force Lt. Gen. William Begert. "If our national interests were threatened day-to-day, people would know about us."

In recent years, the Air Force tried to spread its message with print ads, late-night public service announcements and recruiting officers. Not until the end of 1999 did it try paid television advertising, with a series of spots showing young people discussing how the service had helped them attain personal goals. Even so, the Air Force missed its recruiting goal that year for the first time since the draft ended in 1973.

So last year the Air Force turned to Madison Avenue for a new kind of campaign. Six companies responded, three were deemed finalists, and two ultimately vied head-to-head for the seven-year, $350-million contract. One was Ms. Dufrense's employer, New York's prestigious Bozell Group, creator of the admired "Got Milk?" campaign. The other was GSD&M, an Austin, Texas, upstart known for its comical "Wanna get away?" ads for Southwest Airlines.

Army of One

The winner's product will become public this summer in a series of 30-second TV spots that seek to make plain the Air Force's role in the post-Cold War world. The new campaign comes at a time when other branches of the military are also changing their marketing in an attempt to boost flagging recruiting. Last year, the Army also chose a new ad agency through competitive bidding. And in a controversial move, the service has now killed its "Be all you can be" slogan in favor of "An Army of One." The Navy is preparing new ads as well.

On consecutive mornings in October, teams of executives from Bozell and GSD&M were invited to tell an Air Force panel of two women and seven men how the service could use advertising to engage three target audiences—potential recruits, existing airmen, and the public. Each firm

Roy Spence

came armed with mock-ups of ads, scripts and starkly different ideas about what Americans want in today's military.

They had begun six months earlier with the Air Force's 78-page request for bids. The document detailed formats and procedures, but its thematic guidance boiled down to a statement that Americans "need a deeper understanding of the role and mission of the Air Force." The nature of that mission was left to the agencies to puzzle out themselves.

The pieces didn't fall together easily. Both agencies made presentations to more than a dozen focus groups across the country, showing each roughly 15 story boards—posters with drawings of the ads' key scenes. The responses left them dumbfounded.

Ms. Dufrense of Bozell, a unit of True North Communications Inc., said she had never seen such polarization. Ads showing bombs blowing up bridges offended younger people who worried about civilian casualties. But ads that focused on humanitarian missions drew criticism from older viewers. After seeing a Bozell story board that showed the Air Force delivering food and medicine to war refugees, a man in his 40s fumed, "If I saw that ad, I'd call my Congressman and ask, 'Why the hell are we using military dollars for these types of missions?'"

Divisions were nearly as sharp within Bozell itself. The firm's Dallas office long had handled the Air Force account, including its recent TV spots. But now that the Air Force would be boosting its spending to $50 million a year from about $11 million, Bozell's New York headquarters got more involved. One ad overseen by Ms. Dufrense depicted airmen as angels and included a prayer. The Dallas people hated it. "You talk about God and country in these ads, and you are dead," says Steve Eaker, a senior Bozell manager in Dallas.

Ms. Dufrense wasn't convinced. A week before her presentation to the Air Force, she showed the ad to a focus group of six airmen at a Ramada Inn near Andrews Air Force base in suburban Washington, D.C. Their reaction was mixed. "It gave me goosebumps," one master sergeant said—but not because of the religious overtones. Rather, he said, the spot reminded him of the sense of heroism he felt on his first mission, when he stepped off

(Cont.)

a plane in Saudi Arabia and was surrounded by hundreds of grateful local residents. Other airmen chimed in with similar stories. Ms. Dufrense was riveted.

She left the session and immediately dialed New York. "We've had a major breakthrough," she gushed. She told her colleagues to forget the angel ads—too religious, she conceded—and start work on a series of spots that would capture the heroism and self-sacrifice she had sensed in the airmen's personal stories. The New Yorkers had six days to prepare something for the presentation.

The challenge proved no easier for GSD&M, a unit of Omnicom Group Inc. The Austin firm's 51-year-old president and co-founder, Roy Spence, was determined to grab the Air Force account from Bozell and advance his plan to transform GSD&M from regional player to a national powerhouse.

But pulling that off would be tough. In GSD&M's focus groups, the message seemed to be that folks generally respected the Air Force but didn't think it was doing much these days. "You know what I think of when I think Air Force?" a discount store cashier in her 20s told GSD&M in an Orlando, Fla., focus group. "It's kind of lazy. It's waiting for something to happen."

That wouldn't fly as the basis of an ad campaign, Mr. Spence told his troops. "The idea that we need an Air Force because we might get into trouble doesn't work," he said. "Boring." Instead, the ads needed to change people's perceptions and signal a departure from the military's traditional approach to marketing.

GSD&M's creative director, Daniel Russ, issued an edict: No planes or Air Force personnel in the ads. Some on his staff thought he was nuts. Without a human element, they asked, how would viewers know why this mattered to them? Mr. Russ explained, "Have you ever seen the movie 'Halloween'? It's terrifying. In the whole movie, there are seven seconds of blood. Seven seconds. The message is: We can't allow ourselves to default to the obvious."

A GSD&M team set out to show how the Air Force stays productive when it isn't dropping bombs. At the firm's steel-and-glass Austin complex, in a Western-themed room featuring a massive sculpture of a cow being lassoed, staffers hung photos of weapons like the Predator spy drone and an unmanned spy plane. They also put up a chart showing that exactly 0.2% of today's teenagers say they would like to join the military—about the same percentage that want to be veterinarians.

Mr. Russ and his charges came up with ads laced with technology and attitude. In GSD&M's bloodless, bombless vision, satellites and spy planes would stand in for pilots and streaking jets, and the Air Force would prevent wars by outsmarting future enemies.

Young people seemed intrigued. In a focus group nine days before the Air Force presentation, a teenage boy in a Tommy Hilfiger sweatshirt was asked what he thought about an ad showing a spy drone detecting an enemy camp. "I'd say the Air Force had a serious God complex," he said admiringly.

GSD&M Makes Its Case

On a warm morning in October, the Air Force selection panel assembled in a drab conference room that echoed with the sound of pilots gunning their jets just outside. The nine active-duty and civilian members ranged in age from 37 to 61 and had been chosen from the Air Force's advertising, recruiting and public affairs commands. Their job was to listen and report to Gen. Begert back at the Pentagon, who would make the ultimate decision. Each ad agency was given 90 minutes to present five story boards.

GSD&M was set to go first. Mr. Spence rose and shook his fist. "Make no mistake," he began, speaking in the twang of his native south Texas. "The United States Air Force is not about getting a job. It's not college-lite. Let that be for someone else."

To ensure fairness, the Air Force brass had forbidden the panelists to speak with the bidders or applaud at any time. They were even told not to smile, although that ban was lifted after the airmen complained it was rude. Besides, it was hard not to grin at Mr. Spence, whose evangelical style and blond pompadour prompted some panelists later to refer to him as "Reverend Roy."

Next came Mr. Russ, the GSD&M creative director. He had been working long hours, his gray suit was rumpled, and a faint stain marred his blue necktie. Mr. Russ pointed to a story board that opened with a blank radar screen. In the next panel, three green dots appeared. The idea was that the green dots would move left to right, then three blue dots would cross in the opposite direction. "The green dots don't know where the blue dots are," Mr. Russ narrated in his reedy drawl. "But the blue dots know exactly where the green dots are." In the next panel, the blue dots turned and followed the green dots in tight formation. "Poor green dots," Mr. Russ said. A titter escaped from one of the panelists.

In another ad, men speaking an undecipherable language unloaded missiles from a truck on a mountain road. "At 0700, across the world, a cease-fire is about to be violated," Mr. Russ narrated. The camera cut to a listening device hanging in a tree. "At 0600, we already knew about it." Two other GSD&M spots, including the one with the spy drone that had impressed the teenager in the focus group, also hinted at the possibility of opening fire without showing it.

A final ad broke Mr. Russ's no-airmen-or-planes rule. It celebrated a group of Air Force mechanics who had won a Bronze Star for work on B-2 bombers during the Kosovo war. Mr. Russ had thought the spot old-fashioned and predictable, but Mr. Spence had overruled him.

A GSD&M staffer then described the agency's nontraditional media plan. Rather than running ads primarily on sports broadcasts, as the military typically has done, she urged the Air Force to pound away on MTV, Comedy Central, BET and other networks that target young people. She also advocated buying time on hit shows favored by the 25-to-49 age group, such as "Friends" and "Will & Grace."

Finally, Mr. Spence wrapped up, repeating a voice-over message that would sign off each ad: "The mission of the men and women of the United States Air Force is always to be a step ahead. And when you step up to this mission you'll be a step ahead." He cocked his head and grinned at the panel. "Is that applause?" he joked. "I thought I heard some applause."

The panelists filed out in silence and reconvened in a windowless office where for weeks they had pored over printed materials submitted by the agencies. The reek of coffee and stale French fries hung in the air. The airmen sat on desks and discussed GSD&M's plan.

Several panelists said they hadn't been impressed with the agency's ideas before the presentation. But Mr. Spence had charmed them. "Everyone says the Soviet threat is not there, the Berlin Wall is down," said 37-year-old Master Sgt. Juan Demiranda. "But the mission is there. Reverend Roy gave it to us."

Retired Chief Master Sgt. Dave Smith, 56, agreed. "The threat is diverse," he said. "We can't identify a single threat because there are so many out there we need to track. They hit the USS Cole. They hit the embassy in Nairobi." Heads nodded.

No one liked the ad about the mechanics who had won the Bronze Star. One panelist called it "cheesy." Several panelists also questioned the wisdom of airing ads on "Will & Grace," a sitcom including several gay characters.

Bozell's Turn

The next morning was Bozell's turn. Ms. Dufrense waited on a metal folding chair beneath the fluorescent lamps in the conference room. The rules forbid her to banter with the panelists, as she normally does with prospective clients. But she hoped at least to make the airmen laugh or cry. "If I can do either," she whispered to a colleague, "we're probably in good shape."

Ms. Dufrense began with a slide that said, "Heroes for Global Stability." In today's world, she explained, an environmental catastrophe or a military coup on one side of the globe can trigger problems on the other. Only the Air Force, she said, can bring stability with a combination of high-tech weaponry, fast responses and—most important—selfless heroism.

Ms. Dufrense, a slim woman with dark, shoulder-length hair, lacked the dramatic flair of Mr. Spence. But her message held powerful appeal for the panelists, many of whom believed Americans no longer appreciate the

A New Pitch

Sample illustrations and text from the GSD&M advertising agency's presentation to the Air Force.

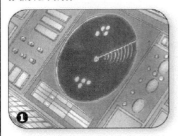

Open on a flat black screen. Suddenly four green dots appear and slowly start moving across the screen. Then, four blue dots appear and start moving across the screen.

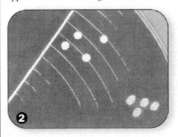

Announcer: *"The green dots don't know where the blue dots are. But the blue dots know exactly where the green dots are."* The four blue dots then change course and head toward the green dots. **Announcer:** *"Poor green dots."*

Cut to a montage of Air Force personnel. **Announcer:** *"The mission of the men and women of the United States Air Force is always to be a step ahead. And when you step up to this mission, you'll be a step ahead."*

Closing logo.

sacrifice military people make for their country. "We want to make the military heroic again," Ms. Dufrense told the panel.

She described the emotional focus group she'd had with the airmen at Andrews. "Before this project," she confessed, "I had never spoken to anyone in uniform, unless you count a police officer, a firefighter or a customs guy." Then she described the tour of Andrews she was given after the focus group. She had clambered aboard an old C-141 cargo plane that was being readied for a mission. Might this plane have flown in Vietnam? she asked. An airman told her the plane had ferried home some of the last POWs freed when the war ended. "I stood there," she told the panelists, "and it hit me: Everyone should feel what I feel right now." As she spoke, she noticed tears welling in the eyes of two men on the panel. She felt her voice catch, and hurried to sit down.

Richard Dahl, Bozell's New York creative director, then narrated three ads developed in New York—"epiphany" spots, as Ms. Dufrense called them, based on her experience at Andrews. Each ended with airmen talking about the moment they realized they were part of something larger than themselves.

One ad opened with an Air Force plane landing in a war zone. In the next panel, airmen unloaded medical supplies that were snatched up by refugees. The scene then shifted to a diner in the U.S., where one of the airmen was sitting with a friend. "The people appeared from nowhere, like out of trees," Mr. Dahl narrated, in the part of the airman talking to his buddy. "Looking back, that is when it hit me: I had a higher purpose here."

'A Great Selling Job'

As the panel filed out of the room, its chairman, 52-year-old Lt. Col. Robert East, whispered, "That gal had my attention. She had me all choked up." Sgt. Demiranda agreed: "She did a great selling job."

They gathered again in their windowless lair. "I loved the concept and the gal did a good job explaining," said Billy Keen, 54, a civilian employee of the Air Force's advertising command. Sgt. Smith, the retired officer who had earlier praised GSD&M's ads, concurred: "She was talking about things we all went through—about that moment when the Air Force's values become your values."

There were problems, though. The panelists thought Bozell's media plan lacked detail, and they faulted the firm for making factual errors, such as showing a picture of air-to-air missiles in a spot involving air-to-ground missiles. And, crucially, while they were drawn to the emphasis on heroism, they wondered if a 30-second ad would be able to capture that sentiment and translate it to a civilian audience.

"I got an emotional thrill out of the pre-

sentation," Sgt. Demiranda told his fellow panelists. "But I don't think people outside the military will relate to it."

Sgt. Demiranda, who works in the advertising command, joined the Air Force 19 years ago because he wasn't earning enough money at a Louisiana pharmacy to support his wife and infant son. Though he talks about the pride he feels wearing a uniform and being "part of an organization that is doing something really important," he worries that most of today's youth wouldn't instinctively be moved by such concepts.

The current generation of draft-age kids is the first whose parents came of age after the armed forces became all-voluntary. As a result, many of them have little or no emotional connection to the military. Even children of military families don't necessarily feel the same call to duty that their parents did. Just last year, Sgt. Demiranda's own son balked after he was accepted at the Air Force Academy, and wound up going to the University of Minnesota instead. "It was best for him and best for the Air Force," Sgt. Demiranda says.

Indeed, none of the panelists had joined the Air Force with such grand objectives as heroism. Two had been mired in dead-end jobs. Three older members had signed up to avoid being drafted and having to dodge bullets in the Army.

Capt. Roger Lawson, 37, had chosen the Air Force for the simplest reason possible. "The Air Force recruiter called me first," he says. The recruiter had painted a picture of the young man living on a Florida beach with his girlfriend. "Sounded pretty good," says Capt. Lawson, a native of Erie, Pa.

It fell to him to write a 500-word synopsis on the effectiveness of the GSD&M and Bozell messages. For several days he struggled. He, too, had grown misty-eyed during Ms. Dufrense's talk. But he couldn't bring himself to endorse Bozell's message, and he didn't understand why.

A Television Moment

Watching television the night before his report was due, Capt. Lawson stumbled across a replay of New York Yankee Don Larsen's perfect game in the 1956 World Series. When the final pitch smacked Yogi Berra's mitt, the crowd rushed the field. Capt. Lawson noticed that many of the revelers were wearing military uniforms. Suddenly, he understood why he and his colleagues were balking at the Bozell ads: The ads probably would have worked with that 1950s audience, but not an audience in 2001.

In Capt. Lawson's view, Bozell had failed to propose a single campaign that would engage all of the Air Force's target audiences—prospects, personnel and the public at large. To do so, he wrote, "would require an additional ad campaign and increase the government costs." GSD&M's ads, on the other hand, didn't demand a deep emotional response from viewers but rather sought to wow them with technical smarts.

Three weeks later, the panel's chairman arrived to brief Gen. Begert in a soundproof conference room at the Pentagon. Gen. Begert, a veteran of more than 300 combat missions in the Vietnam War, sat at a long pine table with a three-ring binder containing the panel's synopses and color-coded ratings of the proposals. He said he hoped to see ads "that would make people come to the Air Force for the right reasons—service to nation and a realistic expectation of what our life is like."

Cut to the Videotape

The general then viewed videotaped excerpts of the presentations. Watching GSD&M's Mr. Russ, he jokingly suggested that the Air Force pay to replace his stained necktie. "I liked that other guy," he said, referring to the agency's Mr. Spence.

When it came to Bozell's presentation, Gen. Begert said he liked the heroism theme, but the ads themselves left him cold. Like the panelists, he was annoyed by factual errors. Like Capt. Lawson and Sgt. Demiranda, he worried that Bozell's plan wouldn't have broad enough appeal. "The ads just didn't quite click," he said.

The next day, he announced the winner: GSD&M. In an interview, he said he especially liked the firm's cool vision of 21st century warfare. Echoing Mr. Spence, he said, "We're the smart service. We're always working to stay a step ahead."

The Air Force and GSD&M are preparing ads for airing in a few months. They haven't decided yet whether to give a starring role to those scuttling blue dots.

Republished with permission of Dow Jones & Company, Inc., from *The Wall Street Journal*, "Target Market: With Recruiting Slow, the Air Force Seeks a New Ad Campaign," p. A1, February 14, 2001; permission conveyed through Copyright Clearance Center, Inc.

7

Marketers put a price on your life
Years of buying matters most

By Greg Farrell
USA TODAY

NEW YORK—The next time you order a Coke, don't think of it as costing $1.25; think of it as a small down payment on the $6,000 you might be worth to Coca-Cola over your lifetime.

Or when you're at a Chevrolet dealer, don't think of that Cavalier as a $15,000 car—think of it as the first installment on the $276,000 you might be worth to General Motors as a lifetime customer.

Even if you prefer not to think of these purchases as down payments on sizable lifetime investments, be forewarned: Marketers across the USA are looking at them exactly that way.

Marketers are focusing on the lifetime value of a loyal customer, not just this quarter's sales.

"It's the new real advance in marketing," says Peter Sealey, an adjunct professor of marketing at the University of California at Berkeley. Sealey, former head of marketing at Coca-Cola, uses the Coke and GM examples in presentations to would-be marketers. "There can't be a marketer who's not brain dead who's not doing this now."

"You don't have to think about all the customers," says Martha Rogers of Peppers & Rogers marketing consultants. "You just have to think about the right customers. If I'm Coke, I really want to know which 6% of customers in the U.K. drink 60% of the colas. I want to get as big a share of those customers as possible. I want them to be Coca-Cola loyalists, not just cola loyalists."

Several developments have pushed marketers toward the lifetime value approach:

▲ Consumers have less time. Marketers know consumers don't want to spend time on brand decisions; most will stick with the tried-and-true.

▲ It costs a lot more to capture a new customer than to care for one you have.

▲ The Internet is giving marketers a better idea of who their regular customers are. More important, marketers can figure out exactly how much it costs to acquire customers on the Web, so they are compelled to figure out how much each of those customers is worth.

"Computers are driving this way of marketing," says Rogers. "If I can build a dialogue with customers, I can get you to tell me something. I can know something about you that my competitors don't know, which makes it possible for me to do something for you that competitors can't do."

The concept of the lifetime value of a customer isn't altogether new. Alfred Sloan assembled General Motors around the principle of a "value ladder," meaning that GM should have a specific line of cars to sell to customers at each stage of their lives.

That principle remains in place today. "We value loyalty at General Motors," says Martin Walsh, general director of marketing for Cadillac. "And we recognize the value of moving customers from one division to another."

What is new is the ability to use the Internet as a tool to deepen ties with heretofore anonymous buyers.

"We're focused on the lifetime value of the customer," says Gateway Computer CEO Ted Waitt.

KEEPING THE CUSTOMER HAPPY — FOR A LIFETIME

The loyal customer is worth more than the sum of her purchases. A faithful General Motors customer can be worth $276,000 over her lifetime, including the 11 or more vehicles bought, plus a word-of-mouth endorsement making friends and relatives more likely to consider GM products.

Estimated lifetime value of a customer for **General Motors:** $276,000

Procter & Gamble   (two or more brands) $10,000

Gateway Computer $25,000

Safeway/Albertson's   (upper income family, with children) $4,800 per year

(Cont.)

"There's a lot more in that relationship than just the box." Gateway is using the Internet to build loyalty. It offers a year's Internet service with the purchase of a new computer.

Executives at rival Dell also are thinking long term. "Hopefully, customers don't view us as one transaction," says Bob Langer, director of Dell.com. "The approach we take is all about building long-term relationships with customers. The end of the transaction is the beginning of the relationship."

Although neither company would give numbers, Aaron Goldberg of Ziff-Davis estimates the lifetime value of a sophisticated computer user—one who buys a new machine and software about every two years—to be about $45,000. A non-technical user who puts off computer purchases as long as possible has a lifetime value closer to $25,000, he says.

For old-line marketers selling several brands, the idea of looking at the consumer's total value doesn't come easily. Procter & Gamble CEO Durk Jager estimated at a recent press conference that the lifetime value of a customer for just one P&G brand could be several thousand dollars, but he didn't know how much that customer was worth across all the company's product lines.

"It hasn't happened in consumer packaged goods," says Sealey. "The Internet is going to permit us to do it far better than ever before. On line, we can order, get customer service, have a dialogue. The Web's going to be an enormous facilitator of this."

Don't snicker at long-time purveyors of toothpaste and soaps. A lot of on-line marketers are even more clueless about the lifetime value of their customers.

"Most Internet firms are fighting for one transaction at a time, and that's an expensive way to do it," says Kathy Biro, CEO of the Strategic Interactive Group.

Hewlett-Packard is trying to make a business of helping Web sites develop customer loyalty programs. It sells "quality of service" software for e-commerce sites.

"If you go to the grocery store, people will wait three minutes in line before getting antsy," says Ann Livermore, CEO of enterprise computing at H-P. "On the Web, people are not willing to look at that hourglass for 30 seconds.

"We allow you to assign a priority to certain transactions and customers. So if the Web gets busy, and it impacts quality of service, your site gives priority of service to certain customers."

"Most of the recipes that made for good business before the Web still make for good business on the Web," Livermore says. "The company that figures out how to have the best customer loyalty on the Web will have the advantage because of how quickly people can jump from place to place on line."

Finding Target Market Opportunities

8

ON TARGET

Retailing stardom: Spritely marketing makes it chic to buy cheap

by Alice Z. Cuneo

Target Corp. is a promiscuous client, with an in-house advertising department and more than a half dozen agencies handling assignments on a project basis.

But after six years working on print ads, Dave Peterson, creative director and founder of Minneapolis boutique Peterson Milla Hooks, was given a plum: Come up with a branding campaign defining Target's DNA.

Mr. Peterson long thought the simple red Target logo had a look reminiscent of an early Gucci or Chanel logo. "It was fun, designery and fashioney," he says. "It was a byproduct of the times we are living in."

The resulting 1999 spots featured "Bull's-Eye World," a funky retro pop culture place where happy blondes serve red target-shaped molded Jell-O and dance in a Target logo wallpapered room wearing a Target logo patterned outfit, all to Petula Clark's "Sign of the Times."

With that, Target hit the bull's-eye. The upscale discounter has established its logo nationally as an advertising icon in a class with those of McDonald's arches and Nike's swoosh.

For that campaign, and for its finely honed marketing position as purveyor of cheap chic, Target Corp. is *Advertising Age's* Marketer of the Year for 2000. Target is the 30th marketer to be honored since *Ad Age* began the award in 1971. It's the fourth retailer on the list, following Amazon.com in 1999, The Gap in 1997, Wal-Mart Stores in 1991 and Kmart Corp. in 1976.

REINVENTING THE DISCOUNT CONCEPT

Target, dubbed by admirers in faux French as "Tarzhay," has "reinvented the whole discount-store concept," says George Strachan, VP-research, Goldman Sachs. Target is managing to stay on top as it competes in a host of categories, bumping against everyone from Wal-Mart to The Gap to Staples to Bed, Bath & Beyond.

Ellis Verdi, president of DeVito/Verdi, New York, whose clients have included Office Depot and Circuit City Stores, says Target is the envy of most marketers in the turbulent retail sector. Target has "been able to carve out the ultimate retail positioning with both a perception of having the highest quality products and at the same time, a perception of being a low price leader."

GOODBY A FAN

One Target customer, Jeff Goodby, co-chairman of Goodby, Silverstein & Partners, San Francisco, says the store's advertising is on target with what the store delivers.

"It's a memorable, clean graphic that represents the place and tells a truth about them," says Mr. Goodby, who frequents Target when he's shooting commercials in Los Angeles and needs to pick up a sweatshirt or pair of shorts, "potato chips and junk food you need for the week."

The sign of the times not only fits but appears to be working at the cash register as well. Target, with $35.3 billion in sales over the last 12 months, expects to leapfrog soon over No. 2 Kmart Corp. in terms of sales to become the second-largest discount chain in the nation behind Wal-Mart. For the first 11 months of the year, Kmart's sales were $28.3 billion, compared with Target's sales of $27.5 billion.

Target reported ad expenditures in 1999 of $791 million. It had $424 million in measured spending, according to Competitive Media Reporting.

SALUTE TO NAME

In a salute to the positioning and strength of its core brand, which now provides an estimated 80% of the corporation's sales and profits, Dayton Hudson Corp. at the start of the new millennium officially changed its name to Target Corp.

The corporation operates Target Stores; Mervyn's California, a 267-store chain with erratic results on its sales of national brands and private-label products for the middle market, and a department store unit that includes Dayton's, Marshall Field's and Hudson's. The department stores are struggling as most traditional retailers are these days, but Target Corp. strives to promote the brands in each locale as "the best store in town."

It was from Dayton Co.'s roots as a traditional, high fashion department store that Target began in 1962 as its discount division. Rivals Wal-Mart and Kmart also opened that year, products of five-and-dime retailers.

"The fact [Target was] spawned by a department store makes a big difference. They don't have a 5-and-dime mentality," says Walter Loeb, president, Loeb Associates,

(Cont.)

a consultancy that publishes the *Loeb Retail Letter.* "Every associate is a team player and they treat customers as guests.

"But don't let the chic advertising in *Vogue* and high-brow image fool you," Mr. Loeb notes. "They show that they're highfalutin, but they're also down and dirty."

ULRICH LEADS WAY

The chain made its biggest strides under Bob Ulrich, who started as a merchandising trainee at Dayton's in 1967 and rose through the corporate ranks. He became president of Target Stores in 1984, then chairman-CEO in 1987. He took his current post of chairman-CEO of Dayton Hudson Corp. (now Target Corp.) in 1994.

Mr. Ulrich, in remarks to investors this fall, credited the company's success to discipline in operations, strategies and finances. "Our consistency of execution . . . gives us the flexibility to be creative in our merchandising, our marketing and our brand identity," he told investors.

That creativity is centered in the stores' marketing department, according to John E. Pellegrene, exec VP-marketing for Target Corp. In many department stores, the merchants often were given the lead on product decisions, with marketers brought in at the end of the process to advertise available merchandise.

Mr. Pellegrene says at Target, it's the other way around. "We don't look at advertising as purely paper and film," he says. "We are a dimensional advertising department. We are not a department that simply deals in conventional media. We deal in marketing programs that will also bring millions of dollars into the company in perpetuity."

CLAIMS BIGGEST REGISTRY

For example, the marketing department initiated Target's bridal registry, Club Wedd.

"We are the largest advertising registry in the world," he claims, surpassing Federated Department Stores' Macy's a year and a half ago. "When other people said, 'Will people buy wedding gifts at discount stores,' my feeling was no, they wouldn't buy them at discount stores, but they would buy them at Target," he says. The Lullaby Club, an extension of the bridal registry, was a natural follow-up.

MONUMENT BUZZ

Another substantial income stream coming from the marketing department was a by-product of a cause-related marketing project, the restoration of the Washington Monument.

Architect Michael Graves designed a translucent sheath to cover the unsightly scaffolding during the restoration, which Target backed as a corporate sponsor. The association with the architect led to a deal through which he launched in 1999 a line of high fashion Target private-label products, such as tea kettles and toasters.

"It came out of marketing, and it migrated to merchandising. And that's the way we do a lot of things," says Mr. Pellegrene. The executive worked in package goods and automotive marketing before he joined the department-store company 31 years ago. He's been with the Target division for 11 years.

EDUCATION PROGRAM

Another marketing department success, he says, was the Target Take Care of Education program through which credit-card holders could designate a school of their choice to receive a donation of 1% of their Target charge card purchases. Not only has the program blossomed to include 17 million cardholders, but also those using the school program spend four times as much as a regular Target customer.

"You have to realize that the advertising department invented a program that is not just cause marketing," says Mr. Pellegrene. "It is the design of a business. And that's what these people have been doing, as well as doing award-winning ads that will win all the regular conventional advertising awards."

Target logo wear, resulting from the "Sign of the Times" commercial, also is doing well. The dog with the bull's-eye logo is the most selected card among the gift certificates, says Mr. Pellegrene. "We're not pushing that—that just happened."

Target also has figured out how to use its co-op advertising dollars to exploit its brand. The so-called "pop art" campaign, which broke this spring, used multiple images of a Tide box to show off a pair of Capri pants worn along a beach. Other spots showed Tums and a woman wearing a two piece Target outfit. "It was the first time I've ever run an advertising campaign where I've had a waiting list in that [Procter & Gamble Co.] and PepsiCo want to be part of it. We're very careful; we actually turned down money and vendors," he says.

COCA-COLA ON BOARD

The campaign resumes this spring with the title, "Color My World," and features for the first time Coke as part of a "red"-themed campaign launching the red line from the California sportswear company, Mossimo. It is a beach and surf line for young men and junior women. A Mossimo black line will feature men's and women's clothing and shoes.

(Cont.)

Another branding effort is expected next year, as well as a campaign dubbed "Spotted at Target," which will feature the work of Mossimo and Mr. Graves and reflect their influence on contemporary art and culture.

"They are product spots, but they function as brand builders," says Mr. Peterson.

Music tie-ins also will be promoted, just as this holiday season has been centered on Tina Turner, with Target sponsoring a TV show of her first and last concert tour, and a CD available only at Target Stores.

But one of the store's most important branding concepts came not from the marketing department, but from the mouth of the customer, Mr. Pellegrene says.

"Tar-zhay, that is a moniker the customer gave Target. It isn't something Target invented," he says. "If you had to do our entire mission statement, that would be it. If you had to say to a buyer, judge your merchandising against that name, Tar-zhay, you would be getting where Target is."

Still, some of Target's successes are due to luck, he concedes. In terms of media, for example, "We try to sponsor the hottest things out there in the media we can sponsor. Sometimes it's luck," he says.

'SURVIVOR STAR'

Target was a major sponsor of the CBS-TV summer ratings phenomenon "Survivor." As part of its ties to the show, it dropped a parachute with the Target bull's-eye on the island, where it was used as a shelter on the beach every week.

Advertising aside, perhaps one of the biggest underlying factors in the Tar-zhay phenomenon is the "massification" of fashion, the shortened length of time it takes for trends to move from designer runway to discount rack. In the past, new looks took months to copy and move down from the higher priced department stores into discount channels.

"Today, customers at all price points can look fashionable quite affordably," concluded a Goldman Sachs shopping study conducted this fall at Roosevelt Field Mall in New York. There, it found Python-patterned pantsuits at Nordstrom's for $447, while a similar-looking outfit at Target had a $41.98 price tag. Nordstrom was selling animal skin cowboy hats for $28, but Target had very similar snake, zebra and other skin styles and colors for $14.99.

Target also has developed a strong line of private-label products, which enhance its fashion edge. Target had developed almost a dozen lines of private-label brands bearing trendy brand names, among them Sanrio's Hello Kitty toys and clothing, Kitchen Essentials from Calphalon, Martex linens and Robert Abbey lamps.

LITTLE OVERLAP

Those products, in addition to providing better profitability, also help Target fight the competition. For example, Mr. Strachan notes only 30% of Target's products overlap with Wal-Mart products.

Beyond the fashion front, Target is making "guest services" a selling point. Ever since Nordstrom raised the bar on customer service, most department stores have enacted lenient return policies.

But Target has gone extra lengths to ensure happy returns for the holiday season. Target provides its guests with free receipt holders at registers; it also will look up receipts for purchases made with most major credit cards.

WEB GAINS

Target also has diligently integrated its clicks and bricks. Starting with extension of its Club Wedd gift registry to the Web, Target has increased the number of items available from about 2,000 at the end of 1999 to more than 15,000 currently. New technologies allow customers to look at weekly circulars by region and provide real-time inventory, so customers will know whether the items they want are in stock.

Target also has realized the value of the Web as an extension of its brand to locales where no stores exist. This holiday, for example, Target.com kicked off an aggressive promotion in New York City, handing out coffee, popcorn and other unexpected treats—including free holiday shipping from the Web site—to Manhattan consumers. This could warm up shoppers for a possible new store as Target investigates real estate in the city.

Beyond its online sales, Target is developing a customer relationship management system within its corporate structure. A database of customers is under development for all Target Corp. stores.

As for Target's sibling retailers, Mervyn's and the department stores unit, corporate execs repeatedly have indicated they will stick with their heritage. "I haven't seen any inclination on the part of management to sell," says Goldman Sachs' Mr. Strachan. "At this point, it doesn't matter."

FICKLE, FAST AND FURIOUS

Still, Target, like all players in the fickle, fast and furious retail trade, is facing challenges. This spring, when sales at Target division stores open more than one year began to slow, critics wondered whether the discounter had gone so far upscale that it was alienating traditional discount shoppers.

Mr. Ulrich, however, has told investors Target keeps its total assortment priced competitively with similar

(Cont.)

items at Wal-Mart and Kmart as well as at category killers such as Best Buy and Toys "R" Us. At the same time, Target also is going to up-market its offerings and product prices to keep pace with specialty and department stores. Still, when Target added a $199 set of Calphalon to the cookware section, it kept a $19.99 Mirro cookware set on the shelves, he notes.

Target also is facing challenges in the apparel aisles, representing 25% of the store's total sales. Target is using the designer name strategy, testing new brands such as Nikki Taylor by Liz Claiborne.

FORMAT CONCERNS

Wall Street has expressed concerns over the next Target format challenge—the rollout of 200 SuperTarget stores over the next 10 years.

The larger stores, like Wal-Mart's Supercenters, will include grocery stores as a way to win repeat visits. An attempt to show off Tar-zhay's take on gourmet from Starbucks to sushi, the new stores have fixtures analysts view as expensive, service intensive departments and reliance on third-party distributors.

Other retail experts, such as Mr. Loeb, wonder when Target will take the plunge beyond U.S. borders. "Ultimately, this company has to go beyond the borders and internationalize," he said.

Mr. Ulrich has indicated no interest in international expansion, noting, "It is still very hard to get profitable returns once you get outside of North America, as Wal-Mart is finding out."

But that's not all. Almost every retailer today, from long-time player Sears, Roebuck & Co. to rising stars Kohl's Department Stores and specialty stores such as The Gap, has its sights set on one place: On Target.

NOW, COKE IS NO LONGER 'IT'

New CEO Daft promises a fundamental shift of focus as consumers flock to bottled water, juice, and tea

Jill Friedman, a 21-year-old college student in Atlanta, says she used to sip Diet Cokes all day long but now prefers bottled water. "As I've gotten older, I've realized that drinking five Diet Cokes a day isn't good for you," she says. Walking away from caffeine and aspartame may have been a smart choice for Friedman, but it's bad news for Coca-Cola Co.

Coke's problem is the countless number of people out there who, like Friedman, have cut way back on their soda consumption. For years, consumers have been moving in droves toward juice, bottled water, tea, and other noncarbonated beverages. Now, after decades of focusing almost exclusively on selling the world a Coke, the company has a new chief executive, Douglas N. Daft, who is gearing up to take on the nonsoda market in a big way.

Coke has a lot of catching up to do. Competitors such as The Perrier Group and Quaker Oats Co., maker of Gatorade, have already made big strides in noncarbonated drinks, weakening Coke's soda sales. After nearly two decades of 7% annual gains in unit volume sales, Coke's global volume grew just 1% last year, while its operating profits plunged 20%, to $3.98 billion. Says Tom Pirko, president of New York consultant Bevmark: "If Coke wants to succeed, [it has] now got to embrace other beverages."

Given Coke's long tradition of focusing most of its marketing clout on its cola brands, that's a tall order. Over the years, Coke has tended to treat its noncarbonated offerings as second-class beverages, giving them far less aggressive marketing than the flagship product. Indeed, one Coke insider acknowledges that in noncarbonated categories, the company has been content to produce what he terms "me-too" or "second-in-the-market" products that have produced small-but-easy profits. "I don't think we've gone at [alternative categories] with our heart and soul," says the executive.

BRIBERY. Making matters worse has been Coke's long-term strategy of subsidizing its noncarbonated beverages to keep competitors off store shelves. In return for cash payments that run into thousands of dollars per store, many stores agree to hand over shelf space to Coca-Cola products, including less popular drinks, such as juice-flavored Fruitopia. Invariably, the practice has left little room on store shelves for rivals such as New Age SoBe and Veryfine juices.

But that strategy may soon wear out its welcome. Some retailers have begun to revolt, scaling back on Coke subsidies in favor of stocking more popular brands. Now, on the shelves of many 7-Eleven Stores, Coke's Nestea, for instance, has had to make more room not just for the better-selling Pepsi brand Lipton but also for Snapple and Arizona Iced Tea. Other Coke products, including its newly launched Dasani bottled water and its Powerade sports drink, are getting squeezed by more popular brands, such as Poland Springs water and Gatorade. Says Jim Jackson, beverage manager for 7-Eleven: "In stores where they're competing on a level playing field, consumers usually choose competitors' products."

That's going to change if Daft has anything to say about it. Departing from years of Coke-centric tradition, Daft says he's ready to give beverage drinkers the variety of products they crave. His goal is to remake Coke into "a leader of the beverage sector, as opposed to a soft-drink company."

Daft and his team agree with analysts that to get back to those halcyon days of 7% annual growth in volume and 15%-or-better annual increases in profits, Coke will have to generate as much as 30% of its future growth from noncarbonated categories. "For us to achieve the growth rate that people are expecting, we have to become more diversified," says Steve Jones, Coke's new chief marketing officer. "We have to move beyond Coke and the carbs."

To that end, Daft, Jones, and other top Coca-Cola executives are pushing hard to shake up the company's culture. In the less than three months since Daft has been in the top job, he has shuffled his management team to promote executives with a track record in noncarbonated products. What's more, Daft hopes that his bombshell move on Jan. 26 to lay off roughly 20% of Coke's workforce will help reduce bureaucracy and allow more new ideas to bubble up from the field.

Next on Daft's agenda is laying out basic guidelines for new products, packaging, and marketing. Then he intends to cut his local managers loose to develop products tailored to local tastes. While Coca-Cola already sells some 300 diverse beverage products around the globe, Daft envisions a day when Coke will offer 2,000 or more, many of which will be new juices, teas, and hybrid products, such as carbonated tea. "We will be trendsetting," he vows.

That would surely mark a dramatic shift from Coke's predicament today. And Daft

> **Will the Coke name mean anything to buyers of mango juice or rice milk?**

has a fighting chance. For starters, Coke's vast global network of independent bottlers, valued by some analysts at $100 billion, gives it a reach that no other beverage company can match. Even so, analysts believe that those bottlers, many of which are financially stretched from costly expansions of the past two decades, may be reluctant to plunge into the nonsoda market. Generating the volume needed "to provide profits . . . is going to be a challenge," says Scott Wilkins, an analyst at Deutsche Banc Alex. Brown Inc.

Even if Coke persuades bottlers to carry its new drinks, some question whether the company will enjoy the same brand equity in, say, mango juice in Latin America or rice-based drinks for Asia as it does with Coke. "Without the Coke name, they're just another brand on the shelf," says Brown Brothers Harriman & Co. analyst Roy D. Burry.

Still, beverage experts say Daft is on the right track. With consumers voting convincingly for new noncarbonated beverages, it would be suicide to cling to cola alone, they say. Just ask Jill Friedman and the many others like her. They're not drinking as much Diet Coke, but they are drinking something. And whether it's juice, tea, or water, Doug Daft is determined that they'll soon start buying it from Coca-Cola Co.

By Dean Foust, with Deborah Rubin in Atlanta

Men Are on the Minds of Hair-Dye Makers

BY JIM CARLTON
Staff Reporter of THE WALL STREET JOURNAL

Gray is increasingly passe in men's hair fashions, and dye purveyors have launched an advertising push to get the word out.

Television and print ads aimed at getting men to dye the gray out of their hair have tripled over the past decade, in line with an explosion in sales of hair-coloring products for men. Those sales soared to $129.3 million last year from $39.6 million in 1989, according to estimates by market researchers A.C. Nielsen.

And while dyed males are still outnumbered about 10-1 by their female counterparts, they are narrowing the gap. According to pollster Roper Starch Worldwide, 36% of men recently questioned indicated they had either tried coloring their hair or were open to it.

Not so long ago, gray hair on men was considered distinguished. That's apparently changing with the business world's increased obsession on youth. "Business is moving so fast it is no longer the gray-haired guy who gets the deference and respect," says Roger Selbert, publisher of Growth Strategies, a trend letter based in Santa Monica, Calif. "Now it's how sharp are you, and are you up on the newest software."

Indeed, many job recruiters are advising middle-aged male clients to dye their hair. "I don't think I would even have gotten in the door if I hadn't changed my hair color," says Dan Lambert, a 45-year-old restaurant manager who followed the advice when he sought a new job recently.

There is also the question of sex appeal. Nearly two-thirds of women responding to a recent online poll by the dating service Datelynx rated as unattractive men whose photos showed them with natural gray hair. But after the same men hit a bottle of dye, the women rated them handsome.

Of course, hair dye isn't for everyone. Actor Richard Gere was named People magazine's sexiest man alive in 1999, despite his silver mane, while TV funnyman Jay Leno frolics with his gray pompadour to no apparent career detriment. Even in youth-obsessed Silicon Valley, many tech companies boast of keeping a few "gray hairs" around, referring to over-40 types hired on to impart wisdom that only experience can offer. "That's mostly because the investors want to see 'em," says Guy Kawasaki, a longtime valley entrepreneur.

And the coloring doesn't always achieve the desired results. "Men will tell me the dye makes them look younger, but it doesn't always," says Anthony Palermo, a colorist at Manhattan's Oribe Salon. "And it can wash out to a strange color. Sometimes you see men walking in fluorescent lights and their head looks purple or red."

Men's hair coloring has been around since 1961, when **Combe** Inc. introduced its Grecian Formula product. But early technology forced customers to spend more time applying the dye with less certain results than today. A combination of technological changes and social advances changed that. Combe, White Plains, N.Y., introduced its Just for Men coloring product in 1987, which touted the fact it required just five minutes to apply.

Meanwhile, the rise of the fast-paced computer industry put younger executives into the work force, heightening society's worship of youth.

"There's a whole new generation right behind us that's pushing real hard, so men want to stay on top of their game," says Dominic DeMain, senior vice president of U.S. marketing for Combe.

Just for Men accounted for $72.4 million in U.S. sales during the 52-week period ended Dec. 5, dominating the men's hair coloring category, according to Information Resources, a market-research firm in Chicago. Meanwhile, traditional women's oriented beauty companies have been attracted to the market. **Bristol-Myers Squibb** Co.'s Clairol unit, for instance, has launched a Men's Choice hair-coloring brand that attained $12.3 million in sales last year, according to Information Resources. French cosmetics giant **L'Oreal** SA is also pursuing the market.

As a result, men's sales have become the hottest segment in the U.S.'s $1.3 billion-a-year hair-coloring industry. According to officials of one national drug retailer, which asked that their company's name not be used, the store space they devote to men's hair dyes has grown to six 3-foot shelves from two over the past decade. Stoking the interest is a barrage of product advertising, which grew to $32 million last year from $10 million a decade ago, according to Competitive Media Reporting.

"Guys will see me do this, and then they will do it," says Rollie Fingers, the retired Oakland Athletics pitcher and a Just for Men pitchman. Another pitchman, former Chicago Bears great Dick Butkus, says dyeing one's hair used to seem unmanly. "Ten years ago, I'd slap the guy who suggested putting color in my hair," says the 57-year-old Mr. Butkus, who recently darkened his salt-and-pepper flattop. "But now, your appearance means so much."

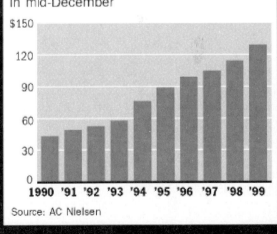

No Gray Area Here

U.S. sales of hair-coloring products for men, in millions for year ending in mid-December

Source: AC Nielsen

TOYOTA: CHASING BOOMERS' BABIES

With its buyers well into middle age, it needs a Gen-Y edge

When Marie Stevenson, 30, went car shopping recently, she thought about a Toyota. After all, she works for an auto insurer, so she knows all about Toyota's reputation for quality. The impulse, however, passed quickly. Stevenson says the new ECHO subcompact "looks kind of goofy." Eventually, she bought a white Nissan Xterra SUV, the perfect stablemate for her husband Brian's dark green Volkswagen Jetta.

That's hitting Toyota Motor Corp. where it hurts. The Japanese auto maker built its fortunes in the U.S. catering to the tastes of baby boomers, starting back when they were buying their first cars. But so far it's been unable to build a similar connection with the next generation. With a median age of 46, according to researcher AutoPacific Inc, in Tustin, Calif., Toyota buyers tend to be older than those of any other Japanese car company. Even though Toyota's sales will be up a healthy 10% this year, the company is worried about what happens when its core customers hit retirement.

Now, Toyota has set a goal of lowering its customers' age by a decade. A year ago, it gathered eight twenty- and thirtysomethings from around the company into a new, ethnically diverse marketing group called "genesis." Their first assignment was to launch three cars meant to pull in younger buyers: the entry-level ECHO subcompact, a sporty new two-door Celica, and the MR2 Spyder, a racy convertible roadster. Under Mark Del Rosso, then a 34-year-old Lexus field manager, genesis began by coming up with a marketing campaign for the ECHO that would speak to people like Stevenson.

FIRST-TIME DRIVERS. The group has an estimated $30 million to spend to get the three cars off the ground. Ads from the new campaign hit TV screens in September, just ahead of the October arrival of the ECHO and the Celica in showrooms. (The Spyder isn't due until spring.) Toyota executives say they're pleased with the results so far. Both the ECHO, a replacement for the Tercel, and the Celica, now in its seventh generation, zipped past their sales targets. More important, the median age of buyers dropped, from 42 to 33 for Celica and to 38 for the ECHO, down from 43 for the Tercel. "We're beginning to see single, young, adult, first-time drivers in our stores," says Steven P. Sturm, marketing vice-president for the Toyota brand. "It's a younger buyer that we haven't seen for a while."

But Toyota is still a long way from its goal. It wants nothing less than a reprise of the strategy that proved so successful with boomers. When that generation was young, Toyota pulled first-time car buyers in with low-priced models such as the Corolla, then moved them into bigger, more expensive models as they aged.

To do the same with the children of the boomers, Toyota needs a car that draws raves from Generation Y. But critics say the ECHO, with its stubby, quirky looks, is the wrong car. Toyota will sell a lot of the model, says George Peterson, president of AutoPacific, "but to older, less-affluent people rather than to younger ones."

To be sure, the built-in-Japan car was designed before the U.S. unit decided to make it the centerpiece of its effort to reach young consumers. Short from back to front but with a high roof, the ECHO isn't winning much applause for its styling. Toyota's advertising, in fact, tacitly acknowledges the shortcomings, using language such as "designed from the inside out" and "funky." Says Peterson: "It's a funny-looking car. That's definitely a problem."

It's not as if Toyota's in trouble yet. Unlike other powerful boomer brands, such as Levi's and Nike, which woke up one day to discover that "relaxed fit" jeans weren't phat, or that teenagers would rather "just do it" in hiking boots than athletic shoes, Toyota is on a roll. The company will sell about 1.5 million vehicles this year, almost 9% of the U.S. market. The Camry family sedan will be the country's best-selling passenger car for the third year in a row. The luxury Lexus brand roared past Cadillac and Lincoln this year and outsold market leader Mercedes until last month. But the competition does better with young buyers. The median age of customers for the Corolla is 45, compared with 38 for the Honda Civic and a mere 31 for the Jetta.

That's where Del Rosso's group comes in. Toyota gave the team its own space in a building across the parking lot from the company's Torrance, Calif., headquarters. To visitors, it could almost be the digs of a dot.com startup, with its wide-open feel and big computer screens. "They gave me the latitude to organize and structure the group the way I wanted it," Del Rosso says, "with the idea of differentiating the Toyota brand and making it relevant to the post-baby-boom consumer."

Right now, Volkswagen is the company to beat when it comes to appealing to younger buyers. "We use advertising to go after the emotional side of the target, with humor, real

AGING APPEAL	Toyota's problem: How to attract younger buyers					
MEDIAN BUYER'S AGE FOR THE 1999 MODEL YEAR						
VOLKSWAGEN	**HONDA**	**NISSAN**	**SATURN**	**TOYOTA**	**CHEVROLET**	**FORD**
36	37	43	43	46	47	47

DATA: AUTOPACIFIC INC.

(Cont.)

people in real-life vignettes, and innovative music," says Elisabeth K. Vanzura, director of marketing for Volkswagen of America Inc. in Auburn Hills, Mich. "We let them discover the rational side of the brand—styling, engineering, product, and features—on their own."

Toyota's attempt to replicate Volkswagen's formula was launched on Sept. 22 with a 45-second spot called "Revolution" that's a virtual remake of the legendary "1984" spot that introduced the Apple Macintosh computer. A casually-dressed youth races against the flow of somber-suited business types and hurls the jack of his boom box cable into the building's sound system. Glass shatters, and the three new cars appear on pedestals. Del Rosso professes not to have gotten the Apple connection until he read it in reviews later. The more recent spots for the Celica employ the all-too-familiar metaphor of sports car as jet plane, photographed on a stark desert road. Only ads for the ECHO are closer to the mark, centered on lifestyle and fun rather than features and specifications.

> **Right now Volkswagen is the company to beat in appealing to younger buyers**

PRICE IS RIGHT. If the ad campaigns are still a work in progress, however, Toyota has gotten the pricing right. The ECHO starts at $10,000, the least-expensive Japanese subcompact on the market and a full $2,200 less than the new Focus, Ford Motor Co.'s similar attempt to lure post-boomers to an aging franchise. The new Celica, at $17,000, is slightly smaller and edgier—and $4,700 cheaper—than its predecessor. And, with the launch of next spring's Spyder, Toyota hopes to recreate the success of its 1984-model MR2, a two-seater sports car. The Spyder will go for around $25,000, well beneath such other premium roadsters as the BMW Z3 and Porsche Boxster.

Genesis has turned Toyota's traditional media buys upside down. Instead of network TV, most of the ads appear on such cable TV venues as MTV, VH1, and Comedy Central. When Take My Picture, the new music video of the band Filter, premiered on MTV on Oct. 15, Toyota's "Revolution" was right behind it. Spliced to the commercial was a 15-second plug for the hot group's first Web-cast—exclusively on Toyota's Web site.

Toyota's new Web site, that is. The genesis bunch pulled out all the stops to create a flashy no-text site full of 360-degree video, edgy music, and what boomers would call "irritating noise." And, in a gentle poke at the corporate higher-ups, they gave it an irresistible address: www.isthistoyota.com. Even the suits across the parking lot are hoping that the answer will someday be "yes."
By Larry Armstrong in Torrance, Calif.

The changing face of Super Sunday

Marketers, NFL focus on game's audience of 40 million women

Michael McCarthy
USA TODAY

NEW YORK—The Super Bowl is becoming the Women's Bowl.

The National Football League's championship game has been the Holy Day of testosterone for three decades. But we've come a long way, baby.

This Sunday, 40 million women will watch Super Bowl XXXV, pitting the New York Giants against the Baltimore Ravens. That's a bigger draw for female viewers than the Academy Awards, with 27 million.

And those numbers aren't lost on advertisers, who know women influence 80% of household consumer purchases. So this weekend, you'll see the nation's top marketers in touch with their feminine sides like never before.

You'll see multimillion-dollar ads and promotions aimed at women during the game, which is the highest-rated TV program of the year. You'll see football-themed shows on female-oriented TV networks. And you'll spot such female celebrities as Marion Jones, Daisy Fuentes, Patti LaBelle, Courteney Cox Arquette and Wynonna Judd invading the once-impregnable male bastion of the Super Bowl.

Anheuser-Busch, the biggest advertiser in the game, has been changing its Super Bowl creative approach to appeal to both genders. "Women are a huge part of this audience," says Bob Lachky, A-B's vice president of brand management. "We've been working hard for five years not to do typical guy jokes."

A-B scored touchdowns the past few games with lovable "Rex," the method-acting dog; two Dalmatian puppies separated at birth; and the "Next Generation" birth of a Clydesdale foal.

The approach has let A-B—dare we say it—show its sensitive side. "It's been a wonderful eye-opener for us. It's taught us that it's OK to be emotional and have a smile—not always go for a gut- laugh," says Lachky.

And this year's game kicks off what looks to be a "Year of the Woman" in sports marketing. Female athletes such as Jones, Venus Williams and Michelle Kwan appear to be taking over as endorsement champions from retired male jocks like Michael Jordan, John Elway and Wayne Gretzky.

"Super Bowl Sunday is as much for women as it is for men," says Heather Paige Kent, star of the CBS prime-time TV show *That's Life*. She should know: Kent will host a Lifetime Television special Friday night at 7 ET called *NFL Stories: Straight from the Heart*. This won't be your father's NFL Films—no footballs spiraling through winter skies; no stirring martial music like *Cossacks Charge;* no exhortations by legendary NFL Films narrator John Facenda to "Be savage again."

Instead, we get a story about deaf Oakland Raiders cheerleader Mona Vierra. And one about Tampa Bay Buccaneers special teams coach Joe Marciano, a 45-year-old bachelor who adopted a baby boy and formed "his own special team" as a single parent.

"The NFL sought us out because they knew Lifetime could help expand their female viewership," explains Harriet Saltzman, Lifetime's vice president of sports programming.

Football shows such as this are about more than X's and O's—they tell the "human-interest stories" that make women watch sporting events like the Olympics, says Kent.

As the rough-and-tumble XFL gets ready to challenge the NFL's dominance in February, Kent thinks the move by the NFL and its sponsors to give women a big hug is a "great" idea. "Everyone needs a few fans—myself included."

Make no mistake, though, the helmeted gladiators on the field love to act macho—one Ravens player declared that Tennessee Titans running back Eddie George should "take his panties off" before the AFC Championship Game.

But the NFL and its sponsors want to show that they "get it." If Bronco Nagurski is turning over in his grave, so be it. It's all part of making the NFL more "inclusive" and expanding the league from "the premier American sport" to "premier sports entertainment," says John Collins, the NFL's vice president of programming and sales.

SUPER BOWL VS. OSCAR

CBS is, however, asking advertisers to pay $2.3 million per 30- second commercial to target women on this most manly of days. One expert, Laura Ries, president of marketing consultancy Ries & Ries Atlanta,

(Cont.)

thinks they are foolishly wasting their millions.

"Most women watch the Super Bowl next to their husbands or boyfriends because they don't have a choice. The guys may be glued to the screen—but the women are talking to their girlfriends or watching the kids." The Oscars are the "real Super Bowl of advertising to women," Ries maintains.

But Betsy Berns, author of *The Female Fan Guide to Pro Football*, counters that "Women can have a conversation and still watch the game—unlike men." Berns says that she has talked with women around the country, from "football widows" to fanatics like one woman who refused painkillers during the birth of her child so that she wouldn't miss a playoff game.

Berns says the best news for advertisers is that "Even women who are not interested in the game are closely watching the commercials. You have to watch—or you miss half the conversations in America the next day."

And advertisers are getting in step with the trend. Gone for the most part are ads treating women as sex objects—the way they often were in the "old days" of Super Bowl spots. Does anyone remember the cheesy 1973 Noxzema shave cream commercial where Farrah Fawcett puts shaving cream on Joe Namath's face? "You've got a great pair of hands," says Broadway Joe, while Fawcett purrs in delight.

Last year, Visa and Southwest Airlines ran commercials showing women as football fans. Oxygen Media launched its women's Web and TV network during the game. Nuveen tugged at the heartstrings with a controversial spot showing actor Christopher Reeve apparently walking again. And Web site OurBeginning.com took aim at brides and expectant mothers. "We did it to reach the female audience. For us, it paid off," says OurBeginning.com chief Mike Budowski .

This weekend, an all-out marketing blitz will target female consumers. The game plan:

▲ A-B will air a mix of heartwarmers, including a couple of possible animal spots. Also, look for a new "Whassup?!" commercial like the one last year showing "Dookie" getting busted by the guys for watching figure skating with his girlfriend. "That ad absolutely resonated with women. Quite frankly, it catapulted the campaign," says Lachky.

▲ Diamond retailer Zales is sponsoring pregame programming to plant the seed that Valentine's Day is only two weeks later.

▲ Breathe Right nasal strips is running a Super Bowl promotion for kids strips "to reach Moms through kids," says Melissa Hanson, senior product manager. "Females and kids follow Super Bowl activities just as much as men," she says.

---

40 million
Number of women who watch the Super Bowl. That's well above the 27 million who watch the Academy Awards and is 45.5% of the game's U.S. audience. The number of female viewers rose 5% for last year's Super Bowl.

375,000
Number of women who attend NFL games on an average weekend. Women make up about 40% of attendees.

30 million
Number of women watching the NFL on TV on an average weekend. Women pick pro football as their favorite TV sport (22.1%) over pro baseball (13.6%), pro basketball (12.6%), figure skating (6.5%) and college football (4.3%).

46%
Percentage of NFL-licensed merchandise purchased by women.

100,000
Number of girls who participate annually in NFL flag football competitions.

12,000
Number of women who attended Football 101 classes offered by NFL teams to teach pro football basics in 2000.

1.3 million
Number of girls participating in the Gatorade Punt, Pass & Kick competition in 2000.

779
Number of girls on high school football teams in 1999, a total up 250% from 1994.

Source: NFL

▲ The NFL will premier an image ad using the Lou Reed song, *Perfect Day*. The spot features vignettes such as a father playing catch in the backyard—with his daughter. The campaign is about football "as a unifying experience."

▲ New York Giants running back Tiki Barber and wife Ginny Barber are penning his and her Super Bowl "diaries" for NFL.com. "Nowadays, when there's a Super Bowl party, it's not just the guys—it's wives and girlfriends, too," says Ginny, 24, a fashion publicist for Italian clothier Ermenegildo Zegna. "We read the

(Cont.)

articles about how much the commercials cost and who will be in them. We talk about the commercials after the game."

▲ Fashion designer—and NFL licensee—Nicole Miller is rolling out a Super Bowl print for the company's 30 boutiques and high-end department stores such as Nordstrom. "I don't think other women's companies have a clue about the potential of these partnerships. And we're not going to tell them," says Shari Grossman, director of licensing.

▲ During CBS' premier of *Survivor: The Australian Outback* after the game, Reebok will launch its first ad with tennis star Venus Williams. The company recently signed Williams to a $40 million multiyear deal, the richest endorsement contract ever signed by a woman. Reebok intends to make Williams its "lifestyle icon," the way Nike used Michael Jordan. "Reebok signing Venus recognizes the increased influence women athletes have," says spokeswoman Denise Kaigler. Stephanie Tolleson, the IMG agent who helped make Williams one of the world's highest-paid female athletes, says: "Companies are finally seeing women as credible, strong spokespersons. For a long time, they just talked the talk. Now, they're realizing female athletes are the link to female buying power."

REFLECTING POPULAR CULTURE

Futurist Tom Julian of Fallon Worldwide says Williams' ascension to Michael Jordan-Tiger Woods territory is an example of the "girl power" trend in pop culture that includes hit movies such as *Charlie's Angels* and *Crouching Tiger, Hidden Dragon*. But Nova Lanktree, president of Lanktree Sports Celebrity Network in Chicago, wonders whether Reebok's multimillion-dollar investment in a "start-up star" from a "niche sport" may be "more about being politically correct—or trying to match wits with Nike," says Lanktree.

One Super Bowl advertiser spending $6 million on media and production believes she has the key to why women pay more attention to Super Bowl ads than guys: Men are more likely to go to the bathroom during ad breaks. "Men get up during the commercials; women only get up during the game," says LaWanda Burrell, vice president of global advertising for EDS.

Maybe for some, but don't tell that to Linda Hempel. The 40-year-old teacher from Minnesota attended the 1967 "Ice Bowl" pitting the Green Bay Packers against the Dallas Cowboys with a girlfriend. "Women are becoming more interested in the game," she says.

Or to Clara Matheson, a 74-year-old grandmother from Stratham, N.H. Her husband, Ron, is the football widow in their family. While she cheers for her favorite teams on fall Sundays, her husband goes fishing.

"I don't know where I found him. It wasn't at a stadium, that's for sure," Matheson says, laughing.

'Mom, the Airlines Don't Like Me!'

BY WENDY BOUNDS AND LAUREN LIPTON

Staff Reporters of THE WALL STREET JOURNAL

Most businesses are wooing kids like crazy—but not airlines. Some are dropping everything from preboarding rights to youth fares. It's even hard to find those little toy wings. Wendy Bounds and Lauren Lipton report.

On a recent United flight to San Francisco, Carol Ann Band brought along her two-year-old son Adam and discovered just how unfriendly the skies can be.

For starters, she wasn't allowed to board ahead of anyone else. Then the family was denied roomier bulkhead seats in favor of passengers with special needs—one of whom turned out to be an able-bodied college student. That left Ms. Band and her husband holding up an aisle of impatient passengers while they struggled to install Adam's child-restraint chair. With the plane so crowded, several passengers knocked young Adam in the head with their suitcases.

Says Ms. Band of her boarding experience: "There was nothing good about it."

What is good about flying with children these days? Today, businesses from Baby Gap to luxury hotels are doing cartwheels to attract kids. But when was the last time you found a youth fare for air travel or saw an airline offering any special assistance to a mother with an infant? And what about saving a few roomier upfront seats for families? These once-popular measures are fading as fast as legroom. And, with the skies only getting more crowded, some airlines are now starting to cut privileges parents have relied on for decades.

Last year, United and Delta Air Lines eliminated preboarding announcements for families with small children; both carriers say it isn't "efficient." Other airlines raised the fees they charge for unaccompanied minors. Even free travel for infants riding on parents' laps—long an industry tradition—may soon vanish completely with an impending government ruling that would mandate child-restraint chairs on airplanes.

All of which means that most kids traveling today are lucky if they get those little pilot wings. And for the parents, the treatment is only more upsetting when compared with the perks the industry keeps lavishing, for example, on business fliers. "The world understands the importance of children," says Keith Waldon with Virtuoso, a Texas-based network of 244 travel agencies. "Airlines are just behind schedule on this."

It's not that airlines are out to get kids; adult leisure fliers usually get the same level of pared-down service. The truth is, much of the change is about economics—and the realities of modern jet service. With 71% load factors, planes haven't been this packed since the 1940s, which only makes it harder for carriers to offer families any special attention or better seats. Airlines also argue that most families these days care more about price than amenities. "Don't get the idea that we don't welcome kids," says Joe Hopkins, a spokesman for United. "The world has changed. It is mass transportation in the sky. We're trying to provide the highest level of service."

Indeed, the bottom line is that kids, who don't typically fly in first or business class, aren't big money-makers. Nearly two-thirds of airlines' revenue is derived from business travelers who take up only about one-third of seats, estimates Sam Buttrick, an airline analyst with PaineWebber. By contrast, child passengers account for as little as 5% to 6% of an airline's revenue. "Airline executives don't sit around thinking about how to improve the travel experience of the average adolescent," Mr. Buttrick says. "And I'm not sure they should."

Still, many travel experts says the airlines may be missing an opportunity here, applying the wrong strategy to a group that's becoming more important to the industry. While still a small portion of overall air voyagers, more kids are becoming seasoned travelers as time-crunched parents increasingly make business trips into family affairs. Children under 18 accompanied adults on more than 26 million air trips in 1998, according to the Travel Industry Association of America, up 30% from just two years earlier. And let's not forget that many of those prized business travelers are parents themselves.

Can't Win

Airlines can't win "by doing bad things to children," says Michael Allen, head of the aviation-information business Back Associates Inc. A parent of two young children, he says any airline that entertained his kids more would "have my business in a second." Indeed, many foreign carriers have noticed this; British Airways has a toy chest in its economy sections, while El Al offers both an in-seat TV channel for kids and a special family-seating section onboard. "It's nice because kids can be together—and drive flight attendants crazy together," says an El Al spokeswoman.

Of course, international carriers typically have more time in-flight to devote to children and bigger planes to hold more amenities. "Young travelers are the future business travelers, and I don't know any company that wouldn't bend over backward to make sure they have a good experience," says Dean Breest with Air France, which operates "Planete Bleue" airport lounges with games and toys. Forced to compete, many U.S. carriers also offer more family perks on overseas flights.

To this day, many parents can still recall the days before airline deregulation when airlines could afford to lavish attention on children. As recently as the late '70s and early '80s, flight attendants would pin metal wings on kids' lapels and invite them to the cockpit. Steep discounts for youth were common, as were onboard diapers and even the occasional sit-down video games. Thom Nulty, president of Navigant International, a large travel agency, still recalls when airlines routinely offered scores of comics and coloring books. "I can't remember the last time I saw those things," he says.

Indeed, in-flight entertainment for children is just one area that's become a sore spot for parents. Of the 36 magazines offered right now on Continental Airlines flights, including Latin Finance and Luxury Golf Homes, none are specifically for children. Several airlines do offer activity books and audio channels for children on certain flights, but the options pale in comparison to, say, the 25 personal video titles available in many American Airlines first-class cabins this month. On United, three of the four movies offered on its domestic flights in February, while edited for airline use, contain either violence, sexual situations or adult themes, according to its company magazine.

That leaves parents on their own during long flights, forced to cart their own assortment of toys, books, video games—anything—to keep antsy children busy in a cramped space. And just trying to bring on the load can be tricky, given the industry's new crackdown on carry-ons. "I've learned not to expect anything from airlines," says Juliett Giordano, who describes the travails of keeping her three-year-old son in check for a four-hour flight to New Orleans. Her tools: Play-Doh, Hot Wheels, crayons and other toys, all in a backpack the family had to lug aboard along with all their other carry-ons.

Happy Meals

A limited selection of airline meals for kids, meanwhile, has forced parents to include kiddie chow in their carry-ons too. United offers 10 meals for passengers with special medical diets; three vegetarian selections; three religious meals and five additional options, including a seafood meal and Obento Japanese. Kids get one choice: a McDonald's Happy Meal, which must be ordered 24 hours in advance. Unhappy with all the junk food options on most airlines, Elizabeth Schimel says she has to lug along juice boxes and carrots on trips with her two young sons. She also complains most domestic airlines make no effort to feed children first, something many foreign carriers do. "Their stomachs are not on the schedule of airlines' feeding plans," says the New York-based executive of Wit Capital.

Another beef: seating. Most airlines now reserve the front of the plane for their top-tier frequent fliers—including the roomy bulkhead seats so coveted by families. On her Thanksgiving trip, Mrs. Giordano says she twice requested bulkhead seats for her family—and still ended up being assigned five rows from the back. Another parent, Renee Berliner Rush, says she inevitably finds herself separated from her nine-year-old son, Wylie, on most flights. "We are always having to call upon the kindness of strangers" to switch seats, she says.

In response, airlines insist they do try to leave some good seats open until the day of departure for families. "You may have a full-fare business traveler who isn't happy with his seat, but we may also rearrange seats to keep families together," says USAirways spokesman David Castelveter.

Teddy Bear Teas

Other parts of travel industry, meanwhile, are going gangbusters for kids, including Amtrak, which offers 50% fare discounts for children up to 15 years old. (On most domestic airlines, children pay adult fares at age two.) In San Diego, parents at Loews Coronado Bay Resort can reach into the "Kids Kloset" to borrow games, car seats, strollers and bedtime books. The Boca Raton Resort & Club in Florida has developed a baby-food menu, while several Ritz-Carlton properties now hold "Teddy Bear Teas."

Compare that to the way some airlines handle the sticky issue of diapers. The last time Holly Hunnicutt flew with her son James, now nine months old, she resorted to laying him on the toilet-seat rim for changing. The reason: Despite having added 25% more leg room to a typical business-class seats in the last few years, many airlines still don't provide changing facilities onboard. Never mind germs, gripes the Langhorne, Pa., mom: "I was afraid he was going to fall in." It's not that planes don't have room. Continental says it offers facilities on every flight, while Northwest and United have refurbished many of their planes to include them.

Right now, the outlook for youth fliers and their parents seems to be getting more turbulent. During the last 18 months, several major airlines raised the fees they charge unaccompanied minors—in some cases doubling the charge to $30 a flight segment and charging extra for connections. And a few, including Northwest and Continental, raised the age for which minors can travel alone without charge to 15 from 12. Divorced parents whose kids fly frequently back and forth are "not happy, obviously," says Seattle travel analyst Steve Danishek. "They thought there were certain costs that disappeared as the kid gets older."

At the same time, as airlines crack down on on-time departure, preboarding for families is disappearing. Delta cut out the practice after finding they typically got a "mass of people at the door claiming to need extra assistance," says spokesman John Kennedy. He notes that the airline will try to preboard anyone who requests it, "time permitting." Same for United, says Lindsey Peterik, who works with the airline's airport-service planning, adding that the new policy "streamlines boarding."

That's little consolation to Kathy Bernstein, mother of two, who always needs the extra time to install a car-seat for her children. With everyone boarding simultaneously, "you're hitting first-class passengers in the head," complains Ms. Bernstein of Studio City, Calif. "I've never had a flight attendant help me. It's a nightmare." What's more, while domestic airlines recommend safety seats, they don't provide them, which means she must carry her own. By contrast, most car-rental agencies rent such seats for $5 a day.

The mayhem may worsen with an impending Federal Aviation Administration proposal that would make child-seats mandatory; the agency is still debating who should supply them. Worse yet, for some parents and their wallets, is that the ruling could end free travel for so-called "lap babies." Major airlines now charge 50% of the accompanying adult's ticketed fare for kids under two riding in safety seats.

"Margins in the industry are thin enough," says Northwest spokesman, Jon Austin, explaining that in a 100-seat plane, one or two full-paying passengers make the difference between a "profitable and unprofitable flight." American Airlines, which was the first to institute the 50% fare, states: "American is a business like any other. We feel our 50% infant fare makes economic sense—both for parents and the airline—and is an affordable way to safely keep infants in their seats."

Yet with all the focus on boarding efficiency and seat revenue, some parents wonder if airlines aren't growing just a bit too uptight. On his last Christmas trip from Jackson, Miss., to Houston, Kevin Schultz was stunned when a Southwest flight attendant chastised him for being one item over the carry-on limit. She counted his baby, who didn't have a seat of her own, as a piece of luggage. Southwest says this isn't standard policy, but Mr. Schultz was soured by the experience.

"Who would consider a child carry-on luggage?" says the father. He's already mulling an alternative route for their next holiday trip: 13 hours, by car.

Pillsbury Presses Flour Power in India

BY MIRIAM JORDAN
Staff Reporter of THE WALL STREET JOURNAL

BOMBAY, India—The Pillsbury Doughboy has landed in India to pitch a product that he had just about abandoned in America: plain old flour.

Pillsbury, the Diageo PLC unit behind the pudgy character, has a raft of higher-margin products such as microwave pizzas in other parts of the world but discovered that in this tradition-bound market, it needs to push the basics.

Even so, selling packaged flour in India is almost revolutionary, because most Indian housewives still buy raw wheat in bulk, clean it by hand, store it in huge metal hampers and, every week, carry some to a neighborhood mill, or chakki, where it is ground between two stones.

To help reach those housewives, the Doughboy himself has gotten a makeover. In TV spots, he presses his palms together and bows in the traditional Indian greeting. He speaks six regional languages.

Pillsbury is onto a potentially huge business. India consumes about 69 million tons of wheat a year, second only to China. (The U.S. consumes about 26 million tons.) Much of India's wheat ends up as roti, a flat bread prepared on a griddle that accompanies almost every meal. In a nation where people traditionally eat with their hands, roti is the spoon. But less than 1% of all whole-wheat flour, or *atta*, is sold prepackaged. India's climatic extremes and deplorable roads make it difficult to maintain freshness from mill to warehouse, let alone on store shelves.

Then there are the standards of the Indian housewife, who is determined to serve only the softest, freshest roti to her family. "Packaged flour sticks to your stomach and is bad for the intestines," says Poonam Jain, a New Delhi housewife.

Pillsbury knows that ultimately it won't make fistfuls of dough from packaged flour. Its aim is to establish its flour business and then introduce new products to carry its customers up to more lucrative products.

That payoff may take a decade or two. "As a food company, we have to be where the mouths are," says Robert Hancock, marketing director for Europe and Eurasia. "We'll get our rewards later."

Starting a flour operation meant turning back the clock for Pillsbury. Though it was born as a U.S. flour-milling company 130 years ago, the Diageo unit all but exited from that business in the early 1990s to focus on products such as frozen baked goods and ice cream. The food giant thought of introducing

high-value products when it first explored India. But it quickly learned that most Indians don't have enough disposable income for such fare. Many lack refrigerators and ovens, too.

Pillsbury is betting that flour will generate sales volumes to compensate for the razor-thin profit margins. "We wanted a product with huge and widespread mainstream appeal," Mr. Hancock says.

Pitching packaged flour meant overcoming thousands of years of tradition. "I'd never met women so intimately involved with the food they prepare," recalls Bill Barrier, who led a Pillsbury team that spent 18 months trying to decode Indian wheat and consumers.

Marketing managers climbed into the attics where housewives store their wheat and accompanied them to their tiny neighborhood flour mills. "Anywhere else, flour is flour," says Samir Behl, vice president of marketing for Pillsbury International. "In India, the color, aroma, feel between the fingers, and mouth feel are all crucial."

Pillsbury had hoped to establish contracts with existing mills, but inspectors found hygiene and safety at some to be appalling. Pillsbury scouts visited 40 plants, where they encountered mice, rotting wheat and treacherous machinery. They often left coated in fine flour dust, whose presence is a severe fire hazard. In fact, when the electricity went out during a visit to one mill, Pillsbury executives were dumbfounded to see one worker light a match in the dark.

Pillsbury eventually found two mills capable of the required standards. But even then, their rollout was delayed by several months because the company rejected 40% of the wheat delivered to the mills after the 1998 harvest.

Many focus groups and lab tests later, Pillsbury came up with its packaged wheat blend, Pillsbury Chakki Fresh Atta. Godrej-Pillsbury Ltd., its joint venture here, launched the flour in southern and western India last year. The blue package, which features the Doughboy hoisting a roti, has become the market leader in Bombay, India's largest city, eclipsing the more established Kissan Annapurna brand from the Anglo-Dutch company **Unilever** PLC.

"People said [prepackaged flour] wouldn't taste the same, but my husband and I don't find any difference," says Shivani Zaveri, a Bombay housewife who was introduced to Pillsbury by a friend who works and so has less time to cook.

Responding to consumers' biggest concern, Pillsbury pitches the flour with a promise that rotis made from it will stay soft "for six hours." Jigna Shah of Bombay, who makes 60 rotis a day and has tried rival packaged brands, is sold. She uses Pillsbury Chakki Fresh Atta to make rotis for her husband's lunch box "that don't dry up around the edges or get rigid."

The company declines to say what ingredients keep the flour tasting fresh, though it says there are no artificial preservatives. The packaging is made of a robust plastic laminate that costs about two and a half times as much as

Doughboy *does New Delhi, hoisting a roti*

the paper wrappers typical in the U.S.

It's too early to declare the Doughboy's foray into India a success. The market is still minuscule, and gains will depend largely on how quickly Indian housewives embrace convenience. Several local companies familiar with Indian tastes have launched branded flour in recent years, only to flounder.

The value of the packaged-flour market in India is $7.14 million. It has expanded by about 45% a year since 1997, according to industry estimates, even though flour made the traditional way costs about 30% less.

To undermine its U.S. rival, Unilever has offered freebies to consumers, such as a free one-kilogram packet of flour with every five-kilogram packet, and a free sample of Surf detergent with every flour pack. Pillsbury has fought back with such promotions as a free sample of sunflower oil with every five-kilogram package of flour. It has also been paying grocers to display a standing cardboard Doughboy with its product in a visible spot in shops. That's a novelty in this market, where most people buy their staples at small, crammed grocers, which have no room for promotional displays.

Unilever, which went nationwide in January 1998, predicts that its sales by volume will double this year to about 100,000 tons. Pillsbury anticipates production of about 50,000 tons in 1999. That's only a drop in the bucket, given that 30 million tons of wheat are consumed as rotis each year.

AN EAGLE EYE ON CUSTOMERS

When Mary Aehlich gave up her career as a weapons controller in an Air Force AWACS spy plane to become casino administrator at The Venetian resort in Las Vegas, she joked that she went from "combat boots and flight suits to sequins and high heels." But now the stay-at-home mom of two babies is again on the front lines, of sorts. As an occasional at-home Web site tester, she's part of an early warning system for e-tailers—helping them figure out what works and what doesn't in the uncharted world of Web commerce.

Take Aehlich's December sortie onto the jewelry site Miadora.com. Following a script prepared by the market research software company Vividence Corp., she shopped for a xen bracelet, a Jordan Schlanger necklace, and a round diamond. Although she enjoyed the site, it was difficult to locate some items. She said as much in an online critique she typed as she worked her way through the exercise. Feedback like hers from 200 testers was priceless for David A. Lamond, Miadora.com's vice-president for business development. Within two days of getting Vividence's report, he ordered changes to make the site easier to navigate. "This is as close as you can get to reading the mind of your customer," he says.

Vividence's product is just one example of a vast array of new software products that are designed to help companies read customers' minds and win them over—whether in cyberspace or on Main Street. The latest advances in software technology make it possible for companies to amass detailed profiles of customers, offer them just the things they're likely to buy, reward them for loyalty, and quell their frustrations. And, thanks to the Web, companies can keep all of their information about customers in a single electronic storehouse, easily accessible through Web browsers for executives at headquarters, salespeople on the road, and service reps in remote call centers. It's all about delivering TLC—Internet style. "Everybody is scrambling to grab the customer and not let them go," says David Caruso, a vice-president at market researcher AMR Research.

It's a mad dash that's creating a vast new software category: call it customer management software. Included is the Old World of so-called customer relationship management software—giant packages such as Siebel Systems Inc.'s program that lets corporate sales forces track their customers and analyze markets. That's now merging with new programs for the Web that manage everything from online sales to customer service. The whole shebang is expected to grow from $4.45 billion last year to $21.8 billion in 2003, according to AMR—a growth rate nearly five times that of the overall software market.

WANTED WIDGETS. Why are companies opening their wallets so fast? The technology promises to transform the way they do business. Gone are the days when they could afford to build products without knowing for sure if customers would snap them up. Now they can learn precisely what their customers want before they design a single widget. Manufacturers can even let buyers specify the key features they would like before a product is assembled. And by using technology to track their every encounter with a customer, companies can easily separate out the best from the bad—and focus their marketing muscle on customers who are likely to buy often and pay their bills on time.

The new software already is delivering cash rewards to its early adopters. For starters, it cuts costs: A self-service package tracking system for customers that IBM built for United Parcel Service Inc. saves the shipping company $450,000 a day in customer service expenses. And this stuff boosts revenues, too: Thanks to call-center software

A GUIDE TO CUSTOMER MANAGEMENT SOFTWARE

SALES-FORCE AUTOMATION
Field sales representatives can track accounts and prospects—plus check goals and inventories—from the office PC or a notebook computer on the road. At the same time, their bosses can keep tabs on their performance. New Net-only versions allow individuals and small teams to handle accounts from Web sites for $50 a month or less.

CALL-CENTER AUTOMATION
Creates customer profiles and provides scripts to help service representatives solve customers' problems or suggest new purchases. The latest versions allow companies to coordinate phone calls and messages on Web sites—plus reps can carry on phone conversations with customers while seeing the Web pages the customers are looking at.

MARKETING AUTOMATION
Helps marketers analyze customer purchasing histories and demographics and design targeted marketing campaigns—then measures results.

WEB SALES AND PERSONALIZATION
Basic e-commerce software manages product catalogs, shopping carts, and credit-card purchases. New features allow repeat customers to keep shopping lists on the Web and quickly resubmit orders. Web shops can create special, on-the-fly prices for specific customers.

WEB CONFIGURATOR
Walks consumers through the process of ordering complex custom-assembled products like computers, and, in the future,

cars. It's even more important for business-to-business transactions. A retailer that brands refrigerators or stoves made by others can specify the features they want.

WEB SERVICE
Self-service packages and e-mail limit the need for live customer service representatives. New artificial intelligence features suggest solutions for problems to customers or service reps.

WEB ANALYSIS AND MARKETING
Warehouses of digital data allow Web sites to track the online activities of individual shoppers and offer them merchandise they're likely to buy based on past behavior. It also enables targeted marketing of individuals via e-mail.

The Goliaths

SIEBEL SYSTEMS INC.

MARKET CAP: $19.4 billion.

REVENUES IN THE MOST RECENT QUARTER: $268 million, up 109%.

NET INCOME: $45 million, up 127%.

WHAT THEY SELL: Software for managing field sales; telesales and marketing departments in large corporations.

STRATEGY: To beef up offerings for Web site sales and service and to provide companies with a single view of their customers on computer screens no matter how they buy—on the Web, or off.

COMPETITIVE POSITION: The leader in the traditional corporate customer relationship management market, it's becoming a force to reckon with in e-business, too.

ORACLE CORP.

MARKET CAP: $170.3 billion.

REVENUES IN THE MOST RECENT QUARTER: $2.32 billion, up 13%. Customer relationship software sales totaled $49 million, up 300%.

NET INCOME: $384 million, up 40%.

WHAT THEY SELL: Products for customer relationship management and e-commerce are relatively recent add-ons for a company whose core products are databases.

STRATEGY: To offer large organizations one-stop-shopping for their key pieces of software that can be integrated with one another.

COMPETITIVE POSITION: Oracle's databases power the top 10 consumer e-commerce sites, so it's in a strong spot to hawk software for Web sales and online service.

NORTEL NETWORKS CORP.

MARKET CAP: $161.6 billion.

REVENUES IN THE MOST RECENT QUARTER: $6.99 billion, up 21%.

NET INCOME: $755 million, up 53%.

WHAT THEY SELL: Telecommunications gear, and, because of a pending $2.1 billion acquisition of Clarify, a suite of customer management software. Clarify revenues were $71.6 last quarter.

STRATEGY: To combine the Clarify products with its software for call-center routing.

COMPETITIVE POSITION: Clarify is the strongest of Siebel's traditional competitors. If the potential synergies with Nortel pay off, it could dominate the call-center software business—and be a strong contender in other markets.

(continued)

competitors in this new land grab: software giants SAP and Oracle Corp. Even Nortel Networks Corp., the maker of telecom gear, wants in on the action. It's about to close a $2.1 billion acquisition of Clarify, the call-center software maker.

While the giants duke it out, hundreds of small fry are cooking up new products for everything from personalizing online sales pitches to customer service software for the Web. Some have solid traction, such as Vignette Corp. and BroadVision Inc., which are each logging more than $40 million in revenues per quarter for Web site software. Many are minuscule—such as Salesforce.com in San Francisco, which just launched its Web-only sales-management site. But even some of the little guys already loom large on Wall Street. Kana Communications Inc., a seller of e-mail systems for customer support, has watched its stock soar from $45 a share at its initial public offering last September to about $240 today—giving it a market cap of $6.9 billion.

Ultimately, expect only a handful of players to claim the lion's share of this market. Siebel and Oracle look like big winners. They already have relationships with thousands of large customers and offer a broad array of software packages. Up-and-comers such as Vignette, BroadVision, and Kana stand a good chance of succeeding, too. They lead in their segments and are rapidly broadening their product portfolios.

With hundreds of others vying for this new software prize, consolidation is a sure bet. Those that survive are apt to be the players that put together the most compelling soup-to-nuts packages. They'll either develop products themselves or buy up smaller competitors—often with stock. It's already happening. On Feb. 7, Kana announced a $4.2 billion purchase of Silknet Software Inc., a maker of self-help software for Web sites. "The companies with the biggest market caps will be the winners," predicts Kevin Harvey, a partner at Silicon Valley venture-capital firm Benchmark Capital.

Some large corporations are already demanding one-stop shopping for customer management software. Honeywell International, for instance, aims to revamp totally the way it does business. Rather than making products and then finding out later if customers will buy them, it's using a software package from Siebel Systems to anticipate more accurately what its customers will want. Honeywell's $5.2 billion air-transport business, which makes jet engines and avionics gear, uses Siebel to track all of its interactions with customers and publishes monthly analyses so executives can quickly spot problems and opportunities. One early result: It noticed that airlines were frustrated with managing parts inventories, so it's rolling out new services that will spare them that headache. "Our focus used to be from the inside out. Now it's the reverse," says division General Manager Lynn Brubaker.

from Clarify Inc., Automatic Data Processing Inc. handed 8,000 customer service reps detailed information about its 80,000 payroll clients—improving the customer retention rate by 5% and upping revenues by $100 million last year. Based on its surveys of six industries, Andersen Consulting estimates that with just a modest 10% improvement in customer management operations, a $1 billion business can reap $40 million to $50 million

a year in pretax profits.

With customers lining up to do business, hundreds of software companies are busy staking claims. Some are well-established players in the customer software arena, such as Siebel, with revenues of $790 million and a 19% market share of the $3.7 billion market for corporate sales and marketing software. But as big as it is in its own market, Siebel has to watch out for even brawnier

---

*The Davids and Goliaths of Customer
Software Square Off (concluded)*

The Davids

VIGNETTE CORP.

MARKET CAP: $11.14 billion.

REVENUES IN THE MOST RECENT QUARTER: $40.9 million, up 512%.

NET LOSS: $5.6 million compared to $9.2 million a year earlier.

WHAT THEY SELL: Software for managing all kinds of Web site information, from stock tickers to product catalogs. E-marketing will be available midyear.

STRATEGY: To broaden from its traditional information-management niche into personalizing e-commerce—studying what people look at on a site and pitching them products that fit their interests.

COMPETITIVE POSITION: The company established a rock-solid reputation by powering high-volume Web sites like CNET. Now it's becoming a major player in e-commerce—though BroadVision Corp. is still the segment leader.

KANA COMMUNICATIONS INC.

MARKET CAP: $6.94 billion.

REVENUES IN THE MOST RECENT QUARTER: $6.5 million, up 650%.

NET LOSS: $90.6 million, due to acquisition expenses.

WHAT THEY SELL: Software to manage e-mail-based customer service and marketing campaigns.

STRATEGY: To fill out its product offerings through stock-based acquisitions like its purchases last December of Net Dialog Inc. and Business Evolution Inc. Target: Customer analysis software for Web sites.

COMPETITIVE POSITION: Kana leads its segment thanks to dot-com accounts like eBay and Lycos. It needs to win in corporate markets to stop giants like Siebel from encroaching on its business.

E.PIPHANY INC.

MARKET CAP: $4.14 billion

REVENUES IN THE MOST RECENT QUARTER: $8.7 million, up 521%

NET LOSS: $6.3 million

WHAT THEY SELL: Software for analyzing customer information and launching marketing campaigns on the Web.

STRATEGY: To create partnerships with e-commerce leaders like BroadVision and Art Technology Group—fitting in with their array of Web site sales software to offer corporations a full package of software.

COMPETITIVE POSITION: Ultimately, the kind of software it makes will be an essential part of every Web site, and most e-commerce software companies will offer it. E.piphany has to get big fast, or sell out.

Westwood, Mass., which sells groceries and household items online and delivers them in Boston and Chicago. "We're really a logistics organization. We've got warehouses and trucks. We're focused on operations," says John Cagno, vice-president for information technology. That's why he bought a suite of software from SAP that includes customer, finance, and logistics software all linked together. When the new system rolls out in March, Streamline.com's customers will be able to chose from its actual inventory, so there's no risk of their picking out-of-stock items and being disappointed with substitutions. The goal: improve customer loyalty and cut down on service calls.

Now, companies want a way to view all customer information in one place. Often companies keep multiple databases for each business and each way of reaching customers—and those repositories aren't easily synced up. This new generation of software offers a way to gather information collected by companies' Web sites, direct-mail operations, customer service, retail stores, and field sales. H&R Block Inc., for instance, is using software from Clarify to combine and coordinate the customer records at its tax offices, discount brokerage, Web site, and customer-service center. Armed with that central storehouse of information, sales people in the stock-trading business, for instance, can look at detailed descriptions of tax customers and size up which of them would be good prospects.

Not every company wants software that will handle the whole enchilada of customer needs. Many—especially dot-coms—shop for single pieces of software that solve problems or boost revenues in a matter of weeks. They shun complex packages that can take months or even years to install. Vignette, for instance, has grown fast because its software allows Web sites to generate pages on the fly that are custom-made for individuals. Web site operators can analyze customers' online behavior and pitch them products that are likely to pique their interest. And the software is relatively easy to get going. Thanks in part to Vignette, Iwon.com, the four-month-old Web sweepstakes portal, was able to launch in just 4 1/2 months.

The more narrowly focused the software, the easier it is for companies to see results. Using Silknet's new virtual sales assistant, for instance, online computer retailer cozone.com created "Jill—the Notebook Advisor." It's a piece of software that walks customers through a series of questions about their lifestyles and what they're looking for in a computer—then makes recommendations. Cozone.com gathers a vast amount of data from cybershoppers and can use it later to target them with e-mail promotions. But mostly, "Jill" is about making customers feel good about their experience so they come back for more.

Often, customers want software to bridge the Web and other businesses. Williams-Sonoma Inc. for instance, uses e-mail soft-

The software giants have taken the lead in assembling packages capable of handling huge jobs such as Honeywell's. Siebel has spent the past two years adding call-center and Web commerce components to its sales-force management software. The newest pieces delivered last year include a package for setting up Web shops and an e-mail marketing product. The empire-building effort is paying off big time: Siebel just landed a deal worth tens of millions of dollars to supply IBM with practically its entire suite of products for 55,000 IBM sales and marketing

employees to use internally.

Oracle and SAP are going further. They're packaging customer software with their suites for managing finances, employees, logistics, and manufacturing. Their pitch: While companies must attach Siebel's suite to the rest of their computing systems manually, Oracle's and SAP's pieces come ready-mixed.

It's not just established companies that want the kind of end-to-end package that Oracle and SAP offer. Many Web upstarts have similar needs. Consider Streamline.com in

(Cont.)

HOW MARRIOTT NEVER FORGETS A GUEST

When retiree Ben B. Ussery Jr. goes on vacation, he typically spends hours beforehand nailing down golf dates, scouting shops for his wife, and making restaurant reservations. But last year, when the Usserys and another Richmond (Va.) couple chose to spend a week at Marriott's Desert Springs resort in Palm Desert, Calif., he let the hotel do the legwork. Weeks in advance, Marriott planning coordinator Jennifer Rodas called Ussery to ask what he wanted to do. When all was set, she faxed him an itinerary. She had even ordered flowers for his wife. "Marriott made it a real smooth experience," says Ussery. "I'm ready to go back."

What makes such velvet-glove treatment possible is Marriott International Inc.'s use of customer management software from Siebel Systems Inc. The hotel chain, based in Bethesda, Md., is counting on such technology to gain an edge with guests, event planners, and hotel owners. The software lets Marriott pull together information about its customers from different departments, so that its reps can anticipate and respond more quickly to their needs. It starts with reservations. Says Chairman J. W. Marriott Jr.: "It's a big competitive advantage to be able to greet a customer with: 'Mr. Jones, welcome back to Marriott. We know you like a king-size bed. We know you need a rental car.'"

Mariott, America's No. 1 hotel chain, is the industry leader in using technology to pamper customers. The company, which manages 1,850 hotels and resorts worldwide, began installing Siebel software in late 1998 and is spending just under $10 million for the initial pieces. A few other hotel chains are dabbling in customer-info systems, but Marriott is ahead of the pack, says analyst Bryan A. Mayer of Credit Lyonnais Securities. "It's a huge advantage," he says.

The biggest boost from the Siebel software is in the hotel chain's sales operations. Marriott is transforming its sales teams from order-takers for specific hotels to aggressive marketers of all Marriot properties. A sales person in Dallas—who understands both the needs of his local customers and the chain's world inventory of hotel rooms and other facilities—can now pitch and book orders for hotels in Hawaii or China.

NO HASSLES. Early results are promising. In 1998, the sales-force software helped Marriott generate an additional $55 million in cross-chain sales. Anecdotal evidence also suggests there has been a jump in bookings from event planners, who find it easier to give business to Marriott, which has their needs on file, than put it out for bid.

Eliminating hassles for guests is the appeal of Marriott's free personal-planning service, too. It's now available at seven resorts, but Marriott aims to extend it to all 32 resorts by 2001. The software tracks guest preferences, so personal planners can anticipate amenities that repeat guests may want. "Our spa is very popular," says Doug Mings, personal planning supervisor at Marriott's deluxe Camelback Inn in Scottsdale, Ariz. "If you don't plan ahead, sometimes you don't get in."

The service also gives Marriott reps an opening to pitch hot-air balloon rides and other fee-generating activities. Happy customers, fatter sales: With that kind of advantage, no wonder other hotel chains, such as Hilton Hotels Corp., are starting to follow Marriott's technology lead.

By Amy Borrus in Washington

ware from Kana to cross-promote its Web site, mail-order businesses, and Williams-Sonoma and Pottery Barn retail stores. Patrick Connolly, general manager of the company's direct-marketing businesses, says he wants to avoid simply transferring sales from stores to the Web site. He can use e-mail addresses collected at stores and on Web sites to send targeted promotions. He recently sent e-mail to shoppers at the company's outlet stores inviting them to come back for 15% discounts. The response rate was 12%—far above the typical 1% response to e-mail solicitations.

BIGGER FASTER. In spite of victories like these, the upstarts can see the writing on the wall. They've got to broaden their portfolios of products if they hope to cement relationships with customers—and compete with the bigs. Even before the Silknet deal, Kana began taking advantage of its outsized market cap by buying NetDialog, for Web self-service software; Business Evolution Inc., for real-time e-mail and chat; and Connectify Inc., for e-mail marketing. "We have to get big fast so when Siebel does come, we're ready for them," says Kana CEO Michael McCloskey.

What could derail the industry giants? The Net is a wild card. All of the major players have converted their applications so they can be accessed via Web browsers. But the newer software companies that built their products from the ground up with Web delivery in mind can offer faster service over the Internet. That could become crucial if corporations and dot-coms opt for the convenience of having applications delivered over the Net by hosting companies. Siebel Systems Chairman Thomas Siebel is convinced that will be only a small part of the market. "None of my customers are asking for it," because they want to control their own technology, he says dismissively.

He better not get too smug. The competitive landscape could change radically in the next couple of years. Siebel charges premium prices for its software—often hundreds of thousands of dollars per sale. Already, competitors such as SalesLogix Corp., a five-year-old company in Phoenix, offer many of the same capabilities for much less. Del Webb Corp., the Phoenix housing developer, bought SalesLogix software to coordinate the activities of 700 salespeople and paid just $600 for each user, vs. the $2,000 that Siebel would have charged. "The big companies haven't rebelled yet, but I believe they will," says SalesLogix CEO Patrick Sullivan.

Siebel and the other high-priced big shots won't have a lock on the ability to give corporations a comprehensive view of their customers, either. The California State Auto Assn. is doing that with a comparatively cheap $1 million purchase from E.piphany Inc., a maker of market-analysis software in San Mateo, Calif. CSAA uses the upstart's software to extract customer information from separate databases controlled by its travel agency, emergency roadside service, insurance business, and Web site. That gives it the capacity to size up customers and give each one a "lifetime value score"—singling out the best customers for special treatment. "It's been a revelation," says Alexandra Morehouse, the association's corporate marketing officer.

Make that an epiphany. If more people have stirring experiences like Morehouse, there could be a revolution in the works for the customer-management software business.

By Steve Hamm in New York, with Robert D. Hof in San Mateo, Calif.

(Cont.)

SALESFORCE.COM: AN ANT AT THE PICNIC

There was a time when Marc K. Benioff could call Thomas M. Siebel and set up lunch. After all, the pair cut their teeth together during the early go-go days at software giant Oracle Corp. These days, though, Siebel won't return Benioff's calls. It may have something to do with the mission of Benioff's San Francisco startup, Salesforce.com Inc., which was officially launched on Feb. 7. "Our objective is to put Siebel Systems out of business," Benioff says flatly.

Never mind that Benioff, 35, was an initial backer of Siebel Systems Inc., the king of software for making salespeople more productive, and that he has pocketed more than $20 million from that 1993 investment. He revels in the thought that Salesforce.com can use the Web to undermine the classic business model that generated $790 million in sales for Siebel last year. Benioff, chairman of Salesforce.com, expects the Internet to change the way salespeople track customers. Right now, his Web site does only a fraction of what Siebel's software can do. But in the future, he believes, instead of buying expensive packages of software, even large companies will pay monthly fees to get what they need from Web sites like his.

With Salesforce.com, Benioff has made a first stab at fulfilling that vision. It's a handy tool for individual salespeople or small groups. For just $50 a month, users click on tabs to move quickly from their contact list to account information to sales leads.

The Web site's simplicity is appealing to customers such as Robert G. Muscat. As head of business development for W.L. Gore & Associates' Industrial Dry Filtration unit, Muscat initially considered Siebel software to link his 15 sales reps. But it would have cost him close to $60,000 to buy and install. "You're talking some big bucks here," Muscat says.

At this point, Salesforce.com is nothing more than an ant at Siebel's picnic. With 150 customers to Siebel's 1,000, it can hardly be considered a threat yet. "Web applications are a compelling story for small startups. But for big companies like General Motors and Microsoft—no way," says David Schmaier, Siebel's senior vice-president for products. To be sure, Salesforce.com isn't for big corporate customers that want all of Siebel's market-analysis features.

SHARED NICHE. Even for small sales operations, Salesforce.com has its shortcomings. Its greatest advantage—being a Web site—could also be its greatest drawback. For sales reps who travel, finding Web connections can be even more difficult than finding a good cup of coffee. "It's not an acceptable solution," Forrester Research Inc. analyst Bob Chatham says of Salesforce.com. He thinks this technology makes sense mainly for small stationary sales forces.

Salesforce.com doesn't have this niche to itself, either. Upshot.com Inc. and SalesLogix Corp. have developed sales-management Web sites. And Siebel is getting into the action too—recently spinning off its Sales.com Web site, which offers some of the features of its core sales-management software.

But Salesforce.com's backers don't seem worried. The company is about to close another round of financing that will bring its total funding to $52 million and value it at $350 million. And Benioff expects to go public this year. If that happens, his $20 million Siebel windfall could seem like pocket change.

By Jay Greene in San Francisco

Evaluating Opportunities in the Changing Marketing Environment

16

Inside Sony, a Clash Over Web Music

Japanese Giant Faced Discord Between Its Record Label And Its Electronics Group

BY ROBERT A. GUTH
Staff Reporter of THE WALL STREET JOURNAL

TOKYO—In the global race to market music on the Web, Sony Corp. has had an unusual rival: Sony.

As both an electronics company and a top record label, Sony wants to capitalize on any musical revolution online, making the latest in listening gadgets for it—just as it has done before, with everything from the Walkman to compact disks.

But the Japanese giant has also had to referee a potential conflict with its own music label—whose artists include Fiona Apple, Celine Dion and Savage Garden—which fears losing out to illegal copying.

For more than a year, it's been a management challenge to push a single strategy through a music house divided. The differences erupted publicly as the two sides argued at industry meetings—even after one of the sons of Sony founder Akio Morita was called in to smooth out organizational differences.

But Sony's campaign to balance their sometimes conflicting interests is beginning to pay off: Sony Music Entertainment (Japan) Inc. last month started selling songs online. Called "bitmusic," the Japanese service will be followed in coming months by a similar service from its sister company in the U.S.

It is Sony's first fully orchestrated effort to cash in on all aspects of the burgeoning Internet music business, from the music itself, to the copyright technologies protecting it, to the devices for playing it. Sony, whose divisions have excelled through autonomy, is the only major company trying to do it all.

To get here, Sony executives have invested in more than a dozen music-related Internet companies, signed technology agreements with Microsoft Corp. and Web-music pioneers such as Liquid Audio and Real-Networks Inc., and rolled out copyright-protection technologies for online music.

For years, Sony and competing labels had been cooking up online music-distribution schemes in-house. But most were caught off guard by the rapid rise of music piracy on the Web. Now they're rapidly laying the necessary technology foundation so that over the next year they can expand their services selling tunes directly over the Internet. Adding to the urgency: America Online Inc.'s plans to merge with Time Warner Inc., which this week unveiled plans to build a music giant by hooking up with EMI Group PLC. Other music companies are hurtling toward selling tunes online, as well.

Sony's race to the Internet started at the foot of Japan's Mt. Fuji in September 1998. At an annual world-wide management retreat there, top Sony officials held their first serious debate over what role digital networks like the Internet would play in Sony's future.

Sony's labs were already brimming with technology and devices for downloading digital music and playing them. The company's hardware side, the spiritual progeny of the late Sony founder Mr. Morita, was eager for a chance to unveil their work.

But the hardware loyalists learned a lesson from the company's attempt in 1991 to market a high-end digital tape recorder. Record companies feared it would be used by music pirates—and they banded together to quash the product.

"That is embedded in everybody's heart here," says one Sony official. "We didn't want to repeat that mistake."

Sony's own record companies in Japan and the U.S. had been planning trials of online music, but thought sales of music over the Internet to portable devices was still some ways off. One crucial voice was Mr. Morita's second son Masao, who was at the retreat. A 45-year-old who spends his days escorting Sony acts such as Aerosmith and Mariah Carey around Tokyo, Mr. Morita is head of Sony Music Entertainment Japan's international business. Having spent most of his career on the electronics side, he saw the long-term potential of the Internet but argued at the retreat that it could smash Sony's music business if mishandled.

The reason: music downloaded from the

Sony just began selling tunes online in Japan. Next stop: the U.S.

Internet is easy to pirate and hard to charge for. Record labels needed more time, he and other Sony music officials at the retreat explained, to figure out how to charge for music online and prevent illegal copies from swamping the market. In the end, everyone agreed that a trial with other major record labels the following year would be a safe first step. "People didn't want to go too fast," says Mr. Morita. "It could have had a lot of repercussions."

Within months, however, the listening habits of American teens were changing fast, making Sony's cautious approach perilous. In the U.S., college dormitories and high schoolers' bedrooms had become hotbeds for a technology revolution called MP3, a type of computer software that made downloading music from the Internet easy. The format offered no copyright protection and rapidly became a standard for music pirates posting tunes on the Net for free.

The format also sparked a new market for portable players that store MP3 tunes on memory chips so they can be listened to on the go—just like prototypes Sony had in its labs. Led by Diamond Multimedia, an army of little-known hardware companies from the U.S. and South Korea seized the opportunity and rolled out MP3 players starting in late 1998.

Rattled, the Recording Industry Association of America, an industry group for major record labels including Sony, moved to halt shipments of Diamond's MP3 player through a court order.

When that failed in late 1998, Tommy Mottola, the chairman of Sony Music Entertainment in the U.S., joined in on an announcement in New York of an industry initiative to settle the piracy problem. The RIAA-led group invited hardware and software makers to propose a single specification for protecting music downloads from illegal copying. It vowed to complete the work in time for that year's Christmas buying season.

Sony's race to the Net was on. Starting in January, Sony's hardware specialists fanned out around the world to make sure their software and devices were compatible

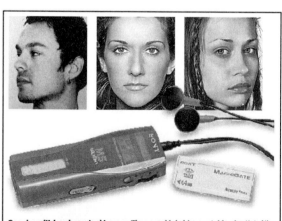

Sony's split-level musical house: *The record label has a stable of artists like Savage Garden's Darren Hayes and singers Celine Dion and Fiona Apple. The electronics division, pioneer of the original Walkman, now offers the Memory Stick Walkman, which can download music from the Web.*

(Cont.)

with an array of programs that protect and allow for the downloading of music.

In February, Mr. Morita was sitting in his office in the piano-shaped Sony Music building in Tokyo when he got a call from company president Nobuyuki Idei. Mr. Idei wanted him to represent the music business on a company-wide committee he was setting up to hash out the issues online music was raising throughout Sony. Mr. Morita then started regular trips to Sony Music Entertainment in New York to help coordinate efforts between the U.S. and Japan.

Meanwhile, Sony's music and electronics divisions publicly faced off at regular meetings of the RIAA forum. In March, at a meeting near Washington, the portable-device makers, including Sony, argued for adding functions like digital recording to their players. But the record companies, including Sony, argued that such features would only enable piracy.

In April, at the launch of a high-end CD player that Mr. Idei himself had started into development eight years earlier, the Sony chief underscored just how willing he was to spotlight Sony's future on the Internet. At the Blue Note jazz club in Tokyo, after a half-hour of live music by Tito Puente and his Latin All Stars, Mr. Idei unveiled the Super Audio CD.

But as he drew to a close, instead of high-lighting the shining CD player, he surprised Sony officials when he pulled out a tiny, purple device that could store music from the Internet. "With this we want to introduce . . . what you might want to call a Netman," he hinted to the crowd.

By November, Sony would showcase the device, formally called the Memory Stick

---

Last March, at an industry forum, Sony's music and electronics divisions squared off on whether to include digital recording functions in players

---

Walkman, at a major computer industry show in Las Vegas. There, Sony also announced another portable player, the Vaio Music Clip, and a string of agreements with technology companies so that Sony devices could work with a range of software for protecting and managing music online.

But as the crucial Christmas season approached, it was clear many pieces weren't in place. The RIAA initiative, for one, was bogged down by infighting over a copyright technology. The issue wasn't settled until November, by which time most major record companies—including Sony Music in the U.S.—had decided to delay the launch of full-blown music download services.

In the U.S., Sony officials say they didn't want to start online music sales until portable music devices with built-in piracy protections came out. Al Smith, senior vice president of Sony Music Entertainment, says these digital players are scheduled to begin appearing on the market here in a few months, with a device from Sony Electronics due out this month or next.

Back in Japan, Mr. Morita didn't want to wait. He wanted his product ready in Japan for the holiday season. Days after the copyright-technology fight was settled, he dispatched one of his staff to Boston carrying a hard-drive loaded with 44 songs. There, Aris Technology installed the protection into each track. By Christmas, Sony Music Japan was selling music on the Internet for 350 yen ($3.30) a tune.

Martin Peers contributed to this article.

Republished by permission from Dow Jones & Company, Inc. from *The Wall Street Journal*, "Inside Sony, a Clash Over Web Music," p. B1, January 26, 2000; permission conveyed through Copyright Clearance Center, Inc.

17

Saving Gracefully

California's Shortages Rekindle Its Efforts To Conserve Electricity

---

Dr. Rosenfeld Tests Solutions He Says Won't Require State to Sacrifice Comfort

---

White Roofs, Digital Meters

By JOHN EMSHWILLER

Staff Reporter of THE WALL STREET JOURNAL

SACRAMENTO, Calif.—With unruly white hair and a mildly absent-minded manner, 74-year-old Arthur Rosenfeld looks like the retired physics professor he is. But these days he has a new career: developing stealth weapons to help keep electricity shortages from short-circuiting California this summer.

Dr. Rosenfeld's humble proving grounds are Building G, a somewhat grimy one-story structure owned by the Sacramento Municipal Utility District, and a spiffier Kaiser Permanente medical office building 10 miles away. There's nothing remarkable about the two facilities—except that both have slashed their electricity demand for lighting and air-conditioning by as much as 30%, largely without their occupants noticing the change.

To cut its consumption, Building G used a combination of digital electric meters and basic physics. The Kaiser office's method was even less sophisticated; it simply replaced its flat dark roof with a flat light one.

Can simple and unobtrusive conservation measures like these be the best way to attack an electrical-power crisis? "That's exactly right," says Dr. Rosenfeld. And, as the newest member of the five-person California Energy Commission, he is in a strong position to influence other energy policy makers in the state.

He may find a receptive audience. That's because the electricity crisis that erupted here last summer and gave rise to rolling blackouts across the state last month has thrust electricity conservation back near the top of the state's political agenda, after a lengthy hiatus. Now, amid the sky-high wholesale power prices and the shortages wrought by the state's flawed 1996 electricity deregulation

law, Gov. Gray Davis has vowed to slash the state's electricity consumption this summer by more than 3,200 megawatts, or about 7%. To set an example, he has sharply turned down his thermostat at home and the lighting in his office.

But Dr. Rosenfeld isn't a big fan of the self-deprivation approach to electricity savings. He argues that the best kind of conservation, and the kind people are most likely to accept, "doesn't affect how you live." For more than a quarter century, he has been pursuing ways to put that theory into practice.

By summer, when Californians switch on their air conditioners and the state's electricity demand peaks, Dr. Rosenfeld hopes to have tens of thousands of commercial buildings outfitted with new meters and vanilla roofs. Though some energy-industry officials say that goal is far too ambitious, Dr. Rosenfeld and others say his plan could reduce electricity demand statewide by hundreds of megawatts or more, possibly enough to avert some rolling blackouts.

'Spectacular Savings'

"Art is a visionary," Loretta Lynch, president of the California Public Utilities Commission, says of Dr. Rosenfeld. His present efforts, she adds, could help produce "really spectacular savings."

Really spectacular savings would be really helpful if California is to weather its electricity woes. Paying for high-priced wholesale power already has left the state's two biggest investor-owned utilities, PG&E Corp.'s Pacific Gas & Electric Co. and Edison International's Southern California Edison unit, on the edge of bankruptcy and put the state on the hook for billions of dollars in power purchases.

In an effort to help stem the drain, the state legislature is looking to roughly double the state's $400 million in annual conservation-related spending. Its kilowatt-cutting plans range from rebates on energy-efficient refrigerators to radio spots urging citizens to do their laundry after 7 p.m., when electricity demand is lower.

With California desperately trying to build electricity-savings momentum, Dr. Rosenfeld is ready with some practical ideas, such as "cool roofs," that he worked on for years at the University of California at Berkeley. His new public role is something of a reprise from a decade ago. Then, as a private citizen, he helped lead a largely aborted statewide search for electricity savings, a commodity one of his associates dubbed "negawatts." If pursued, the program could have left California in a much better power position than it is now, but it ultimately became a casualty of the deregulation push.

Since the mid-1980s, Dr. Rosenfeld has worked with the Heat Island Group at the Lawrence Berkeley National Laboratory to investigate ways to reduce temperatures in urban areas. Researchers there found that a white roof can be as much as 90 degrees cooler than a black one and reduce the energy

Arthur Rosenfeld

needed to air-condition a building by up to 40%. Cooler roofs also mean cooler outside air. That could help reduce smog, which forms more readily at higher temperatures.

Dr. Rosenfeld says white roofs are generally no more expensive than dark ones. Nonetheless, the California Energy Commission is offering $10 million to encourage commercial building owners to switch. The 10-cents-per-square-foot subsidies would help cover 100 million square feet of roof space. Dr. Rosenfeld says more state money might be coming soon. And with about five billion square feet of commercial roofing in California, he believes there's a lot more room for lightening to strike.

The physicist is even more enthusiastic about digital electric meters. Traditional meters, with little clock faces on the dials, only keep a running total of electricity use, to be measured when a meter reader comes calling. The new digital meters can track consumption during intervals of a few minutes and transmit the reading to the utility via phone lines.

Dr. Rosenfeld says that providing something close to "real-time" metering is extremely important, because the cost of electricity varies widely during the day, fluctuating with demand. Under deregulation, retail rates in California have been largely frozen, so that consumers don't see the soaring cost of electricity reflected in their bills. However, he hopes that one day rates will reflect real-time costs and that meters will be part of consumer efforts to regulate demand in response to fluctuating prices.

Though he can't do much about the current retail rate freeze, Dr. Rosenfeld has been pushing for programs to pay electricity customers for voluntarily cutting their consumption during peak demand periods. In keeping with his conservation-without-deprivation approach, he arranged for pilot programs last summer at Building G and at another location.

During test periods in the summer, the thermostats in the buildings were turned up four degrees and lighting reduced 30%. Most commercial buildings tend to be overlit, and the laws of physics dictate that once a building is cool, it will stay cool for a while. So, Dr. Rosenfeld hoped the buildings' occupants wouldn't notice the changes. Indeed, they didn't seem to. "It wasn't a problem," says Harlan Coomes, a senior demand-side specialist for the Sacramento municipal utility who worked on the test.

Armed with his data, Dr. Rosenfeld began proselytizing state and utility-industry officials. With $40 million, he calculates, the state could install 40,000 digital meters at large commercial sites. Combined with financial incentives to get businesses to adjust their thermostats and reduce their lighting when requested, he figures the program could reduce statewide demand by perhaps as much as 2,000 megawatts during peak hours, all without inflicting any hardships.

Partly spurred by Dr. Rosenfeld's efforts, the California Independent System Operator, which runs the state's electricity grid, has begun voluntary demand-reduction programs that pay electricity users for cuts. Under one such program, commercial building owners who agree to reduce their electricity use during peak hours on a tight-supply day are reimbursed a set amount for every kilowatt-hour they save. "Art has been very passionate in trying to get people to pay attention," says Don Fuller, the ISO's director of client relations.

A not-so-brief overview of some of Dr. Rosenfeld's other passions can be viewed on the California Energy Commission's Web site. Entitled "The Art of Energy Efficiency" and initially prepared for an academic publication, it runs 49 pages, including footnotes.

After earning a bachelor's degree in physics at age 18, he received his Ph.D. at the University of Chicago, studying under the legendary physicist Enrico Fermi. He later moved to U.C. Berkeley, where he was part of the research team that helped Prof. Luis Alvarez win the 1968 Nobel Prize for physics.

Dr. Rosenfeld was teaching and doing research in particle physics at the Lawrence Berkeley lab in 1973 when his life took an abrupt turn. The Arab oil embargo and subsequent energy crisis spurred him to begin exploring energy-efficiency ideas. Initially, he thought those ideas would occupy him for only a few months. Then it was a few years. "I completely misjudged how interesting it would be," he says.

At Lawrence Berkeley, he helped assemble a diverse portfolio of energy-efficiency research projects. Work at the lab contributed to the development of electricity-saving compact fluorescent lights and super-insulating windows. And Lawrence Berkley estimates that a research investment of $70 million has produced billions of dollars of energy savings nationwide.

Along the way, Dr. Rosenfeld met Amory Lovins, already well-known in energy circles for his insistence that inexpensive efficiency improvements could eliminate the need for tens of billions of dollars worth of planned power plants. The two men helped persuade PG&E and others that energy efficiency offered substantial potential savings. By the early 1990s, California had established a program that allowed utilities to charge higher rates if they agreed to pay rebates to ratepayers who bought energy-efficient appliances or took other conservation steps.

In January 1991, PG&E announced plans to invest $2 billion over 10 years to reduce projected demand by 2,500 megawatts. Under the initiative, electric customers got rebates for buying more efficient appliances, lighting or air conditioners, and the utility established a $7.5 million center to teach contractors and architects about new energy-saving building designs.

PG&E recruited Messrs. Lovins and Rosenfeld for a $10 million project to apply the best in energy-efficiency ideas to a half-dozen new or existing buildings. "Amory was going all over the country spouting off" about the potential for huge demand reductions, recalls Carl Weinberg, the retired manager of research and development for San Francisco-based Pacific Gas & Electric. "I said let's test it, [and] if you don't prove this, I want Amory to shut up." The project produced electricity savings in the range of 50%, and Mr. Lovins kept talking.

One of the project's most interesting discoveries was "that you could get most of the savings with very basic off-the-shelf technologies" by carefully integrating them, says Chris Chouteau, former head of energy-efficiency activities at PG&E and now an outside consultant to the company. For instance, more efficient room lighting not only uses less electricity but produces less heat. That in turn reduces the amount of power needed to air-condition a building. And, in newer, better-insulated buildings, it might even reduce the size and expense of the air-conditioning systems required to cool them.

Some argued that the rebates unfairly favored the well-to-do, who could better afford to replace their old appliances. However, the effort soon tripped over a much bigger obstacle. Under the California deregulation plan, begun in the mid-1990s, conservation would largely be taken out of the hands of utilities and left to the marketplace. Some people who took part in the process say that years of progress were lost in the transition. Utilities cut back their conservation efforts, but new players didn't immediately take their place.

If utilities' energy-efficiency efforts hadn't been disrupted, California's electricity demand could have been reduced by as much as 1,100 megawatts from its current level, according to one estimate from the state's Energy Commission. By comparison, the recent rolling blackouts in the state were caused by shortages of several hundred megawatts.

18

Mexican truckers face U.S. obstacle course

By Elliot Blair Smith
USA TODAY

HIGHWAY 57, MEXICO—One of the last major fights over the North American Free Trade Agreement unfolds on this road through the mountainous center of Mexico. It follows the path of truck driver Arturo Figueroa, who is hauling 17 tons of textiles bound for New Jersey.

Mexico wants the U.S. government to open its southern border to Mexican trucks. And NAFTA prescribes just that. But the United States argues that Mexican trucks are unsafe and Mexico's regulatory framework too weak to export either its drivers or vehicles.

A NAFTA dispute panel is expected to rule Thursday in Mexico's favor. President Bush then can decide whether to allow Mexican trucks to enter the United States—as Canadian trucks can—or defy the trade panel and face sanctions.

The Mexican trucking industry claims that since NAFTA took effect in 1994, it has lost $2 billion because the U.S. won't let its trucks more than 25 miles north of the border.

About 5 million commercial trucks a year cross the southern border—nearly 14,000 a day—carrying 75% of the $250 billion in total U.S.-Mexico trade. Since NAFTA, truck crossings have nearly doubled at 28 southern border crossings.

But when Figueroa, 45, arrives in Nuevo Laredo, Mexico, just south of Texas, he must hand off his trailer to a U.S. driver who will carry the goods to New Jersey.

Mexico says U.S. consumers pay excessive costs because Mexican goods must be transferred to U.S. trucks at the border. "Today's system is anachronistic," says Luis de la Calle, undersecretary in Mexico's Ministry of the Economy.

If the U.S. doesn't comply with the panel ruling— and if Mexico isn't compensated for the losses it claims— his government will impose tariffs on U.S. imports, de la Calle warns. "We would include industrial products, agro-industrial products and probably services."

The Bush administration wouldn't comment. But as Texas governor, Bush signed a 1996 letter with the governors of Arizona, California and New Mexico that criticized the Clinton administration for denying Mexican trucks access to the U.S. market. "This transborder trucking delay robs the entire U.S.-Mexico border region of the full economic benefits that NAFTA promises," they wrote.

But there is strong opposition in the USA to opening the border. "The U.S. government is going to have to pay sanctions and keep the border closed," says Lori Wallach, head of Public Citizen's Global Trade Watch in Washington. "A basic health and safety matter that affects everybody stands to be undermined by a trade agreement, which most people would think has to do with tariffs and quotas, not whether more unsafe trucks can roll through your community."

Labor is perhaps the strongest opponent. The Teamsters Union, which represents 120,000 U.S. and Canadian freight drivers, plans to rally at the border on Feb. 16, when Bush visits Mexican President Vicente Fox, to protest the prospect of low-wage Mexican drivers coming into the USA. Teamster drivers earn about $19 an hour, more than four times Figueroa's pay.

> **Mexican truck driver Arturo Figueroa makes $300 a week for two 1,500-mile round trips from Mexico City to the U.S. border. His U.S. counterparts earn about four times that.**

BEAT THE CLOCK

At 8:30 a.m. on a Thursday, Figueroa hops aboard his 2001 model Columbia Freightliner truck. He checks his onboard computer and verifies that the global positioning satellite is working. He has 24 hours to reach Nuevo Laredo. If he veers off course or fails to arrive on time, his company will track him via satellite.

Figueroa works for Grupo Easo, Mexico's biggest truck company, 49% owned by M.S. Carriers of Memphis. He earns $150 for the 1,500-mile round trip, which he makes twice a week. He receives medical insurance but does not qualify for a pension or retirement savings beyond government social security.

Figueroa and his new rig represent the best Mexican trucking has to offer. Just ahead looms the other side of the story: a jackknifed truck in a roadside ditch.

In the course of Figueroa's 750-mile drive from Mexico City to the border, he passes a half-dozen wrecks, five involving Mexican trucks. He also swerves past a dead man lying in the road.

Each time Figueroa passes the roadside carnage,

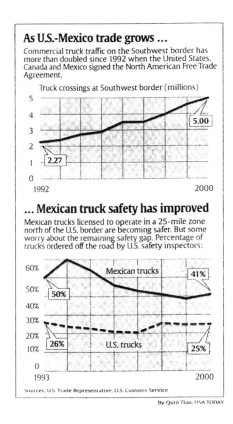

As U.S.-Mexico trade grows ...

Commercial truck traffic on the Southwest border has more than doubled since 1992 when the United States, Canada and Mexico signed the North American Free Trade Agreement.

Truck crossings at Southwest border (millions)

5.00

2.27

1992 — 2000

... Mexican truck safety has improved

Mexican trucks licensed to operate in a 25-mile zone north of the U.S. border are becoming safer. But some worry about the remaining safety gap. Percentage of trucks ordered off the road by U.S. safety inspectors:

Mexican trucks — 41%

50%

U.S. trucks — 26% / 25%

1993 — 2000

Sources: U.S. Trade Representative, U.S. Customs Service

By Quin Tian, USA TODAY

Indians selling snakeskins, live coyotes, deer, even eagles and scorpions to passersby.

Mostly, however, the land is barren. The real difficulty arises at night, when the road is swallowed by darkness. Then the only signs of life are the occasional campfires inviting drivers to pull off the road for peasant offerings of fire-roasted chicken and coffee.

END OF THE ROAD

At 8 a.m. Friday, Figueroa pulls into Nuevo Laredo. He's rested from 7 hours of sleep on a mattress behind his seat. And he's buoyed by the prospect his cargo won't wait long to cross the border at this time of day.

Soon, an American driver will arrive at Grupo Easo's truck yard to hook up a short-haul "drayage" truck to Figueroa's trailer and drive through U.S. Customs. M.S. Carriers then will assign one of its drivers to haul the trailer loaded with textiles to New Jersey.

M.S. Carriers Chairman Michael Starnes says the U.S. and Mexican companies' joint-operating strategy allows them to more efficiently handle cross-border transportation. Most large trucking companies have developed such joint ventures.

But many of the drayage trucks are aging Mexican-owned vehicles unfit for longer assignments. Their smoking exhaust pipes and groaning brakes frequently trigger objections by U.S. safety inspectors.

And they hurt Mexico's efforts to open the border for its long- haul trucks by lowering truck safety averages. The U.S. Transportation Department says 41% of Mexican trucks inspected at the U.S. border were ordered off the road in the year ending Sept. 30, compared with 25% of U.S. trucks as a whole.

"Those vehicles are not safe. We would not want them on a U.S. highway," says Walt Weller, president of Bridgestone de Mexico, which supplies tires to most major Mexican trucking fleets. At the same time, Weller credits large Mexican truck companies such as Grupo Easo. "The improvements in maintenance and equipment I'm seeing from the customers I'm working with here are dramatic," he says.

Grupo Easo President Alberto Anchustegui says substandard trucks and drivers gradually will disappear due to cross-border competition. "Every truck has to comply with all the laws of the other country, or they will not pass to the other side," he says.

The Clinton administration, which didn't act on about 160 applications from Mexican companies to send trucks throughout the USA, said Mexico's efforts weren't enough. "Although Mexico has made substantial progress, work remains to be done," the U.S. trade representative's office said.

U.S. agencies responsible for inspecting trucks are

his shoulders tense and he sighs, thinking of his wife, Susana, 21, who is 8 months pregnant, and their two young children. "A lot of accidents today," he mutters.

Figueroa drives for 14 hours, taking occasional breaks. Because fatigue can cause accidents, U.S. truck drivers must rest after 10 hours. Figueroa crosses five Mexican states and the Tropic of Cancer before stopping two hours from the border.

By then, he has navigated a half-dozen checkpoints staffed variously by the Mexican military, the attorney general's office and federal police. The roadblocks are used to inspect vehicles for illicit drugs and illegal immigrants from Central America, helping to answer another U.S. concern about opening the border.

Mexican authorities last week discovered 7.3 tons of marijuana in a single vehicle on Highway 57. But even with the roadblocks, U.S. Customs' seizures of illicit drugs at the Mexican border have doubled since 1996 to more than a million pounds a year.

During daylight, Figueroa's biggest battle is boredom. The rugged terrain is leavened by stone fences, cactus farms and grazing livestock. In Querétaro state, he passes roadside stands selling strawberries and cream. In San Luis Potosí state, he passes hundreds of

(Cont.)

already overwhelmed. The General Accounting Office says a truck crosses the border at Laredo, Texas, every 30 seconds, 24 hours a day. About 66% of all U.S.-Mexico truck trade crosses in Texas. But, "We inspect less than one-tenth of 1% of the vehicles that cross the border," says Coy Clanton, head of commercial-vehicle enforcement at the Texas Public Safety Department.

While both countries wait for a final ruling from the NAFTA panel—which issued a preliminary ruling in Mexico's favor in December—Figueroa walks the sidewalks of Nuevo Laredo looking for a U.S.-made bicycle for his son.

Because he has neither a Mexican passport nor an American travel visa, he's can't cross into Texas to buy the bike.

How Big Mac Kept From Becoming a Serb Archenemy

BY ROBERT BLOCK

Staff Reporter of THE WALL STREET JOURNAL

BELGRADE, Yugoslavia—During most of the 78-day air war against Yugoslavia, while NATO kept the bombs dropping, McDonald's kept the burgers flipping.

Vandalized at the outset by angry mobs, McDonald's Corp. was forced to temporarily close its 15 restaurants in Yugoslavia. But when local managers flung the doors open again, they accomplished an extraordinary comeback using an unusual marketing strategy: They put McDonald's U.S. citizenship on the back burner.

To help overcome animosity toward a quintessential American trademark, the local restaurants promoted the McCountry, a domestic pork burger with paprika garnish. As a national flourish to evoke Serbian identity and pride, they produced posters and lapel buttons showing the golden arches topped with a traditional Serbian cap called the sajkaca (pronounced shy-KACH-a). They also handed out free cheeseburgers at anti-NATO rallies. The basement of one restaurant in the Serbian capital even served as a bomb shelter.

Now that the war is over, the company is basking in its success. Cash registers are ringing at prewar levels. In spite of falling wages, rising prices and lingering anger at the U.S., McDonald's restaurants around the country are thronged with Serbs hungry for Big Macs and fries. And why not, asks 16-year-old Jovan Stojanovic, munching on a burger. "I don't associate McDonald's with America," he says. "Mac is ours."

This is music to Dragoljub Jakic's ears. The 47-year-old managing director of McDonald's in Yugoslavia was the mastermind behind the campaign to "Serbify," at least during the war, an American icon. "We managed to save our brand," the six-and-a-half-foot-tall Mr. Jakic says with a grin.

That was no easy task. As the fast-food industry's superpower, McDonald's is a global symbol of Western pop culture, Yankee know-how and American corporate cunning. But prominence on the world stage can be a lightning rod for trouble, and the company is often exposed to outbursts of anti-American sentiment and a myriad of political grievances. Last month, a McDonald's restaurant in Belgium was burned down, and animal-rights activists are the suspected arsonists.

The sacking of McDonald's in Yugoslavia came after only one night of air strikes. Whipped to patriotic fervor by the state-controlled media attacks on the "NATO criminals and aggressors," mobs of youths—many wearing Nike shoes and Levi's jeans—targeted three McDonald's branches in Belgrade and restaurants in the cities of Jagodina, Cacak and Zrenjanin, smashing windows and scribbling insults on doors and walls.

The incidents shocked Mr. Jakic, who was more worried at the time about stray NATO bombs than the rage of his fellow citizens. "We have been in Yugoslavia for years, during which time we sponsored schools, sports clubs and children's hospitals," he says. "We're part of the community. We never thought anyone would do something bad to us."

McDonald's, in fact, was once the pride of Belgrade, opening in the capital on March 24, 1988—exactly 11 years to the day before the North Atlantic Treaty Organization began bombing. It was the first branch in Central Europe and quickly became a source of local pride. At soccer matches in the old Yugoslavia, when teams from Belgrade met opponents from Zagreb, the Croatian capital, Belgrade fans would taunt their rivals with chants of "We have McDonald's and you don't!"

In 1996, the company began expanding, opening restaurants in seven other Serbian cities. But on March 26, the day after the mob attacks, Mr. Jakic closed all his restaurants. He then called his top managers to Belgrade for brainstorming sessions to devise a survival strategy.

Within a week, they had launched a campaign to identify the plight of ordinary Serbs with the big burger joint. "McDonald's is sharing the destiny of all people here," read a sign at one branch. "This restaurant is a target, as we all are. If it has to be destroyed, let it be done by NATO."

A key aspect of the campaign was to present McDonald's as a Yugoslav company. Though they are registered as local businesses, every restaurant in Yugoslavia in fact is 100% owned and operated by McDonald's. Mr. Jakic says McDonald's needed to get Serbs to view the company as their own.

It was in this vein that he and his team decided to redesign the logo with the Serbian cap, cocked at a haughty angle over one arch.

Traditional national emblems, like the sajkaca, have undergone a revival in recent years with the rise of Serbian nationalism.

Mr. Jakic says the choice of the cap had nothing to do with politics. "The sajkaca is a strong, unique Serbian symbol. By adding this symbol of our cultural heritage, we hoped to denote our pride in being a local company," he says.

The company also brought back the McCountry pork burger, first released throughout Central Europe in early March, and lowered its price. The economy of preindustrial Yugoslavia was based on the pig trade, and pork is considered the most Serbian of meats. Mr. Jakic says his relaunch wasn't an attempt to pander to local sentiments, but to give people a break during hard times.

There was no time for premarket trials of his plans. "We just jumped in," Mr. Jakic says. In less than a week, McDonald's had printed new banners, tray liners, lapel buttons and posters of the redesigned arches set against the blue, white and red colors of the Serbian flag. On April 17, Belgrade restaurants were reopened and more than 3,000 free burgers were delivered to the participants of the Belgrade marathon, which was dominated by an anti-NATO theme. At the same time, the company announced that for every burger sold it would donate one dinar (about a nickel) to the Yugoslav Red Cross to help victims of NATO's airstrikes.

At McDonald's corporate headquarters in Oak Brook, Ill., spokesman Chuck Ebeling says the Yugoslav campaign was a product of local management and was in no way directed or encouraged by the head office. Mr. Jakic "was functioning as a hamburger guy and not as a politician," Mr Ebeling says. "He was doing what he felt he should do, and needed to do, to be locally accepted and to maintain the support of local government and of his employees. He demonstrated how adaptive he could be under the circumstances."

Mr. Jakic says he was praised by his superiors at a meeting at McDonald's regional headquarters in Vienna. And while he says he is happy his campaign helped McDonald's to

A tray liner *used when McDonald's restaurants in Yugoslavia reopened on April 17—also the date of the Belgrade marathon. The Cyrillic lettering at the top left reads: "Mac is the biggest natural source of energy." McDonald's also began putting a sajkaca, a traditional Serbian cap, atop its coveted golden arches to evoke Serbian identity and pride.*

(Cont.)

prosper during exceptional circumstances, he was also quick to return to business as usual. As soon as the war ended, on June 10, the arches reappeared, without the green cap. "We simply believed that our message was received and there was no reason to continue," Mr. Jakic says.

Asked if the cocky sajkaca had been ditched forever, Mr. Jakic smiles. "We will make an investigation to see how it worked, and then maybe we'll fine-tune it," he says. "We've not abandoned it completely."

The campaign certainly made an impression here. At one McDonald's, a green book for customer comments records the delight of Belgraders when the restaurant reopened and unveiled its new approach. "We are so happy to see the campaign to help people hurt by the war. It's very humane and the only way to justify the business of an American restaurant in Yugoslavia," wrote Andjela, Aleksandra and Dragan, on April 18. The same day, Isidora wrote: "McDonald's is the only American who wished to become a Serb."

—Richard Gibson
contributed to this article.

CYBER CRIME

First Yahoo! Then eBay. The Net's vulnerability threatens e-commerce—and you

The scenario that no one in the computer security field likes to talk about has come to pass: The biggest e-commerce sites on the Net have been falling like dominoes. First it was Yahoo! Inc. On Feb. 6, the portal giant was shut down for three hours. Then retailer Buy.com Inc. was hit the next day, hours after going public. By that evening, eBay, Amazon.com, and CNN had gone dark. And in the morning, the mayhem continued with online broker E*TRADE and others having traffic to their sites virtually choked off.

The work of some super hacker? For now, law enforcement officials don't know, or won't say. But what worries experts more than the identity of this particular culprit or outlaw group is how easily these attacks have been orchestrated and executed. Seemingly, someone could be sitting in the warmth of their home and, with a few keystrokes, disrupting electronic commerce around the globe.

DEAD HALT. Experts say it's so easy, it's creepy: The software to do this damage is simple to use and readily available at underground hacker sites throughout the Internet. A tiny program can be downloaded and then planted in computers all over the world. Then, with the push of a button, those PCs are alerted to go into action, sending a simple request for access to a site, again and again and again—indeed, scores or hundreds of times a second. Gridlock. For all the sophisticated work on firewalls, intrusion-detection systems, encryption and computer security, e-businesses are at risk from a relatively simple technique that's akin to dialing a telephone number repeatedly so that everyone else trying to get through will hear a busy signal. "We have not seen anything of this magnitude before—not only at eBay, but across so many sites," says Margaret C. Whitman, CEO of eBay.

No information on a Web site was snatched, no data corrupted, no credit-card numbers stolen—at least so far. Yet it's a deceptively diabolical trick that has temporarily halted commerce on some of the biggest Web sites, raising the question: How soft is the underbelly of the Internet? Could tricks like these jeopardize the explosive growth of the Web, where consumers and businesses are expected to transact nearly $450 billion in business this year? "It's been war out there for some time, but it's been hidden," says James Adams, co-founder of iDEFENSE, an Alexandria, Va., company that specializes in cyber threats. "Now, for the first time, there is a general awareness of our vulnerabilities and the nature of what we have wrought by running helter-skelter down the speed race of the Information Highway."

To be sure, not even the most hardened cyber sleuths are suggesting the Net is going to wither overnight from the misdeeds of these wrongdoers. But the events of recent days are delivering a shrill wake-up call to businesses that they need to spend as much time protecting their Web sites and networks as they do linking them with customers, suppliers, contractors—and you. Consider just a quick smattering of recent events: In December, 300,000 credit-card numbers were snatched from online music retailer CD Universe. In March, the Melissa virus caused an estimated $80 million in damage when it swept around the world, paralyzing e-mail systems. That same month, hackers-for-hire pleaded guilty to breaking into phone giants AT&T, GTE, and Sprint, among others, for calling card numbers that eventually made their way to organized crime gangs in Italy. According to the FBI, the phone companies were hit for an estimated $2 million.

Cyber crime is becoming one of the Net's growth businesses. The recent spate of attacks that gummed up Web sites for hours—known as "denial of service"—is only one type. Today, criminals are doing everything from stealing intellectual property and committing fraud to unleashing viruses and committing acts of cyber terrorism in which political groups or unfriendly governments nab crucial information. Indeed, the tactic used to create mayhem in the past few days is actually one of the more innocuous ones. Cyber thieves have at their fingertips a dozen dangerous tools, from "scans" that ferret out weaknesses in Web site software programs to "sniffers" that snatch passwords. All told, the FBI estimates computer losses at up to $10 billion a year.

As grim as the security picture may appear today, it could actually get worse as broadband connections catch on. Then the Web will go from being the occasional dial-up service to being "always on," much as the phone is. That concept may be nirvana to e-tailers, but could pose a real danger to consumers if cyber crooks can come and go into their computer systems at will. Says Bruce Schneier, chief technical officer at Counterpane Internet

49

HOW THIS HAPPENED TO YAHOO!, EBAY, AND E*TRADE

Disrupting the Net isn't child's play, but it isn't rocket science, either. And cleaning up the mess takes teamwork.

STEP 1 An individual or group downloads software that is readily available at scores of underground Web sites specializing in hacker tools. The software is easy to use; it's all point-and-click.

STEP 2 They break into scores of computers on the Web and plant a portion of the downloaded program, allowing the hacker to control the machine. Unfortunately, there are plenty of machines on the Net that lack the proper security to stop this.

STEP 3 They pick a target—Yahoo!, eBay, or Amazon.com—and then sit back in the privacy of their homes and instruct the computers they've hijacked to send requests for information to that site. One or two messages won't do it. But send enough of them at the same time and the resulting congestion clogs networks or brings computer servers and router systems to their knees. It's like constantly dialing a telephone number so that no one else can get through.

STEP 4 Responding can take hours. Tracing attackers is hard because they use fake addresses from scores of computers. But as systems administrators sift through the traffic, they can identify the general location—say, an Internet service provider. This takes a coordinated effort involving the company, its ISP, and telecom suppliers. After identifying the machines, the company writes a program to reject the requests—and prays that it doesn't get another flood of messages.

Security Inc. in San Jose, Calif.: "They'll keep knocking on doors until they find computers that aren't protected."

Sadly, the biggest threat is from within. Law enforcement officials estimate that up to

(Cont.)

THE WEAPONS:

DENIAL OF SERVICE This is becoming a common networking prank. By hammering a Web site's equipment with too many requests for information, an attacker can effectively clog the system, slowing performance or even crashing the site. This method of overloading computers is sometimes used to cover up an attack.

SCANS Widespread probes of the Internet to determine types of computers, services, and connections. That way the bad guys can take advantage of weaknesses in a particular make of computer or software program.

SNIFFER Programs that covertly search individual packets of data as they pass through the Internet, capturing passwords or the entire contents.

SPOOFING Faking an e-mail address or Web page to trick users into passing along critical information like passwords or credit-card numbers.

TROJAN HORSE A program that, unknown to the user, contains instructions that exploit a known vulnerability in some software.

BACK DOORS In case the original entry point has been detected, having a few hidden ways back makes reentry easy—and difficult to detect.

MALICIOUS APPLETS Tiny programs, sometimes written in the popular Java computer language, that misuse your computer's resources, modify files on the hard disk, send fake e-mail, or steal passwords.

WAR DIALING Programs that automatically dial thousands of telephone numbers in search of a way in through a modem connection.

LOGIC BOMBS An instruction in a computer program that triggers a malicious act.

BUFFER OVERFLOW A technique for crashing or gaining control of a computer by sending too much data to the buffer in a computer's memory.

PASSWORD CRACKERS Software that can guess passwords.

SOCIAL ENGINEERING A tactic used to gain access to computer systems by talking unsuspecting company employees out of valuable information such as passwords.

DUMPSTER DIVING Sifting through a company's garbage to find information to help break into their computers. Sometimes the information is used to make a stab at social engineering more credible.

THE PLAYERS:

WHITE-HAT HACKERS They're the good guys who get turned on by the intellectual challenge of tearing apart computer systems to improve computer security.

BLACK-HAT HACKERS Joyriders on the Net. They get a kick out of crashing systems, stealing passwords, and generally wreaking as much havoc as possible.

CRACKERS Hackers for hire who break into computer systems to steal valuable information for their own financial gain.

SCRIPT BUNNIES Wannabe hackers with little technical savvy who download programs—scripts—that automate the job of breaking into computers.

INSIDERS Employees, disgruntled or otherwise, working solo or in concert with outsiders to compromise corporate systems.

60% of break-ins are from employees. Take the experience of William C. Boni, a digital detective for PricewaterhouseCoopers in Los Angeles. Last year, he was called in by an entertainment company that was suspicious about an employee. The employee, it turns out, was under some financial pressure and had installed a program called Back Orifice on three of the company's servers. The program, which is widely available on the Internet, allowed him to take over those machines, gaining passwords and all the company's financial data. The employee was terminated before any damage could be done.

The dirty little secret is that computer networks offer ready points of access for disgruntled employees, spies, thieves, sociopaths, and bored teens. Once they're in a corporate network, they can lift intellectual property, destroy data, sabotage operations, even subvert a particular deal or career. "Any business on the Internet is a target as far as I'm concerned," says Paul Field, a reformed hacker who is now a security consultant.

It's point and click, then stick 'em up. Interested in a little mayhem? Security experts estimate that there are 1,900 Web sites that offer the digital tools—for free—that will let people snoop, crash computers, hijack control of a machine, or retrieve a copy of every keystroke. Steve O'Brien, vice-president for information operation assessments at Info-Ops.com, an Annapolis (Md.)-based company that provides intrusion detection services and security solutions, says the number of ways to hack into computers is rising fast. He tracks potential threats both from hacker groups and from the proliferation of programs. Once a rare find, he now discovers at least three new nasty software programs or vulnerabilities every day. And those tools aren't just for the intellectually curious. "Anyone can get them off the Internet—just point and click away," says Robert N. Weaver, a Secret Service agent in charge of the New York Area Electronic Crimes Task Force.

UNLOCKED DOORS. It's an issue that has crimefighters up in arms. At a hastily called press conference in Washington, D.C., on Feb. 9, Attorney General Janet Reno pledged to battle cyber crime. "We are committed to tracking down those responsible and bringing them to justice" and ensuring "that the Internet remains a secure place to do business," she said. But Ron Dick, chief of the Computer Investigations & Operations Section of the National Infrastructure Protection Center, pointed out that Internet security can't be assured by the government alone. Companies need to vigilantly monitor their computers to ensure that hackers don't surreptitiously install programs from which to launch attacks. "For the Internet to be a safe place, it is incumbent on everyone to remove these tools," he says. Using them, "a 15-year-old could launch an attack."

Make that an 8-year-old, once the Internet is always on via fat broadband connections. There are currently 1.35 million homes in America with fast cable modems, according to market researcher International Data Corp. By 2003, the number will grow to 9 million, and there will be an equal or larger number of digital subscriber line (DSL) connections.

That gives hackers a broad base from which to stage an attack. When a PC is connected to a conventional phone modem, it receives a new Internet address each time the user dials onto the Net. That presents a kind of barrier to hackers hoping to break in and hijack the PC for the kind of assault that crippled eBay, Yahoo, and others. In contrast, cable and DSL modems are a welcome mat to hackers. Because these modems are always connected to the Net, they usually have fixed addresses, which can be read from e-mail messages and newsgroup postings. Home security systems known as personal firewalls are widely available for cable and DSL subscribers. But until they reach nearly 100% penetration, they won't prevent intrusions.

In the coming age of information appliances, the situation could get worse. According to many analysts, the U.S. will soon be awash in Web-browsing televisions, networked game consoles, and smart refrigerators and Web phones that download software from the Net. "These devices all have powerful processors, which could be used in an attack, and they're all connected to the Net," Schneier says.

True, broadband customers can switch off their Net connections. But as cool applications come onstream, nobody will want to do that. "There will be streaming music and video, 24-hour news, and all kinds of broadband Web collaboration," says John Corcoran, an Internet analyst with CIBC World Markets. "To take advantage of that, the door will be open 24 hours a day."

Corporations are no better off. There, security is becoming an expensive necessity. "At least 80% of a corporation's intellectual property is in digital form," says Boni. Last year, Corporate America spent $4.4 billion on sales of Internet security software, including firewalls, intrusion-detection programs, digital certificates, and authentication and authorization software, according to International Data. By 2003, those expenditures could hit $8.3 billion.

And still computer crime keeps spreading. When the FBI and the Computer Security Institute did their third annual survey of 520 companies and institutions, more than 60% reported unauthorized use of computer systems over the past 12 months, up from 50% in 1997. And 57% of all break-ins involved the Internet, up from 45% two years ago.

As big as those numbers sound, no one really knows how pervasive cyber crime is. Almost all attacks go undetected—as many as 60%, according to security experts. What's more, of the attacks that are exposed, maybe 15% are reported to law enforcement agencies. Companies don't want the press. When Russian organized crime used hackers to break into Citibank to steal $10 million—all but $400,000 was recovered—competitors used the news in marketing campaigns against the bank.

That makes the job even tougher for law enforcement. Most companies that have been electronically attacked won't talk to the press. A big concern is loss of public trust and image—not to mention the fear of encouraging copycat hackers. Following the attacks on Feb. 8 and Feb. 9, there was a telling public silence from normally garrulous Internet executives from E*Trade to priceline.com. Those that had not been attacked yet were reluctant to speak for fear of painting a target on their site, while others wanted no more attention.

And even when the data are recovered, companies are sometimes reluctant to claim their property. Secret Service agent Bob Weaver waves a CD-ROM confiscated in a recent investigation. The disk contains intellectual property—software belonging to a large Japanese company. Weaver says he called the company, but got no response.

Thieves and hackers don't even need a computer. In many cases, the physical world is where the bad guys get the information they need for digital break-ins. Dallas FBI agent Mike Morris estimates that in at least a third of the cases he's investigated in his five years tracking computer crime, an individual has been talked out of a critical computer password. In hackerland, that's called "social engineering." Or, the attackers simply go through the garbage—dumpster diving—for important pieces of information that can help crack the computers or convince someone at the company to giving them more access.

"PAGEJACKING." One problem for law enforcement is that hackers seem to be everywhere. In some cases, they're even working for so-called computer security firms. One official recalls sitting in on the selection process for the firm that would do the Web site security software for the White House. As the company's employees set up to make their pitch, one person walked into the room and abruptly walked out. It turns out one of the people in the audience was with law enforcement, and had busted that person for hacking.

It's not just on U.S. shores that law enforcement has to battle cyber criminals. Attacks from overseas, particularly eastern European countries, are on the rise. Indeed, the problem was so bad for America Online Inc. that it cut its connection to Russia in 1996. Nabbing bad guys overseas is a particularly thorny issue. Take Aye.Net, a small Jeffersonville (Ind.)-based Internet service provider. In 1998 intruders broke into the ISP and knocked them off the Net for four days. Steve Hardin, director of systems engineering for the ISP, discovered the hackers and found messages in Russian. He reported it to the FBI, but no one has been able to track down the hackers.

As if worrying about hackers weren't enough, online fraud is also on the rise. The Federal Trade Commission, which responds to consumer complaints about bogus get-rich schemes or auction goods never delivered, says it filed 61 suits last year. How many did it have back in 1994, when the Net was in its infancy? One. So far, the actions have resulted in the collection of more than $20 million in payments to consumers and the end of schemes with annual estimated sales of over $250 million.

The FTC doesn't want to stop there. On Feb. 9, commissioners testified before a Senate panel, seeking an increase in the commission's budget in part, to fund new Internet-related policies and fight cyberfraud. The money is needed to go after ever more creative schemes. In September, for example, the FTC filed a case against individuals in Portugal and Australia who engaged in "pagejacking" and "mousetrapping" when they captured unauthorized copies of U.S.-based Web sites (including those of PaineWebber Inc. and The Harvard Law Review) and produced lookalike versions that were indexed by major search engines. The defendants diverted unsuspecting consumers to a sequence of porno sites that they couldn't exit. The FTC obtained a court order stopping the scheme and suspending the defendants' Web-site registrations.

All of this is not to suggest it's hopeless. Experts say the first step for companies is to secure their systems by searching for hacker programs that might be used in such attacks. They also suggest formal security policies that can be distributed to employees letting them know how often to change passwords or what to do in case of an attack. An added help: Constantly updating software with the latest versions and security patches. Down the road, techniques that can filter and trace malicious software sent over the Web may make it harder to knock businesses off the Net. Says Novell Inc. CEO Eric Schmidt: "Security is a race between the lock makers and the lock pickers." Regulators say that cybercrime thrives because people accord the Internet far more credibility than it deserves. "You can get a lot of good information from the Internet—95% of what you do there is bona fide," says G. Philip Rutledge, deputy chief counsel of the Pennsylvania Securities Commission. "Unfortunately, that creates openings for fraud."

And other forms of mayhem. That's evident from the attacks that took down some of the biggest companies on the Net. If blackouts and other types of cyber crime are to be avoided, then Net security must be the next growth business.

By Ira Sager in New York, with Steve Hamm and Neil Gross in New York, John Carey in Washington, D.C., and Robert D. Hof in San Mateo, Calif.

Cellular Industry Braces For Life As Commodity Business

By Peter Venesh
Investor's Business Daily

Volume Selling 101: Sell more widgets and you can lower your prices to sell even more. Get more customers to buy your services and you can lower your rates to get more customers. Fight off competition by cutting prices.

Volume selling corollary: Do the above and eventually your product or service becomes a commodity like personal computers and long-distance phone calls.

The wireless communications industry is facing those same cause-and-effect pressures. Growing numbers of people are signing up for mobile communication services. More are buying cell phones and text messagers and wireless personal digital assistants. Because of these market conditions, the wireless industry's products and services may become commoditized.

Prices have been falling across the board. They will fall further, says Charles Mahla, senior economist in the Sacramento, Calif., office of consulting firm Econ One. "Technology has (gotten) better. Wireless communications is better known and easier to use. As a result, the handset itself has become commoditized."

Unit Growth Still High

While handset manufacturers Ericsson and Nokia recently trimmed their industry sales forecasts, both still expect a healthy 500 million wireless phones will be sold in 2001. A total 405 million were sold last year.

As for the service, or airtime, it has become a commodity, Mahla says. While the carriers have a great deal of money tied up in infrastructure and capital investments, those are one-time expenses. "Because that total cost is fixed, the average cost per user is going to decline with subscriber growth."

Prices To Drop More

How low can prices go? The bottom hasn't been reached, Mahla says. "There's still room for carriers to compete on price and do it with cheap handsets and cheap service."

Prices will drop as more people purchase the wide array of wireless devices coming onto the market, predicts Becky Diercks, director of wireless research at Cahners In-Stat Group of Newton, Mass.

She says the biggest declines will be for the most basic equipment. "Handsets will always have very broad price points. The cheapest will be those that are voice-only. More sophisticated handsets geared to the business person will resist price pressure."

Some new handset features will even push up prices, she says. They include better microdisplays and longer battery life. But one coming technology won't drive prices up, she believes—Wireless Application Protocol, a technology for putting the Internet on wireless devices. "The addition of WAP capability is almost meaningless in terms of dollars," she said. "It costs, literally, almost nothing to put it on the handset."

Among the biggest price drops are those for two-way text messaging devices. "These were originally geared to the high-end business executive. However, now these manufacturers and service providers want to hit the consumer market." Two-way messaging systems that cost more than $500 a few years ago can now be had for under $100, she says.

Some analysts see parallels between the wireless and airline industries. As seats got cheaper, bigger carriers used their bulk to squeeze the discounters to the sidelines and, in some cases, out of business. Then prices soared again.

Consolidation To Continue

Similarly, small operators won't survive against AT&T Wireless, Cingular Wireless, Sprint PCS, Nextel, Verizon, Voicestream, Vodafone and NTT DoCoMo, says Larry Swayse. He's senior vice president of Allied Business Intelligence, a market research firm in Oyster Bay, N.Y.

"There's going to be a price settling at some point dictated by the large conglomerates," he said. "The stronger players will dominate. That's what capitalism is."

One reason he thinks there can't be a price war is that the cost of spectrum, the frequencies auctioned by governments around the world, is rising. The reason for that is the finite nature of spectrum.

Spectrum Is Limited

"People think wireless is endless," Swayse said. "The spectrum for wireless is much more limited than for a wired network. On a wired network, if you need more capacity you just add fiber optic cable."

The logic may seem counterintuitive, he says. "When you look at wireless, you think that it's infinite because it's in the air. You think of wireline and you think it isn't infinite because it's in the ground. Just the opposite is true."

As demand for spectrum rises, so will the capital costs incurred by wireless service providers, Swayse explains. "Eventually you're going to have to come up with a price per minute that will match the capital you've spent and the future capital that must be spent to still make a profit."

Another factor that will sustain prices, he argues, is that added features like data will put more demands on that spectrum. "Due to the number of applications, users and minutes being used, there will always be a spectrum crunch."

Swayse expects the big wireless companies won't compete on price. "It's realistic to think that the wireless price will not go down much further."

He sees wireless as an atypical commodity—a necessity rather than a luxury, much like electricity. And if you must have it, he says, you'll pay the price. "There will be X number of big providers, and they'll pretty much determine the market."

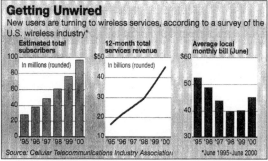

Getting Unwired
New users are turning to wireless services, according to a survey of the U.S. wireless industry*

Estimated total subscribers — In millions (rounded)
'95 '96 '97 '98 '99 '00

12-month total services revenue — In billions (rounded)
'95 '96 '97 '98 '99 '00

Average local monthly bill (June)
'95 '96 '97 '98 '99 '00

Source: Cellular Telecommunications Industry Association   *June 1995-June 2000

A CRACKDOWN ON E-DRUGGISTS

Online pill-pushers are in U.S. regulators' sights

On Nov. 22, a 15-year-old boy in Michigan got on the Internet and visited the Web site of ConfiMed, the self-described "original online source" for Viagra and other medication. He filled out an order for Xenical, a weight-loss drug with side effects including bloating, cramps, and diarrhea. The next day, he got a puzzled e-mail from ConfiMed: "At 5 foot 9, 130 pounds, there would be a question as to why you might need Xenical," it wondered. "Please send further explanation."

Oops, the teenager replied, his weight was really 180. Five days later, on Nov. 29, the pills arrived in the mail, complete with a prescription written by ConfiMed's founder, Seattle's Dr. Howard J. Levine. Unfortunately for Levine, the purchase was a sting set up by the Michigan attorney general's office. In December, the attorney general charged ConfiMed and nine other online companies with selling prescription drugs without adequate medical consultation and proper licenses. Levine denies breaking any laws.

The Michigan crackdown is just one piece of a broad new legal attack on Internet drug-sellers. There have always been doctors and merchants who dispensed prescription drugs out the backdoor. But now the Internet is giving them global reach. Law enforcers estimate that there are now more than 400 online drug peddlers, tapping into the more than $110 billion spent on retail prescriptions in the U.S. each year.

A few sites, such as PlanetRx.com and HealthCentral.com, sell drugs only to those with a valid prescription. But others are freely dispensing everything from Viagra and hair-loss preventer Propecia to steroids and amphetamines with only a perfunctory questionnaire. Indeed, regulators point to the case of a 52-year-old Illinois man who was able to buy Viagra online, despite having chest pains and a family history of heart disease, and who died during sex. Online drug peddling "poses enormous health and safety issues," says Michigan Attorney General Jennifer M. Granholm. "It's the wild, wild West out there."

Now, the sheriffs are arriving—in force (table). Last year, Illinois, Kansas, and Missouri also took action against Web drug merchants, and the National Association of Attorneys General is now establishing a working group to plot a wider assault involving dozens of states. Meanwhile, the Clinton Administration in December announced a new plan to give the FDA $10 million per year to use in tackling online drug peddlers, as well as new authority to impose fines.

ELUSIVE. But even though law enforcers are on the attack, it's not clear they'll ever completely succeed in taming the cyberfrontier. As has already been discovered with online gambling and securities fraud, the Web is much harder to police than the brick-and-mortar world. Many of the worst drug sites, for example, operate outside of U.S. control in loosely regulated foreign havens such as Thailand and the Caribbean. "The foreign sites are...very active, very illegal, and very dangerous," says Carmen Catizone, executive director of the National Association of Boards of Pharmacy (NABP).

Because their companies are built of electrons, the cyber drug merchants are also proving to be very evasive—even when they're based in the U.S. "One of the most difficult challenges has been finding the companies and people responsible," explains Kansas Attorney General Carla J. Stovall. Her staff has had to pierce through a variety of evasive tactics, including multiple-shell corporations and addresses that turned out to be mail drops. In Texas, meanwhile, investigators have found that the sites pay close attention to who visits—and frequently manage to stay one step ahead of the law. "When we go in and look at a site, it logs us in," says Cynthia T. Culmo, director of the Division of Drugs & Medical Devices at the Texas Health Dept. "The next time we try to access it, it's shut down."

AD NAUSEAM. In spite of the difficulties, enforcers say the fight has only just begun. Government gumshoes estimate that sales at the online prescribers are in the tens of millions of dollars and growing. And some of the sites are all but daring authorities to shut them down. The opening Web page for KwikMed, for example, brazenly proclaims: "No prescription? No problem...." KwikMed lawyer James W. Hill says that is just the "grabber"—and that the site goes on to explain "ad nauseam" how buyers must fill out an online questionnaire, evaluated by a doctor, to get Viagra, Propecia, and other drugs. But regulators say such online consultations are woefully inadequate. Indeed, the questionnaires on many sites—including KwikMed's—already have the correct answers filled in.

The FDA is currently investigating 100 sites and plans up to 50 actions later this year. But recognizing the limitations of traditional law enforcement, the agency also plans to attack the problem in other ways. For example, it supports a certification program developed by the NABP that gives a seal of approval to totally legit sites: Four have won approval so far, with 12 more expected soon—and 60 applications are pending. "The certification makes consumers realize there are good and bad guys," says FDA policy chief William K. Hubbard.

Of course, many online drug merchants think the crackdown is unnecessary and unfair. The typical drugs sold by the sites—Viagra and Xenical, among others—are so "benign" that just having "consultations"

(Cont.)

with cyberdoctors is more than adequate to protect the public's health, argues ConfiMed's Levine. "Unless someone grossly lies, the worst that could happen is that the drug won't help them very much," he says.

Online defenders note that a man with a heart condition can get Viagra just as easily by telling a lie to a doctor in person. So why shut down Web sites in a futile attempt to protect people from themselves? Moreover, the Web shields people's privacy—a big concern for many Viagra users, who are embarrassed by the necessity of visiting local doctors and drugstores. "If there wasn't a need for this [type of site], it wouldn't exist," says William A. Stallknecht, owner of The Pill Box Pharmacy, a Houston chain whose online site has been fined by Missouri. (Stallknecht insists that he's trying to comply with the state's laws.)

Nonetheless, the NABP, state attorneys general, and the FDA have drawn a firm line: Prescriptions must come from face-to-face visits with a doctor, or from a consultation with a patient's regular doctor. "Prescription drugs are dangerous drugs," explains Culmo. Online pharmacies "are going outside the lines of safety that were put in place," she says.

That may be the case. But the sites are certainly not lacking for customers. And unless that changes, this problem will continue to plague the regulators.

By John Carey in Washington

DRUGMAKERS: COULD A MOUSE CLICK DRAG THEM INTO COURT?

How's this for a drug company's legal nightmare? A man buys Viagra from an illicit online drug peddler, then dies during sex. An autopsy discovers that he had a heart condition—and should never have been allowed to use the medication. Lawyers scent blood. Knowing it's not worth suing the tiny e-drug merchant, they go after deep-pocketed manufacturer Pfizer Inc. for not keeping the drug from being sold through dubious channels.

PROWLING. Is this hypothetical scenario far-fetched? Not necessarily. "Industry is concerned that, if companies had knowledge that these drugs were being misused . . . they could be deemed negligent," explains Washington food and drug lawyer Marc J. Scheineson.

That's why companies aren't sitting idly by. Pfizer declined to comment on its potential liability for drugs illegally sold online. But the company has been prowling the Web to find sites that offer Viagra. "Once we learned of them, we contacted the medicine or pharmacy board in those states," says spokesman Andrew B. McCormick. That's a smart move. Given the liability threat, "diligent companies should be monitoring the Internet and at least appearing to do something," says drug industry consultant Steven M. Weisman.

Regulators wish that the drug industry would cut off distributors that sell to shady sites. Cynthia T. Culmo, of the Texas Health Dept., believes one reason they don't do so is the fear of losing extra revenue. As this issue continues to generate controversy, the drug industry is likely to feel at least some of the growing heat.

By John Carey

23

Going against the flow
Consumers yearn for the power of old toilets

By Dru Sefton
USA TODAY

Dave Hitt misses his good old toilet, the one that slurped down everything in the bowl in just one flush, every time.

"My wife and twin daughters long for the days when you could flush a toilet and walk away, confident that it would do its job," says Hitt, 44, a computer engineer in upstate Round Lake, N.Y.

The family's water-closet woes began in 1994 when a remodeling contractor installed two ultra-low-flush (ULF) toilets in their house.

Those toilets use 1.6 gallons of water per flush; older toilets use anywhere from 3.5 to 7 gallons.

A week after the remodeling, Hitt's 12-year-old daughter flushed one of the new toilets. The bowl didn't clear, so she flushed again.

The toilet promptly overflowed. The water seeped to the first floor, staining the new kitchen ceiling. That was just the beginning.

"The thing clogs regularly and overflows from time to time," Hitt says.

He wishes he could have installed a larger-capacity toilet in '94, "but by then Congress had decided it should make the choice for me."

Congress did that in 1992, with the Energy Policy and Conservation Act. An amendment requires contractors to install ULF toilets in all remodeling and new-home jobs.

Now, of the 225 million toilets in the USA, nearly 50 million are ULF, according to the Plumbing Manufacturers Institute. More are installed every day.

The ULF toilet is great for saving water, even with occasional double flushes, its proponents say. They cite statistics such as a 1998 study showing that water consumption from toilet flushes decreases from an average of 19.3 gallons per person per day with an old toilet to 9.3 gallons with a ULF toilet.

But the problem with the ULF toilet, critics say, is that it's lousy for getting rid of solid waste.

Manufacturers are busy rethinking toilet designs and now offer options such as power-assisted flushing. They insist that ULF toilets are getting better all the time.

But all the homeowners hovering over toilets, plunger in hand, are growing impatient. They're griping to plumbers: Why won't this gunk go down like it used to? Plumbers are complaining to contractors: Why can't you install toilets that work? Contractors are calling manufacturers: Why don't you make toilets that work better?

And everyone is blaming Congress for plunging America into this swirl of controversy in the first place.

But disgruntled flushers could be getting some satisfaction soon. Rep. Joe Knollenberg, R-Mich., has pledged to see that the issue receives attention in the current congressional session.

After discussing the issue on a radio talk show in early 1997, Knollenberg says, he received "thousands and thousands of complaints from people around the country," prompting him to introduce a bill to repeal the 1.6-gallon requirement.

A hearing on that bill took place in July; Knollenberg's office predicts a vote on the bill this session.

ONE SIZE DOESN'T FIT ALL

The ULF toilets present a double whammy for irritated consumers.

"When they discover that they can't go back to the old-style product, their frustration doubles," Knollenberg says. "So it's a combination of unhappiness over performance and lack of choice."

In June and July, more than 1,400 homeowners and builders logged on to the Web site of the National Association of Home Builders Research Center to respond to a questionnaire about ULF toilets. The nonprofit group, based in Upper Marlboro, Md., reported that 594 of 757 builders in the unscientific survey complained of problems with ULF toilets; 511 of 681 homeowners had problems.

As Knollenberg says: "This particular mandate, frankly, insists that one size fits all. And it doesn't."

The fount of all the trouble is the water spot—what you see when you raise the toilet lid.

Americans like their water spot big. Very big. That causes a problem for manufacturers. The more water in the water spot, the less in the back of the toilet to flush stuff down.

"Cleanliness in the bowl and odor control are factors important to U.S. consumers," and both necessitate a large water spot, says Mike Chandler, associate product manager for toilets, urinals and bidets for the Kohler Co. in Kohler, Wis.

Many countries have a "very small or nonexistent" water spot in their toilets, Chandler says. It's just

(Cont.)

Americans who demand a big water spot.

So Kohler is one of many manufacturers getting creative. The company offers a Power Lite option, with a 0.2-horsepower electric pump inside the tank. " A very powerful but quiet flush," Chandler says.

Or there is the "dual flush actuator": One side of the button flushes 1.1 gallons for liquid waste; the other side flushes 1.6 gallons for solid waste.

Those options are available on Kohler's high-end toilets, which sell for up to $800. Chandler says consumer response has been "overwhelming."

If you're talking about flushing, Tom Kenney is the expert. As director of laboratory services for the National Association of Home Builders Research Center, he determines a toilet's flushability. A good part of his time is spent tossing little round sponges and wadded-up brown paper into toilets, flushing and counting how many pop back up.

Kenney is on the American Society of Mechanical Engineers committee that sets the voluntary industry "hydraulic performance requirements for water closets and urinals." In other words, how toilets should flush.

"There's been concern for several years now about the standard not being as robust as it needs to be," Kenney says.

The committee meets in October to begin revising the recommended standards. After flushing thousands of sponges and paper wads down dozens of toilets hundreds of times, "our data has shown a distinction between water closets. Some do better at flushing than others," Kenney says. That's why performance-testing standards are important.

The ULF toilets pose a tough issue politically.

"Houses with water-conserving fixtures, vs. older fixtures, use less water, there's no doubt about that," Kenney says. "Even with two or three flushes, we're still seeing net savings on water consumption.

"But what we're not seeing in studies is the product satisfaction with the user."

GOING NORTH FOR RELIEF

Dissatisfied toilet users are looking for alternatives.

Canadian retailer Tony Pasqua is happy to oblige. He owns The Master Bath in Sault Ste. Marie, Ontario, and gets about six calls a week from Americans wanting to buy the old-style toilets. On average, he sells three or four a week to Americans.

Some drive up to The Master Bath to pick up their toilets, loading them into pickup trucks or vans; others pay up to $100 for shipping.

Pasqua has sold toilets to homeowners in 42 states.

He has advertised 3.5-gallon toilets for 18 months and says he has been getting calls "since Day 1. It's amazing."

And it is not illegal for a U.S. homeowner to buy a toilet in Canada for use in the USA. Rumors of a "black market" in Canadian toilets have been circulating for years.

The only illegal purchase of a larger-capacity Canadian toilet would be if a contractor brought one back across the border for resale or installation. Such a contractor could face fines of up to $2,500.

So, no, there are no residential "toilet smugglers," says Cherise Miles, a U.S. Customs Service public affairs officer in Chicago.

"All you have to do is declare the toilet, and you're on your way."

24

Here's the Turnoff

In the Market for Guns, The Customers Aren't Coming Back for More

With Hunting on the Wane And Stigma on the Rise, The Pool Is Shrinking

'You Feel Like a Smoker'

By Vanessa O'Connell
And Paul M. Barrett
Staff Reporters of The Wall Street Journal

Michael Maul doesn't have anything against guns; he owns six. But the Houston radio-station engineer hasn't hunted for eight years, and he doubts that he will ever buy another gun. When he wants to shoot animals these days, Mr. Maul, 40 years old, uses a camera.

"It's a lot easier in the city to go to a nature trail or an arboretum," he says.

The gun business is losing customers. Hunters and target shooters—the industry's core market—are gradually walking away from those sports. Subdivisions have encroached on land once used for hunting. Bicycling, kayaking and other hobbies are luring people away from firing ranges.

Most ominously, gun companies' efforts to cultivate new buyers among women and teenagers have failed to stem the erosion. And gun manufacturers face a dramatic shakeout, as recent high-visibility killings have made guns less socially acceptable in many people's eyes.

"Our future is rather tenuous," says Paul Jannuzzo, vice president of the U.S. unit of Austrian handgun maker Glock GmbH.

Mr. Jannuzzo's industry has attracted public attention lately as it attempts to fend off a legal assault by 28 cities and counties across the country. But however that courtroom fight ends, gun companies face the peril of a shrinking consumer market. U.S. gun production and imports have fallen more than 20% since the late 1970s, and despite an unusual buying surge this year, industry analysts predict little to no overall growth in the decade ahead.

Retail giants such as Wal-Mart Stores Inc. and Kmart Corp. recently have reduced their gun and ammunition displays in favor of other sporting goods. The ranks of gun wholesalers—the middlemen between the factory and the store—have thinned by 16%, to about 160, since 1996.

A consolidation wave among manufacturers is already under way. Colt's Manufacturing Co. just this month eliminated its less expensive civilian-handgun lines and is negotiating a possible merger with rival Heckler & Koch Inc. Three small California makers of inexpensive handguns have either shut down or sought bankruptcy-court protection this year. Smith & Wesson Corp., the largest U.S. handgun manufacturer, is diversifying into everything from police bikes to car parts to clothing.

With more than 200 million guns already in civilian hands, industry officials worry that the market is nearing saturation. Just 10 million people own roughly half the national stock, which translates into about 10 guns per owner.

In the 1980s, the proportion of men who said they personally owned a gun held steady at 52%, but by 1998, the figure dropped to 38%, according to regular surveys by the National Opinion Research Center at the University of Chicago. Female ownership has hovered around 11% since 1980.

The lurid massacres of the past two years are statistically an aberration; violent crime has dropped nationally for seven straight years. But round-the-clock reports of gun killings have created a "much broader negative perspective, a tainting" of firearms, says Douglas Painter, executive director of the National Shooting Sports Foundation, the main industry trade group. In the wake of the Littleton bloodshed, his group dropped its first-ever mainstream-magazine advertising campaign, what would have been a $3 million effort to create a wholesome image for shooting sports.

Shooting traditionally has relied on family relationships and word-of-mouth promotion to attract neophytes. But fear of social disapproval is muffling veteran participants, Mr. Painter says. "Does that have a negative impact? You bet it does."

Lory Ambriz bought a new gun every year for more than four decades, displaying his favorites, including an assault rifle, above the fireplace in his La Mirada, Calif., home. But following this year's school shootings, his grandchildren and other house guests questioned why he kept such a potentially dangerous arsenal.

"I began to think I don't need them anymore," says the 68-year-old retired truck driver, who hadn't fired a gun for years. He says he has moved his more than 40 weapons to a neighbor's safe and plans to sell them soon.

To be sure, there are tens of millions of loyal gun users who still raise their children to hunt or target shoot. Mark Anderson, an insurance agent in Columbia, Mo., for example, was taught to shoot by his father and today owns more than 20 guns. A recent purchase was a .22-caliber rifle for his 12-year-old son, who is interested in target shooting. His next purchase is likely to be a quail-hunting shotgun for the boy, Mr. Anderson says.

But in many gun-owning families, these traditions aren't being passed to the next generation. Mr. Maul of Houston learned to hunt with his older male relatives, but they are back in rural Illinois, where he grew up, and as an adult, he hasn't found new hunting buddies. He doesn't plan to encourage his own son, now three years old, to take up the sport. "I expect he'll develop other interests, as I have," Mr. Maul says.

The upshot is that each of the industry's key markets is eroding. Hunting, which accounts for about 60% of consumer gun sales, has declined steadily for decades. The number of adults who hunt tumbled 17% from 1990 to 1998, according to Mediamark Research Inc., a market-research firm. The number of hunting licenses issued annually by states fell 11%, to 14.9 million, from 1982 to 1997, the most recent year for which statistics are available from the U.S. Fish & Wildlife Service.

Target shooting, which accounts for 25%

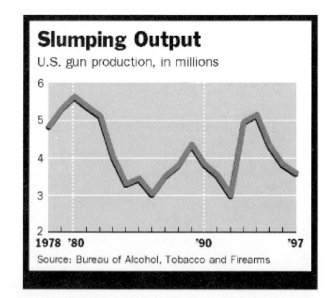

Slumping Output

U.S. gun production, in millions

1978 '80   '90   '97

Source: Bureau of Alcohol, Tobacco and Firearms

(Cont.)

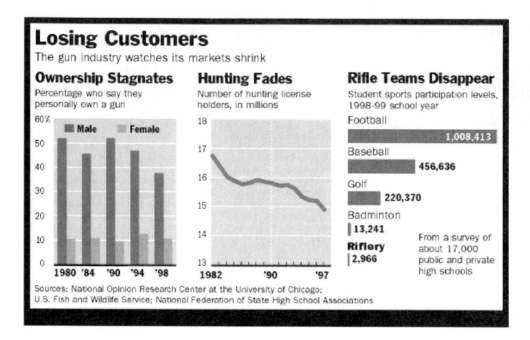

Losing Customers

The gun industry watches its markets shrink

Ownership Stagnates

Percentage who say they personally own a gun

- Male
- Female

```
60%
50
40
30
20
10
0
    1980  '84   '90   '94   '98
```

Hunting Fades

Number of hunting license holders, in millions

```
18
17
16
15
14
13
   1982        '90         '97
```

Rifle Teams Disappear

Student sports participation levels, 1998-99 school year

Football — 1,008,413
Baseball — 456,636
Golf — 220,370
Badminton — 13,241
Riflery — 2,966

From a survey of about 17,000 public and private high schools

Sources: National Opinion Research Center at the University of Chicago; U.S. Fish and Wildlife Service; National Federation of State High School Associations

of sales, is slowly fading, too. From 1993 to 1997, participation fell 5%, to 18.5 million people, according to a survey by the National Sporting Goods Association.

As their ranks thin, hunters and shooters are graying. At last month's New Jersey State Outdoor Pistol Championship, in the town of South River, 66 mostly grandfatherly types fired at paper bull's-eyes. Competitor James Phillips, 72 years old and clad in surgical stockings and orthopedic shoes, describes his fellow shooters as "a bunch of old men." Lone spectator Bill Nolan recalls that in the 1950s and 1960s, the parking lot overflowed with the recreational vehicles of 200 young and middle-age shooters and their families. "Boy, have times changed," says Mr. Nolan, 58.

People who buy firearms for self-protection, mostly handguns, make up the remaining 15% of the market. In an anomaly, sales in this area increased this year, partly because of the threat of stiffer gun-control measures and fear of social breakdown related to year-2000 computer problems. But the larger trend, as crime rates have fallen, is a drop in demand for self-protection guns. In any event, this isn't particularly fertile ground for gun makers because consumers buying only for protection tend to tuck a handgun away in a closet and not return to the gun store for more purchases.

Attitudes toward guns vary from region to region. They are more popular in the South, less in the Northeast. But there is growing anecdotal evidence from around the country that some gun enthusiasts are viewed—and view themselves—as pariahs with an unseemly habit, akin to cigarette smoking. Indeed, the danger for the industry would be

that gun ownership could become as unfashionable and frowned upon as chain-smoking, a habit that as recently as a decade ago wouldn't have raised eyebrows.

Fred Cunnings, a gun owner in Holiday, Fla., felt like such "an outsider" that he sold the pistol he had kept for years in a closet. "You almost feel like a smoker in a restaurant," says the 48-year-old landlord.

Most gun makers seem resigned to the erosion of their core customer base and are focusing on finding new faces. "The No. 1 challenge facing the gun industry is finding nontraditional consumers—women, young people, and suburbanites—to make up for the gradual decrease in traditional male hunting customers," says Ronald Stewart, who was chief executive of Colt's from 1996 through late last year.

Neither Colt's nor the industry at large is succeeding.

Since the late 1980s, handgun makers such as Colt's, Smith & Wesson and Italy's Beretta SpA have tried to convince women that they need to protect themselves and their families. Smith & Wesson, for example, pitched its LadySmith revolver, with pearl handles, as a "personal security plan" for women. But as crime rates eased in the late 1990s, the portion of women who personally own a gun dropped to 10.7% in 1998 from its recent high of 13.8% in 1993, according to the National Opinion Research Center.

Paxton Quigley, a handgun advocate who endorses Smith & Wesson products, recalls a "frenzy of interest" in her all-women handgun self-defense classes following the Los Angeles riots in 1992. Held at gun ranges nationwide, the classes now typically draw only

15 students, down from 35 in the early 1990s, she says.

For years, Dawn Brachmann, a homemaker in Holiday, Fla., kept her husband's .25-caliber Sterling pistol loaded and in a bread box on top of her refrigerator. But she asked him to get rid of it last month after a church sermon on gun violence at schools caused her to worry that her three-year-old son might stand on a chair and get at it. "I don't want to own any more guns," she says, "but I wouldn't mind finding something else to use in my self-defense."

In addition to problems recruiting women, gun makers acknowledge that they are failing to win over enough young people to replace aging shooters and hunters.

In recent years, the gun industry has aggressively courted kids, getting nearly three million a year to participate in rifle programs sponsored by the NRA and groups such as the farming-oriented 4-H clubs and the U.S. Junior Chamber of Commerce. Some manufacturers have tried to capitalize on this activity. H&R 1871 Inc., Gardner, Mass., says that by lending firearms to these programs, among other promotions, it has doubled annual sales of youth guns since 1995, to more than 50,000.

But aside from such small pockets of success, overall efforts to recruit younger customers aren't working, gun executives say. People between the ages of 18 and 24 made up only 8% of all hunters in 1995, down from 17% in 1986, according to the National Shooting Sports Foundation. In one major hunting state, Pennsylvania, sales of junior hunting licenses have dropped 40% during the past three decades, to roughly 98,000.

At a time when participation in scholastic sports is at an all-time high, riflery drew just 2,966 participants in the 1998-99 school year, 47% fewer than in 1974-75, according to a survey of 17,000 schools by the National Federation of State High School Associations. More than four times as many students played on badminton teams.

Robert Soldivera, who coaches shooting teams at three private high schools in Staten Island, N.Y., says that at first, many children "want to learn to shoot because it is the forbidden fruit." But that curiosity tends to wear off quickly, as students conclude that "making holes in paper targets gets boring really fast," Mr. Soldivera says. He estimates that

(Cont.)

fewer than 20% of his students remain active through their senior year; most quit after just a few months.

Like schools, many summer camps are phasing out shooting programs. Kent Meyer, who oversees Camp Chief Ouray in the Colorado Rockies, suspended its 92-year-old rifle program in response to this spring's school shootings in Littleton and Conyers, Ga. Scott Brody, who owns Camps Kenwood and Evergreen in Potter Place, N.H., dropped rifle programs in June and added more woodworking and dance. "They don't have the dangers of the riflery program," says Mr. Brody.

Worried about a stagnant gun market, some major manufacturers are putting more emphasis on military and law-enforcement sales or diversifying into other products altogether. Sturm, Ruger & Co., Southport, Conn., the largest U.S. gun manufacturer,

makes golf equipment. Ed Shultz, Smith & Wesson's chief executive, says he is steering his 147-year-old company, which once made only firearms, toward a 50-50 balance of gun and nongun products.

Other companies are trying more exotic niche-marketing strategies. Smith & Wesson, Springfield, Mass., Colt's, based in West Hartford, Conn., and Mossberg & Sons Inc., North Haven, Conn., are scrambling to be the first to offer a "smart gun" to women and people generally who otherwise wouldn't buy a firearm because of safety concerns. Smart-gun prototypes rely on microchip technology to allow only authorized users to pull the trigger. But the cost and reliability of smart guns are very much in doubt.

Savage Arms Inc., Westfield, Mass., aims to boost sales among aging diehards by designing new guns for older, arthritic hands.

Savage reduced the weight of some of its rifles to 5 1/2 pounds from eight pounds by using plastic parts rather than wood and added devices to reduce the sometimes-painful recoil that comes with firing a gun.

Both modifications appear to be hits with Savage's maturing customer base, says company President Ronald Coburn. But the problem, he adds, is that "as our audience matures, the younger generation isn't coming up behind them."

Buyer Behavior

25

Lost in the Translation

U.S. entrepreneurs have learned a lot about what does and doesn't work; But the lessons may not apply so easily abroad

BY DANIEL PEARL

Staff Reporter of THE WALL STREET JOURNAL

BOMBAY—India is a tough testing ground for e-commerce: Credit cards are still a rarity, only one in 300 adults uses the Internet regularly, and shopping trips are widely considered to be entertainment.

Even the one chief advantage of being a young market—the chance to learn from other people's mistakes—isn't all that it's cracked up to be, because not all of the U.S. lessons apply here. "The funny thing is, I have not even logged on to eBay in the last four months," says Suvir Sujan, co-chief executive of **Baazee.com** Inc., a one-year-old Bombay-based Internet auction site modeled on eBay Inc., the popular San Jose, Calif., Internet auction site. "The market is so different, there's no point."

The Internet may someday create its own global culture, but in the developing world, local conditions are still shaping e-commerce. Baazee, for one, has struggled with problems eBay never had to worry about. Indians tend to equate auctions with bankruptcy liquidations. So Baazee started holding live auctions in shopping malls to promote the idea. Unlike the U.S., India has few nationwide brands that Indians trust enough to buy without seeing. So Baazee is setting up "exchange centers" in different cities, where the seller and the winning bidder can complete their transaction in person after the buyer is assured of the item's integrity.

The one thing Baazee would have liked to have taken straight from eBay—a technology designed to handle great leaps in volume—it had to hire a local company to design. After complaints that people weren't able to place bids, Baazee had to stop all marketing for three months this past fall while building the new system to keep up with bidding traffic.

Market Promise

India's population of one billion, and its

troops of talented software engineers, make it a promising online market for companies looking ahead. But until now e-commerce has been disappointingly small, estimated at half of even China's low level of online sales. Most of India's Internet users and online purchases are concentrated in a handful of large cities. Some analysts expect e-commerce to boom here, as telecommunications improves and credit cards spread, but others warn that personal computers won't become a mass commodity until large numbers of Indians first buy washing machines, color televisions and other big-ticket consumer goods common in developed countries.

Some of the broad lessons from the U.S. have been a help to Indian start-ups. Indian Web entrepreneurs, for example, haven't spent much time promoting content-only sites—like Salon.com in the U.S.—that rely heavily on advertising money. "It took the U.S. seven or eight years" to learn that Internet sites needed direct revenue from surfers, says Dewang Mehta, executive director of the National Association of Software and Service Companies, a computer trade group in New Delhi. "Here, we've learned it in six months."

Other trends have been harder to follow in a country where retailing still lags years behind the U.S. Last year's mantra in the U.S. was "brick-and-click"—that shopping sites should hook up with established retailers and let them handle warehousing and distribution. Witness the link between **Toys "R" Us Inc.** and **Amazon.com Inc.** that was announced this past summer. But in India there are no retailers with nationwide distribution, such as Toys "R" Us or Wal-Mart Stores Inc. in the U.S. "A dot-com in India that depended on somebody else's fulfillment chain would be in big trouble," says Saurabh Srivastava, chairman of the New Delhi-based venture-capital fund **Infinity**

Ventures, which has funded a dozen Indian Internet ventures in the past year.

If anything, Indian sites are moving away from "clicks" toward "bricks" as they struggle to survive. For example, **Indiagames.com Ltd.**, a Bombay-based Infinity-backed site, had 200,000 downloads in 1999 of a free game allowing users to shoot at Pakistani soldiers (India never lost), according to chief executive Vishal P. Gondal. Rather than trying to get people to start buying games online, the company is concentrating on producing CD-ROMs and writing customer software. The Internet is "not a business, it's a business enabler," Mr. Gondal says.

Ashish Dhavan, a Harvard Business

Not Too Deep

India rates low in Internet penetration, compared with the rest of its region (in millions)

	NET USERS	ADULT POP.	USERS AS PCT. OF ADULT POP.
Singapore	1.2	3.4	36.2%
Australia	4.1	15.4	26.3
Taiwan	4.0	17.7	22.8
Hong Kong	1.2	5.9	19.7
S. Korea	6.8	37.8	17.9
Japan	17.7	109.2	16.2
China	8.3	964.9	0.9
INDIA	1.8	695.8	0.3

Hooking Up

Expected e-commerce revenue for India, both business to business (B2B) and business to consumer (B2C), in billions

	2000	2001	2002	2003	2004
B2B	$0.11	$0.27	$1.10	$2.67	$5.42
B2C	0.01	0.03	0.12	0.26	0.67
TOTAL	0.12	0.31	1.22	2.93	6.09

Source: eMarketer 2001

(Cont.)

School-educated partner in Bombay-based venture fund Chrysalis Capital, says **Entranceguru.com,** a graduate-school test-preparation site he helped fund, was having problems because Indians were already too used to getting the information free on the Internet. But when another site printed and bound the same material, it was able to sell it for up to six times the online price, he says.

Suspicious Surfers

Others have found experienced Indian surfers suspicious of anything that happens offline. When banker Harsh Roongta started Bombay-based **Apnaloan.com India** Pte., a consumer-loan site, he used Charlotte, N.C.-based **Lending Tree Inc.'s** Web site, LendingTree.com, as a model, even asking friends with U.S. Social Security numbers to put in applications as a test. But he says he quickly decided that Indian Web users would drop out if he followed Lending Tree's practice of promising responses by e-mail "within one business day." That was too long for his site's skeptical users, who were used to instant responses on the Internet. He had to convince banks to share enough information with Apnaloan to allow it to give loan quotes while the users were still logged on.

"There is a huge degree of cynicism of anything off the Net," says Mr. Roongta.

One reason India's e-commerce market is so quirky is that most of the country's two million or so Internet users are in offices and Internet cafes. So, the office would seem a natural place to seek electronic commerce—except that Indian offices aren't immune from the country's telecommunications problems. **Clips India** Pte., a New Delhi office-supply retailer, has received only a trickle of orders on its Web site, and founder Arun Jain got insight into one of the reasons last month when he bid to supply office products to a U.S. company that he declines to name. "The connections kept hanging up," says Mr. Jain, who spent the day running between two computers hooked up to two different Internet providers, as he made his bids. He had connection problems with both providers.

Pick Up and Deliver

A small market does allow some experimentation that would be hard to try in the U.S. Take the problem of payment: Few Indians have credit cards, and e-shopping sites don't like cards anyhow because the country doesn't yet have good verification systems. One Bangalore-based site, **Fabmart.com,** came up with its own currency, called "Fabmoney," sold in Internet cafes. For gift sites, delivery companies have agreed to pick up cash at one location and deliver the gift to another location to avoid the credit-card problem. With India's low labor costs, the delivery companies charge the e-tailers only about $1 for the service.

Shirish Gariba, vice president of e-business for courier firm **Elbee Services** Ltd., says his Bombay-based company's association with Atlanta-based **United Parcel Service** Inc. helped prepare Elbee for e-commerce, but this particular innovation was home-grown. "We could offer flexible procedures they can't do," he says. "They deliver millions of packages a day."

26

Politics & Society: On the Move

People are migrating at record numbers, as the gap between the haves and the have-nots grows. The big question: Can it continue?

BY BERNARD WYSOCKI JR.

Staff Reporter of THE WALL STREET JOURNAL

Human wandering is as old as humankind, but the world has never seen so much of it.

Yet we will see even more.

The flow of migrants across borders is large and accelerating, approaching four million people a year. Globally, some 125 million people today live outside their country of birth.

But why? And how will mass migration shape the future?

In crassly economic terms, migration involves the poor flowing to the rich. In modern times, that means people go from the sending nations of South Asia, Africa and Latin America to the receiving nations of Europe and North America.

There's little doubt why migration has reached an all-time high. Income inequality between the richest and poorest nations has been rising for well over a century, at least.

The World Bank notes the ratio in average incomes between the richest and poorest countries was about 11 to 1 in 1870, 38 to 1 in 1960, 52 to 1 in 1985, and 49 to 1 in 1998.

"Migration is a result of differences—in demographic growth, in resources and jobs, and in security and human rights," says Philip Martin, chairman of the University of California's immigration and integration program. "And these differences are widening."

Stark Contrasts

At the dawn of the new millennium, these contrasts grow even starker: The richest countries are recording 3% to 5% increases in gross domestic product, while some of the poorest actually slide lower—victims of famine, war, social disintegration, inept leadership, and the flight of their best and brightest.

With ethnic and religious conflict raging in the former Yugoslavia, the Caucasus, Indonesia, sub-Saharan Africa, the Middle East and elsewhere, refugees increase the flow.

WHERE WILL ALL THE BABIES GO?

A powerful demographic fact leaps from the gulf between the haves and the have-nots of the global economy: The have-nots are having the vast majority of the babies.

Birth rates have stagnated or even declined in many developed countries, from Italy to Japan. By contrast, birth rates have exploded in Africa and in South Asia.

The obvious question: Who is going to employ all those working-age people? And just as significantly, perhaps more so, in the long run: Where will the less-fertile nations find the labor necessary to sustain growth?

Consider these numbers from United Nations studies: In 1950, the developed world had 524 million people in the prime working years of 18 to 65. By 1995, the number had risen to 780 million. But the U.N. projects that in the year 2030, this number will actually decline slightly, to 762 million.

By contrast, looking back to 1950, the developing world had 999 million in the 18-to-65 age group. That jumped to 2.76 billion by 1995.

The projections to the year 2030 are staggering: almost another doubling, to 4.9 billion people. In Africa, the number of working-age people will more than double, to 1.01 billion; in Asia, it will rise more than 50% to 3.46 billion; and in Latin America it will almost double to 490 million.

Assuming that home countries can't absorb these kinds of population increases, where will they go? Certainly, the U.S. is projected to absorb many immigrants, from Asia and especially from Latin American, above all Mexico. By the year 2050, the U.S. is expected to have a population of 393 million, of which 24% will be Hispanic (up from 11% today) and 8% will be Asian (up from 4% today). The U.S. has usually been quick to raise or lower borders depending on its work-force requirements, and the influx of immigration could be a godsend in a country full of retirees.

Japan, by contrast, will have to deal with potentially devastating labor shortages amid cultural taboos against immigration. Socially and racially, Japan is virtually homogeneous, with fewer than 1% of its population foreign-born. Even among businesspeople today, opposition to an increase in foreign labor runs at about 80%. The only alternative is a significant pickup in childbirth by today's Japanese women. The average Japanese woman today has 1.39 children during her lifetime.

Demographers predict that if current immigration and birth-rate patterns prevail, Japan's current population of 120 million will shrink to 100 million by 2050 and to 67 million by 2100. By the middle of the 21st century, one-third of Japanese will be over 65, placing a crushing financial burden on a shrinking working-age population.

—Bernard Wysocki Jr.

Nowadays the world counts some 15 million refugees a year, up more than fivefold in just 25 years.

Adding to this strife is separatism, which is spreading fast in this turbulent world. The number of nations has jumped to about 200 today from 75 at the end of World War II, and some futurists think this is only the beginning. Futurist John Naisbitt has predicted that there will be 1,000 nation-states by the year 2150. A fivefold increase in the census of nations would surely intensify migration pressures.

But no one knows for sure whether present trends are going to continue. Will separatist movements really go that far, spilling record numbers of displaced persons into the arms of strangers? Will rich nations, or once-rich nations in decline, turn protectionist, closing their doors on would-be immigrants?

Four Scenarios

Where we don't have certainty, we have scenarios. Consider these four possibilities—drawn from the Millennium Project, a panel organized by the United Nations University—to describe alternative futures for the world between now and 2050.

No. 1: Cybertopia

Technology creates a better world. China and India become software powerhouses. The gap between rich and poor widens, but telemedicine, tele-education and telebusiness partnerships spur developing countries' economies. World Trade Organization-sponsored global social safety nets discourage masses of poor from migrating.

Migration level: **Low.**

No. 2: The Rich Get Richer

Population growth slows everywhere, but remains higher in Africa and South Asia. The sharp disparity in personal income between richest and poorest nations widens, from 50 to 1 today to 80 to 1 by 2025. Migration rises, creating tension. By 2025, global corporations step in to develop more skilled workers, offer venture capital, etc.

Migration level: **High.**

(Cont.)

No. 3: Passive, Mean World

The problem is jobs. Population growth outstrips jobs growth in much of the world. In the rich countries, living standards stagnate. Small "virtual" companies succeed with transient work forces migrating from country to country. "Drifting and dancing" becomes a way of life. By 2025, trade wars envelope the regional economic blocs. Protectionism spreads in many forms, including nontariff barriers and restrictive immigration policies.

Migration level: **High, but resisted strongly.**

"Migration is a result of differences— in demographic growth, in resources and jobs, and in security and human rights," says one expert. "And these differences are widening."

No. 4: Trading Places

The once-booming economies of East and Southeast Asia recover and grow, challenging the U.S., the European Union and Japan. The North-South economic gap disappears, a quaint notion from the 19th and 20th centuries. Regions equalize in wealth.

Migration level: **Low.**

Lasting Trends

It is worth asking amid all this uncertainty whether some trends appear so durable that they're likely to persist as far as the years 2500 or 3000. The answer is: probably. Whatever the future levels of immigration, it's pretty much clear that immigration works for the immigrants themselves, and often for both receiving and sending countries. That's why it has persisted and is likely to continue.

"A permanent migration is successful about 90% of the time," says Richard Meier, professor emeritus of environmental design at the University of California at Berkeley. It has a ripple effect, he says, and this "affects the poorest people"—people whom "public policy is rarely able to target successfully."

Prof. Meier speaks anecdotally of a Guatemalan emigrant who exemplifies a global phenomenon. She arrived in the San Francisco Bay area at age 19 to escape civil strife. She married there and has given birth to two daughters. She sends 40% of her earnings back home, providing a brother and other kin a chance to escape the grinding poverty of her Guatemalan village. Prof. Meier himself has visited this village, and he concludes that her success "pulled about 10 people after her into a brighter world."

Both within and between countries, another seemingly unstoppable trend is urbanization, making the continuing surge of the city, and megacity, look all but unstoppable. The problems will mount, of course. The byprod-

ucts of urbanization include deforestation, depletion of water supplies and toxic levels of air pollution. These already threaten Mexico City and other metropolitan areas. Long term, given that so many cities have been built near seacoasts, the prospects of global warming could cause great migrations inland as coastal hordes flee rising waters.

Either way, few authorities expect the share of urban dwellers to do anything but continue rising.

It will be as if much of the developing world does in the next half-century what South Korea has done in the past 50 years. In the 1950s, Korea was largely rural, and one of the poorest countries in Asia. By the 1970s, it was rapidly modernizing. Seoul grew to a metropolis of 10 million, representing 25% of the population. Yet, as late as 1982, as many as 200,000 Koreans a year left to work in another country. They moved for jobs, mainly to the Middle East.

By the mid-1990s, South Korea had joined the industrialized world. It was prospering and importing labor, and well-educated Koreans who had moved to the U.S. were torn. Kyong Yu, a software manager in Dallas, who came to the U.S. as a student in the 1980s, sat in a restaurant over lunch in 1997, and weighed his decision. His brother had returned to South Korea to be a teacher. He decided to stay. He longed for his homeland and for the camaraderie of after-hours drinking and socializing so common in Seoul. But his economic opportunity, especially at this juncture, lay in the U.S.

Staying Home

Not everyone thinks the pressure or the impulse to emigrate will remain so strong. "People have an attachment" to their homelands, says Graham Molitor, vice president of the World Future Society. He thinks money itself will "be of less interest to people" as

---

CHARTING MIGRATION	

Sending and Receiving
Migration by region from 1990 to 1995

REGION	NET MIGRANTS (in thousands)
■ Sending Regions	
Africa	**−63**
Eastern	−128
Central	+4
Northern	+69
Southern	+2
Western	+10
Asia	**−1,366**
Eastern	−171
South-Central	−664
Southeastern	−485
Western	−46
Latin America	**−392**
Caribbean	−99
Central America	−202
South America	−91
■ Receiving Regions	
Europe	**+739**
Eastern	−109
Northern	+47
Southern	−20
Western	+821
North America	**+971**
Oceania	**+111**
Australia-New Zealand	+122
Other Oceania	−11

Sources: United Nations; World Population Prospects

(Cont.)

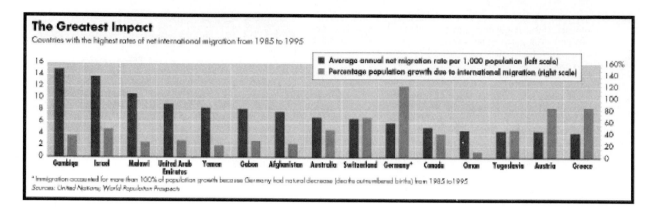

The Greatest Impact

Countries with the highest rates of net international migration from 1985 to 1995

■ Average annual net migration rate per 1,000 population (left scale)
■ Percentage population growth due to international migration (right scale)

*Immigration accounted for more than 100% of population growth because Germany had natural decrease (deaths outnumbered births) from 1985 to 1995

Sources: United Nations; World Population Prospects

wealth becomes more pervasive in the world. A preposterous view? Here's how he sees the next thousand years playing out:

By 2015, the leisure-time era dominates, with recreation, tourism, adventure, the arts, media and socializing (on the Internet and elsewhere) consuming more of people's time in the developed world. Working hours drop, vacation time rises.

The developing world becomes economically enfranchised in the next phase—the life-sciences era, which takes hold in 2100. Developments in agriculture are stunning. Bioengineered crops thrive in hostile environments. Genetic technology produces crop yields far beyond the "green revolution" of the 20th century. With rising wealth, the residents of developing countries are more likely to remain in their homelands.

Then, between 2100 and 2500, a new age of nuclear power provides substitutes for dwindling supplies of oil, natural gas and coal. "Thermonuclear technologies will dominate the economy when obstacles to controlling fusion are overcome," Mr. Molitor believes. The concept of resource deprivation becomes obsolete.

And finally, a new space age emerges in the years 2500 to 3000. Extraterrestrial enterprise becomes an important feature of the world economy, creating, in Mr. Molitor's view, a great new wave of human migration: to long-term residency in space.

It may sound far-fetched to imagine large-scale business operations beyond Earth. On the other hand, imagine how far-fetched the 20th century's technologies would have sounded to someone living in the 10th century.

27

Net company Terra aims for Hispanic connection

By David J. Lynch
USA TODAY

MADRID, Spain – If Juan Perea is right, the next new thing to hit the Internet won't come from a garage in Silicon Valley. It'll spring from a turquoise-accented, faux Greek temple in an office park outside Spain's capital.

This is the home of Terra Networks, Europe's answer to Internet fever and the continent's largest Net company in terms of market capitalization.

With only 9% of Spaniards online, Spain is about the last place you'd look for an Internet powerhouse. After all, this is a country known for Picassos, not portals.

But when Terra went public in November, brokers dubbed the resulting uproar the terramoto, or earthquake. The tiny company, whose Nasdaq shares have more than quadrupled in value since, is valued at more than $27 billion. Pretty good for a 14-month-old outfit that won't see its first dollar of profit for at least three years.

What are investors thinking? Just that Terra could be the play on bringing the Internet to folks who speak something other than English. The company, a spinoff from Spanish and Latin American telecommunications giant Telefonica, is targeting the 550 million Spanish speakers worldwide – including an estimated 31 million in the USA.

"The big players have not addressed in a big way the U.S. Hispanic segment," says Terra CEO Perea, who was in New York on Wednesday to officially launch the U.S. network. "We feel there's still room for us to attack."

Over the next decade, Hispanics are expected to be the fastest-growing slice of the American pie. By 2010, they will be nearly 44 million strong, a 39% gain from today. The Spanish-speaking Internet audience is "where the English-language Net was three or four years ago. It's going to develop fast," Yankee Group analyst Beate Groeger says.

Perea, 36, an investment banker by training, had never used the Internet when he left Bankers Trust at the end of 1996 for a job with Telefonica, which established Terra Networks as a subsidiary at the end of 1998.

But he's learned fast. Through swift acquisitions, Terra has become the No. 1 Internet service provider in Spain, Chile, Peru and Guatemala and is No. 2 in pivotal Brazil and Mexico. In the USA, Terra will sell access through IDT, a long-distance telecommunications company based in Hackensack, N.J.

Thanks to its Telefonica links, the company starts with access to 54 million customers in the Hispanic world. Terra also makes money from advertising and e-commerce on the Spanish- and Portuguese-language portals it operates in those countries.

HUNT FOR MARKETS IS ON

True, the numbers – a worldwide customer base of 1.1 million and about $17 million in annual revenue – are Lilliputian by America Online standards. But as Internet penetration in the Web-saturated USA flattens, companies seeking rapid growth must turn to less-developed markets. That's why AOL has expanded into Europe and Latin America. That's why Terra is going after Spanish speakers wherever they reside.

The growth potential is enormous. In Mexico, today's 1 million Net users (1% of the total) are expected to reach almost 5 million in three years, according to Jupiter Communications. Argentina is likely to see a similar mushrooming. Brazil's online cohort should more than double to 7.5 million over the same period.

Still, Latin America isn't North America. Many homes don't have phones, let alone computers and modems. Transportation networks can be problematic, rendering speedy deliveries difficult or impossible.

So Terra is deliberately eschewing a mass-market approach in favor of a precision appeal to the most

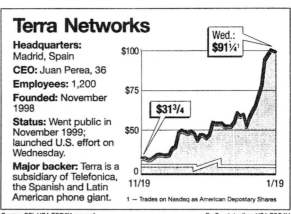

Terra Networks

Headquarters: Madrid, Spain

CEO: Juan Perea, 36

Employees: 1,200

Founded: November 1998

Status: Went public in November 1999; launched U.S. effort on Wednesday.

Major backer: Terra is a subsidiary of Telefonica, the Spanish and Latin American phone giant.

Wed.: $91¼[1]

$31¾

$100

$75

$50

$0

11/19   1/19

1 – Trades on Nasdaq as American Depositary Shares

Source: CSI, USA TODAY research   By Grant Jerding, USA TODAY

(Cont.)

prosperous one-fifth of Hispanics. These urbanites are people with Third World addresses but first world lifestyles.

"Remember, the Internet is all about focusing," says Gary Arlen, a Bethesda, Md.-based consultant.

To date, the Net's pronounced Anglo tilt – an estimated 96% of the Web is in English – may have discouraged Spanish speakers from logging on. About half of all U.S. households are online, but among Hispanics, the proportion is somewhere between one-fifth and one-third.

> **"There's no reason not to believe that one of the largest Internet companies in the world will be one serving the Spanish- and Portuguese-speaking market."**
> —*Juan Perea,*
> *Terra Networks CEO*

Terra aims to combat that disparity with a "global-local" solution providing targeted Spanish- and Portuguese-language content for audiences in eight countries, including the USA. AOL offers the masses Motley Fool investment tips and chats with Rosie O'Donnell. Terra will give U.S. Hispanics immigration forms and Jennifer Lopez.

DEALING WITH DIFFERENCES

But with Hispanic populations split among five different words for "straw," it's not as easy as translating existing English-language material into Español, says Terra content chief Rafael Bonnelly. The former Spanish-language newspaper editor says what works in Chile won't necessarily appeal to Argentines, Mexicans or American Latinos.

"Our Brazilian product doesn't have anything to do with our Mexican product, other than it's under the same brand," he says. "Our U.S. product is not targeted to Latin America. It's targeted to the U.S."

Last week, drawing on its alliance with content providers such as The Miami Herald, Terra's U.S. portal had extensive coverage of the story of Elian Gonzalez, the 6-year-old Cuban boy at the center of a dispute between Washington and Havana. Terra's Spanish and Chilean sites were more interested in the extradition saga of former Chilean dictator Augusto Pinochet.

Perea has a clear strategy, but he concedes success is far from guaranteed. Terra must unite newly acquired Latin American Web sites under its own multicolored brand. Plus, it faces competition from, among others, StarMedia, Quepasa.com, Yupi.com, Prodigy and AOL, which recently launched service in Brazil.

Almost two-thirds of U.S. Hispanics are of Mexican origin. But with sizable groups from each of the countries Terra is targeting, the USA represents an important test.

"The U.S. is a keystone area for us," says Enrique Rodriquez, who oversees Terra's Internet access business. "There are almost as many Spanish-speaking people in the U.S. as in Spain."

QUESTIONS LOOM

Still, there are questions about what proportion of U.S. Hispanics want their Net with a Spanish accent. About two-thirds of third-generation Hispanics speak English exclusively, according to Pepperdine University's Gregory Rodriquez.

It'll also be an additional three months at least before Perea has assembled a Spanish-speaking team of Americans to honcho Terra's U.S. operations. Hiring was slowed by his inability to offer stock options until Terra's IPO in November.

Terra also is under pressure to make an acquisition in the USA to match the Internet companies (and their customer rosters) that it has purchased in Latin America. The company confirms it is actively considering possible U.S. purchases.

So will Perea prove to be a Quixote or a conquistador? He thinks he knows the answer: "There's no reason not to believe that one of the largest Internet companies in the world will be one serving the Spanish- and Portuguese-speaking market."

28

Big Footprints

Hey, Baby Boomers Need Their Space, OK? Look at All Their Stuff

---

They Like Gourmet Kitchens And High Ceilings, Too, So Homes Get Pricier

---

'Not That Anybody Cooks'

By Carlos Tejada
and Patrick Barta
Staff Reporters of The Wall Street Journal

SOUTHLAKE, Texas – The nation's average price for a new home now exceeds $200,000, the Commerce Department reported yesterday. To see why, take a peek inside Rich and Diane Bean's double-decker walk-in closet. It's under the staircase, just down the hall from their two-oven kitchen and steps from the master bathroom, with its vaulted ceiling.

Even though the Beans culled their wardrobes before moving to this Dallas suburb in September they hang some of their more seldom-worn apparel on racks more than 10 feet above the floor. Mrs. Bean, who is 48 years old and of average height, can barely touch the hems. "If you're 10 feet tall, they're great," she says as she reaches up to tug on a skirt.

In the heavily windowed family room of the Bean's new $360,000 home, a Carpenters song on the radio fills the expanse beneath a 20-foot-high ceiling. Mr. Bean, 50, a construction-company president, concedes that the big windows and the house's generous size – 3,800 square feet – may make it less energy efficient than it could be. But, he says, "We just wanted that, whatever the price may be."

More Amenities

Like the American waistline, the new American home is getting larger. Empty nesters, baby boomers at the tops of their careers and the young and options-rich all are buying homes with more bedrooms, more bathrooms and more flourishes than ever before. And it shows: The average new-home price was $209,700 in November, up 4.2% from an upwardly revised $201,300 in October and up 17% from a year earlier. The increase reflects both the demand for more amenities and the higher costs of land, building materials and labor.

Even luxury builders are amazed at the depth and breadth of the demand. "Does anybody need all this? No," says Robert Toll, chief executive officer of Toll Brothers Inc., the nation's largest high-end homebuilder. His company builds some of its homes with recesses designed to display statues or outdoor features such as pillared driveway entrances. "We sell what nobody needs," he says.

In fact, need is hardly a consideration these days. Thanks to low unemployment, relatively low mortgage rates and a long run of stock-market profits, more and more home buyers feel like they can buy what they want, and that, it turns out, is quite a lot.

Though about half of today's new homes sell for $167,400 or less, the average size is 2,230 square feet, about 10% more than a decade ago. Most have at least three bedrooms, and more than half have two stories and at least 2 1/2 baths, roughly one for each member of the average household. "People want incredible amounts of space now," says Leslie Barry Davidson, a Houston architect. They "don't come in and say they want good materials, good labor, good craftsmanship. They come in and say, 'I want space for all my stuff, for my clothes, my skis, my junk.'"

'Showing Off'

To Houston architect William Stern, who builds just two or three large homes a year, the trend is appalling. The bigger-is-better trend is about "showing off to neighbors," he says. "People are saying, 'I can be a 1920s tycoon like anybody else.'"

Perhaps that's why the high end of the market is particularly frothy. In northern New Jersey, builders are putting up as many as 25 speculative homes each month with price tags between $500,000 and $1 million each. Most of the homes are targeted at executives relocating to the New York area, but a handful are designed specifically for Wall Street types with incomes fattened by year-end bonuses.

Whether the buyers will actually be there when the homes are finished isn't clear. "The relocation market makes sense; the magic money market is a little harder to predict," says Patrick O'Keefe, chief executive of New Jersey's builders association.

Though some expect higher interest rates to put the brakes on the current housing boom, the trend toward bigger homes reflects a demographic shift and a general feeling that homes aren't just housing, but an investment. A couple of decades ago, first-time homebuyers were almost forced to turn to the suburbs because that was where they could find cheap land and affordable tract homes. Now, while some new homes are "tear downs" in established urban neighborhoods, the vast majority are in suburban developments often aimed at repeat home buyers who want a bigger piece of land and an escape from the pressures of city life.

With housing prices climbing just about everywhere the last few years, buyers also seem to have forgotten the crashes that devastated home values a decade ago in California, New York and Texas. "Generally, people believe the stock market is more volatile" than the housing market, says Nicolas P. Retsinas, director of the Joint Center for Housing Studies of Harvard University in Cambridge, Mass.

The Beans, for instance, wanted a big, comfortable home to come home to after moving 13 times since the early 1980s while Mr. Bean was climbing the corporate ladder. The upstairs TV room, outfitted with University of Nebraska football souvenirs, has room for a pool table. The oversized bedroom houses exercise equipment. The half-acre lot will get a dog. "We're going to be here long enough, so we made it the way we wanted," Mr. Bean says.

The couple also studied the nation's surging housing market and concluded that a big house would have better resale potential than a smaller one. "Perhaps we got more house than we needed because of that," Mr. Bean says.

The big home isn't a new idea. In the 1890s, economist Alfred Marshall noted that as people progressed economically, they wanted better food, better clothes and larger houses – both for comfort and social standing. In the first two decades of the century, says Houston architectural historian Stephen Fox, home buyers preferred spacious houses with lots of windows, large rooms, and ceilings that exceeded nine feet and often reached 12 feet.

By the 1930s, however, the Depression and changing tastes drove builders to construct smaller homes with smaller rooms and fewer windows. Ceiling heights dropped to what became a standard eight feet. Homes grew again after World War II, but the average new home actually shrank slightly during each recession of the past three decades, according to National Association of Home Builders.

Today, Americans again are feeling confident about buying big. More than 10% of U.S. households had incomes of more than $100,000 in 1998, up from 7.5% in 1992. Then, there's the long run-up in the stock market. Michael Levine, a 43-year-old garment executive, funded the extra amenities in his new home by selling shares of Microsoft Corp. His 5,000-square-foot, $640,000 home, currently being built on an acre lot in the Philadelphia suburb of New Hope, Pa., will include a conservatory with a view of the mountains, as well as a spacious, well-appointed kitchen. "Not that anybody cooks, but it looks impressive," says the New York garment-industry executive.

About two days a week, Mr. Levine commutes more than an hour each way to New York. When he comes home to his new house, his garage will easily accommodate his two sport-utility vehicles. He is also looking forward to the special warming drawer that will keep his supper warm when he works late. Next, Mr. Levine wants to put a piano in his living room, though the room otherwise won't see much use. "Do I need one? I don't need one," he says.

For the same appearance reasons, maple cabinets made up 23% of the wood-cabinet market in 1998, up from 15% four years before, while use of more affordable oak has declined. And Broan-NuTone Group Inc., which sells home accessories, has seen a 50% increase in orders since 1998 for a line of Italian-crafted range hoods selling for $900 to $35,000. "They want a trophy kitchen. They know they're not going to use it, but they want the look," says Karen Collins, a Broan spokeswoman.

Toll Brothers, based in Huntingdon Valley, Pa., has been in business for years, but its high-end market began to soar in the 1990s. For the fiscal year ended Oct. 31, it sold 3,555 homes at an average price of more than $400,000, up from 1,324 homes at an average price below $300,000 in 1993. In recent years, it has piled on the amenities, such as double ovens or twin dishwashers. Master bathrooms often have two sinks and two toilets. It gives the first residents in a new neighborhood landscaping bonuses so subsequent customers will be encouraged to upgrade as well.

Executives lately are studying options for a new line of empty-nester homes that, while smaller, can be just as lavishly accessorized, if not more so. "Will they pay for this?" Edward D. Weber, a vice president, asks one morning as he points to an optional bay window in one design. "Seniors throw money at them. No problem," says Jed Gibson, the company's director of architecture.

Toll Brothers decks out its model homes with its glitziest options in hopes that one will clinch a sale. It might be a 20-foot-tall closet or a circular driveway edging up to the front step. A favorite of Mr. Weber's: a second-floor master bedroom that opens into a walk-in closet with mirrored walls. At the other end of the closet is the bathroom, with a large bathtub below a window. The span from bedroom to tub is 72 feet, or about the length of the typical mobile home.

The builder has been able to make rooms bigger because stronger trusses have eliminated the need of most walls to act as supports. Though ceilings have crept up past nine feet, better insulated walls and tighter windows have made heating and cooling the big spaces less costly.

In part to get around a chronic shortage of skilled labor, Toll Brothers makes the walls and ceilings in a factory and assembles them on site. It builds its developments with the houses at varying distances from the street to avoid a symmetrical, cookie-cutter look. The company plants fatter, three-year-old trees along its streets so they look more impressive than the saplings planted in other builders' neighborhoods.

In a 4,600-square-foot house here in Southlake, Antoine Jenkins is delighted that Toll Brothers keeps raising its prices, which he hopes will add value to the $380,000, five-bedroom home he and wife Karen bought this past fall. He believes the house, with its two staircases, big double doors and embedded alcoves for plants or statues, will do better at resale than his previous home, a smaller one in Manassas, Va. But before investment value, Mr. Jenkins, 36, a human-resources executive at computer-services concern Sabre Holdings Corp., demanded comfort. He enjoys the fact that, because of the space and acoustics, he can't hear his three daughters running the water or flushing the toilet in another room. He loves the bathtub big enough for his stocky frame. Most of all, he loves the den, which has the wall-size bookcase he ordered and a big window overlooking the backyard. "The study is where I'll put my humidor and cigars, with the bottle of port on the side. There'll be a music system. When I come home, that's where Daddy goes," he says.

For the down payment, he rustled up $40,000 from the sale of his shares in Nextel Communications Inc. and American Express Co., as well as shares of Microsoft he received when he worked for the software giant. But he realizes it might not all last. A thus-far successful investor, Mr. Jenkins nevertheless lost money last year while playing stock options. But he isn't worrying. "If it happens, it happens. I'm here today, who knows where I'll be tomorrow?" he says. "If you look for the downturn, you miss the good times. I'll get it now and I'll have no regrets later."

29

Extreme Nesting

Knock knock: Who's there? Your haircutter, the car-repair guy, even the doctor. June Fletcher finds overstressed families staying home and bringing the world to their door.

By June Fletcher

Staff Reporter of The Wall Street Journal

Michael Kempner is buying time.

Two years ago, Mr. Kempner ran himself ragged most weekends, driving around town doing errands. "I was totally on the run," he says. "I always felt stressed." But these days, he hangs around the house most weekends, doing puzzles with his three kids or watching sports on television. The difference? He now pays extra to have everyone from dry cleaners to car washers come to his house. "Life has become so compressed," he says, "that I decided my time with my family is worth more than money."

Now that we've journeyed all the way into the new millennium, a lot of us just want to stay home. Many families have become so overscheduled and overloaded that they're rebelling – by not going anywhere. Exhausted from hectic work schedules, long commutes and family demands, people are increasingly reluctant to go out again, for almost any reason, once they get home. The hunker-down mentality is fueled by the fact that, thanks to the booming economy, many people now have the affluence to fund their stay-at-home fantasies.

As a result, more consumers are shelling out extra cash to have goods and services delivered, or paying other people to run their errands. Feeling that they have more money than time, some Americans are willing to pay a premium for the privilege of being a couch potato.

Mr. Kempner, owner of a public-relations firm, has found all kinds of businesses will come to his Cresskill, N.J., home – for a price. His personal trainer, his car detailer, his wife's masseuse and his children's piano teacher all make regular visits. He bought his wife's birthday present from a jeweler willing to send a selection of watches for him to review in his living room. And last Friday, while others were out celebrating New Year's Eve, he had the party come to him: flowers, sushi, chips and salsa were delivered to his house.

"A year or two ago, I don't think all of these businesses would have been willing to come to my home," says Mr. Kempner, who says the convenience usually adds at least 5% to the price. "But now they're beginning to realize that busy people like me won't buy from someone who won't deliver."

Indeed, plenty of businesses, big and small, are capitalizing on the yearnings of stressed-out consumers to give up on gridlock and let the world beat a path to their doors. Making house calls can be lucrative, even for small entrepreneurs. Stephen Newman, who runs a come-to-your-house brake-repair service, charges up to $200 – more than twice the rates the big chains offer. A car buff and former stockbroker from Fairfax, Va., Mr. Newman says his business has grown more than 25% during the past five years, so much that lately he's been turning new customers away.

Even the doctor's house call, pretty much a thing of the past, is starting to show signs of life: The American Academy of Home Care Physicians says its membership has doubled, to 700 members, during the past two years.

Certainly, the very rich have always enjoyed the convenience of having their tai-chi instructors or dog groomers come to their homes. But now, a whole new group of people can afford – and are willing – to pay for such pampering. Priscilla La Barbera, an assistant professor of marketing at New York University, regularly has an $80 hourlong massage in the privacy of her one-bedroom apartment. At first, she felt it was "self-indulgent." But after a few sessions, she realized how much more she enjoyed home massages than those done in spas, and stopped feeling guilty about the expense. "Afterwards, it's so relaxing not to have to get dressed and go back out into the elements," says Ms. La Barbera, who often drifts off to sleep on the portable table the masseuse sets up in her living room.

In recent years, there's been a "societal shift" in the way people view the worth of their free time, says Ms. La Barbera, and the market has responded. "So many things can be ordered through one toll-free call," she says. "And people are beginning to realize that their time has real value."

The strong stay-at-home sentiment has been a perfect fit for the Internet. Online shopping and Web-based delivery companies play right into the batten-down-the-hatches mentality, which has fueled their growth. According to Jupiter Communications, an Internet research firm in New York, online grocery purchases increased more than 50% since 1998, to $233 million, and should continue to rise rapidly, reaching a whopping $7.5 billion in 2003. While it remains to be seen how many of the new Web-based delivery services will actually survive, it's clear they've tapped into a well of pent-up feelings.

Streamline.com, a Westwood, Mass., delivery service that went public in June, thinks there's money to be made in doing "necessity-based, menial shopping," says Chief Executive Timothy De Mello. For a flat charge of $30 a month, the company delivers groceries, as well as dry-cleaning, repaired shoes, rental videos, fresh flowers, stamps, processed film, bottled water and prepared meals (home-office supplies and liquor soon will be added). In the past four years, the company's customer base has grown to 4,000 households from 200; its revenue for the quarter ended Oct. 2 more than doubled, to $3.62 million, from the same period a year earlier – although, like most Web companies, it has yet to show a profit. "We're banking on the idea that people want to offload a lot of boring activities," Mr. De Mello says.

Time With the Kids

The idea of paying someone else to do the routine stuff is especially appealing to two-career couples. "My day is completely scheduled, every single day," says Valerie Andrews, a Boston attorney, who has two preschoolers. She and her husband, also a lawyer, commute an hour each way to work, putting them under "real time constraints," she says. "I want more time to be with my kids, or work in the office."

Mrs. Andrews, a Streamline customer since 1997, says the system isn't without flaws – occasionally an item has been left out of her grocery order, and the selection isn't as big as it would be in a supermarket. But on the whole, she thinks online shopping has made her more "systematic and efficient." And though she doesn't think the company's food prices are bargains – she describes them as on par with upscale local markets – she's noticed that her grocery bill has actually gone down during the past two years: "When you're buying food online, you can't be tempted with how something smells or looks, so you're less likely to buy it on impulse."

No task seems too special to hire out. At Your Service, a Burke, Va., company, says that during the holidays, several time-pressed customers paid the company to buy, address and mail stacks of Christmas cards – complete with fake "personal" greetings and signatures. "It works well because most people don't know what their friends' handwriting looks like," says co-owner Stacey Both. For rates of $15 to $30 an hour, the company does all sorts of errands for customers, from taking the family dog to the vet to getting a car registration renewed.

Buying more free time is money well spent, some consumers say, even if they don't do much with it. Debra Thomas, a Houston public-relations consultant, pays a personal assistant $75 to run errands and do small tasks four hours each week, ranging from watering the plants to changing the cat litter. Handing off the petty chores gives her guilt-free time to relax, Ms. Thomas says, though she often spends it doing nothing more than lounging in bed and drinking a glass of red wine. "Before, I always had a sinking feeling each weekend that I should be doing this or that," she says. "Now, I just put it on the list for my assistant."

Bringing It All Back Home

*Hankering to hunker down on that cushy sofa with a glass of
Merlot rather than braving the streets? Here's how to find folks
who are willing to deliver their goods and services to your
home – and what you should ask before you sign up.*

DOCTORS Unless you are elderly or too ill to come to an office, you'll probably pay almost double the office rate, out-of-pocket, for the privilege of having a doctor come to your home. But because demand is growing, portable equipment has become lighter and Medicare has increased its payments to doctors who make home visits, that's starting to change. "Physicians are beginning to see that you can give patients better care at home than you can in an office," says George Taler, a doctor in Washington, D.C., who only does house calls, carting around $12,500 of emergency equipment to treat his frail patients.

To find a doctor in your area who makes house calls, call your local medical board or contact the American Academy of Home Care Physicians, based in Edgewood, Md., at 410-676-7966 or www.aahcp.org. Information on other health-care providers such as visiting nurses, physical therapists, pharmacists and dietitians may be obtained from Housecall Medical Resources Inc., Murdock, Fla., at www.housecall.com.

PERSONAL CARE In many cities, you can find bulletin boards covered with fliers from hairdressers, manicurists and skin-care specialists who make home visits. But ask questions before you hire such specialists, especially if they aren't associated with an established salon or spa. Sue Sansom, executive director for the Arizona Board of Cosmetology, Tempe, encourages consumers to ask to see the specialist's license, inquire about disinfectant procedures and find out who will be legally responsible should something go awry. There's a lot more than chipped nail polish at stake – a bad permanent or color treatment can burn your scalp, and dirty tools can spread lice and diseases such as hepatitis. "You need to protect yourself," says Ms. Sansom.

Because not all states allow personal-care specialists to make home visits, "some may be operating illegally," says Jim Cox, executive director of the American Association of Cosmetology Schools, based in Scottsdale, Ariz. (For more information, contact your state's board of cosmetology listed at www.beautyschool.com, or call the National-Interstate Council of State Boards of Cosmetology at 954-389-5302.)

GROCERIES Most online grocery companies currently operate only in limited areas, though expansions are in the works. Webvan Group Inc., Foster City, Calif., delivers both perishables and nonperishables in the San Francisco Bay area through its own network of drivers. Customers can specify a delivery time, but they must be home to receive the order. The company promises delivery, which comes at no extra charge, within a half-hour of the specified time. Streamline.com Inc., Westwood, Mass., installs refrigerators in the garages of its customers in Boston and Washington, D.C., enabling it to deliver perishable goods without having anyone meet the truck. It charges $30 a month for delivery. NetGrocer.com Inc., North Brunswick, N.J., is currently the only company that ships nationwide, but it sells only nonperishables, which it delivers via Federal Express (charges for a $200 order are $16 east of the Mississippi River, and $30 west of it). Though the shipping may take as long as four days, customers don't have to be home when the goods are delivered, according to Mr. Kempner, whose public-relations firm represents the company.

MASSAGE Contact the American Massage Therapy Association, Evanston, Ill., at 888-843-2682 or at www.amtamassage.org. It will recommend legitimate massage therapists who will not only come to your home, but who also have demonstrated proficiency in whatever massage technique you prefer, from rolfing to shiatsu. (Currently, 28 states and the District of Columbia license massage therapists or require them to be certified by the National Certification Board of Therapeutic Massage and Body Work.)

You should ask prospective therapists how many hours of education they've had (look for a minimum of 500 hours), what equipment they provide (some use the clients' own oils and linens) and how big their table is (6-feet-by-4-feet isn't uncommon). "You also need to assess if you have enough space in your home – a massage therapist has to move around," says massage therapist Adela Basayne, past president of the massage therapy association. And of course, inquire about the price; an at-home massage can cost 50% more than one in a salon, according to Ms. Basayne.

(Cont.)

Back to the Future

The demand for home-based services has been building steadily in recent years, fueled in part by the increase in working women. Home-delivered meals – first with the explosion of pizza deliveries, then with more gourmet fare – kicked off the modern trend. But the trend, it turns out, is retro.

Although home delivery was common in the early 1900s, by 1954 it had fallen to 8.8% of food purchases, and by 1986 it was down to 1.2%, according to the U.S. Department of Agriculture. Home food deliveries have increased in recent years, thanks mostly to the delivery of prepared meals, climbing to 2.4% of total food sales in 1998. Other businesses picked up on the niche market for bringing things home; during the fitness craze of the '80s, for instance, personal trainers started holding aerobics sessions in customers' living rooms. By the time e-commerce arrived in the '90s, consumers were ready to be introduced, or reintroduced, to the idea of home delivery.

As Americans begin to rely more on outsiders to deliver goods and services rather than their own efforts, life is starting to resemble the way things were in the early 1900s, according to Jagdish Sheth, a professor at Emory University in Atlanta. Then, even middle-class people relied on servants to provide most services, and nearly all merchants delivered their products. Those practices dropped away about the time of World War I, as servants and delivery clerks sought better-paying jobs in war factories. The move toward hired help and home deliveries began to revive during the past decade, he says, this time spurred not by the availability of cheap labor, but by the rising affluence of time-pressed consumers.

The Home Foreman

Of course, in addition to the extra cost, there are other downsides to having service workers come to your home – like having to wait for them and check up on them. Mr. Sheth and his wife Madhu, who spend about $300 a week on such service providers as landscapers, maids, cooks and caterers, know this all too well. "My wife is like a foreman at a factory," Mr. Sheth says.

But service workers aren't the only ones willing to come to their customers' doorsteps in this competitive, booming economy, Mr. Sheth adds. Some professionals are, too. "My accountant and my lawyer both come regularly to my house now," he says. "I think it's just a matter of time before my doctor will start making house calls again, too."

Indeed, Constance Row, executive director of the Home Care Physicians group, says its members report they're increasingly being asked to make house calls by relatives of their patients – often baby boomers who are trying to care for elderly parents long-distance "and can't fly 1,000 miles to take their mothers to the doctor's office."

Dr. Wayne McCormick, a Seattle physician who's been in practice 13 years, makes about three to five house calls a week, to his most-frail patients. He thinks house calls will increase in the future, in part because of a recent increase in Medicare payments for such visits, but also because affluent boomers won't mind paying extra for the service. "I don't think our own generation will put up with doctors who don't make house calls," he says. Because of new, lightweight medical equipment, most of what he needs fits into a backpack, which he carries instead of a black bag. At a patient's home, he says he can do X-rays, IVs, blood-chemistry tests, ultrasound and many emergency procedures. Medical records are kept on his laptop computer.

Will the growing stay-at-home mindset bring families closer together, or just mean more hours zoning out in front of the TV? As a research experiment, Bruce Weinberg, an assistant professor of marketing at Boston University's Graduate School of Management, has been buying all his family's goods and services online since September. After shopping for everything from a hard-to-find type of glue to a used Rolls Royce (he bought one for $17,000), he's a convert to home delivery. "I used to enjoy shopping at regular stores, but this is far superior," he says. Initially, he thought he'd resent paying delivery charges for everyday items, but now says the "two or three dollars extra" on a typical $70 food bill is far outweighed by the three hours or so a week he saves by not having to drive to a supermarket near his Newton, Mass., home.

"I wasn't aware before how much my time is worth," he says. Now, he has more time to play with his two toddlers, and to spend with his wife, Amy.

Still, all the extra free time at home has had some consequences, Mr. Weinberg says with a laugh: "Amy just told me she's pregnant again."

30

How Baxter, PNC, Pratt & Whitney Make The Internet Work For Them

By J. Bonasia
Investor's Business Daily

It used to take 15 minutes for a worker at Baxter International to put through a change of address. Now it's 90 seconds. Choosing benefits takes three mouse clicks. Buying office supplies took a month. Now it's three days.

Baxter is a company with $6.9 billion in sales. It sells blood-related products and services. It has rebuilt many of its tasks around Internet protocols, and expects to save $50 million a year just on purchasing.

Baxter's plans, performance reviews, employee records and expense forms also are handled faster online.

"This is about changing the mindset of the work force and helping them to embrace the Internet," said Faye Katt, Baxter's vice president of employee services. "When they do, all sorts of light bulbs go on."

Such tools cut across industry lines. They work for Baxter, for banks such as PNC Financial Services and even old-line firms like jet engine maker Pratt & Whitney, a unit of United Technologies.

Jack Staff, an economist at Zona Research, says paper-based purchasing costs $50 to $250 per transaction. Buying online can cut that amount more than 90%.

Real-Time Data

John Moon, Baxter's chief information officer, and Paul Brenner, vice president of e-business, say the Net also has made a big difference in inventory control. Since the Net serves up real-time data on orders and supplies, Baxter can hold less stock.

When a new system is in next year, it will cut stock needs by $45 million.

Baxter, based in Deerfield, Ill., carried $1.12 billion in inventory at the end of 1999. In 2000, it turned 3.4 times vs. 3.2 the year before.

Baxter's e-based customer service lets clients' computers "talk" with its own. This results in fewer mistakes—boosting service and productivity.

Transaction Costs

Chances for savings—and better service—are equally rich in banking. Aberdeen Group says teller transactions cost $1.40 each vs. 30 cents by phone and 20 cents online.

Tim Shack, chief information officer for Pittsburgh's PNC Financial, says e-business staffers work in each of its units to track returns on technology. "I'm not sure anything has had this much potential for the financial services industry in the last 30 years," he said.

PNC linked with Perot Systems to develop a new format for electronic bill payments between businesses. It can be sold to other firms.

Customer Tool

Like Baxter, PNC buys supplies online. That'll save $16 million over the next year. Using online auctions could trim more.

PNC will save another $14 million by automating credit processes for corporate customers on the Web. For instance, the unit that helps businesses manage accounts payable and receivables now fields 10% of its inquiries over the Net.

"This represents real customer value," Shack said.

Some moves are obvious. PNC sites let investors find data about their funds, bonds and loans. Another site lets its fund managers track investments.

Tom Kunz, PNC's directory of e-commerce strategy, says these services build loyalty because clients can get data quickly. They don't have to slog through a slow manual process or a phone tree.

PNC also created Web-based courses that give workers technical and financial training from home or on the road.

And some projects produce sales. PNC Advisors, the asset management arm, created a Web site called unlockingpaperwealth.com. It helps people who may have too much wealth tied up in one company diversify their holdings. Kunz says the unit took in $15 million in new revenue in

its first four months. PNC hopes it will do $30 million this year.

Pratt & Whitney also gets value out of its online systems.

In tearing down an engine, analyzing and sourcing repairs once took 54 hours, but now it takes just minutes.

Peter Longo, vice president of information technology for the East Hartford, Conn., company, says that since going online in 1996, Pratt & Whitney has hiked its on-time delivery rate to 99% from 67%.

"If you can't ship a part, the airline has a $175 million asset on the ground that it can't use," he said.

Documents Online

Pratt & Whitney's maintenance and repair unit is going online because mechanics and managers spend more than half of their time seeking data about specific

E-Business Benefits

Net technology cuts back-office costs . . .

E-procurement of supplies

Prices paid	7.5% savings
Administrative	72.4% savings
Fulfillment cycles	72.8% reduction
Maverick buying	51% reduction
Inventory costs	37.5% savings

. . . and saves a ton on customer service

Bank service costs, per interaction

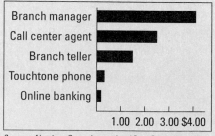

Branch manager
Call center agent
Branch teller
Touchtone phone
Online banking

1.00 2.00 3.00 $4.00

Sources: Aberdeen Group, International Data Corp.

(Cont.)

parts. It's no wonder, as each jet engine contains 50,000 parts on average. Web browsers cut their search time.

David Brantner, Pratt & Whitney's director of e-commerce, says the company developed a Web portal that lets customers and employees create customized windows for online communication.

That gives all parties visibility into Pratt's back-end office systems, using any browser. The portal keeps contract data, repair data, engineering memos and parts orders.

Only The Start

Most important, Brantner says, the Web provides a perfect platform to track the huge amount of technical data that go with engines and parts in the aerospace sector.

"This is a highly regulated industry, so configuration control is tightly managed," he said. "Probably no industry has more to gain from e-business than aerospace."

The actual gains have only just begun. Longo says the reliability of Pratt & Whitney's entire fleet has improved by 15% since it went online two years ago, and he expects greater progress to come.

31

FROM REENGINEERING TO E-ENGINEERING

Companies large and small are racing to revamp operations for the Internet Age

Men and women who have spiced up their sex lives with Viagra can thank the Web for its quick arrival on the market. Here's why: Pfizer Inc. now dashes off electronic versions of its drug applications to Washington for Food & Drug Administration approval. In the old days, it had to truck tons of paper to regulators and thumb through copies of all those pages manually whenever the feds had a question. By managing documents on the Web, Pfizer sliced the old one-year approval timetable nearly in half and sped Viagra into the world's boudoirs.

Post-Viagra, Pfizer's drugs will move through the pipeline even faster. The company's wired researchers now use the Web to mine libraries of technical data and collaborate on new drug development. "We've reengineered our business–digitally," says Vice-President for Research James Milson.

Reengineering. It was all the rage in the mid-'90s. But the vast and speedy Internet is ushering in an even bigger wave of business transformation. Call it E-engineering. Companies realize it's not enough to put up simple Web sites for customers, employees, and partners. To take full advantage of the Net, they've got to reinvent the way they do business–changing how they distribute goods, collaborate inside the company, and deal with suppliers.

This isn't just about saving time and money. The Web gets creative juices flowing, too. Employees who formerly spent their days faxing and phoning basic information to customers and suppliers are freed by the Net's magic to do more valuable work.

NEW BELIEVERS. Technology companies like Intel, Dell, and Cisco Systems were among the first to seize on the Net to overhaul their operations. At Intel Corp., for example, Web-based automation has liberated 200 salesclerks from tediously entering orders. Now, they concentrate instead on analyzing sales trends and pampering customers. Cisco Systems Inc., for its part, handles 75% of sales online. And 45% of its online orders for networking gear never touch employees' hands. They go directly from customers to the company's software system and on to manufacturing partners. That helped Cisco hike productivity by 20% over the past two years. But what grabs attention is sales: The

troika is doing a booming $70 million in on-line business each day.

With numbers like that, it's no wonder the tech jocks are being joined by a second wave of believers, ranging from Rust Belt manufacturing giants like Ford Motor Co. to foreign companies like Mexican cement seller Cemex. Even Corporate America's walking wounded are joining in. Just last month, troubled silicone supplier Dow Corning Corp. appointed an E-commerce czar. "Every businessperson I call on today is filled with greed or fear when it comes to the Internet," says James L. Barksdale, CEO of Netscape Communications Corp. "They're asking, 'How do I do it to them before they do it to me?'"

Doing it is no simple matter. Reengineering projects can be hugely complicated, with technology, business, and organizational upheavals all rocking the corporate foundations at once. There are harrowing risks. Casualties will include some companies that were too bold–but even more that were too timid.

Ford plans to be neither. It's taking on the E-engineering challenge holistically. One executive, Bernard Mathaisel, is both chief information officer and leader of its reengineering efforts. His plan is to fundamentally retool the way Ford operates with the help of the Web, cementing lifelong relationships with customers and slashing costs. "We're bringing new practices into every aspect of the company," says Mathaisel.

Already, E-business has begun to spread through the organization from front to back. Rather than relying on dealers to handle all customer contacts, Ford has put up a Web site that lets tire-kickers pick and price cars–then refers them to dealers. Ford then routes the customer feedback from the Web site to its marketers and designers to help them plan new products.

In the design process, the Web brings 4,500 Ford engineers from labs in the U.S., Germany, and England together in cyberspace to collaborate on projects. The idea is to break down the barriers between regional operations so basic auto components are designed once and used everywhere. When design plans conflict, the software automatically sends out E-mail alerts. Next, Ford's going to roll out a system for ordering parts from suppliers. When all of these pieces are in place, the com-

pany hopes to transform the way it produces cars–building them to order rather than to forecasts.

Other companies need to get wired to defend themselves. In the PC industry, the threat comes from Dell Computer Corp., which has deftly translated its hugely successful direct sales model to the Internet. Other PC companies have to match Dell's efficiencies–or die. Enter Ingram Micro Inc., the PC industry's largest distributor, which has teamed up with Solectron Corp., a giant contract manufacturer of high-tech gear.

TEAM EFFORT. In April, they plan to launch a brand-new way to build custom-made PCs inexpensively for companies like Hewlett-Packard Co. and Compaq Computer Corp. Instead of the PC companies handling orders and manufacturing, Ingram and Solectron will do it for them using a Web-based system that will hasten communications and slash assembly times. The PC companies are still in the driver's seat. They continue to build the value of their brands, designing and marketing their products and handling quality assurance. But now it's a team effort. "Customers are doing business with a virtual company," says Ingram President Jeffrey R. Rodek.

Figuring out what you do best is a crucial piece of Web reengineering. Few companies have pursued that philosophy as aggressively as Provident American Corp. in Norristown, Pa. In December, it took a radical step. It sold off nearly all of its life-insurance business and reinvented itself as HealthAxis.com, an online service that sells insurance products from other companies. CEO Michael Ashker decided the company was best at selling simple, high-volume insurance policies to consumers and taking a commission–rather than managing risk and independent agents.

There are some real shockers in this process. Like: Not all your customers are equal, or worthy. Weyerhaeuser Co. Inc., the forest-products company uses the Web to help it mine information from its suppliers, price products, and measure demand. More down-to-the-minute knowledge paid off: The plant boosted production by 60% to 800,000 doors last year. Weyerhaeuser can also offer more accurate bids to builders. In some cases, it can charge $40 less for certain doors–and still make a profit. That spells entré into some new

(Cont.)

These days, most PCs for business customers are made by PC companies based on sales forecasts and shipped through distributors. The PC company, distributors, and the resellers who deal with customers all keep inventories and often have to reconfigure computers to a customer's specifications. Ingram Micro, a distributor and assembler, and Solectron, a contract manufacturer, have come up with a system that will build computers to order and cut costs substantially. The amount of time a PC sits in inventory is expected to be reduced from months to hours.

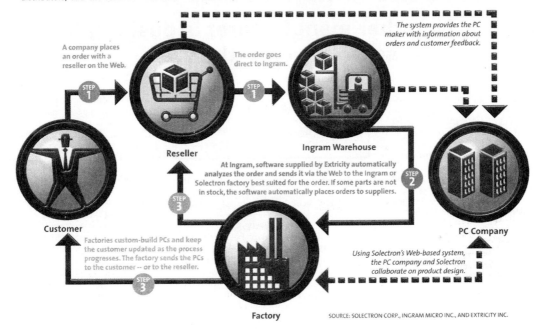

The system provides the PC maker with information about orders and customer feedback.

A company places an order with a reseller on the Web.

The order goes direct to Ingram.

STEP 1

STEP 1

Reseller

Ingram Warehouse

At Ingram, software supplied by Extricity automatically analyzes the order and sends it via the Web to the Ingram or Solectron factory best suited for the order. If some parts are not in stock, the software automatically places orders to suppliers.

STEP 2

STEP 3

Customer

Factories custom-build PCs and keep the customer updated as the process progresses. The factory sends the PCs to the customer -- or to the reseller.

STEP 3

PC Company

Using Solectron's Web-based system, the PC company and Solectron collaborate on product design.

Factory

SOURCE: SOLECTRON CORP., INGRAM MICRO INC., AND EXTRICITY INC.

markets. What's more, it now knows which customers bring in the big revenues and which don't. It can shed the ones that eat up too much time and order little.

That's painful for some customers. But E-engineering, badly executed, is even tougher on organizations. Just ask the engineers at NASA's Ames Research Center in Moffett Field, Calif. They spent $100 million building a Web-based collaborative engineering system to help accelerate development of the space station. Turned out they didn't have the technology plumbing in place to handle the job and lost some valuable data. Among the missing information: the plans for the Saturn V rocket.

Technology isn't always the hangup. In some cases, it's a stodgy corporate culture. "For many older executives, converting to E-business is like changing their religion," says John Thorp, vice-president of DMR Consulting Group Inc. And sometimes resistance comes from a pencil pusher down in purchasing. At Canadian Imperial Bank of Commerce in Toronto, purchasing agents missed the point of a new Web-based system for or-dering supplies. They tried squeezing suppliers for price cuts when in fact the point was for everyone to buy from an electronic cata-log–to land volume discounts. The bank set them straight with tailored incentive bonuses.

Perhaps the greatest danger is that business units will act independently, and the results will be piecemeal. The last thing you want is "tack-on" technology. To work, this effort must be coordinated at a high level–and changes should be fundamental, says analyst Bobby Cameron of Forrester Research Inc.

CHANGE FATIGUE. Citigroup gets it. As an executive vice-president in charge of advanced technologies, Edward D. Horowitz defines his job this way: to get the company's top 200 executives marching to the same drumbeat when it comes to the Internet. Horowitz's first salvo was to send them all copies of Clayton M. Christensen's best-sell-ing book *The Innovator's Dilemma: When New Technologies Cause Great Firms to Fail*, about managing the dislocating effects of technology. Then he gave them a home-work assignment: start banking online. At the time, only a handful were doing it. "The message was you've got to use the product you're selling," says Horowitz.

That's a lot to ask of busy executives who are scrambling to complete the $80 billion merger of Citicorp and Travelers Group. But these days, change is relentless. Many corporate executives are just now finishing up major retooling of their financial and manu-facturing processes. Plus, there's the Y2K problem. After a while, change fatigue sets in. "Companies are exhausted," says Michael Hammer, author of the 1993 book *Reengineering the Corporation: A Manifesto for Business Revolution*. His advice: "Suck it up. You have to face it again." In the era of E-engineering, risking burnout is better than getting fried.

By Steve Hamm and Marcia Stepanek. Contributing: Andy Reinhardt

32

AT FORD, E-COMMERCE IS JOB 1

No other manufacturer is pushing so boldly onto the Web

The Rust Belt is approaching Net-speed. It was just last June, when a Ford Motor Co. task force made a presentation to Chief Executive Jacques A. Nasser and his top managers. Originally assigned to study how the Internet could improve manufacturing, the team had gone all out, showing Nasser a computer simulation of the auto company of the future. The vision was breathtaking: factories that built cars to order, dealerships that reported problems instantly so that plants could make adjustments, and suppliers that controlled inventories at Ford factories–much the way retailer Wal-Mart Stores Inc. does when it gives vendors responsibility for stocking its store shelves. "We were mesmerized," says Alice Miles, a veteran Ford purchasing manager. Nasser gave it an instant thumb's-up. "This is nothing short of reinventing the auto industry," he says.

Since then, the old-line Ford has been latching on to the Net like some new dot-com. In January, Ford showed off futuristic "24/7" concept vehicles packed with cybergoodies such as Internet connections and e-mail. Miles now heads auto-xchange, a newly created online trading mart for Ford's 30,000 suppliers that began taking orders in February. And in an effort to wire up its far-flung workforce of 350,000 people, Ford announced on Feb. 3 that it would offer each of them a home computer, a printer, and Internet access for $5 a month.

Some 90 years after Ford led the world into the era of mass manufacturing, the No. 2 auto maker wants to reprise its trailblazing role–and cash in the way it did decades ago. By using the Net to bust up bureaucracy and unleash radically new ways of planning, making, and selling cars, Ford could become a model of efficiency in the Internet Age. Streamlining suppliers and distribution using the Web could amount to savings equal to 25% of the retail price of a car, says analyst Jonathan Lawrence of Dain Rauscher. The auto-xchange mart could generate $3 billion in transaction fees within five years–of which Ford would get a hefty cut. And that doesn't take into account the monthly service fees of $20 to $25 that Ford could collect if drivers should want to hop on to the Net while roaring down the highway. Says David Bovet, an e-commerce expert at Mercer Management

> Ford's sweeping system, called CustomerConnect, will link buyers and factories with financiers, parts suppliers, and designers

Consulting Inc.: "Detroit will be where the rubber hits the road on the Information Highway, a real acid test for the potential of e-business."

Nasser's vision is a sweeping one. He pictures the day when a buyer hits a button to order a custom-configured Ford Mustang online, transmitting a slew of information directly to the dealer who will deliver it, the finance and insurance units who will underwrite it, the factory that will build it, the suppliers that provide its components, and the Ford designers brainstorming future models. To buyers, it will mean getting just what they ordered delivered right to their doorstep in days.

OUT IN FRONT. Plenty of old-line manufacturers are moving into cyberspace, but none so boldly or so broadly as Ford. And, with the exception of archrival General Motors Corp., none on such a huge scale. This past summer, GM launched e-GM, an initiative to link its suppliers and dealers and to forge Net ties with consumers at their PCs and in their cars. GM, however, has not yet announced plans to wire up its entire workforce. Still, the two are miles ahead of the rest of auto-dom, says David Cole, director of the University of Michigan's Office for the Study of Automotive Transportation. "They're just scaring the liver out of everyone else," he says.

Or are they? DaimlerChrysler and Toyota Motor Corp. are pursuing online ventures and experiments, but on a much smaller scale. Jurgen Hubbert, a member of DaimlerChrysler's management board, says he's not worried about rushing into grand Internet deals: "Why jump into this sort of business when nobody makes money?" he asks.

So far, Wall Street isn't impressed, either. Despite its bold moves, Ford's stock is down 7.5%, to 46, since its sweeping plan was unveiled on Sept. 15. Analysts wonder if Nasser has bitten off more than he can chew. While tantalized by the potential of e-business, they worry that all the cyberdazzle will distract Ford from its bread-and-butter task of design-

ing and building cars and trucks.

Certainly, there are plenty of risks. Skeptics wonder if consumers really want vehicles loaded with costly gadgetry that may be prone to technical problems and obsolescence. "People want to bring their portable communications devices with them," says DaimlerChrysler Chairman Robert Eaton. "Are we going to embed all those devices in every car? No." And some suppliers fret that the big cost savings Ford says will result from its online bazaar auto-xchange could instead squeeze vendors to the breaking point.

And for all its potential, e-commerce may find itself up against the biggest roadblock of all: a century-old industry with an infrastructure that impedes change. Slick new online ways to sell cars directly to buyers collide with an entrenched dealer base protected by tough state franchise laws. And systems that are capable of building custom cars actually clash with the economics of the high fixed costs that prod plant managers to run factories at full tilt.

It's not just ignorance that has made the Rust Belt slow to imitate such tech idols as Dell Computer Corp. Detroit is saddled with a much more complex manufacturing task than that faced by any computer outfit. Starting from scratch allowed Dell to create a state-of-the-art, direct-sales model. Over a 16-year period it has been able to tune its ordering and manufacturing processes–and update them for the Web. That's how it was able to custom assemble more than 25,000 different computer configurations for buyers last year. The company deals with hundreds of suppliers, but about 90% of its parts and components come from two dozen companies. And it works closely with them to make sure the parts are designed for snap-in assembly and for just-in-time delivery to its factories.

But even Dell's level of complexity is mere child's play compared with the challenges in the build-to-order auto business. Cars can contain 10,000 parts and, across Ford's entire line, some 1 million possible variations. Ford's F-150 full-size pickup truck, alone, is offered in well over 1,000 possible combinations of engine, transmission, body style, and color–without counting the truck's optional features.

FORD'S NET STRATEGY: WHERE THE RUBBER MEETS THE INFORMATION HIGHWAY

Ford has launched an e-business strategy to rewire the auto maker. The ultimate vision: To use the Net to do everything from ordering a car to linking 30,000 suppliers. Here is the game plan:

What	How	Goal
RETAILING	Set up BuyerConnection Web site and joined MSN CarPoint site, where consumers can order custom-assembled cars, track their progress, and apply for financing.	Reduce working capital by shrinking excess inventories and wipe out costly rebates needed to move unwanted cars off dealer lots, thus saving up to $650 per car.
CUSTOMER SERVICE	OwnerConnection Web site lets owners get online help, manage their warranty service, and check on financing.	Improve service with 24-hour access. Gather better data on customer problems. And cut costs with automated help.
SUPPLIERS	Launched auto-exchange Web site for online purchasing and swapping of information between 30,000 suppliers and 6,900 dealers.	Save up to $8.9 billion a year in discounts and reduced transaction costs on parts, raw materials, and supplies. Speed data exchange with partners while collecting up to $3 billion a year in exchange fees.
MARKETING	Teaming up with Yahoo!, TeleTech, CarPoint, iVillage, and bolt.com to monitor the interests and buying patterns of Web-surfing customers.	Improve factory efficiency by anticipating customer demand. Funnel data on customer preferences to car designers.
DIGITAL DASHBOARD	Equip new cars with Web access, satellite phone services, and e-mail capabilities.	Make Ford the carmaker for an Internet generation. Collect millions of dollars in fee-based services.
FINANCING	Shift more of the activities of Ford Credit to the Net for online financing and collections.	Cut service costs by 15% to 20%, while boosting revenues by reaching new customers.
WIRED WORKERS	Offering all 350,000 employees a computer, printer, and Net access for $5 a month.	Makes the workforce Web-savvy so it will quickly adopt the Internet initiatives, while enabling the CEO to send weekly e-mail to employees.

To pull off the monumental task, Nasser has created a business group called ConsumerConnect that is driving the e-business efforts across company lines. He also went outside the company to find the team he wanted to lead it. Brian P. Kelley, 39, a former General Electric Co. appliance sales boss who was known there for championing customer communications and launching a GE Web site, was named to head ConsumerConnect last September. Since then, the boyish Kelley has recruited dozens of other Net whizzes from the likes of Whirlpool, Booz, Allen & Hamilton, and Procter & Gamble. Says Michelle Guswiler, director of corporate initiatives: "We see ourselves as a kind of Alpha squad, here to lead change and help make the cultural difference required to bring Ford into the 21st century."

One of ConsumerConnect's most promising efforts is auto-xchange, an online trading site where its 30,000 suppliers can be linked to Ford for quicker communication, better prices, and faster delivery. Analysts say auto-xchange could save Ford $8 billion in procurement prices, and nearly $1 billion more from reduced overhead, paperwork, and other transaction efficiencies each year. Ford owns a majority of auto-xchange, with Silicon Valley giants Oracle Corp. and Cisco Systems Inc. each having a stake.

The troika's plans for auto-xchange are much dreamier yet. They hope it will become so popular that everyone in the auto industry will use it to barter for parts and office supplies. Indeed, Wall Street is expecting that Ford will take auto-xchange public by 2001, when it would have estimated revenues of more than $500 million.

BIRD'S-EYE VIEW. To make Ford's e-commerce ventures robust, there's a lot that must go on under the hood. Oracle is doing the heavy lifting on the software and databases needed to swap information and conduct transactions seamlessly. Cisco, which signed on as a partner on Feb. 9, will provide much-needed networking expertise. And Microsoft Corp.'s CarPoint, an auto sales and information Web site, will help Ford develop a build-to-order service. Internet service provider UUNet, PC maker Hewlett-Packard, and middleman PeoplePC signed on to put Ford's sprawling workforce online, starting in April.

Other tech partners are helping Ford get closer to its customers. Online powerhouses Yahoo! and Priceline.com, along with Denver-based call-center wizard TeleTech, will design systems that deliver highly personalized warranty, loan, repair, and customized services based on more detailed knowledge of driver lifestyles and buying habits. "It could give us a bird's-eye view of what consumers want out of a car before we build it," says Ford design chief J Mays.

Meanwhile, ConsumerConnect and Ford's Visteon auto-parts unit are teaming up to wire future Fords for e-mail and news, voice-recognition systems, and satellite phone

FEAR AND LOATHING IN THE SHOWROOM

Fort Worth auto dealer Cliff Johnson says he's pretty sure that the Internet won't put him out of business anytime soon, but he's wary of e-commerce anyway. Johnson, like many car dealers across the country, doesn't want auto makers and dotcoms getting in between him and his customers. "The Net is making everyone fight for what they perceive as a customer," Johnson says. "And that's a problem."

And not just for Johnson. As auto makers push forward with plans to use the Net to sell more cars, build them more cheaply, and deliver them faster to consumers, traditional dealerships are feeling the heat. Auto makers' motivation to put the squeeze on them is strong: Dealer overhead adds up to $2,000 to a car's price—after it leaves the factory—and adds weeks to order-to-delivery times.

STEALING. Costly, 80-day inventories of cars on dealer lots is also what General Motors Corp. CEO Jack Smith calls "a huge amount of waste. . .and the Internet can help us cut that." Smith and others also want their companies to use the Net to get closer to customers rather than remaining one step removed, as they are now.

For now, though, getting rid of costly middlemen isn't an option. So far, state franchise laws and political clout in statehouses across the nation protected dealers from any head-on digital encroachments. The fiercely protective Texas Auto Dealers Assn., for example, was able to win passage of state laws last fall, thwarting efforts by Ford and GM to sell late-model used cars to customers directly, via the Internet.

But auto makers are finding other ways to get cozier with customers. New dealer-rating systems are being rolled out to reward only those dealers who become more Net-friendly. Daimler-Chrysler Corp.'s Five Star dealership program, for example, only funnels sales leads from the company's Web site to those dealers who meet toughened new standards for service, facilities, and Internet savvy—about half of the company's 4,400 dealers. General Motors sends leads from its GM BuyPower Web site to only 75% of its dealers, including those that answer Net queries from customers within 24 hours.

Failure to comply carries a high sticker price: Slick new e-biz partnerships with Internet service providers give auto manufacturers a way to bypass dealers who refuse. "The manufacturer could steal the lead and steal the customer and give it to whoever they want," say Philadelphia car dealer Geno Barbera.

That's why savvy auto dealers are warming up to the Web. Today, 65% of the nation's 22,600 auto dealerships have at least one dedicated Internet salesperson, 61% have a Web site, and 40% participate in online buying servcies, according to Forrester Research Inc. "There are some dealers who see opportunity in the Net and some who just want it to go away," says Maryann Keller, president of Net company Priceline.com's auto division. The latter, she says, "will go away."

Cliff Johnson, for one, will keep working the Net so that nobody comes between him and his customers.

By David Welch in Detroit

---

services that will, says Kelley, "turn the family car into a Web portal on four wheels." The payoff: a whole array of new services in a marketplace where basic car prices are declining. Better yet, Web services and phones can be sold on a subscription basis, generating monthly fees that keep cash flowing into Ford's coffers for the life of the car.

Given the risks, why does Nasser chance it–especially since Ford is already the most profitable player in the global auto industry? The Net offers a chance to reinvent manufacturing. Forget marginal efficiency improvements. At stake here is the holy grail of carbuilding: Changing from the century-old "push" model to a streamlined "pull" system would save auto makers billions of dollars. Traditionally, an auto plant cranks at full capacity–building a predetermined mix of cars–and ships them to dealers who then rely on strong-arm tactics or fat rebates to move the ones customers don't want.

PINPOINT TAILORING. In a pull model, customers decide what they want built. That could shorten the current 64-day average time from customer order to delivery, freeing a good chunk of the $60 billion now tied up in U.S. completed-vehicle inventories, say Ernst & Young auto consultant Lee A. Sage.

To do this, carmakers would need to deliver those cars swiftly. And they would need to tailor vehicles and pricing with pinpoint accuracy, or high-overhead factories would sit idle. Kelley says Ford hopes to deliver its first high-volume built-to-order vehicles within two years. The company would probably first offer certain popular combinations for quick delivery, taking more time for unusual configurations. Ford hopes to see the results in its bottom line within five years. By then, Kelley says, Ford's Net initiatives could save the company billions in waste.

Reinventing manufacturing while juggling high-tech alliances may be a Herculean task, but Nasser figures he has no choice. Still, Nasser is determined to forge ahead. "We're going to turn the old ways on their ears," he says. "It might not happen right away, but change is inevitable." Judging by Ford's progress since last June, Nasser intends to make sure the company wastes no time making it happen.

By Kathleen Kerwin in Detroit and Marcia Stepanek in New York, with David Welch in Detroit

Getting Information for Marketing Decisions

SAFE AT ANY SPEED?

Online testing: Package-goods companies embrace the Internet despite the dangers

by Jack Neff

Procter & Gamble Co. executives were stunned last month to discover private concept images for its Crest brand posted anonymously on the Yahoo! Finance message board. It took 11 days for the images, which had been used in online focus groups, to be removed.

No doubt about it: Online testing can be highly risky. But even conservative package-goods companies are embracing such methods in record numbers as the breakneck race to market becomes ever more intense.

LOW-COST ALTERNATIVE

Used as a faster, less expensive alternative to traditional tests, the Internet has opened up a new forum for everything from focus groups to real-world market simulation.

"There's a lot of pressure to move as fast as you can with the best possible information," said Ellen Gottlich, associate director of consumer understanding for Unilever's Home & Personal Care unit. That's a leap for an industry where P&G, for example, tested Febreze, Dryel and Fit Fruit & Vegetable Wash for more than five years before launching them nationally. Compare that to the same company's Crest MultiCare Flex & Clean, which rolled out this fall, less than a year after online tests.

But while the advantage of speed is clear—Ms. Gottlich said online focus groups can shrink testing time from the usual two to three weeks to one—it comes with added uncertainty.

"Certainly we are concerned about a brand new product concept ending up in the hands of a competitor" said Bill Reynolds, director of marketing services at Unilever Home & Personal Care. "We have weighed in with that concern [to our vendors], and I'm sure we're not alone in that area."

In the case of the Crest fiasco, Charles Hamlin, president of InsightExpress—an NFO Worldwide unit that shares an Internet server with the NFO//net.discussion service from which the P&G concepts were leaked—said someone hacked into the server to find and post links to the images. He added that NFO, which conducted the P&G tests, is investigating.

'AN ISOLATED INCIDENT'

"This is really a one-time, isolated incident, and steps have been made to ensure it doesn't happen again," said Bryan McCleary, supervisor-oral care, public relations, at P&G. "We strongly believe that Internet testing is a wonderful advance and a powerful new way of getting to know our consumers and that the benefits strongly outweigh the risks."

Research industry observers have long seen risks in sending sensitive concept images to the computer screens of consumers, but the usual fear isn't hackers. "You just honestly can't [provide complete security] on the Web," said Dan Coates, VP-consumer intelligence of online marketing feedback site Planetfeedback.com, and a founder of two interactive market research units. "For every technology we would try to deploy to protect the concepts, there was another technology that could surpass it."

But other testing forms, such as mail, pose risks as great, Mr. Hamlin said. And he doesn't believe security concerns will thwart rapid growth of online testing, which he expects to account for 25% of consumer market research by 2002, up from less than 1% currently.

Lower costs also could be a factor in that rise. Offline testing can cost anywhere from $2,000 for a focus group to more than $25,000 for a concept test run in a shopping mall, Mr. Coates said. When marketers test dozens or hundreds of concepts a year, it adds up.

Marketers, however, are wrestling with the issue of determining how well Internet users represent consumers generally, and whether online tests deliver results as reliable as offline forms.

"We know from years of validation that mall-intercept testing or consumer panel testing correlates with real-world purchase data," said Doug Hall, founder and president of new-products consultancy Richard Saunders International. "But we know that online [test results] don't correlate with mall intercept and there's no evidence that they correlate with consumer purchases."

COMPLETING 'VALIDATIONS'

Aware of such concerns, Unilever is "in the process

of completing a number of validations [of online consumer testing] and the results look fairly good," Ms. Gottlich said.

She acknowledged that Web users score new concepts lower for uniqueness than do consumers tested offline, and that distribution of data is different. But in the end, she said, Unilever executives appear to be making the same decisions using online tests that they would if they used offline testing.

WEB-SAVVY

Even with the growth of the online population, it's too soon to conclude that Web users accurately reflect consumers generally, research executives believe. Online researchers are trying various ways around the problem, including Inter-Survey, a Palo Alto, Calif., company that's putting free WebTV Internet access into a representative sample of households that agree to take surveys regularly.

> *"There's no evidence that [online test results] correlate with consumer purchases."*

But people who agree to take Web surveys tend to be more Web-savvy than others online, one research executive said, meaning that online researchers are getting a relatively sophisticated segment of the online population.

Even the same consumers tend to score concepts differently online than off, according to research from Burke Marketing. That research found consumers grade concepts closer to the middle range online and more at the high or low ends in verbally directed surveys.

Those middle-range responses are probably closer to how consumers really feel, said Jeff Miller, exec VP of Burke. But they can present new challenges in calibrating tests for accurate decision-making and in comparing online results with offline databases, Mr. Coates said.

On the positive side, Burke also found Web participants enjoy taking more surveys, finish faster and are more likely to repeat the process than are offline participants, Mr. Miller said.

MERWYN

As a solution to concerns about Internet testing—as well as to increase speed and lower costs—former P&G executive Mr. Hall has developed Merwyn, software that forecasts consumer acceptance of new products and services using a database of 4,000 concepts that has been tested over the past two years by such companies as AC-Nielsen Corp.'s Bases, NPD Group and AcuPOLL International.

Merwyn analyzes consumer purchase intent for concepts based on how well they measure up to what past consumer tests showed to be "the laws of marketing physics," Mr. Hall said.

Those laws state that the most successful concepts are those that convey overt benefits, real reasons to believe in those benefits and dramatic differences from existing products or services. The software also suggests ways marketers can improve a concept's scores.

Like online market researchers, Mr. Hall bills his product more as a way to screen preliminary concepts than test final ones. But he claims that running hundreds of concepts through Merwyn to find the handful that merit further development can whittle to as little as a day a process that Andersen Consulting estimates now takes 17 weeks.

Using simulation of a different sort, Information Resources Inc. last year launched IntroCast, which can trim time off test markets by forecasting a new product's volume based on past products' results.

IRI clients are using IntroCast to monitor whether a new product's trial and repeat purchase numbers are on pace to meet long-term goals and gauge how various levels of advertising and promotion will affect volume. Using IntroCast can trim the $1 million cost of a traditional in-market test by about 25% and, in some cases, up to 50%.

"With most new products, we can [use IntroCast to] do a decent job of forecasting year-one [national sales] potential after 12 to 16 weeks [in a test market]," Mr. Findley said, a quarter of the time required for a traditional test.

Such speed translates into lower cost and less risk of competitors discovering test markets in time to monitor or disrupt them, he said. IntroCast "also lets you play with alternative marketing plans," Mr. Findley said, without having to use simultaneous tests in multiple cities.

IRI client P&G, which in the past often ran tests in two or more cities to try different marketing support levels, is using just one BehaviorScan market each for such products as Impress plastic wrap and Bounty napkins, though Mr. Findley didn't comment on whether these moves are linked to IntroCast.

UNIVERSAL SIMULATION?

Not every product is ripe for simulation, however, Mr. Findley acknowledged. Repeat purchase rates are difficult to project for products in new categories, such as P&G's Dryel and Swiffer, so marketers generally either have to test longer or supplement their testing with consumer surveys. (While P&G's rival S.C. Johnson & Son didn't test its Swiffer follow-up, Pledge Grab-It, it can be argued that the company had the benefit of monitoring P&G's test results for Swiffer).

IntroCast will likely mean shorter test markets in fewer cities, but the software is still no replacement for in-market testing, Mr. Findley said, adding: "Test market-ing is alive and well."

Unilever's Mr. Reynolds however, believes marketers will keep looking for ways around test marketing.

"If it's a high-risk, high-return idea in one of your key strategic categories, that would argue for deeper testing," Mr. Reynolds said. "But because of the cost and time and visibility to the competition, there will be a general trend to do less in-market testing."

34

CONSUMERS IN THE MIST

Mad Ave.'s anthropologists are unearthing our secrets

The 60-ish woman caught on the grainy videotape is sitting on her hotel bed, addressing her husband after a long day spent on the road. "Good job!" she exults. "We beat the s_ _ _ out of the front desk and got a terrific room."

No, this wasn't an FBI sting operation. Instead, the couple was part of the latest effort by marketers to figure out what consumers really think about their products. By paying regular folks a nominal fee to let them into their homes, their cars, even their hotel rooms, marketers are hoping to learn the kind of detail that just doesn't emerge from focus groups. Calling it ethnographic or observational research, agencies are sending anthropologists and other trained observers into the field and the screening room to chart the hidden recesses of consumer behavior.

For Best Western International Inc., which last spring paid 25 over-55 couples to tape themselves on cross-country journeys, the effort convinced the hotel chain that it didn't need to boost its standard 10% senior citizen discount. The tapes showed that seniors who talked the hotel clerk into a better deal didn't need the lower price to afford the room; they were after the thrill of the deal. Instead of attracting new customers, bigger discounts would simply allow the old customers to trade up to a fancier dinner down the street somewhere; doing absolutely nothing for Best Western. "The degree of discount clearly isn't what it used to be in importance—and we got that right out of the research," says Tom Dougherty, manager of programs, promotions, and partnerships for the Phoenix-based chain.

The technique is hardly new. Nissan Motor Co., for example, redesigned its Infiniti car in the early 1990s after anthropologists helped it see that Japanese notions of luxury-as-simplicity were very different from Americans' yen for visible opulence. A few years later, Volkswagen's ad agency, Arnold Communications, used the approach to reposition the brand toward active users with its "Drivers wanted" campaign.

These days, plenty of other companies are hiring anthropologists who are trained to observe without changing the outcome. Though often more expensive than traditional focus groups, ethnographic research is quickly becoming a standard agency offering. At Avrett Free & Ginsberg, a midsize New York shop, 9 out of 15 large clients have opted for the service, compared with just a handful a couple of years ago, says director of cultural insights Timothy Malefyt.

It's not hard to see why. As products mature and differences in quality diminish, marketers are anxious to hook into subtle emotional dimensions that might give them an edge. This up-close approach can also help marketers figure out how different ethnic and demographic groups react to their products, especially important in a fragmenting marketplace. "Knowing the individual consumer on an intimate basis has become a necessity. And ethnography is the intimate connection to the consumer," says Bill Abrams, founder of Housecalls, a New York consultancy that

---

HOME IS WHERE THE RESEARCH IS

Here's how three big marketers are using ethnographic research

	3COM	BEST WESTERN	MOEN
GOAL	Uncover hidden needs that might be served by an electronic home organizer	Learn how seniors decide when and where to stop for the night	Observe over an extended time how consumers really use their shower devices
OUTCOME	After observing how 64 households juggle complicated schedules, 3Com went with an extremely compact size and simple design for its Audrey device	Videotapes of 25 older couples on three- to-seven-day long drives taught chain not to expand the discounts and to avoid using the tag "seniors"	Watching customers cope with inconvenient design elements uncovered safety problems as well as opportunities for new products

worked on the Best Western effort.

Among the latest converts are technology companies that have grown tired of seeing their engineers design products with whiz-bang gimmickry that doesn't always fill an actual consumer need. 3Com Corp. was determined to avoid that trap with Audrey, launched in October, as the first in its Ergo line of Internet appliances. Audrey was supposed to ease access to e-mail, the Internet, and an electronic calendar. To make sure it turned out that way, 3Com spent four months videotaping 64 households in three cities to see exactly how they used existing devices—from pad and paper to PCs—to organize their days. A crucial insight: It took, on average, an hour and 10 minutes between the time consumers decided to use their PCs and the time they actually logged on, meaning PC use was treated as a planned activity. By contrast, they used their Palm handhelds more like a tool, logging on less than 10 seconds after making the decision. Designing Audrey to be more

like a tool than an activity became an overriding goal, says Ray Winninger, product development director for Internet appliances.

Ethnographic insights can help even with more humdrum products. By videotaping consumers in the shower, plumbing fixture maker Moen Inc. uncovered safety risks—such as the habit of some women who were shaving their legs of holding on with their free hand to one unit's temperature control. Uncovering such design flaws by simply asking questions is almost impossible. "In many ways, these become unarticulated needs," says Jack Suvak, director of marketing research at the North Olmsted (Ohio)-based manufacturer.

DIGGING DEEP. Indeed, focus groups, though still huge in the research arsenal, have many limitations. Stronger personalities can wield undue influence, and participants often won't admit in public—or may not even recognize—their behavior patterns and motivations. Focus groups, for example, told Best

Western that men decide when to pull off the highway and where to stay. The videotapes proved it was usually the women. For some hard-to-reach classes of consumers, any regimented setting may restrict their responsiveness. "If you want to learn about preteens, you have to see them in their natural environment, not a research lab they see as alien," says Hy Mariampolski, president of QualiData Research, a New York-based ethnographic research firm.

Best Western captured such a wealth of customer behavior on tape that it has delayed its marketing plan in order to weave the insights into its core strategy. "The process definitely opened our eyes," says Dougherty. Unfortunately for seniors, that means the rooms won't be getting any cheaper.

By Gerry Khermouch in New York

35

Attention Shoppers:
This Man Is Watching You

Do you breeze by store displays? Avoid narrow aisles? Paco Underhill knows you do, and his methods are changing retail behavior. ■ *by Kenneth Labich*

Retailers are in the throes of a crisis. There are too many retail outlets and too few consumers–experts estimate 20% to 30% excess retail capacity–and the competition for eyes, ears, and dollars is downright savage. It doesn't help that shoppers are behaving weirdly. They have become less loyal to brand names and less predictable in other ways as well; more than half the purchases people make at grocery stores these days are unplanned. Consumers can't even be trusted. In exit interviews and focus groups, says Karen Hyatt, category-development manager at Hewlett-Packard, "people tend to be overly polite and tell you what they think you want to hear."

Enter a tall (6-foot-4), balding New Yorker named Paco Underhill. He doesn't have to trust what people say, because he sees what they do. For more than 20 years, Underhill, 47, has been using hidden cameras and other means to track 50,000 to 70,000 shoppers annually, in an effort to determine why we buy what we buy. Demand for his peculiar brand of research–Underhill calls himself a "retail anthropologist"–has taken off. His company in New York City, Envirosell Inc., now boasts a client roster that includes dozens of top retailers such as Sears, Walgreens, and the Gap; consumer-products giants like Coca-Cola, General Mills, and Johnson & Johnson; and big food-service players like McDonald's, Burger King, and Starbucks. He's even written a hot new book about his work (*Why We Buy: The Science of Shopping,* Simon & Schuster, $25). Jim Lucas, an Envirosell client and director of research and planning at Frankel & Co., the promotion agency for McDonald's and other big retailers, is an ardent fan of Underhill's work. "It's sort of the difference between knowing what people say

they do–and what they really do," says Lucas.

Such plaudits are especially sweet for Underhill, who struggled for years to get his methods accepted and his business off the ground. After graduating from Vassar, he took a job with a New York City outfit called People for Public Spaces, which sends out researchers to follow and film urban pedestrians in the hope of improving the design of public facilities. Underhill played urban geographer for a couple of years, filming people as they waited at stoplights or settled down on park benches. There was, however, one problem. Underhill is seriously afraid of heights, and much of the group's work involves videotaping from the top of tall buildings. One windy day in Seattle, as he perched uneasily on a swaying rooftop, Underhill underwent an epiphany: He had to find a ground-level job or go nuts.

An escape route presented itself a few months later. A friend who helped manage Lincoln Center, the Manhattan arts complex, asked Underhill if his videotaping techniques might help in the design of a customer-friendly souvenir shop. Underhill set up his cameras and made several suggestions that led to the shop's success. More important, the experience sparked the notion that he might make a living indoors using his pedestrian-tracking techniques.

Underhill got his big break in the mid-1980s, when AT&T hired him to help design its chain of retail phone stores. More jobs followed, and as Envirosell staffers studied hours of tapes and analyzed field reports, they found consistent and surprising patterns of customer behavior. After watching countless shoppers breeze past elaborate displays at store entrances, they dubbed the first 30 feet or so of floor space the "decompression zone." They

advised retailers that any attempt to snare buyers before they get their bearings is pointless. Underhill and his employees were also baffled by the fact that nearly all shoppers turn right after entering a store. Was it because most people are right-handed? After working a few jobs in Britain and Australia, they discovered that shoppers in those countries veer left after entering a store. We shop, it seems, as we drive.

Another baffler: After viewing thousands of hours of tapes, Envirosell staffers concluded that most shoppers, especially women, are extremely reluctant to enter a narrow aisle; goods in those aisles generally went unsold. After many interviews, Underhill's troops came to the conclusion that people really hate being jostled from behind and will go to great lengths to avoid it. At Envirosell they call this the "butt-brush factor."

Perhaps the biggest surprise of all was just how often stores were making unpardonable errors that turn off customers and eat into profitability. Says Underhill: "A lot of people in retailing and consumer goods talk about strategy, but not many talk about tactics. And tactics are often about not doing stuff that's stupid." Classic blunders: junk food on high shelves out of the reach of kids; hearing-aid batteries on bottom shelves where the elderly have to bend over to get at them; a drugstore chain marketing hair products for blonds in a Washington, D.C., neighborhood that is 95% African American.

Spying on the American consumer over the years has given Underhill some specific insights that he preaches to nearly all his clients, and you can see the impact everywhere. He advises all manner of storekeepers to keep stacks of shopping baskets around their premises. The results are dramatic: About 75% of the shoppers who pick up a basket buy

(Cont.)

---

some items–usually more than they would have otherwise. Of those who don't pick up a basket, only 34% will buy something.

Underhill is also a strong advocate of the chair. Women who shop with other women spend about twice as much time in a store as when they are with a man, presumably because he's being a pain in the posterior about being dragged along. The solution, Underhill argues, is to make sure that there's plenty of available seating so men can park themselves while the women make their tour. But placement of that seating can be crucial. Underhill cites the folly of the Florida clothing store that placed chairs near a display for Wonderbras. The seats were often occupied by elderly gentlemen who loudly debated the physical merits of women grazing the bra display. Sales plummeted.

Now Underhill is trying to make sense of what seems to him the most crucial retailing innovation of the era, the Internet. He's convinced that Web gazing does not spell the end of actual shopping trips. "We're still a tribal animal," he says. "Movie theaters haven't died because of cable TV." At the same time, Underhill is working with various cyber-age clients to develop more effective Websites. Says Joel Granoff, Internet marketing manager at Compaq, an Envirosell customer: "He puts a new focus on the Internet by looking not just at what technology will do but at what consumers will do." For the moment, Underhill's approach revolves around having staffers test-shop at various sites and report the pluses and minuses of graphics, architecture, and the like. He's soon to begin a program of bringing civilians into his offices, then taping and interviewing them about their likes and dislikes as they surf the Web for specific products and services. There's one big question that's still to be resolved, though: What's the Web equivalent of the "butt-brush factor"?

36

Merry Maids Clean Up Territories With MapInfo System

By Sarah Z. Sleeper
Investor's Business Daily

Rob Sanders played guessing games. The franchise sales manager for Merry Maids, the largest home-cleaning service in the U.S., could never be sure if the territories he assigned to franchisees were equal in size or value. That didn't seem fair.

"Everyone buying a franchise should have a protected and exclusive territory that has boundaries," he said.

Ensuring this was a key goal for the 21-year-old company and its 900 franchises. But that goal wasn't being met.

"When the company first started, they'd go to the corner Exxon and get a map and a marking pencil and draw a franchise's boundaries right there," Sanders said.

As a result, Merry Maids territories often overlapped. Other areas weren't covered at all.

And Sanders/Merry Maids, a brand of ServiceMaster Co., had another challenge. They wanted more demographic data on the areas covered, or soon to be covered, by their franchisees.

As it was, some franchise owners had too much business and others didn't have enough.

Sanders took care of his two problems with desktop software from MapInfo Corp. The software provides detailed, up-to-date geographic data and demographic information.

Clear, Fair Boundaries

"Now all I have to do is plug a ZIP code or a street address into the computer and I know exactly if that territory is open or not," Sanders said. "This fall I sold two franchise territories in Houston, and prior to (using MapInfo) we didn't really know if we had any territory left to sell there."

Sanders did some homework to solve his problems. He says he researched all of the geographic software on the market and met in person with three makers: MapInfo, ESRI and CACI International Inc.

MapInfo won Sanders over. "It was the best balance for mapping and demographics," he said.

Using the MapInfo system required that he attend three training classes. He also needed to draw up maps of Merry Maid's franchise lines to be incorporated into the MapInfo software. For that one-time task, he hired a team of interns. The process took eight months and was well worth the investment, he says.

"We used college students and we were paying them fairly low rates," he said. "Balanced against what we pay full-time people, we got two or three intern hours per regular employee hour."

He won't say what Merry Maids paid for the two MapInfo software products, MapInfo Professional and TargetPro. But, he says, by using MapInfo he can quickly uncover territories that work for Merry Maids, areas heavy in two-income families with annual incomes in the $75,000 to $100,000 range.

"We're trying to find the richest pockets of those people within territories," he said. MapInfo, he says, reveals hidden trends not visible on standard charts or maps.

Tool To Track Trends

Another MapInfo customer, the National Cancer Institute's Dan Grauman, says he paid about $43,000 for the software. It was a bargain, he says.

Like Sanders, Grauman considered several vendors. But when he called MapInfo and ESRI for estimates, ESRI wouldn't, or couldn't, give one, he says.

"I had very detailed specifications,"

On The Map

Functions done by most mapping software

1 **Geocoding:** Match addresses with geographic coordinates, such as latitude and longitude. Can be used to calculate distances or boundaries.

2 **Visualization:** Use lines, points, numbers, words, symbols, shading, colors and coordinates on a map to visualize data patterns.

3 **Spatial analysis:** Use location-specific data to analyze customers.

4 **Routing:** Find out where a customer is and the quickest way to get there.

5 **Geodemographics:** Combine what you know about a customer with what you know about the people in an area. Use that to generate leads, do targeted marketing and boost sales.

Sources: International Data Corp., Integrated Spatial Solutions Inc.

Grauman aid. "We went with MapInfo by default because I needed a number and I couldn't get one from ESRI."

He's glad. "We're getting a big bang for our buck," he said.

NCI uses MapInfo's MapXtreme Web-based product for the online version of its "Atlas of Cancer Mortality." The atlas, Grauman says, shows U.S. cancer death rates from 1950 to 1994.

MapXtreme shows where clusters of cancer cases have occurred in specific areas and segments the data by cancer type for display on the NCI Web site. Users of this online cancer atlas include the Harvard University School of Public Health and the George Washington University School of Public Health. They can click on the site and "draw" maps that include only the types of cancers they are interested in studying.

"The big leap with MapXtreme is that the user isn't limited in the way the map is presented," Grauman said.

The institute is tax-supported, so providing its atlas online saves taxpayer money. Each print version of the atlas costs $15. Grauman says that since autumn, when NCI implemented MapXtreme, 200,000 to 250,000 Web site visitors have saved the institute time and money by creating 750,000 online maps.

That's just one of the returns he's seen on his MapInfo investment, he says.

"Accessibility, cost savings and time savings" are the major boosts NCI gets from MapInfo, he said. "It saves workload here."

Grauman plans to add more options to NCI's online atlas, including animation.

Tech Hot Ticket

The tech industry refers to MapInfo's software products as business intelligence, or BI, software. MapInfo's BI software is easy to use and can handle multiple users at one time, says Peter Urban, an analyst with market tracker AMR Research Inc.

"You just buy the product, and boom—it works straight out of the box," Urban said. "That's a huge differentiator."

He says the company has attracted some big customers through alliances with Oracle Corp. and other well-known companies.

Investors seem to agree. In the last 16 months, the shares of the New York-based company have risen from about 8 to 39. It's been a rare tech-stock winner during a time of big declines for most tech shares.

For its fiscal first quarter ended Dec. 31, the company said per-share profit doubled from the year-earlier period to 14 cents. It said sales rose 26% to $26.5 million.

37

Looking for Patterns

Data mining enables companies to better manage the reams of statistics they collect. The goal: spot the unexpected

By Lisa Bransten
Staff Reporter of The Wall Street Journal

A few years ago, owning a hot Porsche or a zippy Corvette almost guaranteed you would pay more for car insurance. After all, both conventional wisdom and decades of data collected by insurers suggest that drivers of high-performance sports cars are more likely to have accidents than are other motorists.

But upon a closer look at such statistics, insurer **Farmers Group** Inc. discovered something interesting: As long as the sports car wasn't the only vehicle in a household, the accident rate actually wasn't much greater than that of a regular car.

Based on that information, Farmers changed its policy that had excluded sports cars from its lowest-priced insurance rates. By eliminating that rule, "we figured out that we could almost double our sports-car market," says Melissa McBratney, vice president of personal lines at the Los Angeles insurer. Farmers estimates that just letting Corvettes and Porsches into its "preferred premium" plan could bring in an additional $4.5 million in premium revenue over the next two years, without a significant rise in claims.

The pattern Farmers discovered isn't intuitive – it had eluded even most insurance veterans. But that's the beauty of software tools that dig through such data: They can find patterns that people wouldn't dream of hunting for.

Data Filter

"We used to develop a hypothesis and then get the data to prove us right or wrong," says Ms. McBratney. But with this new software, "we put all of our data into a very large database and had it spit out" patterns that it saw.

Much of this new software is based on a technology called data mining, which enables computers to apply sophisticated mathematical formulas to ferret out patterns in data. And companies are finding that it not only allows them to better manage the reams of statistics their systems have been amassing for years, but also helps monitor consumer behavior, catch trends and, as in the case of Farmers, spot the unexpected.

Today, only a small number of businesses use software that incorporates this technology, but analysts expect that to change: According to Forrester Research Inc., Cambridge, Mass., a recent survey of 50 executives from large companies found that only 28% were actively mining their databases, but all planned to do so by 2001.

Based on those figures, Forrester analyst Frank Gillett estimates that spending on database software to accommodate data mining will more than double to $3.56 billion in 2001 from $1.56 billion last year. "It's one of the few remaining places to get a tangible competitive advantage," he says.

Many Web-based businesses are also seeking to capitalize on information about customer behavior with specialized software tools. In many cases, however, they are finding that the potential reach remains far ahead of their actual grasp. The businesses must be wary of Web users' privacy concerns, but there are more basic problems: Effective data mining demands time and resources that many Web-based start-ups simply can't afford to divert to it.

"It's a huge deluge of data, but you really need to have something to help you drill down and analyze it," says Nick Mehta, vice president of marketing at **chipshot.com,** a Sunnyvale, Calif., online seller of custom-made golf clubs.

Companies have been using a variety of technologies to amass and store huge quantities of data from any number of sources for years. But the increasing appeal of data min-

ing now reflects its ability to manipulate information in a new way, unlocking details previously left to rot in "data jails" because processing, organizing and analyzing it has been too difficult.

Consider how some information systems are set up. In many databases, statistics often aren't kept in uniform formats – a customer may be listed as "John Smith" in a retailer's order-entry system's database, but as "Smith, John" in the customer-support database. In cases such as this, it is hard for the computer to know the two entries are the same customer.

Moreover, many databases have been designed as one-trick ponies that let companies very quickly look at specific types of information, such as whether an order has been shipped. That makes aggregating data about customer behavior that lurk in several different databases slow and awkward.

Time and Money

In order to make its discovery about sports cars and accident rates, for example, Farmers first had to combine information from five different databases into an organized central repository. It was a task so complicated it took three times as long as Farmers had expected, according to Ms. McBratney. (Luckily for Farmers, it benefited from an early contact: Because the insurer had agreed to test a program developed by a team from **International Business Machines** Corp.'s business-intelligence unit, it got the software at a substantially reduced rate.)

Another barrier to data mining's use has been that, until recently, the computer hardware needed to store and process so much data was prohibitively expensive for most companies.

Catalog retailer Fingerhut Cos., for example, needed a database that could store nine terabytes of data in order to use a software program it developed to help cut mailing costs. That's no small undertaking: Ten terabytes is equivalent to the entire printed collection of the Library of Congress.

"Two or three years ago...you would have

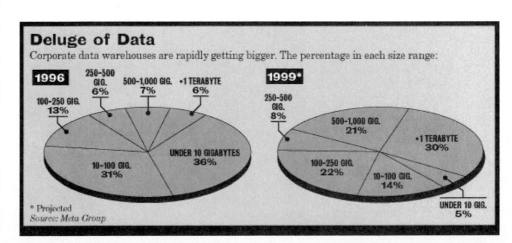

Deluge of Data
Corporate data warehouses are rapidly getting bigger. The percentage in each size range:

1996
- 250-500 GIG. 6%
- 500-1,000 GIG. 7%
- +1 TERABYTE 6%
- 100-250 GIG. 13%
- UNDER 10 GIGABYTES 36%
- 10-100 GIG. 31%

1999*
- 250-500 GIG. 8%
- 500-1,000 GIG. 21%
- +1 TERABYTE 30%
- 100-250 GIG. 22%
- 10-100 GIG. 14%
- UNDER 10 GIG. 5%

* Projected
Source: Meta Group

(Cont.)

had to have had NASA at your disposal to do something like that," says Will Lansing, chief executive officer of Fingerhut, a unit of **Federated Department Stores** Inc. "The hardware is making things happen faster and better."

Mr. Lansing says Fingerhut's investment in data mining – which he declines to quantify – is already paying off.

The software developed with IBM keeps track of the hundreds of items each Fingerhut customer purchases. Since Fingerhut has some products that are featured in all of its catalogs, the company figured it could save money by reducing the number of catalogs sent to its regular customers. Mr. Lansing says that in areas where Fingerhut tested the technology last year, mailing expenses dropped 8% while revenue declined by 1.5%, suggesting that the mail savings can contribute to the company's bottom line over time.

Specialized Software

Other variations of data-mining software gaining popularity help traditional retailers determine how their customers shop by letting them dig even deeper into data culled from cash registers and bar-code scanners. Such products are called "market-basket analysis" tools because they help the retailer peer into a customer's shopping basket and determine what products are typically purchased together.

"Typically in the past, merchandisers could track on a weekly or monthly basis what was sold, but they had to guess at who was buying what," says Lynne Harvey, a senior consultant at Patricia Seybold Group in Boston, a high-tech advisory firm.

Wal-Mart Stores Inc. is generally hailed as a data-mining pioneer, with nearly a decade of experience and a database that trails only the U.S. government's in size. The Bentonville, Ark., retailer uses data mining to supply answers for any number of questions, such as what commonly purchased items should be placed together on shelves and what soft drinks sell best in different areas of the U.S.

And where Wal-Mart has led, other retailers are looking to follow – sometimes too closely for the giant's tastes. Last fall, Wal-Mart sued Internet giant **Amazon.com** Inc. in state court in Benton County, Ark., charging that Amazon stole trade secrets by recruiting Wal-Mart employees and business partners in order to duplicate the discounter's massive computer systems. (To settle the suit, Amazon agreed to, among other things, require all former Wal-Mart employees to return any Wal-Mart property they possessed.)

Meanwhile, **Walgreen** Co. is using data-mining software developed by **Knowledge Discovery One** Inc. of Austin, Texas, to tinker with its own store displays and to measure the success of promotional offers such as 2-for-1 sales, says David Arrington, manager of consumer research at the Deerfield, Ill., drugstore chain.

In the past, the success of such a promotion was judged largely on the product's sales and, by inference, how much traffic it brought into the store. Using the KD1 tool, Walgreen can see what's selling with its promotional items and tune its programs so that it puts things on sale that people tend to buy in tandem with high-margin items.

Web retailers, meanwhile, can theoretically take gathering customer information a step further because they have so much information about not only what their customers buy, but also how they travel around a site. By placing "beacons" on pages within a site, San Francisco-based **Personify** Inc. can help companies match information about where customers travel within the site with information about what they purchase. The company then mines the data for usage patterns that can help Web commerce companies improve their business.

That feature was especially helpful to chipshot.com. One of the hardest decisions for a start-up like chipshot.com to make is where to focus resources; Personify helped the company set priorities, says Mr. Mehta, the marketing vice president.

Chipshot.com discovered that people who added comments to the site's guestbook seldom bought clubs, but people who bought clubs almost always clicked on the customer-service area before buying. Armed with that knowledge, chipshot limited the resources earmarked for developing the guestbook and put more effort into the site's customer-service area.

38

THE INFORMATION GOLD MINE

New software—and the Net's legions of cybersurfers and shoppers—are starting to hand companies opportunities they've only dreamed of

When Harley Dixon clicked on NextCard Inc.'s advertisement for a credit card on the Quicken.com financial Web site, he couldn't believe what he found. It promised instant approval and a choice of terms based on his credit history–all in less than 35 seconds. Intrigued, the retired engineer from Henrietta, N.Y., filled out a short online form with his name, address, income, and Social Security number. Bingo! Seconds later, up popped three offers. Says Dixon: "Next thing you know, I had a new card."

Behind the scenes, the snap approval was a technological tour de force for NextCard. Instantly, NextCard's computers dialed the three major credit bureaus to check Dixon's record. Analyzing that along with his current balances, NextCard in a split second zipped through 30,000 potential combinations of terms in its portfolio and chose three offers tailored precisely to Dixon's profile. The result: Instead of the usual three to six weeks to issue a card and transfer balances, NextCard won a new customer in a heartbeat. "The Internet is the most fantastic source of data the world has ever seen," says NextCard Chief Executive and founder Jeremy R. Lent. "We're creating a brand-new science."

All over the Web, a data gold rush is on. The incredible communications and computing power of the Internet is handing companies an unprecedented opportunity to collect and analyze information. By tracking everything from which advertisements prompt that first mouse click all the way through to the actual sale, they're scrambling to unlock patterns of customer behavior hidden since the dawn of commerce.

Of course, companies have always tried to quantify customers' wants and needs–and largely failed. Department-store pioneer John Wanamaker famously complained 130 years ago that half his advertising was wasted–he just didn't know which half. Since then, companies such as Wal-Mart Stores Inc. have set up huge virtual warehouses full of product and customer data. But those data have been cumbersome to get at and daunting to analyze. Figuring out what customers real-

ly want has remained more of a black art than a science.

LESS WASTE. Now, companies are starting to harness the Net's power to not only answer Wanamaker's question but go far beyond that. They are working away, mining the hidden veins of gold in mountains of data in an effort to prompt customers to buy more, stick around, and, down the road, maybe even pay extra for the tailored products and services that will result. Along the way, the goal is to save money by targeting only the most profitable customers and avoiding the manufacture of costly products nobody really wants. Ultimately, merchants want to tailor unique products and services to each and every customer–so-called mass customization, the unrealized dream of every marketer.

Information gathered over the Net can provide the kind of insight into customers that Wanamaker could scarcely imagine. It's as if he could train cameras on every square inch of a store, with teams in back rooms monitoring how often shoppers touch a rack

of sweaters or turn up their nose at a pair of slacks–and still more legions to make new products on the spot and rush them out to those fussy buyers. Says Chris Halligan, director of Dell Computer Corp.'s E-commerce business: "The Internet has turbocharged our ability to understand our customers."

This ultrapersonal targeting may help E-commerce finally deliver on its promise to revolutionize the business world. Now that Web sellers have all this traffic and millions of customers, they need to find a way to extract the real profits that investors increasingly demand. If they can provide a unique service or product, they can sell more and even charge more. "We want to get to know them the same way a small-town shopkeeper of yesteryear might have gotten to know them," says Amazon.com Inc. CEO Jeffrey P. Bezos. "That kind of personalization is going to be extremely valuable for the customer."

That's why companies are furiously collecting and analyzing the bits and bytes spinning around their computers' fast-growing

E.piphany may just live up to its hifalutin name. The Palo Alto (Calif.) software maker has created programs that let data-hungry companies scarf up and analyze almost any scrap of information on their customers. That has attracted the likes of Charles Schwab, Capital BlueCross, and Hewlett-Packard. With E.piphany's $250,000 software, these companies can suddenly do what has bedeviled marketers for years: ferret out customer behavior to offer just what buyers may be looking for—on the fly. "E.piphany is the railroad track that brings all the information that companies need," says Roger Siboni, E.piphany's president and CEO, who left KPMG International to join the startup. Here's how it works: The software, dubbed E.piphany e.4, pulls

together E-mails from customers, questions at call centers, purchases on a company's Web site, even how a potential buyer responds to sales calls and online advertising.

Businesses use that data to uncover trends and spot the best customers. For example, software maker Visio Corp. was surprised to find that consultants were responsible for 30% of the online sales of one of their software packages for diagramming and drawing. Seattle-based Visio now plans to tailor services and marketing for the consultant crowd. "What's key is that we're able to learn about our customers in real time," says Michael Molendijk, Visio's director of marketing for its online site. With such testimonials, E.piphany may be helping customers see the light.

(Cont.)

WHAT YOU NEED IN YOUR TOOLBOX FOR MINING DATA

MANAGING CUSTOMER CONTACTS

COMPANIES THAT MAKE IT POSSIBLE:
Siebel, Pivotal, Silknet, Vantive

Software programs pull together a wide swath of information on customers based on how they interact with a company–through sales calls, meetings, online and phone inquiries, or buying products and services. Government Computer Sales, for example, combines online sales with traditional sales to keep track of their best customers and what they are buying–helping increase the number of products sold.

CUSTOMER SERVICE

COMPANIES THAT MAKE IT POSSIBLE:
Brightware, Chordiant, NewChannel, HNC

This software lets E-merchants and content sites automatically reply, route, or segment E-mails so companies can be more efficient and effective in responding to customers. Some also pull together info from call centers. It's used by the likes of Suretrade, Schwab, and Ticketmaster Online-CitySearch to automate replies to customer E-mail and forward E-mails to specialized customer-service reps.

AD TARGETING

COMPANIES THAT MAKE IT POSSIBLE:
AdKnowledge, DoubleClick, 24/7, Flycast, Matchlogic, Engage

These services dish up and track ads across a network of sites, monitoring who is clicking on the ads, how often, and whether the ads actually lead to sales. The services often build up profiles that can include information on demographics, tastes, or E-mail addresses of millions of people to improve targeting. Advertisers, including Travelocity, General Motors, and P&G, find these services to be just the ticket.

E-MAIL DIRECT MARKETING

COMPANIES THAT MAKE IT POSSIBLE:
Responsys.com, Annuncio, Digital Impact, Post Communications

The turnaround cycle on these services is what sets them apart. Using lists of E-mail addresses, the services and software can get responses from customers in hours rather than the days and weeks typical with snailmail direct marketing. Companies, such as eToys, Preview-Travel, and Tower Records, target product offers based on customers' interests or what they've bought in the past.

DATA ANALYSIS ENGINES

COMPANIES THAT MAKE IT POSSIBLE:
E.piphany, Manna, MicroStrategy, Blue Martini

Designed to pull together and analyze information from systems that companies already have in place, including inventory, logistics, and sales databases. Used by Schwab, Streamline, and Capital BlueCross to track trends within segments of customers so they can decide what kind of products and services to offer.

SUPPLY CHAIN AND LOGISTICS

COMPANIES THAT MAKE IT POSSIBLE:
Manugistics, i2, Nonstop Solutions, VIT

The last—and, at this point, the weakest—chain in the loop, the goal is to translate an understanding of customers' tastes and purchases into a quick turnaround in making products and working with suppliers. Dell and Cisco are on the cutting edge, though a wide variety of others, including Nestle, Compaq, and Ford, are heading in this direction.

---

arrays of disk drives. Already, for instance, the Web portal Yahoo! Inc. collects some 400 billion bytes of information every day–the equivalent of a library crammed with 800,000 books–about where visitors click on the site. It hopes to figure out what ads and products will most appeal to visitors so it can charge higher rates and garner more E-commerce sales. Likewise, ad-targeting service Engage

Technologies Inc. has gathered some 30 million of its own unique customer profiles.

The shock waves from this new approach will shake not only cyberspace but also brick-and-mortar merchants. Already, unlikely stalwarts such as Consolidated Freightways, investment adviser PIMCO Funds, and industrial parts distributor W.W. Grainger are beginning to tap online cus-

tomer information. "It's at the forefront of how we're growing E-commerce," says Grainger Internet Marketing Vice-President Jim Roots. His customers are largely employees dispatched to make purchases for their companies. Armed with data on the spending caps of each of these employees, Roots targets them with E-mails about products within their price ranges.

What remains to be seen is whether consumers will raise a ruckus about all this intimate knowledge of their secret desires. Although customer data always have been collected, it has never been this easy to connect information within and across networks and to use that data instantly. That's what worries privacy advocates. On June 14, they cried foul when DoubleClick Inc., which runs and tracks ads on 1,500 Web sites, announced that it would buy Abacus Direct Corp., which has purchase information on 88 million households. Their worry: The combined data could reveal so much about buyers that it would violate their privacy. "Privacy will grow as a public-relations and political issue," predicts Martha Rogers, a partner at marketing consultant Peppers and Rogers Group.

"CONNECT THE DOTS." That's not the only obstacle to merchants' mass-customization dreams. Many companies admit they've only just begun to look at the technology they need to most effectively use the reams of information they're collecting. According to a Deloitte & Touche study of 867 manufacturing companies in 35 countries, less than a quarter of those surveyed now use data-mining technologies. Says Deloitte & Touche partner David Brainer: "There is a tremendous amount of work to be done to develop an Internet strategy to connect the dots with customers."

The challenge is particularly acute abroad, where E-commerce hasn't taken hold as fast as in the U.S. Many companies in Japan haven't even digitized much of their marketing and sales data, says Joichi Ito, chairman of U.S. portal Infoseek Corp.'s Japanese unit. Some overseas companies, however, are tiptoeing into mining their data. Matsushita Electric Industrial, the world's largest consumer-electronics company, conducted an online poll of the 8,000 subscribers to its Internet access service about the gifts they had bought or planned to buy online. Now, Matsushita is sharing those results with its clients, such as department stores and mail-order businesses.

What's the magic behind all this newfound data collection? While marketers can't track how much junk mail shoppers throw out, any online merchant with tracking software and database programs can keep tabs on how many times a Web visitor checks out an advertisement or a product–and what they skip over. To do that, Web sites can simply place tags, called cookies, on a visitor's computer disk drive. Those cookies, combined with online registrations, can then be added to information from E-mails and phone inquiries placed by customers. Add in what the cookies and credit cards say about purchases made, and E-businesses suddenly have a treasure trove of insights.

Still, it's only in the past year that companies have used the technology to its fullest. Once the Net reached mass market status, with 100 million cybersurfers and counting,

---

Andrew Brooks, president and CEO of Furniture.com Inc., wants his customers to feel pampered—as if they'd just nestled onto one of the plum-colored velvet slipcovers he's selling. That's why two-year-old Furniture.com overhauled its service in January, adding software and computing power so the company can collect more telling information on its customers. Brooks is betting this will lead to products and personalized services that convince his clientele to snap up everything from Shaker tables to Frank Lloyd Wright lamps.

It has been a pretty good bet. For starters, after analyzing Web surfers' behavior on his site, Brooks found that a high number of visitors were interested in sofas costing $700 to $1,100. The problem was, they decided not to buy when they clicked over and learned that delivery would take up to 12 weeks. So the company persuaded a designer to come up with new couches, available in July, that can be delivered within three weeks of an order.

Staying attuned to customers hasn't stopped there. The Framingham (Mass.) startup now offers a service called My Selections, which lets cyber windowshoppers pick out different items—say, a bedroom suite—and then store those choices on the site so they can mull over the purchase. That's when Furniture.com zips off advice and additional information that might persuade them to buy. "We're extremely close to our customer because every single day, we know what they shopped for, what they liked, and what they didn't like," says the 36-year-old Brooks. Since January, the site's conversion rate of visitors into buyers has more than doubled. That has to feel nearly as good as those velvet slipcovers.

Web site operators began demanding software that would assess what was clicking and what was missing. Now, there is a slew of software to answer their questions–from Responsys.com's $5,000-plus programs that monitor customer orders and tastes so it can create tailored E-mails to E.piphany's $250,000 software modules that track buying trends across hundreds of Web sites, as well as phone calls from customers and in-store behavior.

Many companies already are reaping big benefits from their efforts at using these gobs of data. In a recent survey by Forrester Research Inc., 16% of large companies already expect more effective use of customer information to help them cut costs this year. An additional 34% are banking on savings by 2001.

Just getting info to the right people inside the company is paying dividends for some. "The pressing issue in Corporate America is: 'How do I identify the best customer?'" says Roger Siboni, president and CEO of E.piphany, a Palo Alto (Calif.) software startup that helps companies analyze their customer information.

FATTER MARGINS. That has been a big motivator for Government Computer Sales Inc., a $100 million hardware- and software-procurement service in Issaquah, Wash. The company has created profiles of its customers–3,400 government departments in six states–based on online and traditional sales, marketing and accounting databases, phone inquiries, and other sources. The profiles help GCSI, which does about 60% of its interactions online, track and target the customers that buy the most. That has helped the company persuade its clients, on average, to nearly double the number of software programs and computer products they buy–boosting GCSI's profit margins from 7% in 1997 to 11% in 1998.

Indeed, harnessing the right information offers companies not just a way to save money but also to make more of it. Two months ago, Consolidated Freightways, a $2.1 billion trucking company, found a way to cater to small businesses. When visitors to its Web site look at certain rate quotes or routing guides, a window automatically pops up offering online help. While customers get a speedy helping hand, Consolidated collects info from them–and uses that to target them for more business. The benefit: These small businesses bring in much higher profit margins–10%, vs. a typical 3% for large customers.

Consolidated isn't alone. Forrester found that 20% of large companies expect their use of customer information taken from the Net to boost revenues this year, while 74% expect a lift by 2001. PIMCO Funds is one of those that's seeing results. The investment-advisory firm offers an Internet service that uses each investor's profile and a storehouse of 700,000 records on financial funds to tailor a proposed investment portfolio within two minutes. About 30 daily proposals that average $250,000 are now being generated from the system. PIMCO estimates if half the proposals are accepted, that will add 75% more business than it would have gotten in the past.

The new ability to track results can mean quick payoffs. Online educational retailer SmarterKids.com Inc. used AdKnowledge Inc., a Palo Alto (Calif.) company that manages ad placements, to track every inquiry and transaction that resulted from its $1 million online campaign last December and January. It soon found that a few sites–such as Microsoft Network, Yahoo!, and FamilyEducation

(Cont.)

THE CUSTOMER-DATA MOTHERLODE

How companies plan to use the information they have assembled on their customers

	1999	2001
MARKETING	18%	52%
CUSTOMER SERVICE	16%	48%
SALES	16%	34%
PROCESS IMPROVEMENT	2%	22%
FRAUD DETECTION	10%	14%
PRODUCT DEVELOPMENT	4%	10%
DON'T USE DATA	72%	0%
DON'T KNOW	0%	18%

How companies expect they will benefit from their wealth of customer information

	1999	2001
INCREASE REVENUE	20%	74%
CUT EXPENSES	16%	34%
NO IMPACT	72%	0%
DON'T KNOW	0%	20%

DATA, FORRESTER RESEARCH SURVEY OF 50 OF THE 1,000 LARGEST U.S. COMPANIES

with most buyers, and even those that buyers wanted cost too much. "The value of marketing on the Internet isn't in the clickthroughs," says CNET Chief Executive Halsey Minor about the number of times people click on an online ad. "It's in the data you capture."

That data also can help companies comb their information stashes for clues on how to keep their customers coming back. When Baby-Center Inc., an online baby content-and-products site, opened its cyberstore for business eight months ago, about 100,000 people signed up for bimonthly newsletters about promotions and new items. But results were underwhelming: Only 6% clicked on the links, far below the 10%-plus typical of Baby-Center's other informational newsletters.

FIXING HOLES. So in May, after analyzing what customers clicked on in the newsletter, BabyCenter revamped it around themes such as "Summer Days with Your Baby," with sections targeted at different baby age groups. Since then, the clickthroughs have jumped to 25%, with 1% to 2% of those people buying. Says Duncan Dreschel, Baby-Center's director of marketing: "If you can be smart about your product and are relevant, that's when you can develop loyalty."

One of the best ways to keep those customers is to provide better service. Online upstart Furniture.com Inc., which offers 50,000 products, from couches to Persian rugs, is testing that theory. When customers have questions or want advice, they can hit the Design Consultant icon on the site. Design reps then use product info along with customer feedback and purchasing behavior to make targeted suggestions. This data-intensive approach has helped Furniture.com's revenues jump fourfold, to about $1 million in May. "As customers share specific information about their wants and needs, we can be much more responsive," says Furniture.com CEO Andrew Brooks.

TIGHT COOPERATION. Ultimately, merchants both virtual and physical hope to reach the Holy Grail of manufacturers and service providers: products customized for every single customer. The vast information the Web provides on each buyer has suddenly put the seemingly impossible dream of mass customization within reach. But it requires slick cooperation among suppliers, manufacturers, distributors, and retailers. Dell has led the way with its built-to-order PCs, but it's a whole new approach for most industries–even online merchants. "Our store will be completely redecorated for each and every customer," vows Amazon.com's Bezos–but he says that could take up to 10 years.

That's why, for now, mass customization is happening only in bits and pieces–but intriguing bits and pieces, nonetheless. With Yahoo!'s My Yahoo service, for instance, registered users can set up a home page with their own stock portfolio and news sources–prompting them to spend up to five times longer on the site than other Yahoo! visitors. And Yahoo! can use the registrations to target ads to their interests. Then there's Harley Dixon's personalized credit card. He not only got customized terms, but NextCard let him upload through the Web and stamp on his card a photo of an airplane he's building. For Dixon, the customization helped cinch his decision to apply. And for NextCard? Customers who have personalized cards are more than twice as likely to use their cards as people who don't have them, says Next-Card's Lent.

Nifty enough, but other companies are digging even deeper into their information gold mines. This fall, financial-services company KeyCorp plans to begin offering customized products and services to consumers as they move around its Web site–all based on a data trove of the 7 million customers who frequent KeyCorp's branch offices. When any of those customers visit Key-Corp.'s Web site, it combines the older data with the new information on their Web movements to offer up tailored products–on the fly. For instance, if a customer is looking at mortgage or college loans on the site, Key-Corp will target offers tailored to that customer's financial situation.

Despite the Net's promise, bringing all of this data together and making sense of it remains a huge technological and logistical challenge. In a Forrester Research survey in May of 54 online retail companies, 39% said that combining data from different systems has proven to be difficult. "There is a lot of promise in data management," says Richard Rock, director of consumer insights and analysis for online auction house eBay Inc. "But most companies are drowning in data, and that's the biggest obstacle."

What's more, companies will have to address privacy concerns more directly or face a consumer backlash. Already, those concerns have prompted calls for tighter government regulation. If that goes too far, companies may be hamstrung in what data they can acquire and how they can use it. "These are goldfields, but there are also some bears and

Network–attracted the most clicks on its ads, so the company upped spending on those sites. Result: Half its customers are people who bought after viewing the online ads.

It's also a way to quickly correct marketing nightmares. Gleaning trends from its computer-review guide, technology news site CNET Inc. could show one advertiser–say, a computer merchant–that its offerings bombed

(Cont.)

How do you harness the hurricane of information on the Net and elsewhere to get ahead of your rivals? Ask the gurus. Others sure are. From separate offices in Stamford, Conn., and Bowling Green, Ohio, Don Peppers and Martha Rogers are shepherding Net upstarts, as well as traditional companies, into a brave new world of E-commerce. They've written a series of hot-selling books—*The One to One Future, Enterprise One to One,* and this year's *The One to One Fieldbook*—with a simple message: The big winners will be those companies, like American Airlines Inc. and Dell Computer Corp., that best use the data they collect on constantly shifting customer tastes. "It's a learning relationship that involves interacting with the customer, customizing, and then doing it all over again, says

Peppers. That message is striking a chord: The pair do more than 400 annual seminars, workshops and speaking engagements in places as far-flung as Turkey. Peppers and Rogers pinpoint two key advantages to cozying up to customers. First, by tailoring products and services to a buyer's every fancy, clients will become loyal, shunning the competition. Even better, as customers tell the company more about themselves, sellers can create new products that have built-in buyers. "It's not just using the information I know about a customer to figure out better-targeted harassment," says Rogers. "It's about figuring out what this customer needs next from us, when, in what form, at what price, and how." Now that's not just getting ahead of rivals, but customers, too.

people out there with shotguns," says Jason Catlett, a privacy advocate and consultant on writing privacy policies.

If they can overcome those concerns, says marketing consultant Don Peppers, companies may finally provide the kind of frictionless commerce that both they and consumers have always sought. The ideal, he says: "You already know what I want–I don't even have to tell you." For better or worse, customers may soon find that no one–not even Mom, hubby, or their faithful dog Spot–knows them better than their friendly merchant in cyberspace.

By Heather Green
Contributing: Linda Himelstein and Robert D. Hof in San Mateo, Calif., with Irene M. Kunii in Tokyo

Private Matters

It seems that trust equals revenue, even online

By Andrea Petersen

Staff Reporter of The Wall Street Journal

Corporate America is beginning to take customers' online privacy seriously.

Over the past year, a number of Web sites have been caught in high-profile blowups over how they collect and use data. After online advertising company **DoubleClick** Inc. revealed its now-abandoned plan to cross-reference data about people's offline purchasing behavior with their online habits, the New York company's stock dove. And **Yahoo!** Inc.'s GeoCities home-page service was the subject of a privacy-violation complaint by the Federal Trade Commission. The Commission charged that GeoCities was sharing customer data such as education level, marital status and income with marketers, in violation of the company's own privacy policy. GeoCities denied wrongdoing and the company and the FTC settled the dispute.

Anxious to avoid such messes, companies are taking a hard look at their privacy policies. In most cases, sites aren't giving up on gathering, saving and using information about their customers and their shopping habits. But sites now are much more careful about letting customers know what they're doing.

Many sites are putting their privacy policies in high-profile places, even highlighting them on the home page. There is also a movement toward making the policies easy to understand, a huge departure from the incomprehensible legalese of old privacy statements. In addition, more sites are offering users the choice of opting out of data collection, so a Web surfer can still use a site, but doesn't have to offer up reams of personal information. Other companies are arming their customers with identity-veiling technology from the likes of **Zero-Knowledge Systems** Inc. and **Privada** Inc. that allow users to surf the Web anonymously.

The drive for privacy also is forcing changes in the structure of some companies. Dozens of corporations, including behemoths such as **Microsoft** Corp. and **International Business Machines** Corp., have named chief privacy officers to check for privacy problems. Other firms like travel site **Expedia** Inc. have paid for "privacy audits" from outfits such as **PricewaterhouseCoopers** to prove they are living up to their policies.

"It is the old 'trust equals revenue' thing," says Les Seagraves, the new chief privacy officer of **EarthLink** Inc., an Atlanta-based Internet service provider. "People aren't going to buy stuff if they think their information is going to be bought and sold."

But it's not just the threat of bad publicity that is pushing companies to act. New privacy laws and regulations in Europe are forcing companies that do business overseas to pay attention to their privacy practices and ensure they are in compliance. In the U.S., a federal privacy law seems to be on the horizon, spurring Internet-advertising trade groups such as the Network Advertising Initiative to set up their own privacy standards in an effort to stave off restrictive regulation. Many individual companies are also overhauling their privacy practices in anticipation of a federal law.

Privacy Man

The new corporate emphasis on privacy has made Larry Ponemon, the head of PricewaterhouseCoopers's privacy practice, a busy man. Dr. Ponemon leads a team that is brought in to assess how well a company is living up to its stated privacy policies. He says his company completed 200 audits in 2000, compared with only 20 audits in 1999. Among his clients: Microsoft, Expedia and DoubleClick.

"Companies are beginning to take this issue very, very seriously," he says. "They want to avoid class-action lawsuits and possible shareholder revolt."

During his audits, Dr. Ponemon's team does everything from interviewing employees to sifting through reams of data housed in computer servers. And the results can be surprising. Dr. Ponemon estimates that about 80% of companies don't comply with their own policies. He adds, though, that most problems are the result of human error. Oftentimes, employees don't know the company's policies well and are not trained to follow them.

The audits, which can have multimillion-dollar price tags, often serve as a wake-up call. Many companies make pains to revise their practices to conform to their stated privacy policies. Others, Dr. Ponemon says, have even abandoned certain businesses because of the potential privacy problems. He declines to give examples.

Expedia, the Redmond, Wash., online travel site, underwent a four-month-long audit from New York-based PricewaterhouseCoopers. "They came in-house to our call centers and to our corporate offices to where we handle data to make sure we weren't doing anything improper," says Suzi LeVine, Expedia's marketing director. The audit, Expedia says, proved that the company was in compliance with its stated privacy policies.

Still, Expedia made the language of its privacy policy more explicit. The company also changed its policy for sending out promotional e-mail messages with discounts on airlines and hotels. Before the change, Expedia had an opt-out policy. Users would get e-mail messages unless they specifically said they didn't want any. Now Expedia users have to opt in, or proactively sign up to receive offers. Ms. LeVine says the number of recipients who unsubscribe to the company's e-mail messages actually dropped after Expedia moved to an opt-in policy. "Anything we can do to grow trust is good for our business," she says.

Watchdog Work

Many companies agree—and are appointing executives to make sure their Internet operations keep faith with customers.

At the end of last year, both IBM and EarthLink named chief privacy officers. These executives are charged with following the myriad bills that are floating around Congress, working with their respective industry groups on self-regulatory privacy principles and acting as internal watchdogs. "If you're doing the job right, you should be giving people internally a hard time and taking grief from consumer groups," says Ari Schwartz, a senior policy analyst at one of those consumer groups, the Center for Democracy and Technology, in Washington, D.C.

EarthLink's new chief privacy officer, Mr. Seagraves, says he plans to form an internal privacy council with representatives from all of the major company departments. The council will be charged with overseeing privacy practices and will propose new safeguards. EarthLink is also likely to put together a group of its customers that the company can call on to judge its privacy policies and give feedback on new services and protections. Mr. Seagraves already plans to create Web pages with information on how customers can browse the Web and send e-mail anonymously. The pages will also contain detailed explanations of cookies, those little computer programs that Web sites send to users' hard drives to track their online movements.

But companies are finding that they aren't being judged just on their own privacy practices, but also on those of business partners. Powerful companies that want to keep their sterling reputations are forcing their smaller business partners to beef up their privacy practices. In March of 1999, IBM, of Armonk, N.Y., announced that it would no longer advertise on Web sites that didn't clearly post privacy policies telling people what information was collected, how it would be used and gave them a place to opt-out of providing the information.

"We had some financial leverage, we were one of the largest advertisers, and we could exert some positive influence," says an IBM spokesman. The company gave its partners 60 days to meet the new requirements or risk being dropped. He says that, at the time, about nine U.S.-based sites that were at risk of being cut off instead altered their policies to be in compliance.

DoubleClick—in an attempt to rebuild its tarnished reputation—is getting serious about privacy. In March of 2000 the company hired a chief privacy officer and set up a consumer privacy board. The company began submitting

(Cont.)

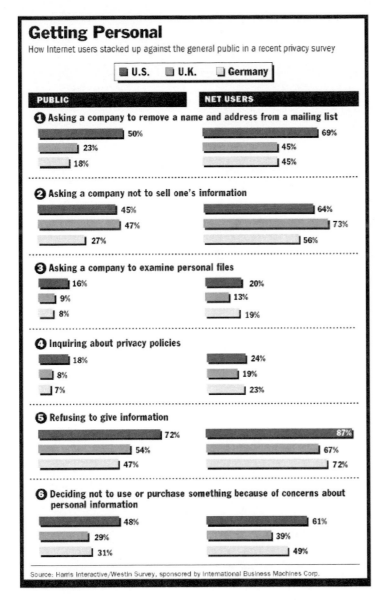

Getting Personal

How Internet users stacked up against the general public in a recent privacy survey

■ U.S.   ■ U.K.   □ Germany

PUBLIC   **NET USERS**

❶ Asking a company to remove a name and address from a mailing list
- 50%   69%
- 23%   45%
- 18%   45%

❷ Asking a company not to sell one's information
- 45%   64%
- 47%   73%
- 27%   56%

❸ Asking a company to examine personal files
- 16%   20%
- 9%   13%
- 8%   19%

❹ Inquiring about privacy policies
- 18%   24%
- 8%   19%
- 7%   23%

❺ Refusing to give information
- 72%   87%
- 54%   67%
- 47%   72%

❻ Deciding not to use or purchase something because of concerns about personal information
- 48%   61%
- 29%   39%
- 31%   49%

Source: Harris Interactive/Westin Survey, sponsored by International Business Machines Corp.

itself to regular privacy audits, ran a banner advertising campaign informing consumers of how cookies work and set up a Web site to let people opt out of DoubleClick cookies. The company now also requires all Web sites it works with to post privacy policies.

"It isn't enough to explain what you do on your site when you've got so many partners," says Jules Polonetsky, DoubleClick's chief privacy officer. "The challenge is to put steps in place to ensure that your partners live up to best practices."

DoubleClick has also added technology safeguards to make sure that it isn't inadvertently collecting information in violation of its privacy policy. The architecture of the Internet sometimes allows information that a Web surfer gives to one site to bleed into another—even if neither company wants this to happen. DoubleClick's technology blocks this kind of transfer. "If you do accidentally throw stuff in our direction, we're closing our window," says Mr. Polonetsky.

Zero Tolerance

Increasingly, companies are turning to technology to bulletproof their privacy practices. There is a lot of anticipation about P3P (for Platform for Privacy Preferences) technology. P3P makes it possible for computers to talk to each other and notify users when a site is collecting information. Microsoft recently announced that its new version of the Internet Explorer browser (available next winter) will include P3P technology.

The new P3P-enhanced browser will work like this: Users will set their privacy preferences, such as what kind of personal information they are willing to share and what kind of cookies they are willing to accept. Then, when they surf the Web, the browser decides if the site meets the privacy preferences. If users come to a site that is trying to get information or send them a cookie that doesn't match their preferences, they will get an alert, and the cookie will be blocked. (The alert will look a lot like the notices that online shoppers get when they visit a site that doesn't have secure encryption technology.) The user can click on an icon to get more information about that privacy alert.

Companies are also buying privacy-enhancing technology and making it available to their users. Zero-Knowledge Systems, Montreal, sells a product, Freedom, that lets users surf the Web and send e-mail anonymously. Most of the company's customers are individuals, but the company also sells the product to about 100 Internet service providers that in turn deliver it to their users. Zero-Knowledge also is selling custom programs to businesses to help them make sure they are following fair information practices and aren't storing more customer data than they need.

"It is only in the last six months that people are saying this is something we really need to invest in," says Austin Hill, Zero-Knowledge's president. "We can't just put up a privacy policy and expect this to go away." Privada, of San Jose, Calif., also sells an anonymous browsing system that American Express Co. is making available to its credit-card holders.

Even in these days of heightened awareness, privacy breaches still occur. And the privacy-advocacy groups aren't likely to close up shop soon. In fact, this is likely just the first act in the privacy debate. New technology, especially wireless services, bring a myriad of new privacy concerns. During the next year or so, when most cell phones will be embedded with global positioning system chips that can track users in the real world, cookies will likely look like kid stuff. "There's a lot of concern about the Big Brother effect that would come from the tracking wireless usage," says Mr. Schwartz, the policy analyst.

Indeed, the FTC recently completed a workshop looking at privacy in the wireless world. On Capitol Hill, lawmakers are busy preparing the first bills.

Ms. Petersen is a staff reporter in The Wall Street Journal's New York bureau.

Product

40

THE WEB'S NEW PLUMBERS

Managed service providers are eager to take jobs away from your expensive staff of techies.

by Dylan Tweney

When some aspect of Web technology is expensive and difficult, you can bet that a better approach will come along fast. Such is the case with Web operations, that pricey combination of techies and technology that keeps the machines and applications behind an Internet site up and running. The improved approach has arrived in the form of a new type of service company, the so-called managed service provider, or MSP, which promises to take on website operations at a fraction of the cost of in-house alternatives—and with far fewer staffing headaches.

For Chris Wong, CEO of Skills Village, the MSP option came in the nick of time. When Wong launched his job site in August 1999, he was in such a rush to open his online doors that he skimped on installing a firewall, a standard part of any business website. It was a bad call. Within two days, hackers had broken into the site. "We had to fork out beaucoup bucks for a security expert to come in, to build a firewall, and to buy [security] hardware," Wong says. He decided that operations wasn't his firm's forte, so he outsourced the task to Loudcloud of Sunnyvale, Calif., one of several dozen new firms that oversee the complicated plumbing of business websites.

In the year since then, Wong says, Loudcloud not only has alleviated security and other management problems but also has saved his company money. Wong's 85-person firm has 30 servers, but only one Web techie on staff—and that person simply coordinates technical issues with Loudcloud. Looking after all those servers in-house would require $3 million to $4 million per year, including staffing costs, Wong estimates, but Loudcloud charges a third of that. Dramatic savings like that are irresistible to Web businesses, which are ever more mindful of the bottom line.

Here's another way to look at the math: Maintaining a no-great-shakes commerce site around the clock requires four to six technical hands. At an average cost of $100,000 per person, that's about $500,000 annually in personnel costs alone. And just try to find and retain those operations people—they're in huge demand. So if you can lose that headache and cut your operations budget by two-thirds, isn't the MSP approach a no-brainer?

Yep, for the most part it is. MSPs offer a great opportunity, which is why research firm Yankee Group estimates that they'll be a $10 billion market in 2001. MSPs are proliferating fast (the MSP Association boasts 88 members), and the leading MSPs already have dozens of customers.

The hard part isn't seeing the value in an MSP; it's the detailed business of selecting one and laying down a clear agreement between your firm and your new partner. MSPs vary widely in how much of a site's management duties they take on, and how they do it, so be prepared to spend some time shopping around. In some cases, an MSP contract will cover just the oversight of the technology (while you supply the hardware and software); in other cases, the MSP provides everything your site needs, from servers to staff.

How do MSPs work? Most use small armies of techies to maintain customers' sites, generally aided by software that allows them to monitor your equipment from their network operations center, or NOC, the MSP's equivalent of NASA ground control. They look after your site's servers, fixing problems, configuring and rebooting the machines as necessary, and coordinating the disparate elements that make up the site's technical underpinnings.

Some MSPs, such as Loudcloud, will work only on certain hardware and software, which makes it easier for them to address problems and expand capacity. That

Fool Disclosure

Why eCompany Now decided to go with an MSP, and how we picked the right one.

Back in November 1999, we had no idea that outsourcing operations was an option (who did?), so we went the obvious route: We hired four techies to handle the job. But by last fall, the lure of the MSP option had us hooked. Our requirements narrowed the choices fast: We needed a partner who was willing to minister to our Sun, Oracle, and Vignette gear, as well as save us at least 50 percent over the in-house option. That brought us to Chicago-based Nuclio, which has been working with us for two months now to prepare for the switch and finalize our yellow-pages-thick service-level agreement. Will it work? We're hopeful, but ask us in a year. What became of our former operations guys? They got sweet severance packages, and employment queries from Nuclio, among others.

—Ned Desmond, eCompany Now president

(Cont.)

The Scoop on Leading Full-Service MSPs

MSP	Services	Average Charge Per Month	Number of Customers
Avasta (formerly Chapter 2) www.avasta.com	Infrastructure and application management and monitoring, and customer support services.	$18,000	20, including Accenture, Novell, PeoplePC
Loudcloud www.loudcloud.com	The whole enchilada: website hosting, management, maintenance, and monitoring. Will work only with certain hardware and software.	$10,000 to several hundred thousand dollars	43, including Britannica.com, Nike.com, Univision
Nuclio www.nuclio.com	Website design, installation, management, and monitoring. Hosting available through its partners.	$25,000	45, including the Chicago Stock Exchange, CVS/pharmacy, Dynegy
SiteSmith www.sitesmith.com	Site hosting and co-location services, architecture, hardware and software implementation, operations, and bandwidth management.	$30,000 to more than $100,000	170, including BP Amoco, Brooks Brothers, Hotmail
StrataSource www.stratasource.com	Website design, management, monitoring, and repair. Will support sites regardless of their hardware, software, or hosting solutions.	$8,000 to $15,000	75, including Footlocker, Fujitsu, 20th Century Fox
Totality (formerly MimEcom) www.totality.com	Website installation, operations, and monitoring of infrastructure and Web applications.	$30,000 to $250,000	20, including BlueLight.com, Smith & Hawken, Tavola

approach works especially well when the MSP is involved from the get-go and can influence early technology decisions. Other MSPs, such as SiteSmith and Nuclio, are more readily able to deal with sites that are already up and running on diverse technologies.

Fees hinge mainly on the size of the site. Some MSPs charge by the server, while others look at the amount of data handled. For a low-traffic site with fewer than 10 servers, you can expect to spend $10,000 or more per month. For larger, higher-traffic sites, monthly fees might run to several hundred thousand dollars.

So when you're ready to hire an MSP, what should you look for? Technical competence and fiscal health, primarily.

Have your IT staff or a trusted consultant perform a detailed examination of the MSP's technical capabilities before you sign on the dotted line. Is it experienced in the technologies your site uses? Lisa Perri, an analyst at the Aberdeen Group, recommends investigating the MSP's procedures for handling site problems or crashes—what's the process for "escalating" problems to the attention of management when something goes wrong?

It's also important to look into the financial viability of MSPs. The sector is new and growing fast, and hosting giants such as Exodus and UUnet are adding managed services to their menus, which will turn up the heat on startups. "There are 60 or 70 vendors calling themselves MSPs, and that just can't last," says Corey Ferengul, senior program director at Meta Group. "There's going to be a shakeout." That means huge headaches for companies that happen to bet on the wrong MSP.

MSPs' service-level agreements, or SLAs, are another area where it pays to ask hard questions. SLAs specify what percentage of the time your site has to be up, such as 99 percent (low) or 99.999 percent (practically impossible). SLAs can also cover other aspects of performance, such as webpage download times. If the SLA isn't met, the MSP typically will owe you a refund on your monthly fee. Setting the terms of an SLA is often a drawn-out affair involving many technical and legal details, as well as weeks—even months—of back-and-forth negotiations.

Once you've contracted with an MSP, you still need to keep an eye on your site—and your MSP. Most managed service providers use automated network-monitoring agents to notify their staff—and yours—when an SLA is not being met. If that seems a bit like the fox guarding the henhouse, it is. For more accountability, consider network-management MSPs (such as Brix Networks, SiteLite, or SiteRock) to monitor your full-service MSP.

One last sobering thought: Don't assume that hiring an MSP means you can forget about your site. According to Sara Plath, VP of About.com (a customer of SiteSmith), success depends on continued communication. "People shouldn't think this goes on automatic pilot," she says. "It takes proactive communication to make your needs, schedule, and business priorities understood." Odds are that you're still going to need a techie on deck to manage your MSP.

41

You've Got Mail (With Cash !)

PayPal Sees Torrid Growth With a Service That Sends Money Across the Internet

By Jathon Sapsford
Staff Reporter of The Wall Street Journal

If your acquaintances are even slightly tech-savvy, it may not be long before somebody beams money into your e-mail in-box.

Don't delete it. The money's good.

It's all part of a new online payment system called PayPal.com, and it's growing by 9,000 new users a day just three months after its official launch. The system responds to many of the needs that led to the creation of virtual currencies with names like "beenz" and "Bippy dollars." But PayPal uses real dollars. And now, instead of just techno-nerds, the service is attracting mainstream users.

Driving PayPal's torrid growth is a simple joining of two proven technologies: e-mail and the credit-card network. Registered users can send a payment to anybody with an e-mail address just by writing a dollar amount into an online form. When the e-mail is sent, the payment is charged to the sender's credit card or bank account. Registration takes five minutes.

If the person on the other end isn't a registered PayPal user, that's OK. The receiver just fills out the form attached to the e-payment to tap the money, which is already waiting in a PayPal.com account in the receiver's name.

Completing the form also registers the receiver as a user. "This is what people in technology call a viral product," says Peter Thiel, the chief executive of PayPal.com. "It's easier than catching a cold. And it is spreading as fast as a virus."

Taking the money out of the system isn't as quick. PayPal will cut a check and send it to you through the regular mail, credit it to your credit card or transfer it into your bank account – all of which can take up to a week. But the big fans of the system keep the money in their accounts to use again.

That last option is the key to how PayPal, based in Palo Alto, Calif., hopes to thrive. The PayPal account doesn't provide interest, so PayPal can invest any money left there until the user wants to spend it. If PayPal keeps growing at its current rate, the company hopes it will soon manage enough customer money to both make a profit and absorb all the fees involved in credit-card transactions. For now, the PayPal service is free, and Mr. Thiel says the company has no intention of ever charging its customers.

Among PayPal's most common uses is the cybersettling of accounts between family and friends. Andrew Brenner, for example, a 31-year-old tech-industry employee, recently threw a big barbecue party with friends. Afterward, he e-mailed $83 to pay his buddy for his share of the burgers and beer.

A few weeks later, another friend was short the cash for his share of a fish dinner at a Palo Alto, Calif., restaurant. Mr. Brenner knew that his buddy did have a hand-held computer with e-mail capacity. So right there in the restaurant, over the remains of prawns and swordfish, Mr. Brenner asked his friend to send him an e-mail for $20.

As the friend sent the e-payment over the red-checkered tablecloth, Mr. Brenner paid the bill knowing his friend's share would be in his account at PayPal. "PayPal is replacing currency," says Mr. Brenner flatly. "This is becoming the payment service of the Internet."

Some heavy hitters in venture capital agree. Wall Street's **Goldman Sachs Group** Inc., together with a fund tied to the West Coast Web incubator **idealab!**, recently invested $23 million in PayPal.com during its second round of venture financing. Its first round came from **Nokia** Corp., the Finnish mobile phone giant, and **Deutsche Bank** AG of Germany. Before that, the company was working with seed money from individuals and a hedge fund run by the current chief executive, Mr. Thiel.

Mr. Thiel, a blond 32-year-old who says "awesome" a lot, graduated from Stanford Law School in 1992 and soon joined the Wall Street law firm of Sullivan & Cromwell. A year later he joined CS First Boston, where he traded currencies for a few years. By 1996 he had moved back out to his native California to start up his own hedge fund. In 1998, he met PayPal's chief technology officer, Max Levchin, who wanted to launch a venture that provided encryption technology.

Mr. Thiel's hedge fund bought into the idea, and Mr. Thiel joined the new venture himself as CEO. Launched in December 1998 under the name Confiniti, the company focused on providing financial institutions with the technology to make online and mobile transactions secure. But the start-up soon saw the huge demand for secure payment systems on the Web.

When the new company hit on combining the credit-card network with e-mail and launched the PayPal service, more investors started to take note. Now, Confiniti is in the process of changing its corporate name to

PayPal, and Mr. Thiel is giving a lot of the company's money away.

That's because PayPal provides a virtual $10 coupon to any user who signs up a friend – and gives the friend a $10 coupon as well. In other words, it costs PayPal $20 for each new user, or $2 million for 100,000. Mr. Thiel says the approach is much more effective – and a lot cheaper – than buying a 30-second ad during the Super Bowl.

Other companies have also deployed or are working on online payment, including **eBay** Inc. and **CheckFree Holdings** Inc.

Since PayPal's launch, 190,000 users have signed up. Some investors value Web-based financial-services companies at $1,000 to $10,000 a customer. Using the middle of that range, PayPal's franchise would now be valued at around $500 million.

The product is a particular boon for online auction denizens because it cuts out the risks of being paid by check through the mail. Lisette McConnell, a 33-year-old graphic designer, sells custom-designed neckties on eBay. She has trusted buyers before, sending goods before checks cleared, only to find out the check wasn't any good. Other merchants spend thousands of dollars and per-transaction fees to be able to accept credit cards. But

---

PAY A FRIEND ONLINE

How to use e-mail and a credit card to send money over the Net.

1 Log onto PayPal.com. First-time users must register, supplying name, street address, e-mail address and passwords.

2 Fill in credit-card number, friend's e-mail address and transaction amount, and send.

3 Friend gets e-mail saying, 'You've got cash.'

4 Friend clicks e-mail link to PayPal.com and registers.

5 Friend asks PayPal.com to transfer payment into bank account, mail a check or leave the money at PayPal.com to use for future e-payments.

(Cont.)

PayPal makes all that unnecessary. "It's like air money," Ms. McConnell says.

There are limitations on bigger transactions, in order to combat fraud and hackers. Cathy Rowekamp, 48 years old, of Winnsboro, S.C., sells antiques online. Once shipping charges are thrown in, her prices are in the thousands of dollars. Buyers of her chests, dressers and rockers must get a form from PayPal through the mail confirming their street address to conduct transactions larger than $200.

That's supposed to take only a matter of days, but the turbocharged growth at the company has caused delays, all of which Ms. Rowekamp is finding frustrating. "I want it to work so bad," she says.

One user, Jim Bruene, had his payments frozen when he tried to get around the limit. The publisher of a financial newsletter called Online Banking Report, he sent a freelance reporter several e-payments that totaled more

---

PayPal has sought to keep its system secure by hiring a panel of encryption advisers.

---

than $200. But the PayPal fraud alarms kicked off, and Mr. Bruene's money was tied up for weeks. "If you're a consumer and a couple thousand dollars disappeared for two weeks, you probably wouldn't want to use" the service again, Mr. Bruene says.

"Sometimes I worry that we're too obsessed with security," concedes Mr. Thiel. Other online payment systems have received bad press over lax security. But long before last week's hacking attacks, PayPal sought to keep its system secure by hiring a board of advisers staffed with heavyweights in encryption technology. One is Stanford University Prof. Martin Hellman, one of the brains behind the most commonly used form of encryption on the Internet. Another is Stanford Prof. Dan Boneh, who leads a team of researchers who specialize in code breaking.

To fire off payments for anything more than $200, a consumer must wait for PayPal to send through the mail an address confirmation, which has a coded approval number. Only after keying in that number can consumers make larger payments online. "Fraud protection is a trade-off," says Mr. Thiel. "If you make it totally airtight, it becomes less user-friendly."

Chinese Officials Force Magazines To Go Without Famous Names

BY MATTHEW ROSE AND LESLIE CHANG
Staff Reporters of THE WALL STREET JOURNAL

Western publishers in China are reeling from a government clampdown that is forcing them to publish magazines without the use of their famous names and logos.

In the stringent new climate, the government has even raised the possibility that many licensing agreements forged between Western publishers and Chinese agencies may be deemed illegal.

China had been a magazine publisher's dream – a place where costs of doing business are low, the advertising market is exploding and rising income levels have produced a vast sea of educated readers. Many industry executives believe China will be the world's biggest magazine market one day.

But it has turned into a nightmare since the Chinese government began strictly enforcing regulations governing licenses that it requires of magazine publishers. Many Western publishers got access to licenses by forming joint ventures with Chinese magazine partners. Since Jan. 1, when the new enforcement took effect, Western publishers must use a direct translation of the often-obscure name that appears on their license, or use no English name at all.

Hearst Corp., for example, is leaving a big blank space on the cover of its Chinese edition of Cosmopolitan, rather than using the name on its license: "Trends Lady." Hachette Filipacchi Magazines, a unit of France's **Lagardere** SA, is doing the same for the Chinese edition of Woman's Day, faced with the equally unsexy name on its license: "Friends of Health."

"I can't believe these guys are doing this," laments George Green, president of Hearst's international magazine division, which also publishes Chinese-language editions of Esquire and Motor. "If a country takes your name off your product, you're gone."

The Chinese government contends that many companies are publishing without the proper licenses. The publishers say they're being penalized unfairly by a regime that keeps changing the rules.

Talks between publishers and Chinese officials have gone on for months. "We just want to go to the status quo ante," says Hearst's Mr. Green, "but no one's counting on it."

Under Communist rule, China cultivated magazine publishing as a propaganda machine. But as it moved toward a market economy, the state withdrew its support. Local government agencies, who had publishing licenses but no money, realized they could form symbiotic relationships with foreign publishers, who had money but no licenses.

Some curious partnerships were born. For instance, Figaro, a magazine owned by French publishing group **Socpresse,** is published in China under a licensing agreement with the Communist Youth League. The flavor is clearly pop, not political, as evidenced by supermodel Claudia Schiffer on a recent cover. Hearst publishes Cosmopolitan and Esquire in China thanks to a relationship with the National Tourism Bureau. And Hachette publishes Woman's Day in conjunction with an organization called China New Sport Magazine.

The government is arguing that foreign publishers abused their partnerships with Chinese entities by printing new magazines without approval and by putting out several magazines under a single joint-venture licensing agreement. Chinese editions of Hearst's Cosmopolitan and Esquire, for example, display the same license number. Hearst says it isn't in violation of the law.

What's behind the timing of the crackdown? Some Western publishers blame it on maneuvering by governmental factions. Inside China, many people see the government's moves as an effort to make good on its promise to clean up inefficient, formerly state-run industries.

In an effort to wipe out money-losing ventures, Beijing has ordered hundreds of magazines shut down and has cracked down on domestic firms for violations, including using book licenses to print magazines. "The regulations target all violators, no matter foreign or domestic," says Wen Bingyuan, an official at the Press and Publications Administration. "Companies that have violated the regulations are required to correct their mistakes immediately."

The clampdown also may reflect official concern at the explosion of fashion and lifestyle magazines touched off by Western titles. The content of many Chinese editions is rather tame by Western standards. Cosmopolitan, known in the U.S. for no-holds-barred sex advice, dispenses mostly fashion and cooking tips in its Chinese-language edition. Still, the magazines' tone may be anathema to China's media mandarins, among the bureaucracy's most conservative.

The sudden change in climate has made the joint ventures unattractive to Western publishers. Under the new rules, not only must the foreign name match the one on the publishing license, it must be "significantly smaller" on the cover than the Chinese name. Publishers now also are banned from using a single license to spin out new publications. Existing foreign magazines must reapply for government approval for their ventures – in effect, putting them at risk of being declared illegal and having their publications halted.

Is China worth the hassle? After all, Cosmopolitan's circulation in China, for example, is only 200,000, compared with almost 2.9 million in the U.S.

"Given the Confucian respect for learning, it is a very viable publishing market," says Patrick McGovern, chairman of **International Data Group,** of Boston, which publishes 19 titles in China, including China Computer World, China Internet Times and Electronic Products China.

Because the Chinese postal service handles so much of the expensive side of the magazine business – sales, marketing, distribution – costs fall to around 3% of revenue, compared with more than 20% in the U.S., Mr. McGovern said, boosting margins to a hearty 40%.

In China, Western magazines are advertiser magnets. Executives estimate advertising revenues for publications linked to a Western title can be almost double those of local magazines, because of demand for ad space from foreign corporations. Magazine advertising in China totaled $860 million in 1998, up 35% from the year earlier, according to the China Advertising Association. Titles affiliated with foreign magazines hold leading spots.

Already there has been some fallout. W magazine, an upscale fashion publication owned by **Advance Publications** Inc.'s Fairchild unit, has put plans to launch a China edition on hold. Fairchild officials declined to comment.

Hoping to avoid such pitfalls, other publishers have been reluctant to invest a lot of time and money in China. **Time Warner** Inc.'s Time Inc. magazine publishing unit sells only two magazines, Fortune and a digest of articles from Time, in China. Time publishes them in Hong Kong using their English-language names and mails them to subscribers in mainland China.

Figaro *magazine, as it appears in China*

WAL-MART STORES GO PRIVATE (LABEL)

Power 'house': Top U.S. retailer takes on the world with own store brands

by Jack Neff

As Sears, Roebuck & Co. built such store brands as Kenmore, Craftsman and DieHard, a little-known Arkansas retailer pursued a different idea.

Sam Walton was creating a discount powerhouse out of cheap small-town real estate, ruthless efficiency and low prices on brand-name goods. Today, with Wal-Mart's sales quadruple those of Sears, Mr. Walton's way has proved superior.

Even so, the victor is borrowing a tactic from its long-vanquished foe in creating its own brands. In the past year, Wal-Mart has rolled out such brands as White Cloud paper products, Spring Valley nutritional supplements, Sam's American Choice detergent and, just last month, EverActive alkaline batteries.

Ol' Roy, named after Mr. Walton's Irish setter, has become the best-selling dog food brand in America. And although those are unadvertised, Wal-Mart's EverStart car batteries have become as ubiquitous on TV sports programming as Sears' DieHard ads once were.

Unfortunately for brand marketers, Wal-Mart's new-found devotion to store brands is where its resemblance to the darker side of Sears' past ends. Wal-Mart's private-label push is steadily stoking up—creating a fearsome rival—even as the chain's overall sales growth remains on fire. Long the nation's biggest mass-merchandiser, Wal-Mart is on pace to become the biggest food-store chain this year.

Brand marketers should be afraid, says consultant Christopher Hoyt, as Wal-Mart transforms itself from their biggest customer to their biggest competitor. The retailer will become even more of a threat as Wal-Mart nears 60% household penetration, making network TV advertising cost-effective, Mr. Holt says.

"They're going to become the marketers of their own brands," he notes. "In five years, the consumer isn't going to be able to tell the difference between a Wal-Mart brand and a national brand."

In some cases, they already can't. Besides Ol' Roy,

Wal-Mart's garden fertilizer also has become the best-selling brand in the U.S. in its category. In vitamins, Wal-Mart's Spring Valley line, launched earlier this year, may soon reach best-seller standing, too, maintains Burt Flickinger, a consultant with Reach Marketing.

PRIVATE LABEL'S PROMISE

Of course, private label is nothing new to Wal-Mart— or to retailing. Neither are dire predictions of its ascendance.

During the recession of the early 1990s, some pundits predicted private-label shares in the U.S. would reach 35% to 50% by 2000, pushing the country down the European path to private-label hell for brand manufacturers. Nothing of the kind happened. In the second quarter of 1999, private-label dollar shares in package-goods categories of food, drug and mass merchandise reached 14.3%, up only marginally from 13% in 1994.

One reason private-label brands didn't grow faster is that the 1990s saw the explosive growth of Wal-Mart, which emphasized private labels far less than its supermarket rivals. While roughly 25% of Kroger Co.'s sales come from store labels, Wal-Mart's private-label sales in package goods are believed to be more in the range of 10%; they are relatively understated because of Sam Walton's commitment to branded products, which has been carried on by current management, Mr. Flickinger says.

So why is Wal-Mart suddenly turning to a bigger, better private-label program?

Besides the obvious lure of better profits, Wal-Mart's private-label push is linked to a number of marketing and strategic forces at play in its plans to expand nationally and globally. Wal-Mart's focus on rolling back prices, which puts the retailer at odds with manufacturers, is one factor.

Record economic expansion or no, Wal-Mart's customer base remains the 60% of consumers in this country who still have not realized any real dollar gain in income

(Cont.)

since 1970, Mr. Hoyt says. To serve those consumers, Wal-Mart claims to have rolled back 25,000 prices in the second half of 1999 alone, saving them $8 billion, Mr. Flickinger says. In the past three years, the price rollback program has helped increase weekly customer counts from 80 million to a brisk 100 million, he adds.

HAGGLING

But the whistling, happy-face price rollback character that has become Wal-Mart's icon has a more sinister countenance for product marketers.

Manufacturers always had incentives to give Wal-Mart the best price to get merchandising support and shelf space, says Paul Kelly, president of Silvermine Consulting. Now, however, Wal-Mart is increasingly haggling even beyond the best offer.

"They've been turning more to manufacturers than in the past for margin growth," he says.

Manufacturers, meanwhile, have generally gotten more aggressive on pricing in the past year to fatten sales amid years of sluggish growth, Mr. Flickinger notes.

Enter private labels, particularly premium-price private labels, which are slightly less expensive than premium brands but look like the exclusive premium products.

"I think the key is that it is premium," says Andrew Shore, analyst with PaineWebber. "I think premium is there to almost forever limit the ability of manufacturers to raise prices. It's really a price cap."

Most consultants see building store brands as a fairly expensive means for Wal-Mart to control prices, even though growing excess capacity is putting more manufacturers into the private-label business. Store brands also play into other Wal-Mart strategies.

"They're going global," says Ken Harris, a partner with Cannondale Associates. "They believe the brands they sell can mean more to international consumers than national brands in the U.S., and they're probably right."

The higher private-label shares and lower disposable incomes in many overseas markets also are likely influencing Wal-Mart's growing interest in private label as it, like many of its suppliers, looks to manage its brand globally.

"Even if [Wal-Mart store] brands weren't successful in the U.S., the potential for them being successful overseas is much greater," Mr. Harris says.

Store brands also provide Wal-Mart with a point of difference that the growing ranks of dot-coms can't match, as it prepares a stronger entry into e-commerce next year, Mr. Flickinger says. They could even figure into Wal-Mart's efforts to expand its presence in the Northeast U.S—which, like Europe, presents such obstacles as high real-estate costs and entrenched opposition

from local governments.

Not only could store brands help offset higher costs for Wal-Mart in potential new markets, but they also could help Wal-Mart compete more like a supermarket as it experiments with its smaller, lower-volume neighborhood market format.

That format could expand in a hurry if—as Mr. Hoyt believes it will—Wal-Mart buys the Food Lion grocery chain, which in turn will give it control over retail chain Hannaford Brothers and an overnight presence in New England without having to struggle with town councils over zoning and permit issues.

Regardless of the motivation, Wal-Mart store brands create major challenges for package-goods marketers.

"They've definitely served notice on the brand manufacturers that if you want to survive, you'd better have a reason to exist," says William Steele, analyst with Bank of America Securities. "Second- and third- and fourth-tier brands that don't bring consumers to the shelves are going to have a very hard time."

Mr. Hoyt, in fact, believes phase two of Wal-Mart's program will be ridding shelves of brands that no longer make sense after Wal-Mart has built successful store brands.

BRANDS' RAISON D'ETRE

In the past, manufacturers' brands could stay in Wal-Mart even if they didn't have a strong consumer following, as long as they delivered a price low enough to let Wal-Mart make a margin. But if Wal-Mart can build store brands that generate better margins than category also-rans with little consumer loyalty, Mr. Hoyt says, it will jettison those brands.

By eliminating some of the other competition, Wal-Mart store brands could even be allies of category leaders such as Procter & Gamble Co. or Kimberly-Clark Corp., says Gary Stibel, a consultant with New England Consulting.

K-C has been monitoring the impact of White Cloud diapers in weekly sales and share data, and has seen no impact on its category-leading Huggies diaper brand, says Kathi Seifert, exec VP at the company.

"Our belief is that [White Cloud] will take share from brands that are less premium, like Luvs and Drypers," she says.

Even major marketers, however, have second-tier brands in some cases. And the success of White Cloud could ultimately push P&G's Luvs off store shelves, Mr. Harris says.

The jury is still out, however, on whether Wal-Mart can move beyond building the brand on its storefronts to building brands on its shelves.

Ol' Roy one of many as Wal-Mart tackles the German market

Not content with simply conquering the U.S. market, Ol' Roy is taking on Germany, too.

Wal-Mart Deutschland is stepping up its private-label presence, preparing to boost its current offerings from 32 to a reported 1,000. Ol' Roy is among the private-label brands already sold in the retailer's 43 German outlets, along with brands such as Special Kitty cat food and Great Value orange juice, cola, iced tea and tissues.

A Wal-Mart spokeswoman in Germany said the retailer is "in the development phase" of additional private-label products but would not confirm the planned number of lines.

The current Great Value brands aren't advertised but the chain's friendly service is highlighted in its general advertising—a novel strategy in that country. The German spots are produced by GSD&M, Austin, Texas.

The mass merchandiser appears to be furthest along in Europe. Just last year, it acquired 74 hypermarkets in Germany from Spar Handels AG and purchased U.K. supermarket chain ADSA Group. Wal-Mart also is rumored to be eyeing the purchase of Casino Guichard Perrachon et Cie in France.

Outside Europe, Wal-Mart has a presence in Argentina, Brazil, Canada, China, Indonesia, Puerto Rico and Mexico—the last largely the result of buying a controlling interest in Mexican chain Cifra.

As a result of its global push, Wal-Mart's international sales for the third quarter ended Oct. 31 were up 100% from the corresponding quarter in 1998 to $5.91 billion. That's 14.6% of Wal-Mart's total $40.3 billion sales for the quarter.

—Dagmar Mussey and Jack Neff

LACK OF 'MARKETING MINDS'

In the U.S., neither Sears nor supermarket chains have seen store-brand programs deliver strong same-store sales growth. One reason, Mr. Harris says, is that retailers "don't have enough marketing minds in their building to pull it off, or they miss trends. They're suddenly relying on themselves to figure out the next big thing, and they can't."

An exception is Target Stores, which has made its private-label merchandise into fashion leaders, Mr. Harris says.

But given its more downscale clientele and down-home image, Wal-Mart doesn't have to be a fashion leader. It could succeed by being a fast follower, Mr. Harris says.

While Ol' Roy has flourished without advertising and EverStart batteries have flourished with it, Wal-Mart still hasn't shown it can build its own brands consistently. The chain abandoned its Sahara Supreme line of towels earlier this year, and its apparel and housewares labels have lagged Kmart's Martha Stewart or Target's Cherokee lines.

Moreover, in other cases such as White Cloud paper products or Faded Glory and Earth Shoe apparel, Wal-Mart has moved to mine residual equity of old brands, but hasn't proved it can build equity on its own.

ASKING FOR HELP

"[Wal-Mart is] a threat, no doubt about it," says one consultant. "But they require a lot of help in developing these brands. They aren't geared to do it. They aren't qualified to do it."

Whether the company is willing to go out and get that help remains to be seen. Though Wal-Mart solicited suggestions from its agencies for a brand name for its new detergent, it ultimately settled on extending its existing Sam's brand, using what several industry observers label as uninspired packaging.

Though he believes Sam's American Choice detergent could rack up $100 million to $150 million in sales and take share from second-tier players, Mr. Shore calls the branding effort behind it "a joke"—one that overseas consumers won't get.

Besides simply not catching on with consumers, Wal-Mart also risks damaging its highly cultivated image if something goes wrong with its private labels.

SPREADING DISTRUST

"The fire can either warm the house or burn it down," says Gordon Wade, a Cincinnati consultant and former P&G executive. "Companies like Wal-Mart don't have their own quality-control labs. They don't have their own manufacturing. And if you have a problem, one category can spread distrust within the Wal-Mart base for various Wal-Mart products."

One scare for Wal-Mart came a year ago, when the chain recalled packages of its Ol' Roy dog food in Dallas after 25 dogs died of liver damage caused by fungal toxins in food made by its supplier. Separately, Wal-Mart wrestled for years over publicity connected to charges its Kathy Lee clothing line was made by child labor overseas. Wal-Mart ended that exclusive relationship last year.

(Cont.)

RIVALS BOOST ADS

But brand marketers aren't waiting for Wal-Mart to stumble. The company's embrace of its own premium brands has been one factor that has led some players to boost advertising in hopes of surviving the onslaught.

Such vitamin brands as Rexall Sundown and Nature Made began to get their first major media advertising in the past year, in part to stem the Wal-Mart threat, Bank of America Securities' Mr. Steele says. Likewise, K-C and Georgia-Pacific have begun advertising their Scott, Angel Soft and Sparkle brands this year as Wal-Mart prepared to roll White Cloud.

Even mid-tier brands can survive at Wal-Mart if they can develop a niche or a consumer following that Wal-Mart's own brands don't serve, says John Bess, consultant with Price Waterhouse Coopers.

"Wal-Mart people are business people first," Mr. Harris says. "They are not going to do something just to cling to the precept that ours is better. If a company is doing it better than they are, they will stay with it."

44

BRAND NEW GOODS

European firms are learning from the U.S. that cultivating a brand can generate bigger profits

By Thomas K. Grose/London

A man walks into a major department store in Paris wearing Caterpillar boots, a Jack Daniels cap, Club Med shades, a Cadillac polo shirt and Marlboro jeans. He smells ruggedly of Chevrolet aftershave. He buys a set of Le Cordon Bleu cookware for his wife and a Jeep radio-CD player for himself. To pay, he flips opens his Harrods leather wallet and whips out a Jaguar Visa card. He's branded to the hilt, and the embodiment of European consumerism for the new millennium.

U.S. corporations, from General Motors to Coca-Cola to Lockheed, have garnered huge benefits from going beyond mere export trade and licensing their brands abroad to manufacturers of high-quality consumer goods, ranging from apparel to toys to foods. Licensing's allure is obvious. It offers companies new revenues that require little if any capital outlay. It's an ideal way to protect trademarks from infringers. And it's an invaluable marketing method because it can enhance a brand's image and lead it to new markets. Corporate brand licensing has grown from practically zero in the mid-1980s to a $26 billion industry worldwide. But while most of the industry is either located in the U.S. or dominated by American brands, international competition is finally heating up–especially in Europe, according to the Licensing Industry Merchandisers' Association.

A growing number of European companies, including Club Med, Harrods, Aston Martin, Pernod-Ricard and Land Rover, have taken up the licensing game and are signing agreements at a furious pace. European companies are beginning to grasp that if they don't act quickly, U.S. brands could soon completely overrun their markets with new waves of licensed goods. Even a pioneer like Coca-Cola, which has been licensing in Europe since 1986, views the continent as wide-open territory. "We feel like we've only scratched the surface in Europe," says Coke spokeswoman Susan McDermott. Equity Management, the largest U.S. licensing agency, which handles licensing chores that include research, legal work and quality control for its client corporations, gives some measure of the new American interest in landing on European soil. Most of Equity's 100 or so clients are eyeing Continental markets or have already taken the plunge. Says GM's trademark-and-copyright counsel Ken Enborg: "Europe is on the verge of a corporate brand-licensing explosion."

A similar boom hit the U.S. in the mid-1980s. Then only one U.S. company in 10 bothered with brand-extension licensing. Now 65% of FORTUNE 500 companies have licensing agreements, says Glen Konkle, Equity Management's chairman. Back then, licensing was primarily the province of Hollywood studios that owned the rights to popular cartoon and movie characters like Bugs Bunny and

> **Corporate BRAND LICENSING has grown from practically zero in the mid-1980s into a $26 billion industry worldwide**

Luke Skywalker; professional sports teams and athletes; and a few fashion designers. But companies like GM had begun to realize that many of their brands had additional value.

Even in those days, GM was spending $2 million to $3 million a year to fight trademark-infringement cases on the periphery of its main line of business, trying to rid the market of unauthorized Chevy baseball caps and Corvette T shirts that were obviously striking a chord with consumers. That's when it hit Enborg that it would be easier–and more profitable–for the automaker to meet the obvious market demand for those goods itself by licensing its brand names to handpicked manufacturers. Today, GM has more than 1,200 licensing agreements generating annual revenues of $1.1 billion. They cover everything from clothes to colognes.

One of the high-profile tycoons looking to follow the American example is Mohamed Al Fayed, owner of Harrods, London's famous department store, who says he wants to copy the success of American licensed goods like the Jaguar Collection and Calvin Klein that are sold in his store. "The American brands really have no assets apart from their names, which they put on other products and designs," he says. "I want to follow that example." This November, Harrods' lines of premium-priced fine jewelry, watches, fragrances, leather goods, foods and linens will be available to consumers. "There is unlimited value in the name Harrods," Al Fayed says. Harrods and Club Med have hired executives with American licensing experience to oversee their efforts.

Jaguar, the British luxury automaker, is one of the godfathers of European licensing, but it is also just beginning a new wave of expansion. Jaguar began with a line of designer eyeglass frames 15 years ago. Today its licenses cover such products as clothes, fragrances and footwear. The company has just opened mall boutiques in the U.S., France and the Netherlands.

"It is a way to let others pay for all the things you'd like to do [with the brand] but your shareholders won't pay for," says John Maries, general manager of the Jaguar Collection. For even smaller but ultra-exclusive companies, like sports-car maker Aston Martin, licensed products can help boost a low profile. Aston Martin has only recently launched its licensing program. And, befitting the producer of a car made famous by James Bond, it's sticking with toys for big boys. Its two initial products are expensive model cars and a Sony video game.

Successful brand-extension licensing operations look easy, but they require foresight and thought. "It shouldn't be misconstrued by companies as a freebie," says Equity Management's Konkle. Every brand has a "core equity," which is its image–what it stands for in the minds of consumers. Is it a premium brand? Does it signal value? What image does it conjure up? "You can't just put out a doodad with a name slapped on it," insists Michael Stone, co-director of New York's Beanstalk Group, another large licensing agency. Missteps abound among those who have held that simplistic view. Take Virgin Clothes: British entrepreneur Richard Branson has successfully etched his Virgin trademark onto a host of products, from CDs to cola. But his apparel line is struggling, mainly because its initial styles were pricey and somewhat conservative, which went against the trendy and value-conscious image originally established by the airline Virgin Atlantic.

Then there are the challenges involved in homing in on your target audience. Though Europe clearly offers new licensing opportunities for its own firms and foreign ones, it still cannot be viewed as one big market of 370 million undifferentiated consumers. Cultural and language barriers are very much a factor in consumer choice. And some brand images vary from country to country. BMW cars, for instance, aren't considered to be particularly top of the line in Germany, but are considered luxury cars in much of the rest of the world. Rovers are commonplace in Britain, but they are seen as classy foreign imports in Southern Europe. There is not even pan-European agreement on what constitutes quality. A T shirt made from a cotton-polyester blend may suit a British shopper, but French and German consumers want 100% cotton T shirts only, please. Licensing executive Gianfranco Mari, head of the agency DIC 2 in Milan, underlines that "what sells in Italy may not sell in France." Then there is the tangle of various legal requirements and trademark laws in each nation, which the European Union has not exterminated. "Those laws can keep the lawyers happy for years," says Jaguar's Maries.

Perhaps the biggest hurdle to overcome in Europe is retailer reluctance. In the past, licensed goods from fellow European companies were often cheap promotional giveaways, so many retailers view licensed products as a form of advertising that doesn't belong on their shelves. That puts the onus on marketers to convince retailers that most of today's licensed products are well-made goods associated with top brands. It's a slow slog. But, says David Isaacs, Equity Management's international director, "it can be done."

Given the new onslaught of licensed goods heading their way, European retailers may have little choice but to change their view. Consumers, after all, like the stuff. As American-style retailing continues to take hold in Europe, shopkeepers are beginning to chant another U.S. mantra: the customer is always right–especially when wielding branded credit cards.

45

Color me popular: Marketers shape up packaging

By Theresa Howard
USA Today

NEW YORK — It is known as the last 5 seconds of advertising, and its aim is to propel a product across the threshold from shelf to shopping cart.

It is package design, and it has become an increasingly important means of product differentiation.

Color, shape and texture offer subtle but tangible cues that don't make it across the airwaves in a commercial. Done well, they make an emotional link to a consumer at the point of purchase, that vulnerable spot where about 70% of purchase decisions are made.

"Product design is one of a few key differentiators you can have" in categories with similar products, says Ed Rice, senior executive director with brand identity and design firm Landor Associates. Maybe that's why just the design of packaging represents a business with more than $100 billion in annual billings and sales.

Some recent innovations:

▶ Grown-up versions of Chiclets under such brand names as Dentyne Ice or Eclipse fetch more, as much as 79 cents a pack, thanks to shiny foil pop-out packaging that highlights stronger flavors.

▶ A redesign of the Salon Selectives shampoo and conditioner line by Helene Curtis elevates the mass-marketed brand to salon-brand status with contemporary colors and names such as "Rain."

▶ Gatorade gets a tighter grip on its market with an ergonomically designed bottle that fits in your hand and mouth.

▶ Lipton Iced Tea makes a break-through with a bottle that fits into a cup holder.

▶ Hidden Valley Ranch turns design upside down with its "Easy Squeeze" inverted bottle.

"More and more marketers are making use of shape and color," says Jim Peters, editor of *BrandPackaging* magazine. Why? The sheer number of products in the marketplace.

Think of those pretty colors and curves as defense mechanisms in response to selection overload.

"We are in an age where there is just a glut of stuff out there," Peters adds. "There are more choices of hand wash and shampoo out there than people can deal with on a rational basis." When making a purchase, "a consumer is in an emotional vs. a rational mode."

Beverage companies have long used packaging as a way to stand out. The spirits industry set a standard for using packaging for brand differentiation. Absolut Vodka built a global brand on the shape of a bottle.

But Coca-Cola was the pioneer in making use of a unique design with its trademark bottle.

While beverage marketers led the way, other industries have followed.

FORM VS. FUNCTION

Gatorade's new EDGE bottle, on sale in some markets, will be available nationally by April.

"It's all about that moment," says Mary Dillon, Gatorade's vice president of product offerings and new brand development. "Consumers take 4 seconds to make that decision, so you really need a package that speaks to them."

EDGE is an acronym for the purported benefits: Ergonomically Designed Gatorade Experience. What makes the bottle special? A resealable top and an "optimal grip, so it fits in your hand really well," Dillon says. "You can throw it on the ground, and it doesn't spill." Among the design considerations: flow rate, lip shape, bottle size.

Yogurt also is getting a new look. The squeezable yogurt category has grown into a business posting $100 million a year in sales. New Hampshire-based Stonyfield Farm seeks its share with its YoSqueeze brand targeted at active youths.

"Packaging-wise, it's great," says MaryJo Viederman, a spokeswoman for Stonyfield Farm. "One of the biggest innovations of the packaging is that it brings yogurt into a bigger part of daily lives. You can eat it in a car or serve it in a lunchbox, and it doesn't require a spoon.

"You can't just add another flavor cup and get space," she adds. "But it has been great for us."

IT'S ALL IN THE LOOK

A gum in any other wrapper wouldn't taste as good. Look at Adams' Dentyne Ice and Wrigley's Eclipse gums, two leaders in the adult gum category. The look says both premium and functional. A 12-piece pack features individual pockets for each piece and a shiny foil overlay (otherwise known as a blister pack). In the four years since its introduction, Adams has moved Dentyne Ice into the top spot with older chewers.

"We have experienced tremendous growth in 2000," says Heidi Dvorkin, senior product manager. "Consumption is up by 48% in volume, and we became No. 3 in the $1.9 billion gum category overall and the No. 1 brand in the breath-freshening category."

Eyeball intrigue

Shelf space is a premium in the retail market, and marketers want as much as they can get for a strong visual effect. But gaining shelf footage means nothing if the product doesn't scream, "Buy me!"

General Foods recently revamped packaging for its International Coffees with help from design specialist The Sterling Group.

In the course of the redesign, the company considered 50 options. The one thing ruled out was retiring the tin pack. With the new look came the addition of a cappuccino line.

"We wanted to optimize the shelf presence and branding so that when customers go to the shelves, they can identify the products easily," says Doug Weekes, category business director for the Kraft unit of General Foods.

"In that aisle, there is still some decision being made at the shelf."

But new designs must be true to the brand image, he warns.

"It is extremely important to be consistent about how you treat your brand and introduce new flavors."

46

Online sales pack a crunch

New products are shaking up shipping plans

By Elizabeth Weise
USA TODAY

Electronic commerce is radically changing the kind of products we buy and expect to have on our doorstep a day or two later. It's not just sweaters from Sears, beef jerky from Hickory Farms, and apples from Harry and David anymore.

Instead, odd-shaped packages containing saws from Amazon's home-improvement section, shovels from Smith & Hawken and bags of specialty potato chips are bumping their way down conveyer belts at FedEx, UPS and Airborne Express.

And that is creating the need for a whole new kind of packaging.

"We're seeing items that would typically not be shipped as small parcels being shipped that way," says Chad Thompson, manager of the UPS package lab in Hodgkins, Ill.

Add a few hundred thousand steaks, pickaxes, orchids and live fish into the mix of the 300 million packages UPS expects to ship in the four weeks leading up to Christmas and the 75 million FedEx will ship "air express," and it's easy to understand why more is involved than packing tape, wadded newspapers and whatever cardboard box happens to be lying around.

Given the ever-increasing volumes they're dealing with, shippers take extraordinary measures to ensure every box arrives intact. A broken box or leaking carton is time-consuming and money-losing: Everything has to stop while a worker retrieves the item, puts it in a plastic bag and reroutes it down the "exceptions" chute, where it ends up in the rewrap area.

To that end, both FedEx and UPS offer free packaging design consultations. At FedEx's Memphis lab, the engineers show off their computer-aided box-cutting machine like kids with a new toy.

The huge Kongsberg cutter dominates the engineering section. It looks a bit like a giant air hockey table: clear plexiglass with hundreds of tiny holes. Air is sucked out, pulling the cardboard flat against the table for the cut.

Engineer Tom Wood uses Laserpoint Page Design software, which offers many basic box designs. He types in dimensions and other choices: tab-closed or telescoping, long and narrow or short and squat.

The design is saved to a floppy disk, which Wood then pops into the Kongsberg. He takes a large, flat piece of cardboard from shelves that hold sheets of every thickness.

The machine first checks to make sure there's enough cardboard for the box: a spinning knife swiftly traces its outlines, cutting out some pieces, creasing others. It takes only a minute to complete.

Wood springs forward, pulls the cardboard out and quickly pokes out the excess pieces. He's left with an ungainly, flapping length of cardboard. He folds and turns it like pizza dough until the flat sheet is transformed into a neat little box with a self-closing lid.

> **FedEx has designed special packaging for shipping laptop computers.**

Companies are invited to send FedEx prototype cartons for testing. Senior packaging design specialist Pati Person carefully cuts open the outer carton to reveal inner cartons full of such things as live plants.

Cardboard a few millimeters thick is all that stands between the timidly waving branches and a House of Horrors of testing equipment. Two giant plates compress a package to determine its crush point, and a drop tester spills all eight corners on concrete to test sturdiness.

A vibration tester creates a mini-earthquake, simulating a truck running through city streets. It then ramps up to mimic a jet plane in flight. Once the "plane" has landed, the platform goes back into truck mode, "driving" the package to its recipient.

Boxes also are tested under real-world conditions. To ensure goods survive shipping, testers routinely slip small microprocessors into boxes to record data such as vibration and temperature changes.

"We can determine from the data whether the package was dropped, thrown or mishandled," packaging lab manager Larry Rutledge says.

All of that is necessary because, if what the customer ordered doesn't show up on time and in perfect condition, a million-dollar marketing campaign is meaningless.

Online merchants "don't have a store, so when

(Cont.)

that package arrives at the customer's doorstep, it's almost the first real, tangible encounter with the company," Thompson says.

As more kinds of stores go online, the items being shipped become more complicated. One company he works with is an online hardware superstore.

"You're talking shovels and rakes, hammers and axes, saw blades," Thompson says. Long-haul freight companies have always shipped by wooden, forklift pallet, but single orders to customers are a different story.

Companies also must prevent sharp implements from flying down conveyer belts and satisfy customers who want shovels to look nice on arrival.

UPS ended up developing protective packaging to blunt sharp edges and created a plastic bag to wrap it in because the paper ones ripped right off.

A few years ago FedEx engineers learned manufacturers were seeing millions of dollars in damage when laptop PCs were shipped for repairs.

FedEx designers developed a special cardboard box with a taut plastic trampoline in the middle. The laptop lies flat between two such pieces, riding in its own plastic hammock, protected from shocks.

"This can be dropped from 3 feet, and it won't be damaged," Rutledge proudly says. "We've had $2 million savings in damage claims."

Another challenge was getting live plants to survive a bumpy, shaky, hot, cold and often very dry trip of 24 to 48 hours to their new homes. Last year FedEx won an award for a seedling package using die-cut cardboard to form four inner holders that stabilize and protect seedling trays on their way to gardeners.

Then there's food. It has to move quickly, stay cold and arrive in one piece. Take the steps involved in shipping cheesecakes, a popular New York and Chicago specialty.

First, they must be frozen solid so they don't "deform" during shipping. Packed in a plastic container to protect them from crushing, they're placed in a Styrofoam cooler box, often with "dunnage" (filler) to keep them from shifting. The entire box is pre-chilled.

Dry ice pellets or frozen gel packs are placed around the box, which goes into another box made of heavy-duty waxed cardboard. This will keep just about anything cold enough to arrive in a cool and sanitary condition within 24 hours.

Even something as simple as dry ice requires serious engineering and chemical expertise or it could kill everyone on a cargo jet. Dry ice, frozen carbon dioxide, is the coolant of choice because of its extremely low temperature – minus-109 degrees Fahrenheit.

But as it warms, the gas displaces oxygen – a serious problem in a confined space. Omaha Steaks ships 2 million filet mignons in 9 million pounds of dry ice from mid-November to late December.

"When we unload the trucks, we have to use fans to blow air into them and swap out the workers pretty often so we make sure they're getting enough oxygen," Rutledge says.

It's harder to step outside for fresh air in the cockpit of a cargo plane, which is why FAA regulations require shippers to track how much dry ice is on board and ensure that it doesn't exceed safety cutoffs. Otherwise, "you'd slowly black out and not even know it was happening," Rutledge says.

Then there's the case of the exploding bags of tortilla chips. UPS' Thompson was approached by a company that was shipping individual bags of them. Chips don't mind getting bumped around, but vibration can lead to a bag of crumbs, and compression could lead to one big, flat tortilla sandwich, not exactly what you want to serve guests at a party.

A series of cardboard dividers takes care of external damage. But there's the problem of the explosions: Bags are normally sealed in factories near sea level, meaning air inside them is at sea-level pressure. But in the small planes used to fly to remote locations, cargo areas usually aren't pressurized. So the air inside the bag is suddenly at 13,000 feet, an extreme difference.

"When it's unpressurized . . . these bags can blow up like balloons until maybe they burst their seams or even bulge the box out," Thompson says. Researchers are still working on a high-altitude chip bag.

47

Why Dow Chemical Finds Slime Sublime

From Monster Slobber to Soup, Some Gooey Stuff Named Methocel Has Many Uses

By Susan Warren

Staff Reporter of The Wall Street Journal

MIDLAND, Mich. – Don Coffey is serious about slime.

Recently, the 46-year-old Dow Chemical Co. scientist mixed up a batch of his newest variety – the kind of slippery, gooey stuff usually found in buckets at Halloween – and plopped a hockey-puck-size glob down on a plate. As it lay jiggling, Mr. Coffey plunged his face in the goo and snarfed it down.

"Have you ever eaten Jell-O without a spoon?" he asks.

For 15 years, Dr. Coffey has devoted his career to slime, convincing food companies that Dow's concoction should be an indispensable part of their recipes. From a handful of products originally, Dow has managed to slip slime into more than 400 foods, from frozen pot pies to whipped toppings, as well as pills, paints, shampoos and special effects for movies.

These days at Dow, slime rocks. Chief Executive William Stavropoulos boasts that the stuff, marketed under the name Methocel, is the premier product in its specialty chemicals and plastics portfolio.

But slime wasn't always so cool. Twice since Methocel's birth 60 years ago, Dow was ready to kill the product. Even its creation is said to have been a laboratory mistake.

In the 1930s, scientists at Dow and elsewhere were experimenting with wood to create a more durable material. By grinding wood into a pulp and then washing it with chemicals to break it down, they were able to create ethyl cellulose, a product used to make the first plastic wrap. It came in handy for things like canteen linings during World War II.

But, as Dow lore has it, someone at the plant goofed one day, tacking an extra carbon atom onto the molecule. The result: an oozing goo called methyl cellulose, an obscure substance previously discovered in Europe. While scientists were excited by the find, Dow managers dismissed the slop as a disgusting disaster. Methocel was quickly sidelined when cheaper, more versatile petrochemical-based plastics came on the scene.

The product gradually found a home as a thickener for tile putty and drywall mud. But business was lousy, and in the mid-1980s, Dow considered selling. With no takers,

though, Dow resorted to trying to save it, slashing costs, raising prices and looking for ways to expand the market.

As a newly minted Ph.D. in food science, Dr. Coffey was recruited to cook up new recipes for Methocel. To the youthful scientist, what was sublime about slime was that, chemically speaking, it is "bass-ackwards." Most plastics get thinner when heated. But Methocel had a unique sticky layer that breaks free when the molecules are heated; the molecules bond together to form a gel with a consistency like cooked egg whites. As it cools, the stuff thins out again into an oozing slime.

Dr. Coffey saw immediately that the tasteless, odorless and calorie-free ingredient, already used in a few foods, could be expanded to thicken soups, sauces and gravies. Added to foods, the stuff has a smooth, buttery texture, compared with the sometimes pasty feel of starch-based thickeners. Though chemicals are used in the manufacturing process, the end product is all-natural wood cellulose.

After trying out recipes in his lab, Dr. Coffey hit the road to convince customers. But food companies were perfectly happy with the corn or potato starches they had been using for 100 years. Besides, food-grade Methocel costs $5 a pound, compared with about 50 cents a pound for starches, though only one-tenth as much Methocel will do the same job.

Dr. Coffey met with a wall of skepticism. On one winter sales call to a Midwestern food company, the customer didn't believe that Methocel would do everything he said it would. He and a salesman were hustled out so quickly, he says, "I'm surprised we didn't end up head-first in a snow bank."

Gradually, some food companies began trying the goo for items like soups and puddings. But most sales still went to industrial and construction product makers. Dow, a chemicals giant specializing in basic petrochemicals, wasn't sure what to do with its slimy throwback to the pre-plastic era.

In the early 1990s, Methocel found itself again on the chopping block. "We still debated whether it had been as successful as it could be," says Michael Parker, an executive vice president then charged with taking a hard look at Dow's less-stellar businesses.

Dr. Coffey, an energetic man with a fondness for food-themed neckties, had a plan. Methocel could be a big player in Dow's expanding specialty businesses, he figured – if only he had a team of food scientists. To win over the food industry, "you need to be able to help them figure out why the cheese sauce is lumpy," he says.

His passionate pitch made superiors worry that there wasn't enough substance to back it up. "The tendency was not to take him seriously," says Gerald Doyle, now the global business director for Methocel.

But the day before Halloween in 1993, Mr. Parker gave slime a reprieve. Dr. Coffey

OOZE NEWS

A few of the hundreds of products that use methylcellulose:

- Wampa drool in 'The Empire Strikes Back'
- Dinosaur sneeze in 'Jurassic Park'
- Twinkies (the filling)
- Lean Pockets
- Citrucel laxative
- Burger King onion rings
- Hidden Valley Ranch salad dressings
- Marie Callender pot pies
- Progresso soups
- Coated medicine tablets and capsules
- Veggie burgers
- Imitation meat
- Breaded frozen vegetables

Source: Dow Chemical

immediately hired three Ph.D.s.

Today, the Methocel division employs 300 people, including 14 food scientists. It boasts double-digit sales growth and produces more than 200 different products. Methocel has been used as monster slobber in "Star Wars" movies and took the title role in the remake of "The Blob." Museums use it as a kind of mud mask to clean artwork, and pharmaceutical companies use it for time-release medicines and coated capsules.

As director of the Methocel food business, Dr. Coffey believes slime's brightest future is on the grocery shelf – though many customers aren't eager to boast about it. Some companies worry about revealing a chemical component in their food products (no matter its natural origins and safe reputation). Others companies want to keep a key ingredient secret. Though Methocel must be listed on the ingredients label, often as methylcellulose, it can also be disguised simply as "vegetable gums."

Incognito or not, Methocel makes cheese

cheesier, gravy creamier and fillings fruitier, says one frozen-food manufacturer who declined to be named. Without it, says a company representative, "you'd have something that was either too soft or too hard or too mushy."

And more food uses keep coming. In his lab near Dow headquarters here, Dr. Coffey, sporting a bacon-and-egg necktie, hovers around lab manager Linda Steinke as she coats pepperoni bits with Methocel powder. Makers of frozen pizza snacks have had problems with oozing grease. As pepperoni heats up in the oven, the Methocel absorbs the grease as it gels.

In another corner of the lab, similar work is being done with pot pies for a manufacturer who wants to reduce "boilover."

The newest Methocel product, dubbed Supergel, can be a substitute for egg whites, working as a sort of food glue to bind vegetable patties together. That appeals to vegans who shun animal proteins. "This is the youngest 60-year-old product out there," Dr. Coffey insists.

It may also be one of Dow's most fun. By filling a surgical glove with Methocel, tinting it greenish-yellow and boiling the mess, lab workers can create a ghastly, gelled appendage. New recruits in the lab have been known to find one sitting in their chairs, slowly melting.

One of the favorite stops on Dow visitor tours is "Slime Time," where school kids can add a pinch of Methocel powder to water to make their own goo. And squeezing it through fingers has its own distinct charm. On some Halloweens, Dr. Coffey buries quarters in a bucket of the stuff and lets kids dig for them.

"Then you can rub it in your hair and make your hair stand up," he says gleefully.

Through it all, Dr. Coffey never stops selling. At a recent presentation to customer service employees, he made his overhead transparencies out of thin layers of Methocel. At the end of the talk, he challenged Mr. Doyle, the global business director, to eat one of the crinkly, ink-stained sheets.

Mr. Doyle politely declined. So Dr. Coffey wolfed it down himself. "You only have one chance to hammer home a few points," he says. "And one of them is that it's OK to eat this. And as a matter of fact, you're *supposed* to eat this."

48

Shelf Life Is Short For Innovations: How To Speed Products To Market

By James DeTar
Investor's Business Daily

Pepsi Bottling Group Inc. plotted the launch of the Sierra Mist lemon-lime soft drink as though it were a wartime invasion.

The bottler mobilized all 20,000 of its salespeople and all route drivers involved. The sales agents got marching orders to prepare such clients as convenience and grocery stores. They loaded point-of-sale displays with free samples.

"We executed on a single Saturday last October," Chief Executive Craig Weatherup said. "We had every single truck, about 10,000 routes, loaded with only one product on that Saturday—Sierra Mist."

In a little more than 24 hours, it accomplished its mission: national distribution of the new drink. It's that kind of execution that allowed the Somers, N.Y., company's stock to nearly double to the low 40s from two years ago, when it went public at 23.

Like other successful companies, Pepsi Bottling knows the value of a smooth, fast product launch. In a changing economy, new products are crucial to growth and profits. And rivals always are eyeing the same opportunities.

Missing a market window can be painful. "It can mean lost customers, lower earnings—read: lower stock price—and becoming a follower, rather than a market leader," said Jim Biolos, president of consulting firm Launch Publishing in New York.

By following some basic rules, firms can cut the time it takes to bring a new product to market, experts say.

First, identify customers' needs. Define, design and test the product. Make sure everyone in the company supports it.

Next, make sure all parts for the product are available in ample quantity. Whether manufacturing is done in-house or by someone else, bring production into the process early on.

Keep lines of communication open internally and with suppliers, outside advertising and public relations and customers. Finally, coordinate all resources for the launch.

The best players are ready to adjust if their plan go awry.

In September, Lisle, Ill.-based network equipment maker Tellabs Inc. was rolling out a new version of its flagship line. The Titan 5500 gear manages and routes traffic on networks. Customers said they needed a product that could manage twice the 500,000 Internet connections handled by the prior version.

When Vice President Rob Pullen got word that the company's software wasn't working in test, his heart sank. He pulled a key software engineer from another project.

Define Problems

"The key was defining the constraint, finding the right person to determine the root cause, prioritizing the project and executing against the fixes," he said.

The new 5500 FP 7.0 made its debut in December, ahead of schedule.

Pullen says one reason Tellabs grew to $3.4 billion revenue in 2000 from $321 million in 1993 was its new-product rollout plan.

First, its marketing people look at customer needs, technology trends and standards. They meet with customers to understand their problems. Then Tellabs' top brass puts together a cross-functional group from engineering, manufacturing and marketing to define the product.

"Then it passes a business case review by our management team, including me," Pullen said. "Then we make a 'go' or 'no-go' decision. Once a go decision to launch is made, we put it into development."

All during this time, the core team prepares the rest of the company to deliver the product. They train the sales staff and installers and set up billing.

No Time To Waste

Researcher James Biolos says a few simple steps can help companies get products to market faster:

1 Ask yourself: Is the product completely new?

- New-product rollouts are complex. Use a strong team of experienced, high-level managers. Define a crystal-clear product concept. Set milestones to keep the project on track.

- New versions of existing products come to market fastest when championed by a lower-level manager. The process tends to be better organized. What's needed is elbow grease, not high-level strategy.

---

2 Quantify the benefits of speed

- Do research on how much more money the company can make if it gets to market earlier.

- Share this information with others. When potential benefits are known, people focus on the project.

- Be open to change. Research may show there's no benefit to getting the product out faster. The cost may exceed possible gains.

---

3 Get just enough money

- Find out how much profit margin is required, and what price you can charge for each product.

- After determining the cost to develop the product, set a budget in stone. But revisit the budget if a lot of new information comes in.

- Make sure the budget isn't too big. Large companies tend to inject too much capital into new products. If the research is accurate, the budget should fit the project.

Source: Launch Publishing

(Cont.)

Tellabs last year asked a consultant to help it set up better benchmarks to measure time to market. It decided to boost its standards.

"We tied individual compensation to it from the executive level on down," Pullen said. "Then we picked strong team leaders. We found experienced people are key to success."

As a result, he says, Tellabs cut its new-product time to market 30% last year.

Pepsi Bottling's Weatherup cites two reasons to cut time to market.

"In most instances, it's a competitive pre-emption before our competition has time to react," he said. "Second, it allows you to better coordinate resources, to get national in a week or in a month instead of 18 months. Whether it's people or media dollars, it's more efficient."

With about $8 billion in sales, Pepsi Bottling Group is the No. 1 distributor of soft drinks for its former parent, Pepsi Co Inc.

EMC Corp. also focuses on time to market. The Hopkinton, Mass., company sells large disk-drive systems. It had the greatest earning growth and stock-price gain of any U.S. company in the past 10 years.

Harness Teamwork

Getting to market first with new product features has been key, says Frank Hauck, vice president of products and offerings.

"The minute we decide to build a new product, we create a product management team," Hauck said. "That team oversees all functions of the project. It shepherds it all the way from idea to shipment."

The group starts out meeting several times a week to coordinate things like the product rollout date, sales force training and the transfer from development to manufacturing. By the time the product is unveiled, he says, the group is meeting several times a day.

49

Crunch Points

Product Development Is Always Difficult; Consider the Frito Pie

7-Eleven and Partner PepsiCo Took a Year to Concoct The Corn-Chip Casserole

The Hurdle: Bag vs. No Bag

By EMILY NELSON

Staff Reporter of THE WALL STREET JOURNAL

DALLAS – Cigarettes and Slurpees are one thing. But 7-Eleven wants to serve dinner, too.

Jim Keyes, chief operating officer of 7-Eleven Inc., thinks America can stomach the idea. Which is why the nation's largest convenience-store chain is not only pushing soft drinks and snacks as never before, but also is challenging fast-food restaurants for the palates of the legions of people who love their cars, love to eat and love to eat in their cars – the people Mr. Keyes calls dashboard diners.

"We're on a journey from the place where you buy hot dogs," he says.

The journey began in 1997, when 7-Eleven began rolling out – literally, in some instances – a line of foods that are as much a main course as they are a munchy: a simple submarine sandwich with a plastic tray for catching crumbs; a Burger Big Bite, molded in the shape of a hot dog, for one-handed eating; the similarly tubular El Taco; a line of Bakery Stix, hollow breadsticks stuffed with meat, cheese and other fillings; and so on.

The expanding menu, managers say, will broaden the appeal of the chain's 5,200 U.S. stores beyond the core "beer and butts crowd." It can only help that at many fast-food restaurants these days, "it's a park-through, not a drive-through," Mr. Keyes says. "We're faster."

Maybe. But the effort that goes into developing hand-held meals is hardly fast. In early 1998, Mr. Keyes ordered up another course: a meal of corn chips, chili and

cheese, all tumbled together into a nachos-style casserole. Only now, 14 months later, is the company's $1.99 "fresh" version available in a 25-store test market.

In the interim, managers, engineers, packaging specialists and others from 7-Eleven and its partner in the project, PepsiCo Inc. and its Frito-Lay snack-foods division, engaged in a process far more complicated than the simple result would suggest. This is the story of the birth of 7-Eleven's Frito pie.

* * *

It's spring 1998, and Jim Keyes has just been promoted to chief operating officer of 7-Eleven from chief financial officer. Several dashboard delicacies are on the market, others are in the pipeline, but 7-Eleven is in a funk. Half the goods in the average 7-Eleven store aren't selling at all each month. While the company is doing a huge business in Slurpees and Big Gulps, the average customer is spending just $3 a visit, and only one of every eight customers who buys a drink also buys a snack.

"That's why fresh food is so central to our future success," Mr. Keyes says. "It will change the way people see 7-Eleven."

But he also figures that customers need foods midway between snack and supper, much like subs and cylindrical burgers, to ease them toward accepting full-blown meals from 7-Eleven. "Even if we put out the best entree to take home, you'd hesitate about that today because we're not known for that," Mr.

Jim Keyes

Keyes says. The Frito pie "is a step as we get there." It also could form the linchpin of an entire line of chips-and-dip entrees that he and other 7-Eleven planners envision.

The Frito pie seems perfectly suited for the role. It's easy, quick and already popular. According to Frito-Lay lore, Daisy Dean Doolin, mother of Elmer Doolin, founder of the original Frito company, concocted the first Frito pie in the kitchen of her San Antonio home in 1932 – an attempt to turn leftover chili into something more. Whatever the origins, the pie had made its way to lunch counters and drive-ins by the 1950s. Now, it is popular across a wide swath of middle America, prepared by the consumer, or bought at mall food courts and the like. Some purists simply pour the fixings into a bag of Fritos and shake.

Mr. Keyes has something a little more presentable in mind when he takes his idea to Al Carey, PepsiCo's senior vice president of sales and retailer strategies. Mr. Carey is a casual

friend whose company is a major supplier of 7-Eleven. Mr. Carey and other PepsiCo executives like what they hear. More-substantial 7-Eleven foods might solve a nagging riddle for PepsiCo: People who eat snacks and soda together seldom buy the two together, whether at 7-Eleven or elsewhere. Putting PepsiCo drinks and Frito-Lay-based entrees side-by-side might boost sales of both.

Within two months, 7-Eleven and Frito-Lay are ready to start work. On June 25, 1998, the Frito-Lay team drives to 7-Eleven's Dallas headquarters from Frito Lay headquarters in Plano. With the group are two chefs hired from a Springfield, Mo., food-marketing agency, Noble & Associates.

Heading up the 7-Eleven side is Sharon Powell, a 20-year company veteran who was promoted to vice president of fresh foods merchandising specifically to develop dashboard dinners. She has been deeply involved in developing smoothies and kiwi-strawberry Slurpees, among other products, and is overseeing a redesign of 7-Eleven stores to give greater prominence to the new foods.

The 10 participants swap business cards and joke about the sweltering heat outside. Then Ms. Powell starts. In the next month, she says, 7-Eleven will be packaging sandwiches with bags of Frito-Lay chips. Now, she says, she envisions a cup of chili and a package of shredded cheese, sold along with bags of Fritos. Eventually, she says, 7-Eleven stores will be stocked with racks of Frito pies, Tostitos nachos and other chips-and-dip dishes.

"We don't know what's possible, but we're ready to explore the options," she says, her formal suit and official demeanor contrasting with the more casual Frito-Lay managers, dressed in khakis and polo shirts.

The Frito-Lay managers and Noble chefs have spent the morning touring 7-Eleven's food-preparation facility in Lewisville, a Dallas suburb. Tim Petsch, a senior account supervisor from Noble who designs recipes for food manufacturers, is excited about the potential of the refried beans and other fixings he saw there – enough for Noble to use to create "a winning food brand," he says. Others chime in with their favorite chips-and-dip combos.

"Are you thinking of trying soup tureens in the stores?" asks Kathy Bassininski, a Frito-Lay senior product manager.

"We tried soup last year," Ms. Powell says, "and it was a fiasco." Among other things, it requires too much attention from store clerks.

As the discussion moves to cilantro and chipotle, Ms. Powell grows impatient. A 7-Eleven customer, she says, is "willing to put ketchup on my hot dog but not much more."

Ms. Powell assures the Frito-Lay team that 7-Eleven wants to move quickly. They break up, agreeing only to meet soon.

A month passes.

On July 29, the two teams gather below 7-Eleven headquarters in a labyrinthine basement of test kitchens. On shelves in glass-fronted cabinets sit plastic beakers of smoothies, bags of shredded cheese, jars of honey mustard. Counters are strewn with plastic cups, trays and lids in all shapes and sizes – including 7-Eleven's new Slurpee cup, clear plastic partitioned down the middle so patrons can buy two flavors at a time. In a room nearby, a group huddles around a woman in a white coat as she slices turkey. In another room, tasters sample Slurpee innovations.

The Noble people have brought a brightly labeled packet stamped "Deli Central Fresh Today" and a list of "menu concepts." Suggestions include a Southwest chicken sub – "succulent grilled chicken breast topped with aged provolone cheese, crisp bacon, shredded lettuce, grilled onions and Tostitos medium salsa on fresh baked bread." Further down appear "Frito-Lay Lunches," which will "offer the taste 7-Eleven patrons trust in a variety of menu choices." Among the entrants is a "FRITO pie with FRITOS Corn Chips."

Noble's Mr. Petsch suggests strategies for advertising and promoting fresh food – for instance, distributing punch cards that allow customers to collect a free meal after buying a certain number. Customers find that boring, the 7-Eleven people say. Joe Horres, 7-Eleven's category manager for grilled foods, pipes in that he already is looking for plastic trays to hold the chips and fixings for the Frito pie. For two hours, menus and marketing dominate. No one mentions pie.

"I want to go back to the original request to have Fritos next to a dip in a case," Ms. Powell says. "But you guys don't seem to be there. So I need to know, is this not the way to do it?"

The room falls quiet. The Frito-Lay managers look to Ms. Bassininski, their product manager. "If you put loose chips in a plastic tray with dip in a well," she says matter-of-factly, "the chips will absorb the dip." Exposed to air for mere minutes, chips lose their crunch. Doused with sauce, they turn to mush. "Today, we can't take anything open where it will share air," she says.

"I knew there was a reason you were leading away from this," Ms. Powell says. Mr. Keyes, 7-Eleven's COO, wants fresh Frito pie, not something in a bag. "This is leading away from his vision," she says.

The planners disperse into the Texas heat, unaware that they have come up against the greatest threat to success: Frito-Lay's concern for the integrity of its chips conflicts with Mr. Keyes's desire to sell foods that appear freshly made. "We are a packaged-goods company," says Harry Walsh, then head of Pepsi soft-drink sales to 7-Eleven. "The consumers are used to getting this," he says, waving a bag of Ruffles potato chips. "They're confident in the bag."

The issue was foreshadowed in 1996, when 7-Eleven began selling nachos – really just trays of Frito-Lay Tostitos and generic cheese sauce. So many chips were broken as workers dumped chips into trays that one worker was busy full-time just emptying

Harry Walsh,
PepsiCo vice president, 7-Eleven team leader:
Consumers, he says, "are confident in the bag," but he nonetheless is willing to consider letting the chips loose for the Frito pie. "This is one of those things we'll try," he says.

garbage pails of tortilla shards. 7-Eleven store managers complained that even more chips shattered during delivery. After a month, the project was halted.

Still, PepsiCo wants to please 7-Eleven, a major customer that can push Pepsi's "Star Wars" promotions and help launch new products such as Pepsi One, a diet soda. But it isn't accustomed to designing products to meet a retailer's whim. "This is so different for us," Mr. Walsh says. "We're consumer driven."

As summer of 1998 slides toward fall, the chips and how they will be packaged in the Frito pie become the central debate. Chips in separate bags? Chips loose in trays, with sealed chili cups and bags of shredded cheese? Bags of chips with sealed cups of chili and cheese combined, all sealed in a tray? Ms. Powell's frustration grows. "They don't get that it has to be out of the bag," she says.

Meanwhile, Mr. Horres, the 7-Eleven grilled-foods manager, is doing his part. A 29-year 7-Eleven veteran who opened the chain's first stores in Australia and Taiwan, he contributed early to the dashboard-dining program by helping to launch the Bacon Cheeseburger Big Bite. The original Burger Big Bite had hit stores nationwide in spring 1997; it soon became clear that the meat tended to dry out and stick to the grill,

Joe Horres,
7-Eleven manager of grilled foods:
Since the Bacon Cheese-burger Bite, he feels pressured to keep rolling out dashboard dinners. "That's why my hair's gray," he says.

prompting adjustments to flavoring and moisture content. Later that year, Mr. Horres was among those who handled the transition to the bacon cheeseburger variation, which sold better in test marketing.

Now, Mr. Keyes is pressuring Mr. Horres to speed the Frito pie. Hot dishes sell best in cooler weather. Worrying about the Texas summers, Mr. Horres wants a small trial run by March 1999. Moreover, the sooner 7-Eleven can finish the Frito pie, the sooner it can add other chips-and-dips.

Mr. Horres calls a meeting. In a windowless conference room at Frito-Lay headquarters in November, he tells the group that they must get a test product in Dallas stores by March 1 so "the heat will be off me." He

Sharon Powell,
7-Eleven vice president
of fresh foods merchandising:
Early on, she frets that the Frito-Lay people "don't get that it has to be out of the bag." That, she feels, threatens 7-Eleven's vision of fresh foods.

adds: "Today is critical."

The 10 people sit around an oval table strewn with bags of chips, plastic trays and paper-cup mock-ups of dipping cups. They grab trays and pair them with cups in various combinations to demonstrate their ideas. Some people put bags of chips in trays; others open bags, pour in chips and consider the result.

The Frito-Lay people mention focus groups. Unnecessary and costly, Mr. Horres says. Instead, executives can sample the product, and 7-Eleven can hold tastings in its basement kitchen for janitors and other building workers. "They're the ones who eat in our stores," Mr. Horres says.

Mr. Horres has brought along an outside packaging engineer who scours the offerings of plastics manufacturers in search of containers for 7-Eleven. Holding a plastic tray full of Fritos and a cup of dip, Mr. Horres suggests 1.75 ounces of chips and 1.5 ounces of dip, based on his own eyeball estimate.

"We did a lot of research on this," Ms. Bassininski interrupts. The research showed that people wanted more dip than chip.

The talk turns to seals. One option is "barrier film" between chips and dip. Another is a plastic lid. Perhaps the entire tray, chips and dip and all, could be covered with heat-sealed film. And there's always shrink-wrap. Mr. Horres suggests "a black tray with a black bottom and a heat-seal top."

Steve Callahan, a Frito-Lay manager of technology, frets that plastic wrap won't be adequate. Only a heat-sealed lid can ensure a shelf-life of 70 to 90 days, he says.

"But we just need two," Mr. Horres says, since the product is supposed to be fresh and will be dumped after two days on display.

As the meeting breaks up, Lisa Merino, a 7-Eleven marketing manager sitting in on the meeting, suggests to a few people within earshot that the Frito pie make use of the chili and cheese-sauce dispensers that 7-Eleven recently began installing in its stores. That way, customers could pump toppings on their hot dogs, and all 7-Eleven would have to do is swap its generic nachos in favor of Frito-Lay chips. No one responds. The dispensers have always been a fallback option with the group, but not a priority; most would prefer a tidier, all-in-one product.

After nearly 2 1/2 hours of talk, the group again agrees only to meet again – this time to let Frito-Lay engineers tour the facility where 7-Eleven assembles trays of no-name nachos.

The Frito pie group gathers Dec. 2 at 9 a.m. The Lewisville kitchens are tucked away off a highway access road, in a bare building that resembles a garage. Inside, the space is broken up into rooms where workers assemble food; they don't cook. For the nachos, about a dozen workers open bags of chips, stuff them into red plastic dishes, snap on clear plastic lids, fasten them with clear tape, slap on 7-Eleven stickers, a bar code and a nutrition label, and load the finished snack into plastic pallets. Workers toss breaks in garbage pails.

Team members don white coats, hair nets and masks before stepping onto the floor. Two Frito-Lay engineers pace about with hand-held humidity readers. Temperature? 48 degrees. Too cold? Customers don't complain after the nachos are in stores. Portions? Workers fill four-ounce trays, working through a two-pound bag of chips at a time. Waste? The plant is proud to lose just 19% of all chips to breaks.

But what if 7-Eleven trucks hit a few potholes? Do the chips break? 7-Eleven doesn't know.

THE MEETING continues in a conference room, where the debate over the form of the Frito pie resumes. Mr. Horres turns to the facility's manager, Craig Weidner. "Option one is very expensive. You guys get chili and cheese . . . and scoop it into a microwavable bowl," Mr. Horres says. "Option two, you do what you're best at, you just do assembly" and receive a sealed bowl of chili and a bag of shredded cheese to package with Fritos. Mr. Weidner says either is possible.

Six months have passed since the group started meeting, and the 7-Eleven Frito pie remains a vague, amorphous thing. 7-Eleven officials are nonetheless encouraged that new foods are helping the company's results. During a morning videoconference call with 7-Eleven field managers, COO Mr. Keyes says merchandise sales rose 7.6% to $5.6 billion in 1998, compared with a 1.9% increase in 1997. Sales at stores open at least a year rose an impressive 5.7%, about one-third of that increase coming from new products. In particular, the new Cafe Cooler, a copy of Starbucks' Frappuccino, produced $50 million in sales.

For Mr. Horres, the quick rollout of so many products has been draining. He put a new item in the stores each month – including a wiener-shaped turkey with cranberry sauce at Thanksgiving – but handling the logistics and the follow-up with store managers was trickier than he expected. And Mr. Keyes is pressuring him to introduce more. "That's why my hair's gray," he says.

Not all the new food is a smash. The sausage-like turkey, sold nationally from the end of October to Dec. 1, 1998, lighted no fires. "We're not doing it again this year. Sales weren't that great," Mr. Horres says. "It wasn't very appealing," he adds. "It didn't look like the turkey you pulled out of your oven at Thanksgiving."

As the new year starts, Mr. Horres is determined to get the Frito pie moving toward stores. He has tasted two types of chili – one for 55 cents a cup and one for 30 cents – and decided the cheaper one tastes just fine. The group needs only to pick a tray to hold the chips – in or out of a bag – and a sealed cup to hold the chili. In a Frito-Lay conference room on a Friday afternoon in January, Frito-Lay's Mr. Callahan and a product manager join Mr. Horres in sorting through plastic trays, cups, plastic wrap and bags of chips.

"That looks pretty hokey," Mr. Horres says of a partitioned black tray with loose chips on one side and a dip cup on the other, sealed with clear wrap. A salsa cup covered in tin foil in a tray next to a bag of chips that is stuffed in to fit "looks so grocery store."

"It's got to look pretty," Mr. Horres tells the Frito-Lay people. "You buy food with your eyes. . . . I'm just not happy with what I see here."

In February, as the packaging problem persists, Ms. Powell is already asking about expanding the menu. She wants Tostitos tor-tilla chips with salsa or Ruffles potato chips with ranch dressing.

Frito-Lay representatives, unsure about selling corn chips outside of a bag, have even stronger feelings about potato chips. Clear bags allow for unsightly grease smears, and potato chips can turn rancid when exposed to light. Also, potato chips are bagged by weight, not volume, because potato density varies from season to season, meaning an ounce of heavier, higher-density chips can look skimpy in a clear bag.

Ms. Powell is nonplused. With her plan for a whole line of chips-and-dip thwarted, she frets that the project has far less sales potential. "I thought we were talking about potato chips all along," she says.

Mr. Horres has doubts about Frito-Lay's commitment. "I don't know how excited they are about this, frankly," he confides. "I don't see them jumping on the table."

Frito-Lay, though, says it is making 7-Eleven more of a priority than ever – so much so that it has created a team dedicated to working only with 7-Eleven. Gone are the two separate sales groups – one for chips and snacks, the other for soft drinks – and the fluid roster of Frito-Lay people who have been working on the Frito pie. Now, one team is dedicated exclusively to 7-Eleven; it is headed by Mr. Walsh, who becomes Pepsi-Co's vice president overseeing relations with 7-Eleven.

Mr. Walsh reports directly to Mr. Carey, the PepsiCo senior vice president of sales and retailer strategies and previously Frito-Lay's chief operating officer. In the past, Mr. Carey says, "we would send over people to call and sell as much as we could. Today, we're trying to solve problems and drive business."

With new members, the next bilateral gathering turns into a rerun of meetings past.

Al Carey,
PepsiCo senior vice president of sales and retailer strategies:
Ultimately, it's his decision to let the Fritos out of the bag. "We're going to do it because we think it's a great opportunity."

Mr. Walsh is surprised that PepsiCo would go so far to tailor its products for a customer – 7-Eleven – that it would even consider letting its chips out of the bag. "This is one of those things we'll try," he says. "We still think a bag is a better way to go." His greater fear is that the Frito pie will inspire retailers to start demanding other customized PepsiCo products. "We're not about to create a 7-Eleven-shaped chip," he says.

(Cont.)

But Mr. Walsh is quick to take the reins when he realizes the group has been stuck on the same problem for months. The conclusion: have their bosses, Mr. Keyes and Mr. Carey, decide whether to let the chips out of the bag.

No one is thrilled about going to the top without a final Frito pie to present. So at a meeting six weeks later, on May 14, they prepare a presentation scheduled for May 25 of what they have – and haven't – accomplished. Again, it comes down to the bag vs. no-bag debate. "We've got a pretty firm foot in the ground that says, going forward, everything we do will be a bag in a tray," says Julie Nelson, a PepsiCo sales manager. "I guess that's something we need to talk about."

"Jim and Al need to talk about that," Ms. Powell replies. "At the meeting on the 25th, we need to say Frito is willing to test [loose chips] in Dallas, but if we go national, our position is bags."

Without a finished product, Ms. Powell suggests presenting their early designs at the meeting. "I want to show him where we started and how ugly it was," she says. Mr. Horres adds, "We've got to get to the bags because Jim's not going to be happy with that."

They discuss preparing mock-ups and having the graphics department come up with labels. Who should lead the presentation?

"I'll lead, but you'll help me," Ms. Nelson says to Ms. Powell.

"Yes," Ms. Powell says.

In subsequent smaller gatherings, Ms. Powell, Mr. Horres and Mr. Walsh retrace their work to prepare a slew of options – from trays of loose chips packaged with cups of chili to the more-primitive unadorned chips for the customer to embellish with cheese and chili from the pumps.

Two weeks later, the group gathers in a room adjacent to Mr. Keyes's 41st-floor office. Outside spread grand views of downtown Dallas. Sipping a can of Pepsi One, Mr. Keyes listens as Ms. Nelson, Ms. Powell and the rest describe their work to date. He then tries to explain what 7-Eleven wants. Mr. Keyes sees a parallel in sushi. Five years ago, he notes, Americans ate sushi only in Japanese restaurants; today, people buy California rolls at the supermarket.

"Could we take a fresh nacho and make it available with eight pieces in a tray like a California roll?" Mr. Keyes wonders aloud. Just as the seaweed shields the rice from the fish in a sushi roll, he says, is there a "cheese seaweed" to keep chips crisp underneath chili and cheese toppings?

Not likely, the PepsiCo team responds politely.

Mr. Keyes points out that the average 7-Eleven store sells 15 trays of no-name nachos a day. Both companies think sales could double or better with the Frito-Lay name on the trays, so why not simply ditch the generic nachos and let the customers buy branded Fritos to adorn as they see fit with the existing chili and cheese dispensers? That would

MAKING THE PIE

1 At $1.99, the unadorned 7-Eleven Frito pie comprises a plastic tray containing approximately 40 Fritos Scoops, sealed to keep the chips fresh.

2 Upon purchase, the customer peels back the clear-plastic seal and adds free chili from dispensers 7-Eleven has already installed in its stores for buyers of hot dogs.

3 After the chili comes the cheese. Unlike the classic Frito pie, which uses cheese that has been grated or shredded, this version makes use of more easily dispensed cheese sauce.

4 The finished pie, to be eaten with one's hands or with plastic utensils that 7-Eleven makes available.

exploit the power of a brand name and eliminate the packaging debate that has consumed a year of work, he figures, and it could be taken to market quickly.

MR. CAREY consults with his director of research and development, and then relents. Frito-Lay will forgo the bag, but for the test only. If 7-Eleven wants to go national later, he will reconsider. "It's not something we do very well," he says, "but we're going to do it because I think it's a great opportunity."

Frito-Lay insists on packaging and delivering the chip trays itself. This time, Mr. Keyes is the one to give in.

Finally, the group has a product: One rectangular tray of large Fritos Scoops corn chips, sealed with clear plastic. Customers will add chili and cheese from 7-Eleven dispensers, the contents provided by Market-Fare Foods, an Austin, Texas, producer of foods for convenience stores and vending machines. Mr. Horres has insisted all along that the pie not sell for more than $2, and at the agreed price of $1.99, the pie will yield a margin of about 50%.

It isn't the ideal pie. The chili and cheese, runny enough to move through the pump, won't please all Frito pie aficionados. Mr. Keyes is frustrated, too, but he also can appreciate why an agreement took so long. "It seems so ridiculously simple in a way. You put chips in a tray," he shrugs. But for PepsiCo, he adds, picking up a bag of Cracker Jack, "this is their business. They see a bag as connoting freshness. We're saying you don't have to stop at the bag. Take it to a new level, a tray."

With a decision from the top, the two teams move quickly. In the next few weeks, Frito-Lay throws about 30 people at the project, including tray vendors, label vendors and staffers from sales, product supply, pur-

chasing, graphics, technology research and marketing.

Mr. Horres wants the chip tray covered with a clear film, printed with both Fritos and 7-Eleven logos. But the printing would take 12 weeks, so he settles for a sticker with both logos that, once affixed to the clear-plastic film, covers half the top. Frito-Lay engineers worry about chip grease sullying the clear cover. Solution: pack the trays sideways, sticker-side down, so that when the chips settle and bump up against the seal, the sticker hides grease spots.

Both companies are getting excited. "Normally, the pre-test is one year," Mr. Walsh says. "We've taken a year's process down to three months." That has meant forgoing, among other things, taste tests with the janitorial staff.

By July, 7-Eleven's Mr. Horres has samples in his office. Late one afternoon, more to soothe his nerves than his appetite, he grabs a tray of Fritos and goes downstairs to the 7-Eleven store in the building's basement. He squirts chili and cheese on a tray of generic corn chips and on a tray of Fritos. He sets his timer.

The Fritos alone pack 640 calories, 360 from fat, before counting the red chili and bright yellow cheese, which together could double the tally. The nutrition label says the tray contains four servings, or about 10 large chips a person. But everyone on the team figures most customers will treat the whole thing as one serving.

After two minutes, Mr. Horres digs in. Still tasty, still crunchy. He continues tasting at two-minute intervals. Both trays turn to goo after 10 minutes or so, but the Fritos "had a little more flavor. Our chips are pretty bland." For dashboard diners, he says, the concoction works. "I was just concerned this thing would turn into nacho soup," he says.

Frito-Lay orders a manual tray sealer about the size of an office copier for the test. On July 30, four line workers practice the process. To reduce the chips' exposure to humid air, they open one bag of chips at a time and pass filled trays to a worker who seals them with a film as sticky as Scotch tape. For a larger rollout, an easier-to-use film will have to be found.

Frito-Lay plans on making 1,700 trays of Fritos for the launch, along with 2,800 trays of Tostitos chips for the new nachos. After that, Frito-Lay will produce amounts based on 7-Eleven sales. "When we start on Monday, it will be hot and heavy. They want the shelves full," says Wendy Smith, a technology consultant to the Frito-Lay plant in suburban Dallas as she oversees a practice run.

At the last minute, there's a mix-up. 7-Eleven is expecting the first delivery Aug. 23, not Aug. 2, and the stores aren't ready. Both sides write it off to crossed messages in the flurry of paperwork that accompanies the launch. And 7-Eleven needs time for the necessary documentation, especially the two-page product-description sheet (ID number, price, photo, description and instructions) to be sent to the 25 test stores. Frito-Lay distributes the extras among staff as samples and sends a few to 7-Eleven.

Three weeks later, Frito-Lay delivers the cases to 7-Eleven's Dallas-area warehouse. The 7-Eleven trucks are loaded and head out into the night with their new cargo.

When one of the delivery trucks pulls up at midnight at a local store, the clerk doesn't know about the test. His store had ordered just two packages of the Tostitos in a tray and no Fritos for the pie. Generics, which were supposed to have been cleared, sit on the shelf. The clerk puts the arrivals on a metal rack next to the old ones.

Later, in a working-class neighborhood in east Plano, night clerk Ric Morgan is thrilled. At a store where the best-selling item is Marlboro cigarettes, customers have been making a mess with impromptu Frito pies, pumping chili and cheese into bags of Fritos, and he doesn't know how to charge for that. A week ago, he started scaling back orders for generic chips, as instructed, and sold his last one the previous night. At 1 a.m., just 20 minutes after the delivery truck, his display case is neatly lined with 10 trays of Fritos and 10 of Tostitos.

"This is one of the best ideas corporate has come up with," he says.

So far, the Fritos and Tostitos trays are selling well in some of the 25 test stores, raising Mr. Keyes's hopes that the Frito pie can go national. At 20 of the stores, daily sales volume of chip trays is up 20% since the in-troduction of the branded products. In mid-November, 7-Eleven and Frito-Lay plan to meet to review the test results.

Down the road, Mr. Keyes sees a more refined product – perhaps in a configuration that is kept warm under a heater, as french fries often are. And he would like nachos packaged like California rolls, in neat, discrete bites. "I want it cleaner," he says, admitting that with the Frito pie's current incarnation, "I can't eat this in my car. It would get all over my tie."

As 7-Eleven adds new foods, he predicts, fresh food for dashboard diners eventually will account for 30% to 40% of 7-Eleven's stock. Already, Ms. Powell is mulling new fruit smoothies. Her store redesign, though "still in the concept stage," she says, will eventually "get the food off the wall" and "speak more to a deli or supermarket style." Mr. Horres, meanwhile, has turned his attention to something for the morning crowd – a variation on the stuffed breadsticks, with an omelet filling.

Republished by permission from Dow Jones & Company, Inc., from *The Wall Street Journal,* "Crunch Points: Product Development Is Always Difficult; Consider the Frito Pie," p. A1, October 25, 1999; permission conveyed through Copyright Clearance Center, Inc.

DO YOU KNOW CISCO?

The company whose routers rule the Web now wants to be in your house and on your mind

by Karl Taro Greenfeld/San Jose

At this Westin Hotel Convention Center, just east of San Jose, Calif., a revival meeting is in progress. Cisco Systems CEO John Chambers, 50, struts across the stage wearing a gray tweed suit and preaching the gospel of the network to a packed, 8,000-strong congregation of the converted. We have made great strides, Chambers drawls in his West Virginian birch-beer-sweet voice, but we need to be ever vigilant, for around the corner, right outside this hall, lurks the enemy–Nortel, Lucent and start-up companies we've never heard of, jesters who would steal our cybercrown.

The audience, consisting of the truest of true believers–Cisco employees–is an easy sell. Chambers and Cisco have made at least 2,500 of Cisco's 23,000 employees stock-option millionaires, which in turn has convinced the rest that they too will be millionaires. Investors have also got Cisco's brand of router religion, as the stock has split eight times and risen about 8,000% in the 10 years since it went public at $18 a share. One share of Cisco bought in 1990 is worth $14,000 today. The company, founded by John Morgridge as a technology-solutions company with a simple idea–hook up networks–has ended up being the baby in the creche of the Internet revolution.

Cisco's principal products are routers—souped-up computers that sort the streams of information packets that whiz throughout the Internet. As it happened, routers turned out to be the indispensable heavy artillery of the digital revolution. As the Internet has grown, so too have the demands for bigger, faster, better routers. Today, Cisco manufactures gigabit routers that can handle a billion bits of information a second. Coming soon, as bandwidth requirements increase and Internet traffic doubles every 100 days–and as we consumers increasingly upload and download video, voice, music and data–Cisco will be ready with terabit (trillion bit) routers and more.

This confluence of technical expertise, market opportunity and ruthless efficiency has made Cisco the fastest company in history to reach $100 billion, $200 billion and, last month, $300 billion in market capitalization, leaving it the third largest company in the world behind General Electric and Microsoft.

Cisco has built dominant market share in a crucial high-technology industry–controlling 50% of the $21 billion business-network market, where it has obliterated once formidable rivals like 3Com, Cabletron and Bay Networks. "We definitely are in the sweet spot," says Chambers of Cisco's prospects. "The whole network business has become a home game for Cisco." Think of it this way: in a wired world where we are just learning to walk, Cisco has become the biggest, best shoemaker on the planet.

In order to maintain Cisco's unprecedented growth rate, Chambers believes he has to remake the company into a great consumer brand. "Three years ago, we didn't care if anyone knew who we were," he admits. "The decisions that mattered were made deep inside companies." Today, making its brand as well known as Intel's or Hewlett Packard's is vital to Cisco's mission of building the New World Network.

Why the change? When it comes to information, homes are becoming much like offices–networks of linked devices connected to a server. In your home, PCs and TVs are linked via broadband Internet hookups such as cable modems or Digital Subscriber Lines (DSL) to the big server that is the Web. As everything from refrigerators (Cisco has just partnered with Whirlpool) to your furnace (Cisco and Samsung) gets Web-capable, each homeowner will become his own chief information officer, making on a household level the decisions corporate executives have been making for a decade: Who will wire the house? Who will power my network? Who will enable the myriad envisioned wireless household appliances?

Cisco anticipates the consumer-network market will be worth $9 billion and plans to take a dominant share, as it has done in 14 of the 15 markets in which it operates. That's why Cisco spent $60 million airing its "Are You Ready?" television commercials and is emulating Intel's successful "Intel Inside" campaign, which made megahertz a measure of computational power. "In order to get to the next level, we need the consumer," says Don Listwin, Cisco's executive vice president.

The first product aimed at the household was launched last week at the Consumer

Cisco's Four-Step Plan

As a Web pioneer, Cisco built its strategy from the top of the cyberpyramid down

INNOVATORS Cisco won the early adapters

ENTERPRISE Big, Web-savvy firms followed

SMALL BIZ Cisco has also captured fast-growth firms

CONSUMERS Cisco's future, the next hot market

Electronics Show in Las Vegas, where the company unveiled the Cisco Home Gateway. That's a DSL home-network hub that converts your phone jacks into broadband Ethernet ports. The company has even introduced a network version of Intel's megahertz gimmick to persuade consumers to upgrade and rewire their homes: PIQ, or Packet Intelligence Quotient. The higher the PIQ, the faster data will zip around your house. Cisco is counting on consumers' rushing out to buy a new networking device upgrading them from, say, PIQ 2 to PIQ 3. Did we mention that Cisco doesn't quite have the hang of this consumer business just yet?

It probably will, though. The culture of success is particularly virulent at Cisco. When you walk around the corporate campus in San Jose today, you get the feeling you are in a tiny, high-technology version of Switzerland, a neutral power–Cisco will partner with virtually any company and employ any promising technology–where the trains not only run on time, they arrive a few hours early. It's a campus of dozens of aqua and

(Cont.)

brown bunker-like buildings that seem to extend to the horizon, differentiated only by banners proclaiming, for example, that this particular building birthed THE FIRST QUALIFIED DOCSIS-COMPLIANT HEAD-END ROUTER IN THE INDUSTRY. "It's a great place to work if you're an engineer," says one. "I can't think of why anyone else would work here."

Actually, Cisco is run by a nonengineer.

John Chambers sits amid the expanse of cubicles in an office as austere and tiny as an entry-level programmer's. His motto is, "Never ask your employees to do something you wouldn't be willing to do yourself." This culture of self-sacrifice and frugality means that Chambers and all top execs fly coach and have no reserved parking spaces. The same quest for efficiency has driven Cisco to make cutting-edge use internally of the networks it sells to other companies. Everything at Cisco–from health-insurance issues to softball schedules–is available on the Web. Already, Cisco makes 84% of its sales over the Web, accounting in 1999 for about $9.5 billion in business-to-business e-commerce. To put that in perspective, mighty Amazon sold about $1.5 billion worth of products online.

Chambers is customer obsessed, a characteristic that will serve the company well as it moves into consumer markets. He discovered the dogma of customer service as a salesman at IBM and and then saw firsthand the cost of losing customer focus when he joined minicomputer maker Wang in the late '80s. As Wang's business eroded–in part because Wang didn't listen to customers–Chambers, the top sales executive, was forced to lay off 4,000 workers. He vows never to do that again, even if it means keeping his company leaner and meaner than seems necessary. "Laying off workers in a tough job market was the worst feeling in the world," he says as he sips his fourth Diet Coke of the day. "It made me physically ill."

Even as the company has grown to become the king of the data network, it has remained, in many consumers' minds, a question mark. Ask most people what Microsoft or Intel do, and they'll tell you. But Cisco? "I don't know," says Harriet Sumner, 30, a customer-service manager for a computer-game company, "but I own the stock."

Chambers thinks it's important that people such as Sumner do know, especially now that Cisco wants to be successful in its other bold strategy: a march into the telecom business, where it will face a whole new level of well-entrenched competition. The $250 billion-a-year telephone-equipment business is where giants like AT&T's equipment-making spin-off, Lucent, and Canadian counterpart Nortel have built powerful, decades-long relationships with telephone companies and service providers. As voice and data networks converge–and data come to account for more than 90% of network traffic– Cisco has boasted that its networks, which are predominantly data or IP (Internet protocol) networks, will also become the leading voice networks.

Consumers, however, are still uneasy about IP telephone service. Do you really want your voice to be as unreliable as your Web connection? Cisco swears it has closed the gap and made its IP networks as reliable as voice networks. What would help, Cisco believes, is for consumers to come to believe in the Cisco brand to the point where they are exerting upward pressure on telephone companies and service providers to run Cisco networks. In other words, for Cisco to be able to apply a two-way squeeze from the corporate side and the consumer side so that your phone company will have no choice but to go with Cisco. "Name recognition and branding are crucial to us," says Chambers. "We want the small business, the medium-sized business and even the consumer to want Cisco-powered networks."

Cisco, in its history, has never gone after a major market and failed. Lucent and Nortel, are you ready?

Place

51

HAMMERING AWAY AT THE WEB

Selling home-improvement products online is an uphill battle, but the combatants are hard at it

I n e-tailing, it's getting pretty tough to hit the nail on the head. But it's especially tricky in home improvement and hardware, one of the last retail categories to move online. This elusive area ranks as No. 16 out of a listing of 20 Net categories tracked according to their potential by Goldman, Sachs & Co. For starters, few consumers want to buy lumber online because it would cost an arm and a leg to ship. Plus, scores of people make urgent trips to the store because their toilet is overflowing or they have a leaky faucet. They're not going to wait for United Parcel Service to deliver the goods necessary to make the repairs. Market researcher Jupiter Media Metrix estimates that online hardware sales will hit $170 million in 2001—up more than double from 2000, but still only a tiny fraction of the $186 billion overall home-improvement market. "It's the crappiest segment of the whole e-tailer sector," says Neil A. Hastie, chief information officer for hardware cooperative TruServ Corp. in Chicago.

Established hardware companies have no dot-com delusions. They know the Internet isn't ideal for selling wrenches and table saws. Instead, they're finding savvy ways to use the Web to cut the inventory costs of stocking big-ticket items in stores and to reach new customers.

Indeed, the Web may be just the ticket for luring buyers into good, old-fashioned stores. Home Depot, Lowe's, and Ace Hardware are using their Web sites to provide online hardware reference guides and how-to libraries, hoping this will help buyers make decisions. "I think online pure play isn't going to work," says Jupiter Senior Analyst Michael May. "But using the Net to enhance the offline experience is of real value to hardware stores."

One way to do that is to bring the Net into the store. Big retail chains such as Ace, Sears, and Lowe's are testing Web kiosks in their stores so customers can get product information, comparison shop, and even buy items— avoiding long checkout lines. North Wilkesboro (N.C.)-based Lowe's, the nation's second-largest hardware retailer with $15.9 billion in sales, has been testing Web kiosks in 30 of its stores since March. "We've had

people tell us it's the fastest shopping they've ever done at Lowe's," says Thomas E. Whiddon, executive vice-president of logistics and technology. He expects half of all kiosk purchases to be take-home buys.

The Web also is helping some Old Economy companies sell products that customers can't carry out the door. At retailer Sears, research shows that its Web site influences 10% of all in-store major appliance purchases. Better yet, Sears.com customers on average made at least one more trip to the store than all other customers. Sears says the content on its Web site—home-improvement tips and product advice—attracts potential customers who then see promos for other products and come into the stores. Although Sears won't reveal the average spending of its online customers, the company says it's 30% to 50% higher than the average spent at its brick-and-mortar stores.

Going virtual may also help hardware companies snag an audience they have failed to attract—women. Ace says its research shows that female buyers are driving most of the big in-home appliance sales. But Ace's in-store clientele is 70% male. That's where its minority stake in hardware e-tailer Our-House.com comes in. Ace supplies 75% of the goods and handles all fulfillment chores for the Web retailer. And Ace is testing a mini version of the OurHouse Web site on kiosks in some stores. The female connection: More than 60% of the buyers at OurHouse are women. For Victoria Stach, 34, a lawyer for the Chicago firm of Winston & Strawn and an experienced e-shopper, buying a light fixture and some Christmas presents like a George Foreman grill at OurHouse was a breeze. "It was easy, no-stress, no-hassle," says Stach, who regularly shops online because she doesn't have the time to wander through stores.

Now Ace wants to get Stach and other women who already shop online into the store. A new national print and TV marketing campaign targeting women based on life stages—buying a first home, having a first baby, becoming an empty-nester—is scheduled to begin in February and also will run on OurHouse.

For Tool Time-type companies, the less risky strategy is to use the Net to strengthen ties to the heavy spenders—professional contractors who typically buy higher-margin products. That's why the nation's largest home-improvement retailer is focusing its Web strategy on the pros. The $38.4 billion

(Cont.)

If I Had a Hammer
(concluded)

Lowe's Companies

Company Revenue: $15.9 billion

Web Site: Lowes.com, with 617,000 unique visitors

Number of Products Online: 11,000

Strategy: In November, Lowe's became the last of the major offline hardware stores to amble online. Lowes.com combines its catalog of tools and appliances with online advice and info on home improvement.

Sears Roebuck

Company Revenue: $41.1 billion

Web Site: Sears.com, with 6.5 million unique visitors

Number of Products Online: 6,000 tools, 2,800 appliances

Strategy: Sears.com offers everything from electronics to lawn mowers to Craftsman tools and appliances. Netizens can schedule deliveries, repairs, and installations. Home-improvement advisers are available online, as are lots of product data.

COMPANY REVENUE AS OF 1999, WEB TRAFFIC DATA AS OF NOV. 2000, DATA: Company reports

Home Depot expects that Web sales will be more attractive to the 30% of its customers who are professional contractors, rather than the typical weekend Mr. and Ms. Fix-It. Home Depot began testing online sales last August to customers in the Las Vegas area. And in recent months, it added San Antonio and Austin, Tex. "Professionals are more likely to use the Internet to buy, along with other channels like phone and fax. We want to give them as many choices as possible," says Home Depot Chief Information Officer Ron Griffin.

Not that the remaining Internet-only hardware sites are ready to close up their tool sheds just yet. CornerHardware.com opened shop in February, 1999, and offers more than 37,000 home improvement products on its site. And in October of that year, Amazon.com Inc. purchased the catalog business of Tool Crib of the North, a Grand Forks, N.D., construction equipment and tools company. One month later, it launched its home-improvement shopping area. Now, Amazon.com offers more than 20,000 products and scores of hardware specialists to its 25 million customers. The company says home-improvement sales this past Christmas were 2.5 times that of 1999.

Still, lacking a partnership with a big bricks-based hardware retailer, or a long-established online brand presence like Amazon.com, pure-play e-tailers face an uphill climb. Watching the growing Web presence of Home Depot and Lowe's, several analysts question CornerHardware's ability to survive the year. The privately held company insists it is doing fine, but its visitors shrank by more than 38% from October through December of last year, according to Internet market analyst PC Data Inc. At the same time, Web traffic at Home Depot and Lowe's shot up 70% and 27%, respectively.

Even having a big backer in the business may not be enough. Under its deal with OurHouse, Ace supplies the bulk of the site's 25,000 listed products. But a dispute between the two companies over who gets manufacturers' discounts has shaken the relationship.

Tool Time

According to surveys conducted by the Home Improvement Research Institute, more people are buying their hardware online.

June, 1999. In a survey of 663 homeowners, **17.8%** say they have made purchases online. Of that group, **2.2%** indicate some of those items were home-improvement products.

June, 2000. In a survey of 684 homeowners, **21%** say they have made purchases online. Of those online buyers, **4.1%,** bought home-improvement items online.

OurHouse Chief Executive Philip Airey isn't predicting when his company will reach profitability, but he says it's on track with more than 750,000 registered customers and average sales figures of $50 for first-timers and $70 for repeat customers. He says sales at the end of 2000 were more than five times what they originally promised Ace and he's confident the two companies will hammer out their differences. Good luck, because being a dot-com in the home-improvement market isn't going to be as easy as hitting the nail on the head.

By Darnell Little

Reprinted from the February 19, 2001 issue of *Business Week* by special permission. © 2001 McGraw-Hill Companies, Inc.

52

A NEANDERTHAL INDUSTRY SMARTENS UP

How the electrical-parts biz got the glitches out

John E. Haluska is a bear of a man whose gray beard makes him look more like Santa Claus than an Internet visionary. But three years ago, while the chief information officer for $2.2 billion electrical-parts maker Thomas & Betts Corp. was visiting a distributor, he passed the accounts payable office and noticed a large stack of documents with his company's name on them. When he asked about the papers, he was told: "It's T&B day." On such days, eight hours are spent crawling through the paperwork, addressing snafus between the distributor and Thomas & Betts–missed shipment dates, damaged goods, and, mostly, price discrepancies. Haluska estimates that it costs his company about $300 to straighten out each gnarly inconsistency. After learning others had the same nasty problem, "That got me thinking," he says.

Good thing. There's bedlam in the $90 billion electrical-parts industry. According to industry executives, upwards of 70% of administrative costs go into correcting order errors. Even highly automated organizations like Haluska's are struggling. In Thomas & Betts's distribution center 35 miles southeast of Memphis, 70,000 different parts–from pipe connectors to light-bulb fittings–are sorted by a mass of conveyor belts and shipped to distributors across the country. It's an efficient operation, but there's one problem: There are scores of distributors like the one Haluska visited that day, lacking the ability to quickly match items they need with the ones T&B ships. So workers instead spend time reshipping wrong orders or chasing down lost ones. The industry has "not had the good sense to back up and understand how to use technology to store and track all of our parts," explains Clyde R. Moore, Thomas & Betts CEO.

All that is about to change. Thomas & Betts and some 225 other companies are shaking their antiquated ways and working furiously to enter the Internet era. In September, the industry launched IDxchange, a cutting-edge private network linked to a massive database that catalogs parts and carries orders between manufacturers and distributors

in a snap. While the new system isn't designed to enable such market-transforming innovations as real-time auctions or comparison shopping, doing business via IDxchange is expected to cut labor and telecommunications costs by some 50% a year. "We're an industry that is certainly a bit Neanderthal," says Malcolm O'Hagan, president of the National Electrical Manufacturers Assn. "But we're taking a quantum leap from the back of the pack to the front of the pack."

The custom network puts the industry light years ahead of its traditional way of doing business. For eons, electrical parts makers and distributors have zapped important sales data to one another using a system called electronic data interchange or EDI. Information on an invoice or sales order was coded based on arcane EDI definitions, then converted to bits and transported through a maze of electronic networks. While each part or category was standardized, the actual way of conveying the categories was not. One company might identify the shipment date with dashes and another with slashes.

That led to a raft of manual errors–nearly 20% of orders had typos or other goof-ups that required at least a phone call to clear up. For example, when a worker at Crum Electric Supply Co. in Casper, Wyo., typed in the wrong part number, the distributor mistakenly ordered a $100,000 motor instead of a set of $2,200 light fixtures. Crum had to ship the motor back and was charged a 25% restocking fee. "It just killed us," says owner David Crum.

Haluska was feeling the same pain. The CIO cringed at EDI costs that hit more than $10,000 a month. Those were the charges for sending data to a kind of electronic post office that forwarded it to designated distributors and vice versa. Many others in the industry had similar, if not higher, costs. "Small players couldn't even play," Haluska says. Add to that this stinger: There was nothing real-time about the old EDI system. Electronic orders didn't automatically pop up in a virtual inbox like they do today. Instead, the EDI system required companies to dial up and fetch data out of their mailbox. That meant most transac-

tions were sent or received at the end of the day, making same-day shipments a rarity.

Haluska dreamed of a network that would bypass the expensive proprietary EDI system and simply speed data along a network using open Internet standards. With cheaper Net gear, costs could be slashed significantly. Indeed, using the new network, T&B now pays a fixed connection and usage fee of up to $2,900 a month.

Haluska's brainstorming paralleled the visions of Crum, the owner of Crum Electric. Crum had been watching enviously as retailers such as Wal-Mart Stores Inc. automated their check-out and distribution processes, while electrical wholesalers were stuck in the "dead tree" world of paper. Crum, along with Haluska, pushed members of the National Association of Electrical Distributors to meet with representatives of the National Electrical Manufacturers Assn. The goal was to synchronize the manufacturers' data with the distributors' so that errors in price and product identification would be wiped out. "We recognized the lack of technology in our business relationships," Crum says.

In March, 1998, the industry's top executives met in Arlington, Va., and pledged about $5 million to construct IDxchange. They commissioned Triad Systems Corp. in Livermore, Calif., to build a database that would store information on hundreds of thousands of parts. With IDxchange, companies like Crum's will be hooked into the database and a point-and-click ordering system, eliminating the time-consuming task of typing in parts numbers. Today, for example, a light bulb has a single part number that identifies it consistently, not by whatever method each company prefers. "Until we talk apples to apples, electronic commerce can't take off," Haluska says.

Now it can. MCIWorldcom Inc. has built the network component of IDxchange. Companies connect using Internet access gear, ranging from sluggish 54Kb modems to speedy T1 lines. The member companies pay a flat monthly fee, from $800 to $2,900, depending on the size of the company and the speed of its connection.

The new system has persuaded some companies to abandon paper forever. Moeller Electric Corp., for example, had been sending invoices and packing slips via snail mail. George Leonard, the company's manager of information systems and logistics, avoided moving documents electronically because the EDI system was too expensive. Now he figures the $840 a month he'll spend on IDxchange will beat paying someone to print an invoice, stuff the envelope, and lug bags of mail to the post office. "There's got to be money saved in that," Leonard says.

With their own private Internet, electrical manufacturers and distributors suddenly have the capability to operate at Net speed. The new network bypasses the clunky EDI network and allows companies to complete transactions in minutes. Connected via IDxchange, a distributor can now send an order at 9 a.m. and have it received by 9:03 a.m. Then, the order can be packed, shipped, and delivered the same day. "That was an impossibility before," says Jeff Kernan, vice-president for information and technology at Lithonia Lighting in Conyers, Ga.

To add even more convenience, several distributors are building Web sites that let them give customers–contractors or utilities–a much higher level of service. In the past, if a plumbing contractor came to a distributor's office to ask about a pipe fitting, the distributor either logged on to a pipemaker's Web site and browsed for a part or, if that took too long, he would pick up the phone. "When you call, the person on the other end is in the bathroom," Crum huffs. IDxchange will eliminate all that. At the touch of a key, the computer will confirm a part's availability.

NOT FAR ENOUGH? Despite the advantages, IDxchange still has its skeptics. Small shops, especially, have fretted over having to adjust to new equipment and ways of doing business. Joseph G. Schneider, president of Madison Electric Co. in Warren, Mich., supports the industry effort, but he's not convinced that it will save his company money. Madison spends about $4,000 a month for phone and data lines that link his branch offices. Schneider worries that expense might not be eliminated, even if he shells out some $2,900 a month for IDxchange. So he's cautious about signing up for the service. "I don't think you go running through the door," he says. "You peek around the corner."

Or do you? For all its merits, there are some who say that IDxchange doesn't go far enough. For starters, it's not set up for buyers and sellers to haggle fast and furiously. That bartering is still going on, but it remains the province of the phone call. Too bad, say Net futurists. John J. Sviokla, a digital strategist at Diamond Technology Partners Inc. in Chicago, says if the IDxchange remains a kind of megacatalog and ordering system, "that's a big thing, but not anything like an electronic market."

For now, the leaders of IDxchange are content to e-engineer their old-line industry this far. After all, IDxchange does catapult them well beyond paper and postage stamps–and past the frustrations of yesterday's poky old technologies.

By Roger O. Crockett

TRANSPORTATION

Last summer Yellow Corp., the No. 1 trucking outfit in the U.S., got a peek into the future of the freight industry—thanks to a youthful wizard named Harry. Scholastic Inc. needed 150,000 copies of the latest Harry Potter book shipped to stores across the country, and it needed them delivered just minutes before midnight on July 8. A late delivery would disappoint thousands of kids lined up for *Harry Potter and the Goblet of Fire;* conversely, if the books arrived too early, leaks about the plot twists might ruin the hoopla that Scholastic had painstakingly built up around the title's release. Only a few years ago, the assignment would have been a real stretch for a general freight hauler such as Yellow. But the Overland Park (Kan.) trucker delivered with flying colors, say Scholastic executives.

Yellow's magic, in this case, was just-in-time (JIT) inventory control. In recent years, this know-how has radiated beyond big manufacturers to the rest of the economy, helping the trucking industry—among others—to improve punctuality. Following up on last July's blast shipment for Scholastic, Yellow's Exact Express subsidiary is now logging thousands of to-the-hour deliveries every day. And the company sees demand only rising, as cost-conscious businesses grow more insistent on receiving orders precisely when they want. "The performance bar is being raised," says William D. Zollars, Yellow's chairman and chief executive—to the benefit of nearly everyone. Facing a slowing economy, transporters might have expected little or no growth in 2001. But industrywide revenues should grow by a healthy 3.2% in 2001, to more than $470 billion, according to forecasts from Standard & Poor's Corp.

DRIVER SHORTAGE. Indeed, Corporate America's rush to minimize inventories is keeping the nation's freight companies rolling faster than ever, effectively turning their fleets into warehouses on the go. Traditional trucking companies such as Yellow and Roadway Express Inc. are pushing into realms once controlled by overnight shipping companies. Air-freight giant FedEx is getting competition for same-day deliveries from United Airlines and American Airlines. Even slowpoke railroads are getting into the act. Burlington Northern Santa Fe Corp. now guarantees on-time deliveries or your money back. "More and more commerce is squeezing into smaller packages with more frequent deliveries," notes William J. Rennicke, a vice-president at Mercer Management Consulting Inc.

Encouraging as the spread of JIT management techniques may be, other factors will keep the transport sector's growth grounded. Across the industry, freight companies are struggling with sky-high fuel costs, while a rippling economic slowdown is cutting into orders. Meantime, the nation's major railroads are still fighting to win back business they lost when they let service erode as they engineered a series of huge mergers in the late 1990s. And on the highway, long-distance trucking companies are wrestling with a driver shortage that shows little sign of easing. "All in all, it will be a challenging year," predicts Samuel K. Skinner, CEO of USFreightways Corp.

But barring an outright recession, 2001 still will be profitable for transportation companies, according to industry analysts. Merrill Lynch & Co. forecasts that earnings will be higher for all but a handful of second-tier trucking companies. One big reason is that the major trucking firms have been able to pass along the higher costs to customers through fuel surcharges.

But more than anything, the cost-cutting potential of the Internet is underpinning a generally upbeat mood within the industry. Linked by the Web from one end of their business to the other, freight companies and their customers now can better manage supply-chain flows, cutting costs by reducing unnecessary inventories. For freight haulers facing a slackening economy in 2001, it's a business boost—just in time.

By Michael Arndt in Chicago

Positives and Negatives

Positives

- The spread of just-in-time business strategies should lift demand for freight haulers.
- Big railroad mergers should lead to smoother service.

Negatives

- High fuel prices hurt smaller operators that can't pass along costs.
- The economic slowdown reduces shipping volumes for long-haul truckers and railways.

Trick or Treat

Hershey's Biggest Dud Has Turned Out to Be Its New Technology

At the Worst Possible Time, It Can't Fill Its Orders, Even as Inventory Grows

Kisses in the Air for Kmart

BY EMILY NELSON
AND EVAN RAMSTAD

Staff Reporters of THE WALL STREET JOURNAL

Just a few days before the biggest candy binge of the year, the Great North Foods warehouse in Alpena, Mich., displayed empty shelves where there should have been Hershey's bars. Reese's Peanut Butter Cups were missing, too. So were Rolos.

The trouble: An order for 20,000 pounds of candy that the regional distributor had placed with Hershey Foods Corp. in mid-September hadn't arrived. Great North earlier this week had to stiff 100 of the 700 stores it supplies on candy orders it couldn't fill. Only yesterday did a Hershey shipment show up at Great North – the first in five weeks – and the distributor still didn't know if Hershey had sent enough to meet its needs.

"No one seems to believe it's Hershey that's having the problem," says Bruce Steinke, Great North's candy buyer.

Spot Shortages

For the nation's largest candy maker, with revenue of $4.44 billion last year, this could turn out to be a very scary Halloween. New technology that came on line in July has gummed up its ordering-and-distribution system, leaving many stores nationwide reporting spot shortages of Kisses, Kit Kats, Twizzlers and other stalwarts of the trick-or-treating season.

In mid-July, Hershey flipped the switch on a $112 million computer system that was supposed to automate and modernize everything from taking candy orders to putting pallets on trucks. Two months later, the company announced that something was wrong. Now, an additional six weeks later – and with Halloween looming – it's still working out the kinks and says it hopes to have everything running smoothly by early December. Some

customers and industry analysts, however, think that based on what they've seen, the problems could persist through Christmas – and maybe even Valentine's Day and Easter.

Already, rivals are benefiting without making much effort. Mars Inc., based in McLean, Va., says sales are up. Nestle USA, the U.S. unit of Swiss food giant Nestle SA, says it, too, has received an unusual spurt of late requests for Halloween treats. "Orders don't typically come in this late," says Patricia Bowles, spokeswoman for the company's candy division in Glendale, Calif. Both companies say they haven't offered any special promotions to boost sales.

The Mars Option

Randall King, candy buyer for Lowes Foods, a chain of 81 supermarkets based in Winston-Salem, N.C., says the delivery delays prompted him to tell stores last month to stop reordering regular Hershey candies. His suggestion: Go with Mars brands.

Hershey says it lost about one-tenth of a percentage point of its still-dominant market share in the four weeks ended Sept. 12. But retailers predict a greater drop for October. And shelf space may be hard to win back, since a typical candy eater is loyal more to type of candy – chocolate, say, or lollipops – than to a particular brand.

"If you don't have my toothpaste, I'm walking out" of the store, says Ron Coppel, vice president of business development at Eby-Brown Co., a Naperville, Ill., candy distributor. "But for a chocolate bar, I'll pick another one." Customers are "not likely to walk out of the store because there wasn't a Hershey's bar. They'll pick another candy bar."

Hershey has taken steps to stay in touch with its largest customers and keep them flush with sweets. Kmart Corp. says it has received 98% of its Halloween orders placed with the company – some of that sent by air freight, rather than the typical and much less costly trucks. Wal-Mart Stores Inc., the nation's largest retailer, won't disclose the impact of Hershey's problems on its own inventories, but says it is talking daily with the confectioner. It also has ordered more than usual from Nestle and Mars for backup.

Information, Please

And John Moser, candy-category manager for Dallas-based 7-Eleven Inc., says a Hershey sales representative is calling him weekly, instead of monthly as usual, to ask what 7-Eleven has received because, among other things, Hershey itself can't tell what the chain has received.

Mr. Moser says that this summer, after 7-Eleven started receiving incomplete lots of everyday items like Hershey's bars, he advised stores to expand their displays of other candies. "If we ran out of Kit Kat or another Hershey item, we might expand facings of Snickers," he says. "We typically used the next-best-selling item."

Hershey officials declined requests to be interviewed for this article. But some details

of the computer glitches have come out as Hershey has spoken in recent weeks with customers and analysts. The company told analysts in a conference call earlier this week that relations with customers are "strained."

Perhaps most galling for Hershey is that it has plenty of candy on hand to fill all its orders. It just can't move some of the candy from warehouse to customer.

Hershey embarked on its computer project in 1996, partly to satisfy retailers who are demanding increasingly that suppliers fine-tune deliveries so that they can keep inventories – and thus costs – down. The company also faced year-2000 problems with its old computer system.

The project called for 5,000 personal computers, as well as network hubs and servers and several different vendors. Under the new system, software from Siebel Systems Inc., San Mateo, Calif., Manugistics Group Inc., Rockville, Md., and SAP AG, Walldorf, Germany, is used by Hershey's 1,200-person sales force and other departments for handling every step in the process, from original placement of an order to final delivery. It also runs the company's fundamental accounting and touches nearly every operation; tracking raw ingredients; scheduling production; measuring the effectiveness of promotional campaigns; setting prices; and even deciding how products ought to be stacked inside trucks. International Business Machines Corp. was hired to pull it all together.

Big-Bang Approach

Despite the complexity of the system, Hershey decided to go on line with a huge piece of it all at once – a so-called big bang that computer experts say is rare and dangerous. Initially, the confectioner planned to start up in April, a slow period. But development and testing weren't complete, and the date was pushed to July, when Halloween orders begin to come in. Retailers say, and Hershey confirms, that the problem is in getting customer orders into the system and transmitting the details of those orders to warehouses for fulfillment.

But no one is taking responsibility. Kevin McKay, chief executive officer and president of SAP's U.S. unit, says the system itself isn't at fault. "If it was a system issue, I'd point directly to a system issue," he says. Mr. McKay says he is in touch with Hershey executives almost daily, and he points out that the companies successfully installed a SAP system in Hershey's Canadian operation last year, though that operation is a tiny fraction of the size of the U.S. operation. IBM spokesman Brian Doyle says the company continues to help Hershey address "its business challenges," adding that "the business process transformation under way at Hershey is an enormously complex undertaking."

Siebel executives say that Hershey officials told them the problem wasn't with their software. "It may have turned out with the big bang kind of installation, they were maxed out there," says Paul Wahl, Siebel's president.

(Cont.)

Candy as Core

The bitter irony for Hershey is that the computer system was part of a broader overhaul intended to sharpen the company's focus on its core mass-market candy business. In early 1996, Hershey sold its Planters nut and Life Savers operations in Canada and its Beech-Nut cough-drop business, as well as stakes in a German praline maker and an Italian candy and grocery firm. In January this year, it sold its pasta business to New World Pasta LLC for $450 million.

In the meantime, it picked up Leaf North America, the maker of Good & Plenty, Heath, Jolly Rancher, Milk Duds, Payday and Whoppers, for about $450 million. While Hershey eliminated about half of Leaf's products, the purchase still boosted its number of specific product offerings by 30%.

Hershey also has been adding variations – king-size, bite-size and such – to its existing products, and has introduced ReeseSticks and reduced-fat Sweet Escapes. It also has created different wrappings and packages for different holidays. Altogether, Hershey estimates it makes 3,300 different candy products.

The proliferation of candies seemed to be working. Hershey sales in recent years have grown faster than the overall industry's, though total candy sales have slowed this year. Hershey was counting on 4% to 6% sales growth this year, but for the first nine months, they fell 2% from a year earlier to $2.84 billion, excluding the pasta business. The computer problems alone clipped sales by about $100 million during the period, the company told analysts.

Hershey had built up eight days of inventory as a cushion against any temporary troubles with the new computer system, but that wasn't enough. By early August, the company was 15 days behind in meeting orders.

In early September, the company told customers to order Halloween candy by Sept. 27. Orders for delivery in October were delayed. And customers placing new orders were told the turn-around time was at least 12 days, more than twice as long as usual. Hershey executives said earlier this week that the 12-day lead time is still in force and that it still can't fill complete orders.

Some retailers and food distributors say Hershey sent them a letter in July saying shipments might be delayed because of computer problems. McLane Co., a food distributor to convenience stores, said it began receiving incomplete shipments in August. "It wasn't any particular item. It was across the board," says Martha Kahler, director of trade relations at the Temple, Texas, unit of Wal-Mart.

Candy companies record about 40% of their annual sales between October and December. Halloween is the single biggest candy-consuming holiday, accounting for about $1.8 billion in sales, followed by Christmas, with $1.45 billion, according to the National Confectioners Association and the Chocolate Manufacturers Association, both based in McLean, Va.

Hershey told analysts that it is looking at a number of fixes, but all of them will have to be tested before they can be used. Meanwhile, the company's stock price has been hammered. In New York Stock Exchange composite trading yesterday, the stock closed at $50.25 a share, up a bit from its 52-week low of $47.50, but well below its price of around $74 a year ago.

Fortuitous Easter

Hershey executives have said they are hopeful sales will rebound in the fourth quarter. The company will get a small break from the 2000 holiday schedule: Easter is later than usual, which means chocolate eggs and the like will be shipped in January and February rather than in December. Indeed, Lowes Foods last Friday placed a Valentine's Day order.

Still, analysts think the company will have to offer retailers special promotions or discounts to win them back. Customers are likely to demand billing changes or shipment changes or other perks because "when retailers smell weakness in a manufacturer, they go for blood," says Andrew Lazar, an analyst with Lehman Brothers in New York.

Mr. Steinke of Great North in Michigan is a little more sanguine than that. He says he received a visit last Friday from his Hershey sales representative and his regional manager. "They understand the problem," he says. They told him they hope the situation improves toward the end of November, "but they wouldn't guarantee anything."

Don Clark contributed to this article.

55

How a Tighter Supply Chain Extends the Enterprise

As companies go to the Internet to cut costs, the boundary is blurring between supplier and customer. ■ *by Philip Siekman*

Many of the brightest ideas for new pieces of computer hardware emanate from companies like Adaptec, a Silicon Valley outfit that turns over most of its production to people on the opposite side of the Pacific. But in a business that can change course in a week, 105 days used to elapse between an order for computer boards from Adaptec's headquarters in Milpitas, Calif., and shipment from its Singapore assembly plant. Then Dolores Marciel, the company's vice president of materials management, saw the light. Treating her suppliers like partners and, not incidentally, installing new computer software and using the Internet, she slashed the cycle to 55 days. Not only did customers get faster delivery, but in addition Adaptec cut its work-in-process inventory, or WIP, in half.

Adaptec is part of a growing vanguard of companies benefiting financially and in other ways from closer ties in their supply chains. Unifi, the leading U.S. maker of synthetic yarn, shares production-scheduling and quality-control information daily with Du Pont, a principal supplier of raw materials. Boeing's Rocketdyne unit uses supplier expertise to help reduce the time and money it spends building engines for space vehicles. And Mercury Marine, the big boat-engine producer, is starting to use the Internet to tighten connections with boat builders and engine dealers as a way to fend off Honda, Yamaha, and Volvo.

In companies that have made such moves, executives speak with the zeal of religious converts. Rocketdyne has cut WIP by $2 million in the past year alone, says general manager Byron Wood. Bigger shrinkage lies ahead, he asserts, along with a reduction in cycle time by a whole order of magnitude. When Adaptec established close computer links with its supply chain, its chip supplier, Taiwan Semiconductor Manufacturing Corp. (TSMC), was so impressed that it created a similar setup of its own. As a result, says Monty Botkin, TSMC's director of customer support in the U.S., he can now "service more customers with fewer people."

Software sellers and consultants say you ain't seen nothing yet. One enthusiast is Dave Cope, vice president of Extricity Software, a private company in Redwood Shores, Calif., that supplied the software being used by Adaptec and TSMC. Get him started, and he paces the room, describing the promised land with the passion of a tent-meeting evangelist. As Cope and others envision it, the future belongs to giant complexes of "virtual companies," tightly integrated from raw-materials suppliers all the way to the consumer, with information flowing front to back and back to front at the blink of a video monitor. More than linear supply chains, these leviathans will be assemblies of companies, tight schools of individual fish with a few always joining and others departing, while the mass moves synchronously in perfect, immediate response to customer demand.

The terminology and details vary with the speaker. Some talk of the "extended enterprise," while others expound on the "borderless corporation." But the gospel is much the same: Integrate the supply chain into some sort of virtual keiretsu and, promises consultant Ann Gracklin, a vice president of Avicon in Natick, Mass., you'll get "lightning-speed responsiveness while cutting a layer of inventory."

More and more corporations are buying in. Extricity's sales, on the way to tripling this fiscal year, are doing the Silicon Valley quickstep. Consulting companies are gathering clients on both sides of the Atlantic. Andrew Berger, a partner in Andersen Consulting's London office, says, "Six months ago it was like talking to fish about land." But no more. Berger says the reason for the interest is simple: "Value is leaking out of the supply chain." That's blood in the water for chief financial officers. Reengineering and continuous quality improvement have already picked up the big gains on the factory floor. The remaining economies must come from cutting the cost of moving, handling, and storing whatever comes in the back door or goes out the front.

At the same time, nearly everybody's encountering the computerized, Internet-connected buyer who, says Douglas Aldrich, a Dallas-based managing director of the A.T. Kearney consulting firm, "decides who gets to play, why they get to play, and, frankly, what price he or she is willing to pay for something." Aldrich has bad news for laggards who delay wringing out supply-chain costs. Lots of businesses, he says, are going to have to deal with "price points that are no place near the sum of costs plus a margin that most people have been used to living on."

Many companies are joining the parade for another reason: A querulous CEO wants to know what happened to the return he was promised on ERP, the enterprise resource planning computer system that took so much money to buy and so many months to install. "A lot of people thought ERP was going to enable them to have a tighter supply chain," says Robert Derocher, a senior manager at Deloitte Consulting. "A lot of them are realizing it doesn't."

ERP programs weren't designed to manage and report usefully on the hodgepodge of machinery and processes in the plant. But that's necessary if suppliers are to anticipate customers' needs and those customers, in turn, are to plan on orders arriving just in time. Dave Cone, CEO of Camstar Systems in Campbell, Calif., which sells a software program he claims does these jobs, says eight out of ten potential customers in recent months had ERP systems that they had put in about four years ago only to find that "the stuff didn't work in the factory." A year ago Camstar's customer base was mid-sized electronics companies plus the occasional early adopter like yarnmaker Unifi. Today it includes big-league players like Dell Computer and Corning.

Improving supply-chain management builds on trends that are transforming much of American manufacturing: outsourcing noncore activities, reducing the number of suppliers, and building only after orders come in rather than for inventory. But supply-chain integration still can't happen without seamless exchanges of order, marketing, and production information. That's well beyond the capabilities of electronic data interchange

(EDI), the inflexible system widely used for years to place and confirm orders but dismissed by Silicon Valley snobs as "glorified fax." Enter the Internet, the Web, e-commerce, and the almost inevitably quoted Forrester Research forecast that the annual value of business-to-business transactions over the Internet will reach $1.3 trillion by 2003.

The Internet brings hazards, of course. By making it easier for buyers to get bids from anywhere, e-commerce could mean that many are called but few are chosen. Deloitte's Derocher foresees that "where specs are tight and turnaround is critical, companies will have strong, deep relationships with partners." Other suppliers will see their products commoditized as nonstrategic items go out for Internet auction among qualified bidders. The low bid today wins this chunk of business. The lowest tomorrow wins the next.

The new environment is already on the way at Solectron, a big Milpitas, Calif., electronics contractor. Kevin Burns, vice president of global material services, says that by the end of 2000 about half of his purchases will be under vendor-managed inventory programs that require close cooperation between supplier and Solectron. For other purchases, it's meet the takedown, that is, the quarterly price-reduction target, or, says Burns, "I'm going to explore other alternatives."

Generally, though, the streamlined supply chain is more aspiration than reality. Sandor Boyson, co-director of the Supply Chain Management Center at the University of Maryland's business school, says, "Lots of companies haven't even begun to get a handle on the supply chain, let alone fashion extended-enterprise concepts." Boyson and his associates found only a fourth of 117 companies in an e-commerce association that claimed extended trading relationships with partners.

And claims can be just that. Says Joe Bellini, president of C-Bridge Internet Solutions, a consulting firm in Cambridge, Mass.: "If you look at most supply chains, even ones that are touting that they are a fully integrated, collaborative environment, in just about every one you can find a point where they're still following the old methods: 'We'll just prebuild what we think the market's going to buy, and then we'll adjust as we get the actual demand coming in.'"

Two major roadblocks are precedent and people. Bellini explains, "The technology is there to tightly couple these supply chains on a daily basis and collaborate, but the management processes, the way contracts are written for supply and demand between the nodes in the supply chain, just aren't able to support it." Moreover, other consultants say, as information filters through any chain, each participant is sorely tempted to adjust or manipulate it for his own reasons or because of prior experience.

Even among Silicon Valley's early adopters, the flow of information from point of sale to basic suppliers like chipmakers is not what it

> **The streamlined supply chain is more aspiration than reality at most companies.**

could be. TSMC's Botkin complains: "I'm at the bottom of the food chain. We're buying millions of dollars of equipment based on information that has been filtered down to me. I'm looking back up the supply chain, and really all I have is what I've read in the newspaper and some comments here and there from customers. It's not part of the culture in electronics to share that kind of information."

For many, sharing isn't what they've been taught. Says Christopher Gopal, an Ernest & Young global director: "They still look at procurement as a semi-adversarial deal where you propose your hardball bids, come up with somebody who has the lowest price, and then try to get that price down." These tough negotiators are now being asked to cooperate and trust. "To work effectively," says Deloitte's Derocher, "you've got to believe that if you make the pie greater, everybody benefits." Accepting that will take time. Adaptec's Marciel has it right: "Although people say they like change, they only like it when it doesn't include them."

Poster children for the cause are big-box retailers like Wal-Mart, which has long required suppliers to manage their portion of its inventory, and a few Silicon Valley players like Cisco Systems, which has a vested interest in expanding Internet use. Any morning after 4 A.M., 7,000 Wal-Mart suppliers can go into Wal-Mart's database and find out which store sold how much of their products for a two-year period ended the previous midnight. In its last fiscal year, Cisco ran up revenues of more than $12 billion with only 500,000 square feet of its own manufacturing space.

Customers now call up Cisco's Website to configure, price, and order $1 billion of its networking equipment a month. Cisco then sends orders back out across the Internet to board producers and assemblers including Celestica, Flextronics, Jabil, and Solectron. Products are built and tested to Cisco standards, sometimes with procedures run remotely by Cisco. Most are drop-shipped to buyers, untouched by human hands on Cisco's payroll.

Wal-Mart and Cisco are so dominant that supply chains follow their dictates instead of functioning as completely cooperative efforts. But lots of collaborative efforts are under way elsewhere to tighten the relationship between buyers and sellers. Chevron, for example, is getting its predominantly independent gas stations to work together. Says C-Bridge's Bellini, who is helping with the project: "Chevron now has the ability to go back to the Cokes and the Pepsis and the cigarette makers, and negotiate for 8,000 locations." The aim is not to hammer down prices, says Bellini, but to raise the question, "Is there a way where everybody wins–suppliers, Chevron, and the retailers?"

Companies working at integrating frequently start by looking in the direction along the supply chain–upstream or downstream—where initial gains are easiest to get. They're in a hurry because they are under stress from new competition or new technology. What follow are the recent experiences of two companies, all stressed, and all reacting by forging closer relationships with suppliers or customers, generally with the help of the Internet.

(This article continues)

UNIFI: Tightening Starts at Home

Little known outside its industry or its home state of North Carolina, where it has its headquarters in Greensboro and plants in eight small towns, Unifi dominates a highly specialized niche in the textile industry. In the year ended last June 28, it generated revenues of $1.4 billion–and a handsome 19.5% return on equity–by "texturizing" partially oriented yarn, a stiff, first-stage polyester or nylon with the look and feel of small-diameter fishing line. Known by its acronym, POY is processed at blurred speeds using heat and tension to condition it so it can be woven. Some is sold that way; more goes through additional steps that alter the yarn's look, feel, and strength, and such characteristics as stretch. The clothes you are wearing or the upholstery on the chair you're sitting in may well have originated in a Unifi plant. The company has more than 70% of its market.

Unifi buys POY from suppliers such as Du Pont and Nanya, an Indonesian company with a plant in South Carolina. But it also makes some in Letterkenny, Ireland, and in a year-old facility in Yadkinville, near Winston-Salem, N.C., which now supplies about a fourth of what Unifi uses in the U.S. The Irish plant starts with petrochemicals. Yadkinville buys solid chips, again from suppliers such as Du Pont and Nanya. Those are melted and extruded in spiderweb-thin filaments that are hardened in air and then spun and entangled together, dozens at a time, to form a single strand of POY.

Yadkinville is close to science fiction's "lights out" factory, where everything is run by computers and there's nobody on the production floor. POY filaments stream down two stories from the melting and extrusion stations at 120 mph or faster. On the ground floor, about a football field in size, 312 winders each feed POY onto six spool-like "packages" that weigh 40 to 45 pounds. When the winder finishes six, the completed packages are automatically rotated out of the way, and six more are started. If the finished packages are not removed from the machine in eight minutes, the new ones will fill up enough to collide with them, jamming the winder and spilling the near-unstoppable flow of POY onto the floor.

Before that can happen, an automated-guided vehicle, or AGV, rolls quietly down the aisle and retrieves the completed material. With caution lights blinking, it shuttles the material to a transfer rack that in turn carries the packages off to an adjoining factory for texturing. Some 12,000 packages make the trip every 24 hours. The only human on the winding floor of the POY plant full-time is a quality-control inspector. It's a lonely job. The lights stay on, but except for the occasional visitor or maintenance person, there is nothing out there except whirring machines and eight AGVs ghosting about.

Unifi's major competitors are Indian and Indonesian companies, including supplier Nanya, that are, in some cases, integrated from oil well to textile plant. When Asia caught the economic flu, these companies aggressively cut prices for yarn, fabrics, and apparel sold in the U.S. Automation and process control systems like those at Yadkinville have helped Unifi survive in this tough climate. The company has also been evangelizing up and down its supply chain, urging everybody to cooperate as though they were vertically integrated.

Several years ago Unifi recognized that a prime requirement for supply-chain integration is to get your own house in order. Says Michael Smith, a vice president of Unifi Technologies, its information technology group: "It all depends on what happens on the shop floor." In what is now a companywide program, Unifi has not only automated processes and machines but has also linked them. Manufacturing information can be gathered continuously, consolidated, interpreted, and "exported" to the ERP system for use in managing the business. Since every batch of chips, every package of POY, and every spool of yarn is tracked and recorded, poor quality in some textured yarn was recently traced all the way back to one of the 1,872 spinnerets used to form POY in Yadkinville.

On a daily basis starting last year, Unifi has been exchanging production and quality information over the Internet with supplier Du Pont (but not with Nanya, which is a rival as well as a supplier). Says Ralph Mayes, president of Unifi Technologies: "We are able to see the inventory Du Pont has. They are able to see our inventory and our demand, so we can both optimize production." In plants where Unifi makes yarn to order, it also sends out work-in-process information daily to customers.

So far, none of these information exchanges is done computer to computer, with suppliers and customers able to peer into Unifi's database. But, says Mayes, "we see ourselves doing more and more of this and moving to Internet access, allowing partners to come in instead of pushing data out." While Mayes' group is working on that, it will also be advising other companies. Convinced that it now knows how to create and install what it calls "integrated manufacturing systems," Unifi is spinning off part of Unifi Technologies as a manufacturing-systems consultant.

(This article continues)

MERCURY MARINE: Focusing on the Demand Side

Mercury's private network is being moved to the Internet to give dealers better access.

The parent, Brunswick Corp., makes a lot of recreational and outdoor equipment: boats, bowling alleys, bikes, and its original product, pool tables. But Mercury Marine boat engines power the company. Last year the Mercury group rang up $1.4 billion in sales, 38% of Brunswick's $3.9 billion, and brought in two-thirds of the company's $340 million in operating income. Mercury makes outboard engines in Fond du Lac, Wis., which serves as group headquarters. It builds inboard, ski, and stern-drive engines, probably accounting for about a third of the group's sales, in Stillwater, Okla.

With sales estimated at 200,000 engines a year, Mercury has about 40% of the U.S. outboard market. Outboard Marine's Johnson and Evinrude brands straggle behind; more worrisome competition comes from Japan's Yamaha and Honda. Honda got a big assist when the U.S. Environmental Protection Agency ruled that emissions by new outboards must be reduced annually between 1997 and 2006, for a 78% overall decrease. The standard two-stroke outboard burning a gasoline-oil mixture won't make it under the limbo bar. But Honda has long made only clean-burning four-stroke outboard engines that meet the EPA target.

Mercury has since caught up, bringing out its own four-stroke engines and a direct-injection two-stroke that is fuel-efficient as well as low in emissions. However, the effort is hurting margins. Both designs are costlier to build, yet competition holds down the price. In the past, Honda's four-stroke had to meet the two-stroke price; now Mercury has to meet the Honda price. That is complicating the supply chain downstream. Some buyers aren't ready to give up old-style two-stroke engines, which put out a lot of power per pound. So Mercury's outboard catalog has expanded to include all three engine types, not to mention horsepower ratings from 2.5 to 250, and special versions for "blue water" and "coastal" use. Counting all variations, Fond du Lac turns out about 400 different outboards.

Until the early 1990s, outboard engines were sold mainly to dealers who mated them to boats. However, the market is changing. There's some consolidation of dealers, bringing professional management to a business that needs it. And about half the engines sold now go to boat builders that provide dealers with a boat-outboard package. Both trends make the business more predictable and manageable. Yet this, too, puts pressure on margins, since boat builders and dealer groups expect and get volume discounts.

The competitive picture is different in the stern-drive and inboard market. Mercury's share is somewhere north of 70%, enough to have made it the target of antitrust and restraint-of-trade suits from dealers and its only important competitor, Volvo. Although Mercury doesn't say, probably nearly half of the Stillwater plant's output is shipped to the two biggest pleasure- and fishing-boat builders, sister divisions of Brunswick, whose brands include Sea Ray, Bayliner, and Boston Whaler. The rest of the production goes to several hundred other boat builders. Market dominance here is not all it's cracked up to be. Business is flat. Politically, Mercury can't increase market share. Nor can it push up prices, since that makes all boats, including Brunswick's, more expensive and encourages potential buyers to do something else with their extra cash.

Anybody who thinks manufacturing has fled the U.S. ought to walk through the Fond du Lac plant. Mercury's outboard production is vertically integrated from the scrap can lids used to make aluminum alloy on down the line to the finished product. Stillwater isn't much different. The plant buys engine blocks from General Motors but modifies them for use on water and adds fuel, electric, and other components. Unswayed by gurus who encourage companies to put a narrow definition on core competency and outsource to the max, Jim Hubbard, Mercury's chief of staff, claims, "We have to have a strategy to compete long-term on cost and quality. So we want to do as much as we can that makes economic sense."

This still leaves room for tightening supplier relations. Among other items, Mercury buys the covers for its outboards, called cowls, and both its plants buy hydraulic components. Fond du Lac recently made a deal with the supplier of the hydraulic device that assists boaters in tilting outboards out of the water. To cut handling and transportation costs, the supplier is going to start consigning truckload lots to the factory rather than shipping in smaller quantities, and will get paid as they're used. The savings will be shared. Mercury says it is going to extend the consignment idea to other suppliers.

Mercury's biggest effort to date has been on the demand side, where the company is trying to make it easier for customers to do business with the company. MercNet, a private electronic network system for parts ordering, has been around since the mid-1980s. Now, says Geof Storm, Mercury's chief information officer, the group "is trying to use technology as a competitive weapon."

MercNet is being moved to the Internet so that dealers can access it with nothing more than a PC and a browser. Along with ordering parts, they can enter an engine type and get all the service bulletins for that model, or search the database for a way to fix a particular problem. Now being planned: electronically sharing forecast information and collaborating on promotions with big dealers.

One thing outboard dealers and boat builders can't do over the Net is buy engines. The reason is not technology, but resistance from Mercury's sales department. Says Gary Tomczsk, an executive charged with introducing supply-chain changes: "They want a more personal touch on that." What he means is that the sales force fears that electronic ordering will eliminate up-selling and cross-selling, that is, the ability of a salesperson to talk a customer placing an order into buying a more expensive engine or adding something else to the order, such as one of the company's inflatable boats. As Storm notes, "There are a lot of culture changes involved when tightening the supply chain."

Such barriers, however, are being overcome at Mercury's inboard operation. Tomczsk has a green light to install a system enabling Stillwater's boat-building customers to buy engines over the Internet. He hopes to prove to the outboard salespeople that "upsale and cross-sale is not as big a problem as they expect it will be."

56

EN GARDE, WAL-MART

Retail rival Carrefour bulks up

All right, so it's not quite as good as winning the World Cup. But the French, dispirited after months of fruitless haggling to create Europe's largest bank, have bounced back by creating Europe's No. 1 retailer with the merger of homegrown chains Carrefour and Promodes Group. Carrefour's $16.5 billion acquisition of Promodes, announced on Aug. 30, does far more than give France a national champion, though: The merger creates a much tougher playing field for Wal-Mart Stores Inc. in its drive to expand internationally.

With 8,800 stores in 26 countries and combined revenues of $65 billion, Carrefour is set to challenge Wal-Mart around the globe. As Europe's new top dog, Carrefour can use its buying clout to extract deeper discounts from suppliers, undercutting rivals and accelerating a push toward consolidation in the industry. The Promodes deal also widens Carrefour's impressive lead in several Latin American and Asian countries. What's more, Promodes brings to the union a reputation for solid inventory and distribution systems, an area where Carrefour has long lagged behind Wal-Mart. "We're creating a worldwide retail leader," says Carrefour Chief Executive Daniel Bernard, who will head the merged company.

CRITICAL MASS. In Europe, the deal puts pressure on Wal-Mart to make another acquisition. The retailer already has holdings in Britain and Germany. But if it doesn't grab

> Buying Promodès gives Carrefour the muscle to vie with Wal-Mart globally

another partner soon, it could be left without the critical mass to become a major European player. Its biggest European holding, Britain's Asda Group PLC, is only one-fifth the size of the bulked-up Carrefour. Likewise, Wal-Mart needs to counter Carrefour's expansion in emerging markets. Only hours after unveiling the Promodes deal, Carrefour announced the acquisition of three Brazilian chains, boosting its market share there above 20%, vs. 1.4% for Wal-Mart.

Certainly, Carrefour isn't about to dethrone Wal-Mart. Now the global No. 2, Carrefour is still far behind Wal-Mart in sales and market capitalization (table). Even if Wal-Mart has trouble growing in Europe, it has room to expand in the U.S., especially in the grocery business. Carrefour, by contrast, has fewer opportunities in its saturated home market. And despite Carrefour's headstart in Asia and Latin America, Wal-Mart has plenty of openings because mass-scale retailing in many countries is only starting to develop. "The scope for growth all over the region is tremendous," says Hans Vriens, a Hong Kong-based vice-president for the U.S. consulting firm APCO Asia.

But Carrefour is a nimble competitor. Since 1963, when it opened the world's first hypermarket, selling groceries, clothing, and other merchandise under one roof, it has been a marketing pioneer. Today, a Carrefour shopper who stops in to buy groceries or a pair of tennis shoes can also get a watch repaired, order mobile-telephone service, rent a car, or book plane tickets and hotel rooms for a vacation. Wal-Mart offers few such services.

Carrefour also has been an innovator in store design, softening the look of its warehouse-size buildings by installing wood floors and nonfluorescent lights in some departments and putting service counters in the food department, where shoppers can get meat, cheese, and bread sliced to order. "Carrefour has incredible depth and breadth of range," says Philippe Kaas, a partner in Paris of OC&C Strategy Consultants. Such services also boost margins: Carrefour's 1998 profits, up 13.6% from the year before, were $755.2 million on sales of $32 billion.

Equally striking has been Carrefour's successful push into foreign markets. It began expanding across Western Europe and into Latin America during the 1970s, opening its first store in Brazil in 1975. During the past decade, it has moved into Asia and Eastern Europe. Merged with Promodes, Carrefour is the No. 1 retailer in Brazil, Argentina, and Taiwan, as well as in France, Spain, Portugal, Greece, and Belgium. True, Carrefour has had setbacks. It made a disastrous foray into

TWO GIANTS FACE OFF

CARREFOUR

SALES $65 billion*

MARKET CAP $47 billion

STRENGTHS Innovative marketer, aggressive, experienced in foreign markets

WEAKNESSES Lacks strong logistical and information systems, crucial to improving efficiency

LIKELY NEXT MOVE Cut costs in Europe while pushing Asian and Latin American expansion

WAL-MART

SALES $160.2 billion*

MARKET CAP $200 billion

STRENGTHS Dominates U.S. market with superefficient supply and distribution network

WEAKNESSES Spotty record on foreign expansion

LIKELY NEXT MOVE Seek more acquisitions to extend its reach in Europe

*Forecast for 1999   DATA: BUSINESS WEEK

(Cont.)

the U.S. market in the early 1980s, when it opened a handful of stores in the Philadelphia area and soon closed them because of weak sales. Emerging markets are risky business, too. Carrefour reported a net loss of $10.4 million in Asia last year. Latin America's economic woes could hit Carrefour's bottom line this year.

A key challenge for Carrefour is logistics. Wal-Mart has clobbered its U.S. competitors by creating tight links with suppliers and fine-tuning its distribution system, squeezing out costs and allowing it to keep prices low. To compete, Carrefour will have to tighten control over its operations, which have been decentralized, says Ajay Hemnani, international retail analyst at Management Ventures Inc. in Cambridge, Mass.

But Carrefour has already proved its mettle in head-to-head combat with Wal-Mart. "They're just relentless—the toughest competitor I've ever seen anywhere," says a retail executive who watched Carrefour ward off Wal-Mart in Brazil and Argentina in the mid-1990s. To counter Wal-Mart, Carrefour slashed prices, remodeled, and even relocat-

ed stores. When a planned Wal-Mart store opening in one Argentine city was delayed by construction problems for four months, Carrefour seized the opportunity to renovate its closest store.

Wal-Mart, by contrast, has taken a cautious approach to foreign expansion, moving into Mexico in 1991 and then Canada before pushing into South America and Europe. It's the No. 1 retailer in Mexico, but foreign sales last year accounted for only 9% of Wal-Mart revenues, vs. 44% for Carrefour.

SHOPPING LIST. Carrefour, saying it sees greater growth potential elsewhere, has stayed out of Britain and Germany, the two European countries Wal-Mart has recently entered. Wal-Mart likewise has stayed away from Carrefour's strongholds in France and southern Europe. But that could soon change as European retailers brace for a shakeout. Governments in France, Germany, and other countries have moved to protect small merchants by placing a near-moratorium on large new stores. So the only way to grow is to acquire stores and squeeze more profits out of them.

Analysts expect Wal-Mart will look for an acquisition in France. That would not only give Wal-Mart a piece of Europe's No. 2 retail market after Germany but would also become a link in a Europewide distribution network. That's key if Wal-Mart is to compete with players such as Carrefour, whose networks are already well-established.

Wal-Mart, however, is a careful buyer and is unlikely to rush into a French acquisition. No matter. Other big European chains, including the Netherlands' Ahold, have said they are eyeing French retailers. "If Wal-Mart wants to get in, it really has to act quickly," says analyst David Shriver of Credit Suisse First Boston. Whether in Paris, Sao Paulo, or Seoul, these two global heavyweights will be duking it out for some time to come.

By Carol Matlack, with Inka Resch, in Paris and Wendy Zellner in Dallas, with bureau reports

U.S. Superstores Find Japanese Are a Hard Sell

BY YUMIKO ONO

Staff Reporter of THE WALL STREET JOURNAL

TOKYO – When **Office Depot** Inc. and **OfficeMax** Inc. entered the Japanese market two years ago, Japan's 20,000 small stationery stores shuddered. The $13 billion stationery industry was archaic, and the stores usually charged full price. The two U.S. companies had grand plans to open hundreds of office superstores, behemoths of a type Japan had never seen, filled with cut-price pens, notebooks and fax machines.

But the U.S. stores proved to be too big and too American for Japanese consumers. Meanwhile, a nimble local competitor came out of nowhere to trounce the U.S. retailers at their own game. Stumbling, the Americans are changing course, testing store formats entirely different from their U.S. formulas.

The office superstores are among a big crowd of American retailers that have run into trouble here. During Japan's great recession of the 1990s, U.S. companies stormed in, aiming to make a killing by revolutionizing a tradition-bound retail industry. They sparked profound changes with their new products, offering better value and wider selections. But only a few, including **Toys "R" Us** Inc. and **Gap** Inc., truly succeeded. Many others are scrambling to revise their strategies, and some are even giving up.

JC Penney Co. is closing its five home-furnishing stores, in part because so many products, from curtains to bedsheets, had to be made differently for Japan. **Spiegel** Inc.'s Eddie Bauer unit, after much prodding from Japanese staffers, is straying from its strategy of selling the same products it sells in the U.S. It recently designed straight-leg pants and stretchy shirts to better fit the Japanese shape. And **Sports Authority** Inc. recently reduced its stake in a Japanese joint venture to 8.4% from 51%. Its Japanese partner, **Jusco** Co., is now opening smaller stores.

"Retailing is such a local business, it's not that easy to succeed," says Kyoichi Ikeo, a professor of marketing at Keio University's business school. However well a retailer fares in the U.S., he says, "you can't just take the same formula and expect it to work in Japan."

The travails of Office Depot and Office Max show why. Like many foreign merchants, the two office-supply giants linked up with local partners that knew the lay of the land, a strategy that permitted quick expansion but limited operational control. Office Depot, the No. 1 office-supply retailer in the U.S. in terms of revenue, negotiated a 50-50 joint venture with **Deodeo** Corp., a Hiroshima electronics chain. OfficeMax, the No. 3 U.S. office retailer, formed a joint venture with the supermarket chain Jusco. Jusco was developing suburban malls and planned to put OfficeMax stores in them. Encouraged, OfficeMax announced plans to open up to 200 stores by 2002.

But the Americans soon hit a wall. Japanese office products are so different from those in the U.S. – just for starters, loose-leaf binders here have two rings instead of three – that they had to buy most products from traditional local suppliers. Because they were selling the same products as their Japanese rivals, they also had to compete extra hard on price. But they didn't always get the best sourcing deals, with some suppliers even insisting on going through costly middlemen for fear of annoying neighborhood stores.

The stores also turned out to be simply too American. Office Depot opened two U.S.-size stores in Tokyo and Hiroshima. They were more than 20,000 square feet each, and featured wide aisles and signs in English. But with rents in Japan more than twice those in the U.S. and personnel costs sky-high, the stores were too expensive to run.

Japanese consumers were baffled by the English-language signs and put off by the warehouselike atmosphere. Tellingly, when Office Depot later reduced the size of one Tokyo store by a third and crammed the merchandise closer together, sales remained the same, the company says.

An even bigger challenge was brewing at **Plus Corp.,** Japan's No. 2 stationery maker. Striving to lift its sagging sales, Plus created a small division in 1993 called Askul to sell discounted stationery by catalog. Askul targeted exactly the same customers as its U.S. rivals: small business owners that weren't getting the discounts that big companies buying in bulk received. Askul's wide selection and catchy name – it means "it will come tomorrow" in Japanese – hooked young clerks who liked the ease of ordering from their desks.

When the U.S. retailers opened shop in late 1997, Askul slashed its prices and boosted selection. Askul also beat the Americans at pleasing core customers. Aware that most small companies put young "office ladies" in charge of ordering stationery, it ran loyalty programs aimed at them: If a company placed orders totaling 100,000 yen (about $920), it won a teddy-bear clock. A 200,000-yen purchase brought a box of chocolates.

The result: Sales continued to soar, despite the new competition and a long recession. In the year ending May 20, Askul expects sales to grow at least 77% from a year earlier to 40 billion yen ($367 million). Twenty percent of those sales are likely to come from an Internet business it started two years ago, an arena Office Depot and OfficeMax haven't yet entered. "We don't think there are a lot of reasons why we should lose" to the Americans, says Hiroyuki Komatsu, vice president of marketing and customer service at Askul.

Last year, as the challenges mounted, Office Depot reversed strategy. It severed ties with its partner, Deodeo, and closed its large store and delivery center in Hiroshima, Deodeo's hometown. That let it act more nimbly and focus more on Tokyo, where it opened four ministores that are about 5,000 square feet, or a fifth the size of its U.S. stores.

Office Depot says that this year it plans to add another four to 10 small stores to the six stores it already has. Its new Depot stores still have American radio programs blaring in the background. But the signs are in Japanese, and the shelves, lining narrow aisles, don't stock as many files or as much copy paper. To compete with Askul, the company is beefing up its two catalogs. Office Depot declines to disclose its sales in Japan but says its losses here last year probably exceeded $30 million.

Meanwhile, OfficeMax, with six large stores in the Tokyo suburbs, says it too is switching to the small-store format in Tokyo. It opened its first "business express store" in Tokyo in November. A spokesman won't provide details of future plans but hints that OfficeMax is mulling further changes in strategy.

Bruce Nelson, president of Office Depot's international business, says his company plans to decide later this year whether its small-store format is working.

The Japanese market "has enormous risk and it has the potential of enormous payout," he says. "It will just be one of the best places where we do business – or it will be one of the worst."

THE BROAD BACKLASH AGAINST E-TAILERS

Brick-and-mortar rivals set up legal curbs all over the place

When Texas-born Jonathan Coon co-founded 1-800 Contacts Inc., a venture that sells contact lenses over the phone, fax, and Internet from an office in Orem, Utah, he made his native state an early target market. But the Lone Star state has given Coon the cold shoulder. In 1997, Texas optometrists successfully lobbied to pass a law requiring out-of-state lens providers to obtain the original, hand-signed prescription before shipping contacts to Texas customers. That makes it more time-consuming to order on the Web, which generated half of 1-800 Contacts' estimated $145 million in sales last year. "Retail optometry has done a good job of striking fear into the hearts of consumers," fumes Coon.

He's not the only online entrepreneur to feel the sting of a brick-and-mortar backlash. Threatened by displacement in cyberspace, retailers, distributors, and other middlemen are waging a surprisingly successful, behind-the-scenes campaign to block e-commerce. While a few cases have come to light, most have occurred under the radar screen at the state level. Now, a new report, due on Jan. 31 from the Progressive Policy Institute, a Washington think tank, catalogs how pervasive the offline rush for protection in everything from autos to wine has become. "The revenge of the disintermediated represents perhaps the biggest threat to the widespread digitization of the U.S. economy," says Rob Atkinson, director of the Technology & New Economy Project at PPI and author of the report.

Atkinson figures that anti-e-commerce efforts cost Americans at least $15 billion a year. And that has consumer groups turning up the heat. The nonpartisan Consumer Federation of America is working on a study showing how consumers are being penalized by state curbs, strongly backed by dealers, on Net auto sales. "This is the kind of fight we really like to take on," says Mark N. Cooper, CFA's director of research.

Of course, industries threatened by economic change have often sought government protection. In the 1920s, the Horse Association of America campaigned to limit the use of trucks and automobile parking on public roads. Independent banks lobbied in the 1930s for a ban on branch banking that was a bulwark against big banks for nearly half a century. But because the disintermediation wrought by the Net is so far-reaching, the reaction has been unusually broad, as the PPI report makes clear.

TELEMEDICINE. Consider radiology. Because X-rays and other forms of medical imaging move easily across the Net, patients can get second opinions from out-of-state practitioners without having to travel. But while this expands opportunities for some doctors, many fear the competition and are pushing to strengthen state licensing laws to raise the bar for out-of-state radiologists. So far, only six states have rules that make telemedicine easier. "Issues around protecting turf do enter in," says Dale L. Austin, an official of the Federation of State Medical Boards, which backs easing the rules.

Wine merchants, music retailers, and realtors have also appealed to lawmakers and the courts to rein in e-commerce. Last year, liquor wholesalers successfully lobbied Congress to let states go to federal court to sue out-of-state suppliers that ship alcohol to consumers in states that ban direct shipments across their borders. "Just the threat of that will diminish online sales," predicts David K. Rher, president of the National Beer Wholesalers Assn. The National Association of Recording Merchandisers is suing Sony for selling compact disks that, when played on a computer, can link users to a Sony-owned Web site where they can purchase more CDs with a few mouse clicks.

Many of those battling shops in cyberspace argue that they just want to level the playing field. Wineries shipping direct to consumers who order on the Web, Rher insists, don't pay state sales and excise taxes and don't take precautions to keep deliveries out of minors' hands. Others say they are acting in consumers' best interest. "With fewer companies controlling too much copyrighted material, there won't be room for choice" or price competition, says Pamela Horovitz, president of the recording merchandisers suing Sony. And radiologists who balk at letting out-of-state specialists make diagnoses from images made locally say patients need to be protected from unqualified practitioners.

What to do about the e-commerce protectionists? Atkinson recommends that the Bush Administration create an e-commerce ombudsman to advocate for cybercompetitors. That's not likely, given Bush's hands-off approach to markets. But the feds already seem to be taking his suggestion that they beef up enforcement against retailers that collude against companies selling directly via the Net. Last year, the Justice Dept. forced the National Association of Realtors to stop requiring brokerages to list exclusively with its Web site, realtor.com. But for now, the brick-and-mortar folks will be keeping the pressure on.

By Amy Borrus in Washington

Car Sales

Putting on the Brakes

Auto dealers thought the Internet would drive them out of business. Not quite

By Karen Lundegaard

Staff Reporter of The Wall Street Journal

GAITHERSBURG, Md.—On the second floor of a Chrysler dealership in this Washington suburb, two college students sort through e-mail on a muggy August morning. Thirty leads have arrived since the previous afternoon, on top of more than a dozen the previous day.

In two days at Fitzgerald Auto Mall, 61 leads will arrive from people interested in a whole range of vehicles, from Jeep Grand Cherokees to Volkswagen Jettas. The young men forward some of the leads to a designated Internet sales staff downstairs whose charge it is to quickly respond, by e-mail or phone to the prospective buyers. Final prices are given. Customers are told if an item is no longer in stock.

Answers over the phone? No stalling tactics just to get consumers into the showroom? Is this the future of car sales?

Perhaps. For many dealers, the Internet, which was supposed to signal their death knell, has instead provided a way to distinguish themselves from competitors down the block.

A Believer

Take Jack Fitzgerald, who owns this dealership and eight others in three states selling some 20 different car brands through 31 franchises. "The Internet is the greatest thing since sliced bread," says Mr. Fitzgerald, whose business last year earned $6.9 million on revenue of $407.5 million.

Mr. Fitzgerald sees the Internet playing a role in most of his future business. It's not the "end-all, be-all" some technology pundits predict, he says. Consumers will still want to test drive vehicles. But it is access to information—particularly his no-haggle price that he posts on a sleek Web site—that he believes will eventually ease the stress of buying a new car. "Our sales are easier," he says. "Our customers are happier."

This year, Mr. Fitzgerald expects online business to account for 10% of his new-car sales, or close to $25 million. But that figure understates "dramatically what the Internet is doing for us," he says, noting that most cus-tomers use the Internet to do research and then contact him the old-fashioned way—by telephone or in person—not online.

All the hype of the online automotive world comes down to dealers on the front line like Mr. Fitzgerald. Here, in the numbers, lies evidence of why some of the automotive dot-coms—which, because of strict regulations, must go through dealers like Mr. Fitzgerald—have begun to disappear. For if the online brokers and referral sites, some of which charge dealers thousands of dollars a month, can't convince him of their worth in producing leads that become sales, they have little chance of survival.

Of course, some analysts and online car brokers argue that if Internet sites had been allowed to sell directly to consumers, as many had hoped to do, they would have cut costs as has happened in other industries, instead of adding to them.

Mr. Fitzgerald, who has been selling cars for 44 years, counters that many of the upstart car dot-coms received undeserved media attention and were run by young people who didn't understand the auto business to begin with. Existing dealers, he says, are "part of the automotive infrastructure. Don't bypass me."

At 65 years of age, Mr. Fitzgerald claims he never feared the Internet. But even today, he doesn't know how to check e-mail or surf the Web. He can't even use the computer sitting in the corner of his office suite, away from his desk, stacked with research and stories of automotive retailing. The computer "sits there and I have someone come in and do stuff for me," he says.

A Dealer's Tale

But he has been testing the online auto waters for four years. He has tried most of the online-referral sites and car-selling services, which he considers an advertising expense, and dropped many of them.

JJF Management Services Inc., the Kensington, Md., holding company over all nine Fitzgerald Auto Malls, used **Autobytel.com Inc.,** the Irvine, Calif., mother of the online-referral industry, several years ago for its Buick and Pontiac franchises when Autobytel was getting started in the Washington area. But Mr. Fitzgerald dropped it after a few months.

"We were getting some business off it," he says. "But it wasn't enough to justify the expense."

That became a familiar pattern. He tried CarPoint, the Redmond, Wash., unit of **Microsoft** Corp., for a year beginning in October 1998. But he discontinued it because the average $25-a-lead fee was too expensive for sketchy returns. He dropped DriveOff.com Inc. after less than three months this spring. The problem: the $250 fee it told dealers to build into their price, says Bill Cash, JJF's general sales manager. The fee would have cut into Fitzgerald's margins or forced it to increase its posted prices for DriveOff clients. In June, CarPoint acquired DriveOff from **Navidec Inc.,** a Denver Web-site developer.

JJF also lasted only six months with Autobytel's used-car listing service. The service didn't update the inventory frequently enough to be useful, says Mr. Cash. Customers would drive to the dealership only to learn the car they were interested in had been sold weeks before.

An Autobytel spokesman says that it's the dealers' responsibility to update online inventory, noting that 65,000 used cars are listed on the site on any given day. The spokesman acknowledges that the service is more expensive than some competitors, but says its benefits, including high-quality leads, make it worth the higher price.

Mr. Fitzgerald says he has found better results going it alone. His own Web site, two years in the making, gives four different prices for each car in stock: the manufacturer's sticker

No Free Ride

Cost analysis for the first eight months of the year of the online fee-based referral services still used by Fitzgerald Auto Malls' Maryland stores

	Total Cost	Cost/Lead	Cost/Sale
AutoVantage.com	$15,705	$12.68	$147
Cars.com	18,295	7.77	124
InvoiceDealers.com	17,043	19.00	243

The chain of dealerships had better luck with its own Web site, FitzMall.com, in the first eight months

	Leads	Sales	Closing Ratios
AutoVantage.com	1,239	107	8.6%
Cars.com	2,354	147	6.2
InvoiceDealers.com	897	70	7.8
FitzMall.com	1,290	220	17%

Source: Fitzgerald Auto Malls

(Cont.)

price and invoice price (the dealer's cost), and Mr. Fitzgerald's two prices (one with $300 of service contracts and the other without). The Fitzgerald prices usually fall between the sticker and invoice prices, though with incentives they can run lower than invoice. And this year he changed the Web address from Fitzgeraldautomall.com to the simpler FitzMall.com. Nearly 35,000 visitors a month logged onto the site in July and August, staying an average of 10 minutes each. That's up from 14,500 in December, just before the name change.

Follow the Lead

Mr. Fitzgerald has created a separate Internet sales staff to handle all of the Internet leads, nearly 1,000 in August alone.

Joe Graves was hired for the Internet staff in May. By July, he was the top Internet salesmen and one of the top salesmen across the chain. He sold a record 22 cars online in July and 20 more in August, compared with an average 6.5 cars sold online per month per dealership, according to a recent study by the National Automobile Dealers Association, a trade group based in McLean, Va.

How'd Mr. Graves do it? Responding quickly and honestly, with complete pricing information by phone or e-mail, he says. "Many dealers are still telling Internet customers, 'Come on down, we'll give you a great price,'" he says. "They're still in the old-school way of thinking of selling a car, and they will fail miserably with the Internet."

During a reporter's two-day visit, 17 of the 61 Internet-generated leads are from Fitzgerald's own Web site. Two-thirds are from the three referral services Mr. Fitzgerald still uses—InvoiceDealers, owned by **Dealix** Inc., in Palo Alto, Calif.; AutoVantage, the referral service of **Auto-Nation** Inc., Fort Lauderdale, Fla.; and Cars.com, a division of **Classified Ventures** Inc. in Chicago. Five are from auto-maker Web sites, including three from Japan's **Toyota Motor** Corp., that get high praise from Internet staffers.

Toyota sends e-mails with potential leads directly to Fitzgerald. By contrast, Detroit-based **General Motors** Corp. requires dealers to log onto its Web site daily and check a mailbox there for leads. A GM spokesman says it's in the process of changing its Web site so that leads can be sent by e-mail directly to dealers.

Now, Fitzgerald is selling cars to 20% of the leads it receives from Toyota, the highest Internet sales rate among all the manufacturers sold by the dealership. (Among the major brands Fitzgerald doesn't sell: Ford Motor Co. and Japan's Honda Motor Co.)

But, Mr. Fitzgerald adds, none of the manufacturers are making Internet sales easy for him. A customer who shops a manufacturer's Web site, and then hopes to link to a local dealer, will never get to FitzMall.com. Instead they'll land on a "cookie-cutter" Web page that the manufacturer suggests all dealers provide. Mr. Fitzgerald says he has little control over the content of these sites and no real choice but to provide them, at a cost of some $50,000 a year.

"It's frustrating," he says. "We pay this extra money to have sites that we don't need."

John Holt, chief executive of Cobalt Group Inc., the Seattle-based company that designs many such sites through relationships with 15 auto makers, says that when he started his company in 1995, some dealer Web sites had incorrect logos, misspellings and wrong vehicle specifications. The auto makers, through a more uniform look, are "insuring the quality of the brand and making sure the leads they create are handled properly."

A Waste of Time

Fitzgerald's manufacturer-linked Web page proved unhelpful in at least one of the potential 61 Internet sales. Rockville, Md., resident Ronald Sheinbaum, in search of a maroon 2000 Jeep Grand Cherokee Limited, had logged onto various Web sites. Those that demanded too much information, he anonymously exited. He tried Jeep's Web site, where he found some valuable information. But the dealership links from there, including Mr. Fitzgerald's Jeep site, offered little beyond name and location. Though he placed a request for more information with the Fitzgerald Jeep site, Mr. Sheinbaum says he walked away from the Internet experience feeling as if he had wasted his time.

"I didn't want to buy the car online," says the 58-year-old supermarket owner. "I wanted to comparison-shop online—anonymously. I [had hoped to] compare apples to apples, and not have a lot of the salesman talk that goes with it."

Bogged down with appointments, Fitzgerald's Internet salesman didn't return the call until two days later, says the dealership. By then, Mr. Sheinbaum had bought a new Cherokee at a dealer a few miles from his house.

Such tales make Bill McClure, one of the car dealership's two Internet managers, cringe. "Speed is king," he says. "Especially on the Internet." He pounds that into the staff in special Internet sales classes. He understands their excuses, but he also knows that delays lose sales.

But, of course, many of the leads turn into sales. John Chmielewski was pleasantly surprised on FitzMall.com to be able to get an exact price—$14,995—on the new Hyundai Sonata he wanted. After finding FitzMall.com through his Web search engine, the Arlington, Va., resident sent an e-mail to the dealership asking for a return call, which he says he received within hours. He then asked competitors to beat or match the quote. But their starting prices were more than $3,000 higher, a difference Mr. Chmielewski says he knew he couldn't dicker away.

"When I was in my 20s," says Mr. Chmielewski, a 50-year-old Navy program analyst, "I kind of enjoyed the sparring between the dealers and me. But at my age, it's just not worth that kind of grief for $500." The Fitzgerald salesman named a fixed price and asked if he wanted to pay it. "It was kind of nice," he adds. "It was absolutely the best car-buying experience I've ever had."

Even Fitzgerald's non-Internet staff say they use the FitzMall.com Web site to their advantage. Scott Ascher, the general sales manager, who admits he's from the old school of car selling, tells all customers as he makes appointments with them to check out Fitzgerald's inventory and prices online before they come in. And Chrysler salesman Howard Haley brings all his customers to the computer kiosk in the middle of the showroom to show them the Web site. "I love it," he says. "It works great."

With the 61 leads, four vehicles are sold by mid-September, but more sales are still possible. Many of the consumers are still researching cars that they might want. Of the four sold, all were handled by the Internet staff in Gaithersburg. Mr. Fitzgerald has been incubating the program here, testing it to make sure it works before taking it to his other dealerships.

He has also changed the advertising focus. He now has FitzMall hats and license plates. In his weekly Washington Post advertisement, instead of listing vehicle price after vehicle price next to blurry car photos, he advertises the Web page address. "Click.Save," the headline reads.

He has his advertising spokesman, Washington Redskins quarterback Brad Johnson, talking up the Web site on local television. "If you're shopping online for your next car," Mr. Johnson says in one television ad, "FitzMall.com is the only address you need."

The Fitzgerald staff closed an average 17% of the leads from FitzMall.com in the first eight months of the year, including a record 35% in July. That compares with the single-digit returns with most of the online car-referral services. Mr. Fitzgerald doesn't want to spend an average of more than $100 a sale. But this year, AutoVantage has cost an average $154 a sale, and InvoiceDealer a whopping $227 a sale.

He's already cut back spending on the referral services, which had been as high as $15,000 a month and now averages about $6,400 a month for three providers.

But even that's too much, he says. He has ordered his general manager to renegotiate contracts with the three providers or drop them. He would rather spend the money advertising his own Web site or trim ad expenditures generally and lower his car prices, he says. Eventually, he predicts, he'll get rid of all the referral services. "I'm pretty sure that's where we'll end up," says Mr. Fitzgerald. "I don't think they're doing anything for me."

Ms. Lundegaard is a staff reporter in The Wall Street Journal's Detroit bureau.

Promotion

60

Does Creativity Count?

Examining the link between good advertising and marketplace success. *An* Adweek *Report By Noreen O'Leary*

For ground zero in the debate about creativity versus effectiveness, look no further than the doghouse at TBWA\Chiat\Day. In the past year, the ad agency that helped make advertising a pop phenomenon—and transformed the Super Bowl into a consumer showcase—has witnessed two untimely deaths. First, the reign of one of the public's favorite corporate mascots, Taco Bell's smooth-talking Chihuahua, ended. Then, Pets.com, the client promoted by TBWA\C\D's spokespup sock puppet, exploded in cyberspace.

The Taco Bell canine was retired last year, and the agency recently replaced. Pets.com, which recently went out of business, left behind the sock puppet as one of its most valuable assets. Both situations may be the result of business problems unrelated to the success of the advertising. But more than any agency, TBWA\C\D—appropriately born in the shadow of Hollywood—epitomizes the prickly tensions inherent in a business melding art and commerce.

TBWA\C\D has created award-winning advertising so entertaining it assumes a life of its own in the larger culture. Some might say that's the problem. Advertising that draws too much attention to itself may also detract from the grittier realities of pushing product.

"I think it's all about having faith in advertising. As a client, you have to believe great creative can give you strategic advantage. Sometimes people get caught in the headlights when they come here. They use advertising as something to save brands when they're in trouble," argues Tom Carroll, CEO of TBWA\C\D in Playa del Rey, Calif., "When things go wrong, how much of the blame can you lay on advertising, and how much of it reflects other things beyond an agency's control?"

Traditionally, the industry's two schools of thought have been divided between advertising that engages consumers in an entertaining way and creates an emotional bond and advertising that offers up boilerplate fact-fueled messages, USP promises and product shots.

"It's absolutely absurd when people try to separate things like creativity and effectiveness. The reason creativity is essential is that it's one of the best ways to connect with consumers," argues Brendan Ryan, president of FCB Worldwide. "I want our advertising to be both funny and entertaining but within the context of selling. It's the ultimate arrogance to think otherwise."

Those distinctions may be blurring. Gary Goldsmith went from running one of the industry's most respected creative boutiques, New York-based Goldsmith/Jeffrey, to heading up the institutional corridors of what is now Lowe Lintas & Partners.

"More and more clients are realizing creative ads work better, are more memorable and make their point more effectively in the marketplace. You can run a good creative ad fewer times. People can remember it after seeing it three times rather than 30 times," says Goldsmith, chairman and chief creative officer at the New York agency. "Any USP advantage is gone in 15 minutes if you don't create an emotional bond with consumers."

That's a notion many of the industry's old-line Madison Avenue shops increasingly agree with.

"I'm of the opinion you should bring together art and commerce," says Steve Novick, chief creative officer at Grey Worldwide. "But you can do some of the most engaging, funny work in the world and if it doesn't motivate me and get me off my ass, stimulate some part of my brain to do something, then it doesn't work."

Part of the historical divide may have been forged in response to the industry's swelling ranks of awards shows, blamed for allowing creative people to toast each other—and boost their careers—at the expense of client production budgets.

"Some clients are a bit suspicious of awards, thinking that all the emphasis on creativity gets in the way of the sales message. They're more of the belief that you state the sales claim and then repeat it seven times," contends Donald Gunn, former worldwide director of creative resources at Leo Burnett and past president of the Cannes Festival. "Commercials which are based on the right message and translate into fresh, charming, engaging and intelligent work are better than commercials with the right message but which lack these creative qualities."

To help boost creativity's status, Burnett and Gunn conducted a study six years ago that combed the rosters of winners from the main international shows to identify the 200 "most awarded" commercials in 1992 and 1998. The agency then contacted the creators of the work, or relevant clients, to measure product performance.

In his arguably unscientific survey, Gunn found that 86 percent of those ads were successful in achieving stated goals—compared to 33 percent "across all advertising on average," according to Gunn.

Gunn, who founded a London-based newsletter that tracks how agencies fare in creative competitions, notes the award-winning ads he researched were two-and-a-half times more likely than average commercials to be linked to marketplace success.

Still, some respected advertising practitioners wonder if the lack of business objectives as a criteria in awards shows—with the exception of the Effies—dulls the edge of creativity as a performance tool.

"[Executive creative director] Chris Wall and I were talking about awards shows, and we were saying there's no degree of difficulty applied to a client's business problem. Most of the ads that win are small stuff that is outlandish and fun," says Ogilvy & Mather chief creative officer Rick Boyko. "Chris says 'If the Olympics were run like these awards shows, Pamela Lee Anderson would win the gold for doing situps, while some Ukrainian doing back flips wouldn't even place.'"

To see how widely recognized creative campaigns fare in effectiveness, Adweek examined three clients. First, we looked at E*Trade, one of the few solid dotcoms built amid the excesses of the past year. The online brokerage brand was built at warp speed, using irreverent humor in a staid financial industry and lost none of its sass in its translation of solid marketing strategy.

The second example is Coca-Cola's Sprite, an astonishing illustration of the pure power of image. The brand's repositioned advertising has quite literally become the product itself and turned around Sprite's fortunes.

Lastly, we studied Pets.com, which offers a sobering glimpse at the reality of life behind a popular advertising facade, where no matter how clever, popular and well-conceived an ad campaign is, it may not be enough to compensate for a flawed business model.

"You can have great advertising but the rest of the organization could be awful, which makes performance hard to judge—except in direct selling, where the ad is the point of distribution," observes Tom Messner, a partner at Messner Vetere Berger McNamee Schmetterer/Euro RSCG in New York. "An ad, to be good, needs to meet an objective. A beautiful building that is washed away with the first rain cannot be good architecture. A good ad is one that meets an objective honestly."

61

Bank on It

E*Trade's ads drew consumers online—and gave the brand its symbolic status.

What running shoes were to the athletic individualism of the 1980's, the Internet is to the financial self-empowerment of the new century. With E*Trade, Goodby, Silverstein & Partners has found one of those enviable, rare marketing relationships comparable to Wieden & Kennedy's with Nike. Like Phil Knight, the sports company's founder, E*Trade's Christos Cotsakos is a chief executive who believes in the power of advertising, invests heavily in it and values its role in defining what he hopes will be the dominant brand in a new industry.

Like Wieden and Nike, Goodby has created aspirational advertising that distinguishes E*Trade through an emotional bond with investors in a commodified category of some 150 to 170 companies. "Fire your broker" is the financial-service company's equivalent of "Just do it."

"In the spring of 1999, we knew online investing and the Internet were about to become a force. We could see it was becoming a lightning rod in the larger culture," said Michael Sievert, chief sales and marketing officer at Menlo Park, Calif.-based E*Trade Group. "To become a brand leader, we knew we had to be effective at seizing that consumer momentum. We had to capture the sentiment of empowerment."

That ambition may be best summed up in E*Trade's appearance on the Super Bowl, before more than 800 million viewers worldwide, last year. The Web company broke through the clutter of dot-com commercials by buying two spots on ABC's pregame show, two spots during the game and sponsored the halftime show itself. E*Trade, a brand many viewers had never heard of, dominated the commercial showcase.

Some of the dot-coms sharing the Super Bowl airwaves are no longer in existence, thanks in part to heavy ad spending. E*Trade also spent heavily at one point pouring nearly half of its revenue into marketing. The difference with E*Trade? One answer may lie in last year's football extravaganza: The company enjoyed a 600% increase in new accounts in the quarter after the Super Bowl, compared to the same period a year earlier.

Underlying the sudden growth was a combination of solid marketing strategy coupled with funny memorable advertising—work with attitude not usually associated with the financial-services category. After Goodby produced its first campaign last year, "It's time for E*Trade" the company became one of the top four most-recognized, blue-chip Internet brands as ranked by Opinion Research Corp.

"In four months, we built the brand," said Goodby creative partner Rich Silverstein. "The advertising wasn't just about preaching. It was about how E*Trade relates to you. Our spots go to the heart of the product. They work because the ads make sense, and E*Trade spends appropriately to their objectives."

Those objectives amount to nothing less than creating the Internet's first pure-play world-class financial-services concern. Accounts rose from 91,000 in September 1996 to 2.94 million in June 2000. E*Trade is now the industry's fourth-largest entity in customer assets and number of accounts and No.3 in trading volume.

The company developed its marketing strategy in three phases, extending its value proposition beyond online trading.

In 1996, E*Trade began building awareness in the online investing industry with the little-noticed tag: "Some day we'll all invest this way." Next came Goodby's work, which focused on developing brand awareness. More recently as the industry became more of a price-driven commodity category, E*Trade sought to pull away from the pack with a new emphasis on diversification. In October, the company unveiled its new marketing theme, "E*Trade. It's your money," to underscore its delivery of a wider range of products and services like banking and asset management. It now has customers in branded Web sites in Denmark, Korea, Japan, U.K., Sweden, Australia, New Zealand and Canada, and has launched a Chinese-language site.

"From the beginning, Christos had a very clear brand scheme. It started with a focus on trading, and he's evolved it from there into banking and personal finance," said Silverstein. "I think they had a matrix and at the appropriate time introduced products and services. It's a lot like FedEx. They started with a basic message of 'cheapest, fastest' and then moved into things like small packages and envelopes and electrical devices."

That comparison is no coincidence. CEO Cotsakos is a former Federal Express executive who has borrowed from the delivery service's marketing strategy.

"Christos is a smart, tough, take-no-prisoners kind

(Cont.)

of guy," said Silverstein. "That's the special kind of sauce that makes advertising work. He's a CEO who loves marketing, wants it and wants it to work."

E*Trade's emphasis on purple and green in its communications, for instance, recalls the heavy use of purple and orange in FedEx's branding.

E*Trade was founded in 1982 as an electronic stock trading service for institutions. After Cotsakos joined in 1996, he took the company public and created its Internet brokerage operations. Like the Internet pioneers at America Online, the Vietnam veteran knew he had to advertise heavily in order to win the battle for brand awareness and early market share in a burgeoning industry.

Cotsakos, who has said "brand building was always first and foremost" in E*Trade's corporate development, hasn't been afraid to sacrifice profits in that pursuit. In fiscal 2000, E*Trade spent almost $522 million on marketing, more than 38 percent of its revenue. (More recently expenditures have slowed. In the quarter that ended Sept. 30, E*Trade spent about $92 million, as compared with $115 million in the June-ending period.) While competitors like Ameritrade and Charles Schwab were already operating online brokerages when E*Trade entered the fray, Cotsakos's aggressive early tactics helped to create the perception of the company as an early innovator.

E*Trade's near-saturation spending has also helped give it category ubiquity. In its efforts to help build awareness, it has become synonymous with the industry itself [netting a *Brandweek* Marketer of the Year nod for svp Jerry Gramaglia in 1999].

E*Trade really established the premium online trading brand, which is frequently cited along with Amazon and eBay," said Jason Lind, e-finance research analyst at investment bank Piper Jaffray, a subsidiary of Minneapolis-based U.S. Bancorp. "They do these blind tests which find that half the time people see an online trading ad they think it's E*Trade. As long as other people continue to advertise, they can just draft on to that message."

E*Trade has used its brand equity to expand into new businesses. The company got into banking through the acquisition of Telebank this year. After retiring that name in May, the company rebranded it as E*Trade and used the teaser line, "Bankers, your brokers should have told you," from the Santa Monica, Calif.-based agency Big Honkin' Ideas.

"The E*Trade brand itself is very unique," said bank representative Debra Newman. "While we haven't adopted quite the irreverent tone as the E*Trade brokerage uses, we do share the same personality and edge. We use a sense of humor in an industry where that seldom happens."

E*Trade's move into banking helps offset stock market volatility and attracts a larger share of the wealth of its customer base. Customers of the company's brokerage operations tend to be younger and have smaller balances in their accounts than those at Charles Schwab.

That may account, in part, for the down-to-earth imagery and scenarios in Goodby's advertising.

"E*Trade feels like the common man with situations everyone can relate to," said Silverstein. "Schwab is Madison Avenue with glitzy celebrities like Ringo Starr and high-price athletes."

Therein may lay the challenge for Silverstein and his creative troops in San Francisco as the edgy upstart increasingly attains institutional credibility.

Just ask Nike and Wieden & Kennedy.

"How do you keep the brand's status over time? You don't do the same thing over and over again," Silverstein said. "You have to keep evolving the advertising. Nike did it the right way for 10 years and then lost its way. You constantly have to stay one step ahead."

A Not-So-New Attitude

Sprite remains true to its brand essence.

Ten years ago, Sprite was a laggard niche brand, as seemingly lost in time as its kitschy "limon" symbol, plucked out of the fertile imagination of a dated Madison Avenue era. While competitors like 7 Up attempted to stand out through initiatives like "The Uncola" campaign, Sprite stuck with selling itself as a clear, lemon-lime soft drink in a category of clear, lemon-lime soft drinks. Then came Coca-Cola troubleshooter Sergio Zyman. As a consultant, Zyman turned his attention to the troubled brand in 1992. He discovered Sprite consumers didn't even like its citrus taste; they drank it because of its cheeky unconventionality. So Coca-Cola threw out the brand's very reason for being—a lemon-lime alternative to the company's core colas—and infused it with attitude. That move quickly resonated with target urban teens and African Americans.

Relaunched in 1994 as a mainstream brand, Sprite became the carbonated-beverage category's fastest-growing brand for five of the past six years. Now it's the country's sixth most-popular soft drink, having slipped behind rival Mountain Dew. En route, Sprite's advertising picked up a slew of top awards, including an Addy, Andy, Effie gold, Clios and an Art Directors Club gold.

Rather than have advertising play off product attributes, advertising became the product attribute. "Image is nothing. Thirst is everything. Obey your thirst," one of Sprite's early repositioning taglines from Lowe Lintas & Partners, New York, served as a sly wink at the role the brand's ads played in reviving its fortunes. Meanwhile, Burrell Communications Group, Chicago, began using hip-hop's Curtis Blow and rappers like Heavy D in Sprite campaigns targeting urban markets.

"In the 1980's, we added a 'cool' factor to the brand" said McGhee Williams, evp-managing director of marketing innovations at Burrell. "It was a fresh approach in advertising for African Americans, but it was bigger than just African Americans. Things like hip-hop, rap and new jack swing are as much a cultural force as they are music."

Sprite's repositioning reaped its biggest rewards in 1998, when former senior brand manager (and former Brandweek Marketer of the Year) Darryl Cobbin took the "Obey your thirst" message to a target audience of young males. Laying the groundwork for rap-inspired and fashion parody ads and a pivotal link to the National Basketball Association, Cobbin helped propel the brand to the No.4 slot in the beverage category.

Sprite's success is now fueling a lemon-lime marketing battle that is quickly replacing the cola wars. In 1999, the citrus category grew 2%, topping the flat results of cola drinks in a sluggish carbonated-beverage market. Lemon-lime sodas now account for $6.5 billion in annual retail sales, or about 11% of the U.S. market for sodas. PepsiCo is eyeing those growth opportunities—and the chance to narrow the gap with Coca-Cola—with last month's national launch of lemon-line competitor, Sierra Mist, the company's first major new carbonated soft-drink trademark in 16 years.

Yet Sprite still commands a 58% category share and continues to outspend its competitors. Pepsi is pouring $50 million into Sierra Mist, while Cadbury Schweppes is increasing 7 Up ad spending 15% to $40 million. Meanwhile, Sprite is putting almost $70 million behind the ongoing "Obey your thirst" strategy.

"With 'Obey' we've become so much more connected with teens," said Pina Sciarra, Sprite's brand director. "It's a straightforward, honest message: 'We're just a soft drink. We're not going to make you a better windsurfer.' We've never strayed from that core message, and we don't plan to now."

This year, Sprite created a contest offering the chance for a one-on-one game with Team USA's NBA players who participated in the 2000 Olympics, and re-upped for sponsorship of the Billboard Music Awards. The soft drink hopes to further solidify its hold on teens through a new partnership with RocketCash, an Internet e-tailer gateway that helped create Sprite.com. Sprite drinkers receive RocketCash codes under bottle caps and can use those codes as online currency. Sprite also has tie-ins with Polo Jeans and Tommy Hilfiger, another brand whose success is tied to the hip-hop culture.

Less clear is Sprite's holiday movie tie-in with *How the Grinch Stole Christmas,* a $10 million on-air and merchandising effort. Coca-Cola execs note that the plot's anti-Santa positioning jibes with Sprite's attitude. The link also plays off mutual association with the color green and the company's preexisting marketing pact with the film's distributor, Universal Studios.

Death of a Spokespup

**Despite the glorified ads, the pooch
is all that remains of Pets.com.**

Around this time last year, Pets.com's wildly popular sock puppet debuted in Macy's Thanksgiving Day parade, a high-flying testament to Internet marketing. This holiday season, the e-tailer's mascot is no less symbolic—now of a deflated industry whose lofty branding ambitions turned out to be a lot of hot air.

Because of the sock puppet's visibility, critics lost little time in holding up Pets.com as emblematic of dot-com companies that burned through market capital only to be extinguished by the Nasdaq's fall in April. But unlike many flaky Web clients that approached ad agencies in the past couple of years, Pets.com was a better bet. For one thing, the online pet-supply retailer enlisted John Hommeyer, a former hot-shot marketing director of baby care at Procter & Gamble. TBWA\Chiat\Day, with its track record of attention-grabbing creative and rapport with entrepreneurial clients, was also brought on board.

Pets.com's prospects looked so good that companies like Amazon.com and Disney became backers. Outsiders became fans as well. The site received rave reviews from Consumer Reports Online.

Pets.com outspent its competitors—spending close to $20 million on advertising last year, according to Competitive Media Reporting—and seemed to get its money's worth. During Super Bowl XXXIV, Pets.com's spot scored the No. 1 recall ranking for the lowest media investment during the game, according to Active Research. Then there was all the free media: Not long after the February 1999 launch, the sock puppet became a celebrity complete with gushing coverage on *Nightline* and *Access Hollywood* and profiles in magazines such as *Entertainment Weekly, Time* and *People.* Under a licensing agreement, the pup's image has been smacked on everything from plush toys to T-shirts and place mats—with royalties split between the Web retailer and the ad agency.

The mascot worked so well that recent media reports about the company dwelled as much on the sock puppet—one of the company's remaining assets being shopped around—as they did on the cause of Pets.com's demise. All of which is bittersweet for its ad agency. In the perennially optimistic world of Madison Avenue, few agencies want to be reminded of their limitations. Yes, advertising can be creative and effective, but brand visibility doesn't necessarily translate into purchase intent.

Awareness isn't able to compensate for the vagaries of flawed operating strategies.

"Business models, market conditions, the Nasdaq, VCs—they're not in my control. This has nothing to do with the success of the advertising." Said-Carisa Bianchi, president of TBWA\C\D in San Francisco. "Ad agencies are hired to create brands, and we did that in spades. Pets.com is one of the few that achieved that in cyberspace. In the Internet space, a lot of business models just needed more time."

Marketing chief Hommeyer, who left the company in May and was not replaced, and top executives at Pets.com declined interview requests.

It's easy to see why the site's senior management feels embattled. The category quickly lost favor with Wall Street, and Pets.com's stock slid from a high of $14 in February 1999 to just 22 cents earlier this month. Even though Pets.com attracted 570,000 customers, it never figured out how to make money in a low-margin business with high shipping costs.

On paper, the founding strategy made sense: Get devoted pet owners to become regular customers for staples like food and kitty litter, with the expectation they'd splurge on pricier pet accessories and toys. That never happened. The bulk of Pets.com's sales was heavy bags of dog food. From the onset of advertising in the fourth quarter of 1999 through the first half of this year, Pets.com spent more than three times in marketing than the $22 million it took in as revenue, according to Competitive Media Reporting. As sales started to slip, the company embarked on heavy couponing promotions through Amazon.com, significantly deflating the level of the average order, which had been around $30 to $40.

Still, as Pets.com unveiled new sock puppet advertising this fall, traffic continued to build on the site. In October, for instance, Pets.com was the category's most popular destination, attracting 1.8 million visitors, nearly double that of its nearest rival, Petsmart.com (which recently bought the Pets.com URL).

Petsmart.com has spent much less on advertising, playing off the association with its storefront retailer parent. While Hommeyer didn't have the built-in advantage of a physical presence, he still approached offline marketing for the Web as he would at a brick-and-mortar entity.

(Cont.)

At P&G, Hommeyer was known for his sharp relationship marketing skills, and at Pets.com he talked about the sock puppet's success in terms of "share of heart" as well as "share of pocket." In developing an early marketing strategy for the pet retailer, he made sure thorough research was conducted in homes and at dog parks to discern the particular likes and dislikes of pet owners.

TBWA\C\D initially offered ideas involving a pet psychic and a scenario linked to Doctor Dolittle. But when the sock puppet was presented, Hommeyer immediately embraced a concept inspired by the tradition of great spokesicons like Tony the Tiger, the Marlboro man and the Pillsbury doughboy. Accompanied by the line, "Because pets can't drive," the sock puppet was deliberately left without a name so consumers would always have to say 'Pets.com' when referring to it. In his view, people knew the character Spuds McKenzie but didn't necessarily relate him to Budweiser. A better example was a character like the Energizer Bunny also from TBWA\C\D for client Eveready. While memorable, many consumers are still not sure which battery company keeps him on the payroll.

That may have also been a problem with the sock puppet, stuck in a competitive frenzy of similar sounding URLs.

"The advertising was great; it featured the brand and connected well with people. But I'm not sure if consumers could say whether the sock puppet was for Pets.com, Petstore.com or Petopia," said Barry Parr, e-commerce research director at IDC, a Mountain View, Calif.-based market-research firm. (That problem may soon be moot, as Petstore.com closed in June and Petopia.com is struggling to stay afloat.)

From the perspective of corporate identity, Pets.com also had its work cut out. In the early days of the Web, such a URL would have been an asset, serving as an easy-to-find intuitive choice for consumers browsing the Internet. But as people have become more sophisticated in their Web searches, the URL might have become a liability.

"Pets.com faced a real challenge in their generic name," said Parr. "While it seemed like a good idea in 1996, it quickly became clear that it's really hard to build a brand off a generic name," Around the same time Pets.com shut down, sites such as Furniture.com and Mortgage.com also ceased to exist.

True to its Chiat roots: the agency is arguably better at entertaining consumers than selling down to them.

"Good creative advertising is effective advertising," said one senior executive at the agency. "But there's no advertising good enough to survive a bad business model."

64

THE CORRUPTION OF TV HEALTH NEWS

Viewers who tune into the local news on Channel 11 (WBAL-TV) in Baltimore will see a series of reports on women's health by Donna Hamilton, the station's health news reporter. In these reports, part of a series called "The Woman's Doctor," Hamilton explains why women should get screened for cervical cancer, for example, or how they can identify the warning signs of ovarian cancer.

Careful viewers might notice that the doctors in these news reports are all from Baltimore's Mercy Medical Center. What viewers do not know is that the reports are part of a promotional deal between Mercy and WBAL. Mercy pays WBAL a hefty fee to get its doctors on these reports. And Mercy officials meet with WBAL staffers every few months to discuss story ideas for upcoming reports.

Such deals involving hospital placements in news stories are increasingly common, hospital officials and television executives say. Many hospitals buy advertising time on TV, of course, but these deals are something different: Mercy wouldn't say what it pays, but hospitals can spend hundreds of thousands of dollars per year to get their doctors and their hospitals on the news.

RIVALRY. It's difficult to know exactly how widespread such arrangements are. Hospitals being offered the deals are sometimes reluctant to talk about them for fear of angering local stations and being locked out of coverage. Hospitals compete ferociously for patients, and loss of TV coverage can be devastating. Gary N. Michael, vice-president for

> **Consumers need unbiased medical information, not paid "news reports"**

marketing and business development at Mercy, says he has received numerous calls from other stations seeking advice on setting up such programs themselves. Medstar Television, a production company in Allentown, Pa., that brokers these deals and prepares the news reports, wouldn't say how many clients it has, but it did say its clients include hospitals, health plans, and TV stations in San Diego, Denver, Hawaii, and San Francisco. A hospital promotion group within the Association of American Medical Colleges (AAMC),

concerned about these new kinds of news sponsorships, has scheduled a panel session to discuss the issue at its upcoming meeting in March.

These promotional arrangements, by creeping into news reports, violate a cardinal principle of journalism–that news and advertising should always be kept separate. Advertising should never masquerade as news. And news outlets should not share undisclosed financial involvement with the subjects of stories. That was what got the **Los Angeles Times** in trouble last fall, when it wrote about the Staples Center entertainment complex and shared ad revenues with the center. "You want the public to trust that a news organization is going to approach any story without bias or favoritism," says Barbara Cochran, president of the Radio-Television News Directors Assn. and former Washington bureau chief for CBS News. "If the content is being selected or influenced by someone who is paying for the privilege of doing that, it is no longer impartial news reporting. There would be no reason to believe that it's honest."

ALARMS. For Mercy Medical Center, the WBAL deal is valuable precisely because it gets the hospital into the newscast. "Ads are limited by the amount of time–there's only so much you can say in 30 seconds," says Michael. "We wanted to showcase our docs as real people and get into the nitty-gritty issues, and I think you do that best through a news story." Mercy spends a third of its promotional budget on its WBAL contract. It employs a full-time public-relations specialist to administer the program, and it has hired a local sportscaster to give media training to doctors before they appear on TV.

The program clearly has proved its effectiveness, Michael says. When "The Woman's Doctor" began airing in 1994, Mercy was "a distant seventh...in the metro area when you asked what hospital you would recommend to a friend for women's health," Michael says. "After one year, we were ranked No. 2, and in 1997, we became No. 1."

For WBAL, the arrangement "was a new opportunity to create revenue," says Ronald L. Briggs, an account executive who works with Michael on the program. It also helped the station attract viewers. "In the beginning, it allowed us to promote our news. We were promoting Mercy, Mercy was promoting 'The Woman's Doctor,' and it was promoting viewership," he says. Mercy "has been on the cutting edge of marketing."

Marianne Banister, a WBAL-TV anchor who sometimes introduces the Mercy reports,

says the practice has alarmed reporters. "It has a lot of people in newsrooms going 'Whoa, whoa–what's going on?'" she says. She "was not particularly comfortable with it to begin with," but she feels the station has not crossed the "fine line between advertising, promotion, and news." News Director

> **"A PR agency or TV sales department can guarantee that an organization's physicians will appear on commercials . . . but they can't guarantee the physicians will be on the news, the most credible source for health information . . . "**
>
> *—FROM A MEDSTAR PROPOSAL THAT PUTS A HOSPITAL'S DOCTORS ON LOCAL TELEVISION NEWS, FOR A FEE.*

Princell Hair does not think the reports compromise the station's standards, because the news staff controls the content. "We decide what story to do, what not to do," he says. "We have complete control over the editorial content. If we didn't, I wouldn't be comfortable with this." What if the relationship with Mercy became known to viewers? "I don't think this would taint our relationship with viewers at all," he says. "It's providing them valuable information."

"RELATIONSHIP." Studies by the Radio-Television News Directors Assn., however, suggest that viewers are concerned about advertisers' influence on news. A poll of 1,007 people in 1998 found that 84% believe advertisers "sometimes or often" improperly influence news content. A similar poll of 300 TV news directors found that only 43% of them agreed.

Not every hospital is eager to pursue such TV deals. L.G. Blanchard, director of Health Sciences News & Community Relations at the University of Washington and the organizer of the medical colleges' meeting on this subject, recently turned down such a proposal. "To the uninvolved observer, it would appear that we were being asked to purchase positive news coverage," he says. He says colleagues at other hospitals have told him that prices for such arrangements can range from $25,000 to $200,000 per year. He says, "I can see a day when nobody is going to get news coverage unless they've paid for it. That's a world I don't want to live in."

Medstar Television Inc. has been arranging such relationships between hospitals and TV stations for more than a decade. "We build a relationship between a local television station and an underwriter in a marketplace," says Vice-President Susan Ferrari. "It could be a TV station and a hospital, or a TV station and a health plan." The "underwriter" pays Medstar to produce two 90-second reports each week, which are given free to local stations. The stations' reporters add their voices, making it appear that the reports were produced by the local station. "It's not advertising. It's really content that's prepared for the newscast," says Ferrari. "The TV station airs the program on its newscast." The reports are preceded or followed by brief advertising spots identifying the sponsor, but the spots do not explain that the sponsor paid for production of the news items.

NO SALE. Medstar would not say how much it charges, but a Medstar proposal obtained by BUSINESS WEEK says the yearly charge for airing two news spots per week for a year is at least $364,000. The figure rises in subsequent years of a multiyear deal. In its proposal, Medstar notes the particular value of featuring doctors on the news: "A PR agency or TV sales department can guarantee that an organization's physicians will appear on TV commercials...But they can't guarantee the physicians will be on the news, the most credible source for health information." Edward C. Dougherty, Medstar's vice-president for broadcasting, defended the company's editorial integrity. "We and the stations maintain total editorial control, from topic selection, research, script writing, final editing," he says.

That's not quite good enough. "Total editorial control" ought to mean the ability to choose the most qualified doctors and researchers to be part of a story–without being influenced by the hospital sponsoring the report. The sponsorship of TV news stories is a problem with an easy answer: TV stations shouldn't offer to sell the news, and hospitals shouldn't buy it. Medical news affects life-and-death decisions every day. It is essential that viewers and patients believe they are getting direct, unbiased information from local TV stations. If television news is prepared for the benefit of sponsors, rather than for the public, all of its credibility is lost.

By Paul Raeburn

Raeburn is senior editor for science and technology.

65

Kick Start

How Sony Marketers Gave 'Crouching Tiger' An Early Leg Up

A Word-of-Mouth Campaign Helped to Generate Buzz; Enthusiastic Hip-Hoppers

'That Whole Karate Scenario'

By JOHN LIPPMAN
Staff Reporter of THE WALL STREET JOURNAL

Rapper Ghostface Killah and author Naomi Wolf don't travel in the same circles. But lately, they've found common ground in a single cause: making "Crouching Tiger, Hidden Dragon" into a box-office hit and Academy Award contender.

The member of rap group Wu-Tang Clan and the feminist scribe have been willing participants in a campaign by Sony Pictures Classics to generate widespread interest in "Crouching Tiger." In one of the most elaborate examples of grass-roots stealth marketing, the studio has transformed director Ang Lee's lyrical period piece from art-house obscurity to breakout film.

This weekend Sony will vault "Crouching Tiger" from its current limited engagements to about 700 theaters around the country. How did the studio create a nationwide buzz for a Chinese-language martial arts film with a cast of largely unknown foreign actors?

In Hollywood, of course, these things don't just happen. In fact, the word-of-mouth is the result of a concerted effort to position "Crouching Tiger," starring Michelle Yeoh and Chow Yun-Fat, to appeal to a broad swath of women, teens, karate fans, action aficionados and foreign-film aesthetes. To make that happen, a crew of public-relations agents with fat Rolodexes targeted a core group of influential viewers for early screenings, hoping they would fan out and create a sort of party-circuit dialogue about the film.

It's a tactic well-suited for a market that's glutted with traditional ads, in a nation heading for an economic downturn. Marketers who sell everything from sneakers to music to vodka are desperate to slip their messages into consumers' ears directly from the mouths of real people. And when the approach works, it's much more cost-effective than buying mass-market ads.

Michelle Yeoh

The marketers of "Crouching Tiger" took the tactic to an unusual extreme. They set up a screening, hosted by Sports Illustrated for Women magazine, aimed at female athletes. The studio arranged Wall Street screenings for people like venture-fund manager Alan Patricof, advertising executive Jay Chiat and CNBC "Squawk Box" host Joe Kernen. Ms. Wolf presented the film to 150 graduates of a women's leadership institute. At $5,000 a screening, the events cost the studio a total of $40,000. Also recruited to the cause: a teenage Internet prodigy and the Tiger Schulmann Karate center chain, which hosted "Crouching Tiger" martial-arts demonstrations.

One of the pioneers of word-of-mouth marketing in Hollywood was Walt Disney Co.'s 1996 hit "Mr. Holland's Opus" starring Richard Dreyfuss. Paula Silver, a marketing consultant on the movie, set up screenings for orchestra leaders, music-teacher associations, instrument makers and congressional spouses to hit the funding-for-the-arts crowd. "We went to the constituents that would really have something to gain from seeing the movie," says Ms. Silver, in the hope they in turn would spread the word. The strategy "magnified the movie outside the realm of movie marketing," she says, resulting in "off-the-entertainment page editorials" in newspapers about the importance of music programs in the schools, and box-office grosses of $82.5 million.

It is an especially effective tactic when a film poses some kind of marketing difficulty. For example, though the DreamWorks SKG and Universal Pictures co-production "Gladiator" became a big hit, initially there were doubts that the public would embrace an old-style Roman epic. But last spring, DreamWorks and Talk Magazine—which was about to put star Russell Crowe on its cover—sponsored a select screening for 150 people at New York's Ziegfeld Theater, followed by a dinner at the restaurant Circo. The screening jump-started talk about the film, and won some nice write-ups from the likes of gossip columnist Liz Smith.

Similarly, Walt Disney Co.'s Miramax unit recently held a special screening of its current film "Chocolat" for Jesse Jackson, on the theory that he would be a good spokesman for the film's underlying theme of tolerance. The strategy takes advantage of a simple fact: Most people are tempted by the offer of a free movie—and the flattery of an early invitation.

Sony's effort began last March, after Tom Bernard, co-president of Sony Corp.'s Sony Pictures Classics and his partner, Michael Barker, saw the first rough cut of "Crouching Tiger." The film was directed by Mr. Lee, a Taiwanese-born director trained at New York University's famed film school whose credits include "The Ice Storm" and "Sense and Sensibility," and produced by independent production company Good Machine Inc.

The movie is a kung fu genre piece, with virtuoso martial-arts scenes. It's also a romance, enveloped in a musical score with performances by cellist Yo-Yo Ma.

The task of selling this odd mixture fell to Mr. Barker, 47 years old, and Mr. Bernard, 48, two executives who have toiled together in the small-potatoes field of independent film for more than 20 years and since 1992 have run Sony Pictures Classics. Their marketing budget for "Crouching Tiger" was $7 million, compared with the more than $20 million that is usually spent on mainstream Hollywood releases.

They started with the obvious maneuver: a noncompetition screening at the Cannes Film Festival in May. David Linde, a partner in Good Machine, said the movie was deliberately not submitted for competition at Cannes "because this film early on needed to be perceived outside the art-house ghetto," which frequently stigmatizes prize winners. Instead, says Mr. Linde, "we wanted to be perceived as entertainment, and expand the audience."

To court teens, Sony executives hired a 13-year-old boy, John Otrakji, of Rumford, N.J., to design a Web site about "Crouching Tiger." Mr. Bernard had run across Mr. Otrakji's skills when his mother brought a printout of the homepage of his Web site, cablejump.com, to a barbecue. The site was devoted to Mr. Otrakji's views of movies and games. An impressed Mr. Bernard dispatched a car and driver to ferry Mr. Otrakji into New York, where he met Sony executives. The Web site, which now focuses almost entirely on 'Crouching Tiger,' has received more than 31,000 hits, with young Mr. Otrakji receiving an initial fee of $100. He declares on the site: "This is a movie everyone in my generation has got to see."

The guts of

Chow Yun-Fat

the push came after Labor Day, as Sony sought to put the film before as many taste-makers as possible. That task was made somewhat easier by the reception "Crouching Tiger" had already received on the festival circuit: It had captured the People's Choice Award at the Toronto Film Festival in September and was the closing night presentation at the New York Film Festival the following month, giving the movie important credibility.

To engineer screenings, the studio hired Peggy Siegal, a New York-based movie publicist and fixture on the Hamptons party circuit. Ms. Siegal has built a database that contains 20,000 names, comprising the New York film and media community, which she uses to mine prospects for movie screenings. Wanting her to branch out, Mr. Bernard told Ms. Siegal: "We only want you to invite people to screenings you don't know."

Ms. Siegal didn't have any links to the hip-hop community, for example. But her partner, Lizzie Grubman, is the daughter of music-industry lawyer Alan Grubman. Through Ms. Grubman's connections, they were able to persuade the Wu-Tang Clan to "host" two screenings on Oct. 4 at Sony's U.S. headquarters in New York where 150 people showed up.

"Crouching Tiger" struck a chord with Olie "Power" Grant, executive producer of Wu-Tang Clan, who says the group's members were influenced by martial-arts movies while growing up and "were pretty much mixed up with that whole karate scenario." The screening had the desired effect: It won a mention in the New York Post's Page Six column, even though it mistakenly reported that the Wu-Tang Clan stars in the film. The movie itself has generated considerable en-thusiasm in the hip-hop community. Vibe magazine, which chronicles hip-hop culture, has had no fewer than four stories or mentions of the film.

On Nov. 6 came a screening for on-air newscasters in New York, hosted by local NBC anchor Chuck Scarborough and attended by local NBC anchor Sue Simmons, NBC legal correspondent Dan Abrams, CNN fashion guru Elsa Klensch and John Stossel of ABC News, among others. Mr. Bernard said he wanted on-air personalities at the screening rather than behind-the-scenes producers, hoping they would feel they had "discovered" the film themselves rather than having had it thrust upon them.

To reach another important group, a Nov. 8 screening was put together for 150 students of the Woodhull Institute, a New York-based organization co-founded by Ms. Wolf to mentor young women for leadership roles. They raved.

"I felt quite euphoric after I saw it," says Ms. Wolf. "It was one of the least exploita-tive, most liberating and most surprising textured portrayals of women in movies in a long time. And besides, she says, it didn't star "yet another thin, white ingenue to emulate."

When arranging for the Wall Street types to see the movie, Ms. Siegal contacted her friend Joe Kernen of CNBC's "Squawk Box," who agreed along with colleagues Mark Haines and David Faber to host a screening at Sony headquarters on Nov. 20. Mr. Kernen, who says his idea of a good movie is "watching 'Unforgiven' over and over again," thought "Crouching Tiger" was "cool. It didn't matter [that] it was subtitled." Mr. Patricof, meanwhile, said he realized after the movie started that he had seen "Crouching Tiger" previews in theaters and "decided I wasn't going to see it. People flying off the walls didn't appeal to me." But after seeing it, he said, "I've recommended it to everyone in the office."

Among those who attended the Sports Il-lustrated for Women screening was pro-bas-ketball star Rebecca Lobo of the New York Liberty. Ms. Lobo says she "would not normally go to a Chinese-language movie." But in this case, she says she has recommended the film widely, telling people "it is action-packed, entertaining and shows positive images of strong, feminine women."

As the film goes into wide release, Sony has minded even the most minute details. For example, it paid Kodak $100 a screen to change bulbs, dust off lenses and tune up screening systems in theaters where "Crouching Tiger" would play, ensuring the best possible projection of the film.

And Ms. Seigal's screening campaign has continued, though not all of her arrows have hit their mark. Last fall, her firm provided "Crouching Tiger" tapes to the New York Yankees, hoping they would be shown on the team plane during the baseball playoffs. That didn't happen, but this week she sent half a dozen tapes to the New York Jets football team, aiming to get it screened for karate en-thusiasts on the team including linebacker and karate blackbelt Mo Lewis.

Bruce Orwall contributed to this article.

Republished by permission from Dow Jones & Company, Inc., from *The Wall Street Journal,* "Kick Start: How Sony Marketers Gave 'Crouching Tiger' an Early Leg Up," p. A1, January 11, 2001; permission conveyed through the Copyright Clearance Center, Inc.

66

Read Their Lips

When You Translate 'Got Milk' for Latinos, What Do You Get?

The Answer Was a Surprise For a Marketing Group Courting Hispanic Teens

---

The Meaning of Biculturalism

By Rick Wartzman

Staff Reporter of The Wall Street Journal

LOS ANGELES – It was late February when Jeff Manning began to focus on a phenomenon he had never had occasion to think about before: slathering peanut butter and jelly on a tortilla.

The executive director of the California Milk Processor Board, Mr. Manning was poring over a report on the Latino community, searching for a way to reverse an industry sales slump in the heavily Hispanic southern portion of the state.

And right there on page 12, the answer seemed to jump out at him: The ranks of Hispanic teenagers, it noted, are projected to swell to 18% of the U.S. teen population over the next decade, up from 12% now. "When you see that kind of number, it's like, 'Wow,'" says Mr. Manning, whose organization is behind the ubiquitous "Got Milk?" advertising campaign.

But appealing to these youngsters, he learned, isn't as simple as cutting an ad in Spanish with tried-and-true Hispanic themes. The kids often live in two worlds: one rich in traditional Latino values such as a strong commitment to family and religion, the other in which they eagerly take part in mainstream teen America. The report described how they bounce between hip-hop and Rock en Espanol; watch "Buffy the Vampire Slayer" with their friends and Spanish telenovelas (nighttime soap operas) with their parents; blend Mexican rice with spaghetti sauce – and spread PB&J on tortillas.

When it comes to "young biculturals," the "conventional model" of straight Spanish-language advertising "is irrelevant," Roxana Lissa, a Beverly Hills public-relations con-

sultant who had prepared the report, told Mr. Manning.

To Mr. Manning, who spent 25 years at major ad agencies before joining the milk board in 1993, Ms. Lissa's advice made perfect sense. Soon, he was talking up the possibility of a "cutting edge" milk ad shot in "Spanglish." He foresaw combining distinctive Latino imagery with sights and sounds that are seductive to teenagers of all backgrounds. "I want to capture both worlds," Mr. Manning declared.

Four months later, a milk spot aimed at Hispanic teens is now ready. It will be aired across California starting next week on the Spanish-language network Telemundo. But the end result is radically different from what Mr. Manning and his team first envisioned –

Jeff Manning

a turn of events that stirred passions and raised a question with broad implications: What is the smartest way to peddle products to one of the fastest-growing demographic groups in the country?

As she sits in her small office one morning in mid-March, ad agency president Anita Santiago is pumped up by the prospect of producing a new style of television commercial.

Since 1994, Ms. Santiago's client roster has included the milk board, for which her firm has generated a series of Spanish-language TV ads tailored to Latino moms. Because "Got Milk?" doesn't translate well into Spanish – it comes out as, "Are You Lactating?" – the moms have their own slogan: "And You, Have You Given Them Enough Milk Today?" With tender scenes centered around cooking flan and other milk-rich Latin classics in the family kitchen (some of the ads were directed by the cinematographer from the film "Like Water for Chocolate"), the campaign has proved popular in its own right.

Yet as Ms. Santiago contemplates the approach that Mr. Manning has in mind, she realizes there is no easy formula to follow. "The word 'bicultural' has been thrown around a lot, but I don't think anybody has really figured it out," says Ms. Santiago, who founded her Santa Monica, Calif., agency 12 years ago.

Not that others haven't recognized the dual worlds of Latino teens. A couple of years ago, for instance, McDonald's Corp. hawked its french fries in ads featuring soccer star Tab Ramos hanging out with basketball's Scottie Pippen. During the 1993 baseball All Star game, a Spanish-language ad for Nike Inc. ran on CBS with English subtitles, a strategy

other major companies have mirrored. And a Levi Strauss & Co. commercial last year fitted a pair of jeans on a hip, young Latina who asserts her independence in Spanish as well as English.

Ms. Santiago imagines pushing the concept even further. "We're going to put ourselves right into that third reality" Latino teens experience, she says.

Meanwhile, up in San Francisco, there is similar excitement at Goodby, Silverstein & Partners, a unit of Omnicom Group Inc. that in 1993 created the "Got Milk?" campaign. Jeff Goodby, the agency's co-chairman, believes that by joining with Ms. Santiago, they can create a bicultural ad that will find a home not only on Spanish television, but on general market television as well. Says Mr. Goodby, whose firm has done work for Nike, Anheuser-Busch Cos., The Wall Street Journal and other big clients: "It's a killer idea."

The next step: Convene some focus groups of Latino teens, and determine which of their buttons to push.

Mana and Korn

At an office building near the Los Angeles airport in late March, Mr. Manning, Ms. Lissa and representatives from the two ad agencies are lined up behind a giant one-way window, noshing on M&M's and observing a group of Hispanic teenage girls relating their likes and dislikes.

"You can speak Spanish or English or any mixture-however you feel comfortable," the focus-group moderator, Horacio Segal, tells the eight 13- to 15-year-old girls seated around him.

As the two-hour session gets under way, the girls move seamlessly between the two languages. They tell of how they tune in to both Spanish- and English-language television, and rock out to the Mexican band Mana and the Anglo group Korn. They characterize themselves as "Latina," while the magazines to which they relate best are Seventeen and Teen People.

They seem, in short, to be the very embodiment of biculturalism that Ms. Lissa had sketched out. But as the girls watch a string of television commercials, something surprising happens – at least in Mr. Manning's view.

The spot they are most enthusiastic about is an ad in English for Kellogg's Corn Pops. It depicts a grunged-out teen being lectured by his parents, when all he wants to do is eat his cereal – a scene that several of the girls say they

Roxana Lissa

(Cont.)

can identify with, though it contains no special message for those straddling two cultures.

At the same time, an ad in Spanish for Mountain Dew with the Chilean technorock band La Ley doesn't resonate much. And the Levi's commercial in which the heroine speaks in Spanish and English doesn't work at all; a few of the girls complain that it's unclear what the ad is even about.

For Mr. Manning, the girls' reactions are eye-opening: They may be bicultural, he thinks, but as consumers of advertising they appear to be completely acculturated. As for language, they don't seem to care – or even notice – whether the message is delivered in Spanish or English or both. They never raise the matter with Mr. Segal.

A little later, the girls' attention turns to "Got Milk?" and, again, Mr. Manning is taken aback. He had always expected that the humorous campaign, which the California milk board licenses nationally, would be well-known and even liked by Latino teens; after all, "Got Milk?" has become part of the American vernacular. But he also anticipated that some in the group would gripe that the ads don't speak at all to their bicultural existence.

Instead, the girls gush over the commercials. They "make you feel like you're thirsty," says Olga, an eighth-grader who came to the U.S. from Mexico 11 years ago. As six different "Got Milk?" ads are played in succession, the room erupts in laughter.

Anita Santiago

Sue Smith, Goodby Silverstein's planning director, leans over to Mr. Manning and whispers: "They really love this stuff." Mr. Manning, clad in a "Got Milk?" T-shirt, beams.

A subsequent focus group, of boys the same age, is a bit less effusive about the "Got Milk?" campaign. But they still find the ads funny, and likewise don't say a word about language or lack of a bicultural perspective. Two more focus groups the next night, of 16- to 19-yearolds, do raise questions as to why more Hispanics aren't being cast in the ads.

By then, however, it's too late. Mr. Manning has all but decided to turn the notion of biculturalism on its head. His new idea: to take the existing "Got Milk?" spots and air them without any changes on Spanish-language television.

What's the Problem?

"Am I missing something? Tell me if I'm missing something."

A week has passed since the focus groups, and Mr. Manning's voice is booming from a speaker-phone on Ms. Santiago's conference table. She and several associates gather around. Ms. Lissa and Ms. Smith are also patched in.

In order to justify a brand-new campaign for Latino teens, "you've got to start with problems, guys," says Mr. Manning, back in his own office in Berkeley. "Where were the big problems with 'Got Milk?'"

The line falls silent for a moment before Ms. Lissa offers up an answer: The teens "didn't think the ads were speaking to them."

"But they did," Mr. Manning says, cutting her off quickly. "They liked them. They laughed at them."

By now, everybody knows where things are headed. Before the meeting, Ms. Santiago had proclaimed Mr. Manning's plan to introduce "Got Milk?" – in English – on Spanish-language television a "disaster." "I have to find a diplomatic way of telling him," she had said.

Yet there is no way. Mr. Manning can't get past the fact that most of the teens loved the "Got Milk?" ads, and showed no special affinity for the spots that were supposed to reflect their bicultural lives. Ms. Smith agrees, chiming in with a strong British accent that, when it comes to advertising, "these teenagers are just like any other teenagers."

Ms. Santiago looks up at the skull mask and other Mexican folk art hanging on the wall and rolls her eyes.

"Got Milk?" is "a very Anglo campaign," she counters. She voices concern that its appearance on Spanish television could conflict with her commercials for the moms. Being deprived of milk – the basis for the humor throughout the "Got Milk?" ads – "is not funny to" an older Hispanic audience, she says. "They've been there too often."

Ms. Lissa raises concerns, too. Unlike previous immigrant groups, she says, many Latinos embrace their language and heritage more strongly as they get older and become more established in America; advertising in English, therefore, may be a lousy way to foster long-term product loyalty. Beyond that, she worries that sticking "Got Milk?" on Spanish-language television could well be perceived as an insult, especially among Latino community leaders. "It shows a lack of commitment," says the energetic Argentine native.

Mostly, she and Ms. Santiago argue that they're letting a tremendous opportunity slip away and that, at a minimum, a lot more research into bicultural teens is needed. "You can say these teens are the same as everybody else, but they're not," Ms. Santiago says after the meeting. "They don't look the same. They don't talk the same."

But Mr. Manning won't budge. He says that he'll certainly look to place more Latino actors in the regular "Got Milk?" campaign. And he may further explore a bicultural ad at some point. But any urgency he had to devel-

op a whole new campaign has waned.

Broadcast Views

"I don't want to look like we're backing off this group of people," he says. "But as a marketer, I can't find a rationale" for launching a bunch of new ads. He is confident that his alternative scheme will "extend the reach" of "Got Milk?" – without having to shell out hundreds of thousands of dollars for new creative work.

As it happens, Ms. Santiago and Ms. Lissa aren't the only ones with doubts about airing "Got Milk?" on Spanish-language television.

Univision, the leading Spanish-language network (and the fifth-largest network in the U.S.), swiftly rejects the ads. It cites a policy against showing a commercial "as it currently airs on English-language television." Univision doesn't even accept general-market commercials with Spanish dubbed in, finding the money-saving technique a slap to its viewers.

Telemundo, a distant No. 2 in the Spanish TV wars, has squishier guidelines. But officials there also express some reluctance. "It seems counterproductive" for the milk board to go on Spanish-language television with commercials that "do not feature Latinos or are in nonrelevant scenarios to a Latino consumer," Eduardo Dominguez, the station manager at Telemundo's Los Angeles affiliate, writes to Ms. Santiago. Instead, he urges Mr. Manning's outfit to devise original ads "reflecting the lives and nuances which Latinos can associate with intimately."

In late April, despite its misgivings, Telemundo warily accepts one ad with no dialogue, save for a voice at the end intoning, "Got Milk?" In the spot, which first ran in 1994, a priest stuffs a hunk of chocolate cake into his mouth and then becomes frantic when he can't get a carton of milk out of a vending machine. Two nuns stumble across him as he flails wildly. Mr. Dominguez says he'll be watching to make sure that, given the Latino community's reverence for the church, there is no "significant public protest."

But Mr. Manning – who held additional focus groups with moms to see if they'd be put off by the ad – isn't worried about a possible backlash. Indeed, he hopes that once this first ad appears on Telemundo next week, additional "Got Milk?" commercials with even more English will follow.

For Ms. Santiago, that's a sour prospect. "This is taking a step backwards," she says. For Mr. Manning, it's something else entirely: "We're breaking new ground."

Cough Syrup Touts 'Awful' Taste in U.S.

BY JOEL A. BAGLOLE
Staff Reporter of THE WALL STREET JOURNAL

W . K . Buckley is proud to say Canadians have hated its cough syrup for 80 years. And now, the company thinks it should be the U.S.'s turn.

Buckley has used a blunt eight-word slogan, "Buckley's Mixture. It tastes awful. And it works," in its advertising campaign to become a household name in Canada.

Buckley, based in Mississauga, Ontario, is trying to stretch a thin ad budget to launch its first national entry into the U.S. Previously, it has run only bus and bus-shelter ads in the New York City area. With just 2.3 million Canadian dollars (US$1.6 million) to spend on ads this winter-cold season, the company is using low-cost tactics, including contests, giveaways and product placements to build a *bad* name for Buckley's brew.

Ads running in the National Enquirer supermarket tabloid, for example, ask people to mail in pictures of their faces as they taste Buckley's Mixture. At the end of January, the company will select the best grimace. The winner will receive US$500 and get his or her picture published in an ad in the paper.

For fans of Buckley's, grimaces come naturally enough. Unlike most cough syrups, Buckley's Mixture contains no sugar or alcohol, the ingredients used to mask the taste. The company says it could improve the taste (and has done so with its Jack & Jill children's brand), but shuns the idea for its main brand. If the taste improved, "nobody would know us anymore," says John Meehan, general manager of the closely held company.

In another bid to get out the word in the U.S. as cheaply as possible, Buckley is giving away samples over its Web site. Also on offer are free T-shirts, refrigerator magnets and coffee cups to Americans who tell six friends or family members about Buckley's and get them to write to the company.

To get Buckley's Mixture showcased on the television game show "The Price Is Right," where contestants guess the cough syrup's retail price, and in other venues, the company has hired **Premier Entertainment Services,** a Hollywood product-placement firm. So far, Buckley's Mixture has landed appearances on 38 TV shows, including prime-time hits "ER" and "The X-Files," and it will be included in a film starring Julia Roberts.

In addition, Buckley said it is spending US$99,000 to run a 10-second TV ad featuring a man shoving cotton up his nose, tasting Buckley's Mixture, and then screaming. The ad will run 23 times over the next two months on shows such as "Jeopardy" and "Wheel of Fortune."

A larger radio-ad campaign, which cost US$435,000, features company President Frank Buckley joking about the elixir's bad taste.

Over the years, plenty of other campaigns attracted attention by focusing on the negative attributes of products. Ads for Listerine mouthwash used to trumpet "the taste you love to hate." Campaigns for the Volkswagen Beetle portrayed it as the ugly duckling of cars.

Ads for Heinz ketchup in the 1980s played on the time it takes for the ketchup to slide out of the bottle. But it stressed the product is so good, it is worth the wait, notes Patrick Dickinson, managing director of Toronto ad agency Publicis SMW, a unit of France's **Publicis,** which is running the current campaign.

Buckley's has a long history of dwelling on the negative, with past ads containing such promises as, "Relief is just a yuck away," and "Not new. Not improved." Those efforts have helped make the company Canada's No. 3 cough-syrup maker, with a 12% market share, according to Advertising Age magazine.

But it trails far behind Benylin, produced by giant **Warner-Lambert,** with 22% of the Canadian market, and Robitussin, made by **Whitehall-Robins Healthcare,** with an 18% Canadian share. According to market-research firm ACNielsen, cough medicine sales in Canada last year totaled C$70 million.

In the U.S., where cough-syrup sales total US$418 million a year, Robitussin dominates with a 52.7% share, according to Information Resources, Chicago. Buckley aims for a 5% market share in five years, the company's Mr. Meehan says.

The U.S. market will be a challenge for Buckley's, where even an audacious but small campaign might simply get lost. Buckley, which has only 28 employees, projects revenue of C$15 million in the fiscal year ending March 31. The company doesn't release profit figures.

Stephen Greyser, a professor of marketing at Harvard University's Business School, says the success of the Buckley ads will ultimately depend on their humor. For a small company trying to gain brand recognition, being funny is probably the best hope, he says.

Buckley's *hopes to win over American consumers by not hiding its awful taste.*

It tastes awful. And it works.

Pitching Saturns to Your Classmates— for Credit

BY ANNE MARIE CHAKER

Staff Report of THE WALL STREET JOURNAL

SANTA ROSA, Calif. – The 18 men and women huddled in a conference room at a Saturn car dealership on a Saturday afternoon are brainstorming intensely. Winding up a pitch for a new marketing slogan – "We Never Sounded So Good" – Tony Emerson says, "You know what? It's a new company that's getting better and better every year." Christina Vorrises expounds on Saturn's "no-hassle, no-haggle 30-day money-back guarantee." Elizabeth Sadlier exclaims, "I'm ready to promote!"

They sound like pumped-up Saturn marketers. In fact, they are students from Sonoma State University in Rohnert Park, Calif., in a marketing class funded by the Saturn dealership, and they will be graded on just how well they promote the cars to their peers.

The long arm of corporate marketing has reached onto campuses in many ways, but corporate underwriting of college classes is a new twist. Saturn's parent, **General Motors** Corp., has funded classes at more than 200 colleges. Others who have paid to have college classes spend a term pitching their products include **Time Warner** Inc., **Wells Fargo** & Co., **Bristol-Myers Squibb** Co. and Ameritech Advertising Services (now part of **SBC Communications** Inc.).

"One reason we signed on was to get in touch with talented college kids who might like to work with our company," says Ken Godshall, senior vice president of partnership marketing and new business development for Time Consumer Marketing Inc., which underwrote marketing classes at five schools last semester. Another goal: to sell a total of 375 subscriptions per school.

For schools, the program typically means money: **EdVenture Partners,** a closely held firm in Berkeley, Calif., that brokers relationships between companies and colleges, says the schools get $2,500 for costs related to the marketing project plus a $500 contribution to the faculty department. Companies also pay EdVenture $12,500 to $17,500 a school.

"A large number of our 106 colleges are engaged in these kinds of relationships," says Christopher Cabaldon, vice chancellor of the California Community Colleges. "A real-world client for students to work with enhances the quality and practicability" of their classes, he says.

Once the class is set up, students typically use their $2,500 budget to plan a promotional party complete with food, games, prizes, music and, of course, marketing come-ons. The end result looks like a corporate-sponsored fraternity bash (minus the liquor) and typically attracts hundreds of students.

At Sonoma State, students began the semester by conducting market research on their classmates. They passed out surveys to 200 fellow students, which revealed that 81% didn't know the name of their local Saturn dealership, Saturn of Santa Rosa. Worse, only 28% rated Saturn an "excellent" car company, compared with 57% who said they thought the same of Honda.

Since Saturn of Santa Rosa wanted the class to throw a party advertising the dealership and its cars, the class began to plan a "Pardi Gras" featuring free food and prizes. Over the next several weeks, students went to work promoting their party by hanging fliers throughout the school and passing them out at campus hangouts.

The class threw the party on a Tuesday afternoon ("Phat Tuesday"), and featured six Saturns parked on Salazar Plaza, one of the busiest spots on campus. About 400 students showed up for free hot dogs, giveaways such as frisbees and compact disks, and a scavenger hunt played inside the racier-looking car models, so that students could get a good look at features like the eight-speaker sound system. Through it all, a GM finance and insurance specialist was on hand, ready to answer students' queries about car loans and credit.

Within two days after the party, the class again polled 200 randomly picked students. Of the students who attended the party, 43% rated Saturn an excellent company. And the students' ability to name Saturn of Santa Rosa as their local car dealership increased to 88% among the students who attended (and even increased to 51% among those who did not attend).

Small wonder, then, that GM considers the program "a bargain," the term used by William Palace, who oversees the company's youth marketing on the West Coast. Students, he says, "are the opinion leaders of the future." Right now, their "aspirational vehicles" tend to be imports such as Mercedes-Benz or BMW. But having them market to their peers can lend GM makes like Chevrolet and Pontiac the cool they now lack. "We see it as a huge competitive advantage," Mr. Palace says.

The underwriting programs outrage critics like Richard Randall, who teaches at North Idaho College. In the spring semester of 1998, when Mr. Randall was an instructor in the philosophy department at Washington State University in Pullman, he protested a campus promotion for Chevrolet run by students in a marketing class. He recalls standing for over two hours clutching a picketing sign that read: "Internships OK – but We Are a University, Not a Car Dealership."

"It was the use of a state, taxpayer-supported institution which was very obviously being used to sell products," Mr. Randall now says. "If this was an academic exercise, then what in the hell were the salespeople doing there?"

The professor of that class at Washington State, David Sprott, is in his third year with

---

BIRTH OF A SALES FORCE

Some classes with corporate sponsors

SCHOOL:	CLASS:	PROMOTION THEME:
Colorado State U. Fort Collins	BK 492 Marketing Seminar	Norwest Cash Cube Contest (Wells Fargo)
Washington State U. Pullman	Marketing 496 Special Topics	Spring into Great Deal! with Chipman & Taylor Chevrolet
Diablo Valley College Pleasant Hill, Calif.	Business 257 Applied Advertising and Promotions	Lehmer's (GMC Trucks) Luau

Sources: EdVenture Partners, Wall Street Journal reports

the GM program in his marketing class and defends it. "There's never enough funds provided by the state," he says. "Any type of external support that comes without work on our part is a good thing." Every spring semester, his students throw a promotional party for a local Chevrolet dealership. He maintains that a program like this is useful in teaching a less theoretical subject such as marketing. "We teach how to sell stuff," he says.

Elsewhere, the program has recently taken a new turn with a different kind of

One college professor complains that for-profit corporations are just using taxpayer-supported institutions to sell their products. He has picketed against such underwriting programs.

sponsor: the Immigration and Naturalization Service, which has just begun classes at four universities. The marketing project for the students: to interest their classmates in working for the U.S. Border Patrol, whose recruiting efforts have suffered because of the strong economy.

69

Just For Feet's 'Kenya' spot during last year's Super Bowl sparked a $10 mil lawsuit and raised a troubling question:

CAN AN AGENCY BE GUILTY OF MALPRACTICE?

by Alice Z. Cuneo

When the fans went home and the lights went out for the 1999 Super Bowl, one image remained for many TV viewers: that of a barefoot African runner fleeing hunters in a Humvee, who captured and drugged their victim to force him into a pair of shoes from Just For Feet.

Amid criticism of racial insensitivity, retailer Just For Feet sued its agency, Saatchi & Saatchi Business Communications, Rochester, N.Y., for more than $10 million in damages for advertising malpractice.

While the status of the case was uncertain at press time, following Just For Feet's move to liquidate last week, the suit has raised a troubling question for the advertising community: Can advertising agencies be held liable for the ads they produce?

'A FRIGHTENING SPECTER'

"It's a frightening specter," said Grant Richards, co-founder and creative director of San Francisco shop Grant, Scott & Hurley. Mr. Richards points out the daunting effect a malpractice threat would have on an agency's creative limits.

Court Crandall, co-partner at Ground Zero, Marina del Rey, Calif., said such considerations would dim the creative spark. For example, he said, beer ads often use beautiful women to sell their product. But Goodby, Silverstein & Partners used lizards, "one of the ugliest creatures on earth," Mr. Crandall said.

The agency gave them a voice and turned them into one of the most effective ways of selling product, he said, adding that the threat of malpractice could change that.

"People would have no choice but to follow what's always been done to avoid a lawsuit," Mr. Crandall said. "Advertising is still an imperfect science."

The case raises concerns in the industry's creative community at a time when agencies have been flooded with requests from dot-com companies for cutting-edge campaigns to build quick awareness in a crowded market.

"With the clutter that is out there, there is certainly an increased exposure for someone [in the agency business]

getting a claim," said Jeffrey Michel, associate general counsel, True North Communications, Chicago.

A MUTUAL MISTAKE

Several executives said the Just For Feet lawsuit is really limited to a mistake made by the client and the agency.

"The agency was a fool for proposing such a thing, and the client was a fool for paying for it," Mr. Richards said. "We live in politically correct times. You have to be careful what you do."

In its lawsuit, Just For Feet said the finished spot, called "Kenya," was entirely different from the concept Saatchi first presented.

The original spot, the company said, would have showed a Just For Feet team coming up to a runner whose shoelace had become untied. The Just For Feet team would tie the runner's shoelace and give him water and a towel, the company said.

The spot was one of two that Saatchi and Just For Feet had been considering using until immediately before Super Bowl XXXIII.

A second spot showed a gymnasium in a school with the fictional name "Ruttenberg High," apparently a reference to Just For Feet CEO Harold Ruttenberg. There, a geeky boy played dodge ball, a school yard game where a player stands alone and tries to dodge a ball thrown at him by other players; the Just for Feet team came in and rescued him by giving him better shoes.

Just for Feet preferred this spot, the company claimed in its suit, but one network rejected it, saying it was "mean-spirited and promotes antisocial behavior."

COST, TIME CONSIDERATIONS

As the clock ticked down toward the big game, Saatchi presented the final "Kenya" spot to the client. Just For Feet said it "expressed strong misgivings and dissatisfaction" over the spot, according to the lawsuit, but Saatchi "then reassured Just For Feet that the commercial would be well received based on Saatchi's expertise and

(Cont.)

experience with national advertising and marketing, and that having committed to advertise in the Super Bowl it was too late to develop and produce another commercial or to reshoot the dodge ball commercial."

The company, out $900,000 in production costs and $2 million for the Super Bowl time slot, said in court documents it had no choice but to run the "Kenya" spot.

But creative wasn't the retailer's only problem.

Just For Feet also planned a sweepstake promotion, the "Just For Feet Third Quarter Super Bowl Win a Hummer Contest." In the weeks leading up to the game, Just For Feet spent $800,000 on promotional teaser spots during the National Football League and American Football League conference championship games.

> *"This is not a doctor who removes the wrong foot. [Advertising] is a shared expertise and a shared responsibility."*

Those spots urged viewers to watch the third quarter and find out how many times the Just For Feet name was mentioned. Viewers wishing to participate in the contest were to telephone or go to the Just For Feet Web site with their answer to enter the sweepstakes.

The spot, however, ran in the fourth quarter, making the contest's correct answer zero. The company's Web site would not accept zero as the answer, so "customers were left with the mistaken impression that Just For Feet was attempting to trick or deceive them," the lawsuit said. Saatchi's sibling, Zenith Media, bought the ad time.

INEFFECTIVE BRAND BUILDING?

Following the Super Bowl, critics lashed out at the "Kenya" spot. Some said it was not only ineffective in building the company's brand, it may even have been viewed as promoting drug use. Advertising Age's Bob Garfield said the spot was "probably racist."

It all came as the retailer was trying to move away from its "Where the 13th pair is free" tagline from agency Rogers Advertising, Birmingham, Ala., and break out as a national advertiser appealing to its core customer base of minorities and women with small children.

The shoe store chain, the second-largest in the nation, also was under duress because of a fashion shift from sweatsuits and white athletic shoes to khakis and brown shoes. It also had been expanding at a rapid rate, buying the Athletic Attic and Sneaker Stadium chains to the concern of some analysts, who questioned the fast

pace of growth.

Just as the dust from the Kenyan runner's shoes settled, Saatchi sued Just For Feet in U.S. District Court in Rochester in late February for failing to pay its $3 million media bill. On March 1, Just For Feet filed its own case in Jefferson County Circuit Court in Birmingham, against Saatchi and Fox Broadcasting Co.

'PROFESSIONAL NEGLIGENCE'

The retailer charged Saatchi with breach of guaranty and warranty, misrepresentation, breach of contract and "professional negligence and malpractice."

"As a direct consequence of Saatchi's appalling, unacceptable and shockingly unprofessional performance, Just For Feet's favorable reputation has come under attack, its business has suffered and it has been subjected to the entirely unfounded and unintended public perception that it is a racist or racially insensitive company," the company said in its lawsuit.

At press time, executives for Just For Feet had not returned phone calls for comment. A spokesman for Saatchi said neither the agency nor its attorneys would comment on the pending litigation. In its legal papers, however, the agency claims advertising is a business that has no explicit guidelines and standards, and therefore, it cannot have committed malpractice.

Still, the litigation and publicity have become an embarrassment to other Saatchi offices, said one executive familiar with the situation. The executive blames Advertising Age's Mr. Garfield for Monday morning quarterbacking the spot in print and in TV interviews and stirring up the controversy.

Before the spot aired, "No one ever mentioned racial overtones," the executive said, noting the client selected the agency and its work in a pitch that included DDB Needham Worldwide, FCB Worldwide and TBWA/Chiat/Day.

"Kenya" "was presented to the networks and it was not rejected. This issue never surfaced," he said.

The executive also said the hunters depicted in the spot were a multiracial group, though it was difficult to determine through the camouflage gear.

The executive also denied that Just For Feet and Saatchi planned to go the "controversy as cheap advertising" route, that is, creating a controversy around the "Kenya" spot to generate talk and subsequent publicity. Such tactics can multiply the reach of a spot far beyond the price paid for its original audience.

Many advertising executives and their legal advisers would agree with the non-culpability of the agency.

"This is not a doctor who removes the wrong foot. It is not a big mistake in auditing," said True North's Mr.

Of contracts and claims:
Agencies face liability issues

While the threat of malpractice may be new, advertising agencies have long protected themselves from other legal and ethical perils.

Many liability issues are handled in agency-client contracts. For example, agencies generally use information provided by clients for advertising claims. In standard contracts, the agency is protected from suits involving the accuracy of those claims.

The contract absolves the agency of responsibility if something goes wrong with the advertised product and consumers suffer damages or other product and liability claims arise.

Agencies also buy insurance to protect themselves from claims brought by third parties. For example, if the music or words of a broadcast spot infringe on a copyright or trademark, the agency's indemnity policy would kick in. It also covers ads that might be libelous, slanderous or might violate the privacy of a living individual or the right of publicity held by the estate of a deceased person.

In addition to legal and financial precautions, agencies can take other steps to protect themselves, attorneys say. For one, attorneys suggest agencies talk with clients to set a clear definition of responsibilities. In addition, agencies can hire attorneys, either as consultants or as part of the agency staff, to screen proposed ads before they run.

At True North Communications' FCB Worldwide, all advertising is reviewed by the company's legal department. "We want to see it all," said Jeffrey Michel, associate general council at True North.

The required broadcast network approval of spots before they run is a good stop gap, as well.

Finally, focus groups and other methods of testing a campaign can alert agencies to potential problems.

"You have the vehicles to test it before you put it on the Super Bowl," Mr. Michel said.

—*Alice Z. Cuneo*

Michel. Advertising, he said, "is a shared expertise and a shared responsibility."

TAKING RESPONSIBILITY

Many clients wouldn't even consider the responsibility shared, but believe it is firmly in their laps.

"I think the client is ultimately responsible," said John Lauck, senior VP-marketing of shoe retailer Footaction, a shoe store chain. "I don't agree with laying the blame on the agency. It speaks poorly of your ability and skills to manage."

Although agencies do carry some legal protection for things that can go wrong (see story at top), most agency executives believe that, ultimately, the client approves the ad and therefore takes responsibility for it. Standing industry philosophy also strongly backs an unfettered creative department.

"How far do we have to go? Build something in [the contract] which says, 'Warning, this advertising might not work' ?" asked one attorney who works for agencies and asked not to be identified.

New York attorney David Lehv, whose firm handles the McManus Group, Omnicom Group and WPP Group, said it is "inappropriate for an advertiser to disclaim responsibility for its message," adding a client "cannot be compelled to do advertising that is illegal, immoral or in bad taste." However, Mr. Lehv said, the agency has a responsibility to tell its clients that "their advertising message may be perceived as in bad taste."

Just For Feet attorney Robert Brodegaard said that's just not the case. "Just about everybody else who holds themselves out as an expert, is," Mr. Brodegaard said. "The agency does have a responsibility . . . And somebody should have said stop."

For an agency to claim it doesn't have any responsibility is the equivalent of saying "we have no expertise," he said.

The issue Mr. Brodegaard raises, along with the "Kenya" spot, may take its place in advertising history. For the retailer, the controversy appears to be a small pebble in the Just For Feet shoe.

BANKRUPTCY FILING

In September, Helen Rockey replaced Mr. Ruttenberg as president-CEO; she left four months later.

By November, the company filed for bankruptcy and began liquidating inventory and closing some stores.

The Alabama Securities Commission also has begun a probe of possible financial irregularities.

Last week, Just For Feet filed a motion in U.S. Bankruptcy Court in Wilmington, Del., to liquidate its assets.

DO E-ADS HAVE A FUTURE?

The race is on to find ways to increase Internet advertising's effectiveness

A palpable tension hangs in the air, as three dozen Excite@Home staffers hunker down in a second-floor conference room, the blinds pulled shut for the Bay Area's chilly December afternoon. At the far end of an 18-foot mahogany table, a steady stream of execs from Internet startups march into the room, taking up the few remaining chairs. Each company eats up every nanosecond of its allotted 45 minutes, hoping to convince the skeptical audience that their technology can provide the much-needed spark to reignite Internet advertising.

For the Web portal, this is a critical meeting. With online ads declining in effectiveness, dropping in value, and failing to live up to their much-ballyhooed potential, Excite@Home is under intense pressure to come up with new, innovative ways of advertising. Nearly half of the company's forecast $653 million in 2000 revenues is expected to come from online advertising. But as an overhead screen displays a whizzy pop-up box that lets Net surfers view 360-degree images of an advertiser's product, including zoom and spin controls, it becomes clear from the gloomy faces around the table that there isn't much excitement in the room today. Even the usual kinetic energy of Susan Bratton, Excite@Home's 6-foot senior vice-president for sales and marketing, is subdued. "I didn't see anything that really pushed the envelope," she says. "The success of Net advertising is critical."

The clock is ticking for online advertising and the Web companies dependent on the dollars they bring. Money that flowed furiously into Net advertising from dot-coms has dried up faster than a 30-second Old Media ad. And traditional advertisers, still uncertain about how to value online marketing, aren't piling in fast enough to take up the slack. One reason for their hesitancy: The so-called "click-through rate," which measures how many people click on ads for more information, has fallen dramatically. Click-through rates on banner ads—billboard-like pitches that account for 50% of Net advertising revenue—have plummeted from 30% for the first banner ad in 1994 to a measly 0.3% today. That's well below the 1% to 1.4% response rate of direct mail. "There's a fear rising up into the boardrooms, and executives are concerned," says Jeffrey Mallett, president of Web portal Yahoo! Inc. "We're doing a lot more hand-holding and spending more time trying to help companies over the wall."

For all the effort, not enough companies are making it over. After rising nearly 100% annually since 1997, the growth of online ad sales is expected to nosedive to 17% in 2001—less than half what Merrill Lynch & Co. was predicting just four months ago. That means overall U.S. online ad revenue will hit only $9.7 billion this year, or 3.5% of total ad dollars. That's a paltry increase of three-tenths of a percentage point over last year and far short of what experts had predicted in the past. "It looks like online advertising is heading toward the low end of aggressive estimates that ranged from 5% to 20% of all U.S. ad spending," says Holly Becker, an analyst at Lehman Brothers.

CLAWING FOR SURVIVAL. It gets worse. Take out the 75% of online ad dollars that Yahoo, America Online, Excite@Home, and six other major portals capture, and that leaves thousands of Net companies fighting for what's left. As unsold ad space piled up, prices in the fourth quarter declined 10% to 15% for every type of ad. At the same time, e-mail marketing prices dropped 25%, to $150 per thousand messages delivered. At those rates, many Net publishers may soon find themselves clawing for survival. Already, entertainment site Pseudo.com and free Internet service provider 1stUp.com Corp., which both relied on advertising revenue, have shut down. Lehman Brothers estimates that it takes $200 million to $250 million in annual revenues for online publishers to break even—too big a nut for most. Apart from AOL, Yahoo, other major portals, and CNET, the Wall Street firm figures only 14 online publishers out of some 10,000 today will survive in their present form.

Already there are signs of more fallout. On Dec. 26, EarthWeb Inc. sold its ad-supported Web sites and e-mail newsletters, choosing to become a recruiting service for tech workers. The number of companies that have missed quarterly estimates, slashed staff, or been downgraded by Wall Street is piling up—including the likes of Yahoo,

(Cont.)

The Wide World of Advertising
(concluded)

Pros: Response rates for skyscrapers, which started being used aggressively in 2000, can be seven times as high as for banners, according to Mass Transit Interactive.

Cons: Just as banner ads were launched with monster response rates, analysts expect the effectiveness of these ads to decline as consumers tune them out.

Streaming Video and Audio

Companies and content networks, including RealNetworks, NetRadio, and MusicVision, insert ads for marketers into music and video clips as consumers listen to them.

Pros: It's much more like the TV that marketing advertisers know and trust. Can get click-through rates of about 3.5%, according to RealNetworks.

Cons: Widespread use will depend on high-speed Net connections, which aren't expected to be adopted by a critical mass of 30 million households until 2005, estimates Jupiter.

Effectiveness Tracking

Upstart DynamicLogic designed a pioneering service to help traditional advertisers gauge the impact of their marketing by placing tiny files, called cookies, on viewers' computers. This helps them track where people go in the days or weeks after seeing ads.

Pros: Offers the ultimate way to gauge the results of brand marketing campaigns.

Cons: Time-consuming—and the cost can cut into the mass use of advertisements.

Minisites, Pop-Ups & Interstitials

These ads burst open on screens, allowing companies such as Volvo and SmithKline Beecham's Oxy acne medicine to dish up games and product information.

Pros: Minisites allow advertisers to market without sending people away from the site they're visiting. This type of advertising also gets higher click rates—on average around 5% of people who see the sites click on them, estimates portal About.com.

Cons: Can be intrusive and annoying. Think AOL's welcome screen.

DoubleClick, NBCi, iVillage, RealNetworks, CMGI, and Ask Jeeves.

What's emerging from this wreckage is a new notion of online advertising that is less ad and more marketing. Unlike dot-coms who spent wildly on banner ads to bring consumers to their sites, companies like British Airways and Unilever see the power of the Net in a new form of virtual branding or digital direct mail. Through mini-sites with useful information or entertainment hooks such as games or contests, corporations are marketing their brands and products to consumers. Last year, H. J. Heinz Co., for example, set up a site that let kids send out e-mails of an exploding digital Heinz ketchup package. Teens latched onto the campaign, sending 50,000 of the "spurt" e-mails to one another in the first two months. Meanwhile, Cheseborough-Ponds USA Inc. has a site that features the Ponds Squad—three animated female characters taking on an evil-doer. In the first month after the site launched, Ponds sent out 200,000 product samples to those who asked for them. Rather than a direct mailing blast, Ponds reached an interested audience and saved 30% in costs.

To drum up interest in these cybercampaigns, traditional marketers aren't even using the Net very much. Last year, when Miller Brewing Co. wanted to increase sales and brand awareness around the Super Bowl, it sponsored games and discussions on its own Super Bowl site. But rather than plastering ads on portals or sports sites, Miller relied almost entirely on TV and newspaper ads to alert people. End result? Miller dished out $9 million on traditional advertising to promote a $1 million online marketing binge. "It's like pizza and Tabasco," says Rishad Tobaccowala, president of ad agency Starcom, which designed the Miller campaign. "Pizza is offline marketing, and you spend more on that. To jazz it up, you add a little Tabasco, but a little bit goes a long way."

No wonder online publishers are feeling scorched. Now, they're scrambling to give online ads the kind of jazzy makeovers that work with the virtual marketing campaigns traditional advertisers are coming to favor. CNET, Disney Internet Group, and Primedia's About.com are working on flashier ads with more information. Technology news site CNET, for example, designed a pilot ad for Dell Computer Inc. that's essentially a small Web site with product specs and forms for requesting more materials—without ever leaving the CNET Web page.

New technologies also are helping to provide more marketing punch.

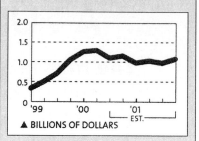

Dot-coms are spending less to advertise online . . .

▲ BILLIONS OF DOLLARS

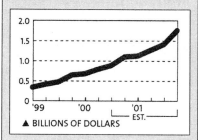

. . . while Web ads by old economy companies are on the rise . . .

▲ BILLIONS OF DOLLARS

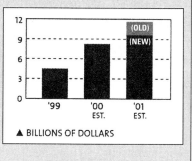

. . . but not enough to pick up the slack

▲ BILLIONS OF DOLLARS

DATA: INTERNET ADVERTISING BUREAU, MERRILL LYNCH

Streaming audio and video ads are being piped into downloaded music and video clips, as broadband connections slowly increase. RealNetworks, for instance, slips 15-second promos for Mitsubishi's Spyder convertible into video clips on the Comedy Central Web site. Others believe bigger is better and are opting for ads called "skyscrapers" that run the length of a PC screen. And pop-up ads, which must be clicked on to disappear, are gaining popularity.

New technologies alone won't cut it. Advertisers say better ways of measuring the impact of online ads and marketing campaigns

(Cont.)

are needed to get them to spend more. Now, Web site operators are sifting through how much time people spend on different areas of a site as a way to size up the impact of ads. That data, along with traditional surveys on brand awareness, are helping to get a better handle on whether online marketing dollars are well-spent. DoubleClick, for instance, is promoting its brand-measurement services, seminars, and case studies with clients such as Coca-Cola Co. "The more we can start integrating these kinds of things with the media buying, the more comfortable traditional advertisers will feel with the Net," says Barry Salzman, president of DoubleClick's Global Media unit.

EARLY DAYS. Reaching that comfortable level will take time. Even one of the biggest online advertisers, Unilever, is feeling its way. The package-goods company, whose brands include Lipton, Snuggle, and Ragu, spends about $144 million annually—or 4% of its ad budget on the Net. In its fourth year of advertising online, the company says it's still learning how to make the most of its online marketing tactics, including e-mail, pop-up ads, and sponsorships of specific content areas on sites such as iVillage. "It's still very early days," says Mark Olney, vice-president of the North American Interactive Brand Center at Unilever. "It's a slow change, and where you hear some of the grumbles about why it's so difficult, it's because people think of the Net as being so very fast."

Increasingly, Unilever is experimenting with online marketing that would be too targeted for a 30-second TV spot. Dove, positioned as a soft, gentle cleansing soap, ran pop-up messages on parenting site BabyCenter, asking visitors whether they knew that Dove was recommended by pediatricians for washing newborns. Those ads got up to triple the response of traditional banner ads.

Clearly, some marketing plays best on the Net. To make a splash with its third car launch this year, Volvo decided to introduce its newest model, the S60, completely online. The extensive multimillion dollar campaign is being done through a partnership with AOL that includes mailing 500,000 CDs, co-sponsoring a sweepstakes for six S60s, and other promotions throughout the online service. Since the Oct. 15 launch, about 21,000 people have configured cars online and asked for quotes, and 3,000 cars have been sold. It will be months before Volvo really knows whether the money was well-spent, says Phil Bienert, manager of e-Business at Volvo Cars of North America. "About 85% of our customers are currently online," he says. "It's a number we think is an advantage. This is an opportunity to prove that out."

So far, online publishers are making only modest gains. Companies such as Visa International and British Airways are standing pat on their online ad spending. "To get me comfortable about investing more, I would need to believe I could accomplish my broader brand-building objectives as effectively as the medium I use now, which is TV," says Liz Silver, senior vice-president for advertising at Visa, which spent $10 million online last year, according to researcher Competitive Media. Despite the latest innovations, online publishers still have much work to do before winning over skeptics like Silver.

By Heather Green and Ben Elgin

71

The Art of the Sale

How the Beauty-Counter Staff Gets Shoppers to Buy More Than They Bargained For

By Emily Nelson

Staff Reporter of The Wall Street Journal

NEW YORK—Any woman who has ever left a store wondering how she ended up spending so much on makeup should watch Muffie Ferrel.

On the ground floor of Macy's huge flagship store in Manhattan, the Estee Lauder saleswoman spots a mother and daughter approaching. "How are you today?" asks the smiling Ms. Ferrel, immaculately dressed in an Estee Lauder-issued navy suit with her blond hair pulled back.

Marilyn Spector and her 21-year-old daughter Erica seem eager, and mom says she's looking for foundation. Ms. Ferrel beckons her to a counter stool by a rack of lipsticks, diagnoses her skin as dry and recommends Estee Lauder Futurist foundation.

Erica Spector, playing with the tester lipsticks, pipes in that lipsticks always look redder on her than she'd like. "I had that problem, too," Ms. Ferrel sympathizes. "Do you use a lip liner?" She doesn't.

Twenty minutes later, Ms. Ferrel is ringing up $82.27 of cosmetics for the two women—including lip liner. Walking away with her unexpectedly large bag, the younger Ms. Spector says, "You get sucked in, but it's a good sucking in."

Estee Lauder Cos. has it down to a fine art. "Beauty advisers" like Ms. Ferrel are the all-important sales agents in the $40 billion global beauty industry, and the key to winning market share. "Good beauty advisers make the difference," says Daniel Brestle, Estee Lauder's president. "I can show you the same product in the same market, and two stores are doing well and one store isn't, and it's [due to] the beauty advisers."

With the economy slowing, beauty advisers are more critical than ever in converting browsers into buyers. Already, department stores have had disappointing holiday sales, and are attracting fewer shoppers. Even so, cosmetics companies typically weather economic downturns better than some other industries—women who cut back on designer clothing can still see paying $16 for lipstick as a justifiable luxury—and beauty advisers play an essential role in that resiliency.

In her sales approach, Ms. Ferrel used classic Estee Lauder techniques, inscribed in a 150-page basic training manual and pounded into her psyche with 100 hours of seminars her first year and annual follow-up classes. For starters, the 30-year-old Ms. Ferrel never crosses her arms—an inhospitable signal. She also eschews the standard clerk's greeting of "May I help you?" Estee Lauder's thinking is that shoppers instinctively decline and leave the store empty-handed. Rather, the company recommends icebreakers including, "I love what you are wearing today" and "Is the weather still nice outside?"

Making people feel comfortable in what can be the intimidating and overwhelming cosmetics area is part of the beauty adviser's role; they are taught to pretend they're hostesses at a party. In the past year, Estee Lauder has also been adding more product displays that people can touch, rather than having to admire through a glass counter.

Indeed, by simply getting the elder Ms. Spector to sit down, Ms. Ferrel increased by 65% her chances of selling two or three products, instead of one, according to the company manual. Her advice to use a lip pencil, for example, was "link selling," or recommending something that fits with the product a customer already intends to buy. Sales clerks are taught to keep asking customers questions to learn about their beauty needs and concerns and then to offer suggestions.

When the younger woman mentioned lipstick, Ms. Ferrel swiped several shades of taupe on the back of her hand. On her other hand, she drew a swatch with brown lip pencil and colored over it with lipstick so Ms. Spector could compare. Ms. Ferrel made a point of demonstrating the makeup on her own hand first because that's less intrusive than on a customer's.

The younger Ms. Spector settled on a Smoky Topaz lipstick and a Chestnut lip pencil. Her mom picked a Cinnamon lipstick but deemed a pencil too costly. Still, Ms. Ferrel neatly wrote the lip pencil color on a business card for her, maintaining Estee Lauder's subtle image by not being too pushy but increasing the odds that Ms. Spector will come back eventually for it.

Estee Lauder has been known for its sales force ever since founder Estee Lauder vowed in 1946 "to touch 50 faces a day." The New York makeup giant runs so many different brands that it now dominates the first floor of most department stores across the country and racks up sales of $4.4 billion. In addition to its namesake line, Estee Lauder also owns Clinique, Bobbi Brown, Mac, Stila, Prescriptives, Aveda and Origins, among others. For each collection, the company creates a distinct image with its sales crew, product packaging and counter display. There are separate manuals for each brand with suggested dialogue and technique to fit the brand's look. Salespeople for Clinique are "consultants" for a dermatological image; at Mac, they're "makeup artists" to be edgier; at Origins, they're "guides" to sound natural. In addition

to navy suits, Estee Lauder beauty advisers wear "minimum" jewelry and "neat, classic" hairstyles. Hair scrunchies are forbidden.

At Macy's, Estee Lauder beauty advisers don't spray passing shoppers with perfume or shout out special offers like salespeople at the neighboring Lancome counter. Those tactics are considered too aggressive. While department stores hire the staff, Estee Lauder has some say over job candidates and trains them for counter work. Estee Lauder and the store share responsibility for compensation, which varies by store; some offer commissions based on sales in addition to an hourly wage.

Industry consultants figure Estee Lauder's 8,800 beauty advisers earn roughly $30,000 to $35,000 a year apiece. Despite the tight job market and modest salary, Estee Lauder says recruiting isn't hard as many women are lured by the glamour, the on-the-job training and the chance for advancement. There's also $1,800 of free makeup each year, given out at training seminars and new-product introductions and as the women's own picks. Turnover runs about 40% to 50% a year, which is better than the 57% typical at retailers, says Mr. Brestle, the company's president.

Mr. Brestle notes that he has made product changes, such as the size of an eye-shadow compact, based on suggestions from beauty advisers who meet him at monthly breakfasts. He strongly encourages all corporate employees to work in the stores one day each year. Many executives got their start behind the counter, including Janet Cook, senior vice president for sales for Estee Lauder USA and Canada.

Ms. Cook, who started as a beauty adviser in 1970, now spends about half her time on the road, checking on the stores and talking to beauty advisers to remind them that a career path like hers is possible. Her presence helps "to keep the beauty advisers motivated," she says.

Ms. Ferrel, who grew up on an almond ranch in California, was drawn to Estee Lauder ever since she got a makeup kit from her aunt each Christmas as a young girl. Without any cosmetics experience, she applied for her first job at the counter in Macy's in Modesto, Calif. A year ago, she and another sales clerk sought transfers to New York. They share a studio apartment, and Ms. Ferrel, a makeup buff who favors brown lipstick and other muted tones, spends her free time at the gym or shopping with her roommate, often browsing other makeup counters. Last March, she was promoted to training director so, in addition to selling, she trains the others at Macy's and checks to see they meet daily sales goals. Her goal, she says, is to land a job at Estee Lauder's corporate office.

The crucial tool for the beauty adviser is her binder, a log of customers with a page for each, recording their purchases and preferences. Sales clerks are trained to ask for a customer's phone number after helping them and to call 10 days after a sale to follow up. (Most customers are willing to give their

(Cont.)

And Here's a Lipstick to Match...

Some sales tips from the 150-page basic-training manual for Estee Lauder 'beauty advisers'

Build a rapport	Link and bridge	Lay a foundation	Lead by the nose	Don't give up
Repeat what the customer says back in your own words to show her 'you understood her needs.' Advisers should make eye contact and hold a product 'as if it were a rare jewel.'	When a customer asks for red lipstick, show her several shades. If she is repurchasing a product, use 'link selling' by showing her a companion item. Use 'bridge selling' by asking what fragrances she prefers, then show her Estee Lauder perfumes.	Hold each product the customer has viewed, explain it and hand it to her. She'll already feel like it is hers. Advisers should encourage the customer to return by mentioning other beauty concerns and scheduling an appointment.	After trying a fragrance on a customer's hand, guide it toward her nose and say 'Doesn't that smell wonderful?' The manual instructs, 'Always have your customer acknowledge the scent.'	If a customer objects to a product's price, don't give up. 'A customer objection is a sign of interest,' the manual says. Advisers should 'first empathize' and then list a product's benefits.

Source: Estee Lauder basic-training manual

numbers.) Clerks should also record products a customer tried but didn't buy so they know to call her about specials. The chart also has space for usage patterns and product sizes so sales clerks can anticipate, months later, when a customer needs a refill and lock in future sales by calling to sell her one.

Ms. Ferrel kept her binder organized with her 30 "best-friend customers," basically people who shop once a month. She recently sent them Christmas cards and, before moving from California, had farewell dinners with many. Her second tier of 100 good customers consisted of people she'd phone about three or four times a year to talk about a new palette of eye shadow or special events like a free gift with a purchase. Even if the call doesn't result in a sale, it's seen as an important relationship builder.

Ms. Ferrel reviews other beauty advisers' books every other week, checking to see that they log in follow-up calls and note each customer's birthday, a prime sales opportunity. One records details like "getting married" or "just moved from L.A., at Columbia U." She reminds them to weed out people and to bookmark their calendar page so they can schedule a consultation without a lot of unprofessional

flipping through pages on the selling floor.

Mary Bush, 38, who started working at the Estee Lauder counter at a Robinsons-May store in Costa Mesa, Calif., in October, is aiming to log in 150 customers her first year. After her first month on the job, however, she realized she was missing her sales goals. One day, Ms. Bush sold $400 of merchandise, considerably short of her goal of $600, she says. Reviewing her binder, she and her training director discovered Ms. Bush was doing a good job getting customers to buy multiple items, but she wasn't waiting on enough customers each day.

"I was talking to each person too long," Ms. Bush says. She now tries to see more people. In her binder, she has customers who are on track to run out of products this month or next, and she plans to call them to sell them refills. "I'm there like a doctor to remind them," she says. "By calling them, that's how they know I'm sincere. I'm not just there to sell $100."

It's hard to know when to abandon a customer who isn't serious about buying. At Macy's, Ms. Ferrel struggles through several lipsticks for two redhead sisters. When one complains the lipstick is "too orangey," Ms.

Ferrel demonstrates lip liners and brushes. Her customer pauses, so Ms. Ferrel, encouraged, hands her a tissue and cleanser to wipe the lipstick so she can try it on her lips. "Maybe I'll leave it on for an hour and see," concludes the customer, walking away. As a last-ditch effort, Ms. Ferrel offers, "can I write down the shade for you?" Having spent 30 minutes with them, Ms. Ferrel hands one a business card with Caffe Latte written on it.

Still, she's philosophic. About 30% of customers who walk away to think about a product actually return and buy it, she says. "You have to be a different salesperson to different people."

The only time Ms. Ferrel says no is when customers ask to look like Estee Lauder's cover model, Elizabeth Hurley. She recommends colors for "harmony" with their own appearance—and confides that Ms. Hurley's look is "helped with some photography."

72

Shopper Turns Lots of Pudding Into Free Miles

By Jane Costello

Staff Reporter of The Wall Street Journal

David Phillips found a lifetime of free plane trips in a cup of chocolate pudding.

Last May, Mr. Phillips was shopping in the frozen-food aisle of his local supermarket when he noticed a frequent-flier offer on the package of a Healthy Choice frozen entree: Earn 500 miles for every 10 Universal Product Codes from Healthy Choice products sent in to Healthy Choice by Dec. 31. Any "early birds" who submitted the UPCs, or bar codes, by May 31 would receive double the mileage – 1,000 miles for every 10 bar codes.

Mr. Phillips, a 35-year-old civil engineer with the University of California at Davis, flies only sporadically each year. Until he made that fateful trip to the grocery store, his largest frequent-flier account had a 40,000-mile balance. "I quickly did the math and realized what this could mean," he says.

With an investment of $3,140 and 50 hours of his time, Mr. Phillips is the proud owner of 1.25 million frequent-flier miles, good for about $25,000 worth of airline tickets. "He's got a lifetime of free travel now," says Mark Kienzle, a spokesman for **AMR** Corp.'s American Airlines.

It's common for consumers to stock up on products to acquire frequent-flier miles. Susan Michael, a real-estate broker from suburban Chicago, bought between 200 and 300 liters of Diet Coke last year to earn frequent-flier miles from Delta Air Lines. "The trunk was so full I'd get worried about the tires on my car," she says. And David Fisher, a computer salesman from Issaquah, Wash., racked up an additional 12,000 **Northwest Airlines** miles by participating in the Healthy Choice promotion last year.

Mr. Phillips, however, is in his own stratosphere. Here's how he did it.

With only three weeks to take advantage of the early-bird offer, Mr. Phillips calculated the best way to maximize his mileage. He contemplated buying an additional freezer to hold the frozen entrees but decided to shop around for cheaper products from Healthy Choice, a brand of **ConAgra** Inc., Omaha, Neb.

While scouring the city for cans of Healthy Choice soup on special, Mr. Phillips happened upon **Grocery Outlet,** a supermarket chain that sells excess inventory to consumers at a discount. He emerged from the store with a full shopping cart and a new identity: Pudding Guy.

"I found the gold mine: cups of chocolate pudding selling for 25 cents apiece," says Mr. Phillips, who subsequently began using the handle Pudding Guy for his online correspondence. "That's when I started to get serious," he says.

He obtained a list of Grocery Outlets from the store manager and set out with his mother-in-law to wipe out the inventory between Davis and Fresno. They went to 10 stores, filling a van with thousands of cups of Healthy Choice chocolate pudding. The manager of the Grocery Outlet in Davis ordered him an additional 60 cases, bringing the final tally to 12,150 cups of pudding.

When it became apparent that he and his wife couldn't possibly remove the labels in time to meet the double-mileage deadline, Mr. Phillips decided to donate the pudding to local food banks. In exchange for globs of free pudding, workers at the Salvation Army in Sacramento and other local charities agreed to peel off the UPC symbols as they dished out the desserts at breakfast, lunch and dinner.

Mr. Phillips incurs no tax obligation from his mileage, which isn't considered income because it derived from a purchase. In fact, he plans to claim the entire $3,140 pudding purchase as a charitable deduction, yielding a tax savings of about $815, bringing down his total cost to $2,325.

A former Internal Revenue Service commissioner, Don Alexander, says writing off the entire purchase might be too aggressive. "Technically, an allocation should be made between the value of the pudding and the value of the frequent-flier miles," he says. "Had he given the charities the frequent-flier miles along with the pudding, he would be entitled to the full deduction."

Another caveat from the ex-commissioner: "Naturally, he can't deduct the cost of the puddings he ate."

A federal tax official declined to comment on whether Mr. Phillips's efforts will fly come April 15. "There is no specific ruling that would address the facts in this case," said a spokesman for the Internal Revenue Service.

Last week, American Airlines posted the last of 1.04 million miles to Mr. Phillips's AAdvantage account. He divided the remaining 216,000 miles between Northwest, Delta and **UAL** Corp.'s United Airlines. He could sell some of these miles to other fliers but says he has no plans to do that. He is planning to take his wife and two children to Europe this spring (flying coach) and is looking forward to a later trip to New Zealand (business class).

Joan Lukas, a spokeswoman for Healthy Choice, declined to comment on the promotion's sales or participant data, except to say that the frequent-flier offer "met and even exceeded expectations."

Healthy Choice purchased the miles in advance from the airlines, as is customary. Most carriers sell blocks of frequent-flier miles to companies for two cents a mile. United has set up a special Web site to spur sales of "Reward Miles." Continental Airlines has a special "Miles of Thanks" section on its Web site to encourage businesses to reward customers with OnePass miles.

American Airlines has more than 3,000 businesses participating in its "American Airlines Incentive Miles" program, which it markets to large and small companies alike. Although officials at the airline maintain silence on the number of miles awarded in total to Healthy Choice participants in last year's promotion, they say they are pleased with the results.

"We're looking forward to working with Healthy Choice again," Mr. Kienzle says. He points out that American benefits twice: companies pay it for the miles and some consumers buy extra tickets for family or friends.

In most instances, miles earned through nonflight-related activities don't qualify travelers for an airline's coveted elite status. But Pudding Guy is now golden at American: The airline confers lifetime AAdvantage Gold status on people who accumulate a million miles, regardless of how they are earned. Gold privileges include access to a special reservations number, priority boarding, upgrades and bonus miles.

All that's enough for Mr. Phillips, who realizes the extraordinary nature of his tale. "It was like a harmonic convergence of pudding and promotion," he says. "That doesn't happen every day."

Price

A Deal No More, Priority Mail Is Prey for Rivals

By Rick Brooks

Staff Reporter of The Wall Street Journal

Last year, **Bear Creek** Corp., the Medford, Ore., parent of catalog retailer Harry and David, could have been a poster child for the rejuvenated U.S. Postal Service. The company sent almost 900,000 shipments of pears, gourmet cheesecakes and other specialty items by Priority Mail, the Postal Service's popular, bargain-basement way to mail packages for delivery in as little as two or three days.

But don't count on the mailman to bring your chocolate truffles and cinnamon swirls this year.

Earlier this month, postal officials—hoping to bolster the bottom line by leveraging Priority Mail's growing popularity in recent years—raised rates for the service an unusually steep 16%. It could be a big mistake.

Bear Creek and other big commercial mailers say Priority Mail suddenly isn't a particularly better deal than its more-reliable private-sector competitors, primarily **United Parcel Service** Inc., **FedEx** Corp. and **Airborne** Inc. Bear Creek expects its three catalog retailers to ship 15% to 20% fewer Priority Mail packages this year. "There's a lot of alternatives out there," says Bill Ihle, a Bear Creek spokesman.

The timing of the rate increase, set in motion during headier economic times a year ago, couldn't be much worse. The post office already is dealing with its steepest quarterly decline in Priority Mail shipments in at least six years—a result of the slowing economy, analysts say. Unlike FedEx and UPS, the post office has little flexibility to quickly adjust prices.

With the Internet pecking away at its core business of delivering first-class mail, and the cost of reaching all 135 million U.S. addresses rising, the Postal Service already had plenty to worry about. It expects to lose more than $480 million for the fiscal year ending Sept. 30, which would mean its second consecutive money-losing year and steepest loss since at least 1994. "This is a tough time," Postmaster General William J. Henderson says.

It could get tougher if the volume of Priority Mail plummets in the wake of the rate increase, which is more than three times the average 4.6% postage increase on most other mail. UPS and FedEx have announced domestic rate increases of between 3.1% and 4.9%, starting next month. Until now, the rapid growth of Priority Mail shipments during the past five years helped the post office withstand a near halt in growth of its biggest business, delivering first-class mail. Priority Mail shipments, which last year brought in

roughly $4.8 billion—or almost 8% of the post office's mail revenue—grew six times faster than first-class deliveries over a period of four fiscal years, ended Sept. 30, 1999. Figures for fiscal 2000 are still preliminary.

The steep boost in Priority Mail rates deals a big blow to the Postal Service's long-running campaign to convince U.S. businesses that services such as Priority Mail, and the Postal Service itself, can be viable alternatives to private delivery companies. Priority Mail's rapid growth has been the biggest success of an enormous blitz to revitalize the 800,000-employee Postal Service. The post office has spent heavily to spruce up the country's 38,000 postal outlets, and it sponsors an international cycling team led by two-time Tour de France champion Lance Armstrong. Through it all, Priority Mail has been promoted endlessly, soaking up much of the post office's advertising budget, even as it enraged UPS and FedEx with ads that the companies felt misled customers by touting its cheap price and ignoring differences between it and competing services. The Postal Service dropped its most controversial ads but still promotes Priority Mail as "the best bargain in shipping."

Priority Mail doesn't match the delivery guarantees or sophisticated package-tracking capabilities offered by private companies, but until the recent rate increase it usually was by far the least expensive way to ship cookies to summer camp or Internet purchases to homes and businesses. Some companies steered a chunk of their packages to Priority Mail just to create more competition for UPS, which has dominated deliveries of ground packages for decades.

This month's rate boost narrows the price gap so much that it can be hard to tell which delivery service is the most economical. For example, it costs $3.95 to send a two-pound box from New York to Chicago by Priority Mail, up from $3.20. UPS charges $3.76 for guaranteed three-day ground delivery of the same package, and it costs $3.71 to ship the box by FedEx, also in three days. Postal officials claim they probably could deliver the box in two days and wouldn't charge an extra $1, as UPS does, for residential delivery.

Priority Mail volume slumped last fall as the economy weakened and e-mail continued to erode shipments, postal officials say. For the quarter ended Dec. 1, Priority Mail volume fell 3.1% to 274.7 million pieces, according to preliminary reports.

Postal officials concede Priority Mail will lose some of its luster as a result of the rate increase. Jim Cochrane, an associate vice president in expedited and package services for the post office, says growth in Priority Mail volume will likely be less than 2% this fiscal year compared with almost 3% growth during the past fiscal year.

Still, the post office maintains that some Priority Mail customers will shift to its even lower-cost and slower parcel-post delivery services rather than to private competitors.

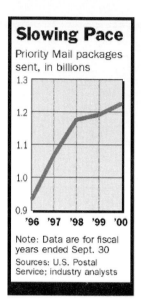

Slowing Pace

Priority Mail packages sent, in billions

'96 '97 '98 '99 '00

Note: Data are for fiscal years ended Sept. 30

Sources: U.S. Postal Service; industry analysts

Other postal customers will be steered to private-sector package consolidators that qualify for lower mail rates by consolidating packages, presorting them and then hauling the parcels to a bulk-mail center.

There isn't much else the Postal Service can do to cushion the blow. It is barred by law from offering discounts, a weapon UPS and FedEx use frequently.

For UPS, the Priority Mail rate increase is a chance to strike back against a bitter enemy, though the company won't discuss what it plans to do. Many big Priority Mail users don't need any bait from UPS or other delivery companies to start retooling their shipping plans. Financial-software maker Intuit Inc. currently ships most packages weighing from 13 ounces to two pounds by Priority Mail. "We're rethinking that," says Ernie Brogdon, mail-services coordinator at the Mountain View, Calif., company. "We have to weigh the customers' interest."

There is hope on the horizon for the post office. Starting in August, FedEx will haul some mail as part of a $6.3 billion delivery contract announced earlier this month. Postal officials say the seven-year deal will speed up Priority Mail deliveries and help the post office cut expenses by more than $1 billion. Those savings should lead to smaller rate increases in the future.

"I think it will do wonders for the performance of that product," Mr. Henderson, the postmaster general, says. "We will see growth rebound."

Airlines

Flying High

Carriers are making big gains by selling directly to passengers on the Web

By Jennifer Rewick
Staff Reporter of The Wall Street Journal

Last year may have been bumpy for electronic commerce, but the airline industry didn't notice.

While many Internet businesses went bust in 2000, airline sites drew a record number of visitors by giving them what they want: bargains. Revenue from airline tickets sold on the Web rose 85% to $8.7 billion last year, according to industry researcher PhoCusWright Inc., based in Sherman, Conn. Web-based sales are expected to rocket even higher this year, the researcher says.

The airlines' gains came at the expense of their fiercest online competitors: travel agencies, whose share of the online ticket market slipped last year in the face of the carriers' offerings. What's more, airlines are reaping huge savings from online deals—about $100 million in 2000 alone, PhoCusWright says. By selling tickets directly to customers on the Web, airlines avoid paying travel-agency commissions that average 5% of a ticket's cost. They can also trim basic mailing and printing charges by confirming transactions via e-mail.

Southwest Sizzle

Leading the pack on the Web is Dallas-based **Southwest Airlines.** Last year, its revenue from Internet sales jumped 46% to $1.3 billion, or 25% of total revenue. Southwest's closest rival, Chicago-based **UAL** Corp.'s United Airlines, pulled in $1.2 billion from Internet sales. Southwest's site also received the most unique visitors of all the major U.S. carriers in 2000, at 1.7 million to 2.3 million a month, the researcher says.

Southwest has spent $5 million to develop and design its site, www.southwest.com, since 1995. In addition to aggressively marketing the site on television—and on cocktail napkins and peanut bags—the company also has an impressive record of keeping customers away from online travel agencies and sites like **Priceline.com** Inc. and **Expedia** Inc. About 90% of Southwest's ticket sales on the Internet came from its own site last year.

Southwest's users are spared the tedious process of having to register online, and the site is easy to navigate. Its home page, for example, offers "Special Double Credit" fares to its frequent fliers who buy tickets online. Under that option, you'd have to buy only four round-trip tickets to get a free trip—compared with the eight round-trips you'd have to buy through real-world channels. It also offers weekly "Click 'N Save" Internet specials of up to 60% off full-fare tickets with a 21-day advance purchase.

Southwest also likes to e-mail its customers. At least 2.7 million Southwest customers have signed up to receive their itineraries and notification of special fares by e-mail. They can also check their frequent-flier status online.

And the airline says it is looking into expanding its online offerings—for instance, by allowing fliers to redeem their credits online, or to check the status of their flight or book tickets with a wireless device.

Southwest won't be specific about how much money the site saves the company, but it does point out that it costs on average only $1 to sell a ticket on its Web site, compared with $10 to sell a ticket through a traditional travel agency.

"One of Southwest's focuses is keeping our costs low," says Melanie Stillings, who runs the Web site's marketing efforts.

Ms. Stillings admits to being surprised by how well Southwest's site has done. "You don't know when you're first doing something that if you build it they will come," she says.

Web Feat

Newcomer **JetBlue Airways** was a bit more optimistic about the Internet when it launched in February of 2000. The New York-based airline, which serves a dozen routes out of John F. Kennedy International Airport, sold 25% of its tickets through its Web site from the start.

"The Web was very important to our initial marketing and distribution strategy," says Amy Curtis-McIntyre, vice president of

---

Click and Soar

The top 10 U.S. airlines, ranked by Internet revenue. At right: How much of the airlines' total passenger revenue came from the Internet in 2000.

Airline	1999	2000*	Pct. of Total
Southwest	$877,000,000	$1,280,000,000	25.0%
United	505,000,000	1,190,000,000	7.4
American	416,000,000	1,060,000,000	6.5
Delta	671,000,000	1,040,000,000	7.5
US Airways	450,000,000	800,000,000	10.5
Northwest	402,000,000	746,000,000	7.5
Continental	408,000,000	710,000,000	8.0
America West	223,000,000	376,000,000	17.0
Alaska	143,000,000	334,000,000	16.0
TWA	118,000,000	280,000,000	9.3

*estimated

The Places You'll Go

Airline Internet revenue, and where it comes from

- ■ Revenue from online agencies
- ■ Revenue from Web sites

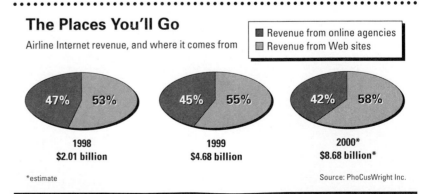

1998	1999	2000*
47% / 53%	45% / 55%	42% / 58%
$2.01 billion	$4.68 billion	$8.68 billion*

*estimate

Source: PhoCusWright Inc.

marketing. "We're a low-cost operator, and direct sales are very important."

A year later, online ticket sales account for more than 30% of tickets sold. Ms. Curtis-McIntyre says that's because the airline knows what makes a Web site easy and fun for customers to use. After all, she says, this is a company that furnishes each plane seat with live, 24-channel satellite television.

The airline says the appeal of its Web site is in its sleek, uncluttered design and humorous writing. For instance, the "Speak Up" section of the site, which addresses customers' questions, quips: "If you have a question, this is the quickest way to get it to us. And no, you can't fly the plane no matter how nicely you ask."

The site also includes an easy-to-read flight schedule and timetable, and a section that lets you track flights, choose your seat and read tips on museums and restaurants in your destination city.

Blue Exposure

Like Southwest, JetBlue plasters its Web address, www.jetblue.com, in as many places as possible—including on the sides of its new planes. The company is currently running its first television commercial to promote the site.

JetBlue offers perks to its customers, such as $2 off each way when passengers book flights online. True, that's not a steep discount, but JetBlue notes that its fares are up to 65% below many of its competitors' offerings. It also says it plans to launch a frequent-flier program this year.

Meantime, airlines that trail Southwest and JetBlue on the Web aren't standing idle. **AMR** Corp.'s American Airlines, Fort Worth, Texas; United; **Delta Airlines,** Atlanta; and **Northwest Airlines,** of St. Paul, Minn., have all reduced the time it takes to book a flight online by moving their reservations option to their home pages. Before that, travelers had to go through the cumbersome process of clicking through several pages to find the reservations page. Over the past 18 months, United and Delta have established separate e-commerce divisions to focus on Web strategies, and many airlines, including American and United, have stepped up their marketing campaigns to focus on their most loyal customers.

So far, their efforts seem to be working. While Southwest's online sales grew 46% to $1.3 billion in 2000, online sales at American jumped 155% to $1.1 billion. Internet sales at **Trans World Airlines,** which sells seats on Priceline and Lowestfare.com, grew 137% to $280 million in 2000, while sales at United—which also has deals with several third-party Web sites—rose 136%.

"All of these airlines have room to grow in 2001, and they'll continue to reap the reward of site upgrades," says Lorraine Sileo, vice president at PhoCusWright. "It wasn't too long ago that a consumer would get bumped off a site mid-way through booking a reservation."

Ms. Rewick is a staff reporter in The Wall Street Journal*'s New York bureau.*

75

WHY TALK IS SO CHEAP

In telecom's new economics, phone rates are just promo tools

How low can long distance rates go? How about zero? You heard it right, free long-distance. That, industry executives concede privately, may be the ultimate outcome as they vie with one another to sign up customers for bundles of communications services–local and long-distance, Internet access, even television. In those bundles, long distance may be thrown in for no extra charge, even though carriers will lose 2 cents a minute on every call. Long-distance upstart Qwest Communications International Inc. already offers 250 minutes of long-distance calling to customers who sign up for a $24.95-a-month Internet service. Phone companies aren't ready to broadcast the idea, but, says Jeffrey Kagan, an independent telecommunications analyst in Atlanta: "They'll be offering long distance for free."

That sort of puts the latest price war among major long-distance carriers in perspective. Unlike previous battles, in which Candice Bergen morphed into the dime lady to help Sprint grab market share from rivals AT&T and MCI WorldCom by promising 10 cents-per-minute calling, the new rate war is heading into uncharted territory. At any amount below 5 cents per minute, the rate that Sprint and MCI WorldCom began promoting in early August, it hardly pays to send out an itemized bill. That means that you'll soon see major carriers offering flat-rate monthly service.

BUCKETS. What's driving all this are the changes in technology and regulation that are erasing the distinctions between types of calling. With today's digital networks, there's not much reason to think about where a call goes or what it carries–voice, data, or video. On the regulatory side, the Federal Communications Commission and state regulators are getting ready to let local phone companies into long-distance (page 173). Once everybody is playing in everyone else's market and the networks are completed, then the battle for telecom bundles will begin: "We can go to a customer and say, 'Here's a bucket of 500 minutes and you can use it for wireless and any other calls,'" says Len Lauer, president of Sprint Corp.'s consumer-services group.

For a sense of how rapidly long-distance is moving beyond the old rules, take a look at what's happening to industry leader AT&T. Ever since C. Michael Armstrong took over two years ago, the charismatic ceo has been trying to get ready for the time when long distance will no longer be the phone giant's cash cow. Consumer and business long-distance services now make up 60% of Ma Bell's revenues, but this percentage will be cut in half by 2004, admits the company. AT&T is facing a steady fall in its long-distance market share, from 80% in 1990 to an estimated 40% by the end of this year, says Rex G. Mitchell, an analyst at Banc of America Securities.

With MCI WorldCom and Sprint announcing 5 cents-per-minute calling plans, Armstrong now has had to pick up the pace. AT&T trotted out its own 7 cents-per- minute plan on Aug. 30, a move that will nearly double the rate at which its consumer long-distance revenues will fall this year, to the 4% to 5% range, rather than 2% to 4%. That

> **Soon, companies will be offering long distance for free to nail down customers for bundles of other services**

will shave some $300 million off AT&T's consumer long-distance revenues, bringing 1999's total decline to about $1 billion. Armstrong told analysts not to worry, however, since healthy growth in data, wireless, and other businesses will more than offset the consumer long-distance decline, which contributes about one-third of the $62.4 billion in total revenues.

AT&T may not be able to hold the line at 7 cents for long. Sprint began offering long distance for 5 cents a minute from 7 p.m. until midnight every day, with 10 cents a minute at other times, plus a monthly $5.95 charge. MCI unveiled nickel calls on weeknights and all day on weekends, and as much as 25 cents a minute during other times, with a monthly $5 minimum. On Aug. 31, IDT Corp., a long-distance upstart, downed the ante–offering 5 cents a minute all day and a $3.95 monthly fee.

These moves aren't as damaging to bottom lines as they might seem. The FCC has been cutting the fees long-distance carriers pay to regional phone companies to carry their calls–from 5.8 cents a minute in 1992 to about 3.3 cents today. "The FCC reduced long-distance carriers' network usage costs, giving them $1.5 billion to pass on to consumers,"

says FCC Chairman William E. Kennard in a statement on AT&T's latest cut. The next step: an industry proposal to cut access fees to 1.1 cents a minute in five years. For now, the race is on to lock in customers with long-distance deals, and then sell a bundle of services–such as wireless and Net access–before other rivals can lure them away. AT&T is already offering discounts on its new long-distance plan to wireless subscribers. And it's gearing up to bundle local, long-distance, and cable services as soon as next year.

Bundling is a key to customer retention. Acquiring new customers is a far bigger cost than long-distance transmission. Lower rates also will make it tougher for Baby Bell companies to compete in long distance, even though they'll have an advantage in not having to pay pricey local-access charges. The Baby Bells, notes Armstrong, "certainly have less room to come in and make a difference based on price."

AT&T is best positioned, by far, to compete in bundled services, analysts say. Having paid $110 billion for Tele-Communications International and MediaOne cable properties, it boasts a suite of wireless, data, Internet, cable-TV, and entertainment assets. In contrast, Sprint lacks its own high-speed Net-access service and cable TV; as does MCI, which also lacks wireless. "AT&T will be the ones to beat," says Blaik Kirby, a principal with Renaissance Worldwide Inc., a management consultant in Boston. "They have a bundle of products that over time will replace the core long-distance revenue."

NO LET-UP. Bundled services guarantee simplified billing. But not all will see lower prices. High-volume users, or those who call mainly during off-peak hours, will benefit. But after paying monthly fees of $5.95 and $2.50 in federal line charges, a consumer who makes, say, only 30 minutes of long distance calls a month under AT&T's new plan would pay $10.55, or 35 cents a minute. That's more than double what AT&T charged the same customer two years ago, says Olivia Wein, a fellow at Consumers Union in Washington.

But downward pressure on rates won't let up. When voice calling over the Net improves, a whole new round of price-cutting could follow. Net2Phone Inc., a Hackensack (N.J.) startup, already sells long-distance at 4.9 cents-per-minute, with a monthly charge of just 99 cents. The savings are even greater internationally. If customers can use soundcard-equipped PCs, Net2Phone charges just 10

LET THE BABY BELLS REACH INTO LONG DISTANCE

With phone rates tumbling, you would hardly think the Baby Bells would be champing at the bit to get into long distance. But three—Bell Atlantic, SBC Communications, and BellSouth—are lobbying state regulators in New York, Texas, and Georgia, respectively, to let them get into the act.

More than three years after the 1996 Telecommunications Act passed, no Baby Bell has won regulatory approval to sell long-distance service within its region. The law requires the Bells to open up their local-calling markets to competition before being able to get into this new business. None has passed muster so far.

But the old test doesn't measure competition as well as it did: Wireless systems, Internet calling, and phone service over cable—and the ingenuity of countless entrepreneurs—have made the arbitrary distinction between long distance and local look like a throwback to Ma Bell days. **"STRONGER STICK."** So it's time to start letting the Baby Bells into long distance. The likely first entrant is Bell Atlantic, which has been working closely with New York regulators to prove itself worthy. In particular, state officials want local-phone customers to be able to switch to a new local-service provider as easily as long-distance customers can today, and Bell Atlantic has been developing a system with this capability.

No doubt, a Bell Atlantic entry will spur the other Bells to become equally cooperative, if only to get the stock market boost that their long-distance entry is expected to produce. Says Robert C. Taylor, president of Focal Communications, a Chicago local phone company that competes with Ameritech Corp.: "Wall Street has a stronger stick than the regulators."

There is also some need to level the playing field when AT&T enters the local market, which it plans to do through the cable systems it has been snapping up. The Federal Communications Commission has already sided with AT&T on one key issue, supporting the giant's stand against "open access" for data services over cable. Internet service providers want to force AT&T to carry all data services on an equal basis, rather than giving favorable terms to Excite@home, in which it is a major investor.

Meanwhile the regulators warn that even with the looming entry of AT&T, Bells still have to comply with the law. "The Bells will get long-distance relief when they satisfy the competitive checklist," says Larry Strickling, chief of the Common Carrier Bureau at the FCC. "What other competitors do in the marketplace doesn't make much difference." But he does concede that "these companies are doing a lot more than they were two years ago."

Many expect state regulators to grant approval to the first Bell sometime this fall and the FCC to move early next year. "Bell entry into New York will be the single most important telecom event of the year," says Scott C. Cleland, an analyst at Legg Mason's Precursor Group.

Ultimately, this is all a prelude to consumers buying telecom bundles from a new generation of megatelecoms. "In the long term, there will be a handful of large companies offering Internet, long-distance, local, and wireless services," says Larry Darby of Darby & Associates, a Washington telecom consultant. A primary goal of the Telecom Act was erasing arbitrary distinctions between service markets. Now that the virtuous cycle of competition between the two sectors is starting, let the games begin.

Yang covers telecommunications policy for BUSINESS WEEK in Washington.

---

cents a minute to ring any phone in the U.S. from overseas.

Although still a tiny niche in the global telecom business, Internet telephony is gaining ground. AT&T is leasing international lines to Net2Phone and running its own limited Internet telephony service in Asia. Sprint has begun trials of Net2Phone's service in Asia, and Compaq Computer Corp. is bundling Net2Phone's software into PCs it sells overseas. Next spring, Net2Phone plans to add voice to America Online Inc.'s Instant Messaging service, an offering that could soon be free, says Net2Phone CEO Howard Balter.

It all adds up to a world where consumers pay a fixed fee to access a network that will provide the full range of voice, video, and data services. As with E-mail, distance will be divorced from price. "Consumers will have choices in what to bundle, and we'll offer discounts and incentives to those who use us more," says H. Eugene Lockhart, president of AT&T consumer services. Long distance will cost pennies, but companies will throw it in for free.

By Steven V. Brull in Los Angeles with Amy Barrett in Philadelphia and Roger Crockett in Chicago

76

GIVING AWAY THE E-STORE

The Web has become a freebie fest. Can firms make money offering something for nothing?

by Karl Taro Greenfeld

Yaron Zilberman, 33, and Guy Blachman, 28, have made all the right moves. They have M.B.A.s from top business schools, $8 million in venture capital and a snazzy Trump Place apartment and office suite on Manhattan's West Side. They also have Gooey, an innovative Web application that allows visitors to any website to chat with other Gooey users at the same site. Zilberman and Blachman will tell you it's a killer app, one that will turn the whole Internet into a billion-voice AOL chat room. So how much is Hypernix, their company, charging for this product?

Nothing. Like hundreds of high-tech and Internet companies, Hypernix has embraced the business of free. You name the product, and someone out there wants you to have it gratis. There are at least five companies giving away PCs, five offering Internet access, a couple promising long-distance calls at zero cents a minute, three passing out voice-mail boxes, one seeking the privilege of doing your faxing and another that wants to give you postage. You want e-mail? Pick from a dozen companies that would love to be your no-cost provider. Once you're online with your free PC, you may want to trade stocks–American Express Brokerage will provide free trading for accounts over $100,000. Amex won't do your taxes, but H.D. Vest, another financial planner, has just volunteered. Other software needs? Linux is a free operating system, and Sun Microsystems' StarOffice is a complimentary office suite.

Why the proliferation of businesses that are literally giving away the store? "We're moving from an economy where people pay directly for services to an attention-based economy," says Joe Krause, senior vice president of content at Excite@Home. "What's valuable for businesses is not necessarily the money being directly paid but rather the consumer's attention." Most of these businesses–like Free-PC, which offers a free computer in exchange for a constant ad presence on your desktop, and NetZero, an Internet provider–are relying on advertisers and marketers to provide their income. They subscribe to the old Net mantra: Get Big Fast. Gather enough eyeballs, aggregate enough consumer-shopping habits and click-through tendencies, and sellers will pay a premium to get at your customers.

One might rightly ask: How much does all this free stuff cost? In the case of PCs, some firms, like InterSquid and PeoplePC, provide quality computers that come with multiyear contracts requiring the user to sign for dial-up Internet access at somewhat pricey rates–a deal many consumers might regret when high-speed Internet access becomes widely available. AltaVista, a free Internet service provider, runs a narrow, scrolling banner across your screen that requires you to click through–interact with the ad–every hour.

Although free everything seems like another Internet innovation, it's actually a century-old strategy. King Gillette gave away his safety razor and made a fortune selling the blades. Perhaps you remember something called broadcast television, which was preceded, in

---

YES, A FREE LAUNCH

New companies are popping up to give away stuff that others still sell

HARDWARE

■ **FREE** Free-PC, InterSquid and PeoplePC give away computers, but there are strings attached

■ **PAY** You can spend up to $5,000 for computers from IBM, Dell and other makers

OPERATING SYSTEMS

■ **FREE** Linux, the OS of the Web proletariat, is popular with programmers and other digerati

■ **PAY** Microsoft's monopoly on the for-profit OS has hurt consumers and slowed innovation, say feds

INTERNET-SERVICE PROVIDERS

■ **FREE** If you will click on demand, such sites as AltaVista, NetZero and WorldSpy will give you Net access

■ **PAY** In the land of the free you still pay Earthlink, WorldNet and AOL, three of the biggest ISPs, for a hookup

E-COMMERCE

■ **FREE** *Bigstep.com* and *OLB.com* will set up your e-store and design your e-commerce site

■ **PAY** Yahoo, IBM and Razorfish have for-profit businesses in e-commerce development

the 1920s, by broadcast radio. RCA created the NBC network to sell radios.

These classic business models are being embraced by an Internet industry that can't dispense money fast enough. "With $60 billion in uninvested capital in the hands of venture capitalists, every gimmick ever thought of will be funded," says Ann Winblad, partner with Hummer Winblad, one of the best-known venture-capital firms. "We have seen free everything walk through our office. Still waiting for Free House."

The Net has always been conducive to giving away high-tech gewgaws. Browsers like Netscape's Navigator and Microsoft's Explorer have long been free. And in 1997 RealNetworks became a new media power by handing out its media player to build market share. Then Sabir Bhatia, co-founder of free e-mail provider Hotmail, sold his company in 1997 to Microsoft for $400 million, or $44 per user. "What hit people when Microsoft bought Hotmail was how much they paid per user," says Diane Greene, CEO of VMware, a Palo Alto, Calif., software firm. "All of a sudden, eyeballs were worth a lot of money."

Entrepreneurs of the pro bono model worship Hotmail–even though the company never made a profit. They overlook the fact that what made Hotmail hot was one of the stickiest applications out there–once you have an e-mail address, you tend to keep visiting the site–and a one-year ramp up to 5 million users. Start-up founders fantasize about that 400 mil. "Now there are so many companies, and you ask them what their revenue model is and they say, 'I don't know. We just want to get big fast and get acquired, like Hotmail,'" says Bhatia. "That's scary when entrepreneurs don't think through how they are going to make money."

Zilberman vows that Gooey will be profitable–he's just not sure when. He says Gooey needs a minimum of 3 million users within a year. Today he's got about 300,000. "Nobody has ever done our business model successfully," he concedes as he heads into Hypernix's next round of fund raising. "But we are talking about really high-quality reach media."

That's another word for targeted advertising. The two-way nature of the Net makes it possible for advertisers to know a lot about you (sometimes without your knowing it) so they can deliver more effective ads. Web entrepreneurs are counting on advertisers paying a higher CPM (cost per thousand) for this rifle-shot data than they do for the old shotgun approach. "We charge more than average because each advertiser can see how their ad is performing with each demographic and can then focus their campaign," says Steve Chadima, founder of Free-PC. Forrester Research estimates that Internet advertising will grow from $2.8 billion in 1999 to $22 billion in 2004. But with click-through rates hovering at under 1%, those ad dollars will support only a handful of the many businesses that are making a go of the giveaway. "It'll be a dogfight," says Chan Suh, CEO of Net advertising operation Agency.com. "People who think that advertising makes up for the lack of a biz model and execution are going to fall by the wayside."

The Gooey guys have no doubts about their model. But neither does their competitor, Third Voice, another free client that allows users to post on websites. These two Internet software firms will be battling it out for eyeballs, advertisers and traffic. One thing you can bet on, however: no price wars.

With reporting by Susan Kuchinskas/San Francisco and Julie Rawe/New York City

77

PENNY-PINCHERS' PARADISE

E-coupons are catching on fast—and companies are learning how to use them

Something about saving a few bucks brings out the miser in almost everyone. Maybe you won't admit it, but Lauren Tascan does. She's among the 80% of Americans that clips coupons every year. The 32-year-old New Yorker accepts her parsimonious streak with an easy shrug. "There's a little thrill that comes from just a little bit of savings," Tascan says.

Get out your piggy bank, thrill seekers. The Internet is becoming one of the hottest spots to save with coupons. Web surfers who clip virtual coupons have risen to nearly 30% of those online from 23% a year ago, says researcher NPD Online.

What exactly are e-coupons? They're discount offers either found on a Web site or that can be redeemed online. Sites such as coupons.com and coolsavings.com, for example, let you print a coupon and redeem it at your local grocer. Just as often, consumers see an e-tailer's coupon bearing a special code in a magazine or on a Net portal. They then enter the code on a Web site to get a discount when buying online.

Virtual coupons have clear advantages over those you clip from the local paper. For starters, they have a "phenomenal" redemption rate, says Charles K. Brown, vice-president for marketing at promotions researcher NCH NuWorld Marketing Ltd. To be sure, e-coupons make up less than 1% of the 256 billion coupons distributed yearly in the U.S., vs. the 80% that are distributed in Sunday papers. But nearly 57% of those who click on e-coupons or get them via e-mail redeem them, Brown says, compared with the 1.2% of Sunday paper coupons that are redeemed.

What makes e-coupons so effective? Merchants can e-mail offers targeted to customers' tastes once they find a consumer who loves the Beatles or Legos or 2% milk. "The manufacturer is able to build a relationship with the consumer in a lot more depth than in any other media," says Steven M. Golden, CEO of coolsavings.com, the Web's most visited coupon mall, with 11 million members.

Like their real-world counterparts, e-coupons help lure new customers, too. During the six months that ended in November, Staples.com jumped from 23rd to 14th among retail Web sites with the most buyers, says researcher PC Data Online. Many new customers were lured by an e-coupon that saved $25 on purchases of $75 or more. Web coupons are "a key tool in the tool kit," says Kelly A. Mahoney, chief marketing officer for Staples Inc.

But Web sites should be careful not to give away the store. In 1999, when the Web teemed with fledgling e-tailers, merchants flooded consumers with "impossible" promotions, says analyst Mike May of Jupiter Communications Inc. Vitamins.com, for example, closed down partly because it was too generous with discounts. The site offered new visitors $25 off purchases of $25.01 or more. Then it added a $15-off coupon for the buyer's next purchase—and delivered it all free.

Better to be wise than bankrupt. Sure, the bigger the discount, the bigger the draw. But the idea is to wean consumers from boffo deals, migrating them from big savings to smaller ones. "If a dollar off works the first time," May says, "the customer should not see that discount again." A good coupon campaign offers just enough savings to give consumers a little thrill.

Reprinted from the January 22, 2001 issue of *Business Week* by special permission. © 2001 McGraw-Hill Companies, Inc.

Click-n-Save

E-coupons obtained on the Web have become a hit. Here are the categories where online coupons are most popular:

Groceries	**59%**	Beauty	**17%**
Books	**32%**	Fast food	**16%**
Health	**30%**	Apparel	**14%**
Music	**26%**	Toys	**14%**

DATA: NPD GROUP INC.

eBay's Bid to Conquer All

For all the dotcom disasters, here's one company that's redefining e-commerce

By Adam Cohen

Let's say you need to get your hands on a 53-passenger school bus with hydraulic brakes and a six-cylinder diesel engine. Or a 1998 Ford monster truck called Wizard that will let you "give rides all day, crush cars all night." Or four pawnshops—plus a half interest in three check-advance businesses—spread across western Kentucky. Where would you start to look?

There's only one place on earth: eBay.

If the name eBay conjures up Bongo the Monkey, Huggy the Bear and the rest of the Beanie Baby clan, you're about three years behind the times. Computer giant Sun Microsystems is listing up to 150 items a day on eBay, including e4500 servers that sell for as much as $15,000. eBay Motors, which launched last April, is the third biggest auto-sales site on the Internet. And eBay's new Business Exchange, which has listings for $6,000 backhoes and $25,000 lathes, has doubled its offerings in the past quarter.

The Internet collapse continues, and even substantial firms like Amazon and Yahoo are struggling to stay ahead of it. But eBay has never had it better. Revenues topped $430 million last year, up 92% over 1999. The auction king now has 22.5 million registered users, a number that grew at a 125% annualized rate last quarter. And it's on track to do more than $6 billion in gross merchandise sales this year.

With stats like that and the stock up 51% since Jan. 1, the New Economy pundits are scratching their heads. How is it that a flea-market auction site has become the most successful company in cyberspace? And when so many other dotcoms are crashing and burning, will this high-tech highflyer come down to earth anytime soon?

At the heart of eBay's good fortune is perhaps the most compelling business model on the Net. As an online middleman between buyers and sellers, eBay is building an empire that bricks and mortar could not have touched. "If Buy.com goes down, you can still go to Circuit City," says Meg Whitman, the Harvard Business School-trained CEO of eBay. But if eBay crashes, there's nowhere else to go. And because eBay's job is connecting people—not selling them things—it isn't lumbered with a traditional retailing cost

structure. No buying, warehousing or shipping. No taking returns or unloading overstock. "eBay is the only e-tailer that really fulfills the promise of the Web," says Faye Landes, an e-commerce analyst at Sanford C. Bernstein & Co. "And the key is its virtuality."

That virtuality translates into remarkable profit margins. eBay's gross margins last quarter were a stunning 82%. Amazon, which actually has to acquire goods and ship them out, has gross margins averaging 20%. And because so much of eBay's customer recruitment is viral—sellers attracting buyers to the site, and buyers attracting sellers—its customer-acquisition costs are just half of Amazon's.

eBay is also the Internet's clearest example of a company that has exploited its "first mover" advantage. The lore among Internet strategists was that whoever nabbed Web space early would have a commanding commercial lead. The failure of a long list of early-bird dotcoms, from CompuServe to eToys, has proved that wrong.

But eBay did benefit tremendously from being first. The key: by locking up the most buyers and sellers in one place, it created a market no one could afford to leave. If you don't like Amazon, you can do roughly as well at Borders.com. If you leave eBay, you'll be going to a site with many fewer products for sale and many fewer buyers.

CEO Whitman and her cadre have leveraged themselves into all but total dominance of the online-auction market. Attempts by other companies to replicate eBay have bombed. eBay controls more than 80% of the online-auction market, with Yahoo and Amazon lagging far behind. eBay lands all the lucrative cross-promotional tie-ins with companies like Visa and Mailboxes Etc. And the auctioneers keep forging new partnerships with name-brand powerhouses like General Motors (which is allied with eBay Motors) and Disney (which uses the site to auction off authentic studio props, like Cruella De Vil's costumes from the movie 102 Dalmatians).

The goal now is to create entirely new markets. Says Whitman: "The best thing to do to grow your company is to extend a proven concept." The company's marketing division had long known that it was missing out on potential customers. Surveys showed that some

buyers are psychologically averse to shopping by auction. They don't like the bidding game, and they are too time pressed. "A lot of people use the Web to simplify their lives," says Landes. "Being involved in an online auction is not necessarily simple."

So when intelligence came back from eBay's Consumer Insights Group that an obscure website launched a year ago called Half.com was a prospective threat, Whitman's gang went to work. Half.com started as a cleverly designed site that allowed people to sell used books, CDs and videos for a fixed price. The eBay investigators recognized immediately that Half's fixed-price system could become a devastating threat to their floating-price auction model. So they asked for a meeting. And then they bought the company.

eBay also experimented late last year with adding a fixed-price option to its auction listings. Items with a BUY IT now logo—as many as 25% of all listings—can be bought immediately for a set price. Buy It Now increased eBay's "velocity of trade," the critical measure of how quickly goods listed on the site are sold. Declared a success (last Christmas it stretched the holiday buying season by 10 days), the program has been extended through this year.

The easiest explanation for eBay's prevalence is that its managers haven't stopped to congratulate themselves. In many New Economy companies, the founders don't step aside easily. But it has now been proved, by billions of dollars in squandered fortunes, that while brilliance may ignite a start-up, it won't necessarily sustain it.

Pierre Omidyar, who founded eBay as a clunky website in his San Jose, Calif., living room, always knew he didn't have the company-building savvy to vault eBay into the corporate big leagues. So in 1998, he and co-founder Jeff Skoll brought in Whitman, who had learned the crucial importance of branding in the trenches of Old Economy powerhouses like Hasbro. Whitman, who combines an upbeat personality with a hard-driving focus on the bottom line, took the company public, grew it and proved adept at exceeding earnings predictions. She culled her senior staff from places like Pepsico and Disney. The kids aren't running this dotcom. The

(Cont.)

BIG TICKET ITEMS that have been auctioned to businesses this month on eBay	
Terex Bulldozer	**$15,099**
Bridgeport Milling Machine	**$1,775**
Sun E4500 Server	**$155,000**

management team's average age is 44, with an average of 20 years of business experience and a strong vision for the company. They've had a knack for making the right calls—and have slain a stream of well-funded companies that tried to move into the online-auction space. And these top managers are relentless about something few dotcoms ever bothered with: pinching pennies.

Whitman and her crew are shedding their sentimental attachment to the stuffed animals and stamps that helped build eBay. Wall Street has long made clear that it is anything but misty-eyed about collectibles. After all, there are only so many coin or toy-soldier aficionados, and eBay was running the risk it might tap out the market. Moreover, the collectibles' average sale price (ASP), a key metric that helps determine eBay's fees on a transaction, is lower than for "practicals," like lawn mowers. The ASP in eBay's computer category, which includes peripherals and software, is $80. The ASP in "Toys, Bean Bag Plush" is $20.

To boost the ASP, eBay is pushing into an array of upscale markets—from autos to real estate to high-end business computers. Buyers were at first a little skeptical when Sun Microsystems started listing its servers on eBay. (Sun received e-mails warning that someone was using the company name to sell its servers.) But in the past year, Sun has sold $10 million worth of equipment, and it now lists between 20 and 150 items a day, making it one of eBay's biggest sellers. The ultimate sign it's working: Sun's competitors have started putting up items too.

Still, for all the good news, eBay has had a few stumbles lately. Great Collections, the high-end antiques-and-art category unveiled with great fanfare a year ago, has been a disappointment in traffic and sales. This month eBay scrapped it and unveiled eBay Premiere, a retooled attempt to capture this lucrative but elusive market. eBay's international strategy, which spans Europe, has yet to take hold in Japan, the world's second largest Internet market.

The company has benefited, though, from some key courtroom victories. It has established a critical legal principle: it is not liable for the sale of improper items on the site by third parties. eBay scored last July, when it extracted a $1.2 million settlement from ReverseAuction, a rival that copied e-mail addresses of eBay users and sent them messages urging them to switch sites. And earlier this month, the company won dismissal of a class action against it for allowing fake sports memorabilia to be sold. If eBay had lost, its entire hands-off business model might have been imperiled.

But preserving its hands-off status has come at a cost: the occasional p.r. black eye it sustains when cases of fraud or sales of offensive items hit the news. Last month a California man was charged with selling $110,000 in computers and consumer electronics on eBay but not delivering. And there was a minor dustup last fall when convicted serial killer Angel Resendez-Ramirez boasted in a television interview that his hair and shavings from calluses on his feet had been sold on eBay.

Given how well it is doing right now, eBay's greatest challenge may be meeting the wildly ambitious goals it has set for itself. Whitman maintains that the company is on track to grow 50% a year for each of the next five years. This means that a lot of things—from an expansive push into international markets to eBay Autos—will need to go right. If eBay does keep growing at its torrid pace, it will amount to more than just the world's leading marketplace. It will stand as convincing evidence that despite the recent spate of bad news, the Internet revolution has changed business once and for all.

Adam Cohen is at work on an independent book about the life and times of eBay

79

Competing Online, Drugstore Chains Virtually Undersell Themselves

Their Web Sites Charge Less Than Their Own Stores, With Some Strings Attached

By Laura Johannes
Staff Reporter of The Wall Street Journal

Cecil Powell Grant didn't want to pay a lot for his cholesterol-lowering medication, so he went online to price shop.

A few mouse clicks later, he discovered that CVS.com, a Web site owned by **CVS** Corp., the big drugstore chain, would sell him his monthly ration of Lipitor for only $78.68 – with free mail delivery. At his neighborhood CVS store, it costs $99.

Waging war in one of the scrappiest battles under way on the Web, the biggest drugstore chains – CVS, **Walgreen** Co., **Rite Aid** Corp. and the Eckerd unit of **J.C. Penney** Co. – have begun offering medicines online at prices 10% to 30% cheaper than those in their own stores. Other drugstore items, from shaving cream to diapers, are also sold at bargain prices online.

"I was shocked to find out that CVS is underselling its own retail stores online," says the 56-year-old Mr. Grant, who lives in Cincinnati. "Why would anybody go to a drugstore when they can get it cheaper from the same company online?"

Many of those who might be beneficiaries of cut-rate prescription prices online lack access to the Internet.

Asking a similar question, retailers of all kinds with a Web presence have approached the Internet gingerly, carefully avoiding online discounts that could ultimately drive down in-store prices.

But there are some notable exceptions. In May, after **Amazon.com** Inc. started offering bestsellers at half the publishers' list prices, **barnesandnoble.com** Inc. matched the discount – even though that meant it was massively underselling stores run by **Barnes**

& Noble Inc., which has a 40% stake in barnesandnoble.com.

J&R Music & Computer World, a New York City music and electronics retailer, offers a handful of special bargains to lure Internet surfers to its Web site. If a customer walks into J&R and asks for the Internet discount, employees are instructed to give him the cheaper price. "We don't want the Web to be a venue that will undercut our bricks-and-mortar stores," says J&R spokesman Abe Brown.

Among the retailers that do undersell their own stores online, none do so as aggressively as the pharmacy chains, where competition is particularly intense. The Web's drug retailers monitor rivals' prices and often adjust their own to match others' discounts. "Prices on the Web are so visible, that you have to be competitive with online providers," says Jim Smith, vice president of electronic commerce at Eckerd.

People with insurance pay the same amount whether they buy the drugs online or in stores. The price differentials apply only to the 70 million Americans who don't have prescription-drug insurance benefits. They account for 10% to 20% of retail medicine sales, but cash customers' prescriptions are high-profit-margin purchases that help offset the discounts given to managed-care and government buyers.

Internet prescription sales in 1999 represented a small slice – about $160 million – of the $101 billion U.S. market, according to Forrester Research Inc., an Internet research firm in Cambridge, Mass. Eckerd, CVS and Walgreen say they have no evidence of cash business defecting from their stores to the Internet. A Rite Aid spokeswoman says that the company's deal with drugstore.com leaves online pricing decisions to the Internet company, while giving Rite Aid a prominent online presence. In most cases, customers must use mail delivery to get the discounts. But Rite Aid, under a deal with Internet start-up **drugstore.com** Inc., allows customers to buy online at Internet prices and pick up their purchases the same day at a Rite Aid store.

Scrambling to Catch Up

Internet start-ups such as Soma.com and drugstore.com launched the first major e-drugstores last year, verifying prescriptions by phone or fax. Conventional drugstore chains scrambled to catch up. In June, CVS bought Soma. That same month, Rite Aid bought a large minority stake, now 22%, in drugstore.com. Eckerd, going it alone, started selling prescription drugs online in August. Walgreen followed in October.

For now, this isn't a price break that's helping the majority of elderly and uninsured cash customers, whose plight has become a major issue with legislators in Washington and state capitals.

Tricia Smith, a health lobbyist at AARP, the big advocacy group for retirees, explains: "Older Americans and those who have no

insurance are the stand-alone groups paying higher prices, and they can least afford it. Ironically, they are among the least likely to access Internet prices so they are left out of the opportunity."

Nationwide, 38.5% of all households have access to the Internet, says Kenneth B. Clemmer, an analyst at Forrester Research. But only 8% of households headed by someone over the age of 65 are online, he says.

The Web Drug Price Gap

A sampling of drug-price savings offered online to cash customers

- ◆ **Claritin** (allergy)
  Dosage: 30 pills, 10 mg.
  Walgreen.com price: $58.99, with free mail delivery
  Price at Walgreen store in Newark, N.J.: $67.19
  Internet savings: $8.20, or 12%

- ◆ **Fossamax** (osteoporosis)
  Dosage: 30 pills, 10 mg.
  CVS.com price: $53.76, with free mail delivery
  Price at CVS store in Akron, Ohio: $69.99
  Internet savings: $16.23, or 23%

- ◆ **Lipitor** (cholestrol)
  Dosage: 30 pills, 20 mg.
  Drugstore.com price: $74.94, with free mail delivery or pickup at Rite Aid stores
  Price at Rite Aid store in Albany, N.Y.: $105.98
  Internet savings: $31.04, or 29%

- ◆ **Zantac** (ulcer)
  Dosage: 30 pills, 300 mg.
  Eckerd.com price: $82.15
  Price at Eckerd store in Dallas: $92.60
  Internet savings: $10.45, or 11%

(Cont.)

A Matter of Convenience

Other patients, even those with Internet access, won't shop online because they like the convenience of drugstore pickup, says Lawrence J. Zigerelli, CVS's vice president for corporate development. Half of CVS's prescriptions are for urgently needed medications, such as antibiotics or painkillers, he says.

CVS.com's Chief Executive Tom Pigott says the Web site is bringing in customers from areas such as California, where CVS does not have stores. Still, Mr. Zigerelli says the company will carefully monitor whether CVS.com is eroding store sales and will adjust online prices – now an average 15% lower than CVS's store prices – if needed.

"We expect there will be fallout and consolidation among smaller players," CVS.com's Mr. Pigott says.

Marie Toulantis, chief financial officer of barnesandnoble.com's, defends the online discounts. "People have to eat the shipping charges and make an investment in a computer. It's a lot of work," she says.

Besides, Ms. Toulantis adds, while online retailers are losing money now, in the long run, it is a cheaper way to conduct business.

For now, the competition is brutal. Mr. Grant ultimately ended up getting his Lipitor at **PlanetRx.com** Inc.'s Web site for $73.97 – $5 less than the CVS.com price.

Republished with permission of Dow Jones & Company, Inc., from *The Wall Street Journal,* "Competing Online, Drugstore Chains Virtually Undersell Themselves," p. B1, January 10, 2000; permission conveyed through Copyright Clearance Center, Inc.

Vaccine's Price Drives a Debate About Its Use

BY GARDINER HARRIS
Staff Reporter of THE WALL STREET JOURNAL

When an influential government health panel meets today, it will face a wrenching question: Should it recommend scaling back the use of a major new childhood vaccine simply because of its unusually high price?

Hopes are still high that the vaccine, called Prevenar, will prevent scores of deaths and millions of illnesses in the U.S. from meningitis, pneumonia, blood poisoning and ear infections. But at $232 for a four-dose series, Prevenar will cost as much as all other approved childhood vaccinations combined.

That price is just too high, say some doctors advising the government. So instead of giving the vaccine to all children up to age five, as it had voted to do in October, the Centers for Disease Control and Prevention's Advisory Committee on Immunization Practices is expected to recommend that Prevenar be given just to the children at highest risk: those under the age of two.

Today's vote also portends a looming problem for government vaccine experts, who rarely worry about price. For decades, research has proved that vaccines save more money than they cost by preventing expensive and deadly illnesses. As most new vaccines came along, government panels readily recommended that all American children get them. And the government has picked up much of the tab, paying for half of all childhood immunizations in the U.S.

But as manufacturers increasingly target less-severe illnesses with pricey medications, government experts will be forced to begin debating if the cure is worth the cost. This same debate has for years roiled adult medical care – and has emerged as central in dis-

cussions over the future of Medicare – but it is only now making its way into childhood vaccines.

"In the past the ACIP has not focused heavily on vaccine cost," says John Modlin, chairman of the CDC committee. "I think we are being forced to do so now." He notes: "Government largesse isn't bottomless."

Many in the medical community don't like making such choices. "A lot of us are very uncomfortable" balancing medical benefits with economic considerations, notes Jon Abramson, chairman of the committee of infectious diseases for the American Academy of Pediatrics and a non-voting member of the ACIP.

No one is disputing Prevenar's medical value. The vaccine targets pneumococcal bacteria that cause about 3,000 cases of meningitis, thousands more cases of blood poisoning, 100,000 to 135,000 hospitalizations for pneumonia and millions of infant ear infections every year in the U.S.

A narrower age range would be a disappointment to **American Home Products** Corp., which manufactures Prevenar. The company expects to receive approval this week from the U.S. Food and Drug Administration to market the vaccine, based on clinical trials on children under the age of two. It says that Prevenar is worth its high price.

While the outcome of today's ACIP vote isn't certain, some prominent committee members predict that Prevenar's price will lead to a change in the recommendation.

The FDA concerns itself only with whether a vaccine is safe and effective. The CDC debates whether a vaccine is needed and, more recently, whether it's worth the price. Critics worry that the government's vaccine committees aren't set up to engage in this kind of cost-benefit assessment.

"The ACIP is mostly made up of infectious-disease experts who see the people who die and suffer from infectious disease. There are not enough people thinking in terms of health economics, where to put health-care dollars," says Richard K. Zimmerman, an associate professor at the University of Pitts-

burgh and a non-voting member of the ACIP.

Several nonvoting members of the CDC's vaccine committee grumbled in October when the committee granted a conditional recommendation of Prevenar before the manufacturer had told any of them what the price would be.

This meant, these members argued, that the CDC had surrendered any power in negotiating a lower price. The CDC should instead insist that manufacturers provide their suggested price with their application, so price can be part of the discussions from the beginning, these members say.

Peter Paradiso, vice president for scientific affairs and research strategy for the Wyeth-Ayerst Laboratories division of American Home, says the price of Prevenar simply wasn't available earlier.

Dr. Modlin says that the ACIP voted in October to recommend the vaccine before it knew the price in part because each week's delay means more preventable infant deaths. "The desire is to have as little delay as possible," Dr. Modlin says. "I don't know whether playing cat and mouse with the company affects the price."

The vaccine has been under development since 1986, and it has seven different types of the pneumococcal bacteria. "That costs a lot of money," Dr. Paradiso says. He also notes that immunizing older kids is more cost-effective than immunizing infants, because children two and older need just one shot, not four. Each shot costs $58.

However, experts concerned about the overall cost of a vaccination program argue that vaccinating kids ages two and older – who aren't as susceptible to illness – isn't nearly as beneficial.

Promotions for Cut-Rate Long Distance Draw Fire

Deluged by Complaints, Regulators to Investigate If Fine Print Is Too Fine

By Kathy Chen
Staff Reporter of The Wall Street Journal

WASHINGTON – When Charles Harris saw a television ad touting a special number that would let him make a 20-minute long-distance call for 99 cents, he thought he saw a sweet deal.

Until he got his phone bill, that is. The 58-year-old retiree from Ooltewah, Tenn., had made some 20 calls to his children out of state using the 10-10-220 number, from **MCI WorldCom** Corp., but got their answering machines. Though each call lasted just a few seconds, he was billed the full 99 cents each time.

"It's not false advertising, but they're not telling you everything," Mr. Harris grumbles. "To me, it's misrepresentative."

Consumers have flooded the Federal Communications Commission with nearly 3,000 complaints since January 1998 about what they view as misleading or confusing promotions of discounted long-distance services from upstarts and giants like MCI and AT&T Corp. The FCC has launched an investigation into such practices, and today it will air the issue in a joint hearing with the Federal Trade Commission, which regulates deceptive advertising.

The companies offer an array of new services from the 10-10 numbers that let callers "dial around" their regular carriers for cheaper rates, to deeply discounted calling plans, such as AT&T's new seven-cents-a-minute offering.

But in the battle to sign up customers, some push too far – often with ads that don't paint a clear or complete picture of the offer, regulators say. "Information that matters to consumers needs to be disclosed in a clear and conspicuous way," says Eileen Harrington, the FTC's director of marketing practices. "What we've found is the ads are all wanting."

In the last three years, the FTC has cracked down on car-lease advertisers, charging them with deceptive advertising and forcing them to revise their marketing and not hide added fees in the fine print. Regulators are looking into the same issues in long-distance phone advertising.

Many "10-10" ads, for example, play up their rates in screaming bold type, then add conditions in tiny print to the side. A billboard sponsored by PT-1 Communications Inc., a subsidiary of **Star Telecommunications** Inc. in Santa Barbara, Cal., proclaims a 7.9-cents-per-minute rate for "long distance, 24 hours, 7 days" in big letters on an orange background. Only by following an asterisk to the fine print in the poster's upper corner does the viewer find that federal tax will be added and that potentially different rates apply for long-distance calls within certain states.

Jerry Ginsberg, Star Telecommunications' vice president of marketing, says the company is "very careful in providing full disclosure and letting consumers know what the offer is." He adds that it has been careful to use a size print that "the average person with average eyesight can read in an average amount of time."

A study last year by the AARP, which represents retired people, suggests many consumers are reluctant to try new long-distance options because of confusion over their terms. One barrier for older consumers is the small print carriers often use to notify consumers of added terms or conditions related to promotions made on TV or in print ads, says AARP legislative representative Jeff Kramer.

"On TV ads, it's difficult to see because they flash it. With print ads, you have to spend time looking at it," Mr. Kramer says.

Mr. Harris, the MCI customer who complained about the cost of calling his kids answering machines, got his money back. But

Many large-type ads detail conditions in tiny print on the side

an MCI spokesman, Brad Burns, says that the company is confident its ads, including the one Mr. Harris saw, are clear.

"More than 85% of our customers on a monthly basis are repeat users" of the dial-around service, he says. "That is our best evidence." He says it's in MCI's best interest to make sure its ads are clear because "at the end of the day, if there's sticker shock, customers won't dial the number again."

One source of confusion is that big carriers like MCI and AT&T, which enjoy a big share of the dial-around market, offer such services under different brand names. That's not only misleading, regulators say, but it also makes it difficult for consumers to figure out where to turn if they have a complaint.

When Ray Lippman of Scottsdale, Ariz., got an unexpectedly high phone bill for a call he placed to Taiwan in June using a 10-10 number offered by Lucky Dog Phone Co., he called the toll-free number listed on the company's flier to complain. He followed up with

---

PHONE TIPS FROM THE FEDS

Advice from the Federal Communications Commission on choosing long-distance service.

■ **Beware of Additional Charges**
Ask if there are monthly, minimum or per-call fees in addition to the per-minute rates. For example, if a dial-around service charges a $5 monthly fee and you make only one 10-minute call that month, then you pay an extra 50 cents a minute for that call.

■ **Be Careful of Comparison Rates in Advertisements**
Consumers should be careful about comparison rates in ads, such as 50% off of a carrier's basic rates, because such basic rates are often not the lowest available.

■ **Check Out the Phone Companies' Web Sites**
Their sites should have specific information on their rates and calling plans.

■ **Tie-Ins and Other Discounts**
Ask your long-distance carrier about mileage tie-ins that they may offer. Many companies now offer frequent-flier miles for the amount you spend on your long-distance bill. Also, some phone carriers provide discounts if you have your long-distance charges billed to your credit card.

(Cont.)

a letter to Lucky Dog but got no response. Neither the flier nor the representative informed him that the 10-10 number is actually offered by AT&T.

Howard McNally, president of AT&T Transition Services, which oversees AT&T's dial-around business, says AT&T decided to offer the service under a different name when it entered the market last year because "some people don't want to buy a brand, they think [10-10] is a better bargain." In addition, he adds, "It allows us to be different...a little cute, very humorous, which isn't in AT&T's brand image."

But Mr. McNally said that while AT&T strives for simplicity in its ads, it can't afford to offer consumers using its 10-10 number the same level of customer service as its core business. He says AT&T will look into Mr. Lippman's case and consider a refund.

Federal officials hope the forum today will bring industry and regulators together to improve long-distance advertising, but are prepared to take enforcement action if needed.

"There's no question any consumer in America today can get cheaper long distance rates than three years ago," says Bill Kennard, the FCC chairman. "But you can only shop around if you get the information you need, and not all customers are getting that information."

82

Soft Money

Private Internet "currencies" and other increasingly abstract forms of exchange may replace government notes

By Sarah Lueck

Staff Reporter of The Wall Street Journal

The global monetary system of the next millennium may amount to a hill of "beenz."

Sure, plenty of dollars, yen and euros will be floating around as paper bills, coins and electronic transfers. But government-backed notes increasingly will vie for wallet space – or its cyberspace equivalent – with private Internet "currencies" that already are cropping up, like the beenz created by beenz.com, along with similar units like "Flooz" and "Ubarter dollars."

"Digicash paracurrencies" is how Internet writer and artist Mark Amerika dubs these emerging coins of the virtual realm. Companies and future celebrities could become the basis for tradable computerized value units backed by their fame and fortune, he believes – like General Electric dollars or Michael Jordan dollars or Picasso dollars. "There are going to be all forms of currencies that coexist with each other," Mr. Amerika says.

That evolution of money over the next millennium would, at one level, mark a logical continuation of the development of cash over the past 3,000 years, from concrete to ever more abstract and diverse. But in taking those trends to a new extreme, the change will raise intriguing questions about the true role and meaning of money in an economy and in society. Why does money exist? Does the system require anything concrete to make legitimate the universe of floating bits and bytes greasing the wheels of exchange? What are the limits of faith that people will place in a promise that they hold something of value? When anybody can issue cash, is anybody in control?

Forward and Back

In some ways, the grand technofuture may look a lot like the past. And it may not be a smooth ride – reminiscent, perhaps, of the chaotic early 1800s, when wildcat banks issued their own currencies.

"People are going to have to be more aware of who handles their money," says Jack Weatherford, author of "The History of Money." "For 100 years, we've been so accustomed to the government taking responsibility. In the old days, people had to weigh coins or bite them to make sure they were real."

Of course, the main purpose of money has always been – and always will be – the same: to facilitate commerce. Business started as barter, when people traded goods of relatively equal tangible worth. But that system had obvious limits. Short-lived items such as food couldn't keep their value for long. Transporting goods, whether five cows or five bags of salt, was difficult. Values varied from region to region.

The first solution was coins, which emerged in Lydia near the Aegean Sea, in 640 B.C. Metal pieces were weighed and stamped with their value, making transactions more convenient and values more standardized – but heavy. Clearly, people needed something lighter as they traveled more frequently. Many began to see advantages to storing money with a money lender and taking away a paper note in exchange.

Paper currency was used in 11th-century China and 14th-century Italy. Yet for centuries after that, people still believed the paper should be fully backed by stores of metal. Through succeeding centuries, there was increasing public trust in gold- and silver-backed paper notes as a form of currency. But in 1933 the U.S. government stopped tying currency to a fixed price in gold, and instead moved to the dollar standard and the elusive notion that the credibility of the U.S. Treasury backed up the notes.

"When you could no longer trust in gold, they invited you to trust in God," says currency artist J.S.G. Boggs, alluding to the phrase on the back of U.S. notes. Quoted in Lawrence Weschler's book "Boggs: A Comedy of Values," Mr. Boggs says "it was like a Freudian slip."

Small Change

Checks and credit cards came into wide use by the 1970s, quickly replacing cash for most large transactions. By the mid-1990s, bills and coins in the U.S. were largely relegated to the smallest of transactions, such as paying cab fare or buying a newspaper. Three-fourths of all cash is now used for transactions valued at $20 or less, says Mr. Weatherford, the author.

With the development of Internet commerce and electronic cash, money has become even more ethereal. U.S. consumers, who spent about $20.2 billion online in 1999, will spend $184 billion in 2004, according to Forrester Research Inc.

Children growing up now are becoming increasingly comfortable with cashless commerce. Several Web sites allow parents to create allowance accounts, which their kids use online.

Convenience is the main advantage of the future system, in which the transfer of money will be effortless. A world traveler may never again have to exchange dollars for euros or pesos for yen, since "value" won't be confined to national borders; instead, international "smart" cards will hold value in a microchip. And workers will be able to say goodbye to being handed a paycheck. Just as spending in the future will deal in intangibles, so will earning – just a slick transfer of data from one account to another.

The touch of a button, or even just a quick scan of the microchip embedded in one's finger, may open the door to the vault that holds their "money." Even pickpockets may have to use new techniques. If they can break the codes that conceal passwords and financial information, they can drain accounts from any distance.

"In 200 years we'll see the elimination of cash in almost all areas," says Tod Maffin, a business-technology consultant in Vancouver, British Columbia.

Technology will facilitate not just the replacement of cold hard cash, but the proliferation of all different sorts of "money." These are the next generation of long-existing reward programs issued by businesses to encourage customer loyalty, like S&H Green Stamps, airline frequent-flier miles and supermarket coupons. But their impact is magnified by e-commerce, which allows for the quick, mass creation and trading of "units" of value.

One such currency is being spread by New York-based Flooz.com, a kind of one-step-removed variation of official U.S. currency. Customers use conventional dollar-backed credit cards to purchase Flooz, then e-mail them to someone else as a gift. This "gift currency" can be spent at 75 businesses, and Flooz.com says it currently has about 150,000 users.

Beenz, launched in March 1999 in the U.S. and U.K., stray even further from the official currency system. People can't buy beenz but must earn them as an alternative form of compensation by performing "e-work," such as providing e-mail or demographic information, reading a document or, in the case of one musical group's site, listening to a song. The businesses awarding beenz pay beenz.com one cent each for them. Beenz are then stored in the user's account and can be spent at retail sites, which receive a half cent for each beenz they honor.

There are even exchange possibilities. Internet users may convert beenz into Flooz, with 200 beenz equaling roughly one Flooz, or about $1. Flooz, however, can't be converted back into beenz.

In the typical setup, a user would have to do, say, about two hours of e-work, such as filling out forms and answering surveys, at about 10 sites to earn the 3,250 beenz, or about $16.25, it takes to buy a compact disk. Users of beenz so far have conducted about 12 million transactions, according to Glenn Jasper, a beenz.com spokesman.

The company says it is mindful of its role

(Cont.)

in creating a parallel currency universe. Mr. Jasper ambitiously describes the venture as a kind of "central bank of the Internet."

Then there are Ubarter dollars, a back-to-the-future blend of third-millennium digital cash and prehistoric bartering. At Ubarter.com, businesses unload their excess inventory and get Ubarter dollars in return, which they can use to buy excess goods other companies post on the site.

"Everybody has something in their garage, and its value diminishes over time and they've gotten their use out of it," says Steve White, chief executive of Ubarter.com. Bartering "is a way for them to recoup part of that asset."

Rough Transition

It sounds like a grand technofuture of unprecedented efficiency. But the transition to that world may not be so easy. The last time America saw such a broad proliferation of currencies was before the National Banking Act of 1863. Back then, any bank that set up shop could issue its own paper exchange notes, backed by whatever it decided was appropriate collateral.

Since many so-called wildcat banks sprang up at that time, they flooded the market with notes, and their value sank. In addition, the banks often had such short lives that a traveler from California, for example, wouldn't know whether the bank note issued to him by one frontier bank would be accepted upon his arrival in Texas.

The Internet could spawn its own wildcats: cyberbanks and companies handling transactions and issuing currencies without regulations or a central bank to guide them.

Take beenz, for example. If 1,000 years from now it is still a popular Internet currency, many people will have accounts holding hundreds or thousands of beenz. Mr. Jasper says beenz will be on safe ground so long as

businesses believe consumers should be rewarded for e-work. Indeed, banks might even start allowing borrowers to use beenz as collateral, and the currency, if enough people are confident of its value, could trade with other forms of money.

But what if several large vendors decide to stop honoring the stuff? Panic could ensue. Banks would call in their loans, and consumers with piles of worthless beenz would lose faith in other paracurrencies. Since national borders wouldn't confine the new currencies, the ripple effect would reach international proportions.

"The thing that has always scared me is a bunch of people issuing digital money who aren't insured and aren't backed up," says Elinor Harris Solomon, author of the book "Virtual Money" and a former Federal Reserve economist.

Indeed, such fears – and other visceral feelings about money – may make the dawning of a digital-cash age less inevitable than experts think. For all the momentum toward replacing coins and bills, there also are plenty of factors to keep them around. Money, after all, has endured to a degree unexplained by the limits of technology alone. It isn't just about exchange. It's about culture. About national identity. About faith.

Limits of Faith

Mr. Boggs, the artist, has, in a sense, made a career out of testing the limits of faith embodied in money – with mixed results. He creates altered versions of national currencies and then attempts to use them to buy things, explaining at museums, restaurants and shops that it isn't traditional money but has its own inherent value. As if mocking the "full faith and credit" claims of government notes, he sometimes labels his bank notes, "I promise to promise to promise." Mr. Boggs amplifies

the test by offering a bill with a larger "face value" than the good he is purchasing, so that he must get change back in "real" money.

At times, Mr. Boggs succeeds in persuading vendors to take his version of cash – transactions aided by the fact that some dealers have valued his money as art worth upward of $100,000.

There are other reasons tangible money may never be fully eliminated. Some may always be needed to legitimize all the digital cash replicating that currency.

"Going way back in the ages, money has always become money because of philosophical and tangible attachments," Ms. Solomon says. "Trust is really at the bottom of any currency.... There has to be something behind it or people won't use it."

"People are very concerned about money," adds Douglas Mudd, manager of the Smithsonian Institution's numismatic collection. "It's hard to convince people to change, even when a change makes sense."

And there are still times when traditional money is useful, even essential. The tooth fairy, for now, deals in quarters, not smart cards. The Salvation Army's bell ringers require coins in their Christmas kettles. And few panhandlers will be accessing digital wallets.

Mr. Boggs thinks people will always want to have cash in some form, especially for making anonymous purchases that can't be picked up by computers. "People will always want some form of private currency," he says. "People do things they just don't want to be on record, like buying dirty magazines."

Marketing Strategies: Planning, Implementation, and Control

Siberian Soft-Drink Queen Outmarkets Coke and Pepsi

By Betsy McKay

Staff Reporter of The Wall Street Journal

KRASNOYARSK, Russia – Yevgeniya Kuznetsova, 60 years old, is a former communist factory director who now espouses capitalism. Does she ever.

As head of beer and soft-drink maker OAO **Pikra**, based in this gray Siberian city of 875,000, she competes with **Coca-Cola** Co. and **PepsiCo** Inc. and airily dismisses both. Coke and Pepsi "are not a problem for us," she declares. "We're a problem for them."

Her weapon: Crazy Cola, an aromatic fizzy concoction meant to ape the global giants. Lighter brown than a Coke or a Pepsi and with a slightly grassy taste, it has a 48% share of cola sales volume in Krasnoyarsk, according to ACNielsen Russia in Moscow.

The success of Pikra illustrates how hard it is for even the world's most experienced marketers to expand in markets with poor and unstable economies. But it also is a testament to the business skills of Ms. Kuznetsova, who was beating Coke and Pepsi at their own marketing game even before the ruble's crash.

In fact, she picked up most of her management and manufacturing techniques from Pepsi, which began bottling its drinks at her state-run plant in 1989. Pepsi even sent her to an executive-education program at Duke University's Fuqua School of Business. "Pepsi was my business school," she says. "They lost out because they taught me so well."

A large part of the U.S. companies' problem stems from last summer's financial implosion, which diminished millions of Russians' savings and paychecks, making price particularly important. At a local grocery, a two-liter bottle of Coke or Pepsi costs the equivalent of 77 U.S. cents; a 1.5-liter bottle of Crazy Cola is 39 cents. The premium is beyond the reach of most consumers.

With these problems, Coke is expected to operate in Russia at about 50% of capacity this year; Pepsi last year took a $218 million charge to restructure its Russian business. Meanwhile, Ms. Kuznetsova's sales volume has doubled since last summer. "Coke may be the world leader," she says, "but we're No. 1 here."

One of only a few female company heads in Russia, Ms. Kuznetsova is also among the very few Soviet-era factory directors who successfully switched gears from the communist to the capitalist system. She took charge of Pikra in 1986, when it was plagued by outdated equipment and, she says, "450 low-paid employees, a third of them drunks." She privatized the plant as soon as the Soviet government would allow her to, in 1990, "so no one else would get it."

Ms. Kuznetsova then set about overhauling the plant and its management. She returned from business studies in the U.S. with "entire notebooks" full of ideas, she says. Among them: Creating a modern marketing department and teaching salesmanship. "I spent a year fighting with my employees," she says. "They didn't know how to sell."

Despite the schooling she got from Pepsi, Ms. Kuznetsova parted abruptly with the company in 1997. The two sides failed to renew their contract in a dispute over expanding distribution of their respective products. Ms. Kuznetsova claims Pepsi wanted her local brands to "die their own death."

Pepsi, which declined to comment on any aspect of its activities in Krasnoyarsk, was left without a local bottler. Now the company has to bring its drinks in from other Siberian regions.

Ms. Kuznetsova's real wake-up call was Coke's sudden arrival in 1996. So eager was Coke to enter the market here in this former prisoners' outpost that it airlifted an entire bottling plant across 12 time zones. Ms. Kuznetsova, a former regional legislator and one of Krasnoyarsk's most prominent captains of industry, had virtually controlled her local market at the time, but Coke's presence threatened all that. Fresh-faced managers began working the stores. They filled shop shelves with Coke and plastered windows with big red signs. Pepsi did the same.

The factory director, unfazed, struck back. She ordered a cola concentrate from a German manufacturer and crafted a new drink that, she says, would "parody" Coke. Calling the concoction Crazy Cola, she drew up an ad campaign that targeted youth with photo contests, prize giveaways and hip advertising: One ad showed teens in gaudy hip-huggers drinking Crazy Cola as they danced in a disco. Another featured two young lovers caught in a kitchen sipping Crazy Cola between smooches.

Then Ms. Kuznetsova followed the lead of Coke and Pepsi and got 20 supermarkets to agree to exclusive deals. Her associates say some of those deals remain to this day.

Ms. Kuznetsova says she rarely thinks about Coke or Pepsi anymore. Her mind is on Pikra's newest recipe for kvas, a Russian traditional fermented drink, and Flash, a new vitamin-laced energy drink.

But the cola wars go on in Russia. Coke introduced a Russian-made, fruit-flavored soda of its own this summer in southern Russia, aimed at consumers who can't afford the premium brands. Both Coke and Pepsi are also cutting prices as much as 50% and running promotions.

"For us, the issue is to make sure we stay highly relevant, and we're being as innovative as we can," says Paul Pendergrass, Coca-Cola's communications director for Europe. "We want the Russian consumer to know we're going to stick by them as they work

Nonstop promotions *have made Crazy Cola's label ubiquitous in Krasnoyarsk*

through the tough economic times."

When times get better, Coke and Pepsi can only hope that Viktoria Pimenova, a 25-year-old graduate student here, is a representative consumer. Ms. Pimenova keeps her eye on the Western brands and hopes one day to be able to afford them again. "Crazy Cola is fun, and it's our local product," she says. "But it's a drink for people who don't have money. Coke and Pepsi taste better."

THE RADICAL

Carly Fiorina's Bold Management Experiment At HP

Since taking over as chief executive of Hewlett-Packard Co. 18 months ago, Carleton S. "Carly" Fiorina has pushed the company to the limit to recapture the form that made it a management icon for six decades. Last November, it looked like she might have pushed too hard. After weeks of promising that HP would meet its quarterly numbers, Fiorina got grim news from the finance department. While sales growth beat expectations, profits had fallen $230 million short. The culprit, in large part, was Fiorina's aggressive management makeover. With HP's 88,000 staffers adjusting to the biggest reorganization in the company's history, expenses had risen out of control. And since new computer systems to track the changes weren't yet in place, HP's bean counters didn't detect the problem until 10 days after the quarter was over. "It was frantic. The financial folks were running all around looking for more dollars," says one HP manager.

One might expect a CEO in this spot to dial down on such a massive overhaul. Not Fiorina. After crunching numbers in an all-day session on Saturday and offering apologies for missing the forecast to HP's board at an emergency meeting Sunday, Fiorina told analysts she was raising HP's sales growth target for fiscal 2001 from 15% to as much as 17%. "We hit a speed bump—a big speed bump—this quarter," she said in a speech broadcast to employees a few days later. "But does it mean, 'Gee, this is too hard?' No way. In blackjack, you double down when you have an increasing probability of winning. And we're going to double down."

The stakes couldn't be higher—both for Fiorina and for the Silicon Valley pioneer started in a Palo Alto garage in 1938. Just as founders Bill Hewlett and David Packard broke the mold back then by eliminating hierarchies and introducing innovations such as profit-sharing and cubicles, Fiorina is betting on an approach so radical that experts say it has never been tried before at a company of HP's size and complexity. What's more, management gurus haven't a clue as to whether it will work—though the early signs suggest it may be too much, too fast. Not content to tackle one problem at a time, Fiorina is out to transform all aspects of HP at once, current economic slowdown be damned. That means strategy, structure, culture, compensation—everything from how to spark innovation to how to streamline internal processes. Such sweeping change is tough anywhere, and doubly so at tradition-bound HP. The reorganization will be "hard to do—and there's not much DNA for it at

HP," says Jay R. Galbraith, professor at the Institute for Management Development in Lausanne, Switzerland.

Fiorina believes she has little choice. Her goal is to mix up a powerful cocktail of changes that will lift HP from its slow-growth funk of recent years before the company suffers a near-death experience similar to the one IBM endured 10 years ago and that Xerox and others are going through now. The conundrum for these behemoths: how to put the full force of the company behind winning in today's fiercely competitive technology business when they must also cook up brand-new megamarkets? It's a riddle, says Fiorina, that she can solve only by sweeping action that will ready HP for the next stage of the technology revolution, when companies latch on to the Internet to transform their operations. "We looked in the mirror and saw a great company that was becoming a failure," Fiorina told employees. "This is the vision Bill and Dave would have had if they were sitting here today."

At its core lies a conviction that HP must become "ambidextrous." Like a constantly mutating organism, the new HP is supposed to strike a balance: It should excel at short-term execution while pursuing long-term visions that create new markets. It should increase sales and profits in harmony rather than sacrifice one to gain the other. And HP will emphasize it all—technology, software, and consulting in every corner of computing, combining the product excellence of a Sun Microsystems Inc. with IBM's services strength.

To achieve this, Fiorina has dismantled the decentralized approach honed throughout HP's 64-year history. Until last year, HP was a collection of 83 independently run units, each focused on a product such as scanners or security software. Fiorina has collapsed those into four sprawling organizations. One so-called back-end unit develops and builds computers, and another focuses on printers and imaging equipment. The back-end divisions hand products off to two "front-end" sales and marketing groups that peddle the wares—one to consumers, the other to corporations. The theory: The new structure will boost collaboration, giving sales and marketing execs a direct pipeline to engineers so products are developed from the ground up to solve customer problems. This is the first time a company with thousands of product lines and scores of businesses has attempted a front-back approach, a strategy that requires laser focus and superb coordination.

Just as radical is Fiorina's plan for un-

leashing creativity. She calls it "inventing at the intersection." Until now, HP has made stand-alone products, from $20 ink cartridges to $3 million Internet servers. By tying them all together, HP hopes to sniff out new markets at the junctions where the products meet. The new HP, she says, will excel at dreaming up new e-services and then making the gear to deliver them. By yearend, for example, HP customers should be able to call up a photo stored on the Net using a handheld gizmo and then wirelessly zap it to a nearby printer. To create such opportunities, HP has launched three "cross-company initiatives"—wireless services, digital imaging, and commercial printing—that are the first formal effort to get all of HP's warring tribes working together.

Will her grand plan work? It's still the petri-dish phase of the experiment, so it's too soon to say. But the initial results are troubling. While she had early success, the reorganization started to run aground nine months ago. Cushy commissions intended to light a fire under HP's sales force boosted sales, but mostly for low-margin products that did little for corporate profits. A more fundamental problem stems directly from the front-back structure: It doesn't clearly assign responsibility for profits and losses, meaning it's tough to diagnose and fix earnings screwups—especially since no individual manager will take the heat for missed numbers. And with staffers in 120 countries, redrawing the lines of communication and getting veterans of rival divisions to work together is proving nettlesome. "The people who deal with Carly directly feel very empowered, but everyone else is running around saying, 'What do we do now?'" says one HP manager. Another problem: Much of the burden of running HP lands squarely on Fiorina's shoulders. Some insiders and analysts say she needs a second-in-command to manage day-to-day operations. "She's playing CEO, visionary, and COO, and that's too hard to do," says Sanford C. Bernstein analyst Toni Sacconaghi.

Fiorina gets frosty at the notion that her restructuring is hitting snags. "This is a multiyear effort," she says. "I always would have characterized Year Two as harder than Year One because this is when the change really gets binding. I actually think our fourth-quarter miss and the current slowing economy are galvanizing us. When things are going well, you can convince yourself that change isn't as necessary as you thought." Fiorina also dismisses the need for a COO: "I'm running the business the way I think it ought to be run."

If Fiorina pulls this off, she'll be tech's newest hero. The 46-year-old CEO already

(Cont.)

THE ASSESSMENT

BENEFITS

HAPPIER CUSTOMERS   Clients should find HP easier to deal with, since they'll work with just one account team.

SALES BOOST   HP should maximize its selling opportunities because account reps will sell all HP products, not just those from one division.

REAL SOLUTIONS   HP can sell its products in combination as "solutions"— instead of just PCs or printers—to companies facing e-business problems.

FINANCIAL FLEXIBILITY   With all corporate sales under one roof, HP can measure the total value of a customer, allowing reps to discount some products and still maximize profits on the overall contract.

RISKS

OVERWHELMED WITH DUTIES   With so many products being made and sold by just four units, HP execs have more on their plates and could miss the details that keep products competitive.

POORER EXECUTION   When product managers oversaw everything from manufacturing to sales, they could respond quickly to changes. That will be harder with front- and back-end groups synching their plans only every few weeks.

LESS ACCOUNTABILITY   Profit-and-loss responsibility is shared between the front- and back-end groups so no one person is on the hot seat. Finger-pointing and foot-dragging could replace HP's collegial cooperation.

FEWER SPENDING CONTROLS   With powerful division chiefs keeping a tight rein on the purse strings, spending rarely got out of hand in the old HP. In the fourth quarter, expenses soared as those lines of command broke down.

---

has earned top marks for zeroing in on HP's core problems—and for having the courage to tackle them head-on. And she did raise HP's growth to 15% in fiscal 2000 from 7% in 1999. If she keeps it up, a reinvigorated HP could become a blueprint for others trying to transform technology dinosaurs into dynamos. "There isn't a major technology company in the world that has solved the problem she's trying to address, and we're all going to learn from her experience," says Stanford Business School professor Robert Burgelman.

Fiorina needs results—and fast. For all its internal changes, HP today is more dependent than ever on maturing markets. While PCs and printers contributed 69% of HP's sales and three-fourths of its earnings last year, those businesses are expected to slow to single-digit growth in coming years, with falling profitability. Last year, HP was tied with Compaq as the leading U.S. maker of home PCs and sold 60% of home printers, according to IDC.

Those numbers make it hard to boost market share. In corporate computing—where the company is banking on huge growth—HP has made only minor strides toward capturing lucrative business such as consulting services, storage, and software. And the failure of Fiorina's $16 billion bid to buy the consulting arm of PricewaterhouseCoopers LLP leaves her without a strong services division to help transform HP from high tech's old reliable boxmaker into a Net powerhouse, offering e-business solutions.

CAREENING. With the tech sector slowing, this may be the wrong time to make a miracle. In January, HP said its revenue and earnings would fall short of targets for the first quarter, and Fiorina cut her sales-growth estimates to about 5%—a far cry from the mid-teens she had been promising. In late January, the company announced it was laying off 1,700 marketing workers. HP's stock, which has dropped from a split-adjusted $67 in July to

less than $40, is 19% below its level when Fiorina took the helm.

It's not just Fiorina's lofty goals that are so radical, but the way she's trying to achieve them. She's careening along at Net speed, ordering changes she hopes are right—but which may need adjustment later. That goes even for the front-back management structure. "When you sail, you don't get there in a straight line," Fiorina argues. "You adjust your course to fit the times and the current conditions." Insiders say that before the current slowdown, she expected HP to clock sales growth of 20% in 2002 and thereafter—a record clip for a $50 billion company. Fiorina won't confirm specific growth goals but says the downturn doesn't change her long-term plan.

Her overambitious targets have cost her credibility with Wall Street, too. While she earned kudos for increasing sales growth and meeting expectations early on, she has damaged her reputation by trying to put a positive spin on more troubled recent quarters. HP insiders say that while former CEO Lewis E. Platt spent a few hours reviewing the results at the end of each quarter, Fiorina holds marathon, multiday sessions to figure out how to cast financials in the best light. Not everyone is impressed. "I grew up with HP calculators, but they don't work right anymore," jokes Edward J. Zander, president of rival Sun Microsystems. "Everything they mention seems to be growing 50%, but the company as a whole only grows 10%." Fiorina says HP has accurately reported all segments of its business and that she makes no special effort to spin the results. "The calculators still work fine," she says.

Fiorina was well aware of the challenges when she joined HP, but she also saw the huge untapped potential. She had grown to admire the company while working as an HP intern during her years studying medieval history at Stanford University. Later, as president of the largest division of telecommunications equipment maker Lucent Technologies Inc., she learned the frustrations of buying products from highly decentralized HP. When HP's board asked her to take over, she jumped at the chance to show off her management chops. While she had spearheaded the company's spin-off from AT&T in 1996, then CEO Richard A. McGinn got all the credit.

"PERFECTLY POSITIONED." Soon after signing on, Fiorina decided the front-back structure was the salve for HP's ills. With the help of consultants, she tailored the framework to HP's needs and developed a multi-year plan for rejuvenating the company. Step One would be to shake up complacent troops. Next, Fiorina set out to refine a strategy and "reinvent" HP from the ground up, a task she expected would take most of 2000. Only then—meaning about now—would HP be ready to unleash its potential as a top supplier of technology for companies revamping their businesses around the Web.

That's where the cross-company initiatives come in. So far, HP has identified three.

There's the digital-imaging effort to make photos, drawings, and videos as easy to create, store, and send as e-mail. A commercial-printing thrust aims to capture business that now goes to offset presses. And a wireless services effort might, say, turn a wristwatch into a full-function Net device that tracks the wearer's heart rate and transmits that info to a hospital. "All the great technology companies got great by seeing trends and getting there first—and they're always misunderstood initially," says Fiorina. "We think we see where the market is going and that we're perfectly positioned."

The first chapters of Fiorina's plan came off as scripted. When she replaced 33-year HP veteran Platt on a balmy July day in 1999, Fiorina swept in with a rush of fresh thinking and made headway—for a time. She ordered unit chiefs to justify why HP should continue in that line of business. And she gave her marketers just six weeks to revamp advertising and relaunch the brand. After a few days on the job, she met with researchers who feared that Fiorina—a career salesperson—would move HP away from its engineering roots. She wowed them. In sharp contrast to the phlegmatic Platt, Fiorina moved through the crowd, microphone in hand, exhorting them to change the world. "There was a lot of skepticism about her," says Stan Williams, director of HP's quantum science research program. "But she was fantastic."

If she was a hit with engineers, it took a bit longer to win over HP's executive council. For years, these top execs had measured HP's performance against its ability to meet internal goals, but rarely compared its growth rates to those of rivals. In August, Fiorina rocked their cozy world when she shared details of her reorganization—and of her sky-high growth targets. She went to a whiteboard and compared HP with better-performing competitors: Dell Computer in PCs, Sun in servers, and IBM in services. She issued a challenge: If the executives could show her another way to hit her 20% growth target by 2002, she would postpone the restructuring, insiders say. Five weeks later, the best alternative was a plan for just 16% growth. The restructuring would start by yearend.

She dove into the details. While Platt ran HP like a holding company, Fiorina demanded weekly updates on key units and peppered midlevel managers with 3 a.m. voice mails on product details. She injected much needed discipline into HP's computer sales force, which had long gotten away with lowering quotas at the end of each quarter. To raise the stakes, she tied more sales compensation to performance and changed the bonus period from once a year to every six months to prevent salespeople from coasting until the fourth quarter. While some commissions were tied to the number of orders rather than the sales amount and contributed to the earnings miss, Fiorina has fixed the problem and accomplished her larger goal of kick-starting sales. "You can feel the stress her changes are causing," says Kevin P. McManus, a vice-

president of Premier Systems Integrators, which installs HP equipment. "These guys know they have to perform."

This play-to-win attitude has started to take root in other areas. Take HP Labs. In recent years, the once proud research and development center made too many incremental improvements to existing products, in part because engineers' bonuses were tied to the number, rather than the impact, of their

inventions. Now, Fiorina is focusing HP's R&D dollars on "big bang" projects. Consider Bob Rau's PICO software, which helps automate the design of chips used in electronic gear. Rau had worked for years on the project, but the technology languished. Last spring, Rau told Fiorina that the market for such systems was projected to grow to $300 billion as appliance makers built all sorts of Net-enabled gadgets. Within days, Fiorina

---

CARLY TO HP: SNAP TO IT

Even before she took charge at HP in mid-1999, Fiorina had formulated a three-phase plan for returning the company to its former glory. Some highlights:

PHASE I, 1999:

Prepare the ground

SPREAD THE GOSPEL Held "Coffee with Carly" sessions in 20 countries to boost morale. Convinced top lieutenants that HP needs to match the growth of rivals.

ONE IMAGE Merged HP's fragmented ad effort under one all-encompassing "Invent" campaign.

SPARK INNOVATION Reoriented HP's R&D lab away from incremental product improvements and toward big-bang projects such as nanotechnology for making superpowerful chips.

PHASE II, 2000:

Improve growth and profits in core businesses

CONSOLIDATE Folded HP's 83 product divisions into four units: two product development units that work with two sales and marketing groups—one aimed at consumers, the other corporations.

SET STRATEGY Created a nine-person Strategy Council to allocate resources to the best opportunities rather than leaving strategy to product chieftains.

WHACK COSTS Lower expenses by $1 billion by revamping internal processes to tap the power of the Web.

PHASE III, 2001 AND BEYOND:

Build new markets

TRIGGER NEW PRODUCT CATEGORIES Establish cross-company initiatives to develop altogether new Net-related businesses.

WOO CUSTOMERS Offer soup-to-nuts solutions for customers by creating teams from across HP that sell to major accounts.

GOOD CORPORATE CITIZEN Use HP's resources to create subsidized or low-cost computer centers and services to make the Net available to everyone.

(Cont.)

created a separate division that operates alongside the two back-end groups and has grown to 250 people. Besides Rau's software, it will sell other HP technologies such as new disk drives to manufacturers. "It was like we'd been smothered for four years and someone was finally kind enough to lift the pillow off our face," says Rau.

ROUGH EDGES. With Phase One of her transformation behind her, Fiorina launched a formal reinvention process last spring. First up: cutting expenses. Over nine days, a 12-person team came up with ways to slash $1 billion by fiscal 2002. HP could save $100 million by outsourcing procurement. It could trim $10 million by letting employees log their hours online rather than on cardboard time cards. And the company could revamp its stodgy marketing by consolidating advertising from 43 agencies into two. That would save money and, better yet, focus HP's campaigns on Fiorina's big Web plans rather than on its various stand-alone products.

But when the big changes really started to kick in, Fiorina's plan started to bog down. In the past, HP's product chieftains ran their own operations, from design to sales and support. Today, they're folded into the two back-end units, leaving product chiefs with a far more limited role. They're still responsible for keeping HP competitive with rivals, hitting cost goals, and getting products to market on time. But they hand those products to the front-end organizations responsible for marketing and selling them.

The arrangement solves a number of long-standing HP problems. For one, it makes HP far easier to do business with. Rather than getting mobbed by salespeople from various divisions, now customers deal with one person. It lets HP's expert product designers focus on what they do best and gives the front-end marketers authority to make the deals that are most profitable for HP as a whole—say, to sell a server at a lower margin to customers who commit to long-term consulting services. "You couldn't miss how silly it was the old way if you were part of the wide-awake club," says Scott Stallard, a vice-president in HP's computing group. "A parade of HP salesmen in Tauruses would pull up and meet for the first time outside of the customer's building."

These advantages, though, aren't enough to convince management experts or many HP veterans that a front-back approach will work at such a complex company. How do back-end product designers stay close enough to customers to know when a new feature becomes a must-have? Will executives, now saddled with thousands of HP products under their supervision, give sufficient attention to each of them to stay competitive? And with shared profit-and-loss responsibility between front and back ends, who has the final say when an engineer wants to take a flier on expensive research? "You just diffuse responsibility and authority," says Sara L. Beckman, a former HP manager who teaches at the Haas Business School at the University of California at Berkeley. "It makes it easier to

say, 'Hey, that wasn't my problem.'"

Indeed, the front-back plan is showing some rough edges. While HP cited many reasons for its troubling fourth-quarter results, the reorganization is probably front and center. Freed from decades-old lines of command, employees spent as if they had already hit hypergrowth. In October alone, the company hired 1,200 people. Even dinner and postage expenses ran far over the norm. Such profligate spending was rare under the old structure where powerful division chiefs kept a tight rein on the purse strings. "They spent too much money on high-fives and setting themselves up to grow the following quarter," says Salomon Smith Barney analyst John B. Jones.

That situation could improve over time. Fiorina rushed the reorganization into place before the company's information systems were revamped to reflect the changes. Before Fiorina arrived, each product division had its own financial reporting system. It was only on Nov. 1 that HP rolled out a new uber-system so staffers could work off the same books. Although it's too soon to say whether it's a winner, HP claims the system will let it watch earnings in powerful new ways. Rather than just see sales for a product line, managers will be able to track profits from a given customer companywide or by region. That way they can cut deals on some products to boost other sales and wind up with a more lucrative relationship.

Another restructuring red flag is the way Fiorina now sets strategy, a big departure from "The HP Way"—the principles laid out by the founders in 1957. Based on the belief that smart people will make the right choices if given the right tools and authority, "Bill and Dave" pushed strategy down to the managers most involved in each business. The approach worked. Not only did HP dominate most of its markets, but low-level employees unearthed new opportunities for the company. "HP was always the exact opposite of a command-and-control environment," says former CEO Platt. Although Platt wouldn't comment on Fiorina directly, he says, "Bill and Dave did not feel they had to make every decision." HP's $10 billion inkjet printer business, for example, got its start in a broom closet at HP's Corvallis (Ore.) campus, where its inventors had to set up because they had no budget.

EYES ON THE PRIZES. Fiorina isn't waiting for another broom-closet miracle. Since the halcyon mid-'90s, the old HP way hasn't worked quite as well. The last mega-breakthrough product HP introduced was the inkjet printer, in 1984. Growth had slowed to just 4% in the six months before Fiorina took over. To give HP better direction, Fiorina has created a nine-person Strategy Council that meets every month to allocate resources, set priorities, and advise her on acquisitions and partnerships. "This is a company that can do anything," Fiorina says. "But it can't do everything."

Again, the move makes sense on paper. By steering the entire company, the council

can focus HP on a few big Internet prizes rather than myriad underfunded pet projects. But this top-down engine could backfire. Experts point out that except for visionaries like Apple Computer's Steve Jobs or IBM's Thomas J. Watson Jr., it's rare for the suits in the corner office to be able to predict the future—especially in a market as fast-changing as the Net. "If we were to go too far toward top-down, it would not be right for this company," acknowledges Debra L. Dunn, HP's vice-president of strategy.

To be sure, Fiorina is quick to embrace ideas from below if she thinks they'll solve a problem. This spring, Sam Mancuso, HP's vice-president of corporate accounts, proposed a team-based plan that advances the front-back approach. Time was, PC salespeople weren't allowed to sell, say, printers. Mancuso has fixed that by pulling together 20-person teams to concentrate on the top 75 corporate customers. The teams create an "opportunity map" for each customer, tracking the total amount of business HP could possibly book. Then the team analyzes what deal would maximize earnings for HP. Mancuso says his operation has boosted sales to top customers by more than 30% since May. "We're taking the handcuffs off, so now we can be more aggressive," Mancuso says.

The shackles may be off, but HP still lags its competitors in many areas. For all HP's talk of becoming a Net power, in the fourth quarter, Sun held 39% of the market for Unix servers preferred by e-businesses, according to IDC. HP is in second place with 23% share, a slight improvement over the year before. But it faces growing competition from third-place IBM, which just introduced a product line that many analysts say handily outperforms HP's servers. "HP is just not making much headway," says Ellen M. Hancock, CEO of Exodus Communications Inc. Her company uses 62,000 servers in its Web hosting centers, virtually none of them from HP. And most of HP's Net schemes, such as Cartogra, a service that lets consumers post pictures on the Web, have failed to catch on.

Even fans of Fiorina acknowledge she has a ways to go. While wireless juggernaut Nokia Corp. just signed a deal to use HP software, Chairman Jorma Ollila questions how successful Fiorina's turnaround is likely to be. "Carly is very impressive," he says. "But the jury is still out on HP." Says Cisco Systems Inc. CEO John T. Chambers, who named Fiorina to his board on Jan. 10: "I'd bet that Carly will be one of the top 5 or 10 CEOs in the nation. But she has still got to get them running faster." Fiorina wouldn't disagree and says she plans to keep upping her bets. "The greatest risk is standing still," she says. She should hope she has picked the right cards, because she's gambling with Silicon Valley's proudest legacy.

By Peter Burrows in Palo Alto, Calif.

85

INSIDE IBM: INTERNET BUSINESS MACHINES

Big Blue is doing a boffo Net business—some $20 billion is driven by demand for e-business. 'They get it,' says a rival. 'Every day they tell a better story'

To prepare for his annual meeting with Wall Street last May, IBM Chairman Louis V. Gerstner Jr. had an assistant pull the financial reports on 25 of the "real Internet standard bearers"–companies like Yahoo!, America Online, Amazon.com, eBay, and E*Trade. Last year, those companies generated combined revenues of about $5 billion–and lost $1 billion. Yet the market value of the Internet 25 together was 50% greater than that of IBM. "Go figure," Gerstner deadpanned when he delivered the news to analysts. "Now, I am not suggesting that you view us as an Internet company, but I think it is worth noting that IBM is already generating more [e-business] revenue and certainly more profit than all of the top Internet companies combined."

Get ready to adjust your thinking. The marquee names of the Internet Age may be dot.com companies, but the big dot in the New Economy these days is IBM. While Amazon's Jeffrey P. Bezos and Yahoo!'s Timothy Koogle get all the Internet kudos, Gerstner has been quietly zipping past competitors, large and small, to emerge as a leading arms supplier to the Information Age. Today, IBM is doing it all: helping merchants hang their shingles online, advising corporate chieftains on how to reshape their businesses top-to-bottom, even wiring local courthouses. "They get it," concedes Edward J. Zander, president of rival Sun Microsystems Inc. "Every day they're telling a better story."

NO CHOICE. And it's one that Zander and other rivals don't much enjoy hearing. Big Blue, despite its dinosaur image, is doing a boffo business from the Net. IBM estimates that 25% of its revenue–some $20 billion–is driven by e-business demand. That's nearly 50% more than Internet darling Sun, whose servers are de rigueur for most Web businesses. Even sweeter: About 75% of IBM's e-business revenue comes from sales of Net technology, software, and services–fast-growth, fat-margin businesses–and not the old mainframe computers for which IBM is so well known.

Just as surprising is how Gerstner is seizing the Internet inside IBM. The 57-year-old CEO, once jeered for his lack of computer industry experience, has done an extraordinary job of weaving the Web's vast reach into every corridor of the company–its products, its practices, its marketing. The results have been stunning: Online sales, mostly of PCs, are expected to top $12 billion for the year, skyrocketing nearly 400% from $3.3 billion last year. The productivity gains from using the Net have been just as profound. The company figures it will save $750 million by letting customers find answers to technical questions on its Web site. And by handling a portion of its internal training over the Net instead of in classrooms, IBM will save $120 million. All told, IBM will whack nearly $1 billion out of its costs this year by taking advantage of the Web.

Suddenly, International Business Machines is looking a lot more like Internet Business Machines. Surprised? Don't be. Gerstner doesn't have a choice. Every company from the tiniest dot.com startup to IBM's biggest rival is using the Net to skin costs to the bone and to reach new customers. And even though Gerstner has been hard at work doing just that, IBM's gargantuan size has made a wholesale Internet conversion tough. PC and server sales, for one, are going nowhere. While competitors Dell Computer Corp. and Sun rack up Internet-fueled sales growth of 25% and 40%, respectively, IBM's revenues have been stuck at an Old Economy rate of 7%. This year, analysts estimate, Big Blue will grow a tad faster–9%, bringing revenue to around $90 billion.

That's not nearly fast enough in the New Economy. But if Gerstner can hook more of IBM's revenue to the Net, he may be able to pull IBM out of the slow lane. With $15

IBM's e-Business Strategy

E-IBM   The best way to learn is by doing. So IBM is becoming an e-business. By moving purchasing onto the Web, the company expects to save $240 million on the $11 billion in goods and services it will buy this year. Similar moves to put customer support online will save another $750 million.

Competitive Landscape: The field is split here. IBM is clearly ahead of rivals such as HP, Sun and Compaq. Others such as Dell, Cisco and Intel have been on Internet time longer than IBM.

E-SERVICES   IBM has 130,000 consultants and an e-service business expected to hit $3 billion this year. IBM has handled 18,000 jobs over the last three years—from Web-site design to hooking older corporate databases into new online systems—for companies such as DHL and Payless ShoeSource.

Competitive Landscape: The giants are plunging ahead—Sun, HP, Intel and EDS—along with upstarts Scient and Lante. Still, IBM has the advantage with corporate databases that need to be hooked into online systems.

E-ENGINEERING   This is where IBM sees e-business heading. Companies will use the Net to cut costs, turning for help on how to do it. United Technologies Corp. has already turned over procurement via the Web to IBM.

Competitive Landscape: Not the usual crowd. Companies with specific skills such as Federal Express will get into logistics, while Andersen Consulting and other Big 4 consultants will help e-engineer business tasks.

(continued)

IBM's e-Business Strategy
(concluded)

PRODUCTS IBM offers everything from laptop PCs to mainframes that plug easily into the Net. Its software, such as MQ Series, is becoming the glue that allows machines from different makers to pass messages over the Net. Other programs such as Net.Commerce handle huge amounts of e-commerce transactions.
Competitive Landscape: IBM continues to stumble in PCs and servers, as pesky Dell Computer and Sun Microsystems roar ahead. In software, Microsoft looms, while upstarts such as BroadVision have been knocking Big Blue out of some key accounts, such as Ford and Sears.

RESEARCH IBM pumps half of its $5 billion R&D budget into Internet-related areas. Gerstner isn't stopping there: He has created the Institute for Advanced Commerce, a think tank that includes outside consultants and academics as well as 50 IBM scientists—all working on electronic commerce. Initial focus: Auction software.
Competitive Landscape: Growing your own takes time. Meanwhile, rivals Microsoft, Cisco and Intel are using their sky-high stock valuations to buy what they need.

E-OUTSOURCING Don't want to run your Web business? Let IBM host it for you at one of their mega data centers. IBM does the works. At Lego, for example, it runs everything, including contracting the Danish post office to handle shipping.
Competitive Landscape: EDS is big, but it has been slow to move its business to the Net. New outsourcing players like Intel and Exodus are piling in. But IBM remains in the lead.

billion of IBM's Net-driven revenues growing at more than 30%, the time may not be too far away when the company's slow-growth businesses such as mainframes and storage systems are no longer a drag.

This is Gerstner's chance for IBM to reclaim the mantle of leadership, and it may be his last. If IBM blows the Internet, which is becoming more pervasive with every mouse click, it blows its franchise–perhaps once and for all–as the leading high-tech supplier to Corporate America. In the Internet Age, it's not just Sun, Microsoft, Hewlett-Packard, or Compaq that Big Blue frets about. Every day, nimbler challengers, ranging from e-consultant Scient Corp. to Net software maker BroadVision Inc., keep chipping away at Big Blue's turf. Says IBM senior vice-president and longtime Gerstner confidant Lawrence R. Ricciardi: "We had to be ready to respond, or we would be dinosaur bones."

Y2K FREEZE. In some markets, IBM is playing catch-up. The company has been slow to woo the dot.com crowd, for instance, leaving that to Sun, HP, and a slew of startups that sell PCs, servers, and software. The trouble is, Web companies will soon buy as much computer gear as traditional companies. "We've had to adapt our model to them," concedes Gerstner. "We were late."

The events of the past couple of months underscore IBM's urgency to focus on e-business. In early October, the company disclosed that it will yank its Aptiva home PC off retail shelves in North America, making them available only through its Web site. IBM also will lay off up to 10% of its PC workforce. The moves, IBM hopes, will stanch the flow of red ink in a unit that lost nearly $1 billion last year. Analysts expect IBM to lose approximately $400 million in PCs this year.

Then on Oct. 20, the company shocked Wall Street with news that sales of large computers–one of its slowest-growth areas, but among the most profitable–had dried up because customers were locking down their operations for the rest of the year to prepare for Y2K. The buying freeze, IBM told analysts, will hurt the company through the first quarter of next year. The news sent IBM's stock tumbling 15%, to 91 from 107. The company also announced another layoff of up to 6% of the workers in its computer server group.

And now IBM's accounting method has come under scrutiny. On Nov. 24 it was disclosed that Big Blue is being criticized for its policy of bundling one-time gains, such as the $4 billion earned from the sale of its Global Network business to AT&T, into operating income. That, critics claim, makes it difficult for the average investor to assess the company's performance because operating income is typically used as an indicator of pure sales success since it excludes taxes, interest and other items.

"VERY AGGRESSIVE." Nonsense, the company says. IBM maintains that it's following Securities & Exchange Commission guidelines and provides analysts with all the data they need to evaluate the company's efficiency. As for Y2K, IBM says, that's a temporary hit on its big iron computers while customers sort out last-minute changes before the new millennium. But Gerstner says demand for e-services and software is strong. And analysts agree. They expect sales for online systems to gain momentum sometime after the first quarter, when companies will have finished wrestling with Y2K. "E-business is the next big thing on the road map for a lot of companies," says Gartner Group Inc. analyst Tom Bittman.

If Gerstner is right, after years of upheaval, Big Blue could once again be on solid terrain. Gerstner believes that the advent of the Internet will befuddle execs already struggling to take advantage of the new technologies. Companies around the globe will spend $600 billion a year by 2003 on e-business, according to market researcher International Data Corp. More importantly, some 62% of that amount will go to consultants and the like who can sort out how to use all the bedeviling technology. By contrast, just 29% will be spent on hardware and 9% on software. "The real leadership in the industry is moving away from the creation of the technology to the application of the technology," says Gerstner. "The explosive growth is in services."

That couldn't be better for IBM. Building powerful computers and software that don't fail, as well as providing tons of services–especially tons of service–is second nature to IBM. Its army of 130,000 consultants in its Global Services unit is unmatched in the industry and does three times more Net work than the $1.9 billion combined revenues of Andersen Consulting, Electronic Data Systems, and Computer Sciences, according to IT Services Advisory LLC, a research and advisory firm in Hillside, N.J. In the past three years, IBM has handled 18,000 Internet jobs for its customers, from shaping an Internet strategy to Web page design to hosting entire online storefronts.

Now IBM's e-business client roster is stoked with the biggest names in industry—from Ford Motor to Charles Schwab, and from Prudential Insurance to the New York Stock Exchange. In a Merrill Lynch & Co. survey last month, 53 chief information officers at major corporations cited IBM as one of only two computer companies–the other was Sun–that are best positioned to handle their Internet projects. "They are very aggressive about building their expertise in the online world," says Rhonda Wells, director of e-commerce for Payless ShoeSource Inc., which chose IBM when it wanted to build a full-fledged e-commerce hub–in three months. "IBM has a strong knowledge of brick-and-mortar businesses, not just Internet businesses."

How did Big Blue catapult itself to such heights after such lows? Credit Gerstner. He

(Cont.)

recognized as early as 1994 that the killer app for the Internet was going to be transactions–not simply having the best browser or the coolest search engine. One of Gerstner's first moves was to shift 25% of IBM's research and development budget into Net projects. He declared that every IBM product must be Internet-friendly. And he began to push all software development toward the Java programming language. There was also a crash effort to tie Lotus Notes software tightly to the Web. "The Internet was a major change and opportunity for IBM. The first person who saw its value was Lou," says G. Richard Thoman, chief executive of Xerox Corp., who worked with Gerstner at IBM, RJR Nabisco, and American Express.

MUSHROOMING SERVICES. To get the massive, 225,000-person organization focused, Gerstner shook things up. He set up the Internet Div. and appointed Irving Wladawsky-Berger, a respected IBM exec and computer scientist by training, to head it. Wladawsky-Berger made sure that every product in IBM would work with the Web. Then he sat down with his staff and figured out what IBM calls the "white spaces"— the empty spots where the company needs to develop products. Indeed, Gerstner looks back on his move as a "bet-the-company decision."

Gerstner's smartest move, though, may be e-business services. Today it seems like a no-brainer, but in 1995, the industry was obsessed with snazzy new products, from network computers to superfast search engines. Gerstner could have focused on trying to gain leadership in Web cruisers or browsers–after all, IBM had its own browser, which it wound up scrapping. Instead, Gerstner decided to use services to distinguish IBM from the pack. "We concluded this [the Internet] was not an information superhighway," says Gerstner. "This was all about business, doing transactions, not looking up information."

Now service is paying huge dividends. The company's e-business services revenue is growing at a galloping 60% and is expected to hit $3 billion this year. And Gerstner says that number could easily double if you include (as he says competitors do) portions of IBM's huge outsourcing jobs that use the Net to deliver software and services. "They have an incredible pool of professional services," says Jeff F. Lucchesi, chief information officer for DHL Airways Inc. IBM helped create DHL Connect, an online shipment scheduling and tracking system that uses IBM software to connect a variety of computers so that customers can get estimated shipping charges immediately. When Lucchesi needed a special Java program, IBM had a team on the job within 24 hours. "That's something that tells me I'll use them again," says Lucchesi.

No wonder Gerstner is adding services as fast as he can. In the past year, IBM has launched 20 new Net-related services including privacy consulting and an online service designed for small to medium-sized business. For as little as $99 a month, IBM will provide all the hardware, software, and services that small businesses need to get online. Big Blue is even in the application service provider (ASP) market, delivering enterprise software from companies such as PeopleSoft, Great Plains Software, and ebank.com over the Net.

Still, the big money is in IBM's traditional customer base–the thousands of big companies that have yet to tap the Net and transform their businesses. IBM refers to such companies as below the e-line. Gerstner isn't just out to help them set up cybershops, he's zeroing in on Web-izing all of their business operations–their supply chains, customer service, logistics, procurement, and even training. "The Internet is ultimately about innovation and integration," says Gerstner. "But you don't get the innovation unless you integrate Web technology into the processes by which you run your business."

Above the e-line, IBM is a straggler. That's why in April, Gerstner created a swat team to focus exclusively on selling IBM products and services to Web companies. It's also trying a novel sales approach. Together with Conxion Corp., an Internet service provider, and the Silicon Valley Bank, IBM is offering up to $1 million in technology and services free of charge for six months to 24 Net startups. The idea is to help incubate startups without them burning through all their funding. At the end of six months, the startup can buy or lease the equipment or simply take a hike.

For all these efforts, IBM's pole position in the Internet race isn't guaranteed. For one, Gerstner hasn't been able to solve his hardware problem. Sure, once companies get past Y2K they'll want more mainframe power to handle massive online businesses. But mainframe prices are falling faster than sales are rising. And in the white-hot Web server business, made up mostly of Unix computers, IBM has been a no-show. That's why its computer business looks anemic compared with Sun's 25% growth. For the year, IBM's sales of Unix systems are expected to reach $3.2 billion, up 7%, says Sanford C. Bernstein & Co. Says Sun Chairman Scott G. McNealy: "They're not nearly the systems provider they used to be."

How IBM Uses The Net

e-Care   Getting customers to use the Net to help themselves means big savings. For every service call handled through ibm.com, the company saves 70% to 90% of the cost of having a person take that call. This year, IBM expects to handle 35 million online service requests, saving an estimated $750 million in customer support costs.

e-Commerce   Through the first three quarters of 1999, e-commerce revenue–from sales of everything from PCs to mainframe software–totaled $9.7 billion, up from $977 million during the same period last year. By yearend, e-commerce revenue is expected to be between $10 billion and $15 billion, vs. $3.3 billion in 1998.

e-Learning   IBM estimates that for every 1,000 classroom days converted to electronic courses delivered via the Web, more than $400,000 can be saved. For the year, the company expects 30% of its internal training materials will be delivered online, with anticipated savings of more than $120 million.

e-Procurement   In 1999, IBM expects to buy $11 billion in goods and services over the Web, saving at least $240 million. So far this year, IBM has plugged more than 6,700 suppliers into its online procurement system. Now, IBM can cut out rogue buying–employees who buy from suppliers that aren't pre-approved.

"UNINSPIRING COMPETITOR." That has left IBM on the sidelines during one of the biggest boom periods for Web servers. "We have been an uninspiring competitor against Sun and HP," admits Gerstner. "We're behind in that arena, and we have to take that share back."

Even so, hardware may be the least of Gerstner's worries. The e-biz field is no longer Big Blue's to romp in virtually uncontested. Sun and Microsoft are beefing up their focus on servicing e-biz customers. A revitalized HP is zeroing in too. Even chip giant Intel Corp. is steering its considerable might there, spending $1 billion to set up rooms of servers to host Web sites. And then there is the raft of hot startups that claim IBM and other big companies are just too bloated to work on Net time. "We have the look and feel of a speedboat," says Rudy Puryear, the former head of Andersen Consulting's e-business practice who now heads Chicago-based e-consultant Lante Corp. IBM, he says, is a "battleship."

Some rivals are even taking a page from IBM's playbook–and using it against them. Earlier this year, HP emulated IBM's hugely successful e-business marketing campaign with its own e-services campaign–even hiring a member of the team that launched the e-business campaign to do it. HP's e-services strategy could be a danger to IBM, if it works. That's because HP, which lacks IBM's consulting muscle, is trying to create do-it-yourself Net technologies. In HP's view, companies should easily be able to add new features and services onto their Web sites, no big consulting contracts necessary. Says Nick Earle, chief marketing officer for HP's enterprise computing unit: "We always bristle when people say we copied IBM. We learned from the good things that they did, but that was over three years ago. In Internet time, that's a lifetime."

That's why Gerstner isn't letting up. He's pumping more than 50% of IBM's huge $5 billion R&D budget into Net projects, up from 25% in 1996. What's next? IBM wants to be the supplier of technology and services to link all manner of digital devices such as pagers, cell phones, and handheld computers. IBM will either license the technology to others or build the infrastructure and rent the capability.

MASSAGE CHAIRS. To present this vision to customers–and within IBM–Gerstner is up to his old tricks. In Feb. of 1998, IBM set up the Pervasive Computing Div., headed by Mark F. Bregman, another former IBM research scientist. Much like Wladawsky-Berger did in the Internet Div., Bregman has spent the past 18 months analyzing the market and working with other areas of IBM to develop strategies centered on devices, software, and services that make the Net accessible anywhere, anytime.

The first offering: software that lets any type of digital device, say a cell phone or Palm handheld, fetch content off the Net. Sounds simple, but it isn't. Right now companies are struggling to deliver pages to screens of any size. Bregman's group has put together a service that companies can rent that will translate content from any Web site and deliver it to any screen. "The idea," says Bregman, "is to offer infrastructure as a service. It's more like a utility. You just pay the bill."

Already IBM is lining up customers. On Nov. 29, PlanetRx, an online pharmacy, will go live with a service that allows virtual shopping via Palm handheld devices. Telecom companies Nokia, Ericsson, and Sprint PCS have signed on, too. "Moving information from 17-inch screens on your desk to where it can be used on the Web from anywhere is an important trend," says John F. Yuzdepski, a vice-president at Sprint PCS. "IBM's technology allows a ubiquity of access to information."

The technology is one thing, but if Gerstner is going to build a new IBM, he has to create an Internet culture. That work began in Atlanta four years ago. When you walk in the door at IBM's Atlanta Web design office–dubbed the "Artz Cafe"–dogs are camped out alongside Web designers and an iguana. Four workers sit astride massage chairs getting worked over by masseuses. Ping-pong tables double as conference tables, and there's a billiard table upstairs where workers can go to clear their heads after long hours toiling at–gasp–Macintosh computers. "To attract the cool, younger people in the Internet business we had to break with the whole IBM culture," says Kerry Kenemer, a creative director who sports a goatee. "We're the only creative bone in the entire IBM body."

Now, IBM is trying to spread the culture throughout its organization. On Nov. 15, the company launched Project Springboard. After pouring $100 million into its four-year-old Atlanta Web design center, it's broadening that approach and opening e-business integration centers around the world. Instead of just design services, these centers will offer customers a place to tap IBM specialists and outside experts to set up next-generation e-business solutions.

The centers reflect a hipper IBM that the company hopes will be able to attract Web-savvy employees. In some areas, IBM is angling to siphon off creative types by setting up shop in cool areas of the country. In Los Angeles, for example, the center will be near the MTV and Sony studios. The company is even lightening up on job titles. One worker in Chicago goes by the title "concept architect and paradoxiologist." (Translation: Someone who works on tough Internet strategies.)

That's not the only Silicon Valley-ish move the company is taking. Like Intel and Cisco, IBM has quietly invested $60 million in venture funds that focus on Web technologies. Of course the company wouldn't mind a big IPO payday, but it is mostly using these deals to provide "headlights" into cutting-edge technologies. IBM has hit pay dirt on at least one investment so far: In August, it invested $45 million in Internet Capital Group, a holding company that funds business-to-business Web companies. That was just before its public offering. Now IBM's investment is worth $619 million.

NEW HORIZON. What's the next e-business frontier for Big Blue? It's getting companies to turn over entire business processes to IBM that are conducted over the Web. "The way we think of e-business is that it's really the opportunity to do the next level of transformation," says Richard B. Anderson, who has been given the task of taking IBM to the Web.

Consider what IBM is doing for United Technologies Corp. IBM uses the Net to handle $5.8 billion worth of general procurement for Carrier Corp., UTC's Farmington (Conn.) subsidiary. The company won't talk about the actual savings of the system, but says it has been a phenomenal success–increasing efficiency, cutting costs, and becoming a gold mine for collecting information about purchasing habits. Now UTC has the data that will allow the company to talk to suppliers and get better discounts. But UTC insists it's not about cutting costs. "This is all about turning data into information and turning that information into action," says Kent L. Brittan, vice-president for supply management for UTC.

That's the sort of phrase Gerstner might coin for his next analyst's meeting. Back in May, for just a few hours after Gerstner's Wall Street meeting, IBM was like a dot.com company: Its shares shot up 20 points, the kind of movement associated with Web giants eBay or Yahoo. But if Gerstner can continue to convince customers that he has truly remade IBM into Internet Business Machines, he may yet join the Internet 25.

By Ira Sager

Contributing: Peter Burrows in Santa Clara, Calif., David Rocks in Atlanta, and Diane Brady in Greenwich, Conn.

(This article continues)

Gerstner on IBM and the Internet

IBM Chairman Louis V. Gerstner Jr. may not be thought of as a tech visionary, but he was remarkably prescient about the Internet. In a conversation with BUSINESS WEEK'S Ira Sager, Gerstner shared his thoughts about IBM and e-business.

Q: *What shaped your early thinking about the Internet?*
A: I commissioned a task force [that] worked for a year on what it really meant to exploit network-centric computing. Their work came together in September of 1995. And we made a very important decision in October. It was the second bet-the-company [decision] that I made. The first was to keep the company together. We said, "If we really believe this, we're going to reprioritize all the budgets in the company." In a period of four weeks, we reallocated $300 million. We created the Internet division. It became the catalyst for change in the company.

Q: *You also made a decision that the Net was about business transactions. How did that come about?*
A: Our work concluded that this was all about business: doing transactions, not looking up information. That came about because every time I'd meet with the task force they would present all this wonderful technology to me, and I would say, "Well,

what's a customer going to do with it?" That's where we really began to believe that every physical transaction in the world was going to be augmented or replaced by a digital transaction.

Q: *When you met with Wall Street in May you compared IBM's e-business to the top 25 Internet companies. Were you trying to get analysts to view IBM as an Internet company?*
A: If you define an Internet company as [one] that is totally committed to transforming its internal business, and in our case, to also have it [the Net] be the basis of our entire product offering, then I think there's no company that's as much an Internet company as we are. Now, if you say an Internet company is [one] that has rapidly growing revenue and no profits, then I don't want to be classified as an Internet company.

Q: *How can companies get the biggest payoff from using the Net?*
A: The Internet is ultimately about innovation and integration. Innovation is what your objective is—in cost structures, selling, marketing, sales, supply chain. But you don't get the innovation unless you integrate Web technology into the processes by which you run your business. And

that's been the rude awakening for a lot of companies. The true revolution coming from the Web is when the Web can get integrated with business processes.

Q: *People talk about the Internet being a landscape-altering technology. Describe how the Net has changed the landscape within IBM.*
A: We discovered what every large company has: When you bring your company to the Web, you expose all the inefficiency that comes from decentralized organizations. Now, when a customer comes to you on the Web, they're expecting to be able to move across those departments. They're expecting to see a common look and feel.

Q: *But what will the Net do to traditional markets?*
A: All we have to do is watch television, see these guys raising their hands in these financial markets, and you say, "This is going to end." There has to be a more efficient way. And so we'll see the emergence of electronic marketplaces that will have powerful effects, real discontinuities, in the existing structure of markets. What we believe is going to be very important is the delivery of traditional software and services and hardware over the Net. That's a form of electronic marketplace.

86

A HIDDEN GOLDMINE CALLED INKTOMI

The Web site supplier could be the Net's toll collector

Three years ago, it was a hard-knock world for Inktomi Corp. The startup set out with grand plans to become as important to the Internet as Microsoft Corp. was to the PC. But its beginnings were anything but regal. The company's six employees were crammed into a 1,200-square-foot office that they could only reach by stepping over homeless people congregating in front of the door. Their conference room was just big enough for a card table and four fold-up chairs–and its porthole-size window peeked out into an elevator shaft.

How times have changed. This month, Inktomi will move into its spiffy new digs–two 100,000-square-foot buildings with breathtaking views of the San Francisco Bay. The company's market cap is $5.5 billion–five times that of Sybase Inc., the onetime software highflier that Inktomi CEO David C. Peterschmidt once led. Its customer list includes such Net heavyweights as Yahoo!, NBC, America Online, and Excite@Home–making it the world's No. 1 search-technology provider. And it's rapidly expanding into promising new markets–like e-commerce. "I want to make sure that when all is said and done, Inktomi will be a company that is core to the Internet," says Peterschmidt.

For now, though, his company is one of the Net's best-kept secrets. That's because Inktomi operates behind the scenes–supplying Web sites with top-of-the-line software in four product areas: searches, directories, comparison shopping, and speeding Webpage delivery.

The company's low profile conceals an astonishing fact, however. While critics feared Microsoft's dominance would make it the toll collector of the Net, that could instead become upstart Inktomi's oh-so-lucrative lot. When someone searches for info on any of the 50 sites that rely on Inktomi's software, the startup collects a fee of around a half-cent per Web page retrieved. And when a Netizen stops by one of 20 sites that use Inktomi's new comparison shopping service–such as J. Crew or Barnes & Noble–Inktomi and its Web portal partners split commissions, ranging from 5% to 20%.

ROSY FUTURE. It's a Net goldmine in the making. The company is on track to ring up

$68 million in sales this year, more than double its 1998 revenues. Analysts estimate sales will again nearly double to $136 million in 2000–when they believe the company will become profitable. Inktomi's stock price has risen from $30 a year ago to about $130 today. "Inktomi is in a great position," says analyst Michael A. Parekh of Goldman Sachs. "Their products are in areas that are key to the future of the Internet." And all indications are that demand for its technology will increase for years to come.

Indeed, if Inktomi continues to live up to its potential, it might start to look more like Microsoft. It's even trying to mimic the software giant's strategy. The key to Microsoft's success is its Windows operating system, for which other software makers have developed thousands of software programs. Inktomi is

> **The number of public Web pages could grow to 8 billion by 2002, so search is a growth business**

attempting to create a similar software "platform" with technology for delivering Web pages ultra-fast–signing up software makers that are using it to improve the performance of their products.

But Inktomi isn't home free yet. While no one competes against its entire range of products, the company's offerings are being attacked on all sides–from networking powerhouse Cisco Systems Inc. to whizzy search engine startup Google Inc. Compounding the problem: While Inktomi made its name in search, its other services are less well known, making its expansion into new markets more difficult. And, longer-term, Inktomi faces an even bigger hurdle: Its continued success relies on its ability to solve some of the Internet's biggest technical challenges, like making the Net as reliable as the telephone.

Fortunately for Inktomi and its shareholders, innovation has always been the company's strong suit. The company was founded by Eric A. Brewer and Paul Gauthier, then computer scientists at the University of Cali-

fornia at Berkeley. Under a federally funded project, Brewer was trying to prove his PhD thesis–that inexpensive desktop computers wired together could match the sheer data processing power of one pricey supercomputer. To test the computer system, Brewer and Gauthier, a grad student at the time, created a Web search engine, software that sifts through millions of Web pages to quickly retrieve information. The search technology worked so well that they decided to quit academe and start a company.

Inktomi, a Native American word meaning "clever spider," could never have gotten this far based on whizzy technology alone. Its founders realized immediately that they would need management help. Six months later, Peterschmidt, the CEO who oversaw database software maker Sybase's growth from $60 million to $1 billion in six years, came on board. At Sybase, Peterschmidt had beefed up the sales force and targeted new markets such as the financial-services industry. From the beginning at Inktomi, he had expansion on his mind. The day he arrived, he asked the company's 13 employees how they could use their technology in new ways. The answer: Caching, the Net speed-up technology. Peterschmidt set an engineering team to work on it the day they finished the search engine.

Peterschmidt's other crucial move was strategic. Search companies like Excite and Lycos decided to mimic Yahoo and become Web directories and, ultimately, gateways to the Web. But rather than turn Inktomi into yet another Yahoo copycat, Peterschmidt positioned it as a behind-the-scenes provider of essential technology that all of the major Web sites needed. "We are arms merchants," says Peterschmidt. That approach has paid off handsomely for Inktomi. By not competing with its potential customers, the company has avoided conflicts, enabling it to sell its products to the fiercest of rivals, like Yahoo and AOL.

Luckily for Peterschmidt, there's no end in sight when it comes to demand for ever more powerful search capabilities. The number of publicly accessible Web pages is expected to grow from 800 million today to 8 billion by 2002, according to researcher International Data Corp. To deal with that

(Cont.)

INKTOMI . . . GETTING MONEY FROM CLICKS AND CACHES

Inktomi's revenues could jump fourfold between 1998 and 2000 if its new products live up to their billing. Here's how:	FISCAL YEAR		
	1998	1999+	2000+
	Revenue (in millions)		
INKTOMI'S TRAFFIC SERVER: Now Inktomi's biggest moneymaker, Traffic Server is software sold at a starting price of $24,000. The software, licensed by nearly 100 companies, allows Internet service providers such as America Online and Excite@Home to speed up the delivery of content over the Internet by caching, or storing, frequently requested Web pages or sites in their high-speed computers. That way they can be dished up instantly.	$8	$40.3	$83.9
SEARCH: If you thought that Yahoo and AOL delivered what you needed based solely on their own homegrown search capabilities, think again. Operating behind the scenes is Inktomi's search service. Sold to more than 50 companies and portals, Inktomi generates revenue by charging every time it returns a page requested by a search query.	$12.5	$25.2	$39.5
SHOPPING: About 20 Web sites offer Inktomi's new shopping service, which allows Web surfers to compare the products of 350 merchants that have partnerships with Inktomi, including J. Crew and Barnes & Noble. When customers buy something found through the shopping service, Inktomi takes a percentage of the sale from the merchant and splits the money with the portal. Inktomi plans to add auctions, local merchants, and classified advertising to this service.	$0	$1.8	$4.1
DIRECTORY: A new portal service launched this summer, Inktomi Directory Engine builds off its popular search to provide portals with neatly packaged subject categories. The directory, for example, will let customer GoTo.com offer cybersurfers categories of information, like health, rather than just bits of information. Inktomi charges the portal every time it serves up a page. So far, it's signed up seven clients, including Knight Ridder.	$0	$1	$4

+Revenue estimates

DATA: Bear, Stearns & Co. Inc.

tsunami of data, Inktomi this summer introduced a new directory of Web pages, called the Inktomi Directory Engine, designed to help speed and improve the accuracy of searches.

WAKE-UP CALL. With the explosive growth in the number of Web pages, though, it's no surprise that new search-engine companies are intent on stealing some of Inktomi's lucre. Earlier this year, Inktomi got a major wake-up call when its first customer, the HotBot Web site, announced it was adding a second search service from Direct Hit Inc., a year-old Wellesley (Mass.) startup. The reason? While Inktomi is considered good at getting results from basic queries, Direct Hit's analysis of many similar searches improves the relevancy of search results. According to market researcher Media Metrix, 53% of all Web searches now use Direct Hit's technology in addition to traditional search engines.

Now comes Google, a new search-technology provider that claims its searches are faster and more accurate than Inktomi's. "We think that there is a lot of room for innovation in the world of search," says Larry Page, co-founder of Google, which is based in Mountain View, Calif. Google has raised $25 million from backers, including the influential Kleiner Perkins Caufield & Byers.

Inktomi isn't running scared. It plans on continually beefing up its search technology. And with the competition in search heating up, Peterschmidt's diversification push is starting to look smart, indeed. Early last year, the company introduced its Traffic Server software, which lets Internet service providers (ISPs) store often-viewed Web pages on

(Cont.)

computers scattered around the world where they're just a quick click from consumers' screens–a practice called caching. Already, more than a half-dozen companies have signed on, including Net video leader Real Networks Inc.

Caching radically improves the performance of Web sites. For Excite@Home, which is using Inktomi's software, at least half of the traffic running on the network doesn't have to travel across the Internet backbone, says Milo Medin, Excite@Home's chief technology officer. On a busy day, that can shave crucial seconds off the time it takes for a viewer to see a Web page.

TROJAN HORSE. Unfortunately for Inktomi, this market is under attack from competitors, too. And they're the giants like Cisco Systems and Novell Inc., which tower over Inktomi in size and resources. The market for caching is now about $100 million and is expected to grow to $1.6 billion by the year 2002, according to the Internet Research Group. So chances are Inktomi will have more adversaries in the future. Even Microsoft is expected to add some basic caching capabilities to its Web server software, something that it bundles for free with Windows NT software.

Wary of all the competitive threats, Peterschmidt is hoping to improve Inktomi's prospects by targeting new kinds of customers–not just the large ISPs and megaportals. Recently, he has inked deals with dozens of smaller, niche players like music site kadoodle.com, set to launch in October. The rationale, say Inktomi executives, is that because the search technology is so flexible, it can be tailored for specialized searches. A music site like kadoodle.com can get a search engine designed by Inktomi to filter out any unrelated Web pages. A search for the rock group REM, for instance, wouldn't return any pages related to dreaming and rapid eye movement, also known as REM.

Peterschmidt's hope is that search is the Trojan horse that gets Inktomi's foot in the door of new customers–making it easier to sell them the rest of the company's portfolio of products. Especially promising in this market are the new shopping service and technology that helps sites build and maintain their own Web site directories. For example, when someone does a search on a site focused on backpacking, not only would the search engine deliver a long list of Web pages based on the key words supplied, but it could also dish up a list of backpack merchants, plus a directory that lists related sites or subjects.

The way the Net is expanding, there's no end in demand for the basic network plumbing that Inktomi supplies. The question is: How quickly can it expand into new markets? For its founders, the pace has been dizzying. "When you hire folks, especially in the early days, you sell them a bill of goods and a promise," Brewer says. "Then you have the on-going burden of making that vision come true." Brewer and Peterschmidt have kept their promises so far. And they no longer stumble over homeless people when they go to work. Now they just have to worry about tripping over themselves as they race to capitalize on what may be some of the sweetest of sweetspots on the Web.

By Michael Moeller

87

The eToys Saga: Costs Kept Rising But Sales Slowed

By Lisa Bannon

Staff Reporter of The Wall Street Journal

LOS ANGELES—Just three months ago, **eToys** Inc. moved into its glitzy new 150,000-square-foot headquarters here with a sense of great optimism: The company planned to double its holiday sales over 1999 levels, secure a final round of financing this spring and reach profitability late next year. Chief Executive Toby Lenk was so convinced that his company would triumph that he kept every one of the seven million shares he received in eToys' red-hot initial public offering of May 1999.

Now, the shiny headquarters stands like a mausoleum to failed Internet dreams. Sales growth at eToys fell drastically during the critical Christmas season and the company responded by laying off 70% of its workers. Mr. Lenk's eToys shares, valued at more than $600 million at their peak in 1999, would fetch about $2.7 million today as the stock has plummeted to about 39 cents a share from its high of $86.

Perhaps more than any other dot-com debacle, the rise and fall of eToys parallels the treacherous ups and downs of early e-commerce. Portrayed as a superstar of the new medium in 1999, the toy retailer's market valuation soared to $7.7 billion the day it went public, 35% more than long-established rival **Toys "R" Us** Inc. Its investors, including **Intel** Corp., **Sequoia Capital** and **idealab!**, pushed eToys to build the biggest, the best and the most expensive toy site to cement its place in the emerging pantheon of Internet stars.

But despite a boardroom full of Harvard and Stanford MBAs and blue-chip backers, eToys wildly overestimated the size of its potential market and the speed at which it would materialize. Its ballooning infrastructure costs required $750 million to $900 million in annual sales to make money—four to five times the $200 million revenue it expects to report for the fiscal year ending in March. Inventing the business as it went along, eToys faced the classic start-up dilemma of whether to build its own infrastructure at great cost or outsource key services to save money. It ultimately failed at both. EToys now tacitly admits that its business is fatally flawed: In December it hired Goldman Sachs Group Inc. to explore a possible sale of the company.

Mr. Lenk won't comment on the reasons behind eToys' woes, citing the company's "quiet period" before it reports earnings later this month. But analysts blame a combination of execution errors, timing, fundamental problems in its business plan and old-fashioned hubris.

For one, eToys' distribution and technology costs ended up climbing so high that many wonder whether any online-only retailer that isn't selling multiple product categories to a broad market can survive. "If you're trying to service a mass market you need to maintain an expensive Web site that costs around $50 million, whether you have $1 or $1 billion" in revenue, says Henry Blodget, an Internet analyst with Merrill Lynch. EToys spent $43 million on its Web site and technology in 1999, for $150 million in sales. **Amazon.com** Inc., by contrast, spent a comparable amount, $47 million, the prior year, but had more than five times the sales.

By building the most parent-friendly Web site with the biggest selection of kids' products, eToys' business plan was predicated on keeping its consumers loyal even after established brick-and-mortar competitors came online. But eToys lost market share to fierce competitors such as the Amazon.com/Toys "R" Us joint venture and **Wal-Mart Stores** Inc., which leveraged their own well-known brands, undercut eToys' prices on some products and incorporated some of eToys' best features. EToys insiders now say they believe the mass market for toys appears to hinge more on price than the quality of the shopping experience.

That underlined another problem with eToys. The 39-year-old Mr. Lenk, a stoic son of a New England fisherman, had always insisted that eToys could continuously decrease its huge advertising and marketing costs—37% of sales in 1999, compared with 11% at Amazon—and not only retain, but increase its customer base. But after many customers stayed away this Christmas, it now appears that the company needed to reacquire many buyers every year, requiring a constant flow of cash to advertise.

EToys could have guaranteed itself a future had it accepted a little-known offer from Toys "R" Us last spring to discuss teaming up, according to people familiar with the situation. But Mr. Lenk, rejecting such "bricks-and-clicks" arrangements as illogical and inefficient, decided to go it alone. Toys "R" Us then teamed up with eToys' archenemy, Amazon.

But eToys' most critical miscalculation, analysts say, was in assuming that Internet growth would continue to soar, enabling it to double its sales year over year until it reached profitability, projected for 2002. Instead, online toy sales in the 2000 Christmas quarter grew only by an estimated 35% to 40%, according to Merrill Lynch's Mr. Blodget, and consumers actually spent less time online in December than in the prior two months. While the general economic downturn is partially to blame, Mr. Blodget says the online toy category may be more mature than other e-commerce categories. Also, the spectacular growth in Internet toy sales in 1999 may have been artificially inflated by the hype surrounding online shopping.

All of this was compounded by the difficulty in raising more money. EToys always assumed that investors would pony up cash until the company broke even. And indeed, Mr. Lenk, a Harvard MBA and former Walt Disney Co. strategic planner, was candid about the massive upfront investment that eToys required. This year, the company was counting on raising $100 million to $150 million. Due to the dismal Christmas, eToys will be out of cash by March.

This outcome is far different than the one envisioned in the heady days of 1996, when Mr. Lenk first dreamed up the idea of providing parents with a hassle-free alternative to shopping for kids in stores. At first, eToys' growth appeared to be unlimited, spiking from $700,000 in 1997 to $30 million in 1998 to $150 million in 1999. EToys figured that if a mere 5% to 10% of the $55 billion U.S. children's product market migrated online, as analysts predicted, the company could comfortably count on a billion dollars in annual sales. International markets, it figured, would add further growth.

"In everything we do. . . we are building eToys the right way: from the ground up, for the long run and always with our customer in mind," Mr. Lenk said in 1999. EToys pioneered parent-friendly innovations, including a sophisticated search engine that lets consumers shop for items based on age, brand and theme, and "wish lists" that allow children to choose gifts and e-mail the wishes to family members. Its site was consistently voted among the highest quality by online shoppers. And despite a horde of online toy competitors, it scored first in revenue, traffic and average order size year after year.

But by late 1999, it became clear that costs were rising higher than the company and investors had expected. During that year's Christmas season, eToys increased its marketing budget by 30% after a flock of unexpected competitors—KBKids.com,

Toby Lenk

Smarterkids.com, Toysmart.com, among others—crowded into the online toy category and spent lavishly on advertising.

The most crucial cost increase, and the pivotal moment in eToys' ultimate crisis, came when it decided to build a new distribution network last year. During the 1999 Christmas season, eToys saved money on packing and shipping by outsourcing the bulk of this work to **Federated Department Stores** Inc.'s Fingerhut Cos. But under this setup eToys failed to deliver 4% of its orders on time, and the resulting bad publicity gave the company its first major black eye. Poor results in the 2000 Christmas season, some eToys executives say, are related in part to unsatisfactory customer experiences the year before.

So Mr. Lenk accelerated eToys' plans to build a giant automated distribution center in Virginia. Although many analysts agreed that the costly move was a sound decision for the long term, profitability would be further postponed, prompting another hit to eToys' stock. Some direct-mail companies subcontract distribution. But unlike books, music or apparel, toys require special handling because of their different sizes, sometimes-breakable nature and urgency for the holidays or other occasions. EToys couldn't risk bungling its distribution again. "At the time of their major expenditures the capital market was prepared to fund everything so it's easy to see why those decisions were made," said Merrill Lynch's Mr. Blodget.

But the distribution decision meant eToys needed to generate much higher sales to justify its costs. The amount of money eToys had invested in property and equipment skyrocketed to $124 million as of September 2000, from $23 million a year earlier. That equaled around 95% of 1999 revenue, compared with about 20% of annual revenue for most land-based retailers (excluding their costs for stores, which generally are leased), and 12% to 13% for catalogue retailers such as Lands' End Inc., says Kevin Silverman, an analyst at ABN Amro.

The company's costs were ballooning just as funding for dot-coms dried up. In another critical misstep, eToys had failed to tap the market for a secondary offering of stock while its shares were still relatively high in late 1999 and early 2000. Last June, eToys was forced to raise $100 million from investors specializing in distress financing. The convertible preferred share deal was structured so that the more eToys' stock price declined, the more common shares had to be issued, diluting shareholder ownership and driving eToys shares down further.

Yet even in such a bleak scenario, Mr. Lenk was betting that by delivering on its holiday sales promise in 2000, eToys might attract one last round of financing. "I clearly, passionately, believe our model works, but we need one more financing to get to break-even," Mr. Lenk said in a December interview. At the rate it had been growing, analysts expected that eToys would hit about $300 million in sales in its fiscal year ending this March, $600 million in the following year, and break even at between $750 million and $900 million in sales in 2002.

D-Day came in mid-December. Despite a spiffy TV ad campaign and an expanded line of goods, there weren't enough customers. EToys expected quarterly revenue of $210 million to $240 million. Instead, it will report closer to $130 million, the company says.

"EToys built an incredible interface, which even the most skeptical people on Wall Street rank as the best," says Mr. Silverman of ABN Amro. "But the mistake everyone made was that you can do all this stuff and still no one might come."

88

Flower Delivery

Pruning Costs

FTD.com turned itself around by following an old rule: Less is more

BY CALMETTA COLEMAN
Staff Reporter of THE WALL STREET JOURNAL

FTD.com Inc. won't be sending itself flowers anytime soon.

Sure, the online floral-delivery company has cause to celebrate. In October, it posted a profit just one year after its initial public offering—months ahead of its own estimate, not to mention Wall Street's less cheerful forecast. But celebrating gets in the way of its new mantra: Don't overspend.

"We weren't going to spend a lot of money to have a party when we still have a lot of challenges ahead of us," says Michael Soenen, the company's 30-year-old chief executive officer.

Frugality was a painful lesson for FTD.com to learn. At first, it followed the dot-com pack by spending heavily on television commercials and print advertising. But by last summer it was bleeding cash, forcing executives to prune overgrown expenses and rethink marketing plans and alliances.

Pushing Daisies

In October 1999, a month after its IPO, FTD.com rolled out a big-budget ad that depicted scenes of a lily opening up to reveal a cityscape, a dancer in a field of daisies and a shower of rose petals.

The commercial was pretty, but it didn't generate profits. FTD.com won't say how much it spent on the spots, but its marketing budget for the fiscal year ended June 2000 was $42.9 million, or 44% of total revenue. "We were very concerned about their high spending rates," says Greg Kyle, a Pegasus Research analyst who tracks the rate at which Internet companies burn cash. "If they didn't cut expenses or get a big infusion from their parent, they risked running out of cash."

That view was shared by some insiders. Sam Hill, a management consultant and former advertising executive who joined FTD.com's board of directors in December 1999, recalls his reaction as he watched the commercial with others in a conference room. "I remember wishing I had gotten here a week before the [ad] agency did," he says.

It didn't take long for FTD.com executives to come to the same conclusion. They began to heed two-year-old research that showed the FTD name already had more than 95% brand awareness among consumers—a legacy of the dot-com's 90-year-old parent,

floral giant FTD Inc., which also runs national television ads. By Mother's Day, FTD.com pulled the plug on national TV and print advertising, and slashed its annual marketing budget by more than half, to between $17 million and $20 million. Still, for the fiscal year ended last June 30, net losses were $34.6 million, or 75 cents a diluted share.

'We Were Wrong'

At the same time it was overspending on broadcast marketing, FTD.com was trying to eliminate the costs of direct mail. In 1999, it dropped its mail-order catalog just before Christmas, the third-biggest season for flower delivery behind Mother's Day and Valentine's Day. It figured Internet banner ads would be enough to draw traffic to its site—another common mistake of dot-coms.

"The conventional wisdom was that everything was going to be online and Internet shoppers wouldn't use catalogs," Mr. Soenen now says. "We were wrong."

The season wasn't a bust, but the drop in customer growth was "significant," the company says, enough so that it quickly resumed its catalog mailings. It now sends out five big mailings a year, centered on major holidays.

The online retailer also ended some of its marketing partnerships. Mr. Soenen declines to name specific failed deals, but notes that the company didn't sell more flowers by advertising with fast-food restaurants and putting inserts in gas bills.

A $2.3 Million Charge

Meantime, FTD.com decided to ax some unprofitable deals with Internet portals, which often required a hefty payout for an "exclusive" presence. The company took a $2.3 million charge to terminate a portal distribution agreement in its fiscal fourth quarter, ended last June. It declines to identify the company with which it had the agreement,

saying only that it continues to be partners with more than 6,000 Internet sites that don't require a payment until after a sale is made.

"If the order's not there, neither is the expense," Mr. Soenen says.

Aside from its marketing missteps, though, FTD.com has fared well at keeping other costs down. For instance, it hasn't built any new office space since being spun off from FTD five years ago. Its home base, including one full-time call center, is tucked inside the Downers Grove, Ill., headquarters of FTD. During busy periods, it outsources additional call-center services and, since its vendors ship flowers and gifts directly to customers, it doesn't need warehouses. With annual sales of roughly $100 million, its office staff consists of just 35 core employees.

Sunny Forecast

FTD.com's move to pare expenses paid off sooner than expected. Some Wall Street analysts figured it would take three years after the company's IPO to turn a profit, while the company planned to do it in two. But less than a year after going public, FTD.com earned $253,000, or a penny a share, in its fiscal first quarter ended Sept. 30, 2000. That compared with a net loss of $3.6 million, or nine cents a share, a year earlier. Last month it posted fiscal second-quarter net income of $2.3 million, or five cents a share, compared with a net loss of $11.2 million, or 24 cents a share, a year earlier.

The surprise was all the sweeter because the first quarter is traditionally the company's slowest, with no major flower-buying holidays falling in the summer months. Its far larger competitor, 1-800 Flowers.com Inc., with roughly $400 million in revenue, has reported a profit but says it expects to incur losses for the foreseeable future.

Mr. Soenen credits the strong FTD brand name and its established distribution network

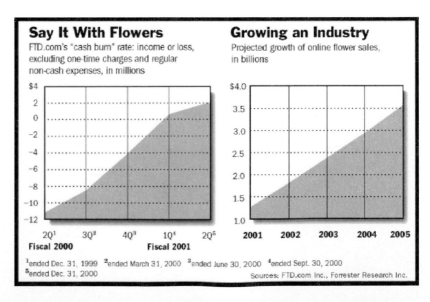

Say It With Flowers
FTD.com's "cash burn" rate: income or loss, excluding one-time charges and regular non-cash expenses, in millions

Growing an Industry
Projected growth of online flower sales, in billions

¹ended Dec. 31, 1999 ²ended March 31, 2000 ³ended June 30, 2000 ⁴ended Sept. 30, 2000
⁵ended Dec. 31, 2000

Sources: FTD.com Inc., Forrester Research Inc.

for FTD.com's blossoming bottom line. FTD's 17,000 florists in the U.S. and Canada process FTD.com's orders using the same Mercury Network order-management system they've used for parent FTD since 1979. FTD.com gets a portion of each sale. "Unlike an Amazon.com that's taking away business from a local bookseller, we're actually pushing more business through existing channels," Mr. Soenen says.

Ashland-Addison Co. in Chicago is a good example of a longtime FTD florist that depends heavily on the Web site. The florist signed on with FTD.com when the online retailer first started. Now, about 90% of its Internet business and 50% of its total business come through FTD.com, though it also has its own Web site.

Because the bulk of the Web business represents existing customers changing the way they place orders, owner Bill Sheffield says his company can't afford not to be online with FTD. "In the flower business, if you turn your back on something like the Internet, other people are going to take it and run with it," he says. "FTD has strong brand recognition."

Next, the company plans to focus on gaining a greater market share in the combined floral and gift delivery business, projected to reach $5 billion by 2004. Last year, it began selling gifts on its site—a way to encourage more purchases for men, who typically favor NFL gift baskets over lilies. Nonfloral gifts, such as baked goods and candles, now account for about 7% of its revenue.

Wilted Shares

It also will have to take a closer look at its stock price, which recently traded around $3 a share, down from its offering price of $8 in September 1999. As other electronic-commerce companies fall by the wayside, Mr. Soenen is hopeful that investors will soon realize his company's value.

"The Internet space is still going through a lot of hard times. As we deliver two or three quarters of profits in a row, our stock will start to reflect it," he says, noting that the company expects to report profitable quarters through the end of its current fiscal year, ending June 30.

He adds, "Then we'll have one big party at the end of the year."

Ms. Coleman is a staff reporter in The Wall Street Journal*'s Chicago bureau.*

89

WHY OFFICE DEPOT LOVES THE NET

Its brick-and-mortar network is a big plus

Warehouses, stores, and inventory are all the kiss of death when it comes to Internet economics, right? If so, someone forgot to tell David I. Fuente, chairman of Office Depot Inc. Since getting into e-commerce nearly four years ago, Fuente has used Office Depot's nationwide network of 750 superstores, 30 warehouses, and $1.3 billion in goods to build the largest office-supply retailer on the Internet, with $250 million in sales. And unlike high-flying Web-based companies that have yet to turn a profit, he gloats over the fact that Office Depot's Net business is in the black. "For us, this has been profitable from virtually the day we opened," says the 54-year-old Fuente.

As the Internet matures, it may be the old brick-and-mortar retailers like Office Depot that have the last laugh. But only if they develop a Web strategy not unlike Office Depot, which is leveraging its strengths in terra firma for success in cyberspace. The necessary ingredients: a solid brand name, extensive local distribution, and hefty purchasing power to match—or even undercut—discount-minded cyber-rivals. "If the traditional retailers would only wake up and use their stores and distribution power, it would be a phenomenal opportunity," says PaineWebber Inc. retailing analyst Aram Rubinson.

Office Depot is a case study in how to avoid being Amazoned. The Delray Beach (Fla.) company is tightly integrating the Net into the heart of its operations. Focusing primarily on business-to-business, it has set up customized Web pages for 37,000 corporate clients, including Procter & Gamble Co. and MCI WorldCom Inc. For each customer, Depot has designed a site with parameters that allow different employees various degrees of freedom to buy supplies: A stockroom clerk might only be able to order pencils, paper, and toner cartridges, while the assistant to the CEO might have carte blanche to order everything the company sells.

Customers also can use the Net to check up-to-the-minute inventory at the nearest store or warehouse to see what's available for delivery the next day. "Office Depot seems to really get it," says Chuck Martin, chairman of the Net Future Institute, a New Hampshire think tank that studies e-commerce. "Rather than just extending their business to the Net,

they've used it to leverage their bricks and mortar."

There's a sweet financial incentive for doing it: Electronic sales cost less than those made in stores or from catalogs. Processing an order taken over the Net costs Depot less than $1 per $100 of goods sold, vs. twice that for phone orders. And since no customer-service representative has to key in the transaction, order-entry errors are virtually eliminated and returns are cut in half. The Web now accounts for some 20% of Depot's sales to corporations—and the company aims to raise that to 30% by yearend. That would help: Last month, the company told analysts that its second-half earnings would come in more than 20% below the Street's estimates, primarily because of rising inventories of outdated office-technology products and the costs of closing underperforming stores.

Office Depot isn't the only one that wins by moving to the Web—so, too, do its customers. The Depot's Web operations help corporate clients reduce their need for costly purchase orders since billing is handled electronically. While the average order for supplies is about $125 at Office Depot, many customers report costs of more than $100 to simply process a purchase order and pay an invoice. Using the Web, that can be slashed to $15 to $25. "We went to Office Depot primarily because of their Web systems, which translated to greater efficiency in ordering," says Urban Sommer, director of procurement at MCI WorldCom. The phone company has seen its $3.5 million annual bill for office supplies shaved by more than 10%.

To be sure, Office Depot isn't the only seller of office supplies on the Net. Staples Inc. in Framingham, Mass., has a site that many experts believe rivals Depot's—and even has certain advantages, such as a partnership with Register.com, a Web site that lets businesses sign up for Net domain names. The third player in the real-world office supply business, Office Max Inc. of Shaker Heights, Ohio, was first to the Web, beating Office Depot by a year. But thanks to Depot's sophisticated approach, it's leading the pack with Web sales that are 25% higher than Staples' $200 million. Office Max doesn't report its Web revenues, but concedes its sales are smaller than the other

---

OFFICE DEPOT'S E-STRATEGY

How it Benefits Office Depot:

Cuts in half the cost of processing an order. Typically, it costs about $2 to process a $100 phone order, but over the Web that drops to less than $1.

Wins new customers. Consumers who weren't close to an Office Depot store can now use the company's Web site to order goods.

Keeps customers. Those that might defect to online competitors can now stick with Office Depot. Less than 1% of sales in the $200 billion office-supply market are generated by Web-only companies.

How it Benefits Office Depot's Customers:

Reduces the cost of purchasing goods. Corporations spend $75 to $175 to issue a purchase order for an item and then pay for it. The Net slices that to $15 to $25.

Businesspeople can place orders from their chairs. Customers tell Office Depot that ordering over the Net reduces phone calls to the purchasing department by 60%

Provides a peek into Office Depot's inventory. Why is that important? If you have a presentation tomorrow, you may want to know whether Office Depot has 40 purple binders on hand.

Lets workers do away with inventory. Because customers can get supplies when they want them, they can ditch the old supply cabinet.

(Cont.)

two. "Depot has done the best job, hands down," analyst Rubinson says.

SMART FRIENDS. Together, the three have occupied the Web early and forcefully enough to neutralize any serious threat from Internet startups, such as At Your Office.com and Online Office Supplies.com. Consider this: Online Office Supplies started operating a year ago and has logged less than $1 million in sales. Anybody would "have a difficult time becoming the Amazon of office supplies," says Paula Jagemann, CEO of Online Office Supplies.com.

Office Depot can credit smart friends for its success. Its push into e-commerce began at the behest of one of the more tech-savvy institutions: the Massachusetts Institute of Technology. The school was looking to ditch an archaic system of requisitioning office supplies from campus stockrooms and outside vendors. "We wanted the school community to use the Internet in a way that would eliminate having to make a call, generate a purchase order, and pay an invoice. Yet they could still have the item the very next day or sooner," says Diane Devlin, who led the MIT team developing the operation.

Depot won the contract and opened the system in January, 1996. Soon, MIT had rid

> With its site for big companies thriving, Office Depot is turning its attention to small business

itself of five stockrooms and a warehouse, allowing redeployment of much of the $1.2 million it had tied up in inventory. And through the Office Depot initiative and other Internet-ordering systems, MIT has reduced employment in its procurement department by roughly half.

Since Office Depot started building similar sites for corporate clients in the autumn of 1996, it has found that the cost of operating on the Web is minuscule compared to the benefits. Because Depot built its Net business on an existing network of warehouses, 2,000 delivery trucks, and phone-order sales to many of the same customers, the upfront cost was less than $10 million. "Our incremental investment to become a Web-based company was almost zero," Fuente says. "We didn't need to buy any different products, we didn't need to build any new distribution centers or order-entry systems. All we needed was a Web site. It's very cheap."

Now, Office Depot is turning its attention

to a public Web site for small businesses and consumers. Individuals can order any of the company's products. Small companies get a poor man's version of the big corporate sites. For example, each visitor can set up lists of authorized users with the ability to purchase specific types of supplies or goods up to a certain dollar value. A company can also authorize a lower-level worker to place orders that will only be submitted after a supervisor, who is notified by e-mail, approves them. The site is catching on: It attracted more than 800,000 visitors in July.

Even though Depot's Net operations are growing 50% per quarter, Fuente believes they will not displace the company's traditional business anytime soon. Even now, the Web accounts for only 3% of the company's total revenues. Besides, he knows how critical brick-and-mortar assets like warehouses are to Depot's Internet future.

By David Rocks
Contributing: Peter Galuszka

90

HOW AN INTRANET OPENED UP THE DOOR TO PROFITS

Weyerhaeuser's door plant was on its last legs—until an in-house information network showed people how to work better and smarter

From its drab, corrugated-metal exterior, Weyerhaeuser Co.'s Marshfield (Wis.) door factory, deep in America's dairy belt, doesn't look like much. But inside, the 100-year-old timber giant is carving out its own piece of the Internet revolution.

Four years ago, the plant was on its last legs–what Weyerhaeuser Vice-President Jerry Mannigel had called a "dead dog" of a door plant, besieged by bloated costs, flagging sales, and bad morale. Even Mannigel, a Marshfield native who initiated a factory redesign in the mid-1980s, had to be begged to return from his job at another facility to see if things could be turned around. "The situation had gotten so bad that Marshfield was operating at half capacity but costing us the equivalent of full capacity," he says. And morale couldn't have been worse. Says Mannigel, whose father also used to work at the plant: "You had to practically beat people with a stick to get them to come back to work every morning."

What a difference the Internet has made. Today, the plant–which cuts, glues, drills, and shapes customized doors according to each buyer's desire–is profitable again, and revenues are growing at an annual 10%-to-15% pace. Better management has been key. But productivity experts give much credit to Weyerhaeuser's installation of a state-of-the-art in-house communications network that uses the Internet to compare prices in a heartbeat, boost on-time deliveries, and track orders as they move through the plant.

NEW RULES. Since phase-in began in late 1995, the technology, dubbed DoorBuilder, has helped the plant to double production–to more than 800,000 doors annually. Tracking software has improved the plant's record for complete and on-time deliveries–up from 40% to 97%. The plant's share of the U.S. commercial door market has zoomed from 12% to 26%. And since 1993, the year Weyerhaeuser thought it might shut down the plant, the factory's return on net assets has grown from -2% to 27%–well beyond this year's companywide goal of 17%.

Now, Weyerhaeuser is taking Door-Builder even further, rewriting the rules of the doormaking industry. In the past year, Weyerhaeuser has begun to experiment with extending its DoorBuilder network beyond the plant's borders to some of its most valued customers–key distributors. That communications link is speeding up the ordering process for customers, while eliminating costly errors, waste, and delivery snafus. The result: Weyerhaeuser can offer faster turnaround and, in some cases, lower prices that rival doormakers may have to match. At the same time, distributors that want to get in on the improvements are being forced to automate their shops so they can hook into Weyerhaeuser's network.

For many of Weyerhaeuser's distributors, the arrival of the Internet to their old-line businesses is jarring, and not altogether welcome. Charles Hummel, CEO of Pleasants Hardware Co. in Winston-Salem, N.C., the nation's largest door distributor and one of Weyerhaeuser's biggest customers, gripes that DoorBuilder will require him to put computers, extra phone lines, and trained tech staff in his 15 branch offices. Hummel is hoping he can hold out but concedes he may have to bite the bullet because of Weyerhaeuser's clout. "It's a love-hate relationship with Weyerhaeuser right now," he says. "If you're not on DoorBuilder, your lead times may actually increase."

Such upheaval is the inevitable by-product of E-engineering in the timber industry and just about everywhere else these days. High-tech and low-tech companies alike are scrambling to remake their businesses from top to bottom so they can tap into the power of the Net. At the heart of these efforts are communications networks much like Weyerhaeuser's, called intranets, that link all the workers in the company while plugging into vast databases of information, factory-floor operations, supplier inventory, price lists, and order-taking. According to International Data Corp., an estimated 52% or more of manufacturing companies with revenues of $1 billion or higher are considering, or already have, intranets. "From its original role as a data repository, the intranet has rapidly grown to become the central nervous system of the enterprise," says a May report from Concours Group, a research and consulting firm in Kingwood, Tex.

As essential as that may sound, not all intranets have paid off. Some companies have stopped with a Web site or have failed to exert the type of leadership and flexibility needed for the technology and the cultural changes it brings. Or, says Ernst & Young consulting's chief technologist, John Parkinson, "they end up costing far more than expected and drown managers in too much information." Even at Marshfield, Vice-President William Blankenship–who persuaded Weyerhaeuser's top brass to O.K. the plant's intranet, admits that "it has been a long haul." Weyerhaeuser's initial $2 million investment has more than quadrupled. And when Mannigel made the system fully operational last February, glitches and worker errors temporarily slowed deliveries and hampered production.

CUSTOM CRAFT. Executives remain committed to Marshfield as one of a handful of examples of E-engineering that is working in the U.S. And Blankenship says Weyerhaeuser is just beginning to discover what DoorBuilder can do.

To understand just how dynamic Door-Builder is, consider the dramatic changes it has brought to the single task of order-taking. At Weyerhaeuser, this has long been a painstakingly complex job, since each door is custom-built, according to an amazing 2 million different configurations–from size, style, and color to the veneer and hardware options. One door might have a round window and a core to withstand 40 minutes of fire; another could be laminated with white plastic stars, destined for a theater on Broadway. Before DoorBuilder, says Mannigel, "we had been buried in information, and our inability to handle it had become the bottleneck of this business. Every six or seven doors or so that we make here are likely to be different from those that come before and those that come after."

DoorBuilder sorts through all that information and calculates the math in seconds. The days when distributors, builders, and Weyerhaeuser reps would haggle for weeks, if not months, to hammer out an order are gone. And, if customers are plugged into Weyerhaeuser's network, they can bypass Weyerhaeuser's reps altogether by typing in their order on the Marshfield plant's Web site. All orders are final once the customer

(Cont.)

pushes the "submit" button on their computer. Sometimes, handwritten substitutions were slipped into the process at the last minute, as a special favor to a particular customer. "Today, there are no special favors," Mannigel says. "Now, every order is equal."

Indeed, DoorBuilder's order-entry software is so sophisticated that it is based on the same system Boeing Co. uses to configure its complex 777 airplane wings. "If a certain hinge can't be used on a certain door in a certain city, then DoorBuilder will reject that as an option and tell you why," says Mannigel.

Converting orders from paper to bits also has reduced the number of errors. Previously, orders were stapled to each door and would inevitably get torn off or lost at various times during production. "We had one guy who used to collect these off the floor and put them in a big bin, and every two weeks or so, he would throw them out. We were having to redo orders like crazy," says Mannigel. Weyerhaeuser figures DoorBuilder has reduced errors drastically, cutting two to three weeks off turnaround times.

The new system is making the company a lot smarter—and tougher—about pricing, too. In the past, prices were based on hunches, special relationships, and haggling with customers and suppliers. "The questions of cost and price every month were a crapshoot," says

Mannigel. With Doorbuilder, there is no more guesswork or favoritism. Thanks to more precise information about costs and lead times, doors are now priced according to what each option actually adds to the total cost of manufacture. Executives who had once prided themselves on their pricing prowess discovered that some of their generations-old calculations were faulty. In one case, Mannigel says, "a distributor who we thought was one of our best customers was actually costing us money." Says Lee Kirchman, the plant's vice-president for marketing and sales: "The machine knew more than we did."

The result: Weyerhaeuser now charges some customers more. If they balk, Door-Builder can instantly offer up different options that are cheaper. "No way that would have worked without the data we got from DoorBuilder," Mannigel says. "For the first time, we had proof some orders weren't making any money, so we set out to fix that. Now we can show a customer precisely why we're asking for a higher price."

Ditto suppliers. Kirchman recalls that in the days before DoorBuilder, the company considered Columbia Forest Products Co. one of its best suppliers of veneers, both on price and quality. "But we did an analysis of them with DoorBuilder, and—surprise—they ranked way, way down on the chain," says

Kirchman. So Weyerhaeuser went back to Columbia, showed the company the data and gave them six months to improve–or it would start buying most of its veneers elsewhere. Now, each quarter, Marshfield's purchasing staff sits down with each key supplier and shows them how they stack up on the value chart, hammering out prices accordingly.

The biggest surprise of all: Armed with this information, Weyerhaeuser actually refuses some customer orders now or redirects them to competitors–unimaginable before. Customers also are ranked by their credit-worthiness, price demands, average order size, and their willingness to go along with the company's new way of doing things. That has weaned Weyerhaeuser's roster of door distributors down from roughly 500 in 1995 to approximately 200 this year–but with more volume and profit coming from each of the mostly larger customers that remain. "This idea of 'whatever the customer wants' is gone now," says Mannigel.

What's more, customers now have to "put some skinny on the table," Kirchman says–just to be able to use DoorBuilder to place their orders. The 12 distributors starting to experiment with having a direct link to DoorBuilder have each shelled out between $3,000 and $5,000 for the software, a dedicated phone line, training, or the hiring of

How Technology Opened the Door to Profits

	Problem	Solution	Payoff
Orders	**Packages of customized** doors were configured manually from more than 2 million options. The process could take months, with time spent on phone, fax, and mail—haggling with suppliers, distributors and buyers. For the distributor, placing an order could take weeks.	**Customers assemble** their own door packages through a "virtual distributor" —a Web site on the Net or direct link by extranet that allows them to tap into suppliers' lists and get instant packages and pricing.	**Orders get placed** in minutes, with fewer errors, faster delivery times, and lower costs to Weyerhaeuser. Turnaround time has shrunk by three weeks or more.
Pricing	**Pricing was based on hunches** and individual relationships between customers, suppliers and distributors.	**A computerized** cost-tracking system now bases prices on customer value profiles— from creditworthiness to volumes ordered over a period of time—and the cost of every option that gets built into a finished door.	**Some prices went up;** some went down. Weyerhaeuser stopped losing money on the production of unprofitable doors, saving millions of dollars.
Customers	**Accepted almost any customer** and order—even though some customers cost Weyerhaeuser money.	**Using new database** and DoorBuilder software, the plant now knows its customers better and can be more choosy about which orders it bids for and which distributors it chooses to do business with.	**At least 50%** fewer customers, but a doubling in order volumes, to more than 800,000 doors this year. That boosted the plant's return on net assets from −2% five years ago to +24% this year.
Tracking Orders	**Handwritten notes** and printed forms stapled to each door for tracking orders through the factory were easily lost, inaccurate, and confusing.	**Computer system** tracks progress in real-time, with no changes in orders allowed after they are submitted by customers.	**Fewer errors,** better scheduling, faster delivery, more precise inventory control.
Delivery	**On schedule** and complete only 40 to 50% of the time.	**Using tracking and scheduling** software and a communications network inside the plant, Marshfield is able to deliver complete orders on time 97 to 100% of the time.	**Door deliveries** are speeded up—and Weyerhaeuser gets paid faster when performance is faster and more consistent.

in-house order-placers. According to some, DoorBuilder has added an extra hour or two to the order-taking process on their end. "What Weyerhaeuser is doing is transferring some of its order work to the distributor," grumbles Hummel.

Other distributors see their investment in DoorBuilder as money well-spent. David Dirtzu, president of Glewwe Door in Eagan, Minn., says the extra expenses are a small price to pay to get on-time deliveries. "You can easily lose what we spent on DoorBuilder if your orders get delivered wrong or are late," says Dirtzu. "We figure DoorBuilder will pay for itself within the year." And it could help make distributors more efficient. Says Gerald Lenger, executive vice-president at H&G Sales Inc., a St. Louis distributor using Door-Builder: "What DoorBuilder has started is like dominoes in this industry. And those who don't keep up will probably be left behind."

> "For the first time, we had proof some orders were not making any money, so we set out to fix that"

DoorBuilder has even had a hand in wiping out niggling problems with inventories. Previously, a shipment of, say, the wrong veneer couldn't be traced back to its supplier. Now, DoorBuilder can pinpoint which manager sold it–along with when and in what condition it arrived. Kirchman, for example, recalls that before the intranet, the plant had been buying 100 very expensive mahogany door veneers each year when they hadn't used up a single sheet of their old supply. "All that our old inventory system told us was that these items were gone and so we ordered some more," says Kirchman. "It's incredible how much this technology can challenge your basic assumptions about things." And DoorBuilder won't schedule any door for production unless the raw materials are available to build it.

Ultimately, E-business is changing the door business. It's not the first industry to feel the power of E-business. But Weyerhaeuser's experience suggests that even the most unlikely candidates for an E-engineering overhaul will have to open their doors to the information revolution–and maybe sooner than they'd like.

By Marcia Stepanek

Reprinted from the July 26, 1999 issue of *Business Week* by special permission.

91

AOL angles for TV viewers

AOLTV marries Net, TV in first salvo of battle for interactive services

By David Lieberman
USA TODAY

NEW YORK — When America Online announced its plan last month to buy Time Warner, everyone saw that joining the No. 1 Internet provider and No. 1 media and entertainment conglomerate would rock the Web.

But many executives and analysts are just now seeing how the deal could fundamentally reshape an emerging business that will touch more people in more ways than the computer-accessed Internet: interactive television.

AOL takes its first step toward this blending of TV and the Internet this year when it launches AOLTV.

The service, expected this summer, could be "profoundly important," says Merrill Lynch's Internet specialist Henry Blodget. If the service is a hit, the company's clout over interactive communications might become "analogous to Microsoft's control of the PC operating system."

"The more ways a subscriber interacts with AOL," Blodget says, "the less likely the subscriber will be to pull up stakes and go with a different provider — especially when the entire family has programmed the service with individual buddy lists, calendars and e- mail accounts."

That prospect terrifies rivals that also want to be interactive TV powers, such as Microsoft, which owns WebTV, and Excite At Home, a cable high-speed Internet service. Their battle could split the cable industry.

"We're sitting on a fault line," says Worldgate Communications CEO Hal Krisbergh, whose company provides Internet access to cable TV viewers. "It clearly portends earthquakes."

AOL declined to discuss AOLTV, although it recently briefed Wall Street analysts and demonstrated the service at a consumer electronics trade show.

What wows observers is the proven appeal of the services AOLTV harnesses. AOL subscribers, now 21 million, wouldn't have to boot up their computers to access e-mail, instant messaging, chats, calendars, and online shopping or investment services.

People could use them while watching, say, Who Wants to Be a Millionaire by pointing a remote or wireless keyboard at a set-top decoder that splits the screen to show online content and the TV show.

Initially, people wanting AOLTV would need a special set-top box to connect the TV to a phone line.

But the deal with Time Warner, the No. 1 cable operator with more than 13 million customers, opens the way for AOLTV to dominate interactive TV. It could become a seamless part of the cable TV package, eliminating the need for a separate set-top box and a phone line.

When AOL and Time Warner announced their merger, "we very quickly had a lot of dialogues with the AOL guys," says Jim McDonald, CEO of Scientific-Atlanta, Time Warner's chief supplier of decoder boxes and systems. "What we want to do now is to port their software into our system as quickly as we can."

They aren't alone.

"Nothing has so excited the (cable hardware) industry in the last year as the AOL-Time Warner deal," says Richard Doherty of The Envisioneering Group. "It's that big a buzz. . . . AOL is out talking to everybody."

Cable operators, who have 66 million subscribers, are just starting to negotiate interactive TV deals. Tests will begin this summer on some systems. Commercial rollout will begin in earnest in 2001.

Key points in the talks include whose name is on the service, who controls the initial online screen users see, and where and how often data and ads appear.

AOL could meet resistance on branding. "AOL wants to be your start page," says Tim Bajarin, president of Creative Strategies. "That's one of the big reasons AOL went ahead with the Time Warner deal."

By contrast, Microsoft and Excite At Home are willing to do software and services and let the cable owner control the face shown to users.

"AOL is its own brand," says Excite At Home Vice President Paul Salzinger. "But in Philadelphia, Comcast is its own brand and it means a lot to them."

The stakes are enormous. Revenue from interactive TV — subscriptions, advertising and electronic commerce — could soar to $20 billion in 2004 from $700 million in 1999, Forrester Research says.

Forecasters are enthusiastic about interactive TV because the country is so addicted to the tube.

"The numbers are staggering," says CIBC World Markets' John Corcoran. "There are still 65 million homes not connected to the Internet, and TV is well-positioned to move into that connectivity gap."

What's more, the average adult spends 126 hours in front of a TV screen each month, while the typical AOL user is online for just 26 hours.

No wonder enthusiasts say cable operators could reap a windfall.

Consider one way it could work. An operator might charge advertisers 40 cents each time a subscriber used the remote control to go to the Web for more information on a product. If a customer clicked on two ads a day, just 1% of the 180 spots airing in a typical home, that subscriber would generate an additional $24 a month.

"That's more than an operator collects from basic cable subscriptions," says Krisbergh. "And that's not a hopeful number. It's a conservative number, and the largest growth opportunity facing the industry today."

OVERHYPED PROMISE?

If it sounds like you've heard this tune before, well, you have. For decades, interactive TV has been one of cable's most over-hyped promises — and embarrassing bombs.

That's why the Yankee Group's James Penhune is "amazed at the degree of attention AOL has gotten for — I don't want to call it vaporware, but something that's pre-market."

> **Television's future?** AOLTV marries TV and the Internet, allowing subscribers to access e-mail, instant messaging, chats, calendars, and online shopping or investment services while watching TV.

Interactive TV could run aground again if viewers see a privacy threat. The tension is there because advertisers relish its potential for tailoring pitches to different viewers.

"We can actually send two different ads to two different TVs in the same house," says McDonald.

Cable operators could also monitor what programs you watch. "There are a few privacy issues there, but the answer is we can technically do that," he says.

Privacy laws may prove insufficient for interactive TV. Most were written for specific media and are ambiguous when applied to hybrids.

"It's problematic when the provisions are applied to old business models," says Dierdre Mulligan, counsel for the Center for Democracy and Technology.

Still, executives and analysts say that interactive TV is finally ready for prime time. People are more at ease with the Web and cable operators are completing long-term upgrades to two-way-capable systems.

To harness that power, they also are deploying more than 30,000 digital set-top decoders a week that can communicate over cable wires. The capacity for advanced services is "ubiquitous across the country pretty much now," says CEO Edward Breen of General Instrument, the leading maker of set-top decoders that is being bought by Motorola.

AOL salivated to reach the all-important cable market, but it was mostly out of reach until its deal for Time Warner. Operators resented AOL's role as leader of an effort to force cable systems to be open to competing high-speed Internet services.

In defense, AOL invested $1.5 billion last year in Hughes Electronics and got a deal to launch AOLTV on its DirecTv satellite service, using phone lines to connect with AOL through a set-top box. The deal to buy Time Warner put AOLTV on fast-forward. And it's a plus for Time Warner's cable systems.

"Beyond offering video on demand, Time Warner has no interactive TV strategy," says Paul Kagan Associates' Leslie Ellis.

Although the launch plans are still unclear, few expect AOL to offer AOLTV only on DirecTv.

"Obviously, Time Warner's going to try to put it up as soon as they can," says Scientific-Atlanta's McDonald. If the service catches on, then "most (operators) will see demand that they'll have to respond to."

Here's where the battle with other interactive TV companies — particularly Microsoft — is joined.

INTERACTIVE BATTLEGROUND

Microsoft says its experience with WebTV gives it a better insight into what consumers want from interactive TV.

"Initially we looked at a TV set as an available monitor," says WebTV marketing director Rob Schoeben. "But we realized that we missed a fundamental point. That monitor is a TV set and people want it to be a better TV, not an alternative to a PC."

That pitch will appeal to cable operators, many of whom already have financial ties to Microsoft.

Last year, Microsoft invested $5 billion in AT&T, which hopes to soon complete its deal to buy Media-One, making AT&T the No. 1 cable operator. In 1997, Microsoft reawakened Wall Street's interest in all cable companies by investing $1 billion in Comcast, the No. 3 operator.

In addition, Microsoft co-founder Paul Allen has recently gone on a buying spree to make his Charter Communications the No. 4 operator. Microsoft also has a satellite alliance with Echostar, which incorporates

Deal boosts maker of set-top boxes

By David Lieberman
USA TODAY

NEW YORK — Scientific-Atlanta CEO Jim McDonald was as surprised as everyone else by America Online's Jan. 10 deal to buy Time Warner. but few benefited more than the maker of cable systems and set-top boxes, 40% of which go to Time Warner.

Scientific-Atlanta stock is up 115% since before the deal, lifting market value to $8.4 billion. This week it announced a 2-for-1 stock split.

To McDonald, the deal vindicated his focus on robust interactive systems, where most of the computing power and memory is at the cable office, instead of set-top boxes that quickly can become obsolete.

"Interactive TV got moved up a couple of years" because of the deal, McDonald says.

His message has resonated with cable operators who put S-A systems in 100 cities passing 30 million homes.

McDonald says S-A will keep growing: "We don't know of anybody else who has even deployed a system."

Not so, says Motorola, which is buying industry leader General Instrument. "We're relying on the infrastructure that all cable operators are using" as they develop a single communications standard, says digital network manager Dave Robinson. S-A's boxes "don't include the (industry standard) high-speed modem."

But McDonald insists his company will have the interactive TV edge. His boxes include the Web's HTML language, which AOLTV uses.

"Our networks and our products can run this unchanged," he says. "No one else can make that claim."

Next up: boxes that control computers and phones as well as TV sets.

"In 18 months, I'll have twice the performance in semiconductors. And in fiber optics, the bandwidth doubles every nine months," McDonald says. "We're in for an extremely rapid rise in what you can do with these networks."

WebTV on some receivers.

Many large cable operators also are friends with Excite At Home, the high-speed Internet service that is controlled by AT&T. And Excite At Home may have some leverage by claiming that interactive TV is part of its multiyear deals to provide high-speed Internet services.

"The most important thing is, we are established today to deliver these services" via cable, says Excite At Home's Salzinger. "We are big promoters of the cable operators offering a service that ties across to the PC. It's all about convenience."

Microsoft and Excite At Home said in December that they're talking about a possible partnership. Those conversations are still under way.

Still, operators know that it would be dangerous to snub AOL and its huge subscriber base.

If they do, then AOLTV could encourage its cus-tomers to cut cable operators out of the interactive TV picture altogether. Use of AOLTV's set-top decoder would keep operators from controlling "many of the next-generation cable services that cable operators had expected to control, including e-mail, the program guide, chat and 'click-to-buy' e-commerce," says Sanford C. Bernstein analyst Tom Wolzien.

The set-top box also could be configured to handle high-speed phone lines — and AOL is exploring accepting data from wireless providers.

Everyone is positioning for a fight that will revolutionize communications and entertainment. "Right now, there's a wall 3 feet thick between the TV and the Internet," says Krisbergh. "And the opportunity to marry the two is awesome."

92

For Sale: Japanese Plants In The U.S.

Some of Japan's biggest names in electronics products are selling out to American contract manufacturers. ■ *by Gene Bylinsky*

Only yesterday, it seems, a choir of journalists, college professors, and management consultants was telling how the Japanese, through their superior manufacturing techniques, would subjugate the world economy by the start of the new millennium. Now, in the biggest flip-flop in recent industrial history, the Japanese–Mitsubishi, NEC, Fujitsu, and soon Sony–are quietly selling some of their treasured U.S. factories to the supposedly backward Americans, who will make Japanese products in them.

Japanese turning to Americans to manufacture Japanese products? Have Eskimos suddenly forgotten how to make igloos? One answer is that, after seven years of recession and poor stock performance, the Japanese have finally begun to give up their cherished dream of keeping everything in the family. They can no longer ignore outsourcing–and outright sale of plants–as a better financial model.

There's a lot more to it. Japan's rigidity has finally caught up with it in manufacturing, at least in electronics industries that require flexible production and fast product introduction to accommodate rapidly shifting demand. An executive of a Silicon Valley diskmaker boasts that, when it comes to speed in turning out a wide variety of complex products, such as computer servers and hard drives, and changing the product mix almost daily, "we can turn on a dime. The Japanese can't do that."

Don't get the wrong idea. Sony, Panasonic, and other Japanese giants still excel at cranking out high-quality consumer electronics products–such as camcorders and TVs–by the millions. And Japanese auto manufacturers still make outstanding vehicles. But it's a different story in industries with short product cycles and factories that must build what customers order instead of churning out products in anticipation of demand. Here Japan's great strength–repetitive manufacturing–is becoming its greatest weakness.

Listen to John Costanza, president of the John Costanza Institute of Technology in Englewood, Colo., and a leading expert on manufacturing: "The Japanese are terrible at building on demand–terrible, terrible, terrible. Repetitive manufacturing works fine if you can sell everything you can build. But the day when they could tell a customer, 'I'll make a product and you'll buy it,' is gone. Building variable products to demand is the requirement for manufacturing today. So now the Japanese are saying, 'We're going to contract manufacturing by selling plants because we don't know how to change our manufacturing culture.'"

This is where a new breed of American supermanufacturers–you could call them the new Japanese–comes in. They are the so-called contract electronics manufacturers (CEMs), which are gobbling up those Japanese plants in the U.S. as well as abroad. A far cry from the grimy job shops found on the bleak back streets of suburban Detroit or Chicago, CEMs use production techniques that top those of the Japanese, in huge, surgically clean, highly automated plants employing thousands of workers. The CEMs now make products more cheaply in San Jose than the Japanese can in Tokyo.

Through supply chains linking dozens of plants around the world, the big CEMs have become the new providers to so-called original equipment manufacturers (OEMs). Though OEM brand names appear on a vast array of products–from computer servers to PCs to cell phones–a growing proportion of the wares emanates from CEMs. The term OEM, in fact, has become dated; today these companies could more accurately be called OBHs (original brand holders).

According to a recent report by the Banc-Boston Robertson Stephens investment firm, the largest brand owners using CEMs include Hewlett-Packard, which relies on ten different CEMs to make its products, Cisco (with nine CEMs), IBM (eight), and Lucent (seven). Technology Forecasters of Alameda, Calif., estimates that 9.5% of the electronic goods sold by the world's OEMs are now put together in CEM plants, and expects this percentage to reach 17% by 2003. Japanese brand owners are just starting to get on the bandwagon.

Thus, the CEMs are the new tailors, shoemakers, butlers, and chambermaids of the brand-holder elite, whose members concentrate increasingly on R&D, product design, and marketing. The biggest contract manufacturers are Solectron of Milpitas, Calif., with projected sales this year of $13 billion, SCI Systems of Huntsville, Ala. ($8 billion), Celestica of Toronto ($6 billion), and Flextronics International of San Jose ($3 billion).

CEMs are one of the fastest-growing industrial segments. Technology Forecasters predicts that their revenues, already $60 billion a year, will hit $150 billion in 2003. Just how good the CEMs are is indicated by the fact that Solectron is the only company that has twice won the Baldrige award for manufacturing excellence. And CEMs excel at running global supply chains and using the Internet.

As the CEMs' stock market performance shows, they are not engaged in a marginal, low-profit activity. Since Solectron went public in 1989, its stock has soared 16,000%, vs. a 7,000% rise for Microsoft and 4,000% for Intel during the same period.

The CEMs' profit margins are not as impressive as those of the brand owners, averaging 4% of sales. But their return on investment, as BancBoston Robertson Stephens puts it, has been "splendid." ROI has averaged more than 20% for the big CEMs, vs. an average of only 6% to 9% for companies that make up Standard & Poor's industrials. The reason is that the CEMs' plants, operating at a high percentage of capacity, are efficient.

The growth of the CEMs has been fueled in large part by their purchases of OEM plants, for which they often bid aggressively against one another. They have turned those plants into more efficient producers by upgrading equipment and by making products for more than one client under the same roof. In 1998 alone, CEMs bought 47 manufacturing plants in the U.S., in the process keeping thousands of manufacturing jobs from leaving the country. Abroad, CEMs run dozens of plants in places like Oulu, Finland; Hortolandia, Brazil; Guadalajara, Mexico; and Kunshan, China. Generally the CEMs make more complex products in their U.S. plants than they do at foreign sites where labor costs are lower.

A big goal of many CEM executives, helped to no small extent by John Costanza's institute, has been to return U.S. manufacturing to its former preeminence. Many who have led this drive are Asian Americans, among them Solectron's former president, Winston Chen, a Chinese American, and its current CEO, Koichi "Ko" Nishimura, a California-born Nisei who spent his boyhood in a World War II internment camp.

Buying Japanese plants in the U.S. could put the CEMs on a new growth spurt. "There's a certain irony in this," says Flextronics CEO Michael Marks. The Japanese plant sales began in 1998, when Mitsubishi sold its cell-phone manufacturing facility in Braselton, Ga., to Solectron. In addition to taking over the manufacture of Mitsubishi cell phones sold in North America–the phones are being made in a new 100,000-square-foot leased facility that it has set up on the Mitsubishi campus–Solectron also manages printed-circuitboard assembly for the phones and new-product introduction. Mitsubishi, for its part, now concentrates on advanced engineering and product development.

Solectron declined to be interviewed for this article, perhaps because of the sensitivity of the subject with both buyers and sellers. But CEO Nishimura is known to be urging Japanese OEMs to sell their plants. "He tells them how Solectron would modernize the plants, reduce their costs, and improve their antiquated distribution system," says a source close to the company. The fact that Nishimura speaks fluent Japanese doesn't hurt.

The changes CEMs make in newly acquired plants, Japanese or otherwise, can be dramatic. Says Flextronics' Marks: "All factories are different. But in nearly every case, we improve the housekeeping and change some information technology functions. We almost always invest in new production equipment."

The CEMs pick their acquisitions carefully, Marks notes: "We buy plants with appropriate geographic locations, to increase customer penetration and to give us technical capabilities we don't have." Flextronics passed on NEC's Hillsboro, Ore., telecom equipment plant, which is on the block, but the company is bidding on another NEC telecom production facility in Sao Paulo. A few weeks ago, Flextronics also acquired a computer-server factory in Paderborn, Germany, which had been jointly owned by Fujitsu and Siemens.

Late last year another big CEM, SCI Systems, bought an NEC Computers manufacturing plant in Sacramento and shipped some of the production tools to Huntsville, Ala., where it has set up a plant that makes laptops and desktops for NEC. SCI will also handle the complete supply chain for NEC Computers in North America. CEO A. Eugene Sapp of SCI hailed the acquisition as providing "the basis for a range of future initiatives between the [two] companies."

What really makes CEM bosses drool is a tsunami of Japanese plant sales expected at the end of March. That's when, according to a spokesman, Sony will announce plans to dispose of 22 of its 70 plants worldwide, selling some and shutting down others. Many other Japanese manufacturing companies are expected to follow suit. "They will be saying, 'If Sony's doing it, we should be doing it too,'" says Sheridan Tatsuno, a Harvard-educated Sansei (fourth-generation Japanese American) who consults with Japanese companies from his Northern California base in Aptos.

The trend is about to accelerate because of pressure from an unexpected source. Says Tatsuno: "Even MITI [Japan's Ministry of International Trade and Industry] is now telling Japanese companies to get into e-business and to sell manufacturing plants." Yes, that's the same MITI that helped engineer Japan's assault on U.S. manufacturing companies in the 1960s and 1970s.

Selling the family jewels–Tatsuno's term for the plants–is a traumatic experience for older Japanese executives, many of whom made their names in manufacturing. "It's a huge loss of face," says Tatsuno, "because they literally grew up on the plant floor. But the younger executives don't seem to care who makes their products."

Handel Jones, a Ph.D. economist and semiconductor engineer who runs a Japan-oriented consulting and data-gathering firm, International Business Strategies, in Los Gatos, Calif., sees nothing but black clouds over the factories of the Land of the Rising Sun. "When we project Japanese strengths and weaknesses out to 2010," says Jones, "it looks very negative for them. They remain strong in the old-style electromechanical, or repetitive, manufacturing. But when it comes to using software intelligence inside new, flexible production systems, they're very weak."

Recognizing a new need, some Japanese companies are now seeking help from American manufacturing experts such as Costanza. Fujitsu, Sharp, and Hitachi are trying to introduce demand-flow manufacturing, a concept he pioneered, in their U. S. plants. Costanza and his staff have installed it in hundreds of U.S. companies, from AT&T to GE to U.S. Robotics.

Demand-flow manufacturing works on principles diametrically opposed to those of conventional manufacturing based on scheduling and forecasts. Not only does demand flow rearrange linear production lines into semicircular cells for more efficient production, but it also does away with that mainstay of Japanese manufacturing, the just-in-time (JIT) delivery of components such as automobile seats or tires. Demand flow substitutes its own concept–raw-in-process inventory, or RIP. This calls for keeping a reasonable quantity of varied raw materials or components on hand to meet changing demand.

Sheridan Tatsuno sums it up: "John Costanza and the CEMs have totally changed the game on the Japanese." Americans teaching the Japanese that it's time for just-in-time to rest in peace? That's how far the world has turned in manufacturing.

Ethical Marketing in a Consumer-Oriented World: Appraisal and Challenges

93

The Omnipresent Persuaders:

Marketing in the future will be everywhere—including your head

By Jonathan Kaufman

Staff Reporter of The Wall Street Journal

As you settle in this weekend to watch the Southwestern Bell Cotton Bowl, the Tostitos Fiesta Bowl and the FedEx Orange Bowl, brace yourself: Pervasive, intrusive, annoying marketing is destined to get worse in the next 1,000 years.

Already, marketers are rolling out technology that attaches to your computer and sprays the smell of a new-car interior or a charbroiled hamburger into your home or cubicle. A Pittsburgh advertising firm is lobbying city officials to turn abandoned buildings into giant outdoor billboards for Iron City beer. And Pizza Hut is planning to put its logo on the rocket that will launch the international space station.

Call it "marketism"—the quest by companies to take every last space that might be commercial-free and brand it with their name and product.

Where will it all end? Inside your brain, if some marketers have their way. As technology advances, futurists imagine a world in which advertisers will "narrowcast" messages directly into consumers' brains, stirring emotional responses that impel us to buy their products.

"The thing you are going to worry about in the future is not Big Brother—the government watching you—but Little Brother—tens of thousands of companies using technology to hijack your attention," says Christopher Meyer, director of Ernst & Young's Center for Business Innovation. He thinks the only way for consumers to fight back will be forcing the government to pass laws treating the expropriation of human attention as a form of theft.

"People will rise up and say, 'They don't have the right to interrupt my brainwaves!'" predicts Mr. Meyer. "Book 'em on Distraction One."

Always in Your Face

The growing intrusiveness of advertising and marketing messages reflects an escalating late-20th-century arms race between marketers and consumers, with technology the weapon of choice on either side. Marketers harnessed the technology of television to beam commercials into people's homes. Consumers fought back by using the remote-control button to channel-surf and the VCR to fast-forward through commercials. Marketers escalated by inserting products into shows and digitally implanting messages into the backgrounds of televised sporting events.

Similarly, consumers armed with caller-identification hookups have pushed back the telemarketing offensive, while computers' filtering software struggles to stymie the ever-more-resourceful e-mail spammers.

In public spaces, consumers have been able to put up far fewer defenses than they can at home. In just the past five years, the number of sports stadiums bearing brand names has soared to 50 from six, according to IEG Inc., a Chicago-based company that tracks corporate sponsorships.

Paradoxically, the more pervasive advertising and branding becomes, the more effective people have become in tuning it out. Several years ago, Coca-Cola Co. did a survey following a race-car event that was festooned with Coca-Cola signs, giant inflatable Coke bottles and the Coke logo painted across the middle of the race track. Only one-third of the attendees named Coke as the sponsor of the event.

"People are so used to seeing Coke everywhere that when they were asked to associate a specific event with the brand, they couldn't tell us," says Scott Jacobson, a Coke spokesman. "That's when we knew it was time to change the paradigm."

'Tune It Out'

"All this signage becomes like wallpaper —you just tune it out," says Lesa Ukman, president of IEG. "The other night, my husband and I went to see something at the new Ford Theatre in Chicago," refurbished and named after the car company. "On the way home my husband asked me, 'Who was Ford in Chicago?' He thought it was named after a local family."

As a result, marketers say, companies may spend the next 1,000 years trying to cut through the clutter they have created in the past 50.

The first wave, already unfolding, is even more invasive marketing. Nowhere is going to be safe, marketers indicate. As companies sell more goods on the Internet, they will try to reach consumers in previously ad-free locations to allow people to see, smell, and touch their physical products. So, watch for auto makers to set up exhibits showcasing a new-car model in a popular dog-walking spot. Look out for mobile "tasting vans" at bus stops and outside schools after parents drop off their children.

Next will be "ambient advertising"— marketing that jumps out of its medium, such as a billboard that speaks to you as you walk by, or a computer that spews the smell of doughnuts into your face when you click on a banner ad. That's the plan of DigiScents Inc., an Oakland, Calif., company marketing a peripheral device to release scents from computers—and eventually from movie houses, television sets and other media outlets.

"Smell is probably one of the most powerful senses in respect to emotion and memory," says company co-founder Dexster Smith. "If a picture is worth a thousand words, a smell is worth a thousand pictures." He envisions a world in which technology begins to replicate touch and other senses with such authenticity that marketers place customers in "full immersion, simulating reality at more and more powerful levels."

Mr. Smith points out that computers are becoming better able to reproduce tactile sensations through the computer mouse, and that visual and auditory stimulation can be taken "far beyond where we are right now." Michael Grzymkowski, lead strategist with Idea Mill Inc., a Pittsburgh advertising firm, envisions companies taking over entire streets and creating a simulated three-dimensional world that consumers will walk through while going from one point in town to another. "More than an advertisement, it will be an experience," he says.

Such immersion will be especially powerful as companies increasingly tailor messages to each consumer, harnessing the massive amounts of information gained from watching people shop online.

Poked by Technology

"More and more, we are going to have software that looks at you as an individual and predicts what else you will like," says Ernst & Young's Mr. Meyer. Over time, he says, this software will merge with technology that allows people to stimulate their brains and recreate memories and emotions—enabling marketers to associate a car, say, with a drive alongside a sunny beach or the thrill you get from bungee jumping.

"Every person is going to be an information wave-front," says Mr. Meyer. "People will want these experiences. Companies will customize responses and give it to them. If it's done wrong, it will feel like 'The Truman Show'—an artificial world that has nothing to do with you. If it's done right, you'll feel like Louis XIV. The market, *c'est moi*. It'll feel like everything is being done for you at your command."

If such a world sounds like nightmarish science fiction, some are betting that consumers will fuel a backlash, responding favorably to marketers who don't bother them. Will it become cool in the new millennium to be discreet?

"One of these days, you won't hear the voice of James Earl Jones everywhere," says Theodore Levitt, the venerable marketing theorist now retired from Harvard Business School. "You'll have promotions that won't intrude."

Jed Pearsall, a marketing consultant, says, "People are telling us they're tired of having advertising in their face. They want it to do something for them. Marketing will become a field that solves people's problems."

Instead of companies relentlessly marketing products, Mr. Pearsall envisions them

(Cont.)

sponsoring environmental cleanups, paying for school systems, funding hospitals. "People will know that Coca-Cola is doing something for them," says Mr. Pearsall, the head of Performance Research Inc. in Newport, R.I. "They'll be driving down the highway and see a sign saying, 'This road toll-free because of General Motors.'"

But to others, the thought of attending Coca-Cola High School is further evidence of marketism run amok.

"Maybe what's going to happen is that those of us who get into a mentally disturbed state induced by brand assault will take vacations in designated market-free zones that will cleanse us for a week," says Philip Kotler, a professor of marketing at Northwestern University's Kellogg Graduate School of Management. "We'll pay for camps, to be cleaned out of brand assault."

Or maybe the camps will be free—paid for by your local sponsor.

94

RUNNING RINGS AROUND SATURN

Rivals are stealing the carmaker's once-loyal customers. Is the magic gone?

No one has to tell Russell E. Hand how badly Saturn Corp. needs new models to sell. The Torrance (Calif.) Saturn dealer has been watching helplessly as rival Toyota Motor Sales USA Inc. and American Honda Motor Co. lure his once-happy small-car customers into roomier Camry and Accord family sedans. "If someone really needed a bigger car, we didn't have a way for them to go," laments Hand.

Small wonder, then, that when the General Motors Corp. division finally delivered the new L-Series midsize car to its long-suffering dealers last summer, hopes were high. After all, Saturn dealers have had a one-car lineup for 10 years. While GM was investing in its other established brands, Saturn was repeatedly passed over for a new model. Even a redesign of its aging S-Series compact was turned down. As a result, the brands' once-legendary popularity has plummeted as Saturn owners defected to the competition's larger cars, sport-utility vehicles, and newly designed small cars.

> The new midsize car was to be a savior. Now, GM is slashing production plans

Falling behind on new models has cost Saturn and its parent dearly. While just 5.6% of GM's sales at its height in 1994, Saturn, with its fresh image and huge customer following, represented one of the few bright spots on the auto giant's horizon. Since then, however, sales have fallen 20%. Last year alone, small-car sales plunged 10%, even though small-car sales industrywide rose 7%. And in J.D. Power & Associates' 1999 sales-satisfaction index, consumers ranked Saturn sixth—the first time in four years the brand wasn't on top.

If all that weren't troubling enough, now comes the lukewarm reception of the new L-Series midsize car. It was to be Saturn's savior, designed to lure new buyers and bring back its old customers. But when dealers finally got an ample supply of LS sedans and LW wagons, the crowds never showed up. "The bloom is off the Saturn rose," says

former dealer David McDavid of Dallas.

Since July, L-Series sales have averaged fewer than 5,000 cars a month, falling far short of GM's projections of 15,000 monthly sales. That forced Saturn, glutted with inventory, to halt production at its Wilmington (Del.) plant for two weeks in January. Meanwhile, Saturn competitors continue to rack up sales in the midsize car market. In January, Toyota Camry sales of 40,285 and Honda Accord sales of 24,241 dwarfed the 4,381 L-Series cars sold. Those numbers are even more startling considering both the Camry and the Accord sell for a few thousand dollars more than the $16,000 to $22,000 price range for an LS sedan. "We get a lot of Saturn trade-ins," says George Black, general manager of Mile High Honda in Denver.

So what's the problem? Uninspired styling of the L-Series hasn't helped matters, analysts insist. But last fall's $82 million-plus "Next Big Thing" advertising campaign somehow failed to make clear the car's roomy midsize dimensions–one of its major selling points. The ads portrayed the car as a fun family sedan, but did little to show that the car was larger than the Saturn compact.

Now, as the L-Series' problems linger, Saturn has quietly moved to slash its production. Suppliers say the company told them in recent weeks it will crank out just 150,000 cars annually, instead of the 200,000-plus originally planned. That means GM will likely have to pay suppliers more for parts, cutting already thin margins–about $2,000 per car. That's only about one-fifth of what auto makers can gross on their bigger sport-utility vehicles, says Rod Lache, a Deutsche Bank analyst in New York who estimates that the Saturn Div. is at best "marginally profitable."

DISHEARTENING." It's all a huge comedown since the days when Saturn was GM's hottest unit and one of the true success stories of U.S. auto makers in the early 1990s. But what bothers Saturn fans most is that clear signs of trouble went ignored for years. "It's been a great franchise, so it's disheartening to see things go awry," says Dallas Saturn retailer Randy Hiley. "The market changed, and Saturn wasn't ready for it."

Saturn's customers and dealers have, in fact, long clamored for more models. But early on, cash-strapped GM was forced to

make tough choices about where to invest its capital. Saturn lost out to Oldsmobile in a debate among executives over whether to kill Olds or revive it at Saturn's expense, says retired Saturn President Richard G. "Skip" Lefauve. "We were a small subsidiary trying to work our way to profitability," he says. "That was more risk than [GM] wanted to take." Instead of giving Saturn a new car when the brand was hot in the mid-1990s, Olds and other divisions got new product money.

Many of the L-Series' current woes stem from the way GM finally agreed to grant Saturn a new model. To save on costs, GM had Saturn share the basic chassis undercarriage with the Vectra sold in Europe by the company's Adam Opel AG unit. The car was designed by the two units at GM's European engineering center in Russelheim, Germany. Saturn, however, didn't do enough early dry runs with workers to iron out bugs in the assembly process. The result was poorly fitting parts and slowed assembly time. There were also shortcomings in adapting the European design for the U.S. market. Tiny cup holders, for example, had to be quickly redesigned to accommodate Big Gulps. By the time Saturn

HARD AT WORK UNDER SATURN'S HOOD

Perhaps the biggest compliment an auto executive can receive is to be called "a car guy." In Detroit parlance, that's somebody as comfortable in an assembly plant as in a high-level corporate strategy meeting. And by that measure, no one is more of a car guy than Saturn Corp. President Cynthia Trudell, say her co-workers and friends.

For Trudell, who came up through the engineering ranks, walking through a factory in work boots with union stewards has long come naturally. But she has also long been a rising star inside GM's corporate elite. A 19-year veteran, Trudell has worked all across the GM universe. Not all business, though, Trudell, 46, also attempts to embody Saturn's fun-loving reputation within GM. She has more than once showed up at auto shows wearing sparkling ruby red shoes, not unlike those worn by Judy Garland in *The Wizard of Oz.*

STARTERS. Of course, it will take more than clicking her heels to turn around what was once a jewel in General Motors Corp.'s lineup. And GM clearly has a lot riding on her abilities. Trudell, a native of New Brunswick, Canada, grew up in the business—her father was a car dealer. Her first post at GM was as an engineer in the Windsor (Ont.) transmission plant. She rose to become head of Saturn's Wilmington (Del.) assembly plant before going overseas to run a British unit that makes sport-utility vehicles. "She's a great businesswoman," says Mark T. Hogan, president of GM's e-commerce business, who worked with Trudell in GM's small-car group.

Nowhere, however, has Trudell faced the kinds of problems she is up against at Saturn. Since becoming president, her reputation has been put on the line, as she deals with both Saturn's falling sales and the botched launch of its new midsize L-Series model. An optimist, Trudell insists she isn't letting Saturn's woes get to her.

Certainly, Trudell has had her share of triumphs since taking the wheel at Saturn. Her biggest to date: cutting a critical deal with the United Auto Workers. Drawing on her earlier days as a plant manager, Trudell was key to inking an agreement that persuaded UAW leaders to support Saturn's longstanding policy for rewarding workers who meet productivity and quality targets. Union leaders, moreover, say they trust Trudell. "She doesn't always side with management," says Scott Farraday, chairman of Local 435, which represents Saturn's Wilmington plant workers.

That's good for starters. But Trudell will have to make Saturn just as popular with car buyers for her plans to pan out anytime soon.

By David Welch in Detroit

---

got the manufacturing problems worked out, it was winter rebate season and rival car companies were laying out deals to move cars off their lots. But that's a practice Saturn has long shied away from because of its no-haggle sales philosophy.

Saturn executives aren't apologizing for the L-Series missteps. "There are glitches in every launch," explains Saturn President Cynthia Trudell, a former Wilmington plant manager hired a year ago to ignite a turnaround at the static division. "Our launch was complex because it was done globally," with production and design spanning three continents. Trudell also blames stagnant sales on last fall's failed ad campaign.

> Saturn is rolling out aggressive new ads, but the company concedes it has lost crucial momentum

CHANGING TASTES. Now, GM is scurrying to undo the damage. "We have to get consumers to see Saturn as more than a small-car company," says Ronald L. Zarrella, GM's president for North American operations. So Saturn is rolling out a new series of uncharacteristically aggressive ads created by Publicis, Hal Riney & Partners, the same ad agency it used before. These ads pit the L-Series directly against the Accord and Camry, even showing them in one commercial. But relaunching cars with new ad campaigns is notoriously dif-

ficult. And Trudell concedes that the company has lost crucial momentum. "You can't change what happened," she says. "You have to make the best of what you have going forward."

It won't be easy. The original subcompact sedan and coupe targeted the Toyota Corolla and Honda Civic head-on. Saturn sold 2 million small cars in the 1990s, and fully 60% of those were snapped up by former foreign-car owners. But this time around, the import lovers aren't biting. "We were hoping for a larger proportion of Camry, Accord, and Taurus buyers," says Mark Pagan, general manager of Saturn of San Francisco, a dealership. "We're not seeing that yet." Current consumer tastes haven't helped Saturn much either as buyers move increasingly toward SUVs and luxury cars, which Saturn doesn't offer.

Typical of the type of Saturn owners who have defected in droves in recent years is Karan Berryhill, 23, who recently traded in her Saturn coupe for a new Honda Civic. Like many other former Saturn owners, Berryhill complains that the carmaker has been glacially slow in upgrading its models. "I liked the Saturn, but it's too rough and noisy," she says. "They'd made some improvements to the new one, but not enough."

With that sort of customer dissatisfaction, it's no wonder that its retailers notice a lot less traffic in showrooms these days. A few have sold their stores. Others are hanging on, hoping for a turnaround. "Now we're making a little or losing money," says Dallas dealer Hiley, bemoaning his 16% drop in 1999 sales and profits.

CUSTOMER CONTROL. With profits down, Saturn dealers are trying to make money any way they can. For example, says J.D. Power analyst Brian Walters, is that the dealers are negotiating harder on trade-ins to beef up their profits. "It hasn't gone unnoticed by Saturn buyers," says Walters. Executives at GM counter that the brands that beat Saturn are customer-pampering luxury marques, adding that no mainstream division has matched Saturn's customer-satisfaction levels.

The carmaker faces another new challenge–a growing number of better-informed buyers with easy access to dealer invoices from the Internet. As a result, consumers are far more willing to haggle and far less impressed with Saturn's once-vaunted no-hassle pricing policy. "Control over negotiating is shifting to the consumer," says Loretta Seymour, a J.D. Power director. "And that's biting Saturn."

GM executives, troubled by Saturn's decline, are anxious to keep the division healthy. So the auto giant, eager for the younger, import-loving buyers that Saturn used to attract, is placing more bets on the division. But has the moment passed? "To me, it's never too late," Trudell says. But many former Saturn owners now driving Japanese cars obviously disagree.

By David Welch in Detroit

95

Foodstuff:

'Genetically Modified' On the Label Means...Well, It's Hard to Say

Attempt at Clarity in U.K. Brings Much Confusion; FDA Studies the Issue

'Non-GM' Isn't 'GM-Free'

By Steve Stecklow
Staff Reporter of The Wall Street Journal

LONDON—It seems simple enough: Let consumers know when they're buying bioengineered food by requiring a label. It's an idea being promoted heavily in the U.S. by groups such as Greenpeace and Friends of the Earth, and even by some members of Congress.

But a trip up and down the supermarket aisles of Britain, which has required such labeling since March, shows the new law hasn't exactly made things easier for discerning shoppers. Rather, it has spawned a bewildering array of marketing claims, counterclaims and outright contradictions that only a food scientist possibly could unravel.

Take cheese. One supermarket chain here labels its cheese as being "made using genetic modification," the European catchword for bioengineering. But other supermarket chains, whose cheese is made exactly the same way, haven't changed their labels, saying the cheese itself contains no genetically modified ingredients.

Then there's Birds Eye frozen beef burgers. The label on a box purchased last week states that one ingredient, soya protein, is "produced from genetically modified soya." But a spokesman for maker Unilever PLC insists that the soya isn't genetically modified. The company has reformulated the product, he explains, but has yet to replace the box.

Yes or No?

Confused yet? Then scan over the small print on a Haagen-Dazs chocolate-covered ice-cream bar. No genetically modified ingredients listed there. But consumers who question the company about it are sent a letter stating that the bar's chocolate coatings, in fact, contain soya oil that "may have been derived from genetically modified soya, but it is identical to any other soya oil and therefore does not contain any genetically modified material." The

letter adds, "We are, however, investigating whether there are suitable alternative oils."

All of this may seem puzzling to American shoppers, who so far aren't up in arms over whether the food they buy includes ingredients that have been tinkered with in a laboratory. After all, that's already the case with many U.S. products. But European consumers, who have lived through such recent food scares as beef linked to "mad cow" disease, salmonella-contaminated eggs and dioxin-tainted animal feed, are taking no chances, even though there's no proof that bioengineered foods pose any health risks.

Monster Mash

The result has been a biotech backlash that at times borders on hysteria. In Britain, tabloid newspapers routinely refer to genetically modified products as "Frankenstein food." One prisoner even went on a hunger strike demanding that no genetically modified food be served to inmates.

Critics say bioengineered foods offer consumers no obvious benefit and that despite industry and government assurances, not enough research has been done to assure they are safe. Environmental groups have expressed concern that genetically modified plants could have unintended side effects, including killing beneficial insects and, through the spread of pollen, promoting growth of herbicide-resistant "super weeds" and antibiotic-resistant "super bugs." Others fear genetically modified foods could cause dangerous allergic reactions in some people.

In response to widespread consumer outcry, the European Union last year approved legislation that required its 15 member countries to begin labeling all foods that contain genetically modified ingredients, namely corn and soybean in which new genes have been added to provide traits such as insect resistance.

American Reverberations

While no such plans have been announced in the U.S., the Food and Drug Administration said last week that it plans hearings around the country this fall to gauge public opinion on the issue. Already, several American health-food companies have begun slapping labels on their products declaring that they contain no genetically modified ingredients.

But before America leaps into mandatory labeling, the government, retailers and consumer groups might want to take a look at the far-reaching impact such a law has had in Britain.

When the European Union introduced its legislation last year, Britain's agriculture minister called it "a triumph for consumer rights to better information." Britain went on to enact the toughest labeling standards in Europe, requiring even restaurants, caterers and bakers to list genetically modified ingredients. Violations are punishable by fines of as much as $8,400, and the government says it intends to conduct surveillance, including independent lab testing.

"This is not a health issue in any way," says J. R. Bell, head of the government's additives and novel-foods division, adding that his ministry believes the latest bioengineered products are safe. "This is a question of choice, of consumer choice."

But, in fact, as a direct result of the labeling law, there's hardly any choice now at all. That's because Britain's new law sparked a mad rush by manufacturers, retailers and restaurant chains to rid their products of any genetically modified ingredients so they wouldn't have to alter their labels and risk losing sales. Even some pet-food manufacturers are claiming their products contain no genetically modified ingredients.

Among the thousands of products sold in Britain that now claim not to contain any GM ingredients are Pillsbury UK Ltd.'s Green Giant vegetables and Old El Paso Mexican food, Kellogg cereals and Unilever's Van den Bergh Foods Beanfeast line. A spokesman for McDonald's Restaurants Ltd., which operates 1,000 restaurants in the United Kingdom, says, "We do not use any genetically modified products or ingredients that contain genetically modified material." He adds, however, that some ingredients, such as soya oil used in hamburger buns, "could have come from a source which itself is genetically modified at some point."

The rush to keep products from being branded as bioengineered is hardly surprising. When J. Sainsbury PLC, a supermarket chain, began selling a bioengineered tomato puree under its own brand in 1996, sales initially exceeded other, more expensive brands by 30%, though the product's label volunteered that it was genetically modified. But as the GM controversy heated up, sales slowed and, by the end of last year, "absolutely fell through the floor," says Alison Austin, Sainsbury's environmental manager. The product has since been taken off the market by its creator and distributor, Zeneca Plant Science, a unit of AstraZeneca PLC.

Having gotten the message that consumers don't want bioengineered foods, Sainsbury's and other supermarket chains, as well as food manufacturers that sell in Britain, launched extensive, month-long reviews of their product formulations. They began changing recipes to eliminate soya and corn derivatives and ordered their suppliers to find new sources of nonbioengineered raw materials in places such as South America and Asia.

"We poured over something like 5,000 ingredients . . . and made changes to 1,800 recipes as part of this process," says Bob Mitchell, manager of food technical policy at Marks & Spencer PLC, which operates specialty food shops. "It was a colossal task."

Supermarkets soon began declaring in advertising that their own house brands, which in Britain can constitute more than half of all sales, no longer contained genetically modified ingredients.

But a close examination of stores' claims,

(Cont.)

based on interviews with supermarket executives, shows that one chain's definition of removing genetically modified ingredients isn't necessarily the same as another's.

Sainsbury's, for example, says on its Web site that it is "the first major U.K. supermarket to eliminate genetically modified ingredients from its own-brand products." Does that include food additives, such as sweeteners and flavorings, which may be genetically modified? Alison Austin, the company's environmental manager, replies, "To be honest, we have focused in on major ingredients" such as soya and maize proteins and oils, as well as lecithin, an emulsifier. As for other bioengineered ingredients, she says, "It takes time for the supply chain to provide alternatives."

'We Mean Zero GM'

Tesco PLC, Britain's leading supermarket chain, says it makes no distinction between major and minor genetically modified ingredients. As a result, 150 of its house-brand products are still labeled as containing GM ingredients. "When we say zero GM, we mean zero GM," says Simon Soffe, a Tesco spokesman.

Maybe so, but laboratories that test for genetically modified ingredients say it is almost impossible to guarantee that a product line contains absolutely no genetically modified ingredients. Many growers don't segregate bioengineered and nonbioengineered soybeans and corn. Moreover, genetically modified materials in highly processed additives or oils often can't be detected in testing. "If there's no way to test, then people are going to bend the rules and they're going to bend the truth," says Bruce Ferguson, president of EnviroLogix Inc., an environmental-testing company in Portland, Maine.

Some inconsistencies in supermarket claims can be attributed to the labeling law itself. At the moment, the European Union and British regulations require labeling only if genetically modified material is detectable in DNA or protein. Additives and flavorings are exempt.

Cheese-Making

That has led to some strange labeling dilemmas in items as simple as cheese. Traditionally, cheese was set using an enzyme called rennet, taken from the lining of calves' stomachs. But to appease vegetarians, many European cheese makers in recent years switched to an enzyme called chymosin that is produced from genetically modified bacteria.

There's no evidence that any genetically modified ingredient remains in the cheese after production. Still, one supermarket chain, Co-Op, decided to place labels on its cheese that say "made using genetic modification and so free from animal rennet." "It's a question of whether the retailer is honest or open in labeling it," says a Co-Op spokesman.

Meantime, Iceland, a small but scrappy convenience-store chain whose chairman coined the term "Frankenstein food," says it has switched to making its cheese with another enzyme that doesn't come from animals and isn't produced from genetically modified bacteria. "We've done them one better," says Bill Wadsworth, the chain's technical director.

European Union officials say they are hoping to clear up some of the confusion in the marketplace. Last week, a panel of government representatives voted to extend the labeling law to cover additives and flavorings, a change that is expected to take effect next year and could force many manufacturers and fast-food restaurants to either change recipes, switch suppliers or begin labeling.

The EU also decided to address the problem of products "contaminated" with trace amounts of genetically modified material despite the best intentions of manufacturers. In a controversial decision, the panel recommended that products don't require labeling if each of the ingredients contains 1% bioengineered material or less. Consumer groups had argued that the limit should be one-tenth of that.

In the future, the EU may also try to define when a retailer or manufacturer may claim that a product is "GM-free," a phrase that already has sprung up in some advertising and promotional material. Many retailers, such as Marks & Spencer, instead use the term "non-GM," which they insist is different. "We would never call it GM-free because you could never guarantee that," Mr. Mitchell says.

And thornier labeling issues loom. In their competitive frenzy, some British supermarkets have begun introducing raw and frozen chicken that they claim was raised on feed containing no genetically modified ingredients–even though there isn't evidence that bioengineered material ends up in the meat. To accomplish this, Iceland convenience stores say they now buy their chickens in Brazil, instead of Britain. Marks & Spencer says it is about to introduce a new line of free-range, non-GM poultry, egg and pork products.

Sainsbury's has yet to join the non-GM chicken and pork parade, but Mrs. Austin says it's probably "inevitable" and adds it may only be a first step. "We are utterly adamant that if you wish to claim you are GM-free, then you are ultimately going to have to go as far as GM-free veterinary medicines," she says.

J&J Unit Pleads Guilty After Marketing Probe

BY RON WINSLOW
Staff Reporter of THE WALL STREET JOURNAL

A **Johnson & Johnson** unit pleaded guilty to federal criminal charges related to its marketing of a defective diagnostic test for diabetes patients, an embarrassing blow to a company that prides itself on being a model corporate citizen.

The decision, which includes an agreement to pay $60 million in fines, sets the stage for litigation already under way that is seeking hundreds of millions of dollars in damages on behalf of thousands of consumers who used the device.

The plea, entered Friday in U.S. District Court in San Jose, Calif., caps a three-year federal investigation into LifeScan Inc., a unit of the New Brunswick, N.J., health-care giant, and its Surestep Blood Glucose Meter, which diabetes patients use at home to monitor their blood-sugar levels. The probe was sparked by two internal whistle-blowers whose repeated warnings about the defective devices had gone unheeded by LifeScan's top executives.

In documents filed in the case, the company admits it knowingly marketed a device that could give erroneous blood-sugar readings and that it misled patients who reported problems with it. It also acknowledges lying to the Food and Drug Administration and failing to provide timely reports to the agency when patients who used the monitors ended up in the hospital with life-threatening blood-sugar levels.

At least 61 patients suffered injury associated with the faulty devices, including some who were hospitalized. Though the FDA said in 1998 that it had received reports that two people who got misleading readings from the monitors may have died, the plea agreement doesn't mention any deaths. (J&J said it doesn't believe the deaths were caused by the device.)

"People with diabetes need to be able to rely on the accuracy of products they use to monitor their blood glucose," said Jane E. Henney, FDA commissioner, in a statement announcing the guilty plea. "Defective products that give inaccurate or misleading readings will not be tolerated." The case was brought by the U.S. Attorney's office for the Northern District of California and the Department of Justice, in addition to the FDA and other agencies.

The Surestep monitor, which the company launched in the U.S. in May 1996, had two defects. In one, a software glitch sometimes caused the device to display error messages instead of the reading "HI" when it detected dangerously high blood-glucose levels. The second problem occurred when patients failed to fully insert the monitor's test strip, a defect that led to readings that were as much as 90% lower than the patient's actual blood-sugar levels.

LifeScan admitted it knew about both defects before it applied to the FDA for marketing approval, but that it failed to describe them in submissions to the agency and failed to inform customers.

In one case, according to the plea agreement, a patient complained three times about getting error messages instead of a blood-level reading from the device. The company knew the error messages could mean that the patient's blood sugar was actually dangerously high, but when it provided a replacement device after each complaint, it didn't tell the patient about the error-message defect.

After the third incident, the patient was hospitalized with ketoacidosis, a serious complication of high blood sugar. Despite the urging of its director of clinical evaluations, LifeScan failed to report the incident to the FDA for more than a year, and then only after the federal investigation had already begun, according to the plea agreement.

Now J&J faces a class-action lawsuit that plaintiffs' attorneys have filed on behalf of what they say are several hundred thousand patients who purchased the flawed devices and test strips that are used with them. Milberg Weiss Bershad Hynes & Lerach is among the law firms mounting the litigation, which also is filed in federal court in San Jose.

For J&J, the LifeScan case stands in contrast to 1982, when reports of seven deaths from poisoned bottles of Tylenol prompted then-Chief Executive James Burke to order an immediate, nationwide recall of the over-the-counter pain relievers. The response was widely heralded as a model for how corporations should manage and behave in a crisis, and it is an important reason why J&J is often included in lists of most-admired companies.

In a statement on the LifeScan matter, J&J said no one at the company "engaged in intentional wrongdoing or intentionally sought to mislead consumers or the government." But "mistakes and misjudgments were made," Ralph S. Larsen, chairman and CEO, said. "We fully acknowledge those errors and sincerely apologize for them."

A spokesman said LifeScan's entire management team was replaced in the wake of the episode, but he declined to identify specific individuals whose behavior led to the criminal charges. He said no LifeScan employees have been indicted as a result of the probe.

LifeScan, based in Milpitas, Calif., generates about $1 billion in annual revenue for J&J from the sale of blood-glucose monitoring devices and the test strips. Only Surestep model monitors marketed to consumers and a similar device sold to hospitals were the subjects of the investigation. The company said it fixed the flaws related to the error messages by July 1997, and redesigned the test strips by early 1998. In June 1998, it instituted a voluntary world-wide recall of all monitors manufactured before July 27, 1997.

The company received more than 2,700 complaints from consumers between the product launch in May 1996 and July 1998, the documents say. The company estimates 290,000 defective units were sold.

J&J shares fell 68.75 cents to $98.56 as of 4 p.m. Friday in New York Stock Exchange composite trading.

Selling Birth Control to India's Poor

Medicine Men Market an Array Of Contraceptives

By Miriam Jordan

Staff Reporter of The Wall Street Journal

Mirzafari, India – From his outpost behind a wobbly desk under a tree, medicine man Sushil Bharati dispenses everything from cough remedies to advice on bad karma. Like thousands of other medicine men throughout the country, he is at the very heart of village life.

Now he is also part of an elaborate new medicine-man marketing network. Known as "Butterfly," its goal is to revolutionize the way the world's second-largest country curbs its soaring population. In return for advocating a formalized birth-control program, Mr. Bharati receives free radio ads and other benefits, like customer referrals. He also profits from selling condoms, prominently displayed in a jar on his little table, and birth-control pills.

It's a revolutionary concept for a village that is far removed from the modern world. Mirzafari's 10,000 citizens have no electricity, and women are confined to the home. Most men earn about $10 a month, mainly farming or weaving cotton. The average couple has eight children.

Plastered on the wall of Mr. Bharati's makeshift clinic are posters with the bright Butterfly logo–the same one that is displayed on billboards and village walls across the giant state of Bihar. There are butterflies, too, on Mr. Bharati's stationery, referral notes and prescription pad.

"We've gone for total branding," says K. Gopalakrishan, the network's director. "This is not only about serving humanity; it's about making money."

That is a significant philosophical shift. For decades, stabilizing population in India amounted to government-ordered sterilization. Policy makers set annual sterilization quotas, which were sometimes achieved by threatening, bribing or otherwise coercing women to participate, other times by fudging the figures. Under pressure from human-rights groups, New Delhi abolished that system three years ago.

Currently, India's census bureau estimates that on May 11, 2000, the nation's population will top one billion. Only China, with 1.2 billion people, is bigger; India is on track to surpass China within four decades. That prospect has spawned Butterfly and other programs–many funded by the U.S. government and U.S. private money–that aim to create networks out of existing commercial enterprises such as the medicine men. In neighboring Uttar Pradesh state, another program recruits milkmaids at village dairy cooperatives to spread the word on family planning.

The hurdles are huge. "Pills collect in your stomach and cause a cancer to grow," declares Lukoh, a pregnant woman in a pink and orange sari at Kharik village in Bihar, who already has had four children and five miscarriages. Another villager, Bebi, chimes in as she cradles her third child: "I have never taken contraceptives. My husband is my master–he will decide."

The northern states of Uttar Pradesh and Bihar are immense and poor. With 165 million people, if Uttar Pradesh were a nation, it would be the world's fifth largest. In neighboring Bihar, 100 million people eke out a living on 5% of India's land, and more than half live under the poverty line. Fewer than two out of 10 women can read and write.

India has made remarkable strides in slowing population growth in southern states, where female literacy is higher and states devote more money to health and education. Three southern states have achieved a replacement-level fertility rate–2.1 children per couple–or lower.

The risk to India is that soaring northern populations will swallow the economic advances made since India introduced market-oriented reforms earlier this decade. "If Uttar

हार्वे बटरफ्लाई प्रोजेक्ट

Pradesh and Bihar don't curb their population, India as a nation will no longer be viable," cautions Gadde Narayana, an adviser to Futures Group International, Washington, D.C., which does population research in India.

Butterfly was born two years ago when DKT International, a Washington, D.C., nonprofit group, created an Indian affiliate, Janani, which hatched the idea of using village medical practitioners. DKT invested $1 million and raised another $4 million from private Indian and U.S. groups.

Eight months ago, Mr. Bharati the medicine man and his wife, Sanju, signed on. They boarded an overnight train to the state capital, Patna, for a crash course on reproductive health at Janani's headquarters, where they learned about basic anatomy and the menstrual cycle. Armed with several tall jars of condoms and birth-control pills, supplied by Janani at cost, the couple returned four days later to northern Bihar.

Standing outside his brick hovel in Mirzafari, Mohammed Khurshid, father of 12, says he would prefer not to have any more children. But he won't countenance birth control. "It's in God's hands," he says. His third wife, Birwira, the mother of four of his children, seems to agree. Later, however, Mr. Bharati says that Birwira, 27 years old, regularly buys birth-control pills: "She doesn't skip a cycle."

That some villagers are even aware of birth-control methods other than sterilization is a tribute to Mr. Bharati and his wife. Typically, it takes several encounters to get a woman to consider birth control, so Mrs. Bharati broaches the subject subtly as she performs her daily chores with other women, such as fetching water at a well.

She is openly proud of her new knowledge. "Word is spreading that I have training," says Mrs. Bharati, who is one of the relatively few women who can read here. "Many women are seeking me to help them have fewer children," she says. Some ask to speak with her in the privacy of her family's dirt-floor home. She encourages the women to bring their husbands to Mr. Bharati.

Mr. Bharati, meanwhile, says he discusses family planning with nearly every customer. The condom jar on his desk stands next to another jar full of birth-control pills, in full view of patients, as required by Janani. "Family planning is my new responsibility," says Mr. Bharati, in his sixth year as a medicine man. "It is good for the village and it is good for my business," he says. A woman in a pink and blue sari steps up to buy a pack of pills.

Mr. Bharati charges about 20 cents a customer consultation, and 40 cents for bandaging a cut, but he doesn't charge separately for family-planning advice. In fact he even has to pay an annual $12 fee to be affiliated with Janani. But he makes a tiny profit from selling Janani's Bull brand condoms and Divine Dancer pills. He also receives a $1 commission for every patient he refers to Janani-endorsed doctors for intrauterine devices or abortions.

His practice, which earns him $70 to $90 a month, most of which comes from selling medicine, is thriving thanks to the free radio ads. He claims he is even winning business away from two competing medicine men. To preserve the brand's cachet, Janani affiliates with no more than one medicine man per village.

Janani has trained about 5,400 rural practitioners in 38 of Bihar's 55 districts. That's a drop in the bucket: There are 150,000 to 200,000 medicine men statewide. But

(Cont.)

encouraging results, such as that about 45% of the condoms and oral pills sold in the state are Janani brands, have prompted the organization to lay the groundwork for similar programs in two other northern states, Madhya Pradesh and Uttar Pradesh.

"We thought that if we could make this work in Bihar, we could make it work anywhere in India," says Mr. Gopalakrishan, the program director.

In neighboring Uttar Pradesh, another approach is under way at one of the world's biggest U.S.-funded population projects. The U.S. Agency for International Development is devoting $325 million over 10 years to an array of grass-roots programs to educate people about birth control. Among them is the milkmaid project.

Looking for an avenue into village society, USAID spotted opportunity in the state's countless dairy cooperatives, which provide a livelihood for women and also serve as de facto social centers. "The cooperative has always offered health care for the cows and buffalo of its members," declares Sumitra Singh, chairwoman of Pradeshik Dairy Co-op in Revri village. "Now, it's taking care of the women themselves."

As the early morning sun warms Revri's mud huts, women with cans of buffalo milk

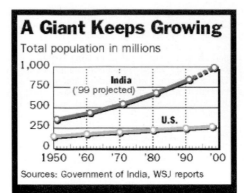

A Giant Keeps Growing

Total population in millions

Sources: Government of India, WSJ reports

line up at the co-op, and Sita Kumari, a co-op member and health worker, canvasses the crowd. Carrying a supply of pills and condoms in her shoulder bag, along with flip charts showing how to use them, she quickly identifies women who might need to restock.

The goods Ms. Kumari gives away are supplied by the government free of charge, though recently she started selling private brands, too.

USAID has trained 4,300 volunteers like Ms. Kumari, and pays them $8 month. In 15 districts of Uttar Pradesh where USAID is operating, the number of couples using family-planning services, such as pills, condoms and IUDs, has nearly doubled in three years.

A few years down the road, the co-op is expected to share the cost of the program by pooling a few pennies each month from members. In the long run, the idea is for each co-op to run the program on its own, and in fact make a profit by sourcing contraceptives for its members to sell.

"Dealing with population in India requires dynamism, flexibility and entrepreneurship," asserts Mr. Narayana of Futures Group. Nevertheless, it may take years before the success of the soft-sell approach can be accurately gauged.

Meanwhile, Ms. Kumari perseveres. Three years into the project, she supplies contraceptives to about 220 out of the 510 couples she has contacted. As for the others, she says, "I keep going back to them with my message."

Republished with permission of Dow Jones & Company, Inc., from *The Wall Street Journal*, "Selling Birth Control to India's Poor," p. B1, September 21, 1999; permission conveyed through Copyright Clearance Center, Inc.

98

BIG CARDS ON CAMPUS

Affinity-card issuers are stepping in with megabucks

You might say that Joseph E. Johnson, president emeritus of the University of Tennessee, thinks like any savvy chief executive officer. When the university hit what he called "a point of crisis" last year because of inadequate state fiscal support, Johnson forged one of the most lucrative corporate sponsor deals ever.

In a $16 million arrangement with First USA, the credit-card division of Bank One Corp., the bank is the sole marketer of the university's Visa "affinity" credit card–a card adorned with the school's picture and logo–to the university's students and alumni. "A lot are concerned that we're soaking our students, but we decided to do this in a reputable way rather than to let just any issuer on campus to solicit. Plus we needed the funds," says Johnson, who retired last month. In addition to the $16 million, divvied up over the course of seven years, the university receives 0.5% of every transaction charge, which could amount to an estimated $4 million annually.

More colleges and universities face similar budgetary problems, and credit-card companies are rushing in to fill the gap. Card companies pay for everything from mentoring programs to lecture series to cap-and-gown rentals. "You're finding much more of a willingness for schools to cut all kinds of creative sweetheart deals with corporations for big money," says Lewis Mandell, dean of the State University of New York at Buffalo's management school and the author of three books on credit cards.

The deals obviously benefit schools, but the real winners are card companies. Credit-hungry students are often a card issuer's best customers, despite the fact that most don't have a credit history or even a job. "If it's the first card you get, chances are you'll hold on to it for a long time," says Robert B. McKinley, CEO of CardWeb.com Inc., a credit-card tracking service. Studies show that students keep their first credit card for an average of 15 years.

Card marketers also like students because 70% of those with cards at four-year colleges have $2,000 or more of revolving debt, according to the Consumer Federation. And ironically, students are less of a credit risk than the general population because their parents often pay their bills.

TOO FAR? Once a bank secures a captive student audience, it can market other products such as first mortgages, car loans, and, in a sinister twist, debt-consolidation loans to help students repay credit-card debt. "They've got

'em and they know it," says Robert Manning, a sociology professor at Georgetown University and author of a recent study on students and credit cards.

Indeed, a growing concern is that affinity-card programs have encroached too far into academia's supposedly hallowed halls. At the University of Ottawa, MBNA Corp., the largest affinity-card issuer, started an alumni-student mentoring program last year. At the University of Hawaii, MBNA provides video production services and airtime to "ensure continuance" of the weekly UH Today radio and TV show. Says Manning: "You can't tell me that having a credit-card issuer controlling student media won't impact editorial decisions." Manning's Georgetown University gets paid an undisclosed sum by MBNA for rights to the Georgetown affinity card. Also, MBNA contributed $2 million several years ago to fund what is officially called the MBNA Career Education Center.

"DANGEROUS." In the face of all of this, student credit-card debt is mounting, due

primarily to aggressive card marketing and students' lack of credit knowledge. According to the Consumer Federation study, debt among college students has almost tripled since 1990. "That's why these mega credit-card deals are more dangerous than, say, whether a college chooses to be a Coke campus or a Pepsi campus or give all of its athletes Nike shoes," says Mandell.

Because of worry over student debt, a growing number of colleges and universities are restricting or banning campus-card marketing by non-affinity-card issuers. Still, most schools, especially large state schools, are not nearly as quick to turn down blockbuster affinity-card deals. "Colleges will say they've done a deal with a single issuer in order to get competing card marketers off campus and to control the process. But what difference does it make if you're a student with $10,000 of debt on an affinity card vs. another type of card?" asks Manning.

One of the reasons affinity cards have become so popular and lucrative for both

The Plastic Invasion

SCHOOL	BANK	DEAL
Georgetown University	MBNA	$2 million for career counseling center
Michigan State University	MBNA	$5.5 million for athletic and academic scholarship program
University of Hawaii	MBNA	$1.5 million for TV and radio shows; athletics
University of Ottawa	MBNA	$0.3 million for alumni mentoring program
University of Tennessee	First USA	$16 million for athletics; scholarships; other needs

Data: Business Week

(Cont.)

colleges and credit-card issuers is that the cardholders are more loyal. "If you've got a card with your college on it, it's like being part of a club. There's pride involved," says McKinley. Part of that loyalty stems from the idea that the cardholder is donating to his or her school or alma mater each time the card is used. In most affinity-card deals, in addition to an up-front flat fee sometimes as much as several million dollars, a college receives half of a percent of the purchase value of each transaction made with the card.

In addition, schools are often paid anywhere from $5 to $20 on each new account that is opened and sometimes a small percentage of loans outstanding. But card issuers emphasize that each deal they make is unique. "We make proposals to schools based on their particular needs and the information they give us," says Jeff Unkle, a First USA spokesman.

For their part, card issuers and schools often argue that affinity cards are tied to the alumni association, not the school itself, but

> **"If you've got a card with your college on it, it's like being part of a club. There's pride involved"**

this can be misleading. "In these deals, the contracts typically specify that issuers have access to student mailing lists and can solicit directly on campus," says Manning.

In a typical First USA or MBNA deal, for example, the bank is the only issuer allowed to market on campus and through student and alumni mailing lists–a coup for any card issuer in these days of cutthroat competition for the college market. At the University of Tennessee, for instance, there are some 270,000 alumni and 26,000 students, in addition to untold numbers of UT fans who are also solicited at sporting events.

Although schools and card companies are pleased with the deals, some factions are not.

This spring, the Tennessee state legislature nearly passed a bill that would have prohibited credit-card solicitations on campuses altogether, thus terminating the university's deal. The bill will be reintroduced next year. As part of the pending bankruptcy bill, Congress is considering a proposal that would allow credit cards to go to people under 21 only if they have parental approval or are financially independent.

"We realize that students may lack credit experience, but most of them are extremely responsible and handle credit cards as well or better than most adults," says Brian Dalphon, a spokesman for MBNA.

As affinity-card programs remain highly lucrative for both colleges and card companies, they will likely continue to remain BMOC–big money on campus.

By Marcia Vickers in New York

99

WRESTLING WITH YOUR CONSCIENCE

Wal-Mart wants to avoid controversy on its shelves, but consumers won't let it

Bill Saporito/Bentonville

Walk into most any Wal-Mart in the U.S. and here are a few of the things you can buy: condoms, birth control pills, hunting rifles, "Western" style toy guns, the movie *There's Something About Mary,* the *National Enquirer,* cigarettes, the video game South Park, the hard-rocking Powerman 5000's hit *Tonight the Stars Revolt.* And here are a few of the things you can't buy: a "day-after" birth control kit, handguns, authentic-looking plastic guns, *Playboy,* rolling papers, the movie *South Park,* the video game Grand Theft Auto and any number of rap CDs.

Inconsistent? Absolutely, and deliberately so. "We're a family store," says Wal-Mart CEO David Glass, and "we try to have something for everyone." And just as in real families, there is conflict about who gets what. Last week the company was pinned by a consumer who demanded that a World Wrestling Federation action doll be yanked from the shelves because both the wrestler it depicted, Al Snow, and the doll carry a prop that looks like a woman's severed head.

It was the latest in a series of controversies in which the company, by virtue of its enormous size and reach, has played an unwanted role as a sort of national conscience, discount division. Wal-Mart has been accused of being both censor and nanny, condemned as a promoter of demon rum and slave labor, and cited as both a friend and a foe of the environment. "We don't want to be America's moral conscience," says Don Soderquist, senior vice chairman. "The watchword for all of our people is 'Do what is right.' That's what we really preach and teach and we want, but there's so much gray."

And wherever there's gray, black, as in ink, is not far behind. Earlier this year, Wal-Mart infuriated some women's groups when it declined to stock Preven, an emergency day-after contraception kit available by prescription. Antiabortion groups hailed the decision as one for their side. But Wal-Mart's rationale was simpler–perhaps too much so: its pharmacies don't stock every drug available; Preven was going to be a small seller, customers were not clamoring for it, and the item was pricey ($25). "You can't carry everything. Sometimes you get credit for making a moral judgment when you're not," says Glass. Similarly, when Glass pulled handguns from the shelves in 1994, the company cited sales

more than ethics, although he notes that by then there were more negatives in stocking handguns than positives.

Glass is certain that some of the books, videos and other products in the stores he would personally find offensive. He just doesn't know what they are. "When you have 100,000 unique SKUs," he says, using the retailer's term for an item–a stock keeping unit–"something is going to irritate somebody."

That would be, for instance, Kevin Clarke, a mild-mannered carpet salesman from Mentor, Ohio, and a loyal Wal-Mart customer, who went ballistic after his son bought a CD by a band named Godsmack that he thought God-awful, particularly a ditty called *Voodoo,* which seemed to be about suicide. Wal-Mart has long had a policy of banning so-called stickered CDs, those carrying a warning label that the content might not be suitable for children. But Godsmack was stickerless, so Wal-Mart stocked it, until Clarke hollered.

The music industry doesn't like Wal-Mart's policy, muttering under its collective breath about censorship and artistic freedom, but it won't buck the system. That's because Wal-Mart's reach is enormous, representing 10% to 15% of all U.S. CD sales. "It's very difficult to have a No. 1" without Wal-Mart, says a record-company executive. That's why even the biggest, baddest acts–Nirvana, Snoop Dogg–often clean up their acts to play Wal-Mart. But even that kind of screen isn't enough for parents such as Clarke, who hold Wal-Mart accountable for everything that ends up on the shelves: "They tout a policy that their stores are a safe haven, but they didn't honor it."

Wal-Mart has a clearly articulated view of its role in society and the economy–to be an "agent" for the consumer. The company views its job as finding out exactly what folks want and getting those products into the stores at the lowest possible cost. It's a strategy that has worked superbly. Wal-Mart earned $4.4 billion last year on sales of $139 billion. It serves 90 million to 100 million customers each week. So while Wal-Mart is a conservative company born of the rural South, it hasn't let that get in the way of some basic considerations of commerce. Years ago, church leaders were unhappy, and unavailing, when the company began to open its stores on Sundays. The customers, not any

other authority, would be obeyed.

This kind of practical morality operates on a larger scale too. Take the sale of alcoholic beverages. Wal-Mart does not sell beer and wine in its traditional discount stores. Yet if you walk into many Wal-Mart supercenters, stores as big as 220,000 sq. ft. that combine a supermarket with a traditional Wal-Mart, you'll find plenty of Budweiser to put in the coolers being sold in sporting goods. Wine and beer are also sold in Sam's Clubs and in the company's new chain of downsized Neighborhood Markets, a.k.a. "small marts."

Why the distinction? Wal-Mart executives attribute the decision to the customers, who say they expect to be able to buy beer and wine in supercenters just as they do at competitors' stores of a similar type. Yet booze will remain verboten in fuddy-duddy old Wal-Mart discount stores. Explains Glass: "What's the difference between selling in a supercenter and a Wal-Mart? I can't tell you I can give you a definite answer. But I can tell you that I have a rationale for it." Nevertheless, within the company and without, there was muttering that Sam–Wal-Mart's late founder, Sam Walton–wouldn't stand for such a thing. Wrong, says Glass. Sam knew better than to buck the customers.

Hence, Wal-Mart is well stocked in inconsistencies. *South Park,* the cartoon television series and recent movie, features a funny but foulmouthed cast of characters and an infinite collection of toilet jokes. The South Park video game got to the shelves but not the film. Reason: Wal-Mart's game buyer figured that customers who purchase it are already familiar with the characters. The video buyer, on the other hand, believed that customers associate animated films with movies such as *Bambi* and not with Cartman and his profane pals. (No doubt the boys would have joyously killed and consumed Bambi.)

In Wal-Mart's world, there is accounting for taste. For instance, the video section stocks the risque comedy *There's Something About Mary.* And there's something in it that more than a few folks would find objectionable. Says movie buyer Eddie Tutt: "It's pretty crude, but [the movie] did $175 million in sales, which kind of tells you that most of the public looked at it and probably felt good about it." Which tells Tutt that unlike, say, Howard Stern's crude movie, *Private Parts,* which Wal-Mart did not carry, *Mary* will light

(Cont.)

up the cash registers.

Yet Wal-Mart customers are not of one mind on some of society's more complicated matters, as it learned with Preven. The primary ingredient in Preven is ethinyl estradiol/levonorgestrel–the same as in birth control pills–given in a high dose. The package also contains a pregnancy test. Although Wal-Mart wouldn't stock Preven, it has always sold birth control pills.

Earlier this year, Planned Parenthood sent women to Wal-Mart stores with "emergency" prescriptions for birth control pills, not Preven by name. A few pharmacists refused to fill them, some apparently under the false impression that these drugs will terminate a pregnancy, as opposed to preventing one.

Planned Parenthood pressed the company for a clarification on its pharmacy policy. Wal-Mart then sent a directive to each of its pharmacists requiring them to fulfill any emergency prescription, which is consistent with the American Pharmaceutical Association's code of ethics. Any pharmacist whose personal beliefs prevented him from filling such a prescription must find someone who will. So day-after contraception is available, even if, for business reasons, Preven is not. "We don't care what their motivation is," says Gloria Feldt, president of Planned Parenthood, who gives the company good marks for its responsiveness. "Our concern is that women can get emergency contraception."

The Preven controversy, among others, has prompted Wal-Mart to reconsider some of its laissez-faire policies. The company recently established an ethics committee, to which buyers and other Wal-Mart employees can refer any knotty issue. As Wal-Mart continues to grow internationally, the committee will no doubt get busier. Certainly the medical-ethics front will get murkier. "We are only at the tip of the iceberg," says Soderquist. "There will be lots of issues that will come up: suicide pills, genetic engineering. Can they prescribe pills that alter the genes?"

And even before we get there, the nation's biggest shopkeeper will be less able to stick to its preferred role as an agnostic buyer for the masses. There's a world full of outraged parents, students, environmentalists, activists, politicians and stockholders complaining with equal fervor about the silly and the serious. Says Glass: "The public in general becomes a little harder to serve all the time. But you have to respond to that." In other words, Wal-Mart is no longer a free agent.

With reporting by David E. Thigpen

WHAT'S ON—AND NOT ON— WAL-MART'S SHOPPING LIST

GUNS

Handguns were booted in 1994. Sales were insignificant. The publicity wasn't.

BUT . . . It sells hunting rifles, part of a strategy to create a dominant sporting-goods department for guys.

MAGAZINES

No adult, or rock titles like Cream. Has pulled individual issues of some mags.

BUT . . . Sells the *National Enquirer* and alien-heavy scandal sheets.

MUSIC

Stocks Top 100 hits, except for "stickered" CDs. Previews lyrics.

BUT . . . Bands will change lyrics to get in. Customers are ever vigilant.

MOVIES/GAMES

Top-seller focus. *South Park,* the movie, is too lewd.

BUT . . . The game is O.K. The company gets an early look at all games, but it's not fussy.

CONTRACEPTION

Won't sell Preven, emergency birth control kit, citing low sales potential.

BUT . . . Sells condoms, birth control pills and spermicides.

ALCOHOL

Not in traditional Wal-Mart stores. Customers don't expect it there.

BUT . . . Superstores are different, so beer and wine are sold where legal.

TOYS

Pulled the World Wrestling Federation Road Rage doll after charges that the character, Al Snow, promoted violence against women.

BUT . . . Still has Stone Cold Steve Austin and others. No complaints.

100

$45 MILLION FOR ONE BUCK

TV, cereal boxes—they're pushing the 'Golden Dollar' like mad

As soon as he heard the new U.S. dollar coins were available at his local Charlotte (N.C.) Wal-Mart, Ron Feuer rushed out to exchange a $20 bill for a handful of the gold-colored coins. "I was one of the first," he says proudly. Feuer, an avid collector, might be more excited than most over the coin's arrival, but that may change.

Starting Mar. 6, the U.S. Mint will unleash a $45 million marketing blitz to sell the new coin to the public. "We want to get everyone talking," says U.S. Mint Director Philip N. Diehl. The mint has dubbed the coin the Golden Dollar, even though it's really a copper and brass alloy. But it might as well be gold, given the glittering launch the mint has planned.

The new dollar has its own public-relations firm, a cereal-box promotional tie-in, and even a catchy slogan: "The Golden Dollar: The Right Change for the New Millennium." Already there are about 200 million of the new coins in circulation and the mint, which projects that number will grow to 1 billion by year-end, just doubled production to keep up with demand. **SUSAN B. FLOP.** Still, the mint isn't taking any chances. Its lavish advertising campaign will hit TV, radio, and the Internet. The coins are already "prizes" in Cheerios boxes and next month, mint officials plan a multi-city coin giveaway, handing out Golden Dollars in front of rail and subway stations.

It might seem like overkill. But the mint is determined not to end up with another Susan B. Anthony, the dollar coin that was introduced in 1979 and quickly flopped. The vending machine industry spent $200 million retooling its machines to accept the Anthony dollar, according to the National Automatic Merchandising Assn. (NAMA). Still, the public shunned the coin because it was often mistaken for a quarter.

Clearly, vending machine operators, including the postal service and mass transit operators, have the most riding on the new coin. NAMA estimates that the industry loses $3 billion a year when consumers try to slip a tattered bill into a vending machine to no avail. "Those are sales that would have happened" if a coin were used, says Thomas E. McMahon, vice-president of NAMA. The mint, on the other hand, didn't lose money on the Susan B. Anthony because it made the coin for only 9 cents, then transferred it to the Federal Reserve for $1. "What the Mint lost was face," says Diehl.

Some argue the wisdom of spending $45 million on an ad campaign for a coin. But in 1997, Congress ordered a new dollar coin. So the mint held focus groups, resulting in a coin depicting Sacagawea, a Native American woman and a member of the Lewis and Clark expedition. Then came

> **The unmitigated failure of the Susan B. Anthony dollar has put pressure on the mint to do this coin right**

> **Selling Sacagawea:** The mint's campaign includes tie-ins with Wal-Mart and Cheerios

the distribution deal with Wal-Mart Stores Inc. and, now, the ad blitz about to hit.

Critics think the mint has lost its bearings. Bankers, for example, feel snubbed by the Wal-Mart deal, since new coins have traditionally been theirs to release. Jerry Ursprung, vice-president of First Liberty National Bank in Liberty, Tex., says he was "caught off guard" when his local Wal-Mart had the first supply of the new dollar coins.

Others insist no amount of marketing will make the coin a success. They point out that the Canadian dollar coin, introduced in 1987, was a success because its paper counterpart was phased out. "With the dollar bill to fall back on, who needs the coin," says Donna Pope, a former director of the U.S. Mint.

Diehl argues that the right coin with the right marketing will work alongside a greenback. "This can be a 'hot' product," he says. Now he just has to convince everyone out there that he's right.

By Ellen Neuborne in New York and Richard S. Dunham in Washington, D.C.

Notes

Notes

Notes

Notes

Notes

Notes

Notes

Notes

Notes

Notes

Notes

Notes